American Association of Collegiate Registrars and Admissions Officers

# The College Admissions Officer's Guide

BARBARA LAUREN, PH.D., J.D. , EDITOR

## *Dedication*

As an educational professional, the college admissions officer must demonstrate a varied set of skills—from counselor to technology expert. The successful admissions officer will continue to seek out the latest concepts, techniques, and strategies regarding the admissions profession in order to remain current within the field. *The College Admissions Officer's Guide* will serve as a valuable resource for you in this endeavor. This book is dedicated to each of you as you strive for professional excellence.

Wanda W. Simpson, Ed.D.
AACRAO Vice President for
Admissions and Enrollment Management (2008)

AACRAO

American Association of Collegiate
Registrars and Admissions Officers
One Dupont Circle, NW, Suite 520
Washington, DC 20036–1135

Tel: (202) 293–9161 | Fax: (202) 872–8857 | www.aacrao.org

For a complete listing of AACRAO publications, visit www.aacrao.org/publications.

The American Association of Collegiate Registrars and Admissions Officers, founded in 1910, is a nonprofit, voluntary, professional association of more than 10,000 higher education administrators who represent more than 2,600 institutions and agencies in the United States and in twenty-eight countries around the world. The mission of the Association is to provide leadership in policy initiation, interpretation, and implementation in the global educational community. This is accomplished through the identification and promotion of standards and best practices in enrollment management, information technology, instructional management, and student services.



AACRAO adheres to the principles of non-discrimination without regard to age, color, handicap or disability, ethnic or national origin, race, religion, gender (including discrimination taking the form of sexual harassment), marital, parental or veteran status, or sexual orientation.

## Acknowledgment of Permissions

Chapter 3, by Professor Michael A. Olivas, originally appeared as "State College Savings and Prepaid Tuition Plans: A Reappraisal and Review" in the *Journal of Law and Education*, Vol. 23, No. 4 (October 2003), 475–514. It is published, in updated form, with the kind permission of the University of South Carolina School of Law.

Chapter 10 originally appeared, in slightly different form, as "Pacing a Web-Savvy Generation: What's New with 24/7 Interactive Web Services," by Joe F. Head and Thomas M. Hughes, in *The Admissions Marketing Report*, June 2005, 17–21.

Chapters 22, 29, 30, and 41 originally appeared, in slightly different forms, in the *College and University* Journal (AACRAO).

Chapter 24, "The New TOEFL," originally appeared, in slightly different form, in the *SACRAO Journal*, Vol. 19, pp. 25-26 (2006).

## Library of Congress Cataloging-in-Publication Data

The college admissions officer's guide/Barbara Lauren, editor.
p. cm.
Includes index.

ISBN 978–1–57858–082–8

1. College admission officers—United States.
2. Universities and colleges—United States—Admission.

I. Lauren, Barbara, 1947–

LB2351.6.C65 2008
378.1'610973—dc22
2008004415

# Table of Contents

## SECTION B: Recruiting in Different Settings

## SECTION I: Data and Institutional Research

SECTION J: Professional Development

# Preface

Once thought of merely as gatekeepers, admissions officers now need to master a wide variety of knowledge and techniques in order to help form the entering classes at colleges and universities. As a professional association, AACRAO is committed to providing exceptional publications addressing multiple areas of this complex and evolving field. *The College Admissions Officer's Guide* is the next volume in a series dedicated to the AACRAO professions.

As vice president for Admission and Enrollment Management of AACRAO (2003–06) and then as AACRAO's president (2006–07), it became my mission to develop a guide for admissions officers to supplement the limited amount of literature available to many important segments of our AACRAO membership.

There were some articles in *College and University*, and there was Swann and Henderson's *Handbook for the College Admissions Profession* from 1998. But there was a lack of more recent, wide-ranging guidance for admissions officers, due in part to the fact that admissions is a relatively "newer" profession within AACRAO, merging with the registrars only in 1947.

Recognizing the need for ongoing professional guidance for AACRAO's admissions officers led to our commitment to publish this *Guide*—to complement and support the professionals in the field, and to serve as the most current comprehensive guide specifically for admissions officers, as distinct from enrollment managers.

When Heather Smith and I requested a call for authors for what was originally intended to be a comprehensive guide for both registrars and admissions officers, the membership response was so overwhelming that AACRAO decided to begin with the registrars' publication and follow with the *College Admissions Officer's Guide*. These two significant books provide current guidance to the two major segments of AACRAO's membership, and allow for additional development of the series or sequence.

AACRAO appreciates the significant contributions of fifty-six authors contributing to the forty-four chapters of expertise. Under the tutelage of Dr. Barbara Lauren, this publication will continue the AACRAO tradition of exceptional professional literature, and will establish a foundation for the admissions profession in the twenty-first century. The AACRAO Board of Directors would like to thank each of you for making this mission a reality.

Angé Peterson, M.S.
Assistant Vice President–Regional Campuses
University of Central Florida

# Introduction and Overview

Newspapers advertise for perfection in our field every day. Here is a composite sample advertisement for a director of admissions.

> *The director is responsible for providing leadership to the institution's recruitment, admission, and retention of undergraduate and transfer students. He or she must have a thorough understanding of enrollment management, data-driven recruitment strategies, promotion and public relations techniques, and assessment/planning skills. Such a person will supervise professional and support staff, and will work closely with the all of the following: directors of the enrollment management division, student affairs, and treasurer's office, and also department heads and key faculty members.*
>
> *Other requirements: Public speaking ability, enthusiasm, knowledge of current and evolving technologies for reaching students, and a commitment to a collaborative approach.*
>
> *The position requires weekend and extended hours.*

The subject of college admissions is a complex one. As the above fictional but realistic advertisement indicates, today's admissions officers must build on their traditional arsenal of knowledge and enthusiasm. They must acquire a comfort with data-driven analysis of targeted student populations combined with the technological savvy to reach them, and they must engage—in many productive ways—with the greater college community.

This book, *The College Admissions Officer's Guide*, follows on the excellent *Handbook for the College Admissions Profession* (1998), by Claire C. Swann and Stanley E. Henderson. So many additional developments have occurred within the past ten years, however, that AACRAO thought it appropriate to create an entirely new work, which would address both new subjects (such as holistic admissions) and new factors affecting traditional topics.

This book is aimed firmly at the admissions officer. Yet we begin with a chapter on admissions in the context of enrollment management, because of the growing interrelationship between the two. As summarized by Stanley Henderson in the opening chapter of this work, the tools of enrollment management can help colleges reach out not only to students of color, but also to what have been called "the New Students"—low-income, first-generation college students. This first chapter discusses statewide partnerships with K–12 education, especially The College Foundation of North Carolina (CFNC), a suite of services for students (beginning in middle school) and parents. The CFNC is designed to be one place, easily accessible on the Internet, where students can plan, apply, and pay for college. Henderson also discusses campus-based partnerships and early outreach, both of which have been productive examples of admissions conducted strategically.

Chapters 2 and 4 present two issues which affect all institutions: financial aid and affirmative action.

In Chapter 3 Professor Michael A. Olivas, of the University of Houston Law Center, discusses the availability of "529" plans for funding college study—both state College Savings Plans (CSPs) and Prepaid Tuition Plans. He also includes a list of programs available, state by state, with Web sites.

We next address what has become a critical concept in recruiting, favorably mentioned by the Supreme Court: holistic assessment. This concept involves taking into account non-cognitive variables as well as more conventional factors such as grades and test scores. In Chapter 5 Michele Sandlin presents "The 'Insight Resumé': Oregon State University's Approach to Holistic Assessment." OSU developed an "Insight Resume," a series of six questions to which every applicant must respond in one hundred words or less (per question). "We emphasized—to faculty and anyone else—that by allowing us to assess how students had set goals for themselves and what steps they were taking to reach them, we were able to consider students based on demonstrated achievements beyond traditional testable scores." In Chapter 6 Ted Spencer of the University of Michigan-Ann Arbor describes how the University of Michigan revamped its admissions procedures after the Supreme Court decisions in 2003, which had involved admissions at the University of Michigan's undergraduate (and law) schools.

After these two chapters which focus on admissions in the state university setting, we include two chapters that discuss "Small Private Liberal Arts Colleges: Recruiting Challenges and Opportunities," and recruiting in the community college context.

The next series of chapters focuses on marketing and outreach. Chapters 9, 10, and 11 address, respectively, "Technology-Enhanced Recruitment Communications" (a challenging tour of everything from instant messaging and chat rooms to "tour blogs" and Podcasts); use of interactive Web-based services for prospects; and making use of faculty in recruiting students.

We then present a coordinated series of chapters on recruiting various categories of students. Deliberately we have started this sequence by addressing the topic of "Low-Income Students: Outreach and Retention" (Chapter 12). These are the low-income and/or first-generation college students whom we first referred to in the opening chapter. Then, in separate chapters, we cover recruiting black, Hispanic, Asian Pacific American students, and Native American students (Chapters 13–16, respectively). Each of these chapters has been written by two authors, representing the blending of two sets of professional experience (one chapter includes perspectives from those who work in student services and retention as well as admissions).

We continue by discussing the recruitment of other distinctive student cohorts: women in Engineering (and by implication, the sciences generally); transfer students; homeschooled students; military students; the adult market; LBGT students; and International students.

Following up on the chapter concerning international students, we present a chapter called "The New TOEFL" (Chapter 24), and a chapter by Professor Olivas on "The DREAM Act and In-State Tuition for Undocumented Students" (Chapter 25).

We next address ourselves to admissions processing, with three chapters: Chapter 26 discusses continuous process improvement and use of technology in admissions processing; Chapter 27 explains the new XML standard for the electronic exchange of admissions applications; and Chapter 28 presents a discussion of yield along various stages of the enrollment funnel, and various techniques for predicting it.

The next five chapters return to the issue of testing. Chapter 29 addresses the topic, "Enhancing Academic Excellence and Diversity." Chapter 30 describes a "Freshman Index" devised by Georgia State University, a combination of SAT score and high school grade point average, and its use in predicting the graduating GPA of white, Asian, and black graduates.

Chapter 31 presents a thoughtful overview of the Advanced Placement exams, including a frank discussion of both the advantages and the challenges involved in using them.

Chapters 32 and 33 present the International Baccalaureate (IB) program. The first of these two chapters provides an overview of the program, its components, and its transcripts by a member of the organization. The second chapter, by an admissions officer at a "receiving" school, discusses (among other topics) how universities can market their schools to take advantage of the strengths of students in the IB program—global perspective, civic/community involvement, extended essays, and capstone projects.

Chapters 34 through 37 will be useful for admissions officers in schools of law, medicine, graduate health studies programs (health care administration, nursing, nutrition, and physical therapy), and graduate work, respectively. But these chapters are, indeed, intended primarily for the undergraduate admissions officer, and may better equip such admissions officers to answer the question: "What are law schools (etc.) looking for in an applicant?" Many of the answers will not be surprising, but they come with particular authority from chapter authors who work in those settings.

Chapter 38 presents a helpful elucidation of the Bologna Process and U.S. Graduate Admissions Practices.

We are proud to present three chapters which focus on the use of data in this field. The study of data is helpful not just for the registrar or the institutional research office! Chapter 39, on "Student Data: The Relationship between the Admissions and Registrar's Offices," covers the following places where a good data relationship is critical: the transition from applicant status to student status; loading data from an online application; two common schedules for "rolling the data," thus creating the student record; and managing data in the "gray period" before the semester begins.

"Ultimately it is all about data," says chapter author Reta Pikowsky. "Data, efficiently gathered and effectively used, can help you significantly increase the quality of your service and interaction with students—the students whom you have worked so hard to recruit and retain."

Chapter 40 offers a unique insight into the use of IPEDS data by admissions officers. It was written by Ira Tyszler, who as dean of Enrollment Management and also as director of Institutional Research has a rare dual perspective. This chapter offers you step-by-step tips on how to use College Navigator, the IPEDS interface which is open to the public. Easy to use, it is full of information about your own school and also about your peer schools (or any other institutions you choose to access).

Chapter 41 discusses how to calculate the freshman tuition discount rate, and how to use the IPEDS Peer Analysis System to compare tuition discount rates.

"So You Want to Be a Director of Admissions?" In this level-headed and practical chapter two current directors and one assistant dean of admission offer you guidelines, which can be modified to fit your unique situation. "The simple (and crucial) truth is simply that the perfect job opportunity comes to those who are prepared," they say. The authors discuss elements to consider in assessing an open position. They then break down your first year and a half in the new position into three semesters, mirroring a typical semester system. They suggest items which you should be observing, researching, and acting on. Their summarizing conclusion is sensible and to the point: "Your goal is to align as many resources across campus as you need to implement the changes you need to make.... All of these efforts should create an environment in which success is the norm, and your value to the institution is without question."

Chapter 43 attends to an issue which every admissions office must face: "Creating a Career Ladder: Motivating and Developing Staff." The two co-authors set forth a three-step interviewing process; discuss the training, mentoring, and assessment of staff; and above all, emphasize that "the most successful admissions offices create [a] sense of achievement—of professional growth—by developing a ladder of success where one is not otherwise apparent."

The concluding chapter ties everything together. Titled "Engaging the Greater College Community," it starts with the premise that "It is all too easy to become disconnected from the campus community. Yet being connected and engaged with the campus community is so critical to doing the job well." Brian Williams, the author, goes on to describe the increasing stages of engagement of an admissions officer, from listener and supporter to influencer and champion, in relation to nine facets of campus life: financial aid; student accounts/bursar; orientation; residence life; student affairs; academic advising; the faculty; business and financial matters; and advancement/alumni.

Brian Williams concludes: "By embracing a spirit of engagement, you will not only find the best way to navigate your current campus, but will also understand the full interaction of different approaches, as staff changes or professional development brings you to new responsibilities. By considering the role admissions plays in the larger academic community, you will begin to intuitively function as an enrollment professional and not just as a recruiter. You will grow. And your office, your campus, and the profession will benefit from your engagement."

We include, as an appendix, three checklists which we reprint from AACRAO's own *College Recruiters' Quick Guide*: "Student and Parent FAQs"; "College Fair Do's and Don'ts"; and "Working with High School Counselors."

I would like to express warm and special thanks to Martha Henebry, AACRAO's Director of Membership and Publications, an invaluable colleague for anyone who creates books at AACRAO. I would also like to thank Jim Graham, our graphic designer, a wizard at making content visually attractive and accessible. All three of us worked together on the companion volume which appeared in 2006, *The Registrar's Guide: Evolving Best Practices in Records and Registration*.

I would also like to express my cordial appreciation to Jill Bogard, director of the Library and Information Service, a library maintained by the American Council on Education, in the National Center for Higher Education at One Dupont Circle in Washington, DC, for associations headquartered there, including AACRAO. Jill has graciously and unfailingly helped us to obtain many obscure print publications, which have illuminated several topics.

Most of all, I would like to pay tribute to the fifty-six authors, all of whom were fully committed to their institutional work, and yet who chose to distill their experience for their colleagues. Our goal has always been two-fold: to add value to the experienced practitioner who specializes in any of these topics, but to do so with such clarity that newcomers, either to the field or to any specific part of the field, can follow the discussion with ease.

During the year and a half in which we all worked with such concentration on this book, I felt that it "belonged to us." Now that it is published, I am glad that it belongs to everyone—to AACRAO members in particular, and to the higher education community, generally.

Barbara Lauren, Ph.D., J.D.
Editor
Associate Director
Compliance and Professional Development
AACRAO

# Author Biographies

### Barbara Lauren, Editor

Barbara Lauren has worked in higher education as a faculty member, lawyer and administrator. She is Associate Director, Compliance and Professional Development, at AACRAO, and works on legal and compliance issues. Her most recent accomplishment at AACRAO has been the shepherding of 35 dedicated authors to create *The Registrar's Guide: Evolving Best Practices in Records and Registration.* Published in 2006, this was AACRAO's first book to offer comprehensive guidance to registrars in more than 25 years.

Barbara has a B.A. from Smith College, a Ph.D. in English literature from Yale, and a J.D. from Georgetown. She practiced law in Boston, and served for seven years as Assistant Dean for Academic Affairs at the Boston University School of Law. Before joining AACRAO, she worked with the Council for Higher Education Accreditation (CHEA).

In 2002–03, she served as President of the Higher Education Group of Washington, a group of people in the higher education associations of the capital region. She has also served as Chair of the Maryland State Bar Association Section on Legal Education and Admissions to the Bar. Barbara has presented on FERPA and other subjects for "Registrar 101 Online," and at numerous state and regional ACRAO meetings

### Mary Baxton

Mary Baxton is Director of Admissions and International Outreach Specialist at The Tseng College of Extended Learning, California State University, Northridge. She earned her bachelor's and master's degrees in business administration at Cal State, Northridge, and has worked there for over thirty years. She is the AACRAO Transfer Credit Practices (TCP) reporting officer for the state of California.

Mary has served on AACRAO's Board of Directors as the Vice President for International Education. She is the author of more than 12 country profiles for the AACRAO EDGE project (Electronic Database for Global Education). In 2006, she served as co-editor of an AACRAO publication, *The Impact of Bologna and Three-year Degrees on U.S. Admissions: A Focus on Europe, Australia and the United Kingdom.*

### Stephen Alan Bischoff

Stephen Bischoff has served as the Retention Counselor for the Asian American and Pacific Islander Student Center at Washington State University (WSU) since Fall 2003. He earned his B.A. in Business Administration (2002) and his Master's in Business Administration (2003) from WSU. Aside from his full-time position, Stephen is a part-time student finishing his Master's degree in American Studies, in which his focus is on Filipino-American youth and social activism. He enjoys working with underrepresented populations in a holistic way. Stephen and his wife Rachel reside in Pullman, WA.

### Tony Campeau

Tony is Director of Admissions at Montana Tech of the University of Montana in Butte, where he has spent most of his professional career. Tony's interests include Enrollment Management and student success, with a special emphasis on students in Montana. Tony frequently presents at AACRAO meetings, and for several years has chaired the Round Table for admissions officers at small colleges. He served as president of the Montana Post Secondary Educational Opportunities Council for two years, and has been active in Montana Board of Regents policy development.

Tony also serves on campus committees centering on student success, including: academic standards, orientation, enrollment management, retention and advising, and also advancement and development. Tony is active in student life as the advisor for the soccer club, and spent six years as a local high school soccer coach. He currently coaches Olympic Development soccer for the state of Montana.

### Rudolph Clay, Jr.

Rudolph Clay earned a Master's Degree in Library Science and joined Washington University Libraries in St. Louis in 1980. He has earned a Master's Degree in Human Resources Management, currently serves as the Head of the Olin Library Reference Department, and teaches a library research methods course in the African and African-American Studies Program. He is actively involved in Washington University's effort to attract a diverse faculty, staff, and student body. Through his involvement with the Black Caucus of the American Library Association and the activities of the Association of Research Libraries, he works with colleagues to attract a diverse workforce to the profession of library and information science. In 2005, Clay was honored with the University's Gloria W. White Distinguished Service Award, for enhancing the research skills of countless students and faculty.

### C. Michael Cook

C. Michael Cook is the Senior Associate Director of Undergraduate Admissions at Michigan State University, where he is responsible for recruitment, operations, and technology. Mr.

Cook has been an active member of the university's Strategic Enrollment Management Group for the past three years. He has presented at a number of regional and national AACRAO conferences and is the vice chair of the association's Institutional Research Committee. He holds an M.S. in Operations and Systems Management.

Prior to joining Michigan State University in May 2003, Mr. Cook served as an aviator and officer in the United States Air Force. During his 21 years of active duty, his career focused on leadership, management, and Continuous Process Improvement. His overall accomplishments resulted in his nomination and selection as the National Image 2000 United States Air Force Officer of the Year. Mr. Cook serves as a member of the Board of Directors for the Lansing Symphony Orchestra and for the Eli and Edythe Broad Art Museum at Michigan State University.

### James M. Croteau

James M. Croteau is a professor in the Counselor Education and Counseling Psychology Department at Western Michigan University and has been involved in research, practice and advocacy efforts in the professions of psychology and college student affairs for over 25 years. He received his master's and doctoral degrees in Counseling Psychology from Southern Illinois University. He was lead editor and author of multiple chapters in the 2005 book entitled *Deconstructing Heterosexism in the Counseling Professions: A Narrative Approach.* He was co-author, along with Dr. Madonna G. Constantine, of a chapter in that book, entitled "Race and sexual orientation in multicultural counseling: Navigating rough waters."

### Susan A. Dewan

Susan Dewan is Assistant Dean in the School of Liberal Arts, and Director of Military Education at Excelsior College in Albany, NY. She earned her Master of Business Administration at the State University of New York University at Albany; she completed her Bachelor of Science degree in Marketing and Management from Siena College; and she earned a second baccalaureate degree from Excelsior College: a Bachelor of Science degree in Accounting–NYS CPA Track.

Susan has been a staff member at Excelsior College since 1980, serving as the College's liaison to the military community since 1989. Additionally, she is currently an adjunct professor with Excelsior College and Empire State College, teaching online courses in strategies for veterans' success, management and organizational behavior. Susan is an active member in many professional associations, including the Council of College and Military Educators (past Executive Board member), National Academic Advising Association, New York State United Teachers Association, and United University Professions. In 1992, she was honored by the National Academic Advising Association as an Outstanding Academic Advisor Certificate of Merit Award winner.

### Michael Duggan

Michael Duggan is the Director of Enrollment Research and Planning at Suffolk University in Boston. He was awarded his doctorate in Higher Education Administration from the University of Massachusetts-Boston, and holds a Master's degree in economics from Boston University.

Michael is one of a cadre of IPEDS trainers who conduct workshops for those who are charged with completing an institution's annual surveys for the Integrated Postsecondary Education Data System. His research interests include retention issues, first-generation college students, and financial aid. Michael is an active member of AACRAO and of the Association for Institutional Research (AIR). He is the father of fifteen-year-old triplets.

### Carl Einhaus

Carl Einhaus served as Assistant Director of Admissions at Western Michigan University, where he earned a Masters in Student Affairs in Higher Education. He is now Director of Enrollment Services, Colorado Community College Systems Office. Carl has presented at national and regional conferences regarding recruiting Lesbian, Bisexual, Gay and Transgender (LBGT) students and has served as the LBGT Caucus Chair for AACRAO.

### Pat Ellison

Pat Ellison earned a bachelor's degree in history at the University of Texas at Austin in 1972. She has worked for the University for 30 years in the area of graduate and international admissions. She is a member of AACRAO, SACRAO, TACRAO, NAFSA: Association of International Educators, and NAGAP (National Association of Graduate Admissions Professionals), and has done numerous presentations at various meetings over the years regarding process automation and imaging.

In 1990, she became Assistant Director of Admissions and helped establish the Graduate and International Admissions Center at UT. In 2001, she became Associate Director of Admissions and Assistant Dean of UT's Graduate School. She has been active in creating the Graduate Coordinator Network at UT and the Texas International Education Specialists, an organization of international credential evaluators and experts for public institutions in the state of Texas. She has been married to Tom Ellison for thirty-some years, and they are the parents of two daughters.

### Angela J. Evans

As the Director of Admissions at Kennesaw State University, Angela J. Evans is responsible for undergraduate recruitment and admissions counseling, along with the management of the home school admissions program. Prior to joining KSU in 1996, she established the recruitment program at Floyd College in Rome, Georgia and served as an adjunct faculty member at Floyd College and North Metro Technical College. Evans received her B.S.A. in Agricultural Communications from the University of Georgia, her Master of Public Administration from Kennesaw State University, and her Doctor of Education degree in higher education administration from the University of Alabama.

Evans has spent the last eleven years advocating for the creation of admissions policies for home-educated applicants in Georgia. She has conducted and published research involving accreditation (certification) for home schooling programs. In 2001, Evans was recognized by SACRAO with the Margaret Ruthven Perry Distinguished Journalism Award for her journal article, "Home school education: Its impact on a state university." She has served on the GACRAO Executive Committee and on its Professional Access and Equity Committee.

### Adriana Farella

Adriana Farella has spent her entire career working with colleges and universities in the use of technology to support their educational mission. Whether working directly on a campus or for a technology company, Adriana has held key leadership positions. Since February 2007, she has served as The College Board's Executive Director, Strategy & Analytics for the Enrollment Division. Prior to that, she was the Director of Product and Industry Strategy at Xap Corporation, and spent eight years at PeopleSoft as the Director of Product Planning for the PeopleSoft Student Administration Solution suite. Before her time at software companies, Adriana spent fifteen years in administrative positions in New England, at the University of Massachusetts-Boston, and at Wellesley, Pine Manor and Hampshire Colleges.

### Carmen Fortin

Carmen Fortin's experience in higher education has included undergraduate admission and financial aid at public and private institutions, and graduate admission at a private college. She spent a total of 21 years in undergraduate admission at the University of Connecticut, Quinnipiac University, University of Tulsa, Hampshire College, and Bentley College. Her experience in graduate admission has been at the School for Health Studies at Simmons College. At the undergraduate level, she has traveled to recruit students in Latin America and Europe, and she has worked extensively with international students.

Carmen holds a B.A. in French from the University of Maine, Orono; a Certificate of Studies from the University of Bordeaux, France; and an M.A. in Higher Education Administration, from the University of Connecticut, Storrs. She is or has been a member of NACAC (regional delegate), NAGAP, NAFSA, and NAAHP (National Association of Advisors for the Health Professions). Her interests include travel, photography, and gardening. She has taught at an international boarding school in Scotland, and has lived and worked in England, Greece, and Israel.

### Dan D. Garcia

Dan García serves as Vice President for Enrollment Management at West Texas A&M University, and oversees instrumental campus departments that include Admissions, Registration, Financial Aid, Scholarships, International Students, and two federally funded TRIO programs that provide outreach to motivate and support students from disadvantaged backgrounds. Prior to joining West Texas A&M University, Dan served as Associate Vice Chancellor for enrollment services at the University of Washington Tacoma. He received his bachelor's degree from the University of Arizona and his master's degree from the University of Houston-Clear Lake (TX).

García is an active participant in the American Association of Collegiate Registrars and Admissions Officers (AACRAO); he has served as the chair of the Latino/Latina Caucus, chair of the Student Access and Equity Committee, and on the Board of Directors as the Association's Vice President for Access and Equity. He is a regular presenter at national and regional conferences on the subjects of marketing, data management, recruitment, and retention, particularly of underrepresented student populations.

### Jonathan Gayles

Jonathan Gayles earned a doctorate in applied anthropology from the University of South Florida in 2003. He is currently Assistant Professor of African American Studies at Georgia State University. His primary research interests include the cultural context of educational outcomes and educational policy analysis. Dr. Gayles has published a number of articles in academic journals that reflect these interests, including *College and University*, *Anthropology and Education Quarterly*, *The Journal of African American Studies* and *The International Journal of Educational Reform.*

### Lynn Gurganus

Lynn Gurganus has worked as an admissions professional for more than twenty years. He has made numerous presentations for AACRAO, SACRAO, and other regional organization conferences. Lynn is Director of Admissions at the University of Montevallo (Montevallo, Alabama) and currently serves as the President of Alabama ACRAO. He and his wife Kim have three children.

### Joe F. Head

Joe F. Head is Dean of University Admissions and Enrollment Services at Kennesaw State University. He received the APEX Innovation in Technology for Admissions Award in 2004 from AACRAO. In 2003 The Board of Regents of the University System of Georgia presented him with its "Best Practices Award" for the Freshman Admission Predictor and the five other innovations described in this book. In 2005 he received a Lifetime Achievement award from the Georgia Association of Collegiate Registrars and Admissions Officers.

### Stanley E. Henderson

Stanley E. Henderson is Vice Chancellor for Enrollment Management and Student Life at the University of Michigan-Dearborn. His responsibilities include change management aimed at combining enrollment services and traditional student services into a comprehensive division of cross-trained professionals concentrating on student academic success.

Prior to coming to U of M–Dearborn in 2005, he held director, associate vice president, and associate provost positions at Wichita State University, Western Michigan University, University of Cincinnati, and University of Illinois at Urbana-Champaign.

A Phi Beta Kappa graduate of Michigan State University in political science, he earned a Masters of Arts in government from Cornell University. He completed doctoral course work in higher education administration at the University of Illinois at Urbana-Champaign. Active at the national level, Henderson was AACRAO's first vice president for enrollment management, admissions, and financial aid, and was a co-developer of the national Strategic Enrollment Management conferences. He served on the Association's Board of Directors for six years and was president in 1995–96. He co-edited the *Handbook for the College Admissions Profession* and wrote what is considered the definitive history of enrollment management, "On the Brink of a Profession," in *The Strategic Enrollment Management Revolution*. He currently chairs the planning committee for AACRAO's 2010 Centennial and has been a frequent national and international presenter and consultant for a wide variety of institutions. In 2007 he received AACRAO's Distinguished Service Award.

### Rob Hoover

Rob Hoover is the Assistant Dean for Admission and Student Services at the Nell Hodgson Woodruff School of Nursing at Emory University. In this role, he provides leadership to the School in the areas of recruitment, admission, financial aid, student records, and student affairs. Prior to coming to Emory he worked at Samford University in Birmingham, Alabama for nine years, ultimately serving as Director of Admission there.

Rob received both his B.S. and M.B.A. from Samford University.

His primary professional focus is on providing leadership through the incorporation of practical and creative business practices in the higher education administration environment.

### Thomas M. Hughes

Thomas M. Hughes retired as Associate Director for Graduate Admissions at Kennesaw State University (GA). He now works part-time as Special Assistant to the Dean, University Admissions and Enrollment Services. Having earned a Ph.D. in political science, Hughes is the former director of the Master of City Management Program at East Tennessee State University. He has a long record of community service as a sponsor of youth organizations, a CASA volunteer, a juvenile court mediator and a community activist.

### Esther Hugo

Dr. Esther Hugo coordinates the Outreach Program for Santa Monica College, a position she has held since 1998. Esther oversees the Office of School Relations, which includes outreach to high schools, campus and community events, and presentations throughout the Santa Monica community. Her experience prior to Santa Monica College includes work as the College Counselor at Westchester High School, a comprehensive public high school in Los Angeles.

Esther serves on the Board of Directors for the National Association of College Admission Counseling (NACAC), and has served as national Chair of the Council of the Guidance and Admission Assembly of the College Board. She maintains her contact with the counseling facet of the profession through her appointments as an adjunct professor in the graduate counseling departments at UCLA and at Loyola Marymount University. Esther holds a doctorate in Educational Leadership from UCLA.

### Dean R. Kahler

Dr. Dean R. Kahler is currently the Associate Vice President for Academic Affairs-Enrollment Management at Western Kentucky University. In his present role, he leads a team of directors from the offices of Admissions, Registrar, Financial Aid, Academic Advising and Retention, First Year Programs, Student Disability Support Services and the TRIO Programs. Prior to this position, Dean served as the Director of Admissions at WKU, as well as the Assistant Director and then interim Associate Director in the Office of Admissions and Records at Southern Illinois University Carbondale.

Dean Kahler has a Ph.D. from Southern Illinois University Carbondale and a Masters degree in Public Administration from SIUC. He received an undergraduate degree in sociology/criminal justice from Winona State University in Winona, Minnesota. Dean has served on various professional committees including the Southern Association of Collegiate Registrars and Admissions Officers (SACRAO) Editorial Journal Review Board, the Kentucky ACT Advisory Council, and AACRAO's Admissions Policies and Practices Committee. He is currently President of the Kentucky Association of Collegiate Registrars and Admissions Officers (KACRAO).

### Christie M. Kangas

Christie M. Kangas is Director of Undergraduate Admissions at Texas State University-San Marcos and has been an active member of AACRAO for almost 20 years, serving on a variety of committees and presenting on a number of topics. Kangas has 21 years experience working in admissions in three states. She previously worked at the University of Southern Colorado (now Colorado State University-Pueblo) and the University of Northern Iowa. Currently she is SACRAO's Vice President for Professional Development, serves on the Assessment Committee for TACRAO and the Texas ACT Council, and Chairs the "ApplyTexas" Advisory and Texas Enrollment Services Efficiency Committees. She has been a contributing author to the *SACRAO Journal* and served as project director for a U.S. Department of Education grant. Prior to working in admissions, Kangas taught at two community colleges.

### Christine Kerlin

Christine Kerlin is currently the Vice President for Enrollment Management and Executive Director of the University Center at Everett Community College (Washington State). Prior to arriving at Everett in 1996, she served as Registrar and Director of Admissions and Records at Central Oregon Community College, and as the Director of Admissions at The Evergreen State College in Olympia, Washington.

Christine holds a B.A. from Western Washington State College, an M.Ed. from Western Washington University, and an Ed.D. from Oregon State University. She is active in AACRAO, a past President of Pacific ACRAO and past Chair of NAFSA Region One, and often makes presentations at those conferences.

Among her contributions to the profession, she has chaired AACRAO's Task Force 2000 and Nominations and Elections Committee, co-facilitated AACRAO's enrollment management workshops at AACRAO's annual Strategic Enrollment Management (SEM) conferences, served as founding faculty of PACRAO's Emerging Professionals Institute, and authored chapters in AACRAO's recent *International Guide, Essentials of Enrollment Management*, and *The Registrar's Guide: Evolving Best Practices in Records and Registration.*

### Lisa Kujawa

Lisa Kujawa has served as the Assistant Provost for Enrollment Management at Lawrence Technological University (Southfield, MI) since 2002. She is a veteran of over 20 years working in the fields of admissions, recruitment and enrollment management. Before joining Lawrence Tech as Director of Admissions in 1998, she worked at Mercy College of Detroit as the Director of Admissions and Scholarships and at the University of Michigan-Dearborn as the Associate Director of Admissions and Director of Information Support Services.

A past president of the Michigan Association of Collegiate Registrar and Admissions Officers (MACRAO) and a current member of the Midwest ACT Executive Council, Kujawa holds a bachelor's degree in industrial psychology and a Master of Arts in training and development. She also has attended the Harvard University Management Development program (in 2002). She chairs numerous committees at Lawrence Technological University on Strategic Planning, Enrollment Planning, Banner Implementation, and Mission Effectiveness.

### Meredyth A. Leahy

Dr. Meredyth A. Leahy, Dean, School of Liberal Arts, Excelsior College has over 35 years experience in adult education at Temple University and the Pennsylvania Department of Education, Cabrini College, and Muhlenberg College, prior to moving to Excelsior in 1994.

Her involvement in military education began in 1979, when she served as V Corps Education Officer under Temple University's contract for the Army Continuing Education Services (ACES) Basic Skills Education Program. Dr. Leahy earned her undergraduate degree at Edinboro State University, and her masters and doctorate degrees in adult education from Temple University, Philadelphia, PA.

She serves on the SOCAD Advisory Council and is a lifetime member of the Pennsylvania Association for Adult and Continuing Education, which named her Outstanding Adult Educator in 1987. She is a charter member of the American Association for Adult and Continuing Education, and a long- time member of the Council of College and Military Educators, which awarded Excelsior its Institutional Award for Excellence in Military Education in 2005. She has presented at a number of state and national conferences, including the 2003 and 2006 DOD World Wide Education Symposium.

### Chidiogo Madubike

Chidiogo Madubike obtained her bachelor's degree in Electronics Engineering from the University of Nigeria in West Africa. She moved to Texas to pursue a Ph.D. in electrical engineering at the Cullen College of Engineering in the University of Houston. As a Ph.D. candidate, she worked for the University as a teaching assistant and instructor in the department of Electrical and Computer Engineering.

She was also involved in the organization of the Women in Engineering (WIE) program and the Girls Reaching and Demonstrating Excellence in Engineering (GRADE) camp for the College of Engineering. Her research was in the area of parallel computations and architectures and involved controlled drug delivery simulations. Chidiogo currently works as an electrical design engineer at Schlumberger in Sugar Land, Texas; she designs Measurement While Drilling (MWD) tools for high temperature and high pressure downhole applications.

### Rebecca Mathews

Rebecca Mathews holds a B.A. in Sociology/Anthropology from Carleton College and a M.Ed. in Higher Education Administration from Suffolk University. She began her career in higher education as a financial aid officer and retains a strong interest in issues concerning financial aid. She has worked in institutional research for seven years.

### James E. McLeod

James McLeod is Vice Chancellor for Students and Dean of the College of Arts and Sciences at the Washington University in Saint Louis. He joined Washington University in 1974 as an assistant professor of German, was named assistant dean of the Graduate School of Arts and Sciences from 1974 to 1977, and then became assistant to then-Chancellor William H. Danforth between 1977 and 1987. From 1987 to 1992, he was director of the African and Afro-American studies Program. In 1992 he was named Dean of the College of Arts and Sciences.

In his position as both Dean of the College and Vice Chancellor for Students, Dean McLeod is concerned with all facets of student life, from admissions through graduation. He oversees all aspects of the College Office, from advising to curriculum to commencement.

### Mark Mitsui

Mark has worked as an Assistant Dean at Green River Community College, Director of Student Success at North Seattle Community College, and Instructor at Renton Technical College. He has been recognized by peers with an Outstanding Faculty Award in 1994 and a Chair Academy Exemplary Leadership Award in Higher Education in 2006.

### Susan Smith Nash

Susan Smith Nash has developed courses, curricula, and distance academic programs for active-duty military professionals since the 1990s. With a special interest in e-learning (including mobile learning), Nash has published articles and book chapters in journals such as the *International Journal of Knowledge and Learning Objects*. Her latest book, *Excellence in College Teaching and Learning: Classroom and Online*, co-authored by George Henderson, was published by Charles C. Thomas. Nash maintains an active edu-blog which contains podcasts on e-learning.

### Michael A. Olivas

Michael A. Olivas is the William B. Bates Distinguished Chair in Law at the University of Houston Law Center and Director of the Institute for Higher Education Law and Governance at UH. Previously, he has chaired the University of Houston's graduate program in Higher Education, and served as Associate Dean of the Law Center. He was named Bates Professor of Law in 1996, Bates Distinguished Chair in 2002, and was selected for the Esther Farfel Award, as the Outstanding Professor at the University of Houston in 2001.

Before joining the faculty at the University of Houston in 1982, he worked as Director of Research for the League of United Latin American Citizens (LULAC) in Washington, D.C.; functioned as Special Counsel to then-Chancellor Donna Shalala of the University of Wisconsin; and served as General Counsel to the American Association of University Professors (AAUP).

Professor Olivas holds a B.A. (magna cum laude) from the Pontifical College Josephinum, an M.A. and Ph.D. from the Ohio State University, and a J.D. from Georgetown University Law Center. He is the author or co-author of eight books, including *The Dilemma of Access* (1979), *Latino College Students* (1986), *Prepaid College Tuition Programs* (1993), *The Law and Higher Education* (2006) and *Colored Men and Hombres Aqui* (2006). His book, *Education Law Stories,* is forthcoming.

A member of the Pennsylvania Bar, he has chaired the Section on Education Law of the Association of American Law Schools three times, and has twice chaired the Section on Immigration Law.

### Alicia Ortega

Alicia Ortega has worked in college admissions since 1997 and is currently the Senior Assistant Director of Admissions and coordinator of Multicultural Recruitment at Oregon State University (OSU). Alicia also worked as an Admissions Counselor and Assistant Director of Admissions at Oregon State University and Portland State University, respectively.

Alicia holds a Bachelors Degree in political science from OSU and a Master's Degree in Educational Policy, Foundations and Administrative Studies from Portland State University. She has served as an Assembly Delegate for the Pacific Northwest region to the National Association for College Admissions Counseling (NACAC), and has also coordinated the region's Summer Institute on College Admission. She serves on the Athletic and Panhellenic Advisory Boards of OSU, and co-developed the university's "START Bilingue" (Bilingual Start) summer orientation program.

### Trevor Packer

Trevor Packer is the College Board's vice president responsible for leadership of the Advanced Placement Program, with overall responsibility for strategic planning, and ongoing development and operations of the program. Named vice president in 2007, Packer previously served as executive director of the AP Program, where for four years he managed its growth and national expansion and worked to strengthen the program's overall quality and reputation. Before serving as executive director, he was manager of the AP Program policy and processes, overseeing day-to-day management of the printing, shipping, and scoring of the AP Exams and the administration of the AP Exams at 15,000 schools annually.

Packer holds a B.A. and an M.A. in English from Brigham Young University. As a former lecturer and instructor in composition and literature at Brigham Young University and at John Jay College, Packer has written a manual on composition pedagogy, has authored works on Willa Cather and abolitionist Sojourner Truth, and is currently working on a book examining Virginia Woolf's relationship to the Pre-Raphaelites.

### Sandra Wade Pauly

Sandra Wade Pauly graduated with a B.A. from the University of California at Berkeley, an M.A. from the Monterey Institute of International Studies (CA), and attended the London School of Economic and Political Science. She served as Assistant Professor of political science at San Francisco State University for five years before embarking on a career in international education at the International School of Manila. There she chaired the Social Studies Department before becoming IB Diploma Program Coordinator and college counselor. Sandra moved to

Singapore in 1999 to serve as Director of Studies at the United World College of Southeast Asia, where she organized the college's first professional development program and developed its first teacher appraisal instrument. She is currently the IB North America University and Government Liaison and works out of the IB North America Vancouver office in Canada.

### Reta Pikowsky

Reta Pikowsky currently serves as Registrar at the Georgia Institute of Technology (Atlanta). She is an active member of AACRAO, having served as a committee member, committee chair, group coordinator, and as chair of the program committee for the 2008 annual meeting in Orlando. She contributed two chapters—on "Graduation, Commencement and Diplomas" and on "Preparing for Accreditation"—to AACRAO's sister publication to this work, *The Registrar's Guide: Evolving Best Practices in Records and Registration.* A frequent speaker at professional meetings, she has presented topics that include managing and using data effectively, assessment of services in the registrar's office, preparing for accreditation, and use of technology in the registrar's office. She holds degrees from Monmouth College (Monmouth, Illinois) and the University of Illinois at Urbana-Champaign.

### Kevin Pollock

Dr. Kevin Pollock received his Ph.D. in Higher, Adult, and Lifelong Education from Michigan State University. He also holds a Master of Arts in Education and a Bachelor of Science in Education, both from Central Michigan University. Nationally recognized as a public speaker, he has spoken at over forty conferences and colleges—including NASPA, NISOD, AACRAO SEM Conference, the League for Innovation, the Small College Enrollment Conference, the First Annual Community College Symposium, and the ACT Planners Conference—on such topics as student success, at-risk students, retention, mentoring, strategic planning, continuous quality improvement, assessment, and organizational transformation. He has written over a dozen article and book chapters and his writings are included in the *SEM Anthology* and *Essentials of Enrollment Management: Cases in the Field.* He is currently Vice President of Student Services at West Shore Community College (Scottville, MI).

### Odie Brant Porter

Odie Brant Porter is a citizen of the Seneca Nation of Indians and a member of the turtle clan. She is currently the Assistant Provost for Planning at Syracuse University, where she also conducts recruiting and outreach for local Native students. In previous positions, Odie has served as the Budget Director at the University of Kansas and as the Advisor to the Provost at the University of Iowa. She earned her M.B.A. from the University of Kansas in 1997 and her B.A. from California State University Hayward (now CSU East Bay). For the 2007–08 academic year, Odie is enjoying a sabbatical at home at the Seneca Nation with her husband, Robert Odawi Porter and two children, Olivia and Elliot.

### Anne M. Richard

Anne M. Richard has been Associate Dean for Admissions and Financial Aid at The George Washington University Law School in Washington, DC, since 2006. Prior to that time, she served as Associate Dean of Admissions at George Mason University School of Law in Arlington, Virginia.

Before entering law school administration, Dean Richard worked as a trial attorney in the U.S. Department of Justice, Civil Division, Commercial Litigation Branch, in Washington, D.C. She also served as an assistant counsel in the Office of Professional Responsibility of the U.S. Department of Justice. From 1984 until 1995, Dean Richard was in private practice in the Virginia law firm, Hazel & Thomas, P.C. both as an associate and as a partner, specializing in commercial business litigation.

Dean Richard earned her J.D. at Yale Law School, where she was a founding editor of the Yale Journal on Regulation. She earned her bachelor's and master's degrees summa cum laude from Boston College, and is admitted to practice law in Virginia, the District of Columbia, and Florida.

### Jane Rohrback

Jane Rohrback is the Director of Admissions at Lawrence Technological University. She has been working in the field of admissions, recruitment and enrollment management for 18 years. Her career began at Lawrence Tech in 1994 as an Admissions Counselor; she became Assistant Director of Admissions there in 1999, and Director in 2002.

Before 1994, Ms. Rohrback had worked in placement and admissions departments in two Michigan private postsecondary institutions. She received her Bachelor of Arts in psychology from Central Michigan University in 1987, and her Master of Arts in Instructional Design and Performance Improvement from the University of Michigan-Dearborn in 2006. Ms. Rohrback has been married for 17 years and has three children, Samantha, Austin and Jack.

### Michele Sandlin

Michele Sandlin is the Director of Admissions and the Campus Visitor Center at Oregon State University. Michele has been with Oregon State for over 11 years, and during that time the enrollment of the university has increased by over 40%. She first served as the Senior Associate Director for five years, her expertise being operations, non-cognitive and holistic admissions, personnel and team building. Before coming to Oregon State, she served at Western State College in Colorado, University of Oregon, Pacific University, and Portland State University. She completed her Master of Science degree in Higher Education Administration at Portland State University, and her Bachelor of Science degree in Human Sciences from Colorado State University.

Michele launched and served as the Chair of the AACRAO Admissions Institute, which provides practical training across the country for new professionals; has been a President of

Oregon ACRAO; recently served as Program Coordinator for AACRAO Group 1 Admissions and Enrollment Management, and is the current President-Elect of PACRAO. In 2005–06, she was the recipient of the AACRAO Bilger Outstanding Service Award. Michele currently serves on the North America College and University Recognition Board for the International Baccalaureate Organization.

### Luke David Schultheis

Luke David Schultheis is Dean of The School of Hospitality Management and The Culinary Arts at Monroe College, which has campuses in New York City, in Westchester (New Rochelle), and on the island of St. Lucia in the Caribbean. He previously served the school as Director of Admissions and Director of Outreach.

Luke has an M.S. from New York University in Hospitality Industry Studies: Asset Management, and holds two degrees—an M.A. and an Ed.M.—in Higher Education Administration, both from Columbia University.

Luke has researched and presented widely on issues related to urban colleges, college access for the poor and retention issues. Currently, a core part of his duties includes working with urban populations so that they can enjoy the benefits of a college education.

### Catherine Solow

Catherine Solow is Assistant Dean for Student Affairs and Curriculum, and Director of Admissions at the University of Iowa Carver College of Medicine. Ms. Solow received an M.A. in Higher Education Administration from the University of Iowa and has held leadership positions in student services for over twenty years in undergraduate, graduate and professional degree programs. She joined the Carver College of Medicine in 1999, where her primary responsibility is oversight of the M.D. admissions process.

Ms. Solow currently serves on the Advisory Board of the American Medical College Application Service (AMCAS), and is a regional representative to the Committee on Admissions of the American Association of Medical Colleges (AAMC).

### Theodore L. Spencer

Ted Spencer is Associate Vice Provost and Executive Director of Undergraduate Admissions at the University of Michigan-Ann Arbor.

He is co-chair of the Enrollment Working Group, the body that manages undergraduate enrollment numbers, and oversees all functions related to the undergraduate admissions procedures. Ted is a Lieutenant Colonel in the United States Air Force, Retired. Prior to his responsibilities at Michigan, he was an Associate Director of Admissions at the USAF Academy. After graduating from Tennessee State University (Nashville) with a B.S. in political science and from Pepperdine University with an M.S. in sociology, he received his commission through the AFROTC program and entered the intelligence career field.

In the professional arena, Ted has served as a member of the Secondary School Committee of the Michigan ACRAO. He has also served as a Legislative Representative and a member of the ACT Executive Counsel, Midwest Region, of the Michigan Association of College Admissions Counselors (MACAC). Ted has given presentations at numerous professional conferences and garnered the John B. Muir Editors Award, given by the National Association of College Admissions Counseling (NACAC) for an article published in the Association's Journal entitled "Why Admission Directors are Social Engineers." In the Fall of 2001, Ted was featured as a hero in the article entitled "Point Man on Diversity Defense" in the *College Board Review*. Ted also served as a College Board Trustee from 2002–2006.

### Eric Staab

After earning his bachelor's and master's degrees from Indiana University, Eric began his career in higher education at the University of Chicago as the Assistant Director of the Office of International Affairs. Subsequently he worked for St. Olaf College in the Office of Admission as the Assistant Director of International Student Admissions, and then for Grinnell College, where he served for ten years as the Associate Dean for Admission and Coordinator of International Admission. Currently he is the Dean of Admission at Kalamazoo College (MI). Eric has been an active member of AACRAO for over ten years, and has served on the Board of Directors for the association.

### Robert J. Sternberg

Robert J. Sternberg is the Dean of the School of Arts and Sciences at Tufts University and Professor of Psychology. He is also Director of the Center for the Psychology of Abilities, Competencies, and Expertise (PACE), at Tufts. Sternberg served as President of the American Psychological Association in 2003. He is the author of more than 1,100 journal articles, book chapters, and books and has received more than $20 million in government and other grants and contracts for his research. The central focus of his research is intelligence, creativity, wisdom, and leadership.

### John T. "Tom" Stewart

Tom earned a Bachelor of Chemical Engineering and a Master of Science in Teaching from the University of Florida. Prior to joining Miami-Dade Community College in 1966, he worked as a research chemical engineer at Dow Chemical Company and as a lieutenant in the U.S. Air Force in France. He became the first registrar for the Kendall Campus, and later served as director of admissions as well as campus registrar. In 2000, he became the college registrar and was responsible for implementing the touchtone telephone registration system, an imaging system, and the current student information system. He was also involved in the creation of the Florida system to exchange electronic student records.

Up until his retirement in 2003, Tom was active in both the Florida ACRAO and Southern ACRAO, serving as president of each. He has been active in AACRAO since his first conference in 1968. He has served on the Task Force for the *Academic Record and Transcript Guide,* was chair of the AACRAO SPEEDE Committee from 1989 to 1993, and received the AACRAO Distinguished Service Award in 1992 as well as SunGard Higher Education's APEX award, and Honorary Membership in AACRAO in 2003. He still serves on the AACRAO SPEEDE Committee.

### Julie Martin Trenor

Dr. Julie Martin Trenor is the Director of Undergraduate Student Recruitment and Retention in the Cullen College of Engineering at the University of Houston (UH). She is also Instructional and Research Assistant Professor there. She holds a Ph.D. in Materials Science and Engineering from Virginia Tech and a B.S. in the same field from North Carolina State University. Dr. Trenor founded and now directs the UH women-in-engineering program, WELCOME (Women in Engineering Learning Community for Maximizing Excellence), and develops and teaches freshman engineering courses. Her research program focuses on increasing the diversity of undergraduate students in engineering.

### Ira Tyszler

Ira Tyszler is Dean of Enrollment Management and Institutional Research and Review at Touro College/Touro University (New York and California). He received his B.A. in English from the City College of New York and an M.A. in English from New York University. Ira has over thirty years of experience in various registrar, admissions, and enrollment management roles. He is a past president of two regional ACRAOs and has been an officer and member of several other professional organizations.

### Wanda L. E. Viento

Wanda Viento is the Associate Director of Student Development and also the Women's Center Coordinator at Boise State University (Idaho).

She holds a Master of Social Work from the University of Michigan and a Ph.D. in Student Affairs in Higher Education from Western Michigan University, with a specialty in multicultural issues. She served as a counselor at Kalamazoo College where she advised the LBGTQ student group and was the coordinator of Lesbian, Bisexual and Gay Student Services at Western Michigan University for two years.

### David R. Wallace

A native of Knoxville, Tennessee, Wallace received a Bachelor's degree from the University of Louisville (KY) in 1967 and a Master's degree from the University of Tennessee at Knoxville (UTK) in 1972. After completing the coursework for a Doctor of Education degree at UTK in 1974, he accepted a position as Director of the Office of Admissions at The University of Memphis (then Memphis State University). His duties there have included the centralized admission of all applicants: undergraduate, graduate and professional; domestic and international; degree and non-degree seeking; and new and readmitted. In addition, the recruiting and orientation functions were part of his responsibilities, as well as the evaluation of transfer credit and the assigning of residency classifications for fee purposes. Currently, his office processes more than 26,000 applications each year.

As a member of Tennessee ACRAO (TNACRAO), SACRAO, and AACRAO since 1974, Wallace has served as a presenter and facilitator numerous times on many subjects. He has also been elected to several offices at the state level including President of TNACRAO in 2000–2001.

In addition to serving on many SACRAO and AACRAO committees, he is presently a member of the Auditing Committee for SACRAO and is chair of the Admissions Policies and Practices Committee for AACRAO.

### Stephanie J. Waterman

Stephanie J. Waterman (Onondaga tribe, turtle clan), worked at Syracuse University (SU) for almost 27 years. Her dissertation was the first study of Haudenosaunee (Iroquois) college experiences. Her research interests are Native American college experiences, the role staff play in student retention, race and gender in higher education, indigenous methodologies/pedagogy, and college transition. Dr. Waterman is an Assistant Professor in Educational Leadership at the Margaret Warner Graduate School of Education and Human Development at the University of Rochester, teaching courses in higher education.

Dr. Waterman was a 2005 National Academy of Education/Spencer Post-Doctoral Fellow. In addition to teaching in the SU school of education, she served as Faculty Associate with the Native Student Program (NSP) through the Office of Multicultural Affairs. She has published articles in the *Journal of American Indian Education* and the *Journal of School Violence*. She serves on the Onondaga Nation Higher Education Committee and is a member of the Central New York Native American Consortium.

### Robert Watkins

Robert Watkins is Assistant Director of Admissions in the Graduate and International Admissions Center of The University of Texas at Austin. He has been in Admissions at UT–Austin for 28 years, predominantly in international student admission and credential evaluation. Robert holds a Bachelor's and Master's in history from The University of Texas at Austin.

A member of NAFSA: Association of International Educators since 1983, he has served that organization in a number of capacities: As ADSEC (Admissions Section) Regional Representative 1984–86; ADSEC National Team Member and Chair 1992–97; NAFSA

Representative to the National Council on the Evaluation of Foreign Educational Credentials 1992–2000 (Chair of the Council 1996–2000); and Chair of NAFSA Region III 2000. Robert has served on the NCAA Foreign Student Records Committee since 2000, chairing that committee since 2001. He is also a member of AACRAO and serves on the International Publications Advisory Committee (IPAC).

### Rupert Wilkinson

Rupert Wilkinson, Emeritus Professor of American Studies and History at the University of Sussex (UK), is the author of *Aiding Students, Buying Students* (2005), a history of financial aid. He has written about financial aid for the *Chronicle of Higher Education*, the *College Board Review*, and the *Journal of Student Financial Aid*, and was the 2007 recipient of the Robert P. Huff Golden Quill Award from the National Association of Student Financial Aid Administrators (NASFAA).

Rupert spent his early life in the Philippines, has an A.B. degree in government from Harvard and an interdisciplinary Ph.D. in history and the social sciences from Stanford, and has taught at several American colleges and universities. Co-founder of the International Summer School at Sussex, he has visited over a hundred American colleges and universities as a study-abroad administrator, combining that work with research on student aid.

### Brian Williams

Brian Williams serves as Vice President for Enrollment at John Carroll University (University Heights, Ohio), working in various capacities across the institution. Prior to joining the University, he had worked at Providence College since 1998, most recently serving as Dean of Enrollment Services. Additionally, he has prior work in admission and financial aid at both La Salle University (Philadelphia, PA) and Saint Louis University (St. Louis, MO). Mr. Williams holds an M.A. in Higher Education Administration from Boston University and a B.A. in English from the University of New Hampshire. Over the last five years, he has presented at over twelve regional and national conferences on the admission process, enrollment management systems, and trends in degree audit, scholarships and financial aid.

/ CHAPTER ONE /

*by Stanley E. Henderson, M.A.*
*Vice Chancellor for Enrollment Management and Student Life*
*University of Michigan-Dearborn*

01

# Admissions' Evolving Role: From Gatekeeper to Strategic Partner

American higher education has always been about a tenuous balance between quantity and quality of students. "The challenge of maintaining a class size large enough to safeguard financial solvency while maintaining a class profile high enough to be able to comprehend the faculty's instruction has preoccupied colleges and universities since long before admissions offices appeared. Enrollments cycled through feast and famine, and standards followed the same roller coaster ride. As colleges faced the uncertainties of their times, they became eminently resourceful in turning aside adversity.... Enrollment management was a practical necessity before it became a theoretical basis for organizing recruitment and retention" (Henderson 1998).

## The Rise of the Admissions Office

Admissions offices—and their staff—are a relatively new development in higher education. They—and other areas of specialization—grew out of a recognition that the increasing complexity of collegiate institutions required specialized services and time to manage them that could no longer be handled just by giving faculty added work.

As the rise of the high school movement at the end of the nineteenth century began to fuel enrollments, one of the first administrative positions to develop was the registrar. The registrar, complained an early twentieth-century writer, was a person "whose authority is supreme, whose methods are autocratic, [and] whose ways are beyond the highest research" (Veysey 1965). The responsibilities of early registrars were in fact so broad as to encompass many of the responsibilities of today's admissions officers: registrars "often corresponded with prospective students, conducted high school visitations, sent and received application forms, oversaw scholarship and financial aid awards, greeted freshmen and transfer students, conducted their orientation, advised them on programs and courses, counseled them on vocations and careers, scheduled classes, forecast enrollments, predicted tuition income, analyzed teaching loads, responded to questionnaires, conducted other institutional research, suggested curriculum revisions to the faculty, signed diplomas, and even shook hands with graduating seniors at commencement" (Conner 1979).

Before the start of World War I, some private institutions were employing admissions directors to bring their campuses to the attention of prospective students. Indeed Columbia University established what may have been the first Office of Admissions in 1915. (Rudolph 1962) Still, not until 1937 were admissions offices widespread enough to warrant the formation of a professional organization—the Association of College Admission Counselors, now the National Association for College Admission Counseling (NACAC) (Quann *et al.* 1979).

The shrinking college enrollments caused by the Great Depression were creating a market for recruiters who could specialize in finding scarce students to fill empty seats. However, it would be 1949, as returning GIs flooded campuses, before the registrars' association, the American Association of Collegiate Registrars (founded in 1910), added "and Admissions Officers" to its name and created gatekeepers to manage the student influx that threatened to overwhelm higher education (Constance 1973).

Whatever the terminology involved, every era of higher education has had someone to fill the role of admissions director. "...Sometimes it was the clergy of a particular sect, sometimes the institutional president, sometimes the registrar. In every case the person playing the role filled by the admissions director today has been involved in determining the requirements for institutional survival, reading the mood of the public, ascertaining the size of the applicant pool, and creating a product. Whether to educate the clergy; attract the self-made frontiersmen; entice the sons of merchants and farmers; or welcome the high school graduates, the GIs, or the baby boomers—the admissions function has shaped the quantity and quality of institutions, and borne the burden of balancing the two" (Henderson 1998).

By the 1950s admissions was becoming truly institutionalized as "a theory of administrative action based upon knowledge of the interaction between a given college environment and various crucial characteristics of the applicant population. Selection and guidance represent the techniques and procedures through which this 'philosophy' is implemented" (Fishman 1958). Standardized approaches to this "administrative action" were important to the gatekeeping function of admissions in times of plenty. Grades and the Carnegie unit, the standardized instructional unit, became the iconic tools of the admissions officer. "Indeed, [grades] are undoubtedly becoming more, rather than less, difficult to eliminate. Increasing numbers of young people are attending college, and grades based largely upon achievement examinations are a part of the traditional bureaucratic machinery for 'processing' these students" (Fishman 1958).

## The Gatekeeper Becomes a Recruiter

While higher education burnished the role of admissions as gatekeeper during the Baby Boom years of the 1960s and early 1970s, at least one institution was signaling a change in admissions philosophy—a change toward targeted recruiting—that would have a profound impact when synchronized with business practice in the 1980s and 1990s.

An example from the state of Michigan will illustrate this change. In the early 1960s, Michigan State University (MSU) embarked on a decade-long mission to move out from under the shadow of its cross-state rival, the University of Michigan in Ann Arbor, by *targeting a specialized segment* of the burgeoning student market: National Merit Scholars. The National Merit Corporation, funded by private business, industry, and foundations, was broadening its ability to recognize outstanding high school students by developing college and university sponsorship of Merit Scholarships. Michigan State saw the opportunity to attract a different kind of student and use that as leverage to change the "cow college" image that its Land Grant heritage had given it. By the end of the 1960s, MSU would become the largest sponsor of collegiate Merit Scholars in the country.

There was considerable risk involved in such a strategy. Enrollments were burgeoning, with waves of Baby Boomers enveloping campuses across the country. At the time, there was a decidedly distasteful cast to the notion of actually recruiting students. This view was particularly common among faculty, and even some leading admissions professionals. The emphasis on merit scholarships, rather than the comparatively new concept of need-based aid, which was just then being introduced in federal financial aid programs with the National Defense Student Loans after Sputnik, also flew in the face of prevailing admissions philosophy. Having more Merit Scholars than any other school carried little weight in many quarters because, cried the naysayers, these students were seduced—"bought"—into coming to MSU. The critical voices asserted that such students were choosing based on institutional merit aid, rather than on institutional merit alone. Nevertheless, in spite of the criticism, MSU's foray into National Merit sponsorship represented the first time a public institution had become an active participant in the college selection process, rather than sitting passively while the student exercised all of the choice.

In fact, a clearer understanding of the MSU National Merit strategy shows that it represented far more than just an exercise of buying power. Instead the university popularized a new motto for college admissions: "They recruit best who serve best" was both a training mantra and a guiding principle for MSU admissions officers through the better part of a decade.

Under the leadership of a communications professor turned vice president, Gordon Sabine, the admissions team at MSU devised a suite of personalized services that beat the opposition every time. Picking up the list of National Merit semi-finalists at National Merit headquarters in Evanston, Illinois the day it was released to the public allowed MSU to have its own congratulatory letter arrive at the same time the official notification went to the student. Being first communicated a sense that MSU was more interested, and would be more attentive to student needs. Compared to the experience where other institutions might send a letter recognizing the student six to nine months later, MSU had a decided jump on other schools in making its own particular case to the student.

Using the entire admissions staff to personalize semi-finalist letters (in the days when "Dear Student" letters were the norm) established a personal relationship between school and student. Information sessions (on campus and in cities throughout the country), newsletters, and personalized recruitment—all were utilized to tell prospective Merit Scholars about how MSU could help meet their needs and goals.

MSU's recruitment through service went beyond mere personal contact and relationship building. *Structure* was also an integral part of providing service in a strategic way to new students. "New student" financial aid and scholarship programs were pulled from the financial aid office and combined with admissions to create an Office of Admissions and Scholarships, surely an ancestor of one-stop shopping. Through collaboration with the counseling and testing office, Gordon Sabine also created an orientation program. MSU's communications, relationship building, and integrated structuring of services "ensured consistency of service to students throughout the recruitment process and provided a bridge to enrollment" (Henderson 2001).

In spite of the misgivings of faculty and admissions professionals at other institutions, MSU's National Merit strategy played a significant and positive role in changing the profile of students attracted to the East Lansing campus. Five years after MSU began its National Merit sponsorship—and the accompanying changes in communications and structure—high-ranking University of Michigan administrators were reportedly asking what had happened to the Ann Arbor campus's traditional lock on Michigan high school valedictorians and salutatorians.

"In that era of proliferating Baby Boomer applications, many admissions officers' chief responsibility was to discourage or deny. Michigan State was perhaps the first public university to target and recruit a *specific population* in order to change the mix of students on campus. [Emphasis added.] As a strategy, it was based on providing service to parents and students without benefit of being informed by market research or techniques. It actually proved to be one of the earliest precursors of what we now refer to as *enrollment management*" (Henderson 2001).

As the Baby Boom of the 1960s and '70s slipped into the Baby Bust of the 1980s, more and more colleges began to emulate MSU's practice of targeting specific segments with strategic services. "The decline in the college-age cohort...places all but the most selective institutions in the position of recruiting, rather than admitting students..." (Stewart 1992).

A significant change was occurring in college admissions. "[I]nstitutions turned increasingly to business methods, initially adapting commercial direct mail strategies and techniques, then moving to telemarketing and telecommunications methods, [and finally] targeting market segments of high-ability students, students of color, specific academic majors, children of alumni, and so forth" (Henderson 1998). College admissions found itself in a new landscape with new language, new technologies, and a new culture.

So great was the change that "admissions practitioners of the late 1960s and early 1970s would probably recognize only the general admission objectives and some of the admission folkways that have persisted to the present. Much that is done now on the admissions landscape would be foreign territory to many of them" (Stewart 1992).

## The Birth of Enrollment Management

Enter Jack Maguire and Frank Campanella at Boston College in 1974. Maguire, a physics professor named dean of admissions, and Campanella, a Harvard-educated executive vice president, tackled almost insurmountable odds that had actually led BC at that time to consider abandoning its private status for the public sector.

As these two colleagues struggled to meet ever-growing deficits through intense academic planning and reengineering of processes and policies, Campanella came to the conclusion that admissions alone could not meet the challenges facing the campus. Enrollment needed a broader perspective than Maguire and his admissions staff could provide, Campanella believed. Administrative oversight, attention to faculty matters such as teaching loads and schedules, sources of tuition generation, and pricing strategies all needed to be integrated into a new approach to enrollment planning. Campanella could see relationships between market demands and academic planning that people in traditional office silos missed. His comprehensive view took him to a new level. "Managing enrollments was a way of managing the business of higher education" (Maguire 1999; Scannell 1999).

In 1974 Campanella told Maguire that he wanted to restructure the way in which BC handled enrollment planning and call it "enrollment management." On November 11 of that year, he wrote a memo "to introduce the idea of 'enrollment management'" (Campanella 1974). He envisioned enrollment management as directing admissions resources, minimizing student attrition, predicting market demands, and developing financial aid strategies. "I am convinced," he wrote, "that enrollment management will shortly be the 'name of the game.' I am equally convinced that it will require a coordinated and integrated effort of the highest order." The rest, as they say, is history (Henderson 1998).

Maguire became the chief implementer of this new paradigm at BC. In breathing life into enrollment management, he fundamentally changed admissions in higher education. "Simply stated," he wrote, "enrollment management is *a process that brings together often disparate functions* having to do with recruiting, funding, tracking, retaining, and replacing students as they move toward, within, and away from the university." [Emphasis added.] It was, he said, a "grand design" (1976). Years later he would say that "enrollment management was developed to bring about a *synergy* among functions such as admissions, financial aid, and retention, which too often were viewed as independent and working at cross purposes" [Emphasis added] (Britz 1998).

Maguire put together a team of specialists in these disparate functional areas to look at their work with a new lens. Their collective experience and perspectives allowed a deeper and broader approach to tracking prospective students and influencing their choices in order to solve BC's enrollment problems. The enrollment management team "spent a lot of time trying to figure out how these functions interacted. And instead of viewing them as four separate functions [admissions, financial aid, retention plus marketing], we realized we were also managing six different interactions for a total of ten. This realization led to a very careful management of these important interactions, such as admissions/financial aid and marketing/retention, and ultimately to the success of enrollment management at Boston College" (Henderson 2001). Maguire took Campanella's concept and created the components of an enrollment management system: outstanding people using the right information in the right organizational structure.

### A Campus-Wide Model

Don Hossler, a professor of higher education at Indiana University, expanded the components of enrollment management beyond the Boston College model. Student marketing and recruitment, along with pricing and financial aid, were essential elements of Hossler's enrollment management model. In addition, the enrollment management area would need to exert strong influence on academic and career counseling, academic assistance programs, institutional research, orientation, retention programs, and student services (*e.g.*, athletics, activities, career planning, counseling, residence life). "It is not simply an administrative process. Enrollment management involves the entire campus" (Hossler 1986).

More important, Hossler was turning the field toward a research base. The competition and the smaller applicant pools intensified the imperative for those in enrollment management to understand such issues as higher education demand and college choice; pricing; fit between student and institution; retention, and outcomes. Hossler (1986) was challenging enrollment management officers to recognize the "need for a new level of professionalism vis à vis a sound knowledge base and the need for a strong research and planning effort for enrollment managers."

In fact Hossler was describing a new kind of enrollment management professional—more than "just" an admissions officer (although an admissions officer could bring a solid knowledge of recruitment and marketing). Indeed, many enrollment managers in this period would come from the ranks of the faculty (such as Boston College's physicist-admissions director Maguire).

### Identifying an Enrollment Manager

Hossler (1986) was specific:

> *It is evident that enrollment managers should have public relations skills in addition to good administrative skills. Those, however, will not be sufficient. Effective enrollment managers will also have to be comfortable with data analysis and knowledgeable about non-profit marketing. They will also need to be comfortable with institutional research techniques and methodologies. Enrollment Managers need not be able to actually conduct the research, but they should know the right questions to ask, and they should be able to understand the findings that emerge from their questions.*

In fact, Hossler sees enrollment management as benefiting from a focused view of the total student experience. Each of the parts of enrollment management—admissions, financial aid, retention offices, orientation, etc.—sees students from a particular vantage point. Decisions in these areas are made in different parts of the campus, in different divisions, with different administrators. It is little wonder that the resulting views vary considerably, and even conflict! Applying the enrollment management lens enables the institution to see its students from a wider, more comprehensive, angle. It also helps the institution see itself through the eyes of students, thus providing a student-centered view (Henderson 2001).

In 1990 Hossler and Bean defined enrollment management as:

> *An organizational concept and a systematic set of activities designed to enable education institutions to exert more influence over their student enrollments. Organized by strategic planning and supported by institutional research, enrollment management activities concern student college choice, transition to college, student attrition and retention, and student outcomes. These processes are studied to guide institutional practices in the areas of new student recruitment and financial aid, student support services, curriculum development and other academic areas that affect enrollments, student persistence, and student outcomes from college.*

## Focus of Strategic Enrollment Management on Academic Context

By 1993 Michael Dolence, a former strategic planner at California State University–Los Angeles, was defining *strategic* enrollment management (SEM) as "a comprehensive process designed to help an institution achieve and maintain the optimum recruitment, retention, and graduation rates of students, where 'optimum' is defined within the academic context of the institution. As such, SEM is an institution-wide process that embraces virtually every aspect of an institution's function and culture."

Dolence (1993) introduced the "linking" of academic programs and SEM: "An institution's academic program is inexorably co-dependent on enrollment management. The quality of the academic program can only be developed and maintained in a stable enrollment environment, and stable enrollments are only possible through sound planning, development, and management of academic programs. The alignment of institutional academic policies with SEM goals and objectives is essential to successfully structuring the SEM process." Dolence believed the focus on academics to be the "heart and soul" of SEM (Dolence 1999). His view of SEM is not just student-centered, but learner-centered (Henderson 2001).

Dolence's primary contribution to enrollment management may have been framing the concept for consistent implementation and evaluation. All those who preceded him agreed that the look and feel of enrollment management systems would vary greatly. Dolence, on the other hand, set forth criteria for every enrollment management system to work toward, both as a goal and as a means of being evaluated, no matter what the system's "look" or "feel." The Dolence model provided a template for measuring the success of enrollment management systems while providing sufficient flexibility for institution-specific development. By suggesting a set of primary goals that all enrollment management systems would share, regardless of the unique institutional features that created and drove the systems, Dolence standardized the field while respecting its inherent variability (Henderson 2001).

### A Roadmap for Campus Units

Dolence's (1993) Strategic Enrollment Management goals showcased the comprehensive nature of enrollment management and provided a roadmap for how every component of the campus, from admissions to the faculty to the groundskeepers, could participate to:

- Stabilize enrollments (stop declining enrollment, control growth, and smooth out fluctuations)
- Link academic programs and SEM (align the principles of SEM with those of the academic nature of the institution)
- Stabilize finances (eliminate deficits, pay off debts, and reinvest strategically)
- Optimize resources (contain growth in the number of employees and redirect and refocus employees)
- Improve services (shorten response time, increase satisfaction, and reduce paperwork)
- Improve quality (eliminate errors and increase student quality ratings)
- Improve access to information (put information systems online)
- Reduce vulnerability to environmental forces (mitigate the negative impact of local and regional events and expand the pool of qualified prospects)
- Evaluate strategies and tactics (track what works and change what doesn't).

### Critical Success Factors

After setting out the SEM goals as a framework, Dolence went on to develop a set of critical success factors against which institutions could evaluate their SEM plans and practices:

- LEADERSHIP: No enrollment management system or organization can be anything more than incremental without support and understanding from the top.
- STRATEGIC PLANNING: Enrollment management is a form of strategic planning and must be tied to the institution's strategic plan.
- COMPREHENSIVENESS: Enrollment management cannot operate as a silo. The enrollment management system must be embedded in the total university system in order to function, which means that everyone must be involved in enrollment management.
- KEY PERFORMANCE INDICATORS (KPIs): Institutions must identify and track progress against metrics that reflect the institution's goals. KPIs are measures of institutional health.
- RESEARCH: Analysis of data and information must inform strategies and decision making.
- ACADEMIC FOUNDATION: Enrollment management must function in the academic context of the institution. As academics are at the heart of an institution, so they are at the heart of enrollment management.
- INFORMATION TECHNOLOGY: State-of-the-art information systems are essential to provide service, track data, and inform decision making.
- EVALUATION: Assessment of strategies' effectiveness is essential to allow feedback for change.... (Henderson 2001, adapted from Dolence)

## Admissions in the Enrollment Management Environment: Higher Profile, Higher Expectations

"No matter what fancy name you call it, it will always be Admissions!" (Statement to author at 1990 AACRAO Annual Meeting, New Orleans). The director of admissions who spoke those words thought enrollment management was just an extension of admissions. She personified the era of the admissions officer as the "roadrunner," moving down the highway from high school visit to college night, without a thought as to the interest or fit of the prospect. alternately playing the stern gatekeeper of quality or the "y'all come" seeker of numbers. As that era faded, an increasingly complex higher education environment would dictate a new role for the admissions office in enrollment issues, a role at once more comprehensive, more collaborative, and more strategic. The admissions office in such a *strategic* enrollment management process would find itself with more power and more success in its institution.

However, while the enrollment management environment ostensibly raised the profile of admissions as part of a go-to operation, EM would also raise the expectations of the campus community. With the strategic initiatives, technology, and data of EM in place, campus presidents began to look for a successful enrollment season much as they would expect a championship football season. And successful enrollment would not be just about numbers in seats; it could also mean leapfrogging the opposition in the rankings, raising the average ACT/SAT scores, improving diversity-a plethora of KPIs that would demand performance, or else. One enrollment manager, let go the same year as his institution's football coach, said, "The only difference between Coach X and me is that he'll be making $3 million on his contract for each of the next two years!" That position inevitably raises questions about compromising professional standards and leads quickly to concerns about misplaced institutional priorities and diminished access for students who don't measure up. "...The pressure put upon admissions personnel to meet enrollment goals often puts them in a position of working against the best interests of the college" (Stewart 1992).

By the early twenty-first century, enrollment management was in the center of a passionate debate over its role in higher education and its treatment of students through the admissions and financial aid processes. Wildly popular among many campus CEOs and board members, EM was not uniformly embraced by faculty, advocates for underserved students, high school counselors, and even a number of professionals in the field. A significant—and vocal—segment of higher education was beginning to see this new EM paradigm as a blight upon higher education. "Enrollment managers are ruining higher education" (Quirk 2005).

## Enrollment Management's Dark Side

If the early days of enrollment management promised more power and success for admissions, some would say that the reality of advanced EM has put admissions—and financial aid—offices on a par with the airlines: crass pliers of data mining and pricing tactics.

The changes wrought in college admissions by enrollment management led some admissions officers from back in the day to shake off the dust of comfortable retirement to rail at the ills of enrollment management tools. One highly respected director at two top-tier institutions, packed a New York hotel ballroom with twenty-first-century admissions directors and enrollment managers to decry the use of merit-based financial aid: "It's wrong to give money to people who don't need it," he said, "if that means turning away students who do." The audience erupted in applause. But the challenge of changing back was obvious when one of his former protégés, himself now a director at a national research university, rose to agree with his mentor's views and then say, "I have a hard time with unilateral disarmament."

High school counselors see enrollment management as a nefarious device to uncouple them from the college process. Repeatedly, they carp at the introduction of technology-driven service mechanisms embedded in admissions offices which are themselves part of an enrollment management system. Online applications? They remove the high school counselor from the application process. Interactive Web sites and portals where students can tailor their information searches? They remove the human touch from the college selection process. Demographics, predictive modeling, and financial aid leveraging? Tools of the EM devil.

### Impact of Merit-Based versus Need-Based Financial Aid on Access

The next chapter in this book discusses "The American Way of Student Aid," including the role of merit-based as opposed to need-based financial aid. This chapter will focus specifically on the role, or alleged role, of enrollment management in distorting or mis-prioritizing the system.

Haycock (2006) gives voice to widely held perceptions:

> *Through a set of practices known as enrollment management, leaders in both public and private four-year colleges increasingly are choosing to use their resources to compete with each other for high-end, high scoring students instead of providing a chance for college-qualified students from low-income families who cannot attend college without adequate financial support. In institution after institution, leaders are choosing to use their resources to boost their "selectivity" ratings and guidebook rankings rather than to extend college opportunities to a broader swath of American young people.*

Similarly, after interviewing attendees at a recent AACRAO annual meeting, Matthew Quirk (2005) wrote in the *Atlantic Monthly*, "At its worst, enrollment management employs a host of ugly tactics to deter low-income students and to extract as much money as possible from each entering class."

Quirk continues: "The ACT and College Board don't just sell hundreds of thousands of student profiles to schools; they also offer software and consulting services that can be used to set crude wealth and test-score cutoffs, to target or eliminate students before they apply." Descriptions of predictive modeling evoke a distasteful interpretation of enrollment management data analysis: "A student who lists a school first when asked where to send test scores, files for financial aid with that school, and then visits campus has tipped his hand, and some schools will figure, why waste money to attract a sure thing?" (Quirk 2005)

Those who lament the rise of enrollment managers as a class point to the fact that by the early years of the twenty-first century, nearly 75 percent of four-year institutions had an enrollment manager integrating operations between admissions and financial aid offices ostensibly for the good of the institution, not of students. "No longer pre-occupied with ensuring ability to pay, institutions primarily [use] enrollment management strategies for two very different purposes: (1) to 'purchase' the high school talent that would enhance their prestige in ranking guides and (2) to shield middle-and upper-class students and their families, who [are] reluctant to pay full price, from the rapidly escalating cost of attending the nation's colleges and universities (Haycock 2006).

There is, say EM's critics, a college arms race underway. Escalating costs of technology, recruitment strategies, and financial aid leveraging burden institutions that feel they cannot afford *not* to join the headlong rush to shape their class. Money for academic programs or for student access is sucked into enrollment management schemes, often with the explicit support, if not the pressure, of the institution's president or Board of Trustees. Some see recent data detailing the cost of recruiting a student in the enrollment management era as an appalling commentary on institutional priorities: Public colleges spend an average of $455 per student on recruitment, and private colleges spent an astounding $2,073 *per student* on recruitment in 2005, up more than $150 per student from the year before (Noel-Levitz 2006a).

With special emphasis on the use of financial aid leveraging, EM is frequently criticized most severely for the role that it has played in transforming institutional financial aid from "a tool to help low-income students into a strategic weapon [used] to entice wealthy and high-scoring students" (Haycock 2006).

> *You can tell a lot about fundamental values from the ways leaders decide to use the resources they do have. So when college leaders, too, choose to join politicians in catering ever more to the most privileged Americans, their actions represent a sorry retreat from the values that drew many of them to education in the first place. It is important to take stock of the cumulative effect that choices like these have on the hopes, dreams, and effort of America's high school students* (Haycock 2006).

And what is the result of this situation? Among high-achieving math students from low-income families, 75 percent went to college but only 29 percent graduated. Among high achievers from high-income families, 99 percent went to college and 74 percent graduated (Baum and Payea 2005).

There are similar statistics as to level of college attendance by income sector: Among the best-prepared American high school students, 20 percent of those from low-income families do not go directly on to college. Among high achievers from high-income families, however, only 3 percent do not enter college right away (Haycock 2006).

Mortenson (2005) suggests that those initial college-going rates will not improve after the low-income student leaves high school. By age twenty-four, a student from a home in the top quartile of family income would be 8.7 times more likely to have a bachelor's degree than a student from the bottom quartile of family income.

Statistics about Pell Grants offer another insight into barriers to entry. In 1975 the maximum Pell Grant covered 84 percent of costs at public colleges; by 2006 it covered only 35 percent, "effectively blocking access for thousands of aspiring college students from low-income families" (Haycock 2006).

"The demand for revenue and prestige also increasingly controls the earlier mass-marketing and recruitment states of the admissions 'funnel,' by which a student goes, in the industry lingo, from 'suspect' to 'prospect' to 'admit' to 'matric' " (Quirk 2005).

In the final analysis, the naysayers in relation to enrollment management see the academy as held in thrall to the enrollment management "devils": "Any aspect of university life that bears on a school's place in the collegiate pecking order is fair game: academic advising, student services, even the curriculum itself. Borrowing the most sophisticated techniques of business strategy, enrollment managers have installed market-driven competition at the heart of the university" (Quirk 2005).

"We must begin to think very differently about what constitutes 'quality' in higher education. At the moment, colleges and universities get a lot of their status from things that have very little to do with the fundamental purposes of higher education. Things like how many applications they get for every one they accept, the average SAT or ACT score of their freshman class, or how well their sports teams do. Indeed, new college presidents are often charged with improving their institution's performance on these rankings, and retiring presidents' accomplishments are often celebrated in much the same way.... If higher education is to play the role of widening opportunity that the nation needs it to play, we need very different metrics for assessing quality" (Haycock 2006).

## Enrollment Management's Hidden Virtues

The indictment is damning against EM, but practitioners such as Bob Bontrager manage to mount an eloquent and elegant defense: Charging that the critics are too often simplistic in their characterization of EM as worshipping at the altar of material gain at the expense of academic values and kids' best interests, Bontrager outlines the level of complexity in EM that critics often miss. When an institution begins to lay out its enrollment goals, "a focus on aggregate numbers will evolve into detailed analyses of the 'mix' of students that best fulfills the institution's mission. A single goal for overall enrollment becomes multiple goals for undergraduates, graduates, residents, nonresidents, first-year students, transfer students, students of color, retention and graduation rates, and any number of other student subgroups depending on an institution's unique circumstances" (Bontrager 2006).

Bontrager further argues that institutions can use EM to achieve clarity on enrollment goals and institutional priorities, redefine academic ability, potential, and success, and realign institutional financial aid programs. If some in this profession abuse the trust of students and institutional mission, unscrupulously seducing presidents and boards into the enrollment arms race, the true professionals, far from "checking their morals at the door," are looking at how to use EM for "other things, like needy students" (Tally Hart, quoted in Quirk 2005). Even some of those quick to criticize will acknowledge that "although competition increasingly threatens a university's principles, the most innovative work in the profession comes from enrollment managers who attempt to align market with mission" (Quirk 2005).

It is that innovative spirit of service in enrollment management that will "guarantee enough revenue to support the academic mission, or even to expand low-income access to higher education. Indeed, the sophisticated methods of enrollment management may be the only way for schools to hang on to their principles while surviving in a cutthroat marketplace" (Quirk 2005).

## Enrollment Management and Admissions in the Academic Context

It is, indeed, in the academic mission of institutions that EM will thrive and where admissions can find its place within enrollment management.

This view of EM as embedded in the academic mission and principles of the institution reshapes the whole EM concept. Technology and data-mining exist not as ends in themselves but as expressions of what the institution is all about. Admissions is not the nest of vipers using financial aid leveraging methodology to recruit full-pays at the expense of access but rather is a player in expressing the academic mission of the university. Enrollment management professionals—and senior officers in the institution—need to ensure that they view EM through an academic lens. A re-defined EM ethos—the underlying fundamental character and spirit of a higher education institution's culture—gives new import to Dolence's definition of "optimum" as being defined in the academic context of the institution.

Looking at enrollments through the academic lens of the culture and principles of the institution provides that integration that Campanella and all the early EM theorists and practitioners sought as a way to combat the scourge of the "silo mentality." Isolation from the academic mission into a separate EM structure was the first step down the road to abuse of the technology and research that EM could bring to bear. By contrast, a more broadly conceived "EM ethos" is at work in that institution which seeks students who will graduate, rather than merely those who will fill empty seats. Such an EM ethos will guide an institution to define its market niche according to its academic strengths. In addition, thinking in terms of the academic context will lead EM to develop enough net revenue increases to plow back into access for the benefit of the "new" students emerging from high schools today. "The academic ethos of EM will set the tone for a comprehensive approach. The academic enterprise will, by definition, by its underlying assumptions and values, encompass all components of the institution" (Henderson 2005).

"The academic lens not only confirms the comprehensive nature of EM, it reshapes every fundamental element that gives EM its identity. To rethink these EM principles in the academic context ensures that the EM ethos on any campus will be consistent with the institution's academic being" (Henderson 2005). Enrollment structure will follow an institutional commitment to the EM ethos, and each of the separate offices of any enrollment management structure will reflect the nature of the academic culture. Admissions' role takes on new meaning in these principles.

### Shared Responsibility

If enrollment policy and practice reflects the academic culture of a campus, then responsibility for the success or failure of enrollment efforts must belong to every member of the community. No longer does the fickle finger of blame point solely at the admissions office when enrollments decline. To be sure admissions will bear the responsibility for the execution of recruitment strategies. But faculty must look to the program mix; business affairs officers must look to tuition policy; staff must look to client relationships. It takes a village to raise a child, and it takes an academic community to ensure enrollment health for an institution.

### Integrated Institutional Planning

The admissions role in institutional planning is much like the Roman god Janus, who faced in both directions. On the one hand, admissions speaks as the voice of the campus, representing the academic strengths and messages to various external constituencies. On the other hand, the admissions staff also functions as the eyes and ears of the institution. Admissions officers have access to data and experience that tells the institution what students and parents want and need. The integration of their input into institutional planning both informs and enriches the EM ethos of the campus.

### Focus on Service

In the EM ethos, service is more important than structure. Business practices flow from the academic foundation of the institution, and the business of a campus becomes student academic success. The campus community should want to test its students' talents in the classroom rather than their patience in navigating the institutional bureaucracy. In the EM ethos, the admissions function becomes the first step in retention. The EM-focused admissions office *recruits graduates*, not just freshmen.

The academically centered EM reshapes the view of admissions away from an isolated and insulated silo into a part of the whole—a big tent approach to enrollment. The big tent, where students access those services they need and ignore the others, provides an intuitive way to look at student service. Do policies and practices make sense to students? Do they meet student expectations? Admissions in an EM environment will be focused on service from the student perspective. Why is the student drawn to the campus? To find a mate? To have a good time? To join a fraternity? To play sports? To save money? To prepare for a job? Or, possibly, to get an education? In any event, the EM-oriented admissions office will recognize that the only way a student stays in school is if he or she is successful *academically*. Recruitment in the academic context looks for strategies that will allow prospective students to see how they can be successful on the campus. Once again, "They recruit best who serve best."

### Key Performance Indicators

Key Performance Indicators (KPIs) are placeholders for the institutional values of the EM ethos. If the driving force for the admissions office is "get the bodies, not the fit," the process is out of sync with the academic values of the institution. We have in too many places put the emphasis on *how many* students rather than *which* students. The academic culture should define the appropriate characteristics of the enrolled student. Those characteristics, then, become what the admissions office will track in suspects, prospects, applicants, and admits.

### Research and Evaluation

The people who go into admissions or other enrollment management units are not always predisposed to research and evaluation. These are "people people." If they had wanted to do research, they would have become faculty. They are more interested in spending time with prospective students and with those students' families than in doing research on student choice or evaluating recruitment programs. "However, the industry standard is more and more based on data, surveys, research—all the tools of the academic enterprise. Without a data-driven approach to practice and process, the logical outgrowth of a major dip in enrollment is disappointment, recrimination, and finger-pointing. EM units cannot continue to do "feel-good" programs where the evaluations say everybody thought it was a great program, and staff felt so positively about how things went. If it didn't make a difference in reaching the institution's academic goals, then it wasn't successful, no matter how positively everyone felt about it" (Henderson 2005).

### Long-Term Commitment

EM is never finished. Just as academic disciplines evolve with the discovery of new knowledge, the infusion of new research interests, or the development of new pedagogy, so EM will remain fluid and responsive to its external environment and institutional culture. Within this environment, the successful admissions office must follow the deliberative, purposeful path of the long-term academic, not the quick fix of the repairman.

These principles, applied to admissions as a participant in the EM ethos, will guide the practice of an enrollment management-based admissions office.

## The Admissions-Faculty Partnership

Chapter 11, "Faculty's Role in Recruitment" (on page 179), specifically addresses the role of faculty in the recruitment process. This chapter will briefly speak to how an admissions office with an understanding of the EM ethos can use faculty more positively and productively when enrollment efforts are in sync with the academic side of the house. Highlighting just a few examples of faculty interaction with admissions work can show how to avoid certain "traps" in interacting with faculty as partners in an enrollment management-centered admissions operation.

Clayton Smith (2007) notes that "admissions counselors and financial aid staff are less effective in the post-admission cycle. Faculty, on the other hand, have the potential to be extremely effective in helping the student to choose your institution. Faculty members can make the 'experience' more real by sharing their passion for their academic disciplines and the institution to which they have committed to working."

Unfortunately, too often traditional, or silo, admissions officers merely ask faculty to write a letter to students. With no guidance as to content, format, focus, or institutional message, faculty may resort to the tried and true: "I'm happy to know you have been admitted. Please let me know if you have any questions. Sincerely, etc." How much more effective would be an admissions request for a letter that suggests broad themes such as faculty expectations of freshmen, why the faculty member is passionate about teaching or research, or how the faculty member engages with students. Positive faculty letters could be based on four or five bullet points that include institutional messages that position the school in the most favorable academic light. The admissions office could offer to draft a letter for the faculty member's review. The admissions officer who operates with a sense for the academic context of institutional enrollment management can do a good job of outlining the faculty member's messages, because the "non-silo" admissions office will understand the academic underpinnings of the campus community. The admissions officer thus becomes the faculty member's partner in the recruitment. The admissions office can emerge as facilitating a positive experience for the faculty in enrollment management.

Faculty who are involved in telethons often express frustration and disappointment in the experience. The faculty member asks, "What questions do you have?" The student says, "None." The conversation limps along for a brief, but painful minute, and the faculty member hangs up, convinced that the quality of the incoming class has sunk to new depths and vowing never again to be sucked into "doing admissions work."

To make the most of the faculty's strengths, admissions should, instead, structure the phone calls. Perhaps faculty should phone only the very strongest students, those more likely to share the faculty member's passion about the discipline or at least ask questions. Or faculty could target parents, who are never at a loss for conversation and endless questions. In any case, admissions should work to select faculty who talk easily, and who will feel at home in a situation where they do not know the person on the other end of the phone. In a structured situation, a carefully chosen faculty member will have a positive experience, convey a positive impression to the parents, and leave as a willing return volunteer.

The ability to harness the power of the faculty in the recruitment process will position the admissions office as a major player in enrollment management. It will inoculate against the silo mentality that suggests that faculty should stay out of the admissions process, and it will enrich the practice of admissions with the academic culture of the institution. "[F]aculty members who participate in enrollment management influence the size, the academic quality, diversity and values of the student body" (Smith 2007). Admissions officers who facilitate the involvement of faculty will be seen as part of the whole enrollment management enterprise. And students will be better served as a result.

## Enrollment Management's Redemption?

In the last years of the twentieth century, American higher education looked with unabashed delight at the waves of a new Baby Boom stretching out to fill enrollment coffers through 2018. However, the initial glee at having so many more students has been tempered by a more careful examination of who they are. Not only is this Baby Boom Echo—students leaving high school for college—the offspring of the original Boomers; many others are the children of new immigrants and minorities who have not traditionally been represented in higher education. "The nation's high schools are graduating a far more complex and varied group of students than we've seen in the past. The data...should be a wake-up call, urging us to look closely at where we're doing well and where we need to do much better in terms of retaining and graduating our young people" (WICHE 2003).

While African-American and American Indians/Alaska Natives will increase their share of the high school graduating class in 2014 only slightly from where they were in 1994, Asians/Pacific Islanders will increase from 4.5 percent of the class in 1994 to about 7 percent in 2014. The two groups with the largest changes will be Hispanics and Whites. The proportion of Hispanic students will grow the fastest, increasing from a 9.3 percent share of public high school graduates in 1994 to nearly 20 percent in 2014. White students will decline as a percentage of the high school graduating class, going from 72.4 percent to 58 percent in the same time period (WICHE 2003).

When seen in the span of time of fifty years, the change is truly remarkable. "The minority share of high school grads has grown from about 7 percent in 1960 to 31 percent by 2002 and will grow further to 45 percent by 2018" (Mortenson 2002).

In addition to the fact that so many of what might be called the "New Students" will be students of color, many will also come from financially disadvantaged families. Over 16 percent of the 2007 class will come from families with incomes under twenty thousand dollars per year (WICHE 2003). The New Students will be the first in their families to go to college. Many will come from academically weak schools. They will not be students who have traditionally been represented in American higher education. What will be the response to them by our admissions officers embedded in enrollment management?

## Pioneering New Forms of Access to Information

The stages of the path to college begin with aspiration and end with choice:

> *Student aspirations precede the development of college plans, college preparation precedes college choice, and all of the foregoing are the precursors to college enrollment. Along the pathway to college and over the course of elementary, middle and high school, students pass through predisposition, search, and choice stages where they decide whether to attend college, search for information, consider specific colleges, and finally choose a college destination* (Hossler, Braxton, and Coopersmith 1989).

The less familiarity students have with the byways and highways of college, the more barriers they encounter to deter them from enrollment. The College Board Task Force on College Access for Students from Low-Income Backgrounds[1] suggests that students with

[1] A publication from the Task Force, to be titled "Removing Barriers to College Access for Students from Low-Income Backgrounds: A Framework for Success," has been announced for release by the College Board.

low aspirations and expectations and lack of rigorous academic opportunity and preparation would be especially at risk without adequate and early information and planning.

If, as the research shows, students who are "groomed" for college at home begin, as early as elementary school, to develop the aspirations they need to spur them to seek a college education, the traditional approach to college admissions will not work with the New Students. Tierney (2005) suggests significant new directions for building access:

+ *A key to successful college preparation [programs] is that the programs are long-standing, begin by the eighth or ninth grade, and they focus on academic achievement....[T]he key indicator for student success in college is that [students] are academically prepared.*
+ *College admission officers would provide an enormous service if postsecondary institutions coordinated with one another to offer a series of progressive seminars in every high school in their area. The objective of the seminars would be to explain the in's and out's of applying to college and how to get financial aid without incurring a mountain of debt* (p. 147).

Torres and Marquez (2005), in a study of parental outreach programs that seek to develop access for underrepresented students, identify common characteristics of successful programs. Each program identified as exemplary had a committed program champion who could garner support and move the program's development. Cultural considerations were essential in ensuring success: each of the successful programs had worked with and within the cultures of the students' communities. Program evaluation that led to feedback loops for change and improvement were present in every successful program studied. Successful programs had stable funding sources. And, perhaps of greatest significance, were the partnerships that nurtured, guided, and supported the programs.

## State-Wide Partnerships with K–12 Education

The research suggests new ways of reaching the New Students: In order to ensure that students are, first of all, directed to college and secondly, ready to be successful there, productive partnerships with K–12 education are being developed that put higher education in the trenches with teachers and administrators. It will take committed faculty and staff at the university, as well as administrators and teachers in the schools, to accomplish this—and probably committed parents, as well. A one-time faculty dog-and-pony show will not accomplish this kind of outreach. Can one institution do it by itself? We have to take a broader view to get to students in the earlier grades.

### The College Foundation of North Carolina: A Suite of Services for Students and Parents

One program that embodies the partnership concept is an ambitious state-wide effort in North Carolina. The College Foundation of North Carolina (CFNC) is designed to be one place, easily accessible by Web, where students can plan, apply, and pay for college. CFNC is a state-funded program encompassing the University of North Carolina System, the Department of Public Instruction, the North Carolina Community College System, and the North Carolina Independent Colleges and Universities.

The essential service provided by CFNC is its suite of services for North Carolina students and parents. CFNC Access Services provide technology and Internet resources for information and application, a central Resource Center staffed to take phone calls and dispense answers, and a GEAR UP program, funded by an $8.8 million, six-year U.S .Department of Education grant reaching eight thousand-plus students in twenty North Carolina counties with programs aimed at improving preparation and access.

These state-wide CFNC services have created a one-stop shopping environment that provides students and parents with a simpler, easier to understand college preparation and access pathway, based on research about student choices. The following goals are implemented by the following elements:

- To develop student aspirations, via an online Career Planner module;
- To help academic preparation, via an online Student Planner module;
- To build a sense of affordability for college, via an online Paying for College module;
- To build a level of comfort around availability of opportunity, via a College Fair online module; and
- To simplify the actual application process, via online applications for all colleges and universities in North Carolina.

Market research shows the success of the CFNC.org resources in penetrating the target audiences: 80 percent of high school and middle school parents in North Carolina are aware of CFNC.org, and of those 80 percent, 84 percent anticipate using the services (George Dixon 2005).

CFNC is an example of enrollment management writ large in its offering of a suite of services supporting college preparation and selection by North Carolina students. It is, in many respects, a new evolution of enrollment management in its comprehensive, collaborative approach to the issues of admissions, financial aid, and enrollment services for students and parents. Certainly the admissions role in CFNC has moved out of the campus environment to become a player with a broader interest than just the institutional perspective. Students are the beneficiaries, but one expects that the institutions will be as well.

## Campus-Based Partnerships

However, while such a state-wide effort as CFNC may be the ultimate example of the type of partnership needed to ensure access for the New Students, there are other, campus-based instances of programs expressing the academic mission of their institutions through a thoughtful and imaginative application of enrollment management. At the University of

Michigan-Dearborn (UM-D), a metropolitan campus centered on Southeast Michigan, a partnership program, led by an enrollment management-focused admissions office, reaches younger students via a non-traditional service orientation.

A new UM-D admissions staff inherited a traditional recruitment program that recruited only the senior class with an excessive use of mailed letters (172,000 annually) and a reliance on high school visits and college fairs. Applying an enrollment management approach, the staff looked at the data on New Students, recognized the need to reach students earlier, and saw an opportunity to be more strategic in recruitment while enhancing institutional enrollment.

Linking their work to the campus mission of a student-centered learning environment, the staff worked to meet four primary SEM goals: improve services, improve quality, improve access to information, and increase enrollment. They designed a program to recruit three freshman classes at once (starting with high school sophomores), to better prepare students for college, to start thinking about college selection earlier, and to engage students on a campus to validate their aspirations of seeing themselves in college.

Working with data on teens, they created "a sense of participation and [built] a relationship with a brand" while appealing to students' need to belong to a community, and their interest in trying new things, meeting diverse people, and having fun (STAMATS 2006).

The result: "Thinking About Tomorrow," a strategic recruitment and communication program, targeted to ninth through twelfth graders, using print media, technology, telephone contact, and on-campus events "to recruit and stay in constant contact with students" (Tremblay *et al.* 2006).

The program begins in the ninth or tenth grade as a "soft-sell" concentrated on providing services related to college preparation, college choice, financial aid, and careers. As students move into the junior and senior years, the recruitment becomes more targeted and specific to the University of Michigan-Dearborn.

The integrated communication plan relies on a mix of traditional and technological contacts: a Web site with a home page and sub-sites, a tri-fold brochure (1), postcards (4), net-posts (5), letters (13), on-campus events (4), phone calls (5), and even posters and letters to high schools (4).

Communications vary from introductory, to time sensitive, to calls to action, to program specifics. University staff use e-mail to wish students good luck on finals, and also include study tips in the e-mail. At the end of the sophomore year the program sends college search tips. College fair schedules and gentle nudges to take the ACT mark the junior year. Recognizing that it is necessary to recruit families, not just students, "Thinking About Tomorrow" includes letters to parents and targeted financial aid and career information designed to answer family concerns.

The program embodies the collaborative nature of enrollment management, as well as the student-centered mission of the UM-D campus, through the involvement of faculty and staff in a series of on-campus program elements. A Leadership Symposium includes staff from the

Women's Resource Center, Career Services, Student Activities, and ROTC. "Transitions: A College Prep Workshop" involves English professors teaching how to write a college essay, staff from Financial Aid and Career Services, and even the participation of a vice chancellor! Maize and Blue Day includes faculty teaching sample classes and staff from every student affairs office.

Response to programs is a key indicator of need. The return to the initial mailing for "Thinking About Tomorrow" exceeded the goal by 50 percent. The original goal of having one thousand participants by March 2006 turned into an actual number of 6,848 (Tremblay *et al.* 2006).

## Conclusion

The partnerships and enrollment management efforts to reach the New Students, as just discussed, and to ensure their access to college all have a familiar ring: the successful ones are all about providing service to students.

> *...the over-riding concern should always be in helping students and their families make the decision that is right for the student. The challenge is to empower students and their families to make the right choice, and once that choice is made, to ensure that students have the requisite academic and socio-emotional skills to succeed, and that they understand how to navigate the application process and pay for college. Such challenges are considerable, but they are not impossible. The solution lies in a coordinated, sustained effort and a reinvigorated commitment to the public good* (McDonough 2006).

When admissions is seen as part of the enrollment management perspective, it is all about service. Whatever the configuration, whether the admissions officer approaches a traditional student or a New Student, "They recruit best who serve best."

/ CHAPTER TWO /

*by Rupert Wilkinson, Ph.D.*
*Emeritus Professor of*
*American Studies and History*
*University of Sussex*

02

# The American Way of Student Aid

Most American college undergraduates—over 60 percent of them—receive financial aid of some sort, mainly grants and loans from federal and state governments, private donors, and colleges themselves. Financial aid lies at the heart of political and popular concerns about social opportunity and fairness, most obviously college access and affordability. At the same time, for many colleges it is a business pricing operation, involving strategic decisions about who should pay what so the institution can prosper. As in so much of modern life, market motives and influences are powerfully pervasive.

This chapter is written for college administrators, especially admissions officers, encountering the wheels-within-wheels of financial aid for the first time, but also for the experienced enrollment manager who would like to reflect on the essential nature of financial aid and the many issues it raises. The chapter focuses on undergraduate aid at public and private nonprofit, four-year colleges, largely excluding formal athletic scholarships as these are usually paid for out of separate, athletics budgets. The term "college" is used throughout to include the undergraduate parts of universities as well as liberal arts colleges and other, primarily undergraduate institutions.

## Trends

Let's start by picking out some trends behind the issues—the shift from grants to loans, increasing student debt and "unmet need," tuition escalation, and the growth of "merit" scholarships.

In constant dollars—controlling for general inflation—financial aid has grown enormously, and not just because more people are going to college. In the ten years from 1995 to 1996 through to 2005 to 2006, annual grant aid per student (based on total undergraduate and graduate student numbers converted to full-time equivalents) went up by 46 percent from $3,034 to $4,443. However, this increase in grant aid did not stop a long-term shift from grants to loans, though grant aid to undergraduates actually grew more than loans between 1996 and 2002 (College Board 2005a, pp. 5, 23). The push to expand student aid through loans—justified to the student as a good investment—started among elite colleges and private philanthropies in the early twentieth century, and the federal government later joined in. In recent years, about 80 percent of college education loans have been federally financed or sponsored. As in other countries, government and colleges have coped with mounting demand for student support by turning some of their costs back onto students themselves, as loans to be repaid after they graduate.

The result of all these shifts has been a rise in the debt incurred by graduating students—a development much remarked upon by commentators on American higher education. The commentators seldom mention that rising personal debt is not confined to students, but the facts are stark. Although average student borrowing briefly declined in the early 2000s, the median borrower graduating from a four-year public college in 2004 came out with a debt of $15,500, an increase of more than three-quarters in constant dollars from 1993. At private nonprofit colleges, median debt was $19,500, up by nearly a half. Nor does this include extensive credit card debt (College Board 2006a, p. 12).

Rising debt reflects rising "net cost of attendance"—tuition, room and board, and other college expenses, *less* grant aid. The movement of net costs has varied for different types of colleges and students; but the trend over the past fifteen years has been up, compared with general inflation. Net costs have grown especially as a proportion of the incomes of poorer families, which have risen less than the incomes of wealthier families. In 2003–04, college charges and basic estimated expenses, after subtracting grant aid, averaged 47 percent of family income at public four-year colleges for the poorest quartile of students. At private nonprofit colleges, it was 83 percent (College Board 2005b, pp. 18–19; Wilkinson 2005, p.274 note 27).

Family resources and financial aid have not covered all college expenses. Some colleges, especially the richest and most selective private ones, do put together enough aid, in the form of grants, student loans, and "work-study" jobs, to cover "financial need" (what students are figured to need on top of family resources to pay for college). But most colleges do not achieve this coverage, and the gap has been growing since the 1980s. In 1999–2000, according to one calculation, "unmet need"—defined here as the difference between college expenses and federal estimates of what families could reasonably afford plus financial aid—was over 20 percent of financial need at both public and private four-year colleges (College Board and NASFAA 2002, p. 24). To fill the gap, many students get extra help from relatives, take out additional, private loans and/or do more paid work, perhaps going to college part-time if the college provides for this. (The gap's growth was not just due to a freeze in the amount of federal loans that students could take out, but estimating total unmet need is particularly tricky: *See* Choy 2004, pp. 16, 30–33.)

The relationship between student aid and college costs goes to the heart of student aid. College "sticker prices"—charges for full tuition before grant aid—have grown faster than increases in median family incomes since the 1980s. The reasons for this have been much discussed; they are not entirely the same for public and private colleges, but they include the competitive drive by colleges to spend more and more on expensive programs and facilities. A much-publicized charge by U. S. Secretary of Education William Bennett in the 1980s that increased federal student aid encouraged colleges to jack up their prices has been sharply challenged, though not totally discredited; the same applies to state aid (Dynarski 2000, p. 31; Gladieux 2004, pp. 36–37; Rizzo and Erhenberg 2004, p. 339; Wilkinson 2005, pp. 58, 146–148; Long 2006, pp. 3–6). It is true, however, that grant aid given by colleges themselves is a form of price discount; it enables them to raise the full prices charged to non-aided students by discounting the price to those students they want who are unable or unwilling to pay full price. This is particularly true for private colleges which generally charge higher prices and give more grant aid than do public colleges.

But why, then, have the grant-aid discounts given by colleges to needy students not, on the whole, kept pace with their full charges? One reason is that colleges have traditionally viewed their grant aid as a virtuous but painful expense to be contained. When their full charges go up faster than incomes, so that more students qualify for "need-based" aid, the impact on the financial-aid budget can look alarming.

Another, broader reason for the lag between grant aid, especially for the needy, and rising charges lies in the varied demands placed on student aid: it has been used for many purposes rather than simply helping poor students. The word "scholarship" itself carries over from seventeenth-century England, where it had had the dual meaning of *provision* and *prize*: support for the needy but also reward for ability, piety, and diligence. In the open country of the New World, the purposes of student aid fanned out. Numerous constituencies, from churches to veterans groups to ethnic minorities, have gotten behind student aid, pulling it this way and that to suit their own purposes and members, while appealing to a public interest. Their members have often had some financial need, but not always.

This brings us to the perennial issues swirling about "merit" aid, given to students on the basis of academic or other achievement, not financial need. More will be said about this later, but the merit proportion of all grant aid has steadily grown since the 1970s, though most grant aid is still geared to financial need or income. Worries that merits were stealing aid that should be concentrated on the needy go back to the late nineteenth century; there was a backlash against a new movement among state governments and elite colleges to use merits ("open competition" scholarships, they were often called) to enroll talent and encourage good work. Merits, however, became more of a class issue after World War II. The rise of a new professional class, more serious about academic study than the old upper classes, meant that richer, educationally advantaged students became likely to win the merits. This said, some merits do go to lower-income students, and some are awarded for service rather than talent, as, most famously, in the post-World War II G.I. Bill (Wilkinson 2005, pp. 48–50).

One reason why student aid is so complicated in America is the diversity of its sources. A student's aid package, processed by the campus financial aid office, will commonly include grant aid, loan, and a campus job. And it will often put together money from three levels: the federal government, the state government, and the college itself. In addition, besides using its own funds, the college may fold into the package an "outside scholarship," awarded the student by a private donor or organization. Each type of provider has spawned its own controversies.[2]

In the rest of this chapter, we will look in turn at federal aid, state aid, and "institutional aid" provided by colleges themselves. A final section, "Fault Lines," confronts the fact that in the American system colleges themselves are ultimately responsible for meeting (or not meeting) student financial need. "Fault Lines" explores issues of equity and good practice in the way colleges handle that responsibility amid the pressures of market competition.

## Federal Aid

In addition to funding or underwriting the bulk of student loans, the federal government provides just under a third of all grant aid (author's calculation; *see* Figure 2.1, on page 30). It also gives money to colleges for student jobs, and its six Trio programs (originally three) contribute to "access" organizations and to colleges themselves, to help disadvantaged students get to college and graduate successfully. One Trio program even subsidizes campus child-care for student parents.

Many critics have decried the "grown like Topsy" proliferation of federal aid programs, each protected by vehement constituencies with power bases in Congress. It would be clearer for needy students, they say, to have fewer programs with more "philosophical coherence"—and less red tape (Hearn 2001; U.S. Secretary of Education's Commission 2006). The critics may underestimate America's mix of system with creative disorder. Aside from the original U.S. Constitution, very little in American life is the product of a master plan.

With the exception of aid to veterans and other military-related aid, each of the different types of federal aid was originally "campus-based" aid, funds given to colleges to allocate within guidelines and on a "matching" basis, *i.e.*, requiring the colleges to contribute too.

[2] The impact of private scholarship providers needs much more study and is not discussed here. On their variety and purposes, see Wilkinson (2005), pp. 18, 119–20.

The first federal aid for needy students in general was the campus-based work-study program of the 1930s Depression. Campus-based aid respected college independence and more or less allayed fears of federal "dictatorship." When federal forces grew bolder and directly funneled aid to students (though it was still processed by campus administrators), the new programs were added to the old ones, not substituted for them.

So, the Pell grant program, started in 1973–74, did not *replace* the campus-based Educational Opportunity Grants of 1965, nor were they intended to. Likewise, the government's Ford Direct Loan Program of 1994—loans made directly from the government to students—did not replace the Perkins campus-based loans; nor could they dislodge the government's indirect loans, made via private lenders in return for federal subsidies and guarantees to the lenders. The result was more programs. The government has, however, made some response to calls for simplifying aid applications and giving earlier information to students about aid and college costs.

With the exception, again, of military-related aid such as ROTC scholarships, almost all federal grant aid has been need-based. Pell grants, much the biggest category, are targeted to low-income students: they seldom go to students with family incomes above $50,000. The maximum Pell grant, for students a lot poorer than this, was $4,310 in 2007–08, so the grants are obviously much less helpful to students at high-priced colleges than at low-priced ones.

In 2006, however, Congress and the Bush administration created add-ons for some Pell recipients, giving extra money to freshmen and sophomores who had done a specially "rigorous" high school program, and even more (up to $4,000 a year) to juniors and seniors studying specified sciences, technology, or foreign languages. The added grants for sophomores and above required a 3.0 GPA.[3]

These additions have drawn fire for introducing a "merit" element to Pell grants, allegedly discriminating against the most disadvantaged students and schools and indeed excluding part-time students (though that exclusion may end). The new additions have also excited fears of federal interference in high school curricula, while colleges have objected to the added costs of checking that applicants' high school programs qualify for extra Pell money. From World War II on, however, the government has used financial aid to promote science and language training and more rigorous school work when the strength of the nation seemed to need it. The spark for such programs today is the belief that only a strong "knowledge economy" can withstand globalized competition.

[3] The freshman-sophomore supplements are called Academic Competitiveness Grants (ACG). The junior-senior grants are named Science and Mathematics Access to Retain Talent, or SMART grants. This choice of name and acronym was not very smart. The program was created not long after the Department of Defense set up another, SMART program (Science, Mathematics and Research for Transformation). In 2006 this highly selective program gave stipends of $22,500 p.a. to undergraduates (more to graduate students) plus free tuition, books, and paid summer internships, in return for an equal period of working for the Defense Department after graduation. Recipients are students in science, technology, and mathematics. The whole panoply of military-related aid today, including the Montgomery GI Bill, is largely neglected by policy reports on student aid and college access.

An older criticism of Pell grants and other federal aid is that they have lagged way behind rising college charges since the 1970s, though Pell grants rose somewhat in relation to general inflation and many college tuitions between 1996 and 2003 (Kantrowitz 2007). In August 2006, the federal Commission on the Future of Higher Education (the "Spellings Commission") recommended raising the average Pell from the current 48 percent of average tuition at four-year state colleges for in-state students to 70 percent. The question of spending such money turns partly on your view of college price escalation, and to what extent government grant aid should compensate for it. The proposed increase in Pell grants looks more reasonable if you see most of the escalation as inevitable, a result of the skilled-labor-intensive nature of education, rather than waste and inefficiency (Wilkinson 2007). That also became a hot issue in the early 2000s. There is also of course the question of how much the federal budget can afford. In the meantime, the College Cost Reduction and Access Act of 2007 extended Pell grant funding for fiscal years 2008 through 2017, and also authorized appropriations which would increase maximum Pell grant awards by set amounts for those fiscal years. Those funding levels could be increased (or conceivably, decreased) as budgetary circumstances permit. The increases authorized by the Act average out at 5 percent per year, above general inflation but still below the rate of growth in college charges since the mid-1990s (College Board 2006b, pp. 10–11).

Federal student loans, like federal grants, have been criticized for not keeping up with college prices. The limits per student stayed unchanged for more than a decade, until Congress raised some of them in 2006. As aid in general fell behind college prices, students turned increasingly to private loans, not sponsored by the government and often incurring interest at commercial rates. Between 1995 and 2005, private loans to students grew from the equivalent of 5 percent of federal loan volume to 25 percent (College Board 2006a, p. 2).

Federal loans divide into "subsidized" and "unsubsidized" categories. "Subsidized" loans require proof of financial need (which can include families with over $150,000 income at a high-priced private college) and are interest-free through college and for a short "grace period" afterwards. "Unsubsidized" loans have no interest-free period and do not require financial need. The government holds down interest rates for both types, and both include government loans made directly to students (the Direct Loan program mentioned above) and FFELP loans made indirectly via private lenders.[4]

The government's use of commercial firms for disbursing most of its student loans is unique among developed countries. Especially unusual is the extent to which the lending companies compete for student and college business. Whatever the merits of FFELP versus

[4] FFELP is an acronym for the Federal Family Education Loan Program, a public-private partnership originating in 1965. It includes several kinds of loan, largely paralleled in the Ford Direct Loan Program. Thus, the largest type of student loan, Stafford Loans, has FFELP and Ford versions, both subsidized and "unsubsidized." Lending companies taking part in FFELP include some nonprofit organizations as well as banks, etc. The industry has a complex food chain. It includes a "secondary loan market" for buying and selling student loans; and nonprofit "guarantee agencies" which insure federal loans (Direct Loans as well as FFELP) against default, monitor them, and administer debt collection, often through collection contractors. During 2007 crossfire intensified between Direct Loan defenders on the one hand and proponents of the loan industry and FFELP on the other. The controversy lacked, in my view, a full and fair comparative assessment of the two systems, distinguishing between taxpayer costs and costs and benefits for different kinds of borrowers and colleges.

direct lending—controversial from well before the Direct Loan program started—the creation of a competitive student loan industry through FFELP was a pre-condition of the "loan scandals" exposed by New York's Attorney General, Andrew Cuomo, in 2007. Lending via industry did not simply cause the undue favors given to colleges and financial aid administrators by lenders to get themselves recommended to students, but it was a necessary factor, along with the rise of "alternative," nonfederal loans.[5]

Scandal aside, burdening students and young graduates with loans has been controversial at different times in American history (Wilkinson 2005, pp. 75–76, 130–31). Critics stress the daunting effect of college loans on low-income, non-college families. They worry too that the costs of repaying loans are steering graduates away from low-paid social service careers (Rothstein and Rouse 2007). In response to this criticism, government agencies have expanded the "forgiveness" provisions of some federal loans, canceling all or part of them if the students go on to work in areas such as inner-city schools and rural pharmacies (Gertner 2006). Many economists, though, argue that the income differences between graduates and non-graduates still make borrowing for college a good investment even at current levels of student debt. And they were saying this well before the College Cost Reduction and Access Act (CCRAA) of 2007 provided for cuts in some interest rates, easier repayment terms, and new loan "forgiveness" for students going into public-service jobs.

The CCRAA was a landmark piece of legislation, uniting several different strands of reform. In addition to the Pell grant increases and student loan provisions already mentioned, the architects of the Act—Senator Edward Kennedy (D-MA) and Representative George Miller (D-CA), chairmen of the two relevant committees—sought to strengthen the links between financial aid and preparing for college. The Act established new TEACH grants (Teacher Education Assistance for College and Higher Education) for undergraduates and graduate students planning to teach sciences, languages, and other selected subjects in disadvantaged public schools. The Act also authorized matching grants to states for "outreach" and aid programs targeted at "underserved student populations." To finance these and other provisions, the Act[6] reduced federal subsidies received by student loan companies. Following the loan scandals, opinion prevailed in Congress that the loan companies were getting too much subsidy.

For all its range, the CCRAA did not address another, controversial type of federal aid: tax credits. Introduced toward the end of the Clinton administration, special tax credits reduced a family's income tax to help pay college tuition and fees. Critics, who seem to include most public commentators on higher education, say the tax credits do not really extend college

[5] Federal tax credits can only apply to tuition less aid grants. There have also been educational *deductions* from taxable income, phasing out above $170,000 family income in 2004 (not available to tax-credit recipients) and tax-free federal and state college savings plans. This chapter is not an exhaustive survey of all federal aid issues, which range from loan systems, interest rates, and loan subsidies to the treatment of aid under "welfare to work" rules. More generally, too, it does not get into technical issues of aid administration. For a glossary of federal and other financial aid, and related admissions terms, see Wilkinson (2005, pp. 219–26).

[6] See NASFAA, "College Cost Reduction and Access Act Resources" page, which gives a link to both a summary of the law and the full text, available at <www.nasfaa.org/SubHomes/2669Resources/HR2669Resources.html>.

FIGURE 2.1

Financial Aid Outlays

In Billions of Dollars, 2005–2006 (excludes work-study funds and private and other non-federal loans)

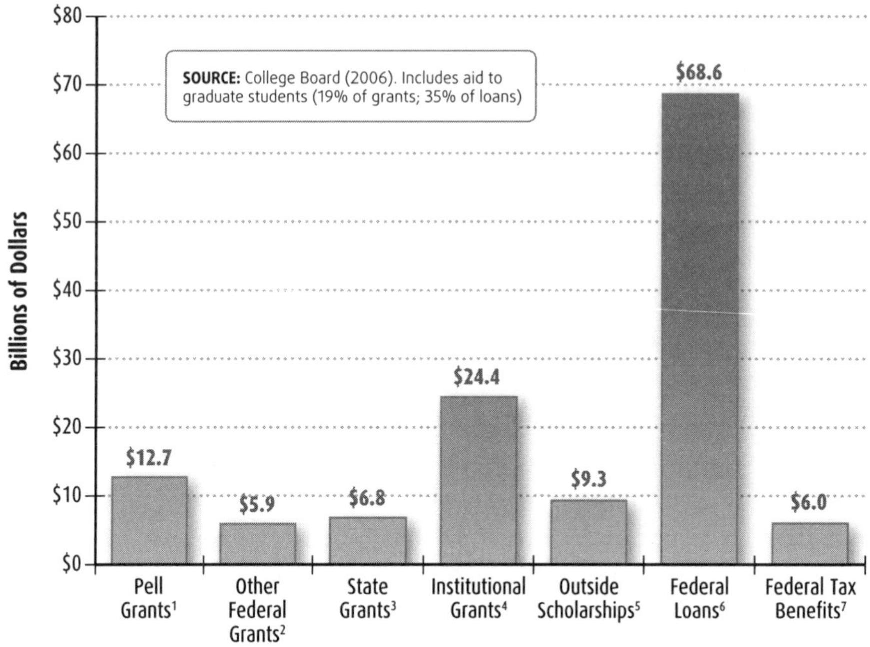


1 Basic Educational Opportunity Grants, named for their architect Sen. Claiborne Pell (RI)

2 Includes campus-based grants and LEAP aid grants to states

3 Excludes state loan "forgiveness" and tuition waivers

4 Aid by colleges, including some campus-based state aid

5 Awards by employers and other private donors

6 New loans, including PLUS loans to parents

7 Tax credits and tax deductions

access since they mainly benefit middle-class students with significant taxable income, who would go to college anyway. And families do not get the tax benefits for up to sixteen months after paying tuition (Dynarski and Scott-Clayton 2006, p. 7). Defenders of tax credits stress the overall burden of paying for college on many middle- and upper-middle income families compared with the easier ride of much richer families. In 2004, just under half of the tax credits went to families with less than $50,000 income, and such credits did not apply to families with incomes above $105,000 (College Board 2006a, p. 25).

Looking at federal student aid as a whole, three purposes stand out: extending access and opportunity for low-income students; rewarding recruits to important service occupations and skill fields; and easing middle-class burdens. All of these efforts need help from other sources beside the federal government. (*See* Figure 2.1.)

## State Aid

State governments give just over 10 percent of all grant aid. In addition many states fund a variety of programs, including campus employment, loans, and loan forgiveness for service occupations such as nursing, and "tuition waivers" for veterans and dependents of firefighters and police killed in the line of duty. (These variations add about 20 percent to the reported state grant total; they include monies which are really grant aid but which are not officially reported as such.)

The states vary enormously in the amount of aid they give.[7] Requirements for aid and its target populations vary too. Some grant aid, officially classed as "need-based," should really be called "need-related" aid in that it requires, say, a 3.0 GPA in high school as well as financial need and/or relatively low income.

The states also differ on merit scholarships. In 2004–05 twelve states—half of them southern—plus the District of Columbia did not require financial need in most of their grant aid to students. The great bulk of this grant aid was merit aid. At the other end of the pole, fifteen states required need or income qualifications for over 99 percent of their grants.

A surge in state merits started in the mid-1990s. Through the 1980s and early 90s, non-need-based grants stayed at about 10 percent of reported state grants. By 2005–06 they had grown to 27 percent (author's calculation). The surge reflected a growing concern with developing "human capital" for state economic development, led by high tech and other "knowledge industries." State merits, it was hoped, would develop talent and keep it in state. The movement also tapped into an old, nineteenth-century idea that state scholarships could provide a carrot in the classroom, encouraging high school students to do better work to get into college.

The main criticism of state merits, as of other merit aid, is that they favor richer, well-prepared students, most of whom could go to college anyway. Two studies of Georgia's much-publicized HOPE merit scholarship program provide points for both sides here. HOPE scholarships go to all state students with a B average in high school. (As with many other state merits, the academic requirements are not stellar). The merits provide free tuition and books at a state college or a fixed amount at a private one, but other grants are deducted from the scholarships. The studies did not entirely agree as to the effects of HOPE scholarships, but on balance they indicated that the HOPEs increased college attendance, disproportionately among richer students as a whole but also among blacks generally more than whites. They raised college-student SAT scores and kept more college students in-state (Dynarski 2002; Cornwell *et al* 2006). One advantage of state merits is that they are usually simpler to understand, qualify for, and apply for than need-based aid. (Dynarski 2004, p. 95).

In spite of this apparent link between state merits and college access, at public colleges across the land, state aid which is not need-based seems to have increased college enrollment much less than need-based aid (Baird 2007). David Longanecker, an expert on public higher education finance, has argued that state merits have not generally *replaced* need-based aid: *i.e.*, they have not captured money that would otherwise have gone into it. In actual dollars, too, state need-based aid has grown more than non-need-based aid since the volume of need-based aid was larger to begin with.

---

[7] See Schmidt (2007, p. A21).

And not all non-need-based awards are really merits anyway (Longanecker 2002). For example, North Carolina gives non-need-based aid to students planning to be school teachers. It also gives "tuition equalization" grants to all state students at private colleges in the state, in order to extend student choice of college and make fuller use of private colleges' capacity, as well as for other, more political reasons.

This said, the growth of state non-need-based aid is part of a broader cultural shift toward merits, albeit stronger in some parts of the country than in others. Where a state government gives a lot of merits relative to need-based aid, public colleges in that state tend to do the same (Doyle *et al* 2004).

## College Financial Aid Policies

About 40 percent of all grant aid comes from colleges themselves, though some colleges, especially public local ones, give virtually no aid of their own, aside from campus jobs. But the role of colleges in financial aid extends way beyond their own "institutional" aid. It is the college that helps the student put together a package of aid from different sources, and in the many cases where colleges do give substantial aid, campus administrators decide how to combine outside aid with their own, and which students should get the best deal.

We will look first at private non-profit colleges, since they generally give more aid and have led the way in developing complex aid policies. Public colleges have traditionally relied more on state-subsidized low tuition to widen access, though that is now changing.

### Private Colleges

Unselective private colleges tend to have the biggest aid "discount rate"—cutting full tuition by the biggest percentage per average student. With a relatively weak market position and difficulties getting enough students, they need to offer a lot of grant-aid discounts to survive, even though they post lower full-tuition prices than more selective colleges. As a group, small, lower-tuition private colleges give grant discounts to more than 90 percent of their students (June 2006a; Redd 2000, p. 13).

The alternative for such colleges would be to cut their full-tuition prices. A few colleges tried this in the 1990s, but even at this market level, the "Chivas Regal" principle operates: higher official prices signal quality, while producing more revenue from those students who do pay full price.

In addition to maintaining or expanding enrollment, most private colleges, and many state ones, use aid to buy good students, so as to improve their freshman SAT/ACT averages in college consumer surveys and to contribute to other students' education. Unlike the customers of commercial firms, some of a college's customers are also *suppliers*, enhancing what economists call the educational "product." So students tend to get more aid if their test scores are above the college average (Clark 2006). Colleges make this happen through merit aid and/or "preferential packaging," a.k.a. "merit within need": sweetening a needy student's aid package by expanding the grant proportion and reducing the need for a loan or job.

Colleges also use aid to buy social diversity; this too is regarded as valuable educationally for all students. Since the 1960s civil rights movement, most colleges have defined "diversity" by visible ethnicity rather than social class; they often give extra grant aid to "under-represented minorities," which in practice usually means black and Hispanic Americans. This usually costs a college less in aid than meeting the need of all low- income students.

These of course are generalizations. Depending on their market position and ideology, private colleges divide into four types of student aid culture, with some overlap at the margins.

### PRIVILEGED PURITY

This type is mostly confined to about thirty, highly endowed and selective colleges, including all eight Ivies. They claim to practice "need-blind" admissions—admitting students without regard to their financial need—and to m*eet all* need, filling in the big gaps left by other sources of aid. Their attractiveness to top students enables them to eschew merits, but some of them sweeten their aid packages for needy students in hot demand elsewhere. Since at least the 1980s, some of them have also practiced "differential packaging"—the same as "preferential packaging" described earlier but targeted to low-income or first-generation-college students.

Starting with Princeton in 1998, concern about not enrolling enough low- and middle-income students propelled a competitive move to give these students much more. Huge endowment increases in the 1990s reduced the financial pain. So did the fact that these institutions still had relatively few low-income, aid-expensive students. Among both public and private colleges, the more selective academically a college is, the fewer low-income students it tends to have, not so much because of price but because lower-income students tend to have less academic preparation and lower test scores. A study in 2003 found that low-income students who did have high test scores were not under-represented at the most selective, "name" private colleges, though middle-income high scorers were under-represented (Hill and Winston 2006).

### TRADITIONAL MIX

The grant aid given by such colleges is mostly scaled according to financial need, but such colleges also give some merits and usually some preferential packages. They may also do some differential packaging for disadvantaged students. Many of these colleges do not meet all need. The more selective ones are more apt to meet all need but may do so through "need-aware" ("need-conscious," "need-sensitive") admissions: that is, they limit their intake of high-need students by favoring full payers or low-need students among their academically weaker applicants.

### YIELD-BASED DISCOUNTING

Some colleges base their aid policies on yield and cost-effectiveness: on what it takes in aid, and no more than that, to enroll the students they want. Financial need is a consideration, but the colleges gear their grant discounts more to what a student *will* pay than what they *should* pay. Here as much as anywhere, strong academic students, attracting enticing offers from other colleges, will get the biggest grants in relation to their need (if they have any). Some colleges in this category fold need-based aid, preferential packaging, and merits into an almost seamless mix. These policies are usually based on extensive analysis of admitted applicants' responses to aid offers.

Priorities vary among colleges. For some, the overriding aim is to increase tuition revenue by increasing enrollment. Using grant aid as a discount to do this goes back to the early nineteenth century. Against the more established view of scholarships as a charitable cost, the presidents of small, struggling colleges used aid as a revenue lever: better to get that extra student paying half-tuition, or even just room and board, than no extra student and no extra dollars. Modern discounting has fine-tuned this, targeting different amounts of grant aid on different students to yield the most "net tuition revenue" or NTR (revenue net of grant spending).

Many colleges, however, use yield-based discounting for more than one purpose. A college may, for example, want to raise its freshman SAT averages overall, enroll more minorities, and attract women to its engineering program while maintaining or even increasing NTR.

To analyze their yield from aid, colleges often use sophisticated statistical techniques, especially econometric modeling based on regression analysis. Much of this comes from commercial marketing, analyzing the response of different types of customer to different prices and messages. Computer technology has made it all more feasible.

College price discounting has in fact developed its own industry. Consulting firms provide colleges with statistical modeling and advice on how to use it in the light of the college's goals and market position. Financial aid may be part of wider recommendations by the consultants on admissions policies and how to retain students once they are enrolled.

### MINIMUM FUNDING

In contrast with the above, a small but significant minority of low-tuition, private non-profit colleges give minimum grant aid of their own, perhaps just a handful of merits. They rely for access on their relatively low full prices plus federal and state student aid. Often they have found a local or regional clientele by offering well-targeted, well-taught vocational courses. Their offerings may well include part-time programs, catering to older, "nontraditional" students. Their approach to pricing and aid is somewhat like that of for-profit colleges, though their cultures are very different.

The lines between these four types of private colleges, especially the first three, are not hard and fast. Many a college embodies features of more than one type. For example, an essentially "traditional mix" college, basing most of its aid on financial need, may use studies of yield and net revenue in designing an array of merits.

### State Colleges

State colleges range from institutions, often smaller, local ones, that give no grant aid of their own, to some major universities that combine endowed scholarships with yield-based discounting. For those that do give aid, much depends on how much leeway the state gives them to set their own tuition and vary it with discounts.

In the 1990s pressure from faculty to get better students, and general ambitions to upgrade, encouraged state universities to create more merits, which were often attached to special honors programs. Though some aid programs increasingly focused on disadvantaged students, state college aid generally shifted in favor of higher SAT/ACT scorers and wealthier students (McPherson and Shapiro 2006, pp. 70–73).

Most state college aid, like that of low-tuition private colleges, is not need-based. Some state college merits and athletic scholarships go to needy students, but in 2004–05 only 50.5 percent of grants given by state flagships and 45 percent at other four-year state colleges went to students with financial need (Baum and Lapovsky 2006, pp. 3–5).

At four-year public colleges as a whole, and two-year ones too, low- income students get more grant aid from federal and state government than from their own institutions.

Some state colleges, however, are paying closer attention to financial aid strategies, including yield-based discounting. As their subsidies from state appropriations have fallen behind their rising costs and full charges (even in years when the appropriations per student rose in relation to general inflation), the colleges have come to depend more and more on tuition revenue. As in the private sector, this has driven many state colleges toward the cost-benefits of grant-aid discounts (Longanecker 2006; Hossler 2006; Jaschik 2007a).

These similarities with tuition-dependent private colleges have raised an old question: should major state universities deliberately go for a "high-tuition/high-aid model," charging much more to their richer students while giving more back to their poorer ones? The question has generated heated arguments. The main pros and cons are these:

- PRO: Taxes paid by non-college families help subsidize relatively low in-state tuition, which in turn subsidizes richer families who can afford to pay more for the advantages of college education. The same is true of state lottery payments in some states. A big increase in full tuition could be partly spent on more aid, reducing the current net tuition paid by the neediest.
- CON: This would alienate the middle and upper classes whose financial and political support is needed by state colleges. The colleges' activities, including research and public extension programs, serve the whole state. There is also the political reality that state colleges and governments cannot always be trusted to match big tuition raises with

increased aid for the neediest. Endorsing a high tuition/high aid model might encourage a drift to higher tuition without commensurate aid.

Almost all state colleges do, of course, charge higher tuition to out-of-state students. Some leading state universities concentrate their tuition discounting on this market, largely to recruit superior students and increase net tuition revenue by increasing enrollment. The higher full-tuition rates for out-of-state students give the colleges more money to play with, and state governments often permit more variation in charges to non-state residents. In the 1980s and 90s, state flagships sought out-of-state students more for student quality than revenue, but the revenue motive has become more pressing since then (Rizzo and Ehrenberg 2004, p. 339; Hossler 2006).

At the same time state politicians and others have moderated the pursuit of out-of-state students by reminding the universities of their historic obligation to provide access inside the state. In that spirit, several state flagships, and state governments too, have in recent years joined top private colleges in giving low-income students extra help, ranging from free tuition to bigger grants in the place of loans.

## Fault Lines

The historic decentralization of American higher education, the freedom to create brave new campuses on the frontier as well as in the city, produced today's rich variety of institutions funded from diverse sources—gifts and endowments, public subsidies, and tuition fees. The system needs extensive financial-aid discounts, especially in the private sector, to keep under-enrolled colleges in business at one end of the market and offset high sticker prices at the other. In its ideal form, the system is just: students pay according to their means for the life advantages of a college education.

The downside of decentralized freedom is that responsibility for meeting student need is left ultimately to the individual college, and the college's leaders may not be willing or feel able to fulfill that responsibility. Oregon's move in 2006 to underwrite aid packages meeting all financial need for its public college students was highly unusual at the state government level (Lederman 2006). At the federal level, proposals to expand the use of "incentivizing" grants, giving extra aid money to colleges in return for more spending by them on lower income students, recognize the primary responsibility of colleges for meeting need.

The expansion of merit aid exposes the potential mismatch between the interests of individual colleges and the claims of a wider public interest. In 2003–04, just over half of grant aid by colleges did not require financial need (Heller 2006). Some of the non-need-based aid in fact did go to needy students; on the other hand, more and more need-based aid has gone to students from prosperous families to offset escalating tuition at the more expensive private colleges. And at private colleges with relatively low tuition, merit aid was so important that they gave more grant aid per student to wealthier students than to poorer ones (College Board 2005a, pp. 20–21).

Up to a point, merits serve everyone. They enable colleges to recruit a quality of student they could not otherwise get; this benefits other students. And for the many colleges that are under-enrolled, merit scholarships, if not set too high, can increase net tuition revenue by increasing enrollment. Some of the added revenue may fund more need-based aid.

But merit aid has, arguably, gone beyond the point of educational and social virtue. Some merits are "full ride" (full tuition, or even more), which does nothing for net tuition revenue. And many colleges that give merits to some students without financial need, as well as preferential packages that favor low need students, do not meet the full financial need of their lower income students. Nor do they always plough back much merit-earned revenue into aiding low-income students.

Much the same situation, in which some students get more than they need and others a lot less, led the College Board more than fifty years ago to create the College Scholarship Service (CSS). The new agency promoted need-based aid and offered colleges a collective service for assessing financial need. The formation of CSS was also prompted by bidding wars, in which colleges wasted financial aid competing for strong students without need.

There are similar fears today of what is often called an "arms race" (or more wittily an "alms race") in merit discounts, at the expense of longer-term investment in college programs and faculty. Some colleges have accordingly cut back on merits and floated the idea of easing the antitrust law on college price and aid agreements, so that they can more easily get together to limit non-need-based aid (Tomsho 2006). Informally, too, some colleges target their merits at students who are just above the line of qualifying financially for need-based aid but still feel the burden of college costs. The fact remains that regressive aid policies, favoring the non-poor over the poor, serve the market position of many colleges, especially when the policies are fine-tuned by market research.[8]

Market factors have also entered into the way colleges handle "need analysis," the assessment of financial need. The methodologies used for this resemble tax law, involving detailed financial information from students and families. The aim is to produce an "expected family contribution" or EFC: an estimate of what a student and family can afford to pay. Virtually all colleges use the "Federal Methodology" (FM), at least for federal aid and often for state aid, but many selective private colleges use versions of an "Institutional Methodology" (IM), developed by the College Board, for their own aid.

---

[8] My book, *Aiding Students, Buying Students*, gives a fuller analysis of arguments for and against merit aid; and it includes a fictional debate between "Mike Merit" and "Alison Antimerit." It discusses the hypothesis of Michael S. McPherson and Morton Owen Schapiro that merit-aid moves some student talent down the college selectivity pecking order (Wilkinson 2005, pp. 152–56). A study of Southern state merits found the opposite; they concentrated talent upwards (Cornwell and Mustard 2005). Among selective colleges meeting all need and not looking to increase enrollment, giving small merits can pay for themselves by recruiting more academically strong students instead of academically weaker students who tend to need a lot of aid.

Through the 1990s and into the 2000s, FM tended to produce lower EFCs than IM, but this is by no means always true: the two methodologies handle different financial circumstances differently (Padgett 2007). For most students, both methodologies are demanding. In 2006–07 under IM, a couple with an income of $65,000, assets of $110,000 mainly invested in their home, and one of two children in college, would usually have had to pay an EFC of about $6,300, in addition to the student's expected summer earnings of, say, $1,800.

If a college really wants a student, however, it may practice what one insider has called "preferential need analysis," trying extra hard to find new information, *e.g.*, about family medical expenses, so it can lower the EFC, or applying whichever methodology (FM or IM) qualifies the student for most need-based aid. Or it may just raise the grant aid offered, especially when the student's aid application shows that he or she has applied to other, strong institutions. (The federal and College Board aid application forms, FAFSA and CSS/profile, both require this listing of colleges.)

Estimated financial need itself depends on what a college decides is its total "cost of attendance," or COA, over the school year. To minimize "need" and look more affordable, colleges have incentives to give low estimates for the most variable and subjective components of COA, especially "books and supplies" and "personal and miscellaneous expenses." Colleges do not always increase these annually in line with inflation, and some college Web sites do not show them at all. In 2006–07, many private colleges allowed $1,000 or less for personal expenses. On the other hand, some low-tuition public colleges have boosted their estimates for books and personal expenses so that their students can qualify for more need-based federal aid.

Colleges also vary in what they treat as financial aid, especially regarding loans. Institutions espousing best practice do not count commercial loans or federal PLUS loans, designed to help parents pay EFCs, as part of their aid packages. Some colleges do, however, without always saying so clearly (Burd 2006). Some students, in fact, take out private loans without exhausting their eligibility for cheaper federal ones—a problem that some colleges and legislators have started to address (Danenberg 2007; Luebchow 2007).

This brings us finally to issues of transparency (College Board 1997, pp. 23, 30–36; Clark 2006). Most colleges publish basic information about financial aid and how to apply for it. At the next stage, however, the financial-aid award letters sent out to admitted students have been criticized for sometimes using terse, unexplained jargon when listing the types of aid offered (Clark 2007). And claims abound that students and families do not understand the process by which different colleges determine aid offers. Among commentators on higher education, the complaints come not just from those who distrust the impact of market economics on financial aid but from those who want to make the market work better, providing more rational consumer choice through improved customer information.

Looking at the information flow from the other direction, colleges get more information on their prospective customers than just about any type of business, except maybe life insurance. On top of the academic and biographical information collected through admission applications, student aid applications give colleges huge amounts of data about their customers' resources. Even those students who do not apply for aid are thereby saying something about their ability to pay. The educational and caretaking duty of colleges that justifies their collecting so much data on prospective students give colleges market power—information power—over their customers.

Could the information flow from college to customer be made more equal to the reverse flow? We should distinguish here between what students are told about their individual packages and what is announced as general practice. Except for aid based purely on financial need, students are seldom told exactly how their aid is affected by academic, demographic, and competitive factors. Whether and in what detail they can and should be told this is a matter for further debate. At the level of general practice, though, there is a strong case for saying that colleges should do nothing that they cannot defend and disclose publicly. The same might be asked of any institution but it applies with special force to institutions which receive tax breaks and public subsidies—and are, after all, in the business of truth! This means that colleges should disclose all the factors that shape their admissions and financial aid practices.[9]

Administering financial aid is demanding work. "My job," a seasoned financial aid director told me, "is 50 percent calculator and 50 percent Kleenex." College financial aid offices handle intricate numbers, mounds of government regulations, and an almost infinite range of personal circumstances. As part of enrollment management, financial aid directors also have to make their professional ethics, stressing need-based aid, jibe with the market interests of the institution that employs them (NASFAA 1999). These two considerations overlap but are not identical, as this chapter has shown. The sheer versatility of student aid, the fact that it can be used for different purposes, makes it at once an asset and a problem.

[9] This is not as easy as it looks. For example, colleges which practice need-aware admissions in order to meet all need often do not declare this. How does one do it without sounding self-destructively exclusive? For a model statement showing it can be done, see "FAQs for Prospective Students" (as of 2006–07) on the Web site of Mount Holyoke College, which has a high proportion of low income students relative to its selectivity. Some colleges, too, are open about how they respond, or do not respond, to competitive aid offers. Mount Holyoke's statement is at <www.mtholyoke.edu/offices/sfs/5804.shtml>.

/ CHAPTER THREE /

*by Michael A. Olivas, J.D., Ph.D.*
*William B. Bates Distinguished Chair in Law and Director of the Institute for Higher Education Law and Governance*
*University of Houston Law Center*

03

# State College Savings Plans and Prepaid Tuition Plans:
## A Reappraisal and Review

If college savings plans (CSPs) did not exist, someone would have to invent them. As I travel through various states, I almost get a lump in my throat seeing public service ads for CSPs on late night television. Texas has one that features a pretty young Mexican American, who asks her mom if she will be able to go to college—fade to a Florida family standing around a cake, celebrating a grandchild's birthday, complete with prepaid tuition certificates as popular birthday gifts—fade to another state's public service announcement that I think is for its lottery, when it is revealed that all the hullabaloo is about the new prepaid tuition plan. Certain ticket holders even will receive scholarships—yet another state will give fully paid CSP awards to the first five children born in the upcoming year—I find myself mentally backdating nine months from the due date, and realize I missed out.

By the end of 2002, every state plus the District of Columbia has a CSP, either the prepaid version, in existence since the 1980s, or a pooled-investment savings trust program.[10] Several states have both, prompted by the 1996 legislation that created 529 plans, named after their IRS tax code provision.[11] The prepaid plans, operational in twenty states, work on a very

[10] For a complete listing, download the Institute of Higher Education Law and Governance's "List of State Prepaid Plans" from <www.law.uh.edu/ihelg/stateprepaid.pdf>. See also College Savings Plans Network at <www.collegesavings.org>.

[11] IRC 529 (2001)

simple premise: parents or grandparents place a lump sum in a contract (or they make monthly payments) that guarantees the money will be sufficient for an equivalent of tuition and fees in a set period of time in the future. Thus, if 2003 tuition at a Texas public college is $10,000 for each of four years, that $10,000 (plus a small fee) invested in the Texas Tomorrow Fund (TTF) in 2003 will be guaranteed to cover my newborn daughter's four years of tuition and fees in 2021—eighteen years from now. The state can guarantee the return by virtue of pooled assets, economies of scale, and careful actuarial practices. Some states even assure the full-faith-and-credit (FF&C) of their state (Texas being one) to these plans, pledging state funds to cover any eventual shortfall.[12] In other states, you take your chances with the markets.

States have also created a kissing cousin to CSP's—savings program trust funds, which enable persons to invest in a state-operated investment fund. While they are state-operated, they are often managed by private investment firms or large financial institutions, which are contracted to perform these tasks (Hurley 2002, p. 16). With recent federal legislation, these funds have gained tax exempt status, covered additional college expenses (such as room and board), and allowed parents to defer the gains made from the investments and to delay and transfer the earnings to the beneficiary children, who are taxed at lower rates than are wage-earners. Many states have also given state income tax exemptions to the plans.[13]

This panoply of state and federal tax treatments for both types of plans turned the tide: a decade earlier, these plans had no statutory tax exemption and were not even considered tax exempt by the Internal Revenue Service. In the 1980s, the IRS challenged the Michigan Education Trust (MET). The MET lost its case at the trial level, but then won an important victory in the Sixth Circuit Court of Appeals.[14] When the IRS decided not to appeal, the way was cleared for Congress to act (p. 12). Since then, both types of plans have prospered. Florida has over $3.5 billion in prepaid contracts, while the TTF sold nearly 50,000 contacts in its first year of operation (Sidoti 2002, p. 28; Jennings and Olivas 2000, p. 18). Additional developments have whirled by, as states make provisions for investments in private institutions, as the Teachers Insurance and Annuity Association-College Retirement Equities Fund (TIAA-CREF) has established a program to manage several of these state investments, as states have added FF&C (as in Texas[15] and Ohio) or declined to do so (voters in Oregon voted down such a proposal in 1998), and as even private colleges have formed consortia to pool prepaid investments for their institutions (Kristof 2002, p. C3; Hurley 2002, pp. 16, 108–109; Schmidt 1998, p. A53; Dale 2003).

When I first examined these plans in the early 1990s, I wondered how these programs could survive the MET experience and thrive as taxed, essentially for-profit organizations.[16] As

[12] Sometimes, these "guarantees" are not true FF&C (Hill 2002).

[13] See Hurley (2002, pp. 35–39; p. 110).

[14] See *Michigan v. United States*, 802 F. Supp. 120 (W.D. Mich. 1992) and *Michigan v. United States*, 40 F.3d 817 (6th Cir. 1994).

[15] See Texas Constitution Article 7, Sec. 19(b).

[16] See Olivas (2003).

it turns out, reports of the death of these programs were exaggerated, and I am glad to have been wrong. My concern was who would be required to pay for burying these programs: I thought it wrong for states to use general tax revenues to bail out programs that served the relatively well-to-do.

However, these plans placed their bets on a bull market, and won. Even conservatively managed funds (some bound by state investing practices that limit equity stocks and innovative investment vehicles) have outstripped higher education's annual rate of inflation, which has consistently doubled the consumer price index in the 1990s. As long as the stock market or bond market does well, these plan managers will look like geniuses, especially in light of the long term nature of the portfolios (usually requiring at least two or three years of investments and often covering children who will use the money a dozen or more years hence). The rising tide has floated many boats. Of course, as the markets refused to defy gravity in the 2000s, several of these plans have not done as well. As I note, this has placed several funds in trouble.

In another salutary development, these plans have attracted competent managers, and given rise to a strong infrastructure of technical and government support mechanisms, both in the public and private sectors. The College Savings Plan Network, an arm of the National Association of State Treasurers, holds regular workshops and conferences for the industry.[17] Private consulting firms and financial services exist to assist and manage programs for the states. Some of the most successful plans have privatized the operations and investments of CSP programs. The flexibility of the private sector has allowed the investments to build up, with few new public employees added to state rolls. As noted, TIAA-CREF, Fidelity, and other money managers have recently begun to make their investment and insurance underwriting expertise available to state plans. Other states have hired the College Savings Bank (CSB) to administer their investments. (CSB is the country's only bank devoted solely to college prepaid tuition financing.)[18]

Thus, state plans have networked, established well-run organizations, lobbied for tax relief, and gained the confidence of investors and state officials. Ohio, for example, not only accorded the state's FF&C to the CSP program, but invested over $1 million, enabling it to bring its operating costs down (Jennings and Olivas 2000, p. 8). In California, discussions with legislative officials have suggested that two political considerations have kept this pacesetter state from enacting its own prepaid plan: FF&C considerations, especially after the Orange County fiscal disaster,[19] and the fact that development of a CSP was a major plank in the gubernatorial campaign platform of then-State Treasurer Kathleen Brown, making it an untouchable initiative for the eventual winner, Pete Wilson. Moreover, liberal State Senator Tom Hayden introduced the legislation, making it dead on arrival in the Republican-

[17] For more information on these conferences and workshops, see the College Savings Plan Network at <www.collegesavings.org>.

[18] For more information on the College Savings Bank, see the College Savings Plan Network at <www.collegesavings.org>.

[19] See Hofmeister (1995).

dominated legislature. Nonetheless, it is only a matter of time before California resolves these older issues and enacts a CSP, as it has the perfect, fertile climate for such a plan: many students in excess of the state's capacity to build new institutions, a thriving private sector system of independent colleges, several elite and nearly-elite public institutions, a large economy, and very low tuition in the public institutions. These characteristics, plus California's "good-government" climate will soon combine to produce a solid prepaid plan, with or without FF&C, and then the remaining states will follow. As of early 2003, such a plan still has not materialized, although California has had a state savings plan since 1999.

As for the next generation of such plans, such as those likely to grow up in California and New York, two states with new college trust fund programs but not prepaid tuition plans, the programs will become very innovative and flexible, should strong investment markets continue. (Even bear markets provide solid investment opportunities in bonds and other high-grade debt instruments. Over the long haul of college investments, the long-term nature of such portfolios, combined with the economies of scale and tax exempt status of the plans, virtually assures their financial viability.) Moreover, as the plans spread, more innovative program features will likely result, such as multi-state compacts (especially for regions with small populations, such as New England or the Pacific Northwest), increased reciprocity among states (letting the beneficiaries take portable plans across states), relaxed residency requirements (in an attempt to sell the plans, letting purchasers or beneficiaries be residents of another state), increased participation by private institutions (guaranteeing returns on investments but not guaranteeing that the plans will cover private college cost increases), and offering attractive consumer options (single course purchase options, mix and match plans for inter-institutional mobility, room/board/book/fee/tuition/allowance packages—the whole enchilada, not just tuition), and other finance options (such as increased use of indexed debt mechanisms, refinanced home mortgages, credit-scoring, and income-contingent payment or repayment schemes). Acquiring an education is sure to become more like home buying, with the full range of purchase and finance options. College prepaid and savings plans, as likely as not, will be seen as the catalyst for such creative approaches to this field.

## State Policy Issues

Prepaid and savings plans were creatures of state law, with Wyoming inaugurating the first prepaid plan in 1986,[20] and with Kentucky's pooled-assets trust serving as the prototype for 529 savings plans.[21] In the early 1980s, these plans were at considerable risk, both because they had not caught on as popular investment vehicles and because of the uncertain tax treat-

[20] The Wyoming state prepaid plan closed shop in 1995, less than a decade after its 1986 start. According to observers I have interviewed, the plan was just too small, considering the state's small population and single public university. Wyoming has enacted a savings program, run by the state treasurer and administered by a private investment company.

[21] The Kentucky Education Savings Plan Trust, begun in 1990, was substantially reconstituted as a 529 plan in 1999. The current savings plan is administered by TIAA-CREF. The state also has a prepaid contract program. See also Hurley (2002, p. 73).

ment. This culminated when the Michigan prepaid program lost in court in 1988. The issue was whether or not the interest earned on the MET was taxable (Williams 1993, p. 55, 66). The Sixth Circuit reversed the district court, and the IRS decided not to appeal the ruling against it (Jennings and Olivas 2000, pp. 7–8). When Congress acted in 1996 to provide the requisite tax treatment to the plans—making them 529 plans, for the revised statutory code chapter—the second problem was solved (Hurley 2002, pp. 11–13). The first problem, however, which was that the programs had not caught on, quickly resolved itself after the law provided an attractive tax shelter. Of course, there had been longstanding tax breaks available to the public, particularly the wealthiest tax-payers, but the vehicles all had unattractive features: for example the Uniform Gift to Minors Act (UGMA) sheltered and transferred resources to students, but did not require the recipient to spend the money on college expenses.[22] More than one wealthy child has blown his UGMA inheritance on a muscle car or another lifestyle that did not include college, as the donor parents or grandparents exercise no control over the gift, once made.

Even with the substantial federalization of prepaid and savings plans, they remain state creatures, established and maintained by state legislatures and agencies. As of the end of 2002, all fifty states and the District of Columbia have established savings plans, and nearly two dozen also administer state prepaid plans. (Vice President Al Gore proposed a federal savings plan during his 2000 presidential campaign, but there have been no other serious efforts to reformulate the state plans into a comprehensive federal system.)

That the programs vary among themselves is an inevitable byproduct of their state-ness, as is the variability of the plans' success, measured by the wide fluctuation in participants, the financial reserves, and the overall efficacy of the plans. Florida's Prepaid College Tuition Program has over 375,000 contracts in play, and over $3.5 billion in total assets; [23] Wyoming's prepaid program, the country's first, closed its doors in 1995. Florida's demographics, with its many low cost public colleges and community colleges, its growing population, its many retirees who choose to invest in their grandchildren's futures, and its savvy and aggressive marketing of the plan have made it the Cadillac of prepaid plans. Contrast these advantages with small Wyoming, which has a single public college and a static population base. In this case, all the states can array themselves along this ladder, with favorable features or built-in headwinds. In addition, states have begun to gain competitive advantages relative to each other by fashioning programs that are more attractive that those of the competition—usually by transcending borders and adding program elements that offer more competitive terms and features such as lower fees, more portability, tax exemptions, or guarantees. These extremely attractive dimensions also have serious drawbacks to states left behind or to consumers who

[22] See also the Alaska Uniform Transfer to Minors Act (AS 13.46.010–13.46.999).

[23] For more information on the Florida plans, see Florida Prepaid College Board at <www.floridaprepaidcollege.com>.

do not gain access to the considerable comparative information available in the public domain through Web sites and publications (Frankie 2002; Kristof 2002).

Notwithstanding, these programs are state entities, even as they must meet 529 federal eligibility criteria for federal tax treatment purposes. As such, policy analysis requires attention at the state level, as well as at the federal level. Three major state level issues have emerged in the decade and a half since these plans began, and especially in the half dozen years since the enactment of the Taxpayer Relief Act of 1997:[24] finance and financial stability, system complexity, and the proper role of states in a federal financial aid system. (Additional issues of state taxation in the federal tax regime are treated separately in the following section, and mirror the parallel tracks of state/federal program design and implementation.)

## Finance

The financial success of state prepaid and savings programs is not a slam-dunk assured matter. After all, Wyoming closed the country's first such program, and others have found it a rocky road to program solvency. When inflation is low and when the stock market is rising, even modest state programs make geniuses of their managers. After all, most investors are in it for a long haul, purchasing their children's contracts that do not come due for many years: a newborn's payout will not come due for eighteen years, allowing a variety of investment strategies to states—including a mix of stocks and bonds, invested on an age-basis that becomes more conservative in the later stage of the transaction. Bundled together with many thousands of such contracts, a state's investment portfolio has many advantages, doing business as tax-exempt entities and having access to sophisticated markets that risk-averse individual investors do not possess. In a number of instances, states provide substantial public funds to establish or operate these programs; much of their cost is subsidized. In 1994–95, for example, Ohio underwrote its prepaid program by investing $1 million to reduce the cost of its prepaid contracts and to provide a FF&C guarantee to the program (Jennings and Olivas 2000). Virtually all the programs have been subsidized by the sponsoring state at some point in their operation, even those administered or operated by private investment companies or financial institutions. These state contributions have surely enabled the programs to become established and operational.

But it is one thing to operate a program in the 1990s, when the stock market defied gravity, and it has proven to be another in the slowed-down, self-correcting stock market of the new century. In 2002 alone, Morningstar reported that average 529 stock funds it monitored had fallen by 21.2 percent, a better performance than the year's S&P 500-stock index, which performed even more poorly, at a 21.8 percent loss for the year (Kimelman 2002, p. 7). In 529 bond funds, the average 529 programs performed better, gaining 2.5 percent for the year; however, age-based bond funds keyed to five-year-old children (with thirteen years left

[24] Pub. L. No. 34, 111 Stat. 788 (1997)

before they cash out and attend college) declined by an average of 16 percent (p. 7). And this occurred in a year when college tuitions rose by almost 10 percent, leaving even the most successful funds losing ground. In its first year of operations, the TTF planned for a (9%) payout in its prepaid program, and then discovered that the aggregate Texas public college tuition and fees rose by 19 percent (Jennings and Olivas 2000, p. 12).[25] Such a one-year shortfall can be made up over time by improving estimates and adjusting program charges, but no portfolio can sustain long-term losses even if college costs did not increase. Sometimes, states have even discounted the costs, in order to attract program participants, as the Michigan Education Trust (MET) program did in its early period (Lehman 1990). This mistake and the early tax problems caused the state to suspend its sales operations for a time until financial stability was restored.

But even with the favorable tax treatment meted out to the programs in 1997, and with several years of a robust market, the 2000s have seen substantial losses across the states. News reports and annual program reports have noted losses by most state plans, both prepaid and savings programs.

As a result, states have substantially increased the costs of these programs, added additional fees, and reduced benefits. As one example, in Maryland, the one-time payment to cover a four-year degree in the Maryland Prepaid College Trust rose 30.5 percent for an infant and 20.2 percent for a ninth-grader (whose contract would ripen in three years after twelfth grade). The 2003–04 cost increases will be almost 10 percent, with 6 percent increased each year after. The College Trust's fiscal year 2001 reserves were $238 million, with an "actuarial deficit" of $30.5 million. These paper losses show that if the revenue/ expenditure continues without correction, it will be short $30.5 million on already-existing contracts when they come due. In fiscal years 2000 and 2001, the portfolio lost 7.8 percent and 8.8 percent; respectively (Baker 2002).

Maryland's situation is not unique. Ohio projected a $46 million deficit after its portfolio performance in 2001–02, and in four separate increments, raised the cost of each credit unit a total of 53 percent.[26] Virginia raised the cost of its plan by 25 percent in 2001–02. Washington increased prices by 24 percent in fiscal year 2001–02. Pennsylvania maintains several investment funds, and in the first three months of the funds performances, the returns ranged from a high of plus 1.88 percent to a low of minus 19.06 percent (Cooper 2002, p. E1). New Jersey's losses ranged from up 1.6 percent to down 7.34 percent (p. E1). In most of these plans, any losses to be made up will affect new subscribers, who will be charged more to subsidize the losses in earlier fund participant portfolios.

Some states are so concerned about their prepaid or savings programs that they are closed (Wyoming), are considering closing (Florida, Tennessee, Colorado), are limiting or delaying

[25] In program year 2002–03, the TTF suspended operations. See <www.texastomorrowfunds.org>.

[26] In addition, Miami University (Ohio) changed its tuition schedule in 2003. Increasing all tuition to $18,000 and giving $9,000 rebate scholarships to Ohio residents will likely throw off Ohio prepaid calculations (Stephens and Theis 2003).

enrollment period (West Virginia, Colorado, Maryland), or are allowing dissatisfied participants to withdraw without the usual penalties (Colorado)(Jennings and Olivas 2000; Sanko 2002; Powers 2002; Baker 2002; Kurdi 2002). Conflicting reports have even suggested the enormously popular Florida Prepaid College Plan could be in trouble (even with its 750,000 contracts and $4-plus billion reserves), and even as the state finally enacted a state savings plan in 2002, the Florida College Investment Plan (Powers 2002). While the total investments in 529 plans have grown ($9 billion in 2002 alone), and while there is evidence that more parents and other donors have heard of 529 plans, these stutter—steps, program restrictions, and losses do not appear to bode well overall, especially in a market downturn. One saving grace is that most of us are risk-averse and unlikely to do better in the stock market than are the major investment firms currently operating state program portfolios. And who knew bonds would perform well (Fuerbringer 2003)? Evidently, the lower transaction costs (for some funds), market advantages due to large size, and tax savings still make these funds attractive to many investors seeking a diverse portfolio for their children's college expenses.

## System Complexity

A good way to appreciate the complexity of 529 plans is to consider traditional retirement plans or 401K programs, and then make them more complicated. Virtually no state operates its prepaid or savings plans the same way as does another state. For example, Joseph F. Hurley, whose annual book, *The Best Way to Save for College*, rates state plans, records the following criteria for each:

- Eligibility, or who can open an account
- Time or age limitations on beneficiary or on use of account assets
- Age-based investment options
- Static investment options
- Underlying investments
- Fees and expenses (annual/enrollment/withdrawal)
- Broker distribution
- Contributions (maximum/minimum)
- Account changes (beneficiary changes, transfer ownership, successor owners, rollover/transfer assets, investment options)
- FF&C
- State income tax deductibility
- Exemptions from creditors
- Subject to involuntary transfer or alienation
- Reciprocity with other state plans[27]

[27] See "What to Look for in a 529 Plan: A Checklist" in Hurley (2002. pp. 79–113).

In addition, there are many other complicated features, such as whether programs involve a state's private colleges (Texas); whether a state plan's withdrawal provisions conform to federal law (California, Arkansas); where there is a cancellation penalty (Illinois); whether payroll deductions are permitted (Idaho); whether tuition alone is covered, or tuition and college fees (Virginia); whether receipt of a scholarship provides special refund provisions (Texas); whether there are special provisions for death, military service, disability, state financial aid eligibility, and a myriad of other conditions (Hurley 2002).

Of course, these many options reflect the maturity of investment markets and make the various plans extremely popular with parents and other investors, especially those plans that offer enhanced portability and tax benefits as program choices. Additionally, investors have many choices among investment funds, especially in state savings plans: Alaska offers eight age-based options and four static portfolios, while Tennessee and Vermont offer eleven age-based funds, all managed by TIAA-CREF (pp. 186, 274, 279). Texas maintains thirteen fund options.[28] Each state also maintains at least one major diversified investment portfolio for its base funds. California even offers a "social investment" portfolio, one that invests only in stocks considered socially and environmentally progressive, such as not including alcohol or tobacco interests (p. 195).

As attractive as these choices are, an observer cannot help but question whether a state program really requires eleven or thirteen investment choices for contract purchasers, each with a different fee structure, investment mix, or tract record. The marginal advantages may not be evident in any annual review, while the state's supervisory role is made more complicated by the extremely complex bid and review process, especially in states with intricate procurement and investment regulations. This lack of transparency is the clear disadvantage, held up to the mirror of enhanced investor choice. Most likely there are too many choices for most investors, the system's complexity rendering comparable choice shopping too complicated for most investors, particularly for those who participate because they are risk-averse and do not feel comfortable simply investing in traditional instruments and beating the markets. I have a law degree, a Ph.D., have studied these state programs since their early versions, have written two books on the subject, own contracts in five states, and still cannot compare the plans across various states. There is almost too much dynamism in the plans, as states vie with other to offer more plans and more complex options so as to attract more contract purchasers. A system can have too many choices, and can intimidate or paralyze unsophisticated buyers, especially in such churning markets (Opdyke 2003; Schwanhausser 2003; Appleman 2003).

This system complexity can become a barrier to market entry for some. The early state prepaid programs did not pose this issue, as purchasers simply bought into a contract that

[28] The newly established Texas Tomorrow's College Investment Plan was too new to be included in the Hurley study. See Texas Tomorrow Funds, at <www.texastomorrowfunds.org> for more information on the new Texas plan.

either performed well or did not, and in states with guaranteed state FF&C, the investment results literally made no difference to the purchasers (save for their concern about overall program efficacy, as in the Wyoming case). Consumers of state savings and trust plans, however, invest both for the substantial state and federal tax advantages, and for enhancing their investment returns. This lack of transparency is another result of system complexity and too many choices.

Yet another issue is that the range of investment options may have unintended consequences. Diverse plan options may encourage purchasers to place all their eggs in one basket. I have been concerned about the rise of single mutual funds as state options, both with and without brokers, in several state plans, such as those in Utah, Texas, and Nebraska.[29] My concern is that many people in traditional marketplaces might choose mutual funds due to their broadly-based mix of stocks (or bonds, in some instances), when individual contract purchaser needs may be poorly suited for such vehicles. For example, a neutral fund will likely track the performance of the Dow-Jones or Standard & Poor markets, when an investor with a teenaged or middle school child will need to better today's disappointing market performance. Use of a single mutual fund may not be a well balanced choice for college going plans: college attendance will likely come soon after high school, whereas retirement age is subject to many features and can be postponed in real life. Joseph Hurley (2002b) made this point dramatically in an October 2002 editorial to his service subscribers to the Savings College Plan Network, when he noted a similar concern in this Utah Educational Savings Plan, a single 100 percent equity mutual fund option, offered by the private Vanguard Institutional Index Fund. While he notes that he is, in principle, for "greater investment choice," he is also concerned that such options will lead parents to place all their CSP eggs in one basket, rather than diversifying across several options, especially age-based ones that shift their investment mix as the beneficiary approaches college age. No doubt, he was also influenced by the mutual fund's poor performance in 2001–02, when it lost over 30 percent, but his overall point is a good one, a situation exacerbated by system complexity. Whenever information, such as how to best allocate and invest in state programs, is at a premium, the persons least likely to participate or prosper are the less well educated, the poor, and minorities. Thus, system complexity in state prepaid and savings programs—even in states with low barriers to entry and monthly payment options—attract and reward the most advantaged and knowledgeable participants, much like the college application process itself, which so clearly serves the interests of advantaged and wealthier students. If information and investor savvy are needed for these dynamic investments, state prepaid and savings plans will widen the gap between wealthy and poor, majority and minority, street-smart and book-smart.

[29] These plans can be reviewed at: Utah Educational Savings Plan Trust (www.uesp.org); Texas Tomorrow Funds (www.texastomorrowfunds.org); and College Savings Plan of Nebraska (www.planforcollegenow.com).

## Role of the States

As noted earlier, these prepaid and savings plans are creatures of state law, even if it took federal tax deductions and exemptions to breathe life into the plans. (In 1993, my book on prepaid plans worried about who would pay for the funerals of the plans then in existence; my 2000 book raised fundamentally different questions about the runaway success of the savings and prepaid programs.)[30] A subtle thing happened on the way to success, following the 1997 Taxpayer Relief Act:[31] Qualified State Tuition Programs morphed into Qualified Tuition Plans. What will become of the state role in state plans? Was this change symbolic, either because of the federalization of the programs (after all, it was 529 plans in play) or preceding the 2002 legislative changes that made it possible for private institutions of higher education to offer their own plans, either singly or grouped into college consortia, or because private investment firms now perform much of the heavy lifting in state plans?

There is some truth to all three scenarios, and states may further confuse audiences by camouflaging or dismissing the state role in the plans. Consider a recent advertisement for New Mexico's "The Education Plan's College Savings Program," which appeared in the Start Capital's daily *Santa Fe New Mexican*.

As in Arthur Conan Doyle's *The Hound of the Baskervilles*, this publicity piece is more interesting for what it does not show: nowhere does the official, legal name of the program appear ("The Education Plan's College Savings Program"), nor is there a local or state address for the program itself. The plan is presented as "Scholar's Edge," a trademarked program of Smith Barney/Citigroup, Schoolhouse Capital, LLC, and Oppenheimer Funds. There is a local phone number, and the very-fine caveat that New Mexico non-residents need to investigate their home state's "alternative tax advantages." However, there is no other reference to the state, and this advertising is so generic it could appear in almost any state.

This savings plan was established in 2000, along with a state prepaid plan ("The Education Plan's College Savings Program"), also subject to The Education Trust Board of New Mexico and administered by Schoolhouse Capital, LLC. If one calls the phone number, a Santa Fe exchange, at a time other than regular office hours, there is no recording to identify the program; the program is not listed in the 2002 Santa Fe Phone Directory. The Web site is not located on a Santa Fe server, and the program information requires a toll-free long distance call. Where is the "New Mexico-ness" of this New Mexico state program?

I do not mean to pick on the New Mexico plan, as I am certain nationalization of these plans has led to similar generic advertising in many, if not most of the states: And no savings plan is offered by any state without the active involvement of private investment funds or banking institutions, certainly a salutary development, especially as the plans allow non-

[30] See Olivas (1993, pp. 1–14) and Jennings and Olivas (2000, pp. 20–23).

[31] P.L. 105-34, 111 Stat. 788 (1997).

residents to purchase shares or enroll in state institutions. This evolution has been a good thing, to be sure.

But my cynical side cannot help but characterize such programs as ones that rent-a-state, operating these programs as branch offices of a larger network of financial services institutions. TIAA-CREF, the immense insurance company/financial services company that recently lost its federal tax-exempt status due to congressional action, administers and operates over a dozen state plans (Kimelman 2002). Again, I stress that there is nothing unethical or even suspicious, but state programs outsourced to private markets and operators cloud discussions about the proper role of states, state agencies, state regulations, state taxation, and state-ness. My late father was a certified public accountant in New Mexico, where he had several Indian tribes and gaming companies as clients. During the last years of his life (he died from a car accident in 1997), he told me several times that New Mexico's Indian tribes and gaming interests, who subcontracted tribal gambling and casino operations, but who did not build up or develop an infrastructure of Indian self-reliance or self-determination, were disserving pueblos.

Of course, Indian gaming interests (or another similar state program, state lotteries) may not be the perfect analogy, but there is a genuine public policy question of whether such a privatized infrastructure fully serves the state host interests. In the alternative, it diminishes arguments that these are truly state programs if they are turnkey operations, simply state-located. And closing a privatized program is clearly easier than would be closing a genuine state program. One has to wonder about the staying power of such operations.

While there are open questions concerning the state-ness of state prepaid and savings plans, there can be no doubt that there are state investments at play. Several states offer FF&C on their prepaid plans; most states offer tax exemptions or tax deductions in their plans, although details vary widely. These investments are both real and imagined, in the form of foregone tax revenue or credit guarantees, should the plans fail to meet their contractual obligations at some point. And even in states that do not offer the state-guaranteed FF&C, such as with the MET prepaid plan, state officials may maintain a "political FF&C" policy. When the MET was under attack by the IRS to render its operations taxable, then-Michigan governor John Engler publicly pledged to backstop the program's reserves, if need be, even without any legal requirement to do so (Lehman 1993). The New Jersey Better Educational Savings Trust (NJBEST), a savings plan rather than a prepaid plan, has a formal "moral obligation" provision that requires the NJBEST program to request legislative funds in the event of a shortfall (Hurley 2002a, p. 98).[32] Other states also have ambiguous status for their prepaid plans, such as Pennsylvania's which is called the Guaranteed Savings Plan, but which does not have the state's backing of FF&C. The program, begun in 1993, has published a detailed, twenty-eight page booklet so that persons considering joining the $493 million fund are

[32] See <www.njbest.com> for more information on the NJBEST program.

fully on notice that the plan, despite its name, is not actually "guaranteed" (Hill 2002). In 2002, Pennsylvania's plan had an actuarial shortfall of $26 million (Hill 2002). A similar situation occurred in Colorado's Prepaid Tuition Fund, which required a $7.7 million infusion into the $62 million program in June 2002, by the fund's parent, the Colorado Student Obligation Bond Authority. Since that time, the Fund has allowed purchasers to opt out of the program without penalty (Schmidt 2003; Sanko 2002; Block 2002; Yip 2003). This cannot shore up purchasers' or investors' confidence.

By the end of 2002, only eight states offered state prepaid plans with the FF&C backing of the state, a guarantee that the state would honor its contracts even if the fund reserves were not available: Florida, Illinois, Maryland, Massachusetts, Mississippi, Ohio, Texas and Washington. In 1998, Oregon voters went to the polls and voted down extending FF&C to its savings plan (Schmidt 2003).

Another function exclusively reserved for state determination is that of residency and reciprocity. First, by establishing rules to determine who is eligible for in-state residency and by charging tuition differentials for non-resident students in public institutions, states play the crucial role in residency determination. Cases going back to the nineteenth century, a number of U.S. Supreme Court decisions, and substantial research literature all chart this well-established role for the states.[33] While the details differ, often wildly, most states require a twelve-month period of residence, as well as domiciliary intent to make the state the student's true, permanent, fixed abode, evidenced by voting, paying taxes, holding licenses, working, and other indications of residence and domicile (Olivas 1988). Designation as a resident entitles a student to pay lower (resident) tuition and to be eligible for special admissions considerations (such as in limited-enrollment curricula or programs). States also provide many exceptions and exemptions for persons not able to fully establish or document their residency, such as military personnel, certain aliens, fiancés, and others with unusual personal circumstances (Olivas 1995).

These determinations are important in the state prepaid and savings programs in several crucial ways. First, the amount of public colleges' tuition charged varies substantially between residents and non-residents: at the University of Texas Law School, for example, 2003–04 resident tuition and fees were $12, 216, while non-resident tuition and fees were $20,789.[34] Second, for 529 program participants, this residency determination may determine eligibility for the state plan. For instance, beneficiaries of the TTF, the state's prepaid contract plan, must be either Texas residents for at least twelve months preceding the late of the TTF application or even more unusually, the non-resident child of a purchaser who is a Texas resident.[35] In addition, if a beneficiary moves from the state before she attends college and withdraws TTF

[33] See *State v. Regents of University of Wisconsin* (11 N.W. 472 [Wis. 1882]) (upholding non-resident tuition policy).

[34] See University of Texas System (www.utsystem.edu) for information on tuition rates.

[35] See Texas Tomorrow Funds (www.texastomorrowfunds.org) for a description of eligibility criteria.

funds, she may retain her classification as a resident, even though by Texas residency criteria, she would not be eligible to claim residency status. This is an enormous windfall, one nearly unique to the Texas prepaid plan.[36] In virtually every other state with a prepaid plan, students must be deemed residents at the time they enroll in a public college to be eligible for the lower tuition. I have served as faculty chair of the University of Houston's Residency Appeals Committee for seventeen years, where we hear dozens of appeals from unsuccessful non-resident claims each year, and this feature trumps all the usual criteria for establishing Texas state residency. A savvy Texas parent who purchases a TTF contract and who may plan on moving away from the state can, with modest sums, guarantee their child a resident student contract even should the beneficiary not be eligible for the lower tuition by virtue of the child's domicile in Texas. Given Texas' relatively high barriers to residency (for example, requiring that the applicant be "gainfully employed"), this is an extraordinarily generous benefit.[37] (Some border states award in-state benefits to foreign nationals in Canada or Mexico.)[38]

In truth, both savings and prepaid plans have become more portable, both within states and across states. For example, students in most states can use the 529 funds to attend public or private institutions into which they are accepted, with the dollar amounts pegged to an aggregate amount, either the mark of public college tuition (as in Ohio and Alabama) or an amount up to the estimated average costs of an undergraduate education in the state's private colleges (as in Texas). In this fashion, the beneficiaries of state plans can apply to colleges in almost any other state.

These developments have been for the good, since earlier plans had more geographical restrictions, which discouraged some potential purchaser parents who were unwilling to restrict their children's options to in-state public colleges, and therefore chose not to purchase 529 plans with such restrictions. As private institutions make plans to enact their own programs, this portability and mobility should increase, since private colleges do not differentiate tuition on a resident/non-resident basis. One could also expect additional developments that will lessen state residence barriers, as there will likely appear state exchanges, reciprocity, and multi-state consortia to allow regional compacts. Fully developed plans could even include reciprocal state tax deductions or exemptions where both states (the home state and receiver state) have state income taxes. Now that all states have college savings plans in operation, negotiating these reciprocal compact programs is the logical next step.

Reviewing these state-level policy issues, an observer need not be Delphic to comment upon the general "privatizing" of this movement, in light of the development of private markets and financial institutions actually implementing many states' savings and even prepaid plans, the involvement of private and even proprietary institutions of higher education as

36 Utah has a similar provision though it requires eight years to lock in Utah residency. *See* Utah Educational Savings Plan at <www.uesp.org>.

37 See 19 TAC 21.23(b) (2003).

38 See 19 TAC 21.26(b)(6)(C) (2003).

recipients of students enrolled with 529 plan resources, and the relaxed residency requirements for purchase options that allow parents who live in nearly any state to buy contracts for beneficiaries who will want to attend colleges almost anywhere. I raised questions about the diminished "state-ness" of state savings and state prepaid tuition plans and forces at play will likely lessen the states' roles in these state programs. Additional forces include the success of private sector savings plans such as that of the College Savings Bank (CSB), 529 eligibility of private institutions to establish individual or consortia savings plans, and similar devices (such as UPromise)[39] that allow consumers to save college funds by retail purchasers that generate "frequent flier"-like points towards college tuition and other clever options such as college tuition gift certificates and college gift registries, pledging programs that are likely to grow as parents seek ways to pay their children's future tuition bills. When they get married, buy them a china setting or two English literature courses.

There can be no doubt that the private market incentives and public tax advantages have stimulated these state college savings and prepaid programs. In 2002, nearly $20 billion had flowed into these investments, even in a depressed stock market. This development has been a public/private sector collaboration that has exceeded most observers' expectations, especially those who remember the tax problems of the early prepaid programs and the period before the 1997 federal law changed the landscape entirely.

A number of policy issues remain unresolved, but they will likely be worked out as the plans expand and mature. The interaction of state and federal taxes is one such issue. Problems include reconciling the complex and overlapping 1997 Taxpayer Relief Act[40] college provisions and those of the 2001 Economic Growth and Tax Relief Reconciliation Act of 2001,[41] especially the complex education provisions of tax credits, tax deductions, and tax exclusions that are included in the Hope and Lifetime Learning Credits, deductions of educational expenses and student loan interest payments, Education Individual Retirement Accounts, and Employer-Provided Tuition Assistance provisions.[42] These complicated and detailed provisions present the same system complexity that was seen as problematic in the 529 Qualified Tuition Plan provisions, only more so.

Because of the different state-level income taxation issues at play in the fifty-plus jurisdictions, a variety of taxation issues have arisen, including state plans that penalize non-resident 529 purchasers (as in Illinois) and actually favor non-residents (as in New York) (Hurley 2002c; 2002d).[43] Some state plans exclude state tax on payouts, while others have no such exclusion, rendering comparability almost impossible, either for purchase price comparisons or actual use calculations. In some plans, such as in Virginia, the state may lose money on

[39] See UPromise at <www.upromise.com>.

[40] P.L. 34, 111 Stat. 788 (1997).

[41] P.L. 107-16, Sec. 203, 115 Stat. 38 (2001).

[42] See Hurley (2002a, pp. 11–20, 50–55).

[43] See also Lauricella (2003).

resident beneficiaries because of the way state contracts are drafted, but will likely come out ahead on all beneficiaries who attend colleges outside of the state (Hurley 2002a, p. 280).[44]

As technical as these state tax issues appear, additional federal tax issues have also arisen, and have not been addressed by the IRS or Congress. Some of these include how Medicaid "countable resources" count,[45] tax reporting provisions for income reported on form 1099,[46] income averaging,[47] how to treat 529 plans when the student receives a scholarship (the "scholarship penalty"),[48] criteria for qualified higher education expenses,[49] "self-help" provisions,[50] and issues involving saver's credit.[51] Not all these issues affect a large number of contract-purchasers or beneficiaries, but two tax issues continue to vex all participants: interaction with financial aid programs and 529 sunset provisions.

It has been five years since the 1997 legislation that created 529 programs, and it is still unclear how prepaid or savings plans will affect the beneficiary's financial aid package. This entire process is extraordinarily complex, and turns on whether or not the student is a dependent, has siblings in college, has assets, or has parents with earned income. In traditional arrangements, parents are expected to pledge a certain percentage of their income and assets to their dependent children's college education; the calculations turn upon the parents' submitting a financial aid form, the Free Application for Federal Student Aid (FAFSA). If the child is under consideration for private colleges, the parents will also likely be required to complete and submit an "institutional methodology" form called the PROFILE, administered by the College Board's College Scholarship Service. This form, an extremely detailed review of assets, is used to dispense institutional aid.

The FAFSA formula roughly measures the individual college's Cost-of-Attendance (COA), a composite of tuition, fees, and other expenses needed to enroll in that institution and live for the academic year. A given student's financial need would be calculated by subtracting the Expected Family Contribution (EFC) from the COA. Herein lays the crux of the problem: are 529 plans counted in financial aid determinations (such as the EFC)? The answer is yes and no. Federal law requires that prepaid tuition plans reduce the COA, meaning that in most instances, the assets of the contracts will reduce the "financial need" of a student (Hurley

[44] For more information on the Virginia plan, see Virginia College Savings Plan at <www.virginia529.com>.

[45] For example, a parent's or grandparent's 529 plan assets may be considered as "a countable resource" in Medicaid eligibility, due to many 529 plans' revocable feature (Hurley 2001).

[46] Joseph Hurley (2002a) reported on the complexity of filling out income tax forms, and reporting deduction from 529 plan contributions (pp. 42–44).

[47] See Hurley's (2002e) article describing the complexities of income averaging.

[48] Michigan is one example of a state prepaid plan that will give a weighted refund if the beneficiary receives a full tuition scholarship. Ohio's College Advantage Plan also has such a provision, see Ohio Tuition Trust, at <www.collegeadvantage.com>.

[49] See (IRS 2007, p. 40).

[50] Some of the 529 plans can be "gamed" in a way that allows parents to minimize taxes by changing beneficiaries, naming themselves as beneficiaries, or by willing over accounts. This should not be tried by amateurs.

[51] The 2001 Economic Growth and Tax Relief Reconciliation Act enacted a "saver's credit" that can be counted against investments in retirement accounts (P.L. 107-16, Sec. 203, 115 Stat. 38 [2001]).

2002a, pp. 64–65). However, assets from 529 savings plans do not count on the COA side, but shift to the EFC ledger for parents who hold the contracts, and are counted at a lowered rate; even better, if a grandparent owns the contract, it is as if it doesn't exist at all (p. 65). In some instances, however, such as if the parents are relatively lower income (with an adjusted gross income of less than approximately $50,000 in tax year 2001–02); no 529 assets will be counted (p. 65). This differential treatment is as confusing as it is meaningless—to parents, putting money into a 529 plan should not turn on whether it is an asset, forcing their hand into a prepaid or savings plan on the basis of whether the child ends up in a public or private college, whether it is the grandparents or parents who actually fund the plan, and whether or not they will, at some future date, be eligible for asset reduction due to the fine print. Again, this system complexity reduces public understanding and confuses choices.

As daunting as this system complexity is, and as much uncertainty as is built into the system, at least until Congress, the IRS, or the Department of Education acts authoritatively, the biggest threat to all state prepaid and savings plans is a simple one. All federal 529 legislation provisions of the Economic Growth and Tax Relief Act[52] will sunset or expire on December 31. 2010—a point that will likely impact most 529 contracts in play now and until that time. Unless Congress acts to extend the 529 provisions (and those of Coverdell accounts and other financial aid programs), there is no guarantee that the favorable tax treatment of Qualified Tuition Plans will continue. It is almost inconceivable that Congress will not extend the sunset provisions, as it is certain that a great deal of political pressure will be brought to bear on them. However, until Congress does act, there will be this sword of Damocles hanging over 529 accounts and the fifty states.

In all, it has been a remarkable five years since 529 plans were given their federal status, and the widespread developments have greatly strengthened through the comprehensive financial markets and investment firms that operate the plans and sell most of the contracts. Since late 2002, every state and the District of Columbia have college savings plans, while a small but growing number of states (20) have established college prepaid programs, including twelve with a form of FF&C.

Despite the phenomenal growth and comprehensiveness of these state plans, a number of questions and policy concerns arise. I would argue that this movement, while salutary in its overall stimulation of college attendance and initiation of parental planning and contribution to their children's college payment, has troubling seeds that have been built into its system, ones that may not be evident for several years to come, and will certainly appear many watches from now. These concerns fall into three categories, which I label Equity Implications, Institutional Implications, and Legislative Implications.

[52] P.L. 107-16, Sec. 203, 115 Stat. 38 (2001).

## Equity Implications

The bottom line for supporting CSP plans such as the Alabama Prepaid Affordable College Tuition plan or the TTF is that they provide an investment vehicle for parents or grandparents (or other "givers," like those saving for nieces, nephews, and godchildren), one that guarantees a return on the investment sufficient to pay for a specific amount of tuition in years to come. By pooling the funds and gaining certain market leverage, a well-run fund can get a better return on the money than can you or I. Further, the program can anticipate future tuition levels and predict with relative certainty how much has to be paid out at a certain time in the future. Thus, run properly, it almost cannot lose: the state takes in the money up front and pays out at the back end, and over time. Program costs are either included as a cost of doing business—as part of the long term "float"—or by a premium (for example, a set or sliding percentage fee). Unless bond markets go haywire or something cataclysmic occurs (a la the Mexican Bolsa or Orange County), program actuaries can predict the cash flow, program participation ratios, and other technical details. Texans have participated in record numbers, far surpassing the first year experience in Florida, the country's premier program, run with excellent management, low cost colleges, and almost 750,000 contracts to date (Tomsho 2002; Shah 2002). Of course, poor market performance, at least over the short haul, has hurt virtually all stock investments.

But it is very likely to be wealthy and upper-middle class Texans who profit from this venture. The equity issue is not far-fetched, but both intuitive and evident from programs in other states. Take Michigan, which sold its first contract in 1988. In 1990, Professor and Law Dean Jeffrey Lehman published an influential article in the Michigan Law review, "Social Irresponsibility, Actuarial Assumptions, and Wealth Redistribution: Lessons about Public Policy from a Prepaid Tuition Program." In 1993, he followed with a careful study of the MET's decision to expand its subscriber base by offering a monthly payment option. In his earlier article, Lehman had charted the redistribution of state subsidy benefits upward to the most-advantaged Michigan residents. In 1990, partially in reaction to this criticism, the MET board changed its way of selling contracts to allow purchasers to spread the payments over a set period of time—on an installment plan. It was anticipated that this would permit families with lower incomes to participate, especially since the size of monthly payments is often more salient to low-income consumers than is the total obligation. (I am reminded here of my brother, a former car salesman in New Mexico and California, who marvels at how customers seem more concerned with their monthly payment rates than they were with the total price of the cars he sold.)

Lehman found that the availability of the monthly payment option reduced the "skewedness" of the original MET purchaser profile, but not by a substantial margin, and measurement discrepancies between the periods before and after the change made exact comparisons difficult. Even so, in 1990, the richest two-fifths of the Michigan population with children had purchased 61 percent of the MET monthly payment option contracts

(Lehman 1990, p. 35, Table 3.2). More recent figures for Florida and Texas suggest that purchasers in these states also constitute their more advantaged citizens.[53] When the purchaser profile is combined with the original state investment to start the program, it is a remarkable and remarkably regressive redistribution of state resources to the wealthy.

Any subsidy or bailout of a CSP would come from that state's general revenues—requiring all to pay for the advantaged purchasers' continued advantage. Even in Michigan, where there was no legal FF&C provision, the governor said the sate had a "moral full-faith-and-credit" obligation (p. 34). A variant of this scenario happened in Ohio recently, where general state revenues of $1 million were used to reduce the price of the state's tuition units (Jennings and Olivas 2000, p. 8). In the first year of the Texas operation, before the voters approved a Constitutional amendment to extend FF&C to the state's CSP, the program underestimated costs by 10 percent (p. 22). A shortfall has to be made up from somewhere, and now the state's citizens will foot this bill.

Paradoxically, the clear indication of state investment, willingness to use a state's FF&C, and incorporating general revenues into the program are signposts that the IRS (and judges) will look to in determining whether a CSP will be tax exempt (Hurley 2002, p. 93; Williams 1993, p. 24). It would seem fair if all the program participants share proportionately in a loss (as in bad investments or a shortfall). I urge legislatures to constitute CSPs so that the states' taxpayers will contribute very few general fund dollars to either the startup or any bailout provisions. On equity grounds, it seems very unfair to tax those who cannot afford or who are unable to attend college, so that their more advantaged neighbors can do so more easily. I do not know where the fair tipping point is, but it may be some "borrowing against" the future and repayment to the state for out-of-pocket startup costs.

I know and respect the Biblical admonishment that we will always have the poor among us, but I do not believe they should have to ante up just so that wealthier parents can have an additional savings vehicle for their children to go to college and more easily consume the consideration state investment already in place. This is particularly true in a time when the federal government is in a pell-mell rush to create similar tax subsidies, which are decidedly regressive. At the least, states should not under-price their product, as occurred in Michigan (Lehman 1993). Why should any state's CSP purchasers receive a 20 percent discount? Indeed, I believe a surcharge for program fees is a better way to raise operating funds, and this has been the practice for the most recent startups.

## Institutional Implications

I also fear that at some point institutional behavior will change, so that admissions might be predicated upon ability to pay. Let me project a plausible scenario, based on Texas and

[53] In Florida, more than half the prepaid purchasers in 2003 had annual incomes over $50,000. In Texas, by 1999, only 16 percent of the prepaid participants had annual income of less than $50,000 (Jennings and Olivas 2000, p. 22). Texas legislators were so concerned about the skewed participation levels that they enacted a special scholarship fund for low-income families who participated in the prepaid fund.

Florida, whose demographics are similar. Florida's CSP has sold over 750,000 contracts, and soon will have over a million contracts in play, spread over approximately twenty-five years; this includes children just born all the way to college seniors consuming the paid-for benefits. If this were in Texas, and meant that 15,000 contracts were coming due each year, let us say that two-thirds of them actually wished to attend college in Texas; the others did not enroll or went of out state. This would mean 10,000 funded freshmen competing for spots in Texas institutions. Let us say 500–1,000 wanted to attend Rice, Trinity, Baylor and Southwestern, the elite private institutions in the state. This would leave 9,000–9,500 funded students applying to University of Texas, Texas A&M University, Texas Tech University, the University of Houston, and the state's other public and private two- and four-year colleges. The admissions pressure upon the University of Texas and Texas A&M University, already evident as they scale back to more manageable size, will be enormous.[54]

Now say you are the President of University of Texas, considering two exactly-equally qualified students—let's say Mexican Americans from the Rio Grande Valley in South Texas. But one is fully funded and the other will require a combination of state, federal and scarce institutional funding. Who are you going to admit? Mind you, the fact that one student has been lucky enough to be born into a family that saves for her college education is no reflection as to her personal character; indeed, growing up successful in a family without financial resources has often been seen as a plus in admissions decisions.[55]

And I do not exaggerate the admissions pressures: in a strictly enrollment-driven system such as we have in Texas, there is some slight current under-utilization of higher education, some "excess capacity." But Texas Coordinating Board (2003) data conservatively predict that in a mere twelve years, there will be 155,000 more students clamoring for higher education in Texas. If we get lucky and minority achievement increases, we could have 400,000 more students by 2015. (In 1999, Texas public universities alone enrolled over 400,000 students.) Let's say we split the difference: by 2015 we will have 290,000 more students then we do today. This is nine *additional* University of Houstons. Moreover, a college savings tuition plan will stimulate savings and likely stimulate college attendance. (And I would argue that any of the "higher education–lite" proposals for televising distance learning would be inadequate to deal with this problem.) Even if the savings go to substantially the same students who would have enrolled without a TTF, its existence is bound to increase—in fact, it is *designed* to stimulate—college attendance and college investment. That is, a successful plan will likely stimulate a greater need for college seats in Texas. You could do the same calculations for Florida, and see the pressures those 50,000 contracts each year will have on Florida International, the University of Florida, or Florida State University. The seduction to acti-

[54] The Texas Top Ten Percent Plan has put additional pressure on state institutions, particularly the University of Texas at Austin (Kay and Jyson 2003).

[55] See Olivas (1997).

vate the CSP electronic funds transfers will be very powerful, and the Florida institutions will ignore the pressure at their peril.

Thus, I believe my admonitions about the merging of admissions and ability to pay are conservative and the pressures at the institutional level will prove to be irresistible. While no CSP guarantees admission, all will certainly guarantee higher expectations about admissibility on the part of purchaser parents, who are likely to become an angry cohort of taxpayers. No warning label or disclaimer about admissions standards will serve to placate this group.

## Legislative Implications

This leads to my third major concern, the legislative fallout from a successful CSP. After ten years of a successful TTF, widely advertised in English, Spanish, and Vietnamese, there will be a very large accumulated pool of money, completely dedicated to higher education. For example, in 1998 alone, Florida earned a pooled fund of almost $500 million; even Michigan, with its originally adverse tax ruling and a year of suspended sales for reorganization, sits on over $500 million.[56] Will the state legislatures continue to appropriate state general revenues for an enterprise that has so many potential guaranteed-paid applicants in the pipeline? In other words, will this program *supplant* state support rather then *supplement* appropriations? And just to make it interesting, what will happen if the answer is for free tuition levels to rise to "market levels" (Robinson 2003)?

Again, I will use Texas as an example, but could use almost any other to make my point. The TTF, actuarially premised upon steady, predictable tuition rates, will find it difficult to stick with its careful figures—which drive the plan's engine—if tuition rates exceed investment rates. Any ratcheting effect here will doom the careful equilibrium necessary for balancing both ends of the equation. And again I ask, where will Texas get the funds to build the nine new University of Houston campus-equivalents in fifteen years? State support for higher education in Texas has declined as a portion of overall expenses, and the state historically ranks low in per capita support of post-secondary education. The TTF, instead of being a wonderful device for stimulating parental savings, could become an attractive nuisance—either by dampening legislative support for general institutional appropriations or as a large, unintended ratchet to keep up tuition rates unrealistically low. As I noted earlier, Texas undershot its costs in its first year by nearly 10 percent, leaving the shortfall to be amortized across all latecomers.

As a corollary concern, fees, also guaranteed by the TTF, have virtually no control. A cynic might observe that the Texas legislature has enacted a silent fee system to guise its political unwillingness to take the heat for raising tuition rates (Nissimov 2002). One good thing to come from this legislation may be a more open consideration of fees, tuition, fees, and residency structures in the states. All of these details have real institutional consequences. Now

[56] Discussion with Florida prepaid staff and MET staff (Summer 2000).

there is in place a governmental counterweight to keep tuition levels low, even though they should probably rise in states such as Texas and Florida, who charge too little for their product. In Virginia, the year 2000 saw smaller actual dollar appropriations for public colleges than the 1999 levels.[57] This does not even take inflation into account, or a stagnant federal economy that has led to state deficits and falling support for higher education.

Moreover, if legislators do the right thing and substantially increase public tuition, these plans may lose over the long run, or one year's class will subsidize the others. There is nothing inherently wrong with this, but several years of imbalance, a market correction, or a long bear market could certainly erode any plan reserves.

## Other Policy Concerns

Section 529 plans pose all these concerns, and additional ones: parents might do better in their own investments than will these state-run programs, and so these savings plans will simply reallocate parents' overall savings, not actually stimulate new college savings. With the tax breaks now in place for the plans, it is unlikely that any amateur investors will do better, and many parents are risk-averse, so professional money managers may be the better investors. As of January, 2003, only a handful of states had both a prepaid tuition and a college savings plan, but the next several years will see growth of both plans in remaining states.

Another issue is what to do when a program ends, as happened in 1995 with the eight-year old Wyoming Advance Payment of Higher Education Costs Program, which closed due to poor participation rates. Because the state is obligated to honor all the contracts sold during the life of the program, the program may become the equivalent of a Civil War widow's fund—one that has to function until the last participant dies or chooses not to enroll in college. Perhaps the program can be absorbed into a regional pact or neighboring state's plans. Washington, for example, began a CSP in 1997, and it would likely benefit both states to combine their resources. As stock values have declined, other states have seriously considered pulling the plug on their programs (Block 2002).

My views on post-secondary prepaid tuition plans grow out of extensive research on the subject, familiarity with the national and state trends in this complex area, wide consultation with prepaid fund and trust fund officials, and discussions with a large number of legislators and treasurers in states with such funds or those contemplating either program. My thinking on these programs has evolved to the point that I believe them to hold great promise but also to hold far-ranging implications—a number of which have been unanticipated and which could undermine general public support for the programs.

Earlier, especially during the pending complex litigation over the Michigan fund's tax status, I was concerned (like many observers) with the viability of the programs, However, this corner has been turned. It is almost unpatriotic to be against a program that assists par-

[57] Discussion with University of Virginia President John Casteen (February 2000).

ents in saving for their children's college educations. Rather I now fear the programs' likelihood of "success."

For the reasons I have explained here, I want more information on the plans, and more evaluation. Most of the plans have shown little concern for evaluating their results or for conducting research on their portfolios. Success has been measured largely in the numbers of contracts or in how many dollars are invested in the plans. Surely these cannot be the sole markers of success. Why are there no post mortems on the Wyoming experience, analyses of Michigan's resurgence, research on Texas' under-estimation of first year costs? For these programs to be genuinely successful, they need to undertake critical, searching self-analysis. I conclude by offering a partial research agenda, one that would likely answer nagging equity concerns, institutional implications, and legislative questions.

First, this is a field where there has been strangely little introspection. Each state needs to undertake evaluation plans on a regular, even annual basis, both to see the results of their targeted information and to plan for future products and services. Once they have established a baseline data set, they can model simulations, test innovations, and experiment. The availability of data would be an important first step.

Second, more sophisticated research, such as the zip code analysis of MET contract purchasers, should be possible (Lehman 1993, p. 35). Many other such initiatives would be possible if the data were made available to scholars and researchers seeking to understand financial aid policy. Program and legislative staff contemplating legislation would find data extremely useful in proposing legislation or regulations, as would public policy analysts generally.

Finally, the more the public understands these programs, the more likely such programs are to gain public support. People recognize that the finance mechanisms for college are changing, as they are in private markets, generally, and building public support is essential for such plans, especially with the complex and confusing options. Analyzing Wyoming's under-participation or Michigan's problems or Florida's possible over-participation could lead to policy changes and program improvement. One thing is clear: these programs have become popular because they address an important social issue. Staying ahead of this curve is an important byproduct of these plans, one that may enable them to gain the long-term support and confidence they will require.

## Developments Since 2003

In some respects, the recent story of 529 plans has resembled Dickens' *A Tale of Two Cities*: "It was the best of times, it was the worst of times...." While the U.S. economy has had its peaks and valleys, nearly every state has contributed less of its resources to public higher education appropriations, and as a result, tuition costs have increased to record levels, even outstripping inflation and cost indices.

These pincer movements have clearly been the worst of times for 529s. The resultant rising tuition has made it impossible for states with 529 prepaid tuition plans to gauge pricing for those plans or to meet targets for guaranteeing plan terms.

As a result, states have closed programs entirely, as in Wyoming, or closed plans to new participants, put plans on hold, or suspended operations until the plans can be restructured. For example, in Summer, 2006, Wyoming (which earlier had closed its 529 Prepaid plan) also closed its 529 savings plan, called the College Achievement Plan, and coordinated with the Colorado CollegeInvest program for those who chose to keep their contracts.

Eight of the nineteen states with prepaid plans (of either the guaranteed or the unit variety) are either closed or not open in 2007, and more are sure to restructure. Even those states that have full faith and credit guarantees have had to reorganize their plans, as in Texas, which has suspended the operations of its popular Texas Tomorrow Fund (a prepaid plan) until the predicted $3 billion actuarial shortfall can be dealt with. Maryland accountants have predicted at least a $70 million actuarial shortfall, and other states will be found to have similar deficits. In some states, such as Illinois and Texas, these public funds and their kissing-cousins, public lotteries, have even been seriously discussed as candidates for sale and privatizing. Several states have tightened up criteria, added "fees," reduced coverage for expenses, or "decoupled" tuition and the payout, in the hope of making the programs more sound.

One issue that observers will be watching carefully in the prepaid/college tuition area is whether some states might decide to "privatize" these assets in order to gain a short-term, lump-sum buyout or lease by private investors, as has happened with some public transportation authority programs. Such actions are very troubling public policies, and raise many complex policy issues (Schwartz and Nixon 2007).

In addition, fraud and poor management have reared their head in this market, as in criminal charges brought against the head of the otherwise-successful Utah 529 plan, where the state not only lost money due to embezzlement by the director of the program, but had to pay a Securities and Exchange Commission (SEC) fine due to poor institutional oversight.

Indeed, the industry has imposed new self-governing rules and policies to fend off greater regulation by the federal government, and Congressional hearings were held, at which there were calls for increased oversight. In 2004, the SEC found widely-divergent investment policies and results among the plans it studied. On November 15, 2006, the SEC imposed sanctions and issued a cease-and-desist order against 1st Global Capital Corp. for sales practices relating to 529s and for supervisory failures.[58]

Even an international prepaid plan, based in the Philippines, gained notoriety when its assets disappeared and left thousands of Filipino contract-purchasers without recourse, in a nation where there are no such things as student loans or work-study programs (Overland 2006a).

[58] The SEC found that 1st Global had violated MSRB (Municipal Securities Rulemaking Board) rules in its sales of 529 plans, between 2001–2004, by its agents selling C-class units when A-class units would have produced better returns over the expected time period of investment. In 2006, the MSRB amended advertising and supervision rules to align with those of the SEC and NASD (National Association of Securities Dealers).

Litigation has arisen in several settings, as in the SEC case against the Utah thefts and in the 1st Global Capital Corp. matter. In Kentucky, the state's Attorney General sued to prevent the state Legislature from allocating surplus state funds to the State's "Kentucky Affordable Prepaid Tuition" program (KAPT), which in 2007 is not accepting new participants. In state court in Illinois, litigation has arisen concerning the issue of state tax deductions for non-residents who purchase the plan for resident beneficiaries; in response, the State revamped its program in August, 2007 (H.B. 376), which removed the state tax on qualified distributions to an Illinois taxpayer from a non-Illinois 529 plan.

However, as in Tale of Two Cities, these have also simultaneously been the best of times for 529 plans, especially with developments at the federal level. The Deficit Reduction Act of 2005[59] wrote important changes in parental assets determinations for federal financial aid purposes. In the Tax Increase Prevention and Reconciliation Act,[60] a technical loophole (in the "Kiddie Tax") reconstituted how money set aside in college-savings plans is to be counted in determining a dependent student's eligibility for need-based financial aid if the account is in the student's name. Prior to this change, beginning in 2006, contributions made to college-savings plans, even under a student's name, would act to shrink a student's financial-aid award. Most importantly, the sword of Damocles was removed from the head of 529 programs when President George W. Bush signed into law the Pension Protection Act of 2006,[61] which removed the plans' original sunset provisions, which would have ended their life in 2010. As a result, the financial services industry has moved much more aggressively into the market, extending the reach and scope of the 529 savings plans.

In Congressional hearings in 2007, the Bush Administration proposed to make all 529-plan contributions tax-deductible on federal income tax (by adding to the existing "saver's credit" provisions). While not yet enacted, there is no doubt that the 529 plans are faring better at the federal level than they are at the state operational level, especially in those states where both types of 529 plans co-exist in a single agency or department.

TABLE 3.1: **Known Prepaid Tuition Programs, by State**

| State | Program | Plan Type[1] | Start Date | Administrative Agency | URL |
|---|---|---|---|---|---|
| **Alabama** | Prepaid Affordable College Tuition (PACT) | P | 1990 | Alabama State Treasurer | www.treasury.state.al.us |
| | Alabama Higher Education 529 Fund | S | 2002 | Alabama State Treasurer | www.treasury.state.al.us |
| **Alaska** | University of Alaska College Savings Plan | S | 2001 | University of Alaska and the Alaska Trust | www.uacollegesavings.com |

[1] P=Prepaid; S=Savings

[59] P.L. 109-171, 129 Stat. 4 (2006).

[60] P.L. 109-222, 120 Stat. 345 (2006).

[61] P.L. 109-280, 120 Stat. 780 (2006).

TABLE 3.1: **Known Prepaid Tuition Programs, by State**

| State | Program | Plan Type[1] | Start Date | Administrative Agency | URL |
|---|---|---|---|---|---|
| | T. Rowe Price College Savings Plan | S | 2001 | University of Alaska and the Alaska Trust | www.troweprice.com/collegesavings |
| | John Hancock Freedom 529 | S | 2001 | University of Alaska and the Alaska Trust | www.manulifecollegesavings.com |
| **Arizona** | Arizona Family College Savings Program (CSB) | S | 1999 | The Arizona Commission for Postsecondary Education | http://arizona.collegesavings.com |
| | Arizona Family College Savings Program (SMR) | S | 1999 | The Arizona Commission for Postsecondary Education | www.smrinvest.com |
| | Waddell & Reed InvestEd Plan | S | 2001 | The Arizona Commission for Postsecondary Education | www.waddell.com |
| **Arkansas** | GIFT College Investing Plan | S | 1999 | Arkansas Tax Deferred Tuition Savings Program Investment Committee & Executive Director of the Arkansas Teacher Retirement System | www.thegiftplan.com |
| **California** | Golden State Scholar Share College Savings Trust | S | 1999 | ScholarShare Investment Board | www.scholarshare.com |
| **Colorado** | CollegeInvest-Prepaid Tuition Fund | P | 1997 | Colorado Student Obligation Bond Authority and State Treasurer | www.collegeinvest.org |
| | CollegeInvest— Scholars Choice College Savings Plan | S | 1999 | Colorado Student Obligation Bond Authority and State Treasurer | www.collegeinvest.org (Colorado Residents); www.scholars-choice.com (national) |
| **Connecticut** | The Connecticut Higher Education Trust Program (CHET) | S | 1999 | The Connecticut State Treasurer | www.aboutchet.com |
| **Delaware** | Delaware College Investment Plan | S | 1998 | Delaware College Investment Board | www.fidelity.com/delaware |
| **Florida** | Florida Prepaid College Program | P | 1987 | Florida Prepaid College Board | www.floridaprepaidcollege.com |
| | Florida College Investment Program | S | 2002 | Florida Prepaid College Program Board | www.floridaprepaidcollege.com |
| **Georgia** | Path 2 College 529 Plan | S | 2002 | Georgia Office of the Treasury and Fiscal Services and Georgia Higher Education Savings Plan | www.path2college529.com |
| **Hawaii** | Hawaii College Savings Program Tuition Edge | S | 2002 | The Hawaii Department of Budget and Finance | www.state.hi.us/budget/college/ |
| **Idaho** | Idaho College Savings Program (IDeal) | S | 2001 | Idaho College Savings Program Board | www.idsaves.org |
| **Illinois** | College Illinois! | P | 1998 | Illinois Student Assistance Commission | www.collegeillinois.com |
| | Bright Start College Savings Program | S | 2000 | Office of the State Treasurer | www.brightstartsavings.com |
| **Indiana** | College Choice 529 Investment Plan | S | 1997 | Indiana Education Savings Authority chaired by the State Treasurer | www.collegechoiceplan.com |
| **Iowa** | College Savings Iowa 529 Plan | S | 1998 | State Treasurer | www.collegesavingsiowa.com |

[1] P=Prepaid; S=Savings

TABLE 3.1: **Known Prepaid Tuition Programs, by State**

| State | Program | Plan Type[1] | Start Date | Administrative Agency | URL |
|---|---|---|---|---|---|
| **Kansas** | Learning Quest 529 Education Savings Program | S | 2000 | Kansas State Treasurer | www.learningquestsavings.com |
| **Kentucky** | Kentucky Education Savings Plan Trust | S | 1990 | Kentucky Higher Education Assistance Authority | www.kentuckytrust.org |
| | Kentucky's Affordable Prepaid Tuition (KAPT) | P | 2001 | KAPT Board of Directors & the Office of the State Treasurer | www.getkapt.com |
| **Louisiana** | Student Tuition Assistance and Revenue Trust (START) Savings Program | S | 1997 | Louisiana Office of Student Financial Assistance, Louisiana Tuition Trust Authority, and State Treasurer | www.startsaving.la.gov |
| **Maine** | NextGen College Investing Plan | S | 1999 | Finance Authority of Maine and State Treasurer | www.nextgenplan.com |
| **Maryland** | Maryland College Investment Plan | S | 2001 | Maryland Higher Education Investment Board | www.collegesavingsmd.org |
| | Maryland Prepaid College Trust | P | 1998 | Maryland Higher Education Investment Board | www.collegesavingsmd.org |
| **Massachusetts** | U. Fund College Investing Plan | S | 1999 | Massachusetts Educational Financing Authority | www.fidelity.com/ufund |
| | U. Plan | P | 1995 | Massachusetts Educational Financing Authority | www.mefa.org. |
| **Michigan** | Michigan Education Trust | P | 1988 | MET Board of Directors and Department of Treasurer | www.michigan.gov/setwithmet |
| | Michigan Education Savings Program | S | 2000 | Michigan Department of Treasury | www.misaves.com |
| **Minnesota** | Minnesota College Savings Plan | S | 2001 | Minnesota State Board of Investment and Minnesota Higher Education Services Office | www.mnsaves.org |
| **Mississippi** | Mississippi Prepaid Affordable College Tuition (MPACT) Program | P | 1997 | Mississippi Treasury Department | www.collegesavingsmississippi.com |
| | Mississippi Affordable College Savings (MACS) Program | S | 2001 | Mississippi Treasury Department | www.collegesavingsmississippi.com |
| **Missouri** | Missouri Saving for Tuition (MO$T) Program | S | 1999 | Missouri Higher Education Savings Program Board, chaired by State Treasurer | www.missourimost.org |
| **Montana** | Montana Family Education Savings Program | S | 1998 | The Montana Board of Regents of Higher Education | http://montana.collegesavings.com |
| **Nebraska** | College Savings Plan of Nebraska | S | 2001 | State Treasurer and Nebraska Investment Council | www.PlanForCollegeNow.com |
| | AIM College Savings Plan | S | 2001 | State Treasurer and Nebraska Investment Council | www.aiminvestments.com |
| **Nevada** | Nevada Prepaid Tuition Program | P | 1998 | Bd of Trustees of the College Savings Plan of Nevada and the State Treasurer's Office | http://nevadatreasurer.gov |

[1] P=Prepaid; S=Savings

TABLE 3.1: **Known Prepaid Tuition Programs, by State**

| State | Program | Plan Type[1] | Start Date | Administrative Agency | URL |
|---|---|---|---|---|---|
| | America's College Savings Plan | S | 2001` | Bd of Trustees of the College Savings Plan of Nevada chaired by state treasurer | www.americas529plan.com |
| | American Skandia College Savings Program | S | 2002 | Bd of Trustees of the College Savings Plan of Nevada chaired by state treasurer | www.americanskandia.com |
| **New Hampshire** | UNIQUE College Investing Plan | S | 1998 | State Treasurer | www.fidelity.com/unique |
| | The Advisor College Investing Plan | S | 2001 | State Treasurer | www.advisor.fidelity.com |
| **New Jersey** | New Jersey Better Educational Savings Trust (NJBEST) | S | 1998 | Higher Education Student Assistance Authority & the New Jersey Dep't of the Treasury, Division of Investment | www.njbest.com |
| **New Mexico** | The Education Plan's Prepaid Tuition Program | P | 2000 | The Education Trust Board of New Mexico | www.tepnm.com |
| | The Education Plan's College Savings Program | S | 2000 | The Education Trust Board of New Mexico | www.theeducationplan.com |
| | CollegeSense 529 Higher Ed Savings Plan | S | 2001 | The Education Trust Board of New Mexico | www.collegesense.com |
| | Scholar's Edge | S | 2001 | Education Trust Board of New Mexico | www.scholarsedge529.com |
| **New York** | New York's 529 College Savings Program | S | 1998 | Office of the State Comptroller and NYS High Education Services Corporation | www.nysaves.org |
| **North Carolina** | North Carolina's National College Savings Program | S | 1998 | North Carolina State Education Assistance Authority | www.cfnc.org/savings |
| **North Dakota** | College Save | S | 2001 | Bank of North Dakota | www.collegesave4u.com |
| **Ohio** | CollegeAdvantage Savings Plan | S | 1989 | Ohio Tuition Trust Authority | www.collegeadvantage.com |
| | Putnam CollegeAdvantage | S | 2000 | Ohio Tuition Trust Authority | www.putnam.com |
| **Oklahoma** | Oklahoma 529 College Savings Plan | S | 2000 | Board of Trustees, Chaired by State Treasurer | www.ok4saving.org |
| **Oregon** | Oregon College Savings Plan | S | 2001 | Oregon Qualified Tuition Savings Board, chaired by State Treasurer | www.oregoncollegesavings.com |
| **Pennsylvania** | Tuition Account Guaranteed Savings Program (TAP) | S | 1993 | Pennsylvania State Treasury | www.pa529direct.com |
| **Rhode Island** | CollegeBound Fund | S | 1998 | Rhone Island Higher Education Assistance Authority and the State Investment Commission | www.collegeboundfund.com |
| **South Carolina** | South Carolina Tuition Prepayment Program (SCTPP) | P | 1998 | State Treasurer | www.scgrad.org |

[1] P=Prepaid; S=Savings

TABLE 3.1: **Known Prepaid Tuition Programs, by State**

| State | Program | Plan Type[1] | Start Date | Administrative Agency | URL |
|---|---|---|---|---|---|
| | FUTUREScholar 529 College Savings Plan | S | 2002 | Office of State Treasurer | www.futurescholar.com |
| **South Dakota** | CollegeAccess 529 | S | 2002 | South Dakota Investment Council | www.collegeaccess529.com |
| **Tennessee** | Tennessee's BEST Prepaid College Tuition Plan | P | 1997 | Treasury Department and 9 member Board chaired by State Treasurer | www.treasury.state.tn.us/best.htm |
| | Tennessee's BEST Savings Plan | S | 2000 | Tennessee's Baccalaureate Education System Trust and State Treasurer | www.tnbest.org |
| **Texas** | Texas Tomorrow Fund | P | 1996 | State Comptroller's Office and the Texas Prepaid Higher Education Tuition Board | www.texastomorrowfunds.org |
| **Utah** | Utah Educational Savings Plan Trust (UESP) | S | 1997 | Utah Higher Education Assistance Authority and State Treasurer | www.uesp.org |
| **Vermont** | Vermont Higher Education Investment Plan | S | 1999 | Vermont Student Assistance Corporation | www.vheip.org |
| **Virginia** | Virginia Prepaid Education Program | P | 1996 | Virginia College Savings Plan Board and its Executive Director | www.virginia529.com |
| | Virginia Education Savings Trust (VEST) | S | 1999 | Virginia College Savings Plan Board and its Executive Director | www.virginia529.com |
| | CollegeAmerica | S | 2002 | Virginia College Savings Plan Board and its Executive Director | www.americanfunds.com |
| **Washington** | Guaranteed Education Tuition (GET) | P | 1998 | Washington State Higher Education Coordinating Board | www.get.wa.gov |
| **West Virginia** | West Virginia Prepaid College Plan | P | 1998 | State Treasurer's Office under the authority of the West Virginia College Prepaid Tuition and Savings Program Board of Trustees | www.wvtreasury.com |
| **Wisconsin** | EdVest College Savings Program | S | 1997 | Wisconsin College Savings Program Board and the Office of the State Treasurer | www.edvest.com |
| | Tomorrow's Scholar | S | 2001 | Wisconsin College Savings Program Board and the Office of the State Treasurer | www.tomorrowsscholar.com |

[1] P=Prepaid; S=Savings

/ CHAPTER FOUR /

*by Barbara Lauren, Ph.D., J.D.*
*Associate Director*
*Compliance and Professional Development*
*AACRAO*

04

# Affirmative Action: What Is Next?

From at least the era of the Civil War, access to higher education in the United States has been tied to social mobility and a trend toward greater inclusiveness.

Some exceptions to this pattern—such as the long period from the 1920s through the 1950s, when some elite Eastern colleges imposed a "Jewish quota"—were corrected gradually. At the public school level, another glaring exception to inclusiveness—enforced legal segregation by race in the public schools of some states—was corrected by the courts, specifically by the U.S. Supreme Court in *Brown v. Board* (1954).

Nearly twenty-five years after *Brown*, the Supreme Court for the first time addressed "race-conscious admissions" in higher education. In the *Bakke* case (1978), the Court outlawed race-based quotas and separate admission tracks for minority applicants, but it did allow race to be considered as "one factor."

In 2003 it returned to the issue of race in college admissions when it decided *Grutter v. Bollinger*. In *Grutter*, the Court stated that the admissions practices of the University of Michigan's Law School would pass muster, because the Law School "engages in a holistic review of each applicant's file, giving serious consideration to all the ways in which each candidate might contribute to a diverse educational environment." Moreover, the Court stated in *Grutter* that "in order to cultivate a set of leaders with legitimacy in the eyes of the citizenry, it is necessary that the path to leadership be visibly open to talented and qualified individuals of every race and ethnicity." Nevertheless, the Court issued an unusual conclusion: "We expect that 25 years from now, the use of racial preferences will no longer be necessary to further the interest approved today." Moreover, in a companion case, *Gratz v. Bollinger*, involving the undergraduate school of the University of Michigan, the Court found that the scheme being used was too mechanical, in that it awarded points for race to all minority candidates who were members of certain minorities.

Higher education has been so preoccupied with having won the "landmark case" of *Grutter* that it has failed to observe that race-based affirmative action is nevertheless on the defensive. Class-based affirmative action is a more inclusive form of outreach to a broad range of students who have not grown up being "groomed" for college. In fact, several advocacy groups have been successful in opening up various ancillary programs—summer bridge programs, journalism programs, and so forth—to all "at risk" students, not just to minorities. (These results have been achieved either by threat of lawsuits by such advocacy groups, or administratively, by their filing of complaints with the Office of Civil Rights within the U. S. Department of Education.)

It is important to remember that in *Grutter*, the Supreme Court stated only that the U. S. Constitution *does not forbid* race-conscious admissions; the Court *did not state* that *Grutter* requires such programs. Thus, the ruling in *Grutter* does not prevent the voters of a state from adding such a prohibition to their state constitutions, as is already occurring. Indeed, since *Grutter*, the focus of attention has shifted to the states, via referenda or executive action in at least four states which have barred considerations of race in public college and university admissions.

There are other sources of distortion in the applicant pool which even the "win" in *Grutter* does not address. Above all, many students, of whatever race, go to secondary schools which are insufficiently funded and which do not adequately prepare them for college. This case has been made both by Bob Laird, former Director of Undergraduate Admission at the University of California at Berkeley, and by Douglas S. Reed, a political science professor at Georgetown University who has studied the efforts of states to equalize, or more nearly equalize, their funding formulas. Reed concludes that the long drawn out battles in state legislatures have produced some progress, but not as much as reformers had hoped.

A constructive way of dealing with an artificially constricted applicant pool is by making a concerted effort to inform students of their options at a much younger age—in junior high, for example. The first chapter in this volume highlights the effort of North Carolina to present to its students, from seventh grade on, a suite of online services which will make it easier for them to plan, both academically and financially, to go to college or to pursue post-secondary training.

In the meantime, however, some other states are, in effect, de-funding their systems of public higher education. When funding goes down, tuition (or fees) go up, thus excluding many students, especially at the community college level.

Finally, there have been calls to create a new, "post-Iraq" G.I. Bill. The G.I. Bill helped to underwrite post-World War II prosperity, and a fuller development of the talents of many Americans. In *Grutter*, Justice Sandra Day O'Connor, writing the opinion of the Court, stated: "Effective participation by members of all racial and ethnic groups in the civic life of our Nation is essential if the dream of one Nation, indivisible, is to be realized." There are so many barriers to achieving this goal on a state-by-state basis that a national effort would seem to be required. Reviving and modernizing the G.I. Bill—a national tool which has already proven its effectiveness—would seem appropriate.

## From the Morrill Act to the G.I. Bill

From the Morrill Act of 1862 which established the Land Grant colleges to the G.I. Bill, education has provided the means for Americans to improve their position in life, and also to participate more fully in civic life. The first Morrill Act, signed by President Lincoln in 1862, became the basis of 106 "land-grant universities" aimed at making "liberal and practical education" available to farmers and "the industrial classes."

For every step forward, there is a step back. The second Morrill Act (1890) was blighted by "separate but equal" racial provisos,[62] and starting in the 1920s, the Big Three of the Ivy League (Harvard, Yale, and Princeton) enforced anti-Jewish quotas even at the height of the Depression, when the admission of such high-achieving students would have helped fill the class.

The next important Federal statement about race and higher education came some 60 years after the second Morrill Act, in Supreme Court rulings on two paired cases in 1950: *Sweatt v. Painter*, 339 U.S. 629 and *McLaurin v. Oklahoma State Regents*, 339 U.S. 637. Neither of these cases ruled on a broad admissions scheme, per se. Instead, they addressed inequities involving individual black students.

Both of these cases construed the Equal Protection Clause of the Fourteenth Amendment to the U.S. Constitution.[63] In *Sweatt*, the State of Texas had denied admission to a black applicant to its law school at the University of Texas, because the State was in the process of establishing a separate "law school for Negroes." (Future U.S. Supreme Court Justice Thurgood Marshall was one of two co-counsel who argued for the petitioner, *Sweatt*.) The Supreme Court ruled that *Sweatt* had to be admitted to the University of Texas Law School.

[62] The second Morrill Act, which was aimed at extending the 1862 Act to the former Confederate states, actually provided that "No money shall be paid out under this Subchapter to any State or Territory for the support or maintenance of a college where a distinction of color is made in the admission of students"—but it also provided that "the establishment and maintenance of such colleges separately for white and colored students shall be held to be compliance...if the funds received...are divided equitably" between both sets of institutions. See 7 U.S.C. 323, at <http://caselaw.lp.findlaw.com/scripts/ts_search.pl?title=7&sec=323>.

[63] See *Sweatt* at <http://caselaw.lp.findlaw.com/scripts/getcase.pl?court=us&vol=339&invol=629>; *see* McLaurin at <http://caselaw.lp.findlaw.com/scripts/getcase.pl?court=us&vol=339&invol=637>.

In its ruling in this case, the Court held by implication—four years before its landmark ruling in *Brown v. Board of Education*, 347 U.S. 483 (1954) regarding elementary and secondary schooling—that in higher education, "separate" is not "equal."

In *McLaurin*, the issue was unequal and stigmatizing treatment of the petitioner by the graduate school which had admitted him only after having been sued. Citing *Sweatt*, the Supreme Court concluded that "the conditions under which this appellant is required to receive his education deprive him of his personal and present right to the equal protection of the laws." The appellant, having been admitted to a state-supported graduate school, "must receive the same treatment at the hands of the state as students of all races."

On a different front, the 1920s saw the advent of Jewish quotas in the Ivy League; Yale did not abandon its Jewish quota until the class which entered in the fall of 1962. (Karabel 2005, p. 331).[64]

The 1960s saw the beginning of "affirmative action"—in higher education and other settings. The Supreme Court eventually ruled in the *Bakke* case that quotas or separate tracks for minority applicants were unacceptable, but that race could be "taken into account" in postsecondary admissions.

This formulation obviously left many questions unanswered, and in a pair of cases 25 years later—*Grutter* and *Gratz*—the Court ruled in 2003 that if the admissions process considered applicants "holistically," *i.e.* as a whole person as the University of Michigan Law School did, with race or ethnicity as only one factor, the admissions scheme would (or at any rate, in this case, did) survive "strict scrutiny." However, if the school considered applicants solely as the representative of a group, as the University of Michigan's undergraduate school was deemed to have done (by awarding points for various racial categories), that type of plan would not survive scrutiny.

In 2006, the Supreme Court revisited the *Grutter* ruling in the course of considering race-based school assignments at the K–12 level in Seattle and Kentucky. The Court struck down both these race-based school assignment schemes, but did explicitly uphold *Grutter* at the college level.

In a speech at the National Press Club in Washington in 2007, retired Justice Sandra Day O'Connor, author of the majority opinion which sustained affirmative action in *Grutter*, stated that in the long run, it would probably be better to improve elementary and secondary schools, so that race-conscious admissions policies would no longer be necessary (Schmidt 2007a).

Indeed, that is the way events are moving. Several advocacy groups which oppose affirmative action in its race-based form—groups such as the Center for Individual Rights (CIR) and the Center for Equal Opportunity (CEO)—have filed, or threatened to file, complaints with the Office for Civil Rights in the U.S. Department of Education, and have succeeded

[64] Beginning in 1922, Harvard had added the following question to its application form: "What change, if any, has been made since birth in your own name or that of your father? (Explain fully.)" (Karabel 2005, p. 94). Like Harvard, Princeton added a question on its application form in the 1920s about religious affiliation. It did not delete that question until 1950. (p. 243).

in opening many scholarships and programs which had hitherto been open only to minorities, to students of any race who might need a "bridge" program, or other assistance (Schmidt 2007b, p. 129).

Finally, three states (California in 1996, Washington in 1998, and Michigan in 2006) have passed state ballot measures banning the use of racial, ethnic and gender preferences by public colleges, and other public entities. Florida has achieved the same effect by action of the governor in 1999. In addition, Ward Connerly,[65] who was instrumental in getting the first three referenda passed, is aiming to get similar measures on state ballots in 2008 in Arizona, Colorado, Missouri, Nebraska, and Oklahoma. The three states which have passed such bans—California, Washington, and Michigan—together account for about 17.7 percent of the nation's population. "If the five states being eyed by Mr. Connerly pass such measures, the share of the U.S. population living in states with such bans will rise to just over 25 percent" (Schmidt 2007c).[66]

Beyond the impact of Supreme Court decisions and state referenda, it is clear that admissions at the college level have been made to bear burdens resulting from inadequate education at pre-college levels. Put more bluntly, there is a lack of investment in education at elementary and secondary levels in many minority or simply poor neighborhoods. Bob Laird, former Director of Undergraduate Admission at Berkeley, makes this point passionately. We will elaborate on this later in the chapter, and will mention some state-wide outreach to children of junior-high age who would not normally be thinking of college. In addition, there are some innovative programs which pair high school students with meaningful job-related work; we will mention one that was highlighted by Robert Reich, when he was President Clinton's Secretary of Labor.

In addition, it is extremely difficult to equalize spending on schools systems within states, although there have been some heroic efforts to do so. One illuminating book is *On Equal Terms: The Constitutional Politics of Educational Opportunity* (2001), by Professor Douglas S. Reed of Georgetown University. Reed discusses lengthy battles in New Jersey and other states to achieve something approximating a more equal distribution of state resources to local school systems. The Reed book also contains a list of "Significant State Supreme Court Rulings on School Finance," which is very useful for rulings up to 2001.

The result of all these factors is that, as more and more slots in classes in competitive institutions are taken by students with "hooks"—legacies, athletes, faculty children, early action candidates and now (even after due modification) affirmative action considerations—stu-

[65] In his book *Creating Equal: My Fight Against Race Preferences*, Connerly (2005) writes that as a black man, "I saw an additional and unexpected group of victims—the members of 'underrepresented groups' who worked hard and gained entry to [the University of California system] on their own merits and then saw their accomplishments degraded by policies implying that all minority students get where they do only because of preferential treatment" (p. 145).

[66] Schmidt (2007c) continues: "Add Florida—where the former Republican governor, Jeb Bush, curtailed affirmative action preferences in state government and subsequently persuaded the governing board of the state universities to follow suit—and the share of Americans living where public colleges cannot consider applicants' race now stands at about 23.7 percent and could rise to just over 31 percent as a result of the 2008 vote."

dents without a "hook" are limited to competing for a smaller part of the pie. This has led to a sense of frantic competitiveness. Some parents are hiring private financial aid counselors to advise them on how best to arrange their finances so as to (legitimately) qualify for the maximum financial aid package for their child. Other parents are hiring "packagers" who advise on everything from essays and test-taking to how to get in off the wait-list. And some parents are even hiring specialists to advise their children on how to make the best impression during the interview.

Finally, and most importantly, the erosion of public funding of higher education is distorting the whole concept of responsibility for education. As many commentators have pointed out, education used to be thought of as a public good. Great state university systems were funded—universities which became engines of prosperity for the state, and of individual social mobility. California is perhaps the outstanding example, but the pattern was repeated nationwide. Today, as a former president of the University of Wisconsin system has observed, there is a "de facto privatization" of American public universities.

This shortsightedness is having all sorts of untoward effects, many of them already visible. First, some students are being priced out of four-year schools, and even community colleges. This is a grievous loss—both for the individual and society. Second, some schools are beginning to charge students more to major in popular "practical" majors (such as business) (Glater 2007). Thus, the students who most need to major in a field which is in demand, are (anecdotally, at least) being priced out of a choice which should be theirs to make.

It is not surprising that there are calls now to enact a new "post-Iraq G.I. Bill." When one considers that the post-war success of "the greatest generation" was in large part funded by the far-seeing generosity of the Servicemen's Readjustment Act of 1944 (to give it its formal name), it seems that an extension of it tailored to meet the needs of today's servicemen and women would be timely and wise.

Since the Civil War, every generation has risen to the challenge of extending education, and opportunity. This generation needs to take its place in that tradition.

## Education and Social Mobility: The Move Toward Racial Inclusiveness

The land grant universities established by the first Morrill Act, enacted in the darkest days of the Civil War, aimed to "promote...liberal and practical education" for working people "in the several pursuits and professions of life." The animating idea behind the Morrill Act was to make both liberal and practical education available to the non-elite of society (Harl 2003, p. 1). The mechanism was that the federal government made available federal land to each state in the Union (as of the census of 1860). The states' intended sale of the lands then funded a network of "land grant colleges," now existing in every state.[67]

The second Morrill Act, of 1890, extended the benefits of the land grant system to the 16 Southern states. That second Act required that states which maintained "separate but equal" colleges had to propose a just and equitable division of funds received under it. The second Morrill Act thus served to establish black land-grant colleges throughout the South.

As demonstrated by this brief history, the Morrill Acts illustrate both the ideal of higher education for all, and some of the difficulties in living up to that ideal.

Nevertheless, the trend of American higher education has been toward greater inclusiveness. Specifically, two cases in 1950, already briefly mentioned, were omens of things to come. Both addressed the predicaments of applicants with undisputed good qualifications—one a law student, and the other a graduate student. The first case, *Sweatt v. Painter*, rejected the concept of a "separate but equal" law school. The Court ruled that the Equal Protection Clause of the Fourteenth Amendment to the U.S. Constitution required that a qualified black student be admitted to the University of Texas Law School, rather than to a separate "law school for Negroes" which the state was going to establish for him, and others.

And a companion case, *McLaurin v. Oklahoma State Regents*, required that the institution not sequester or ostracize a black student, once he had been admitted to a state institution. The Supreme Court actually had to hear that case twice. The first ruling required the Regents to *admit* the student—a qualified black graduate student in education; the second ruling required the Regents to cease their practice of *sequestering* the student from others. (The school had required the student to take classes only by sitting at a designated desk in an anteroom adjoining the classroom; to use the library only by sitting at a designated desk on a different floor from the regular reading room; and to sit at a designated table and to eat at a separate time from the other students in the cafeteria.)

## Selectivity

### "Leadership Material"

It is interesting to note that even the most prestigious Eastern schools were not always as highly competitive as they are today. In the nineteenth century, admission reflected high status in society, rather than high performance on exams. The elite universities on the East Coast did not recognize many of the subjects taught in public high schools, while their own requirements, especially in classical languages, could not be fulfilled in many of them (Karabel 2005, p. 22).[68] Thus, for those who had gone to the "right schools," it was surprisingly easy to get in.

[67] Later on, other colleges such as the University of the District of Columbia and the "1994 land-grant colleges for Native Americans" were awarded cash by Congress instead of land, to achieve land-grant status. See <http://en.wikipedia.org/wiki/Morrill_Act>.

[68] Harvard did not abolish its Greek requirement for freshman admission until 1898 (Karabel 2005, p. 23); Yale did not eliminate its Greek requirement until 1904 and its Latin requirement until 1931 (p. 52).

The schools Karabel (2005) calls the "Big Three"—Harvard, Princeton, and Yale—considered themselves to be "in service to the nation," *i.e.*, involved in the molding of leaders for the nation. It was understood, of course, that such leaders would be in the mold of Rhodes Scholars—white, male, Protestant, and "manly." The emphasis was on the liberal arts—nothing too specialized. In the wake of Sputnik in 1957, however, Harvard scientist George Kistiakowsky led a "revolt of the faculty" in relation to admissions. The nation needed more scientists, Kistiakowsky said, and Harvard was not producing enough of them. "He proposed a far more academically rigorous admissions policy limited to the top 1 percent of the nation's high school seniors, with the SAT playing a central role in determining who would belong to this elite group" (p. 264).

William Bender, Harvard's Director of Admissions and Financial Aid from 1952 to 1960, and something of a liberal for his time and place,[69] nevertheless abhorred what he called the "Ecole Normale" model—the concept of the university as an oasis for the upper intelligentsia who would be chosen exclusively for academic prowess. Bender warned that such a policy had already been shown to yield "a lot of singularly unimpressive human beings" (Karabel 2005, p. 284). Indeed, Karabel notes, "in the aftermath of [Bender's] historic assault, the forces at Harvard favoring selection on academic criteria alone were routed, never to recover" (p. 285).

"Perhaps," Bender mused, "the time has come...to define our purpose as the production of chemists or economists or anthropologists rather than educated men" (p. 264). This musing was sarcastic; "a future student body made up largely of prospective Ph.D.'s will not add largely to our endowment," he wrote in a confidential report to the Dean of the Faculty of Arts and Sciences (p. 281). On second thought, Bender did admit that perhaps " the 'gentleman' will disappear anyhow," and that "the big money will be in the hands of other kinds of people, possibly including Harvard Ph.D.'s who come to us as bright, impoverished scholars from small town high schools" (p. 281). But above all, Bender believed in the concept of a balanced class, including "healthy extroverts" in the formulation of Harvard Provost Paul Buck in 1948: "A student body balanced in its composition and its potentialities for later contribution to all phases of American life" (p. 185).

## The "Jewish Problem"

In the early years of the twentieth century, Harvard, Yale and Princeton, as already noted, administered their own exams. "But the tests were not especially demanding, and a young man with modest intelligence from a feeder school like Groton could usually pass them with ease" (Karabel 2005, p. 22). Even if such applicants did not pass individual exams the first time, a liberal re-take policy existed.

[69] Karabel (2005) suggests that Bender's history as a transfer student into Harvard—from Goshen College, a Mennonite institution in Goshen, Indiana—gave him a residual sympathy for people who had entered Harvard in atypical ways (pp. 181–82).

"Even the unfortunate applicant who failed to pass exams in enough subjects could still be admitted with 'conditions.'" Indeed, "at each of the Big Three, admission with conditions became a common pathway to the freshman class." At Harvard, 55 percent of those admitted had otherwise failed to fulfill the entrance requirements (in 1907); at Yale, 57 percent had (in 1909); and at Princeton, the figure in those years ranged from 56 percent to 65 percent (p. 22).

Things moved along smoothly until the 1920s. That was the first decade in which significant numbers of Jewish students applied to the leading Eastern universities.

Columbia, because of its location in New York City, was the first to be significantly affected by having large numbers of well qualified students applying who were not WASPs. This became known as "the Jewish problem."

Indeed, "by 1914, the 'Jewish problem' was so great at Columbia that its dean, Frederick Keppel, openly acknowledged the widespread perception that the large number of immigrants had made it 'socially uninviting to students who come from homes of refinement'" (p. 87).

Nor were Catholic students notably more welcome. In his book *The Big Test* (1999), Nicholas Lemann recounts that Yale's Catholic chaplain told William F. Buckley, Jr. when he was an undergraduate in the late 1940s, that "Yale maintained a [combined] ceiling of 13 percent on Catholics and on Jews."

As to black students, six years into the tenure of progressive Harvard President James Bryant Conant (1939), blacks made up less than one quarter of one percent of the student body. (Karabel 2005, p. 173–74).

Administrators were acutely aware, as Conant put it, of "the size of the pond in which the privately supported colleges are fishing." Drawing on government statistics, according to Karabel, Conant set out to estimate the number of "potential freshmen (white, male) each year" from families with incomes (in 1938) over $5,000—the floor for students able to pay Harvard's costs without financial assistance. He estimated that there were only about 15,000 such young men in the country, and that not more than 50% of them would be "good bets" for Harvard—leaving 7,000–8,000 potential Harvard applicants out of roughly 1,000,000 young men of college age (Karabel 2005, p. 174).

Given such statistics, it is especially remarkable that administrators made a clear and conscious choice to exclude Jewish students even during the Depression, when admitting them would not only have filled the classes, but would have raised the academic average. In 1933, the Dean of Admissions at Dartmouth reported to Ernest Martin Hopkins, who served as President from 1916 to 1945, that Dartmouth faced a shortage of students as a result of the Depression. The admissions dean recommended raising Jewish enrollment *by 1 percent* [emphasis added], rather than lowering academic standards by admitting poorly qualified non-Jews. President Hopkins replied, "Life is so much pleasanter in Hanover, ...and friends of the college visiting us are so much happier with the decreased quota of the Hebraic element, that I am not enthusiastic at all about your suggestion" (Freedman 2000).

There is no doubt that such attitudes are no longer common. But such attitudes have left vestiges in admissions applications (such as "mother's maiden name"), in ways which most people are not even aware of. For example: When Columbia adopted admissions quotas in 1914, it took care to ask for a photograph, for the parents' place of birth, and for the mother's maiden name. By such means, "Columbia reduced the proportion of Jewish students enrolled from about 40 percent in 1914 to 21 percent in 1918, and eventually to 15 percent during the 1920s, despite the size of the Jewish population in the city around the college" (Freedman 2000).

Yale did not drop its Jewish quota—of 10 percent of the class—until the spring of 1962, for the class entering that fall (Karabel 2005, p. 331; *see also* p. 115).

The author of this chapter does not imply that there were no other schools with such unfortunate attitudes. The prominence of these schools, however, has drawn a greater number of scholars to examine their admissions histories.

Although these overtly exclusionary quotas are now a thing of the past, the dilemmas raised by allocating a limited number of slots have been the source of ongoing litigation and continuing concern.

## Affirmative Action in the Courts

### The Bakke Case

In 1978, the Supreme Court issued a ruling on affirmative action—*Regents of the University of California v. Bakke*, 438 U.S. 265—which defined the field for 25 years (until the two University of Michigan cases in 2003).

Alan Bakke was a white candidate who was twice rejected (in 1973 and 1974) for admission to the University of California-Davis Medical School (UCDMS). The Medical School, which had opened only in 1968, had an entering class of 50 students, which in the years in question became an entering cadre of 100. The first class contained three Asians but no blacks, no Mexican-Americans, and no American Indians. Over the next two years, the faculty devised a program to produce some changes in this situation.

Sixteen slots were reserved for "disadvantaged" or "minority" candidates. The minority groups listed on the application form were "blacks," "Chicanos," "Asians," and "American Indians." Candidates who identified themselves as either disadvantaged or minority were considered by a special committee (a majority of whom were members of minority groups). In addition, they were not ranked against candidates in the general admissions process; and they were competing for sixteen slots which were set aside for people in those categories.

Bakke applied in the general admission category. In both years, special applicants were admitted with lower scores than his. When Bakke sued, a trial court in California ruled in his favor, finding that the special program acted as a racial quota, because minority applicants in that program were rated only against one another, and 16 places in the class of 100 were reserved for them. Bakke appealed to the California Supreme Court because the trial court had declined to order him to be admitted (on the ground that he had failed to prove that he would have been admitted "but for" the special program).

The California Supreme Court held that the special admission program was invalid because it violated the rights guaranteed to the majority by the Equal Protection Clause of the Fourteenth Amendment of the United States Constitution. Moreover, the state supreme court held that since Bakke had established that the University discriminated against him because of his race, the burden shifted to the University to demonstrate that he would not have been admitted, even without the special admission program. Since the University conceded that it could not meet that burden of proof, the California Supreme Court directed the trial court to enter a judgment ordering Bakke to be admitted.[70]

The Medical School then appealed to the U. S. Supreme Court. The Court invalidated the Medical School's admission system as a quota, but also held that some consideration of race is permissible, as long as it is "only one of many factors."[71]

In *Bakke*, four justices voted to uphold a remedial use of race. Four others concluded that race *cannot* be the basis of excluding anyone from participation in a federally funded program. Justice Powell cast the "swing vote." Powell agreed with four of his colleagues that USDMS's special admissions program unlawfully discriminated against Bakke,[72] but he agreed with another four of his colleagues that universities could consider race in their admission programs.

What admissions officers took from the *Bakke* case was that quotas, set-asides, and separate admissions tracks were out—but that they could consider race as *one among many* factors, in order to achieve a "diverse student body." Such a composition of the incoming class would ostensibly improve the educational experience for white students, as well as for the more obvious beneficiaries of affirmative action.

Peter Schmidt (2007b), deputy editor of *The Chronicle of Higher Education*, points out that "none of the briefs by colleges or higher education associations [in the *Bakke* case] offered any empirical evidence to back their claims that racial diversity produces educational benefits. Nonetheless, their arguments were good enough for [Justice Powell], who was looking for a way out of a bind. Powell was too conservative in his temperament to go along with the four justices on the court who thought colleges should be completely barred from considering race. At the same time, he was too conservative in his political ideology to join the four liberal justices who argued that colleges should be allowed to use racial preferences to remedy societal discrimination. By seizing upon the idea that racial diversity has educational

[70] See *Bakke v. Regents of University of California*, 18 Cal.3d 34 (1976), available at <http://login.findlaw.com/scripts/callaw?dest=ca/cal3d/18/34.html>.

[71] The result for the litigant was that the Supreme Court ordered him to be admitted. Alan Bakke completed medical school and, according to Ward Connerly (2000), subsequently worked "in a hospital in Minneapolis with a multiracial working class clientele" (p. 125).

[72] Four of the Justices (Stevens, Chief Justice Burger, Stewart and Rehnquist) relied on Title VI to reach this conclusion; one (Powell) relied on the Fourteenth Amendment's Equal Protection Clause. See Kaplan and Lee (2006), *The Law of Higher Education*.

benefits, Powell was able to allow the continued survival of race-conscious admissions policies without giving colleges license to engage in social engineering" (p. 164).

Schmidt (p. 163) further points out that "the educational benefits of diversity had not even been discussed in the first dispute over college affirmative action that came before the Supreme Court, the lawsuit that the rejected white applicant Marco *DeFunis* had filed against the University of Washington's law school in 1971. Had the justices actually decided *DeFunis*'s case, rather than declaring it moot because a lower court had already ordered the law school to admit him, the entire debate over affirmative action might have been framed in...different terms"—in terms of social justice rather than of benefit to (white) students.

What was merely a dismissal for mootness[73] provoked an interesting dissent from Justice Douglas. In *DeFunis v. Odegaard*, 416 U.S. 312 (1974),[74] he stated that the Court should have reached the merits—that is, the substance—of the case. Even more to the point, he in fact offered some suggestions as to how schools could evaluate minority or disadvantaged applicants.

Specifically, he stated that the Equal Protection Clause of the Constitution "does not prohibit law schools from evaluating an applicant's prior achievements *in light of the barriers that he had to overcome*" [Emphasis added] (*DeFunis*, 312 U.S. at 331). This approach—an approach which attempts to assess what challenges applicants have faced, and how they have overcome them—is becoming a preferred way to assess the merits of candidates of all races and socioeconomic status, especially if their grades and test scores are less than stellar, but other aspects of their record indicate that they have promise.

Justice Douglas's comments in *DeFunis* do not have the authority they would have if this had been an adjudicated case—his opinion, as already noted, was merely a dissent from a dismissal for mootness—but his observations provide useful perspective nevertheless. Justice Douglas offered a specific example of his recommended approach—an example which is familiar to any admissions officer:

> *A black applicant who pulled himself out of the ghetto into a junior college may thereby demonstrate a level of motivation, perseverance, and ability that would lead a fair-minded admissions committee to conclude that he shows more promise for law study than the son of a rich alumnus who achieved better grades at Harvard. That applicant would be offered admission not because he is black, but because as an individual he has shown he has the potential, while the Harvard man may have taken less advantage of the vastly superior opportunities offered him.*

[73] Faced with a ruling by its state supreme court that it had to admit DeFunis, the Washington University School of Law did so, but appealed the ruling to the U.S. Supreme Court. By the time the U.S. Supreme Court considered taking the case, DeFunis was about to graduate. Hence, the Supreme Court was able to duck the issue (in 1974). Four years later, however, in *Bakke*, the Supreme Court did, for the first time, address the issue of affirmative action in college admissions.

[74] Available at <http://caselaw.lp.findlaw.com/scripts/printer_friendly.pl?page=us/416/312.html>.

*...a poor Appalachian white, or a second generation Chinese in San Francisco, or some other American whose* ***lineage is so diverse as to defy ethnic labels*** *[emphasis added], may demonstrate similar potential and thus be afforded favorable consideration by the committee* (pp. 331–332).

All of these comments have turned out to be prophetic.

## Defining American Citizens by Race: Legacy of Two World War II Cases

The issue of defining American citizens by race received its most eloquent repudiation—at least in words—in two Supreme Court cases during World War II. In the first case, *Hirabayashi v. United States* (320 U.S. 81 [1943]), Chief Justice Stone declared, in a much quoted statement: "Distinctions between citizens solely because of their ancestry are by their very nature odious to a free people whose institutions are founded upon the doctrine of equality" (320 U.S. at 100).

Ironically, that was the case in which the Court upheld a night-time curfew on all persons of Japanese ancestry in certain designated military areas. Citing the danger of sabotage and other possible "menaces to safety."

The next year, the Court reiterated in *Korematsu v. United States* (323 U.S. 214 [1944]) that "all legal restrictions which curtail the civil rights of a single racial group are immediately suspect. That is not to say that all such restrictions are unconstitutional. It is to say that courts must subject them to the most rigid scrutiny. Pressing public necessity may sometimes justify the existence of such restrictions; racial antagonism never can" (320 U.S. at 216). Based, as in *Hirabayashi*, on the pressing public necessity of combating the "twin dangers of espionage and sabotage" (320 U.S. at 217), the court upheld the relocation of citizens and aliens of Japanese ancestry, from certain "military districts."

Thirty years later, in his dissent in the *DeFunis* case in 1974, Justice Douglas noted: "This Court has not sustained a racial classification since the wartime cases of *Korematsu* and *Hirabayashi* [citations omitted]" (*DeFunis*, 416 U.S. at 339).

The Supreme Court's admonition, in *Bakke*, to weigh race as "only one factor" was a cryptic formulation which offered little guidance to admissions officers. One harbinger of future directions, between *Bakke* in 1978 and the two University of Michigan cases in 2003, was the case of *Hopwood v. Texas*, 78 F.3d 932 (5th Cir. 1996). The facts were these: The Law School of the University of Texas Law School had an affirmative action program which gave preferences to African American and Mexican American applicants. Four white students filed suit in federal court after being denied admission, claiming that they had been denied admission to the UT law school on the basis of their race. The U.S. District Court (the federal trial court) found that the UT admissions program served a "compelling state interest," both in ensuring diversity in the student body, generally, and specifically in remedying discrimination by the State of Texas in its entire K–12 school system.[75]

However, a three-judge panel of the Fifth Circuit (the federal appeals court for Texas, Louisiana, and Mississippi), reversed this decision.[76] The immediate result was that UT's policy of admissions preferences fell. The larger result was that, during the years between *Bakke* and *Grutter*, the three states just named were under a ban on using race-based affirmative action in admission to state institutions.

### THE UNIVERSITY OF MICHIGAN CASES: *GRATZ V. BOLLINGER* (UNDERGRADUATE) AND *GRUTTER V. BOLLINGER* (LAW SCHOOL)

The following two cases establish the parameters admissions offices operate under as of the writing of this chapter (2007).

The cases were neatly paired. In the *Gratz* case—*Gratz v. Bollinger*, 539 U.S. 244 (2003)—rejected white applicants appealed their rejection from the undergraduate school [the College of Literature, Science and the Arts (LSA) of the University of Michigan], and challenged the affirmative action plan at LSA. In the *Grutter* case—*Grutter v. Bollinger*, 539 U.S. 306 (2003), argued concurrently at the Supreme Court—applicants to the University of Michigan Law School appealed their rejection, based in turn on the law school's affirmative action plan for admissions.

The Supreme Court rejected the undergraduate school's affirmative action plan (by a vote of 6-3), but upheld the law school's plan (by a vote of 5-4).

We will discuss the undergraduate case first, since the *Gratz* case offers a template of what will not be found acceptable.

In Chapter 6, "Holistic Methods of Assessment: The View from the University of Michigan," we learn that at the time of the lawsuit, the Office of Undergraduate Admissions was dealing with about 25,000 applications for an undergraduate target enrollment of 5,400. It is probably understandable that with such volume, any school would wish to create some sort of matrix to sort candidates, at least in a preliminary way. Although the University changed its admissions guidelines several times during the period relevant to the litigation, the essence of the discussion—as Chief Justice Rehnquist noted in his majority opinion invalidating the undergraduate school's admission schema—revolved around the fact that the undergraduate college (LSA) automatically distributed 20 points to every member of an

[75] See Kaplin and Lee (2006, p. 789).

[76] The reason the Fifth Circuit panel arrived at this unusual result, in effect negating a critical part of a Supreme Court decision as it applied to the states within the Fifth Circuit's jurisdiction, was that it did not regard that part of Justice Powell's opinion—that furthering student body diversity was a sufficient underpinning for allowing an institution to have racial preferences in its admission plan—as, in fact, the "opinion of the court." In support of this conclusion, the Fifth Circuit panel pointed out, quite correctly, that no other Justice joined in that facet of Powell's judgment. Thus, the Fifth Circuit panel concluded, that as to "the diversity rationale," Justice Powell "wrote only for himself." See <www.nacua.org/documents/hopwoodvsstateoftexas.html>.

"underrepresented minority" group, out of a total of 150, where 100 points was normally considered enough to guarantee admission.

Although 20 points were available to nonminority students for other factors—athletic ability, socioeconomic disadvantage, or "at Provost's discretion"—and lesser numbers of points were awarded for other factors (10 points for being a resident of Michigan, six for residence in an underrepresented Michigan county, five for leadership and service, and so on)—the case hinged on the fact that all minority applicants were automatically awarded 20 percent of the points needed for an automatic admission.

In addressing the operation of the affirmative action plan at the undergraduate school (LSA), the Supreme Court ruled that "the current LSA policy does not provide the individualized consideration Justice Powell [in *Bakke*] contemplated." The Court also stated in *Gratz*: "The fact that implementation of a program capable of providing individualized consideration might present administrative challenges does not render constitutional an otherwise problematic system."[77]

In *Grutter*, by contrast, the Supreme Court held (in a 5-4 vote) that the admissions practices of the University of Michigan's Law School were constitutional because each applicant was evaluated "holistically" as an individual, and that race or ethnicity was not the defining feature of the admissions decision.[78]

Toward the end of her majority opinion upholding "race-conscious admissions programs," Justice Sandra Day O'Connor noted: "It has been 25 years since Justice Powell first approved the use of race to further an interest in student body diversity in the context of public higher education. Since that time, the number of minority applicants with high grades and test scores has indeed increased. We expect that 25 years from now, the use of racial preferences *will no longer be necessary* to further the interest approved today." [Emphasis added.][79]

Peter Schmidt (2007b) has addressed this question directly. "In a 2005 study," he writes, "three well-known economists—Alan Krueger and Jesse Rothstein of Princeton and Sarah Turner of the University of Virginia—used economic and education data to subject Justice O'Connor's 25-year deadline to a reality check (p. 224). [They] concluded that black students still will need admissions preferences to remain at least as represented on selective college campuses in 2028 as they are today" (p. 251).[80]

[77] See <http://caselaw.lp.findlaw.com/scripts/printer_friendly.pl?page=us/000/02-516.html>.

[78] In Chapter 5, "The 'Insight Resumé:' Oregon State University's Approach to Holistic Assessment," Director of Admissions Michele Sandlin describes a six-question short-answer instrument which Oregon State has devised, to gain insight into how students have met challenges, and managed commitments over time. Students must answer all six questions, each in 100 words or less (see page 101). "Because this writing exercise was intended to give us far more insight than we ever had before, we call this part of our application the Insight Resume," Sandlin writes. Moreover, since the questions so specifically ask the students to describe or draw upon their own experiences in a personal way, "answers that are vague or second-hand are easily apparent, and receive low scores."

[79] See *Grutter v. Bollinger*, available at <http://caselaw.lp.findlaw.com/scripts/printer_friendly.pl?page=us/000/02-241.html>.

[80] See Krueger, Rothstein, and Turner (2005). Schmidt notes that a "separate study by a University of Chicago economist [Neal 2005] has projected that, absent major changes in public policy or in the economy, the earliest the black-white skills gap will close is 2050, and it is equally likely the gap will remain significant for the rest of the twenty-first century."

## INFLUENCE OF "THE MILITARY BRIEF" ON *GRUTTER*

One of the most remarkable parts of the background behind the Supreme Court's granting affirmative action a limited reprieve in *Grutter* concerns a highly influential friend-of-the-court brief, submitted on behalf of the university by 29 former leaders of the U.S. military, both uniformed and civilian. President Gerald Ford, himself a University of Michigan graduate, worked with James Cannon, a former Ford operative and former chairman of the Board of Visitors at the U. S. Naval Academy, to orchestrate a brief[81] which emphasized that recruitment and integration of minority officers into all military services is critical to national security.[82]

Groner (2003) characterized this brief as "one of the most important amicus curiae briefs ever submitted to the U.S. Supreme Court." The brief made several points: In 1973, 2.8 percent of military officers were African-American; in 2002, 8.8 percent were. Minorities now constitute 19 percent of the officer corps, the brief stated (p. 17). These long-serving but retired military officers reminded the Court that in the 1960s and 1970s, when the percentage of minority officers was so low, "perceptions of discrimination were pervasive" (p. 6.) This discrepancy between the composition of the officer corps and the enlisted ranks was a leading cause of "low morale and heightened racial tension. The danger this created was not theoretical, as the Vietnam era demonstrates." (p. 6) The officers asserted that they then came to the conclusion that "equal opportunity is absolutely indispensable to unit cohesion." (p. 17.)

Moreover, the brief stated that as of 2003, each service academy was associated with a federally-funded preparatory academy that was the single most significant source of minority candidates for that academy (p. 23). "For example, the Military Academy Preparatory School accounts for 20–40 percent of African-American students and 20–30 percent of Hispanic students at West Point, and these students are highly successful after admission" (p. 23). Specifically, "78 percent of [preparatory school] alumni graduated from West Point in four years, a half-percentage point higher than average" (p. 23; Dickerson 1998, p 15).

During oral argument, Justices O'Connor, Ginsburg, Kennedy, Stevens and Souter all asked questions reflecting their appreciation of the factors raised by the military brief, which stated in essence that "the [relative] absence of minority officers seriously threatened the military's ability to function effectively and fulfill its mission to defend the nation" (Consolidated Brief 2003, p. 7). Through the use of preparatory academies and other ways, the military "has expanded the pool of highly-qualified minority candidates in a variety of explicitly race-conscious ways" (p. 7.)

If there is one sentence which summarizes the rationale, in *Grutter*, for Justice O'Connor's upholding the law school's narrowly-tailored use of race in admissions decisions, it is this one:

[81] See <http://supreme.lp.fndlaw.com/supreme_court/briefs/02-241/02-241.mer.ami.military.pdf>.

[82] See also "Gerald Ford's Affirmative Action," by Jeffery Toobin (2006).

*In order to cultivate a set of leaders with legitimacy in the eyes of the citizenry, it is necessary that the path to leadership be visibly open to talented and qualified individuals of every race and ethnicity* (539 U.S. 306 [2003]).

Ironically, as of 2007, it appears that the Defense Department is considering stripping the military's ability to use these preparatory schools to bring in black, Hispanic and American Indian candidates for admission (Schmidt 2007d).[83]

### Criticism of Affirmative Action from Within the Courts

In 1974, in the *DeFunis* case, Justice Douglas had commented on the arbitrariness with which certain groups are listed for affirmative action protection, while others are left to fend for themselves. The University of Washington, he observed, included Filipinos as one of the selected minority groups; why, he wondered, did it exclude Chinese and Japanese? Would a Court "need to attempt to assess how grievously each group has suffered from discrimination, and allocate proportions accordingly?" he mused (*DeFunis*, 416 U S. at 338–339).

Similarly, the Federal District Court Judge who first ruled in the *Grutter* case—and who found the use of race in law school admissions by the University of Michigan to be unconstitutional, before the Supreme Court reversed his ruling—was critical both of the lack of a time limit for the racial preferences and, like Justice Douglas, of the arbitrariness as to "why [the school] has singled out particular groups for special attention." "Certainly," Judge Bernard A. Friedman wrote, "other groups have also been subjected to discrimination, such as Arabs and southern and eastern Europeans to name but a few, yet the court heard nothing to suggest that the law school has concerned itself as to whether members of these groups are represented in 'meaningful numbers'" (97-CV-75928-DT [2001], p. 52).

Judge Friedman continued: "If the law school may single out these racial groups for a special commitment today, there is nothing to prevent it from enlarging, reducing, or shifting its list of preferred groups tomorrow without any reasoned basis or logical stopping point" (p. 53).

An even more piercing observation was made by Justice Clarence Thomas, one of the dissenters in *Grutter*. "It is uncontested that each year, the [University of Michigan] Law School admits a handful of blacks who would be admitted in the absence of racial discrimination. Who can differentiate between those who belong [on their own merits] and those who do not? The majority of blacks are admitted to the Law School because of discrimination, and because of this policy all are tarred as undeserving." The Law School, he added, wanted only

[83] The proposed revision in the Defense Department's directives would eliminate a reference to "minorities, including women" among the groups that should be given "primary consideration for enrollment" in the preparatory schools. Schmidt cites the Air Force Academy's Director of Admissions, who notes that about 40 percent of the black, Hispanic and American Indian students who enroll in the Air Force Academy each year gain admission through a 10-month program which the Academy operates on its campus. The program involves both academic preparation and some fitness and military training.

to improve the "esthetics" in its classes; but the "aestheticists will never address the real problems facing 'underrepresented minorities'" (539 U.S. 306).

We will return to that theme later in this chapter.

## The Real Push-Back: Complaints Filed with the Office of Civil Rights

Within 18 months of the "dodge a bullet" victory of *Grutter*, reporter Jeffrey Selingo (2005) wrote an article in *The Chronicle of Higher Education* called "Michigan: Who Really Won?" Selingo's answer was telegraphed in the sub-title: "Colleges' cautious reaction to the Supreme Court's affirmative-action decisions may have snatched defeat from the jaws of victory."

In reality, as Selingo himself points out, the real battle against race-conscious admissions policies has been carried out—and quite effectively—by various conservative advocacy groups. In a "second wave" of the battle of affirmative action, they have proceeded to work through administrative agencies, as well as through the courts. In particular, they have filed complaints with the U.S. Department of Education, specifically its Office for Civil Rights.

Their goal is not to "shut down" various kinds of programs, but the far more reasonable goal of making internship programs, "bridge" programs, and scholarships available without regard to limitation by race. For example, Selingo (2005) reports that "dozens of institutions, including Carnegie Mellon, Harvard, and Yale Universities, ...have quietly opened a range of what were once exclusively minority scholarships and programs to students of any race."

Similar changes have come about under threat of lawsuits. For example, a summer journalism program operated by the Dow Jones Newspaper Fund agreed to open its workshops to college students of all races, after the Center for Individual Rights, an advocacy group, threatened a lawsuit under Title VI of the Civil Rights Act of 1964, and the 14th Amendment to the U.S. Constitution—the same two sections of law and the Constitution which were at issue in *Gratz* and *Grutter*. The fund also agreed to rename the 20 summer journalism workshops it conducted, to drop references to minority members as the sole targeted participants.

The fact pattern alleged in the journalism-related complaint illustrates why the Center for Individual Rights (CIR) (and the Center for Equal Opportunity) have been effective. The CIR lawsuit, which led to a settlement, alleged that Virginia Commonwealth University, one of the universities offering the summer program with Dow as one of the sponsors, originally notified Emily Smith, a high school junior, that she had been accepted for the workshop, but then rescinded its offer after one of its faculty members called Ms. Smith, asked her her race, and learned that she was white (Schmidt 2007e).

It seems likely that "who [or what] really won" after Michigan is in fact a concern for individualized evaluation of candidates, without either automatic points awarded to minorities, or automatic exclusion of white students from programs such as occurred in the journalism program.

## State Referenda Banning Preferences in Admission to Public Colleges

Another major factor in curtailing the use of "affirmative action" as it was discussed in the Michigan cases—*i.e.*, generating an incoming cohort of students of various ethnicities large enough to produce a "critical mass" on campus—is the passage of a series of three referenda: one in California (Proposition 209 in 1996), one in Washington State (Initiative 200 in 1998), and one in Michigan (Proposal 2 in 2006).[84] Each of these referenda, now effective as law in their states, bans the use of racial, ethnic and gender preferences by public higher education (and other units of state and local government).

In addition, a similar result was achieved in Florida in 1999 by Executive Order of Governor Jeb Bush (followed by additional implementing action in 2000 by the governing board of the state's universities.) The Florida plan banned use of race-based preferences in higher education, but also instituted a "One Florida" program, which guaranteed admission to students in the top 20 percent of every public high school in Florida, if those students had passed 19 core courses in high school (Saunders 2000).[85]

Percentage programs have also been instituted in Texas (top 10 percent in public or private high schools) and California (top 4 percent of same).[86]

When Ward Connerly (2000), the member of the University of California Board of Regents who spearheaded Proposition 209 in California, was asked for his reaction to the passage of I-200 by a large margin in the State of Washington, he said: "Two down, forty-eight to go" (p. 245).

In addition, Connerly plans to spearhead a so-called "Super Tuesday on affirmative action" in November 2008, with referenda planned for Arizona, Colorado, Missouri, Nebraska and Oklahoma. Peter Schmidt (2007) points out: "The three states that have already passed such bans, California, Michigan and Washington, together account for about 17 percent of the nation's population. If the five states being eyed by Mr. Connerly pass such measures, the share of the U.S. population living in states with such bans will rise to just over 25 percent." Moreover, Mr. Schmidt states: "Add Florida... and the share of Americans living where public colleges cannot consider applicants' race now stands at about 23.7 percent and could rise to just over 31 percent as a result of the 2008 vote."

[84] California's Proposition 209 was approved by 54 percent of the voters; Washington's Initiative 200 and Michigan's Proposal 2, each by 58 percent.

[85] Critics of the Florida program point out that students who are in the top 20 percent of their high school classes almost always gain admission to a public institution anyway (Hebel 2003).

[86] Critics point out that the programs in California and Florida have had limited effects on those states' most selective campuses, such as the University of California at Berkeley and the University of Florida, since those states' plans guarantee access to a public college, but not necessarily to a student's preferred campus.

## Race-Conscious Assignments Stricken at the K-12 Level

Four years after *Grutter*, the Supreme Court struck down race-conscious assignments of some schoolchildren in public schools in Seattle and in Jefferson County, Kentucky (metropolitan Louisville).

The Court took care, on several occasions in its majority opinion, to make clear that the principles of race-conscious but "holistic" admissions practices, as enunciated in *Grutter*, can survive scrutiny at the college level. However, the tenor of the majority opinion, written by Chief Justice John Roberts, is not encouraging for race-based remedies. The concluding sentence of Justice Roberts' opinion is: "The way to stop discrimination on the basis of race is to stop discriminating on the basis of race."[87]

It is notable that both these school districts were acting voluntarily to try to ensure that the racial balance at public schools fell within certain ranges. When the racial balances in certain schools did not fall within the prescribed ranges, the Seattle district used race as a "tie-breaker," and the Jefferson County school system assigned students who would "unbalance" a school (the plan required all non-magnet schools to maintain a black enrollment of not less than 15 percent and not more than 50 percent) to a different school.

The Seattle public schools had never been segregated, and the Jefferson County schools had been under a federal court order to integrate in 1975, but that order was finally rescinded in 2000, because the federal court found that although some racial imbalances still existed at that time, there was no evidence that they were any longer caused by an *intentionally* segregated system.

This latter fact was very important to Chief Justice Roberts. Historically, there have been two ways of overcoming "strict scrutiny," which is normally seen as a great barrier to classifying Americans by race. The first justifiable reason for sustaining an action based on race is that of "pressing public necessity" (as we have seen in the *Hirabayashi* and *Korematsu* cases of the 1940s). The second, of which the most famous example is the "school desegregation case" of *Brown v. Board of Education* (1954) and its progeny, is for the purpose of overcoming de jure segregation (*i.e.*, deliberate racial segregation *accomplished by law*). The third way of surviving "strict scrutiny"—a way enunciated most fully in *Grutter*—is to present one's program as benefiting the educational experience of one's college students by exposing them to a "critical mass" of students different from themselves. (There has been a small cottage industry of law review articles as to whether race-based diversity can in fact be assumed to represent "viewpoint diversity," as well. If it does not, then implying that all black students think alike comes very close to subscribing to the "group rights" theory of the Fourteenth Amendment.)

Chief Justice Roberts criticized Justice Breyer, the spokesman for the four dissenting Justices, for "seek[ing] to justify the [race-based assignment] plans at issue under our prece-

[87] See *Parents Involved in Community Schools v. Seattle School District No. 1* and *Meredith v. Jefferson County Board of Education*, at <www.supremecourtus.gov/opinions/06pdf/05-908.pdf>. The two cases were argued together and decided together, and are reported under the rubric of *Parents Involved*, etc. Decided June 28, 2007.

dents recognizing the compelling interest in remedying *past* intentional discrimination" [Emphasis added]. "Not even the school districts go this far, and for good reason," the Chief Justice added. "The distinction between segregation by state action and *racial imbalance caused by other factors* has been central to our jurisprudence in this area for generations" [Emphasis added].

Parents of students denied assignment to particular schools under these plans solely because of their race brought suit, contending that allocating children to different public schools on the basis of race violated the Equal Protection Clause of the Fourteenth Amendment. The respective federal district courts and federal appellate courts upheld the plans. The Supreme Court reversed those decisions.

In a long and eloquent dissent, Justice Breyer, speaking for three other Justices as well, wrote: "Just as diversity in higher education was deemed compelling in *Grutter*, diversity in public primary and secondary schools—where there is even more to gain—must be...a compelling state interest."

He concluded: "This is a decision that the Court and the Nation will come to regret."

A month after *Parents Involved* was decided, Derrick Bell (2007)—who as a lawyer for the NAACP Legal Defense Fund had supervised 300 school-desegregation cases—wrote in *The Chronicle of Higher Education*: "Justice Stephen G. Breyer's dissent properly condemns the court for undermining the half-century-old promise of integrated primary and secondary schools proclaimed in *Brown*. [But] his long and ringing dissent may become the elegy of the school-desegregation era." Bell continues: "The resilience of civil-rights groups is praiseworthy, but future litigation, even if successful, is not going to alter the fact that most poor children, regardless of race, are attending schools that are not meeting their educational needs." He adds: "The plain fact is that a great many white Americans, including many with otherwise liberal views on race, do not want their offspring attending schools with more than a token number of black and Latino children."

Bell concludes: "It is painful for many of us, but it is time to acknowledge that racial integration as the primary vehicle for providing effective schooling for black and Latino children has run its course. Where it is working, or has a real chance to work, it should continue, but for the millions of black and Latino children living in areas that are as racially isolated in fact as they once were by law, it is time to look elsewhere."[88]

## Student Preparation Lacking at Pre-College Levels

After he was appointed to be one of the Regents of the University of California system, Ward Connerly (2000) discovered that when the previous regent, a white man, had been appointed, an agreement had been reached between Governor Pete Wilson and the State Senate, which

[88] In a companion piece, Arthur R. Coleman and Scott R. Palmer (2007) take a more optimistic view of the legal outlook, as is evidenced by the title of their assessment: "A More Circuitous Path to Racial Diversity."

had the power of confirmation, that future appointments would reflect greater "diversity." Connerly wrote: "I'm sure that Pete was aware that if [that idea] had been mentioned [before the position was offered], I would have walked" (p. 106).

Connerly was introduced to the arcane world of affirmative action when he was approached by two parents, physicist Jerry Cook and University of San Diego faculty member Ellen Cook, whose son was outstanding in every respect, but who was rejected by all five UC medical schools. Upon further investigation, Connerly found not only that UC schools, then under a self-imposed affirmative action program, were accepting minorities whose scores ranked in the lowest one percent relative to Asians and whites (p. 121), but that poor whites who needed a boost, were "never given a break under affirmative action" (p. 122), and that no effort was made to distinguish between minorities who were truly needy, and those who were not.

Ultimately, the Cooks' son James obtained a Master's degree at Cal Tech—the first student in the department ever to earn a Master's degree in one year—and was finally admitted to the medical school at UC-Davis. (Ironically, this was "the campus whose rejection of Allan Bakke fifteen years earlier had led to the growth of the affirmative action establishment in the U.S.") (p. 120).

As he investigated the plight of the Cooks, and found that it was only the tip of an iceberg, Connerly became indignant at the unfairness visited on students of any race whose upbringing in low-performing schools was impeding their progress, but in ways which a race-based system of preferences could only erratically ameliorate. He concluded that a system of race preferences is "altruism on the cheap" (p. 229). Corporations which proudly wear "diversity" as a badge," he said, "do very little to improve the lousy schools inflicted on black kids, say, or to provide college scholarships for poor students whatever their color.... Instead, they hide behind the fig leaf of diversity" (p. 229).

As Stanley Henderson makes clear in Chapter 1, those states which make a methodical outreach to junior high students are creating the conditions—via early outreach and academic/financial aid/career counseling—for students to prepare themselves for college. To accomplish this kind of outreach via an *individual* college or university is admirable, but it is a challenge to both financial and human resources. In the late 1960s, for example, a suggestion was made to Chancellor Heyns that UC Berkeley itself become involved in K–12 education reform. One of his advisors urged caution: " 'If handled as a direct service operation, this could be extremely costly, and the requirements could be far in excess of our available talent and manpower' " (Reuben 2001, p. 218).

This was probably a prudent reaction. The needs are immense—usually larger than what one university could handle on its own. Bob Laird (2005) wrote an impassioned book, *The Case for Affirmative Action in University Admissions.* He is particularly eloquent on the impact of differential funding among California school districts. "The passage of Proposition 13 in 1978 was a major force in stripping public schools in California of adequate funding, but well-off communities, as they almost always do, have found their own ways to compensate, often by passing local initiatives for their own tax districts" (p. 187). He adds that the critical importance of early education is underlined by studies by the National Institutes of Health (NIH), which indicate that "students who are behind in reading in grade three have only a 12 to 20 percent chance of ever catching up" (p. 186).

Since education at the primary and secondary school level is primarily a local and state matter, it makes sense that the ultimate route to creating a larger pool of qualified applicants, of all origins, is to more fully and equally fund public schools districts (on a state-by-state basis). A fascinating book, already referred to, by Georgetown professor Douglas S. Reed traces several efforts which have been made within the states, and how hard-fought those battles have been. The title, *On Equal Terms: The Constitutional Politics of Equal Opportunity* (2001) gives a good description of the scope of this short but enlightening work.

As has become apparent from our previous discussion, the role of the federal courts in expanding educational opportunity, by race, in the public schools is well known. The role of the state courts in helping to equalize state funding in public schools, across wealthy and poor districts, is much less known.

Although *On Equal Terms* concentrates on K–12 education, the story it tells is pertinent to college administrators because even advocates of affirmative action have conceded that there is a "pool problem"—that there are not enough high-achieving minority applicants at the college level.[89]

In the first section of the book, a review of the historical background, Reed makes it clear that at one time, it appeared that the Supreme Court might declare public primary and secondary education a "fundamental right," thus subjecting disparities in spending to "strict scrutiny." The landmark *Brown v. Board of Education* decision (1954) contained language which could be read to imply that. Two decades later, however, in *San Antonio School District v. Rodriguez* (1973), the Supreme Court explicitly rejected that possibility.

Starting in the early 1970s, therefore, education activists began to look to the state constitutions to find rights which they could vindicate. Reed states that 49 of the 50 states have some sort of "education clause" in their constitutions. Moreover, Reed notes that state legislatures appropriate nearly half of all public school expenditures in the country. Accordingly, starting in the early 1970s, 42 of the state supreme courts have ruled on the funding mechanism for the public schools within state. Nineteen state courts have found the state system of funding unconstitutional. The other 23 have either found the funding schemes constitutional, or have declined to rule, in deference to the legislature.

[89] Indeed, one of the arguments of Maureen Mahoney, representing the University of Michigan Law School in the oral argument in the *Grutter* case, was that affirmative action need not be a permanent feature of the admissions landscape "because…the number of high-achieving minorities will continue to grow, and the law school will be able to enroll a sufficient number to have a critical mass…without taking race into account." See Transcript of the Oral Argument in the *Grutter* case, at <www.supremecourtus.gov/oral_arguments/argument_transcripts/02-241.pdf>.

As we have seen, the Supreme Court cautiously endorsed race-conscious admissions with the caveat that such a program would not be necessary in 25 years.

In the second section of the book, Reed studies how some of the battles have actually played out. In particular, in Chapter Seven ("Regimes of Inequality"), he describes in detail the interplay between the courts, the legislature and the taxpayers in New Jersey—the scene of a nearly twenty-year battle over school finance. The state at first attempted to mandate equity—*i.e.*, equal or near-equal funding of all school districts. This course of action would have required a hefty tax increase. In the face of predictable howls from all sides—wealthy suburbs, teachers' unions (because of the impact on teachers' pensions), and even from New Jersey's 30 poorest urban areas (they would have had to raise local tax rates to qualify for certain increases in state aid), the immediate result was that the Democrats, who were most identified with this initiative, lost the governorship and both houses of the state legislature.

The longer-term result, according to Reed, was in fact a somewhat increased level of funding. The New Jersey experience highlighted the dilemma: "How do you reconcile a court order mandating equality [of funding] with an existing system of financing that virtually guarantees inequality" (Reed 2001, p. 153)?

## Sources of Pressure on Students

### New Kinds of Preferences?

In 2004, William G. Bowen, president of the Andrew W. Mellon Foundation and former President of Princeton University, called for the addition of what is in effect an additional preference—this one for low-income students (Schmidt 2004). At some schools, such extra consideration is currently in use, but only for the most extreme cases of poverty combined with high SATs. Peter Schmidt (2007b) quotes some scholars who call this the "knighting effect"—where students have combined SAT scores of 1,300 or above, plus very low family income ($24,000 in 2003 dollars) (p. 36). In the study of 28 colleges from which these statistics are drawn, Schmidt notes, however, that "the knighting effect" appeared to play no role at all among students who had SAT scores below 1300 or whose families earned more than $24,000 per year (p. 36).

It seems unlikely that Bowen's suggestion will be formalized any time soon. For one thing, he himself admits that implementing it would probably reduce minority enrollments—at the 19 selective colleges Bowen studied (p. 36).[90] For another, he concedes that such a policy would be costly. The private colleges in the study would need to increase their spending on student aid by about 12 percent, assuming that they maintained their current financial-aid policies (p. 36).

Finally, if colleges not in the referendum states referred to above wish to maintain their commitment to race-conscious admissions, and if they also do not wish to curtail access to

[90] The institutions studied include five private Ivy League universities (Columbia, Harvard, Princeton and Yale Universities, and the University of Pennsylvania), four leading state institutions (Penn State University, the University of California at Los Angeles, the University of Illinois at Urbana-Champaign, and the University of Virginia), and ten selective, private liberal-arts colleges (Barnard, Bowdoin, Macalester, Middlebury, Oberlin, Pomona, Smith, Swarthmore, Wellesley, and Williams Colleges).

those who can pay their own way, the remaining strategy "almost invariably call[s] for the squeeze to be put on those in the middle." (p. 213). It could be argued that the confluence of these two factors accounts for much of the frantic quality seen in the admissions process at the most selective end of the spectrum.

The rise of the private admissions consultant is common knowledge in the admissions profession. About a decade ago there were about 400 independent college counselors in the United States; now there are closer to 3,000 (Kahlenberg 2004). According to Kahlenberg, the president of the Independent Educational Consultants Association says that costs typically average about $2,600 (2004); but one college counselor charges up to $36,000 per student for advice (Tergesen 2006).

In addition to the classic services—helping students "brainstorm ideas" for the personal essay, and editing drafts—at least one counselor videotapes practice interviews, and another suggests that students submit history papers to *The Concord Review*, a journal that publishes high school authors. An experienced admissions consultant can often think of unusual ways of making a candidate stand out. One consultant encouraged a female candidate intent on getting into the Massachusetts Institute of Technology to enroll in beauty pageants—an activity, as Tergesen (2006) noted, "which is not typical of the school's applicant pool. She was accepted."

## The De-Funding of American Public Higher Education

### FOUR-YEAR UNIVERSITIES

Another source of great anxiety to students is what Lyall and Sell (2005), two administrators at the University of Wisconsin system, have called the "de facto privatization" of American public universities.[91]

The American Association of State Colleges and Universities (AASCU) has calculated that as of 1980, states contributed approximately 80 percent "of the dollars needed on average to operate the nation's public four-year universities," but as of 2007, that amount had declined to 64 percent (Hurley 2007, p. 2).

In many states, the declines are even steeper. In Massachusetts, over the past two decades, the proportion of state funding for the state university system has dropped from 40 percent to 20 percent (Powers 2006). And in Michigan, state appropriations from the 1960s to 2005 declined by a factor of ten—from almost 70 percent of the University's operating budget to 7 percent. James J. Duderstadt (2005), President Emeritus and University Professor of Science and Engineering, goes on to state: "Over the past three decades, UM has evolved from a state-supported to a state-assisted to a state-related to a state-located university" (p. 7).

It goes without saying that tuition increases made necessary by decreasing state funding are "leaving many students behind" at four-year public institutions.

[91] See also Clark (2006).

### COMMUNITY COLLEGES

The impact on community colleges is even more disastrous for the students—or potential students—affected at that level. George Boggs (2004), president of the American Association of Community Colleges, reports that nationally, such institutions receive an average of 60 percent of their revenues from state and local funds. If funding cuts occur, community colleges are much less likely to be able to turn to federal research grants or alumni fundraising than are universities. The result: "Stretched to the limit, the 109 community colleges in California turned away about 175,000 prospective students last fall, while an estimated 35,000 went unserved in Florida"(p. 9).

### CONNECTION BETWEEN SCHOOL AND WORK

Finally, there is a hidden issue: the urgent need to connect schooling to meaningful work for the many thousands of students who neither need nor want a college education, but who do want to be connected to real skills which will lead to a good job.

In *Locked in the Cabinet,* an interesting book which was not as widely commented on as it should have been, Robert B. Reich (1997), Secretary of Labor under President Clinton, wrote about a Machine Training Institute which he visited in Detroit (pp. 153-155). The students, many of them high-school drop-outs, were learning computer-aided design, statistical process controls, and other skills which would allow them, once they completed the program, to be hired as precision machinists. The computers and machines are state of the art.

The building, in an otherwise blighted area of Detroit, "is modern, clean, spacious. It occupies an entire city block." The Institute is privately run (by a Catholic priest). Reich asked the priest, Father William Cunningham, how he had managed to create such an inviting program. Father Cunningham said that the program was receiving funds from the Defense Department. "Let's just say there's a senator who's very fond of us, who sits on Defense Appropriations. He's one *hell* of a guy, pardon my expression."

This anecdote is not necessarily a preface to a call for Defense Department funding for skilled young technicians. But it does suggest that a new version of the G.I .Bill would be in order.

### A NEW G.I. BILL?

Two Senators have recently suggested the need for "A Post-Iraq G.I. Bill." Senators Jim Webb (D-VA) and Chuck Hagel (R-NE) wrote in an Op-Ed piece in the New York Times:

> *Members of Congress and other political leaders often say that the men and women who have served in our military since 9/11 are the 'new greatest generation.' Well, here's a thought from two infantry combat veterans of the Vietnam era's 'wounded generation': if you truly believe that our Iraq and Afghanistan veterans are like those who fought in World War II, let us provide them with the same G.I. Bill that was given to the veterans of that war.*

*...Veterans today have only the Montgomery G.I. Bill, which requires a service member to pay $100 a month for the first year of his or her enlistment in order to receive a flat payment for college that averages $800 per month. This was a reasonable enlistment incentive for peacetime service, but it is an insufficient reward for wartime service today. It is hardly enough to allow a veteran to attend many community colleges.*

*...We must put together the right formula that will demonstrate our respect for those who have stepped forward to serve in these difficult times. First-class service to country deserves first-class appreciation.* (Webb and Hagel 2007)

Suzanne Mettler (2005), author of *Soldiers to Citizens*, points out that ten years after World War II, 2.2 million veterans had attended college under the law's provisions. "And for every veteran who used the G.I. Bill to attend college, more than twice as many—a total of 5.6 million—seized the opportunity to acquire training below the college level. By attending G.I. Bill-financed vocational or business schools or by utilizing the bill's subsidy of apprenticeships, on-the-job training, or on-the-farm training, they gained preparation and credentials for a wide array of occupations" (p. 7.).

Such an act suited for our times would honor veterans and serve the nation.

/ CHAPTER FIVE /

*by Michele Sandlin, M.S.*
*Director of Admissions*
*Oregon State University*

05

# The "Insight Resumé:" Oregon State University's Approach to Holistic Assessment

In his path-breaking book *The Big Test*, Nicholas Lemann (1999) describes the evolution of the Scholastic Aptitude Test: it was intended by James Bryant Conant, the distinguished chemist who served as President of Harvard from 1933 to 1953, to open the path to elite education to students who would really benefit from it—not just rich preppies,[92] but bright young men of modest circumstances who would seriously engage with the curriculum.

Lemann continues:

*To the extent that Harvard already had an admissions screening device, it was a weeklong battery of essay examinations in various subjects, called "the college boards." These exams were offered by the College Entrance Examination Board, a tweedy, clubby association of a few dozen private schools and colleges.... The boarding schools wanted a uniform admissions test that all the colleges would accept, and the colleges wanted to impose some curricular order on the schools so their students would arrive reliably prepared.*

[92] According to Lemann (1999), "rich young men at Harvard conducted a life barely recognizable today as college students. ...[They] customarily did not attend classes, and enrolled briefly in special tutoring schools at the end of each semester so they would be able to pass their exams" (p. 27).

*From Conant's point of view, the problem with the college boards was that they were so much a test of mastery of the boarding-school curriculum that they couldn't be used to size up the Midwestern public-school boys he wanted to bring to Harvard.* (pp. 28–29)

Accordingly Conant seized on the comparatively new Scholastic Aptitude Test (which had first made its appearance in 1926, with 8,026 takers) to serve as a vehicle for testing scholarship applicants in the 1930s (Lehman 1999, p. 41).

It is ironic that the adoption of a test which was intended to break the hold of one aristocracy—the old Eastern seaboard "first families"—has now, according to critics such as Lemann, operated to the disadvantage of a new class of underserved students: students who, for whatever reasons, do not perform to advantage on standardized tests.

## Attempt to Assess Noncognitive Variables

In *Beyond the Big Test* (2004), a book which builds on Lemann's critique of testing as the sole or preponderant assessment mechanism for college admissions, psychologist and statistician William Sedlacek sets out his case for incorporating "noncognitive variables" in college admissions.

"The term *noncognitive* is used here to refer to variables relating to adjustment, motivation and perception," he states, "rather than the traditional verbal and quantitative (often called cognitive) areas typically measured by standardized tests. Noncognitive variables are useful for assessing all students, but they are particularly critical for assessing nontraditional students, since standardized tests and prior grades may afford only a limited view of their potential" (Sedlacek 2004, p. 36).

Sedlacek (2004) makes the following case as to the problems with over-relying on the validity of scores on standardized admissions tests (SAT, ACT):

+ *They predict first-year grades fairly well for traditional students (that is, white middle-class and upper-class males).*
+ *They predict first-year grades less well for nontraditional students (cultural, racial, gender groups).*
+ *They do not predict grades well beyond the first year for any students.*
+ *They do not predict retention or graduation well for any students in any year* (pp. 60–61).

Sedlacek's critique is bolstered by the now-famous admonition from the Supreme Court, in *Grutter v. Bollinger*, that college student applicants should be assessed "holistically"—given a "highly individualized" review, so as to "[afford] serious consideration to all the ways an applicant might contribute to a diverse educational environment" (539 U.S. 306, 337 2003, p. 10).

Instead of relying primarily on cognitive factors (verbal and mathematical) which have traditionally been the objects of testing, Sedlacek suggests eight noncognitive variables which, he argues, allow students to present themselves more fully, and which also allow colleges to make offers to under-served students on the basis of a fuller knowledge of their strengths and weaknesses.

Sedlacek's eight noncognitive variables involve the following qualities:

- Self-Concept
- Realistic Self-Appraisal
- Handling the System/Racism
- Long-Range Goals
- Leadership
- Strong Support Person
- Community
- Non-traditional Learning

Even before the Supreme Court's Michigan rulings, however, Oregon State University (OSU) was attempting to create a holistic form of assessment of student applications. OSU created a six-question set of essay questions—actually very short-answer questions (one hundred words or less)—which applicants now have to respond to. Those six topics, all of which applicants must address, are:

- Leadership/group contributions
- Knowledge in a field/creativity
- Dealing with adversity
- Community service
- Handling systemic challenges
- Goals/task commitment

The rest of this chapter will discuss how OSU incorporates noncognitive variables in its holistic assessment of applicants.

## The "Insight Resumé" Model

It seems paradoxical that the targeted populations we are trying to attract to our institutions—to diversify and create a richer learning environment for all our students—are the same populations that we are in danger of closing our doors to. This is because we have not had a reliable way for non-traditional students to demonstrate their knowledge in order to be admitted to our campuses. Holistic admissions proposes to add the other measures of knowledge to the formula, rather than to take away the existing measures of cognitive intelligence.

After creating and testing various instruments, we concluded that eight questions based on the original eight noncognitive variables were too numerous for an undergraduate writing assessment, so we ended up in our final product with six questions intended to elicit the following information: how were students participating in activities, meeting challenges, and managing commitments over time; what did they learn; and how did they grow from the experience. Because this writing exercise was intended to give us far more insight than we had ever had before, we now call this part of our application the "Insight Resumé" (IR).

## Abandoning the Long Essay

The IR is not an essay; it is a series of short answer questions—six specific, short writing pieces, which allow (and indeed, expect) a student to talk about his or her own experiences in a very personal way. Answers that are vague or secondhand are easily apparent and receive low scores.

Of course colleges have long required essay-style components in their applications, both as a means for students ostensibly to reveal more about themselves and (possibly) for the college to predict their ability to write and think (the latter assumes that the essay was really written by the student).

It is useful to know, as background, that before we added the requirement that students respond in writing to six questions in one hundred words each, OSU did not have any essay requirement or written response as part of the application. Admissions requirements for public institutions of higher education in Oregon were limited to a record which showed a minimum course pattern of fourteen academic areas in high school; a GPA of 3.00 or higher; submission of the SAT or ACT; and high school graduation.

As part of our attempt to make up for the limits of traditional admissions writing instruments, we explored with other universities their experience in requiring an essay as part of their admissions requirements.

Many schools were willing to state candidly, off the record, that the "essay," as such, was not working. The four main complaints about admissions essays were:

- Admissions staff could not determine if the essay was the student's own work or whether it was just lifted off the Internet.
- It did not provide the admissions staff with any additional information or insight about this student.
- The essays were difficult and time-consuming to read and score, and the whole procedure added to the turnaround time to process the application.
- Most schools did not have a fair, legitimate scoring guide to fall back on if they were challenged.

## Impetus for the Insight Resumé

As with the University of Michigan at Ann Arbor, it is useful to have some historical background to understand our development of an admissions process which would give us enhanced insight into a student's personal strengths or needs.

At the start of the academic year 1999–2000, OSU was beginning to grapple with two main issues surrounding the admissions process. The first was the incredible growth that had occurred at OSU in the previous four years. Ironically 1996 had seen one of our lowest total enrollments in recent years, and was of major concern to the university. However, with the hiring of a new President and new administrative staff in Enrollment Management, OSU was able to reverse the previous downward trend significantly within four years. In fact, by 1999–2000, enrollment had grown by approximately 30 percent, and we had achieved our largest enrollment.

With this success also came opposing concerns: oversubscribed classes, filled dormitories, multiple space issues, etc. So of course, the issue of capping enrollment and moving towards greater selectivity in admissions now became the focus of concern. Accompanying these discussions was the university's goal of continuing to diversify the student body.

## Developing the Model

The model's goal was to simultaneously support: 1) diversifying the student population and 2) improving student retention (OSU 2005x). To move us forward, we convened a committee that had a cross-campus representation of major stakeholders, including faculty, one of whom was an Associate Professor of Statistics.

The first year we met regularly and focused on three areas:

- Reviewing current research on admissions requirements with regard to selectivity and diversity;
- Conducting a phone campaign to other universities that had developed additional measures beyond the traditional admissions criteria for assessing the potential for student success; and
- Looking at the research data from Adelman's (1999) *Answers in the Tool Box*, and running the same correlating OSU data.

Table 5.1 shows the results of the College Board data and OSU data.

As one can see from Table 5.1, the correlations to first year GPA of such predictors as high school GPA alone, SAT alone, and GPA and SAT combined—even in the best case (which is for Native American students with combined GPA and SAT score)—were still not good, at

TABLE 5.1: **College Board/OSU Data (Correlation with First Year OSU GPA; $R^2$ Values)**

| Variable | Data Source | African American | Asian Pacific American | Hispanic | Native American | Caucasian | Total |
|---|---|---|---|---|---|---|---|
| **High School GPA** | College Board | 0.08 | 0.14 | 0.120 | 0.18 | 0.14 | 0.15 |
| | OSU | 0.12 | 0.28 | 0.150 | 0.38 | 0.29 | 0.28 |
| **SAT** | College Board | 0.09 | 0.15 | 0.070 | 0.12 | 0.10 | 0.13 |
| | OSU | 0.04 | 0.23 | 0.004 | 0.17 | 0.15 | 0.14 |
| **GPA+ SAT** | College Board | 0.14 | 0.23 | 0.190 | 0.30 | 0.20 | 0.23 |
| | OSU | 0.15 | 0.37 | 0.170 | 0.46 | 0.33 | 0.31 |

46 percent for OSU and even worse in the College Board data at 30 percent. It was clear to our committee that reliance on traditional admissions criteria was insufficient.

The *Answers in the Toolbox* research also makes clear that the strength of the high school curriculum is the strongest indicator of college success.

It was during this first year of research that we re-found Dr. William Sedlacek's research on noncognitive assessment in higher education. I say re-found, because we already knew of Sedlacek's noncognitive variables. Our Financial Aid and Scholarship Office was already applying the variables to scholarship awarding, and the Office of Admissions, in partnership with our Undergraduate Admissions Appeals Committee, was using the eight noncognitive factors in decision making involving appeals of denied admissions decisions. (The concept of NCV criteria was useful in order to fairly assess non-academic criteria that were referred to in a student's personal statement when he or she was appealing a denied admissions decision.)

In the second year we focused on William Sedlacek's noncognitive variables, and developed a subcommittee to work with the eight variables and come up with a noncognitive instrument that could be used for admission. The subcommittee worked with Sedlacek's eight noncognitive variables for a year, and tested multiple versions within the first two weeks of the start of term with incoming first year students in a first-year experience class. It was important to test new students while they were still "green" and not OSU-acclimated. By spring of 2003 an instrument was developed, ready to be implemented in the fall of 2004 for that year's incoming class.

It was at this time that the name "Insight Resumé" was bestowed on Oregon State's short answer writing piece, based on what it was and was going to do—a resumé that would provide personal insight about a student.

Originally the author of this chapter pushed hard for capping responses to seventy-five words per question in order to be sensitive to processing turnaround times and to continue to meet enrollment/financial aid deadline goals, but the results after a couple of rounds of testing proved that the richest answers were around one hundred words per question.

By the beginning of the third year we were ready to launch. Appropriately communicating to major stakeholders—high school counselors (at annual meetings and fall visits), community college advisors, parents and students—*before* you launch is crucial to unveiling a new admissions requirement. Hosting informational sessions of all sorts greatly aided in our successful launch of the Insight Resumé. Also critical is campus buy-in. Having the original committee composed of stakeholders across campus was very helpful, but in reality it was our faculty who needed the most persuading to accept a noncognitive component in admissions.

### Incorporating Noncognitive Variables

We emphasized—to faculty and anyone else—that by allowing us to assess how students had set goals for *themselves* and what steps they were taking to reach them, we were able to consider students based on demonstrated achievements beyond traditional testable scores.

Once the "Insight Resumé" part of the application is read and scored, it is electronically filed with the applicant's other submissions, and the whole file is reviewed as a whole: the strength of the curriculum within the context of the school the students attended; their academic credentials (GPA, test scores, rank); and their IR scores.

### The Scoring Mechanism

Each IR is read by two readers, who award each question from one to three points; the IR will go to a third reader if there is a difference in scores by four or more, out of a scale of six points (minimum) to eighteen points (maximum).

Whether a reader logs in online to read and score, or is reading on paper, they do not know or have access to the full file or even the student's name. Our research has shown that even a name can trigger a personal bias. In many of the Insight Resumés students disclose very personal information, more than we ever would have imagined, and they do occasionally disclose ethnicity and gender. During the trainings it is amazing the assumptions that are sometimes made by IR readers about the gender or ethnicity of the student, and how many of those assumptions are often very wrong.

## Evidence of Success[93]

The statistics professor who was an original member of the committee conducted the following research as to the usefulness of the Insight Resumé after its first year of operation.

The success of the IR was most significant with regard to retention. OSU examined 2,783 complete[94] data records for students who were in attendance in spring 2005, and who had completed the IR in the fall of 2004. Of the 2,783 students represented in the dataset, 2,244 were "retained" from spring 2005 to fall 2005.[95]

Using a logistic regression model,[96] we examined the effect of the IR on retention, after accounting for GPA, gender, ethnicity (coded as white/non-white), and a proxy for socio-economic status (coded as Pell eligible or not). After accounting for these factors, we concluded that the IR does have a *significant* effect on the odds of retention. In fact, for a given gender, Pell-status, and ethnicity (white/non-white), and a given cumulative spring '05 GPA, a one-unit increase on the IR is associated with a 10.6 percent increase in the odds of retention. A 95 percent confidence interval for this increase is 3.8 percent to 17.9 percent. More data will be needed to determine whether this result holds in the longer term, although we find it quite encouraging to have obtained a measurable effect of the IR in the available data.

93 Data for this section was acquired from OSU's *IR Summary Statement* (2005b, p. 4).

94 "Complete" denotes no missing values for GPA, IR, gender, or ethnicity.

95 That leaves 539 who were not "retained." We know that they did not return in that semester, but we did not track the reasons.

96 In a logistic regression model, the long odds of retention is modeled as a linear function of the explanatory variables; see for example Chapter 20 in Ramsey and Schafer's (2002) *The Statistical Sleuth*.

Also statistically noteworthy was the effect of the IR on admissions appeals. Although the success of the appeals decisions is not totally attributable to the IR, the IR did in this process not only provide more personal information about the student, it also changed the weight given to undergraduate recommendations (which the committee had previously felt were not overly helpful; many were standard form letters), based on the depth on information now available to the committee. The results are shown in Table 5.2.

## Implementation Costs

One of the first questions I am always asked about our Insight Resumé is, What was the cost to implement? Since OSU Admissions received no additional funding to implement this new process, we paid extremely close attention to making this an efficient process.

Over the first year of implementation in 2003 for the 2004 fall class, we did most of the work manually, on paper. To build and launch the Insight Resumé required additional hours from professional staff, and I was very proud that the commitment was there to make the process a success. But clearly, in the first year, we knew we needed to automate as soon as possible in order to survive year two—which we did successfully.

TABLE 5.2: **Results of Admissions Appeals Based on Extenuating Circumstances**

| | Year of Appeal | | |
|---|---|---|---|
| | 2005-06 | 2004-05[1] | 2003-04 |
| Admitted on Appeal and Enrolled (n) | 61 | 90 | 76 |
| Success Rate[2] of UAC Decisions (%) | 85 | 70 | 63 |
| Success Rate for Students of Color (%) | 31 | 23 | 22 |
| Denials (% of Total Appeals) | 55 | 52 | 39 |

[1] New admission requirements pilot and implementation of the Insight Resumé (IR) began in 2004-05; UAC Committee was approved to use the IR and holistic admissions review in admit decisions.
[2] Success Rate is measured by retention from first to second year and student in good academic standing.

OSU receives approximately 90 percent of its undergraduate applications via the Web, and we are an SCT Sungard Banner school, as is the entire public university system in the State of Oregon. So, during year one, we built the IR into the Banner Web application; once the IR is submitted to OSU, there is a direct feed of the IR and scores into the Banner application. In year one, the Admissions Office did have to reshuffle work-study students to manually enter IR scores, but by year two that was no longer needed. If you are looking at adding a noncognitive instrument—definitely the first step is to get it online with your application!

The other cost issue relates to the individuals who read and score the resumé. OSU's staffing model for IR readers is voluntary (and without stipend). A reader must go through a day-long training, which was developed by OSU and has been extremely successful. The training focuses on the research, history, and development of the instrument; the cultural competency needed to read it; and a segment on recognition of our personal biases, and learning how to keep those in check, so as to be as fair as possible when reading and scoring. The training concludes with actual scoring of IRs in a group setting and in pairs. OSU tracks weekly number of incoming reads by term, including those waiting to be read and those scored, and notifies readers via a list-serv so we can meet our in-house turnaround policy goal—providing student notifications on complete files within two weeks.

In three years OSU has trained over 120 readers, with about sixty to seventy active per year. Trained readers represent ages ranging from twenty-two to sixty years of age; ethnicities of readers include Hispanic, African American, Asian, Pacific Islander, Native American, International, and Caucasian; we have male and female readers, and readers who are of various sexual orientations. The youngest IR readers come from OSU's master's level program in College Student Services Administration. That program offers variable one or two credits; it requires participation in all training and feedback sessions, a learning outcomes writing component, and a minimum number of IR reads per credit. Working with assessment of the Insight Resumés is a perfect fit for this master's program which develops future enrollment management leaders—and the IR assessment program attracts five to eight master's level students annually.

## Special Considerations

### Effects of FERPA

The IR is a permanent part of the application, so that it constitutes a permanent record (along with the application), according to state record retention law. As a part of the student's education record under the Family Educational Rights and Privacy Act (FERPA), it is subject to access by "school officials" (*i.e.*, other offices on campus) with "legitimate educational interests."[97] Other offices that have been involved are the admissions appeals committees, academic success center (tutoring and placement), the Disabilities Office, the Student Conduct Office and the Dean of Students.

### Depth of Disclosure

We were not prepared for the depth of what students are disclosing in their Insight Resumés. Insight into a student's personal strengths or needs affords OSU an opportunity to provide intervention, if necessary, or to make referrals to services or connections to learning communities designed to maximize the student's education experience.

### Effect on Application Rate

When we called other institutions initially to ask about the success of their essays, many spoke of a 10 percent drop in applications the first year they added an additional writing piece to their admissions requirements. At OSU we experienced the same 10 percent drop in fall 2004 applications, but our yield was consistent with previous years. The second year we rebounded back in the number of applications received annually.

[97] See 20 U.S.C. 1232g(b)(1)(A) and 34 C.F.R. 99.31(a)(1).

## Summary

The purpose of OSU's Insight Resumé, and our move to holistic admissions assessment generally, is to promote student success through more accurate assessment of student preparedness and academic potential. In addition to making more accurate admissions decisions, this holistic assessment has provided OSU with more information on applicants earlier in the process than we ever had before. The IR is allowing us to be better prepared for students before they come to campus, helping us connect them to support services an earlier stage. We want them to learn, as early as possible, how to be successful and how to make the best use of needed services once they get to campus. We have been able to proactively connect students to services early in their career at OSU, rather than waiting to intervene once they are in a crisis state.

We are in the infancy of our holistic admissions assessment and still have a journey ahead of us, but we are confident in the measures we have taken so far and are secure in addressing future challenges.

/ CHAPTER SIX /

*by Ted Spencer, M.S.*
*Associate Vice Provost*
*and Executive Director of*
*Undergraduate Admissions*
*University of Michigan*

06

# Holistic Methods of Assessment:
## The View from the University of Michigan

Let me begin by restating what many others have said about diversity on most college campuses, and that is that minority students, especially African American, will continue to be underrepresented on most majority campuses for the foreseeable future. And, if voter initiatives like Proposition 209 in California and Proposal 2 in Michigan, in which affirmation action programs are described as giving preferential treatment to minorities, continue to pass in other states, then we may run the risk of re-segregating both K–12 and higher education over the next twenty-five years.

The University of Michigan, like most other universities, realized very soon after it began to aggressively identify and recruit underrepresented students that the history of segregation, unequal public schools, and huge gaps in test scores all significantly limited its ability to achieve a "critical mass" of minority students.

So the University of Michigan developed statewide and national recruitment programs to recruit, admit, and encourage the enrollment of African American, Hispanic, and Native American students. The students who were recruited and admitted to the University of Michigan were exceptionally bright and very well rounded. Like many other students who were admitted to the University of Michigan, some of the minority students were not as competitive as others. But all were considered by the University to be qualified based on the mission of the University, its academic guidelines, and many other factors that predict success at the University of Michigan.

Therefore, when selecting students from among this qualified and competitive pool, admissions officers decided which of the applicants, considered individually and collectively, would take fullest advantage of what the University of Michigan had to offer, and would also contribute the most to the educational values and mission of the University.

The process that was used to admit students prior to the U. S. Supreme Court decision in *Gratz v. Bollinger*[97] in 2003 was one in which students were given points based on information they provided to the University. There was a possible maximum of 150 points per applicant. Members of underrepresented minority groups automatically received twenty points, as did those who attended a predominantly minority or disadvantaged high school, or were recruited for athletics. Residents of Michigan received ten points, and alumni children received four.

At the time of the lawsuit, the Office of Undergraduate Admissions (OUA) employed twenty full-time admissions counselors who spent much of the year reviewing almost twenty thousand applications, while also developing and attending outreach and recruiting programs; making phone calls; writing letters; meeting with students, parents and counselors during visits; and, of course, making individual contacts with admitted students in an attempt to convince them to attend the University of Michigan.

Therefore, the volume of applications, coupled with the recruiting effort and a rolling admissions notification process, required procedures and routines to promote fairness, consistency, and uniformity in this review, while preserving the counselors' ability to exercise judgment.

Consequently, in the review of applications, a point system was utilized in which counselors considered a broad range of academic and other factors in order to calculate a "selection index." The index reflected the University of Michigan's commitment both to Michigan residents and to broader geographic diversity, as well to students from categories including socioeconomic disadvantage, membership in an underrepresented minority group, attendance at a predominantly minority or socioeconomically disadvantaged high school (regardless of race), recruited athletes, or "at the provost's discretion." At the center of the diversity debate was the number of points given to each of these categories, in particular the twenty points given to underrepresented minority groups.

[97] *Gratz v. Bollinger* (539 U.S. 244 [2003]) addressed and rejected some of the admissions practices of the University of Michigan's undergraduate school (the College of Literature, Science and the Arts); *Grutter v. Bollinger* (539 U.S. 306 [2003]) addressed and upheld the admissions practices of the University of Michigan Law School.

## Court Decision Guides a Change in Process

Although we argued that our undergraduate point system complied with *Bakke*,[98] and we relied, as well, on the fact that the federal district court in Detroit had previously ruled our undergraduate admissions process to be constitutional, the U.S. Supreme Court disagreed. However, in doing so, the high court still allowed us to consider race—but in a more individualized, flexible manner. With the *Grutter* decision,[99] which allowed for the use of race holistically, we in the undergraduate school were able to use the law school decision as a roadmap in developing the new undergraduate admissions process.

In making its decision, the Supreme Court also addressed considerations as to the "critical mass" of minority students in the undergraduate student body, in such a way that added clarity to the affirmation action discussion. The Court stated that "critical mass" does not entail a specific numerical target. Rather, it is an educational concept that refers to enrolling enough minority students to be able to achieve the educational benefits of diversity—the opportunity for all students, majority and minority alike, to have meaningful and unstereotyped interactions in the classroom, in the residence halls, and in social and extracurricular settings.

So, as we developed our new admissions guidelines, we wanted a process that would help us achieve a "critical mass" of minority students on campus, but one which also asked for more information from the students, in order to make a complete, individualized, and holistic review of each applicant.

Following the Supreme Court's decisions in *Grutter* and *Gratz*, the undergraduate admissions office worked with the faculty of each school and college, and with the general counsel's office, the law school, and the provost's and the president's offices to determine the criteria for admission into the specific academic units.

Our new undergraduate admissions process essentially continues to examine most of the same factors we used in the past, but the review process is substantially different.

### New, Expanded Application

Applicants for the first year following the *Grutter* and *Gratz* decisions, the 2004–05 academic year, were asked to provide additional information about themselves that would assist the admissions counselors and readers to better understand if the University of Michigan would be a good fit for them.

The additional items included information about:

- The student's intellectual interests, expected contributions to the campus community, significant intercultural experiences, or unusual life circumstances;

[98] *Regents of the University of California v. Bakke* (438 U.S. 265 [1978]) held that race could be considered in university admissions if it was considered as only one factor among many.

[99] *Grutter v. Bollinger* (539 U.S. 244 [2003]) held that the admissions practices of the University of Michigan's Law School were constitutional because each applicant was evaluated "holistically" as an individual, and that race or ethnicity was not the defining feature of the applications decision.

- The student's most notable awards and meaningful activities or achievements;
- The educational backgrounds of the applicant's parents, grandparents, and siblings;
- The student's household income; and,
- Clarification of shortcomings in the student's educational record (if applicable).

Additionally, for the essay that is required of all applicants, specific topics are suggested for the student's consideration. While still allowing students wide latitude, these topic suggestions were designed to give evaluators the richest possible picture of the student's intellect, character, and personal values. Although we have made use of essays in the past, the new essays required students to spend more time to complete this portion of the application. The new essays do receive more consideration than before because they were designed to give us more insight into the student's interests, concerns, and obstacles overcome.

Also added was a revamped high school counselor form, and we introduced for the first time a requirement that a *teacher recommendation* be presented.

### Multiple Blind Application Reviews

The present evaluation process begins for an individual freshman student application as soon as all the relevant documentation has arrived in our office, and the student's application file is complete. At this point, under the new process, each file will receive a minimum of two very thorough, individualized reviews that will consider many factors. Each review is blind; in other words, the second reviewer is not able to view the first reviewer's evaluation and recommendation, so as not to bias the second review by the first. Each review will result in an admissions recommendation, which is then validated by a member of our senior management staff, who will make the final recommendation.

There are also several standing faculty committees which are used when a senior OUA staff member cannot resolve the difference between recommenders.

During the evaluation process, readers and counselors will consider a broad range of criteria. As with many other colleges and universities, we look for factors that exemplify the student's academic achievements and potential:

- High school grades
- Standardized test scores
- The choice of curriculum
- The student's educational environment
- Geographic location
- Personal achievement
- Leadership
- Alumni connections
- Socioeconomic status
- Underrepresented minority identification

- Scholarship athlete
- Special skill or talents
- Unique experiences
- The quality and content of the student's essay and short answers
- Counselor and teacher recommendations

## Staffing, Training, and Resources

Justice Sandra Day O'Connor wrote in her opinion in *Gratz*, in paraphrase, that although the undergraduate program received a large volume of applications, seemingly making individualized review impractical, that fact does not relieve the University of its constitutional responsibility to conduct individual review. So we understood that to mean that if we wanted to continue using race as one of many factors in the admissions process, we would need to find the resources to make truly individualized determinations.

The University of Michigan budgeted approximately two million dollars in additional one-time startup costs and budget funding to develop new materials, initiate hiring and training, and revamp our information technology systems. Now, after the initial startup costs, the new system of admissions evaluation adds an additional (approximately) eight hundred thousand dollars per year to the undergraduate budget.

We added sixteen part-time readers to our staffs, who conduct the initial review. We also added five new counselors. Because the new application requires additional information and paperwork from the student, we also added additional staff for data entry, filing, and processing.

We realized that training was extremely important in order to provide a high degree of consistency. So, the readers and counselors go through an intense training program that involves review of sample applications in accordance with our admissions guidelines, followed by discussion sessions and by progressively challenging sample file reviews, in an attempt to help them calibrate their ratings. The results of this training have been remarkable, with fewer ratings needing additional reviews.

In 2004–05, the first year after the Court decisions, our staff managed to process 21,297 applications using the new, more labor-intensive system in about the same time as we did the previous year. In 2005–06 our application volume rose to 25,806, and we were able to review and to notify students in about the same time as it took us prior to the Court rulings. In the fall of 2006 we moved to an all-paperless Freshman application process, and the efficiency of that process helped us to process promptly an equally large volume of applications. It should be added that the overall undergraduate target has remained fairly constant, at approximately 5,400 students each year.

In addition to turning the corner on the timely processing of a large volume of applications, we have also experienced record increases in yield. For example, in 2002–03 (the year prior to the Supreme Court cases), our selectivity rate was approximately 65 percent, but in

2006 we admitted only 46 percent of the applicants to the undergraduate school. The reason we admitted fewer students reflects the fact that a record number of students enrolled in the fall of 2004 and 2005. With such large enrollments, we had to reduce the total number of students we admitted.

We can only speculate about the various factors which may have contributed to such dramatic increases in enrollment, but it is possible that our new holistic review process may have attracted precisely those students who were more seriously interested in Michigan.

However, it was not all good news, because while our overall selectivity and yield rates were increasing, in 2004 our underrepresented student application and yield rates decreased. At first we thought that perhaps the decrease was due to our more extensive application requirements. But when the application yield rebounded over the past two years, we think that the temporary drop may have been caused by the chilling effect of the Supreme Court decision, rejecting the admissions process of the undergraduate school at that time, coupled with the often negative media coverage.

## Recruitment and Marketing Programs

The focus of OUA's recruitment and marketing programs is to support the mission of the University of Michigan. Our part of that mission is to recruit, admit, and encourage enrollment of applicants who are academically excellent, accomplished in extracurricular endeavors, and broadly diverse.

Consequently our overall strategy is first, identify potential students, then develop and maintain relationships with them throughout the admissions funnel from prospective to enrolled student. We accomplish this through a complementary blend of on- and off-campus programs and regular communications. In addition, we focus much of our efforts on top scholars and students from geographically underrepresented areas within Michigan, as well as underrepresented minority students, students from disadvantaged or low socioeconomic backgrounds, and first-generation college students. Much of the recruitment success we have experienced over the years has been due in large part to the commitment we make every year to what we consider to be fundamental priorities:

- Providing superb customer service
- Making use of personalized recruitment to all the various underrepresented students and their parents
- Maintaining and strengthening collaborative relationships with the schools and colleges, and with the offices involved in undergraduate recruitment and admissions
- Continuing a strong presence in feeder schools
- Drawing upon alumni to complement and reinforce our recruiting efforts
- Developing and strengthening relationships with high school counselors
- Integrating all forms of communications, particularly when attempting to encourage the enrollment of minority students

- Utilizing data to assess and quantify potential markets for the more difficult-to-recruit students.

Finally, with the passage of Proposal 2 in the fall of 2006 in the State of Michigan, the University of Michigan has a number of new challenges to face. What is not clear at this point is how the law will be interpreted to allow us to achieve our goal of diversity without using race.[100] But what *is* clear, is that our office is developing and preparing ways to achieve diversity in an environment that is race neutral, but not race blind.

[100] On March 7, 2007, the Michigan Civil Rights Commission (MCRC) released a report entitled "'One Michigan' at the Crossroads: An Assessment of the Impact of Proposal 06-02."

The MCRC was charged with investigating how the passage and implementation of Proposition 2 would or could affect state laws and regulations, state educational institutions and programs, and state economic development efforts. The Commission stated that "Michigan's public educational institutions will face a huge challenge in maintaining diversity under Proposition 2" (p. 25), but added that "outreach to groups based on race, sex, color, ethnicity, or national origin is permissible, as long as that outreach is not exclusive to groups on these bases." (p. 32)

The MCRC also stated: "Michigan is a state where not just the largest, but the only projected population growth in the next 20 years will be realized in racial and ethnic groups with the lowest levels of educational attainment. [Footnote omitted.]" The report added: "Minority populations are overwhelmingly underrepresented in higher education. Insofar as educational attainment is strongly correlated with average earned wages, it is safe to presume that if all ethnic groups had the same educational attainment and earnings as whites, total personal income in Michigan would be approximately $3.9 billion higher, and the state would realize an estimated $1.4 billion in additional tax revenues."

See "'One Michigan' at the Crossroads," <www.michigan.gov/documents/mdcr/FinalCommissionReport3-07_1_189266_7.pdf>.

/ CHAPTER SEVEN /

*by Eric P. Staab, M.A.*
*Dean of Admission*
*Kalamazoo College*

07

# Small Private Liberal Arts Colleges:
## Recruiting Challenges and Opportunities

What is a college without students? A bankrupt think tank perhaps. Most colleges might be successful in enrolling some students without an office of admission or a recruitment strategy, but a college without either of these opens its doors to destiny and loses all control of class composition and financial planning. To ensure that the college fulfills as many of its often contradictory goals as possible, active recruitment of students is a must.

An admissions dean is usually expected to achieve several goals at once, and at times the goals can appear to be at odds with one another: Improve the SAT/ACT average. Enroll more students from outside the state/region. Increase the number of African American/Hispanic/Native American/Asian students. Bring the gender balance closer to 50/50—and by the way, ideally the campus would have a broader socio-economic representation, and could we reduce the discount rate by three percent in the process? An admissions dean is wise to probe these interests further and to assess if there is a ranking of these desired outcomes.

When the institution involved is a small private liberal arts college,[101] it becomes even more of a challenge to pursue—much less to achieve—all of these objectives. Liberal arts

[101] Typically defined as colleges with enrollments of 2,500 or less.

colleges (LACs) face a variety of hurdles in enrollment, but they also offer distinctive strengths. In this chapter, we will discuss some of the hurdles first, and then move through the stages in crafting a class: building the prospect pool; moving prospects to applicants; shaping the class; the use of the wait-list; and some concluding thoughts.

This chapter will focus on colleges which offer four-year bachelor's degree programs, with a liberal arts focus, and which draw on (or aspire to draw on) a national applicant pool.

## Financial Structure

At their core all private colleges are a business with expenses and revenues, assets, and capital. If the college fails to cover its expenses with revenue, it must erode its assets and capital. Persistent failure to cover its expenses ultimately results in the failure of the business or, in this case, the closing of the college.

Private colleges typically have four sources of revenue: interest earned from an endowment, tuition received from enrolled students, donations from alumni and friends of the college, and grants received (for special projects) from the federal/local government or private sponsors. Only through the various programs of student financial aid will a private college receive any direct assistance from the federal government. Occasionally, a state will make funds available to private colleges for capital projects, but this is rare.[102]

Thus, with the exception of a few dozen private colleges which enjoy the benefits of a large endowment, the vast majority of small liberal arts colleges are highly dependent upon the revenue from tuition received.

The amount of tuition received is dependent upon the number of students enrolled and the amount of financial assistance needed to achieve that enrollment:

*No. of Students × Rate of Tuition – Institutional Financial Aid = Net Tuition Revenue*

The percentage by which an institution "discounts" its tuition is calculated by averaging the amount of financial assistance expended on the enrolled students and dividing that by the cost of tuition:

*No. of Students ÷ Institutional Financial Aid = Average Financial Aid*

*Average Financial Aid ÷ Tuition = Discount Rate*

Chapter 41, "Tuition Discount Rates: Using IPEDS for Comparative Analysis," discusses tuition discounting in more detail. For the purposes of this chapter, the three variables affecting Net Tuition Revenue can be adjusted, slightly and yet achieve the same desired budgetary effect:

[102] Maryland is an exception: It funds some capital improvement grants for construction and renovation at the state's 16 private institutions (MICUA 2007).

- Slightly fewer students at a lower discount rate; or
- Slightly more students at a higher discount rate.

However, there are limitations to how much either of these options can be allowed to slide. Most private colleges are small and therefore not in a position to absorb large numbers of new students and provide the same level of service. There may not be enough residence halls to accommodate the increased demand on housing (especially for a college that has residency requirements), or enough classrooms or faculty to accommodate a larger student body. Conversely there can be consequences to under-enrolling, even if the institution is successful in meeting its budgetary goals. Too small a student body may limit the range of opportunities on campus: A reduced enrollment may under-utilize certain departments, thus putting into question their necessity; it may cause difficulties in fielding a football team, marching band, orchestra, etc. There is also the potential public perception that a college is too small, and therefore unappealing. As a result the board of trustees and the administration may set a desired total enrollment goal to remain viable and attractive.

For this reason, in this "tuition-driven" model, colleges must walk a fine line in achieving the right balance of students enrolled, scholarships awarded, and the size of the budget the college constructs. A larger budget may yield many attractive options: a larger faculty (thus driving down the average class size), more academic departments (attracting a greater number of students with different interests), more physical capital (new science building, new athletic center with a climbing wall, a wireless campus), and more benefits, such as grant money for student research, paid internships, free movies, concerts, and events. But the larger budget drives up the cost of attendance, or it requires driving down the discount rate. Most likely the "larger budget" option would require a combination of the two.

## Unique Challenges

### Meeting Rapidly Changing Market Demands with Limited Resources

Most LACs are targeting their efforts on students about to graduate from high school: the indecisive seventeen- to eighteen-year-old, strongly influenced by peer pressure and the media. Each year a new cohort of seniors, with subtle (and sometimes not so subtle) differences between themselves and the previous year's class, graduates from high school. This makes for a moving target for the admissions office.

Over the course of a few years the favorite methods used by prospective students to do college search can change significantly. In the early 1990s, for example, the Internet was not yet even in the toolbox of resources used. In the early 2000s the blog was just making its debut. These challenges are common among all institutions of higher learning—big, small, private or public.[103] All institutions are scrambling to keep up with their applicants in terms

[103] See also Chapter 9, "Technology-Enhanced Recruitment Communications."

of using technology to reach them. But smaller colleges are especially challenged with these shifts, since resources needed to keep up with the changing market are typically lean. LACs will have a recruiting staff between seven and twelve and a support staff of three to eight.

### Overcoming False Assumptions and a Lack of Brand Power

In addition to the ever-changing challenges of technology, small liberal arts colleges have several other hurdles to overcome. First of all, the general populace does not always comprehend what a liberal arts college is, misled by the terms "liberal" and "arts." Families want to ensure that their children are prepared for the workforce upon completion of a bachelor's degree, and "liberal arts" is frequently misinterpreted to mean that only impractical subjects are taught at LACs.

Limited name recognition is another hurdle for LACs. Small private colleges are rarely household names. An eighteen-year-old is less likely to know someone who has attended an LAC, since their alumni bases are a fraction of the size of the larger public universities. Moreover, small colleges will not have the advertising budget that larger universities have, and rarely will a small college have athletic programs that merit national television appearances. All these factors can result in lower name recognition, and a resulting conclusion that "If I haven't heard of it, it must not be any good."

Finally, LACs are also, on average, more expensive than their public counterparts. The sticker price shock can deter applicants in droves, especially if they are not provided, at an early stage, with information about financial aid opportunities. Some families will apply to LACs and public universities, intent upon paying no more than what it would cost to attend their local public university. When faced with a higher out-of-pocket expense to attend the LAC, the family must assess if the private college is worth the cost difference. The LACs must be prepared to make that argument.

Certainly, even among LACs there are considerable differences. Some colleges enjoy sizeable, if not wildly impressive, endowments, while many others survive on a very lean budget and live hand to mouth. Not always in correlation with endowment size, but frequently the case, colleges will have varying degrees of reputation. Logically, the stronger the reputation, the broader the radius from which the college's students will come. While even "regional colleges" might attract a handful of students from across the country, they are, for the most part, highly reliant upon high school graduates within close driving proximity of the school. As already discussed, some LACs attract students on a national and even international basis, but these colleges do not represent the norm for their size.

## The Funnel: Identifying and Developing Prospects

An admissions officer is frequently reminded that the system within which we work is a funnel. Of the hundreds of thousands of graduating high school seniors, how do we get them into our database? How do we get them over the rim of our funnel and into our system and make them a "prospect?" Once we have them into the system, that battle has only just begun. You may have their attention, but now you must convince them to apply and enter the "applicant pool."

Now the real fun begins as the admissions office reads, evaluates, assesses, and makes its final decisions, moving the student further down into the restrictive neck of the funnel to enter into the "admit pool." Even here the game is not over. More work must go into the effort of educating the eighteen-year-old that your college is the right one for him or her. The student is now firmly in the driver's seat, possibly with a few offers in hand and finances to consider.

Now, the May 1st reply deadline has come, and once the mail has finally been opened, the admissions office knows where it stands. And yet, the process is still not quite done. With months to go before the beginning of the fall term, students change their mind, get cold feet, financial situations change, or family emergencies alter plans.

An admissions office must be aware of all parts of the funnel, and careful attention must be given to each step along the way. However, a dean of admission must decide how to allocate the office resources, and make strategic decisions as to what part of the funnel merits a larger portion of the office budget and staff's attention. The following sections will examine the funnel segments and probe the question of how to make best use of finite time and resources.

The main goal of an admissions office is to deliver a message to the soon-to-graduate high school student. A carefully planned and crafted communication stream must be developed using printed and electronic media. The student must be exposed to enticing and accurate information about the college to help distinguish it from the thousands of other college choices the student has before him or her. To deliver this content, the admissions office must establish a database of names and addresses. This prospect pool can be built through both *passive* and *active* methods.

## Active Prospecting

### WORD OF MOUTH

There is often no better means of advertising than general word of mouth. All colleges benefit from this to some degree or another. Even regional colleges will enjoy a local following, or at the very least, a general name recognition, due to proximity alone. Students will therefore voluntarily step forward and submit their name for consideration by the college. Referrals from alumni and people in the community will also be a small source of names to a college. High school guidance counselors and teachers will also refer students to your college. This source of referrals can be cultivated to a greater extent through visits made to the high schools by the admissions staff, and through special programs (on or off campus) for high school guidance counselors.

### HIGH SCHOOL VISITS

Active recruitment activities will entail a lot of travel, requiring a sizeable admissions staff to simultaneously cover the responsibilities in the office and on the road. Traveling to high schools, as just mentioned above, can be used as an opportunity to speak with the guidance counselors with the goal that they will pass the word on to their students about your school. Additionally there is the goal of actually meeting with students at the school—students who may already have been in the college's database, as well as new prospects. Travel is, however, time-consuming and expensive, and the effectiveness of the high school as a channel to students seems always to be in question in the admissions profession. Rarely will a public high school have a counselor solely dedicated to college advising, or a staff of counselors that has the time to learn the nuances of the college and university choices available. High schools are also reluctant to release students from their classes to meet with a visiting college representative. A high school visit can all too often entail meeting with no counselors and few, if any, students. However, especially for the LAC which already has a national reputation and wishes to maintain that status, and the regional LAC which is attempting to establish a broader name recognition, establishing a personal relationship with high school guidance counselors, with information flowing in both directions, will probably continue to make high school visits a staple of admissions outreach.

### COLLEGE FAIRS

High schools as well as state and national organizations will host college fairs. Some fairs will cost the college nothing but time and travel expenses, while others will charge fees ranging from a few dollars to several hundred dollars. These formats can be a great opportunity to meet, albeit briefly, with prospective students and to get an institution's name out to the public, but an admissions office must assess which fairs are best suited to its college.

College fairs can have their limitations. With sometimes well over one hundred institutions represented, distinguishing oneself in a sea of college representatives can be daunting. With precious little time or patience, and so many tables at which to stop and gather information, a prospective student is less than inclined to spend very much quality time with a college representative. In this format, perfecting the thirty-second elevator speech becomes an art, if not an imperative. The small LAC with limited name recognition is unlikely to experience a lot of foot traffic in front of its table.

### GROUP EVENTS WITH OTHER SCHOOLS

As an alternative, colleges may band together in small groups and hold an event that will enable them to present their institutions in a more favorable setting. Videos or PowerPoint presentations (gone are the days of the slide show!) are frequently used, or perhaps a panel presentation drawing on alumni or faculty members. These groupings may be organized around various themes or premises. Colleges from the same state or region may be promoting the concept of their location. Schools with similar curricula, such as engineering or studio arts, may choose to travel together with the goal of attracting students with defined interests, and as a means of distinguishing themselves from one another. LACs with strong regional foundations, hoping to expand their reach, may band together with like LACs from other regions. Each college knows it is exposing its market to a potential competitor, but each college benefits from the others' name recognition.

## Passive Prospecting

### PURCHASING NAMES

For many years now, colleges have been augmenting their prospective student database through the practice of purchasing names. A college-bound student, in preparation for the application process, in most cases must take an academic assessment examination, typically the SAT or the ACT. However, the author will note here that there is a growing (albeit small) trend among colleges not to require either of these examinations—but, for the purposes of this chapter, the author notes that even those schools which do not require either the SAT or ACT do stand to benefit from those prospective students who choose to take either exam. An institution can go to the College Board, which administers the SAT or ACT, and place an order of names.

There is a real science to this process, since there are multiple variables the institution must consider when placing an order. Suffice it to say that when purchasing names, an institution can focus on variables such as academic achievement based on self-reported GPA and actual SAT/ACT scores; or ethnicity, gender, academic interests, or geographic information. In addition juniors and sophomores (as well as seniors) are sitting for these exams—and an institution can decide to focus on these younger examinees with the prospect of cultivating their interest over several years, thus strengthening the bonds.

As one can imagine, this tool can be very powerful when an institution plans to influence the composition of an incoming class. A dean of admissions must plan several years in advance if he or she wants to increase the number of female students from the Southwest who want to study the sciences. An institution cannot enroll such a student if she is not in the applicant pool, and chances are she will not be in the applicant pool unless she was in the prospect pool. But getting her into the prospect pool is not as simple as just purchasing her name.

There are hundreds of thousands of names an institution can purchase, and only a small fraction of the names an institution will purchase will have any serious (rather than merely a passing) interest in your school. Once an institution sets its parameters and decides how many names to purchase (note that here again, an institution's budget will dictate its purchasing power), a letter is mailed out to those prospects, inviting them to join your mailing list, typically by returning a postcard or going online to register. The return on one's purchase will depend heavily upon an institution's reputation, the effectiveness the letter has in commanding attention, and the parameters used to conduct the search.

This latter point merits additional attention, for an institution could set highly unrealistic parameters, which can result in a very poor return, regardless of how colorful or creative the mailed letter might be. For example, a private college in a less-than-desirable location with only a regional draw will likely have limited appeal to a valedictorian at a private boarding school in New England. Because there is a great deal of expense involved in purchasing the names, designing a mailing piece, and mailing out tens of thousands of letters, only to get what might be a return of ten percent or less, an institution must weigh all these variables before deciding what parameters to use to conduct the search. A dean of admissions must also take into consideration the cost of one's success. Adding thousands more names to the database will ultimately cost the institution more in postage, assuming that a prospect in the database is slated to receive a stream of mailings. Postage and material mailed can be a serious cost burden; this must be taken into consideration when deciding to build a large prospect pool.

### WEB PORTALS

With the maturing of the electronic age, a new source of prospects has emerged. A growing number of Web portals are being developed by entrepreneurial individuals who are providing college search engines and self-assessment Web sites to today's Web-savvy teenagers. These portals can attract tens, if not hundreds of thousands, of users, all of whom must register to use the Web site's free services. Colleges are then courted by the portal designers to advertise on their Web sites or to "mine" their databases for names. Much as with SAT and ACT name purchases, the college can set specific parameters to narrow the focus and to attract an appropriate prospective student.

## The Stealth Applicant

Today's millennial generation, ever leery of spam, identity theft, and perhaps with an understandable need to be in control, has become increasingly hesitant to divulge information unless it is absolutely necessary. The advent of the Web has made data collection easy for this generation, and gone are the days when a prospective student had to "surface" in order to learn more about a particular college. Instead, these "stealth applicants" lurk just below the surface, reading college ranking information, the occasional printed material their parents may toss in front of them, but frequently checking the Web sites of their favorite, select-few colleges. They may blog, chat, and even revert to that ancient technology of e-mail to share with their friends, and even complete strangers, their reactions to the various colleges they are considering. All the while College X is never aware that Max Millennial is even contemplating their college as an option until the day Max submits his application for admission.

Colleges will code all the students in their database with their "first source of contact." How did this prospective student get into our database? Was it a college fair, high school visit, alum referral, or a purchased name? The "application" as the first source of contact is by no means a new phenomenon. As a percentage of the applicant pool, more traditionally this figure would have been in the single digits, but today those figures can be well into the thirtieth or fortieth percentile.

Chapter 9, "Technology-Enhanced Recruitment Communications," will cover the uses of technology in recruitment, and thus that subject will not be touched on in detail in this chapter. However, this observation about the stealth applicant drives home the importance of the Web site. It also raises other questions, and suggests new uses for old means of communication. For example, the viewbook is not as old-fashioned as it at first seems. How useful is the viewbook, and to whom is it mailed? The parents are, for the time being, more inclined to read what arrives at the front door. Developing a mailing stream for the parent may be more effective than sending material to the prospective student.

## Turning Prospects into Applicants

Once a college has successfully established a sizeable prospect pool, the next goal is to convince the prospects to take that next big step of actually committing the time and the money to send the college all of the necessary documents to be considered for admission. Wooing an applicant is not too unlike dating. A college wants to make the process easy, perhaps by limiting the number of documents required, such as asking for only one letter of recommendation or none at all. However, if the applicant deems the process to be too easy, this could be misconstrued to mean that the college is not selective, and may discourage higher caliber students from applying. Walking the fine line is challenging.

Online applications have certainly gone a long way in recent years toward simplifying and expediting the application process. Joining a consortium of other colleges that use a common or universal application has also helped to streamline the process. These improvements, however, have also resulted in students applying to more colleges than their predecessors did, thus calling into question the seriousness of some of the applicants.

Once a student enters into the prospect pool, the college begins to focus on the next step—convincing the student to submit an application for admission. With a name, physical mailing address, e-mail address, telephone number, and perhaps information about the student's academic and extracurricular interests, the admissions office is armed to reach out to the prospect with the primary goal of winning over the heart of the student by mailing targeted information.

A mailing sequence will be designed to inform the prospective student of the distinguishing features of the college. The small LAC will focus on the benefits of having very few large lecture-oriented classes, and the opportunities to foster close bonds with the faculty who are committed to teaching. To exemplify this aspect, the admissions counselor will e-mail, call, and write to the prospective student, in hopes of opening a productive channel of communication. The student will be encouraged to come to the college campus for a tour, an interview, and to sit in on a few classes. Special programs will be organized in the fall to invite large numbers of prospective students onto the campus. These open house events will showcase the campus and provide access to the faculty and the campus. Such open houses can even be tailored for special cohorts within the prospect pool such as student athletes, intending science majors, or students of color. However a college feels that it can best present itself and highlight its strengths, an open house event can be built around it.

An admissions office is limited only by its own imagination and resources when it comes to creating methods to move the prospect along in the admissions funnel. From blogs, chat rooms, e-mail blasts, text messaging to interactive Web sites, the varieties of electronic resources available are impressive, and are covered in much greater detail in Chapter 9, "Technology-Enhanced Recruitment Communications." Not to make use of at least some of these techniques would be a great mistake in today's market.

In the fall the admissions staff spends a lot of time on the road. Informing the students in your database of a visit to their school is imperative. Even if the student is unable to get out of class to meet with the admissions counselor, the effort has been made to establish contact, and the student is reminded about the college. Offering interviews off campus provides yet another opportunity for the admissions counselor to establish a relationship with the prospective student.

## Crafting a Class

The main objective of an admissions office is always to achieve the institution's enrollment goals. If the college's budget is built around a model that requires 515 freshman at a discount rate of 35 percent, that is the bottom line that must be met. Rarely, however, does a president or board of trustees ask only so little of an admissions office, as noted at the outset of this chapter. The "required goal" entails filling the freshman class with the correct number of bodies. For a small private college, that target can be very narrow: "We need a minimum of 515 students at a 35 percent discount rate, but don't enroll more than 535 students total, or we'll have to find more faculty members to teach the Freshman Seminar, and rent additional housing at the local Motel 8."

But there are always additional mandates handed down to the admissions office to achieve "desired goals" of the institution: "Ideally the incoming class will be 60 percent out-of-state students, and the class needs to be more diverse than last year's class." Others on campus will come to the admissions office to make their requests, as well. The football program needs a new quarterback, and half of the defensive line will graduate this year. The orchestra program has been small in recent years, and the new conductor has asked that special attention be given to applicants who play the violin and oboe. The German department has been shrinking in recent years, and while they have a steady stream of students taking introductory classes, they desperately need more majors, or the department might be cut.

Small private colleges are especially pinched by these demands, since there are fewer students in the community who already fulfill all these demands, and there are limited numbers of slots in the admitted pool. To find an African American male applicant in the top 5 percent of his graduating class, who plays the French horn, swims the breast stroke, and has an interest in philosophy is extremely rare. And once you have found him, of course you will have to wait in a long line to vie for his attention, as other colleges across the country are offering him large scholarships.

Crafting a class, however, does not begin at the time of admission. It begins at the very top of the funnel. The goal is to fill the prospect pool with the right composition of students to increase the chances of matriculating the kinds of students the college hopes to enroll. The college will not increase its Hispanic enrollment if there are no Hispanics in the applicant pool, and the chances of having Hispanics in the applicant pool will be minimal if the college fails to populate the prospect pool with Hispanic students. How does the college achieve that?

- When purchasing names, the parameters used to build the dataset should be narrowly defined to target Hispanics.
- Using demographic data, identify the states and cities with a higher concentration of Hispanic students and actively recruit in those regions.
- Design publications for the mailing sequence to appeal to the cohorts desired.
- Work with Hispanic alumni to assist in recruitment efforts.

Academic departments and programs at the college can help in hosting special, on-campus programmatic events such as open house programs or leadership workshops. The football program, for example, could collaborate with the admissions office to host a visit program. The music department could organize a competition on campus, inviting prospective students to compete. The foreign language department could host a cultural event for prospective students who have indicated languages as a potential major.

Any number of creative concepts could be put into place to help move the prospects move down the funnel.

The college may take the additional step of creating special scholarship opportunities for targeted students, such as music or art scholarships. In addition, financial assistance for international students will go a long way in establishing an international presence on campus. Merit-based scholarships can be established to attract high academic achievers. While these strategies do little to reduce an institution's discount rate, they can be highly effective in achieving diversified enrollment targets.

Once the applicant pool has been narrowed down to a smaller and more manageable size, the admissions office can focus its efforts on recruiting special cohorts within the admitted pool as a means of improving the chances those applicants will accept the offer of admission. Here again, special programs both on and off campus can be created to appeal to certain groups to increase the chances of matriculating a higher percentage of these students. Paying for an admitted student's travel expenses to attend an on-campus event is an excellent method, not only to ensure that the student will see the campus, but also to convey to the student that the institution is very serious about enrolling him or her.

Influencing the composition of the prospect pool, and thus the applicant pool, is just the first step in the process. Ultimately a college that hopes to craft a class, and meet multiple objectives set forth by its administration, strives to achieve two goals in the application pool:

① Build an application pool larger than is minimally required—in other words, not be in a position where the admissions office must admit 100 percent of the applicants to achieve enrollment goals.
② Populate the application pool with enough applicants in the various cohorts that the administration wants to see on campus (out-of-state applicants, students of color, tuba players, intending foreign language majors, male applicants, etc.).

The first goal is paramount. As a college becomes more selective—receives more applications than is minimally required—the admissions office becomes more reliable in terms of meeting enrollment targets and crafting a diversified (however defined) student body. A college compelled to admit nearly all of its applicants will almost certainly fall short of building an applicant pool with just the right proportion of out-of-state students, Hispanics, tuba players, and linebackers to achieve all of the institution's enrollment targets. Therefore, a college will strive to become more selective, thus enabling the admissions office to craft a class to meet the institution's needs.

Deciding who to admit is one thing. Deciding how many to admit is quite another. This point is clarified in greater detail in Chapter 28, "Predicting Enrollments and Yields," a process that is complicated and highly unpredictable. Failing to accurately predict yield can be catastrophic for a small college, and for this reason a small college will want to build into its enrollment projection model a pressure valve, also known as "the wait-list." A wait-list, however, can only be achieved if there are more applicants in the pool than a college needs.

## Wait-Lists

LACs that enjoy application pools larger than are necessary to enroll a class will typically establish a reserve of potential students at the time of admission. These applicants are placed on a waiting list and informed that they will learn of the college's admission decision in May, after all of the admitted students have responded to their admission offers. This practice, while unpleasant for the wait-listed applicant, is necessary to safeguard a small college from under-enrolling.

A tuition-driven LAC that fails to meet its enrollment projections can suffer the consequences of cutting staff and/or faculty members, or eliminating academic programs or services, to name just a few undesirable alternatives. The wait-list functions as a pressure valve in this highly unpredictable procedure. Yield rates for an institution can fluctuate from year to year, influenced by many variables, many of which are outside the college's influence. Having a pool of admissible applicants on the wait-list provides a source of insurance that the LAC will meet its enrollment target, if not the desired composition of the matriculating students.

## Summary

Private liberal arts colleges share many of the same challenges that their larger public peers experience. All institutions must enroll a group of qualified freshman each year, and virtually all of them are striving to achieve a certain balance of men and women and students from all ethnic backgrounds. However, by virtue of their small size, which serves as both their strength and weakness, LACs typically face challenges which are distinct from those of the large public universities. Lack of name recognition (in some instances); a wariness by both parents and students as to small colleges that generally do not offer highly specialized, career-focused programs; and "sticker shock" when compared to public college tuitions are but a few of those challenges in recruiting students.

The challenge in recruiting students to the small private liberal arts college is that the tuition-driven institution, which most private LACs are, must walk a fine line between over- and under-enrolling. The skills required to recruit a student to an LAC, namely the ability to communicate effectively with many different kinds of people, must also be employed within the college setting itself. A successful director of admission must know how to work with trustees, who may have a narrow understanding of the admissions profession; presidents, who are under pressure from trustees and faculty; and faculty, who see the successes and failures of the admissions offices as impacting them most directly. However, this author has yet to meet a dean of admission who got into the profession because it was easy. A successful and "happy" dean is a person who loves a challenge and thrives on the idea that he or she is providing an opportunity for young minds to be exposed to great ideas.

/ CHAPTER EIGHT /

*by Christine Kerlin, Ed.D.*
*Vice President for Enrollment Management*
*Everett Community College*

08

# Community College Admissions:
## Keeping the Door Open

Admissions work in the community college setting takes place within the context of each individual college. Its history, location, size, budget, programs, regional demography, and management structure will affect the type of work it calls "admissions." This chapter will focus on fairly common practices and processes in community college admissions, and on several trends and issues that face the wide variety of community college practitioners and leaders.

At the outset, though, the author wishes to acknowledge that the perspective of this chapter is largely focused on publicly funded community and technical colleges with multiple missions.[104] This is not to dismiss other two-year colleges which may be independent or singular in their mission; they, too, may find resonance in the issues in this chapter.

## Background

Many community colleges bundle admissions, registration, and records. Thus, an office may be called "Admissions and Registration" or "Enrollment Services," in either case carrying out

[104] AACC (2007) reports that there are 991 public community and technical colleges, 180 independent colleges, and 31 tribal colleges. Alternatively, NCES lists 1061 public institutions and 622 private two-year institutions (Snyder, Tan, and Hoffman 2006, p. 421). The difference may be due to a disparity in data methodology—NCES includes private proprietary colleges (those that offer two-year programs as well as short-term training programs).

multiple functions. This is a reflection of the fact that for most community colleges, with their open door mission, admission is an automatic process without the complications of lengthy application forms, transcripts, test scores, essays, letters of recommendation, selective admission criteria, deadlines, deposits, and waiting lists. Except for some selective programs in community colleges, such as nursing, admission may roll up to the first day of class (or later) on a first come, first served basis and requires perhaps a transcript, if that. In many cases, an admission process is dispensed with and a new student flows directly into a registration process—a process which may include placement testing, orientation, and advising prior to registration as a new student.

The admissions and registration office, or enrollment services as it will be referred to in this chapter, is the front door for many types of students, and many types of programs. In a single day processes may be directed toward students interested in the programs of Adult Basic Education, English as a Second Language (ESL), GED,[105] pre-college, high school dual enrollment, university transfer, technical training, and personal enrichment, all of which may be credit or non-credit, short-term or regular term, on-campus, off-campus, or online. Some of these programs may have their own staff at separate locations to process and induct new students, and their admission-cum-registration is a matter of referral and internal coordination by staff in a back office.

Increasingly, though, community colleges are emphasizing a more recognizable "admissions" function. This move might be ascribed to several factors: 1) reaction to fluctuations in enrollment that may be caused by competition, employment rate swings, or population declines (or increases); 2) opportunities available through adopting new technologies, such as Web portals and integrated information systems; and 3) budget pressures that focus administrative attention on the need to manage enrollment.

In simplest terms, admissions functions can be seen as "recruitment" and "intake." In the early years of most community colleges, recruitment was often handled by counselors, usually located in a counseling and career office, and sometimes by faculty, and was focused on visiting local high schools and participating in local college fairs. Recruitment was also accomplished through mailing out the class schedule to the district, advertising in local papers, and perhaps having good contacts with local unemployment, vocational rehabilitation, and social service agencies. Intake was handled as a paperwork process, either accepting an application form and responding with registration directions or responding to walk-in new students with immediate directions about how to register. It is no longer that simple.

[105] Test of General Educational Development (GED), i.e., high-school equivalency test. See definition of GED in the IPEDS Glossary at <http://nces.ed.gov/ipeds/glossary/>.

## Themes and Issues

### The Open Door

Community colleges are cast as the open door to higher education (Boggs 2004; Vaughan 2004). Typically, persons who are age eighteen or older, or who have graduated from high school or earned their GED (high school equivalency) are eligible for admission. Special programs, such as GED classes or shared programs with high schools, may enable persons younger than eighteen to attend. State or local policies may exercise slight variations on this pattern, but, in the end, community colleges take almost all comers.

As concern about accountability and effectiveness in higher education has grown, the results of an open door posture have come under some debate. Some argue that the open door is actually a revolving door and that community colleges should take greater measures at the front door to assure ultimate success for students who may be eligible to enroll, but may arrive unprepared in one or more ways (Barefoot 2004). Accurate information, mandatory orientation, enforced course placement, and other services are seen as necessary tools that should be employed as the student enters the community college. The enrollment services office should be involved in these discussions, since often these types of interventions will be the responsibility of the enrollment services office.

### Enrollment Management

Enrollment management has its own special application to community colleges. While many would think that the open door would make a sufficient number of students enroll every term, factors such as budget pressures, population swings, and shifting demographic characteristics require a more strategic and intentional type of enrollment planning than the "build it and they will come" posture. This more deliberate approach requires a focus on admissions functions, including considerations as to program mix, marketing, and retention, and the employment of professionals specifically charged with such responsibilities.

In many ways this evolution toward a more specialized staff has edged out the counselors who, for many colleges, traditionally had made outreach visits as an adjunct to their counseling role.[106] Indeed, in some cases colleges have expanded the functions of their enrollment services office, or perhaps have even developed separate but related "Outreach" or "Enrollment Development" offices. As with universities, the strategies of building prospective student interest, transforming inquiries to applications to enrollment (the "funnel"), and establishing effective and responsive intake processes have been developed through a more specialized and professional staff, with a correspondingly elevated position for the admissions functions.

This development represents a challenge to some community colleges, which have mechanisms and formulas for evaluating the need to add faculty based on course offerings, but may

[106] The professional counselors, usually associated with the college's "counseling" office, find themselves with more than enough to handle as students increasingly bring significant personal problems with them, and faculty need more support in handling disruptive situations in class.

have less experience in determining whether or when to add staff for recruitment and intake, much less engage in a more holistic enrollment management approach. Increasingly, however, we are seeing community colleges moving toward adding positions with an enrollment leadership focus, such as Associate Dean, Dean, or Vice President for Enrollment Management. In a related development, we see some community colleges following a university model, where the enrollment management purview is extended to financial aid, orientation, registration, and other functions seen as pertinent to entry and retention.

The role of enrollment services in enrollment management should be that of a partner with other units and divisions within the college. Because the community college serves such diverse audiences, connections with various instructional programs should be strong, so the prospective students are informed and guided in the appropriate direction. And, in light of the community college mission to serve its local area, the enrollment services' ability to field the inquiries of prospective and entering students enables it to discern trends that affect enrollment and success and to provide feedback to other campus sectors.

## Access

In the community colleges, the chief mission of the enrollment services staff is to assure access. Among the many strategies employed to assure access, several are prominent, especially in addressing diversity and affordability.

The increasing *diversity* of the American population alone (not even taking into account students from abroad) challenges us to assure sensitivity to the range of cultures we encounter. Our publications, staffing, and related services must be attuned to the different backgrounds and needs of our potential students. For many community colleges, publications (either in print or electronic) may need to be offered in several different languages. In addition, it may be appropriate for the staff to include members who speak languages other than English. Similarly, outreach efforts may be tailored to the different cultural communities within the service area.

As administrators at open door institutions, we often find that many prospective students with whom we come in contact have little clear idea or understanding of the world of higher education. Thus professionals associated with the admission functions must also serve as *entry advisors*. Their mission should not be solely to recruit and enroll students, but also to inform and guide students who may need conversations about financial aid, skill level and appropriate placement, and program options, as well as referrals to other professionals at the college who can provide career and personal guidance.

The type of persons hired for admissions work, the training they receive, and their accountabilities should include strong consideration of their function as holistic entry personnel (*i.e.*, persons with multiple skills and a high level of "cultural competency"). In this way, such professionals help prepare community college students for true access to higher education, as well as contribute to their success and retention.

*Affordability* is a critical determiner of access. Enrollment services personnel are in a unique position to collaborate with several sectors of their college on this issue. Most obvious is collaboration with the financial aid office. It is not unusual for prospective community college students to approach the community college late in the game, making it difficult to complete the financial aid application and award process in time for registration and payment deadlines. Developing communication strategies and joint processes can reduce some of the barriers. A collaborative effort can also be initiated with the student accounts or bursar office. For example, delayed payment plans and clear billing and payment procedures can help a student manage his or her finances. In addition, work with the college's foundation, if one exists, can build scholarship programs and "emergency loans" that are applicable to all types of students, not just the 4.0 high school valedictorians.

### Recruitment Strategies

Community colleges are uniquely positioned to engage many audiences in higher education. Given the continuum of educational programs from basic literacy, ESL, high school completion, GED and pre-college skill remediation, to college-level technical and university transfer programs, every part of a local and regional community can be touched. Many strategies for good practice are described by the experienced professionals who have contributed to this book. Strategies that can be particularly well suited to the community college—given its mission to provide access to both the well-qualified and the academically marginalized populations—include developing community agency and business relationships; outreach to middle schools and high schools; creating various types of events, including financial aid workshops, that bring prospective students and their families on campus; and making available special programs that appeal to under-prepared students.

### Relationships with Business and Industry

Many community colleges have joined with business, industry, and local chambers of commerce to reinforce their mission to serve as the locus of workforce development. Demographic projections indicate shortages in the labor market as Boomers retire and the younger population cohort is either too small to refill those slots or is, in some cases, unprepared without further training to meet the technology and skill demands of future employment slots.

Relationships between faculty and business enterprises can yield partnerships that not only serve the community's needs, but also engage under-prepared youth and adults who might otherwise not emerge from the usual recruitment channels. In many states, additional funding is available for these types of enrollments. These workforce development programs might be managed from a different office, but linkage between enrollment services and such offices can maximize institutional coordination and the intake and entry processes of those students. Often special processes are called for, such as off-site entry services, special advising, and non-standard financial processing. Large local and regional businesses may also have opportunities for periodic employee fairs, where local educational programs are encouraged to participate.

### Outreach to High School Students

Outreach to high school students is a special challenge for community colleges. For many students, a community college represents their second choice, even though it is their eventual destination. While community college educators can advocate repeatedly for the community college as the best choice for a substantial percentage of high school seniors—and, in the end, many students realize that that is in fact the case—along the way there are many barriers to overcome, and chief among them is the late application behavior of the students.

Outreach activities to the high schools need to encourage early application for admission and financial aid—a result which is more likely to be accomplished if there has been careful timing of visits and communications. For example, the following activities, arranged by the community college, can help students get into the "stream" earlier: working with high schools to make college decision-making presentations to juniors; pursuing contact with parents early in the school year; offering financial aid workshops; and creating "instant admission" opportunities. All these activities can raise the profile of the college, as well as plant the expectation that early application is beneficial. ("State-Wide Partnerships with K–12 Education," on page 19, refers to The College Foundation of North Carolina [CFNC]—a one-stop state-funded program, easily accessible on the Web, where students, starting from middle school on, can plan for college, academically and financially. The CFNC includes the North Carolina Community College System among its partners.)

On the other side of the coin, the community college inevitably is also a destination for "late bloomers": seniors who wake up in May and realize that they need a school to go to in the fall. Working with the high school to reach these students—through mailings and on-site visits—can help these students get on track.

### Outreach to Middle School (and Younger) Students

Many educators now realize that college aspirations need to be formed much earlier than the high school years. For that reason, outreach to, and partnerships with, elementary and middle schools are assuming prominence within both baccalaureate and community colleges as strategies for reaching students. Such programs generally have dual purposes: first, they attempt to reach marginalized or underrepresented populations who may not have an understanding of educational pathways in general, thus boosting high school completion and college enrollment behaviors; and second, they attempt to establish a feeling of affiliation for the particular college. Most often these programs bring young students on to the campus for one or more days of tours and activities that build motivation and interests. Some programs provide skill-building and emphasis on academic preparation for college and careers.[107]

### E-Tools

Technology brings constant change to the outreach environment. Chief among the current strategies are interactive Web sites, customer relations portals, chat rooms, blogging, and podcasts. They will soon be joined—and eclipsed!—by other innovations in communications. While baccalaureate institutions are aggressive in implementing these recruitment technologies, community colleges may be less so. Think twice; the competitive environment has eroded the "build it and they will come" position of local open-door colleges, and prospective students are using new tools to support their enrollment decisions.

Community colleges should carefully assess their outreach strategies and partnerships that enable prospective students to learn about their options and find smooth entry. New organizational configurations and specialized professionals may be the key to success.

### Age and Role Diversity

While traditional baccalaureate institutions generally work with adults as the parents of their students, community colleges work with adults at many stages of their life: older adults who are themselves returning to school for basic education, college transfer, job and career skills, or continuing education; middle-aged adults who are the parents of young students enrolled in high school dual credit programs or college level programs; and young adults who are themselves parents at a very early age. For all these reasons, outreach and response systems need to be sensitive to the wide diversity of the experience of such students, as well as their role.

This diversity presents itself foremost as a challenge to managing college outreach and recruitment activities with limited resources. Brochures, the Web site, and campus events all need to take into consideration the varying needs and interests of their target populations, with the result that a single event or publication might well be replicated in several different formats to appeal to different audiences. Such diversity also challenges our staff as they work with any or all of the following scenarios: parents of underage students who demand access to the student's records; mature adults who may still be very naïve about college procedures and processes; or the adult student who is balancing job, family, commuting, sick children, and his or her own college planning process at the same time.

[107] Example progams include: Northwest Missouri State University's "Challenge U" program; Everett Community College's (WA) "I Am Going to College" and IDEAS Summer Science Camp programs; and Westminster College's (UT) AWE+SUM Camp. See <http://people.westminstercollege.edu/faculty/tshepherd/As.html>.

### Proliferation of High School Programs

There are several types of dual enrollment relationships that community colleges can have with high schools. A 2002–03 study by the National Center for Education Statistics (NCES) found that at least thirty-eight states have some sort of state policy regarding dual enrollment, with the majority of students in those programs enrolled at community colleges.[108] Growth in these types of programs is significant. As an example, a recent article cites Iowa as having 25,578 high school students enrolled in a community college in 2006, compared with 15,633 in 2002, a 63 percent increase in four years (AP 2007).

Running Start[109] programs, funded by high school districts, enable selected high school juniors and seniors to leave the high school setting and enroll as regular college students, earning both high school and college credit. The aims are to accelerate and challenge students, and to save public funds by reducing "time to degree." Studies indicate remarkable success in reaching these goals. The challenge to the "open door" community college is to determine whether or not selective admission criteria are appropriate in this situation. Research conducted at Everett Community College (WA) found that high school GPA and placement test scores are useful in assessing the potential success of these students. Since these types of students are typically using the college courses to satisfy high school requirements, the students' success in the college courses is doubly important.

"College in the High School" or "College High School" programs, in such states as Washington and Oregon, enable high school students to remain in their high school, by pairing high school faculty with college faculty for several purposes: to examine the curricula of advanced high school classes (such as AP English or advanced foreign language); identify those that have equivalence to college-level courses in terms of content and credentials of the instructor; and articulate them with college classes for the purposes of earning college credit.

Tech Prep,[110] sometimes called 2+2, is similar to College in the High School, except that that the articulation is usually with the community college's technical courses. The goal of this type of program is to engage students who are learning specific job skills in high school and to provide them with an efficient transition into community college technical programs. The Tech Prep courses are placed on the college transcript. Enrollment services staff can then formulate strategies for engaging these students in continuing their education at the community college, since they have already earned college credit.

108 A study of 812,700 high school students who took college level courses at 2,410 Title IV degree-granting institutions during 2002–003 revealed that 77 percent of those students were enrolled at a community college (Kleiner, Lewis, and Greene 2005).

109 "Running Start" is a frequently used title for these programs, and was first developed as a shared high school-college program by Minnesota as PSEO, Post-Secondary Education Options. See <www.revisor.leg.state.mn.us/data/revisor/statutes/2004/124D/09.html>. For background information as to such a program in Washington State, see <www.k12.wa.us/RunningStart/default.aspx> or 1990 Parent and Student "Choice" Act (Chapter 9, Laws of 1990, 1st Ex. Sess.). Other states with this type of program: Illinois, Hawaii, Oregon.

110 "To date, roughly 47 percent of the nation's high schools (or 7,400 high schools) offer one or more Tech Prep programs. Nearly every community and technical college in the nation participates in a Tech Prep consortium, as do many four-year colleges and universities, private businesses, and employer and union organizations" (ED 2007a).

"Youth re-engagement" programs may be designed to appeal to students who have left high school, or are at serious risk of dropping out. Funded by the high school or district, these types of programs often focus on individualized case-management and clear enrollment guidelines at the community college to maximize student success.

Such programs may or may not be managed in the enrollment services area. In any event, linkage to other community college programs is important. Traditional outreach programs to high schools should be developed with "youth re-engagement" programs in mind. They represent opportunities to develop pathways for students to continue their relationship with the community college, once the original program ends. They also represent opportunities to collaborate with high schools on a wider variety of initiatives. Community colleges without such programs may want to review models that currently exist, and adopt ones that best fit the local circumstances.

### Expanded Missions

The movement to expand the community college mission toward adding baccalaureate degrees presents unique challenges and opportunities to the enrollment services functions of the community college (Floyd, Slolnik, and Walker 2005). Community colleges in a number of states (*e.g.* Florida, Hawaii, Nevada, Texas, Washington) have been authorized to add bachelor's degrees; in some cases the community colleges involved have quickly transformed themselves into traditional baccalaureate institutions, while in other cases the community college has remained primarily a two-year institution, although it may offer selected degrees in professional areas.

In either case, such an expansion affects the enrollment services area in a number of ways. First, it provides more options to prospective students, and thus may attract new populations; this development calls for an enhancement of traditional outreach functions, publications, and response systems. Second, it requires a re-thinking of traditional processes; it may change matriculation procedures, entry advising, and entry points. Third, it affects the professional qualifications and development of staff, who now must grapple with a new vocabulary, new standards, and added relationships with other entities. Finally, the scope of accreditation must be expanded, which requires significant work on the part of enrollment services to demonstrate the capacity to meet new expectations.

A number of community colleges in the U.S. have been aggressive in creating "university centers" on their campus.[111] The motivation is to provide baccalaureate degree options for those students who are placebound, and advanced education programs (bachelor's, master's, and certificates) to their local residents. Enrollment services offices may be involved in expanding their outreach messages and sharing one-stop services with the university entry

[111] Examples include: North Harris Community College District (TX), Macomb University Center (MI), Edmonds Community College (WA), and Everett Community College (WA).

personnel, as well as participating in articulation advising. In some cases, coordination of admission and financial aid practices may occur, such as in dual admission processes, and when verifying concurrent enrollment for financial aid purposes.

### Selective Programs

While the community college itself may be open door, some programs make use of selection criteria. Administrators and staff should be well aware of caselaw and state regulations that prohibit discrimination based on race, sex, age, and other types of status subject to special scrutiny by the courts. At some colleges, faculty may manage the selection process, and might not be fully attuned to compliance issues. Enrollment services staff should collaborate to assure that processes are correct and that information and advising for prospective students is clear, particularly where competition is keen, prerequisites are complex, and the outcomes of the selection decision are high stakes. In particular, the management of documents and transcripts used in the application process should be carefully monitored. While community colleges are not usually the recipients of fraudulent transcripts, students faced with high stakes competitive admission processes, particularly in professional programs that lead to valuable careers, may be tempted to submit them.

Enrollment professionals can assist by serving as the neutral party in the consideration of applicants for selective programs. Often, eager applicants are in direct contact with the faculty of selective programs, and this contact could bias the faculty toward or against their selection. In addition, bias can be minimized by utilizing objective criteria validated by research on the characteristics of successful students in particular programs—characteristics such as grades, prerequisites, and test scores. The use of objective research criteria, as well as the participation of neutral third party admissions staff, can help to create not only the reality but also the perception of objective consideration for all applicants involved in selective programs.

### International Enterprises

Community colleges engaged in international student admission and other international exchange programs follow procedures which are usually fairly comparable to those of their university counterparts. Differences which occur may center on the location of the services, the stringency of the admission criteria, and the nature of the services provided.

Community colleges vary in their configuration. Some locate all services and personnel related to international student admission in the enrollment services area. Others create an entirely separate division to handle international students. Others split the recruitment and advising function from the application and admission processing. These organizational structures usually reflect the size of the international enrollment, as well as the campus culture. Sometimes, however, they simply reflect how the institution did it twenty years ago, without regard to changing aspects of international student admission.

Due to the increasing complexity of the admission process in international admissions, and the need for compliance with frequently-changing immigration regulations, it is wise to analyze the work flow within a college's configuration to determine if ongoing communication with prospective students is speedy, and if the application and admission are processed in a timely and accurate way. Colleges should ensure, in particular, that communication about application and admission includes the most current information about pertinent visa requirements. The complexity of those regulations requires that admission personnel be fully aware of the different requirements for each type of visa situation. Furthermore, the interface with the college's student information system is crucial, in that the admission and enrollment data are linked to the SEVIS reporting system. In sum, it may be most appropriate to consolidate all functions of international recruitment and admission either within, or closely affiliated with, enrollment services.

Community colleges can vary in their admission criteria for international students. Some community colleges may maintain an open door by having few requirements for high school grades or TOEFL (Test of English as a Foreign Language) level. (*See* Chapter 24, "The New TOEFL.") Others may set higher criteria.

Admission criteria should be driven by several factors. First, those colleges which maintain an ESL program for international students may decide that a minimum TOEFL score is immaterial, because they can place a student at virtually any level; alternatively the college might decide that it is important to advise students as *part of the admission process* as to the likelihood of their placement in ESL or college-level classes. Second, the college may have fewer student support services than desirable, and feel that only well-prepared international students would survive. Community colleges whose programs have a wide array of prerequisites may require extensive documentation and ability to meet certain standards.

There is no single rule. Instead, it is advisable for community colleges to examine the best match between their services and programs and the capabilities of incoming students, and to translate that into admissions criteria. Furthermore, the professional staff managing the programs and processes should ensure that all staff are well trained in the most current best practices and regulations.

### New Technologies Demand Increasingly Creative Computing Skills

Colleges are continuously engaged in seeking technology solutions that respond to student information management needs. In some cases, community colleges share a statewide system that enables the centralization of enrollment data (and thus funding). In other cases, each community college has its own system and, depending on the structure of any particular public system to which it belongs, may distill its data into a standard format supplied to a state and/or local agency for accountability and funding purposes.

Off-the-shelf software solutions for recruitment may not always meet the needs of community colleges, primarily because most such programs are designed for university systems.

Challenges lie in the software's ability to support simultaneous clock-hour and credit systems, variable data entry requirements depending on specific programs, course funding categories, and varying fee codes depending on program and student status, etc. Community colleges that wish to employ new web-based student prospect systems may find that those products have templates that use the word "university," or have pre-programmed options for fraternities, sororities, and dormitories in their menus—services that are fairly unusual in the community college sector. Pricing structures for such software are sometimes beyond the reach of community colleges, which typically do not have the expansive budgets of the universities that recruit nationally and expect to spend large sums on recruitment. Frequently software prices are based on enrollment, which can be large at a community college, while budgets for recruitment may be relatively small due to a local or regional focus.

For these reasons, selection of an information system and other vendor services should be embarked on deliberately; a diverse team of users should evaluate institutional or divisional options and purchases. Volunteering to serve as a pilot site for new software or to assist a developer in modifying software can be an avenue for lower cost and more effective adaptation.

The rise in software applications and other electronic forms of communication is placing new pressures on enrollment services offices in community colleges. Increasingly, forward-looking colleges are considering new or revised staff positions that emphasize creative computer program development skills. We have moved beyond the days when data entry was the chief technical skill and into an era of innovation, rapid response, and complex tasks that require the ability to mix content with technology in order to communicate with prospective and new students, keep our Web pages up to date, and transform our records into digitized media. This is not to say that "people skills" are unimportant, but rather that enrollment services offices in community colleges must be able to use and support emerging technical tools, either via their own staff, or in partnership with their information technology department.

### Professional Development

The difficulty in writing about enrollment services at community colleges is that the context is always changing. In that light, it is important to emphasize the value of continued professional development for community college staff. The agility of the community college curriculum is often cited and envied, and the same should be true of student and enrollment services. Enrollment leaders should be connected at state and national levels with their peers and within professional associations in order to lead their community college in accordance with evolving concepts of good practice.

Front-line staff need to be trained to relate well to their diverse clientele. Since community colleges are often under-funded and thus are not able to simply add staff as the college grows or adds programs, the quality of the staff is an especially important asset. The ability to deliver enrollment services does not necessarily require expensive bells and whistles each year, but it does require staff who know the best way to use limited resources to meet new challenges.

## Conclusion

Different institutional cultures and demographics will shape the community college's organization, and its policies and practices. Nonetheless, the overarching focus of an enrollment services division in the community college is on access. Outreach and admission processes should be designed to assure access. The needs of special populations (high school, traditional, adult, culturally diverse) must be accommodated by appropriate processes as well as skilled staff. External influences, such as state regulations, federal mandates, and funding may provide both opportunities and constraints. As acknowledged by many professionals, enrollment services functions are both an art and a science. The science is in assessing the demands and needs; the art is in the execution of high quality services and processes to assure access.

/ CHAPTER NINE /

*by Dean Kahler, Ph.D.*
*Associate Vice President for Enrollment Management*
*Western Kentucky University*

09

# Technology-Enhanced Recruitment Communications

Today's technologies and the increasing portability of new media open up many creative and potent ways of communicating with prospective students. This chapter will discuss some of the ever-evolving uses of technology in the admissions process, including: data collecting as a tool for relationship-building; the ongoing relevance of printed materials; communication by e-mail; instant messaging and chat rooms; the Internet, with uses ranging from "tour blogs" to Podcasts; the contribution of current students to recruitment; telephone communications; cell phone text messaging; CD-ROMs and DVDs; and other applications limited only by your own imagination—and common sense.

But be warned: These new media *must* be used with care. Elizabeth Farrell's (2007) article, appearing in *The Chronicle of Higher Education,* offers the following anecdote that illustrates this point—

- The director of enrollment services at a state university thought it would be a good idea to incorporate text-messaging lingo into the viewbook the university sends to prospective students. Its cover had read: "You belong at [State U]." The director changed it to: "U belong @[State U]." His younger staff members thought the brochure looked dated, because many people no longer use shorthand language in their text messages.

After all, as Farrell noted, most cellphones now have a feature that automatically spells out words. This year, according to Farrell, the university once again printed the cover of its viewbook in plain English, though the text-messaging phrase still appears on the enrollment office's Web site.

## Building Relationships

As market overlap becomes an increasing factor in various market segments, the need for efficient processes and effective outreach strategies becomes even more critical. Leveraging new technologies to communicate—with what appear to be personalized methods—allows universities to process large quantities of inquiries, applications, and supporting documents without requiring an increase in staff to handle the data. Without such techniques, the volume of data that flows into and out of recruitment divisions could overwhelm even a generous allotment of staff.

The creative use of technology is a necessity for colleges and universities that wish to reach the expanding field of potential students—prospects who are looking for "just the right school" in which they *feel* they fit. The demand for this emotional connection highlights the importance of schools creating meaningful linkages with both prospective students *and* prospects' parents. As a result, relationship-building via one-to-one marketing should be a priority in every communication or outreach initiative that the college undertakes in communicating with the student.

### One-to-One Marketing

One-to-one marketing, put quite simply, means building a relationship with each customer in a way that responds to his or her individual needs or desires (Peppers, Rogers, and Dorf 1999). A communication plan that addresses all students with the same message is different from one that is driven by the college's perception of the customer. A one-to-one marketing communication takes into consideration whether the student will be a freshman or a transfer student, the major in which he or she has expressed an interest, and many other individual characteristics. *Technology* allows recruitment to take place on a one-to-one level.

Even before considering how to use the data, the admissions officer should give some thought to the capacities of the college's student information system (SIS). Such systems can range from quite robust, commercially built systems to home-grown systems devised in-house. In any case, the more robust the data that is collected, the more likely it is that the data can be used to respond to a broad range of queries.

### Automating Data Collection

Thus, after taking into account the capacity of your information system database, the first step for recruitment divisions is to begin collecting the data from prospective students. Traditionally, such data has been collected by having prospective students fill out information cards, which are then entered into the SIS at the home institution. This method, although commonly used, requires a substantial amount of time to key the data from the cards into the computer, and can delay the institution's response to the student with follow-up materials.

To reduce the effort and staff time required to key in student data, many schools are now automating data entry. Newer methods for collecting data include *optical character recognition* (OCR) scanning. In this method, prospective students fill out information cards on special forms which can be scanned into a computer system using OCR software. An alternative OCR-based technology allows students to write with special pens that collect the characters that each student writes—characters which can then be downloaded to a computer for upload to a database. This technique, like the scanning technique, eliminates the need for staff to key in the student data.

Of all automated methods to collect student data, utilizing the Web to collect information online is probably the easiest. It is well known that students surf the Internet around the clock and on weekends. Online inquiries allow the student to type data into a form at any hour, and then transmit it to the colleges at their convenience. Web-based data forms, generated by students, can then be loaded into a database for further use by the staff. As an added bonus, automated responses can be generated immediately, and sent back to the student regardless of whether members of the office staff are available at that time. Products like Hobson's Enrollment Management Technology (EMT), for example, allow colleges to collect information from prospective students and to respond back almost instantaneously with highly developed customized messages and e-mails. The costs for such products usually include an initial customized set-up fee, as well as annual maintenance fees.

## Refining Prospect Communications with Predictive Modeling

After the admissions office has collected data from prospective students, the essential next step is to track all such communications, assess levels of interest, and act on a plan to maximize the effectiveness of future contacts.

Institutions can better target their marketing messages by predicting the students' level of interest in the institution. Predictive modeling allows institutions to build a statistical model in which students' demographics are used to explain the probability that they may apply to or even enroll in that college. The demographic attributes of each student—whether relating to socio-economic status, geographic setting, academic achievement, attendance at recruitment events, communications to the school, or even time and method by which they entered the enrollment funnel—all these variables may contribute to the model.

A predictive model will provide scores ranging from zero to one. In a very reliable model, the closer the score is to "one" the more likely the student's chance is to apply (let us say) to that school. Predictive models can be built to assess a student's likelihood to progress though the different stages of the enrollment funnel. Such models are particularly useful in tracking a student's likelihood to move from inquiry to enrolled status at that school, and thus suggesting to the institution how best to allocate its resources in recruiting.

In short, by using predictive modeling and stratifying the students, the institution can identify those with a very low probability of enrolling, as well as those with a very strong likelihood of doing so. Sending materials to a group of students with a very low enrollment probability—let's say 0.01 to 0.33—would yield very low results and may not be desirable. Similarly, although at the other end of the scale, students with a high likelihood to enroll, let's say 0.85 to 0.99, may not need to have all the recruitment materials sent, because they are most likely to enroll regardless of the communications received.

The students who are the "fence-sitters" or "shoppers," let's say 0.34 to 0.84 in the predictive model, may be the most subject to persuasion. Thus, recruiting those students with *middle scores* under predictive modeling may produce the greatest return on the institution's marketing investment—while saving resources formerly devoted to students at either end of the predictive scale.

By using predictive modeling the institution can grade and qualify students, and, therefore allow the different administrative units to communicate at different levels and intervals with them. At a threshold level, it becomes apparent that students who have inquired frequently, or who have responded to certain messages even if not to others, show a stronger interest level than those who show a lower level of engagement.

At the next level of complexity, it is apparent that students who possess highly desirable characteristics, such as strong leadership capability or strong academic achievement, can be sought in a different manner from others.

Thus, one "lesson learned" is that institutions that make use of predictive modeling should be prepared to communicate in non-uniform ways to their prospective students. In other words, not all students will receive invitations to every event, and not all will receive certain brochures at all.

In short, predictive modeling is a method for conserving resources, including staff resources, while targeting the most desirable students who are likely to enroll. Admissions staff using predictive modeling may receive pressure to communicate equally with all students. However, deviating too far from use of the model, which would normally suggest full targeting of only some students, will tend to undermine any savings realized by employing the model.

Identification of a predictive model can be accomplished "in house" by someone with a strong understanding of multiple regression models, or else a third party can be hired. The strength of the model is determined by its ability to factor in pertinent variables. The reliability of the model may change over time, if significant changes are adopted in the marketing and recruitment strategies of the institution. Thus, the model should be reassessed from time to time, as appropriate.

Monitoring follow-up communications also allows institutions to determine which further messages should be transmitted to the student, and in what sequence. Automating follow-up communications makes it easier for institutions to communicate with students via a well-thought-out plan customized to the student.

For example, once a student receives an admissions letter, an automated system can generate follow-up communications to be sent at defined intervals—often more effective than sending one packet with many miscellaneous messages. Such follow-up messages could include a congratulatory letter from the president or a department head, or a message related to housing, and other useful information. The benefit to sending multiple communications to students is two-fold: it confirms the institution's interest in them, and it regularly reminds the student of the qualities and strong points of the institution.

### Customer Relationship Management Software

Once data has been collected from the prospective student, the creativity of recruitment staff can be very helpful in identifying uses for the data, in addition to uses suggested by Customer Relationship Management (CRM) software.

CRM software allows institutions to build and monitor relationships with students using the data collected. Such software allows the enrollment manager to analyze student data, manage contacts, integrate individualized marketing plans for each prospective student, and even conduct event management. The manager can view performance indicators using the CRM software to adjust recruitment strategies that might be needed (Ciffarelli and Cullen 2004).

## Hard-Copy Considerations

Sending printed materials to prospective students has been a staple of recruitment strategies for quite some time. However, the number of printed materials sent by institutions has grown exponentially, so that prospective students are receiving, literally, basket loads of them. In some cases, students and their parents are becoming overwhelmed by the volumes of glossy brochures they receive from colleges and universities, all extolling the wonderful qualities of their campus and academic programs.

Most campuses describe their campus as beautiful and their academic programs as some of the best in the region, state, or nation. The messages sent to the students quickly become indistinguishable from one another. As a result, colleges are searching for strategies, many of them technology-based, to enhance the marketing impact of their materials and to stand apart from the others.

### Personalizing Communications

Customers respond to materials which catch their eye, and letters referring to the individual student's interests—potential majors, sports, and other extracurricular activities available at the school—should be a high priority. The best message sent to the student is one that is personalized: one-to-one marketing. With the introduction of word processing software, messages to students can be merged with data reflecting the student's interests to create what appear to be customized letters.

Once the student has been offered admission, a personal letter from a faculty member, in a subject of potential interest to the student, is often an effective follow-up to the president's letter, which broadly welcomes all students who have been offered admission.

Colleges are now applying the merging of data to the rest of their publications, as well. Viewbooks, the glossy premiere brochures sent by colleges and universities, are now merged with the data collected from the student to personalize and customize the messages in the materials. Students' names are merged into the text. In addition, rather than describing all of the majors and minors offered, the brochures address the disciplines in which the student has expressed an interest. The personalized viewbook can also be targeted according to student status, whether as a first-time freshman or as a potential transfer student. For example, a recitation of general admissions criteria can be replaced by a helpful listing of requirements specific to first-time freshmen or to transfer students.

Such viewbooks, reflecting the specific needs of a particular student or groups of students, and based upon previous communications and expressed interests, are often more effective than sending a static, one-size-fits-all brochure.

### Driving Inquiries to the Web with Print "On-Demand"

Applying the "just in time" inventory concept to printed materials, the admissions office can make sure that pertinent publications are printed "on demand," thus allowing for dynamic ongoing publications, rather than issuing all publications on a rigid pre-set (and non-customized) schedule.

Because printed materials can have a very short shelf life, they should direct or push the audience toward online sources of information, which can be updated with ease. In some cases the student can be offered a choice. In the case of Web inquiries from prospective students, for example, the institution can offer the student a personalized viewbook sent electronically as a portable document file (PDF)—or, if the student prefers, he or she can receive a hard copy by mail.

### Offering User-Friendly Forms

Preprinting the student's name on applications is another way of using technology, at a low-tech level, to assist the application process. High school students embarking on the college search process frequently experience frustration in having to complete so many forms during the college search. This frustration often expresses itself at college fairs, when students often attempt to use preprinted address stickers to complete information cards, rather than manually writing the same information repeatedly at each college representative's table.

To respond to that frustration, the savvy admissions officer will see to it that preprinted applications are included in the college admission applications that are included in viewbooks, whether hard copy or online. All the student has to do is to complete the missing information, and review the preprinted data for errors. Preprinted inquiry forms also promote the return rate of inquiry cards.

### Cost-Benefit Considerations

Customized or personalized viewbooks, brochures, and applications printed on demand are initially somewhat more expensive than the standard one-size-fits-all publications. However, the low level of waste, since all publications are printed on demand, can offset the initially higher cost. Additionally the higher start-up costs may well be justified by the increased impact of the tailored marketing messages.

Moreover, bear in mind that personalized publication materials do not necessarily have to be printed individually for each student. Identifying data by categories—such as academic interests, specific needs, and extracurricular interests—can allow information about those areas to be sent to larger groups of students. "Gang printing" of brochures to targeted audiences allows the institution to channel such information to target audiences larger than just one student. Although the use of "gang printing" does not build relationships to quite the same extent as truly individualized communications, such publications still provide information in areas of interest expressed by the student, and in a very cost-effective way.

### Sharing Recruitment Data Internally

College departments outside of the recruitment division should also be encouraged to make use of the data collected by admissions officers. The admissions office, on its own or working in concert with other pertinent offices on campus, should make sure that relevant and useful data is forwarded to the respective departments to allow them to follow up with prospective students.

For example, data as to students who have high levels of academic achievement should be forwarded to the honors program or the scholarship office for additional follow-up. Such practices can be automated by transmitting the students' names, contact information, and qualifying information on a daily basis via FTP.[112] Student information systems can have rules set to send such data automatically to the e-mail addresses or networked printers of the respective departments, thereby eliminating any additional human intervention. Efficiently transmitting and sharing the data between departments is critical in enhancing the communication program that the marketing or recruitment department is undertaking.

[112] FTP or file transfer protocol is used to connect two computers over the Internet so that the user of one computer can transfer files and perform file commands on the other computer.

### In-House Printing versus Outsourced Printing

Printed materials are expensive to produce as well as to mail. However, historically their impact has been substantial. Moreover, in some target audiences, print material is the only way to reach the intended audience.

Although it is usually expensive to print recruitment materials on campus, there are some circumstances in which "in-house" printing may be appropriate, especially for material which needs to be customized. When sending letters to students, for example, as already discussed, the communications should be addressed to each student individually, preferably with content personalized to some extent.

Letters can be sent using the merge capabilities that word processing software allows. Multiple drawer printers allow the operator to print documents in different formats, including different colors of paper and envelopes. There are also printer systems, such as Pitney Bowes' Documatch system, which can merge processes to accomplish the following: print data fields onto a letter, thereby personalizing the letter; print custom information onto brochures; address a letter; fold multiple sheets of paper; and insert the sheets of paper, brochures or flyers and a return envelope into another envelope and address that envelope.

Merge capabilities of word processing software are also available to sort the data by zip codes, and to print barcodes. Barcoding a mailing campaign and sorting and bundling by zip codes allows for a significant savings on the postal costs of most materials. Another software feature will allow the operator to check the addresses of all addressees to determine if the address is correct. Those that are not correct will be sent to another location so that the user can manually check those addresses for typographical errors or other problems and therefore save on postal costs for returned undeliverable mail.

For materials which do not require customization, there are, within most communities, mass mailing businesses that will print, stuff, sort, and mail materials at a cost that would be substantially less than what an admissions department may be able to achieve. Such companies require that the institution or admissions office supply such raw materials as letterhead, brochures, or other copy to be printed, and the electronic address file for merging the data.

## E-mail Communication

E-mail communication exists in two forms: *one-on-one*, and in *batch* form.

The most basic e-mail communication involves a staff person communicating one-on-one with a student or parent. In many cases, this is the most effective method for transmitting information between the school and a prospective student. However, that mode of communication is labor-intensive and reaches only a very small audience. Having to type the same information repeatedly may not be necessary.

E-mail communication can, in fact, reach very large numbers of prospective students through batch e-mails. In basic batch e-mails the sender types a message once and saves that message to be sent out to multiple recipients. Using software packages such as ColoradoSoft's Worldmerge, the sender can merge data into fields on the saved message and thereby customize the e-mail to the receiver.

A batch of "Dear Student" e-mails can now be addressed directly to each prospective student, using the student's name as well as any additional information that is saved into the data file. Entire paragraphs can be changed to give personalized information to prospective students about their respective major, extracurricular interests, and so on. The e-mails can be scheduled to be sent during non-peak times, such as during the evening. Thus, one-to-one marketing can be achieved through mailings to large numbers of students simultaneously.

Student information systems can also be enlisted to allow for e-mail communication, both with applicants and with admitted students, in personalized ways. As already mentioned, e-mails can be scheduled to be sent when specific benchmarks for a given student have been reached. For example, e-mails asking for missing information can be scheduled for transmission when an application is incomplete. In addition, an e-mail can be sent to a student inviting him or her to a special event, after the student has been admitted. Once established, the rules for those e-mails need not be revisited until they require updating.

The impact of sending large batch e-mails is substantial, and thus users should follow some important guidelines.

- OPT-OUT PROVISIONS: All batched e-mails must allow the user to "opt out" of receiving any messages in the future, in an easy manner.
- CONTACT INFORMATION FOR THE INSTITUTION: All batched e-mails must have contact information for the institution readily apparent in the e-mail, so that recipients can easily communicate with the institution if they wish. Sending what would otherwise appear to be anonymous e-mail is inappropriate, and reduces the credibility of the information that is sent. The e-mails in question can be sent from a specific user account, but can have a "reply to" address other than that of the person who is actually sending the message. However, the principle is that the student should always be able to respond back to the institution, in the form of a specific person.

## Instant Messaging and Chat Rooms

Other forms of electronic communication that have become popular in recruitment have been the use of instant messaging and chat rooms. Both of these methods can take place in structured campaigns, as well as in ad-hoc situations.

In the formal structured campaigns, a campus may announce to prospective students that staff, faculty, parents, and even currently enrolled students will be available to "chat" with prospective students in chat rooms, or by instant messaging, at specific days and times. In those sessions the staff sign into specific accounts and then type in responses to conversations and topics brought up by prospective students and their parents. Especially in campaigns involving faculty, the professors are guaranteed to be available for specific time intervals; it is important that those appearances be scheduled and carefully followed up on. The windows, as to days and time, are usually strictly limited.

In instant messaging situations, the staff and faculty at a university or school go about doing their business while being logged into an instant messaging session. Should a prospective student inquire with a message, the staff or faculty members involved can briefly interrupt their work to respond to the student's inquiry, and then return to their work. In such an arrangement, staff and faculty are *not* scheduled to be available to communicate with the students on a real-time basis (in other words, as soon as the inquiry comes in).

In both arrangements—chat rooms and instant messaging—the exchange involves one-to-one communication between the prospective student and a staff member. However, unlike instant messaging, the chat sessions can also be observed by others who may want to join in the "conversation." Chat sessions can be set up by the institution for very little or no cost; alternatively, the sessions can be coordinated by an outside agency for a fee.

## The Internet

Even casual observation suggests that today's college-bound youth are more familiar with surfing the Internet than with visiting libraries, reading newspapers and magazines, watching television, or listening to the radio. The use of the Internet—a medium that appears to enjoy a higher level of trust for its perceived "unmediated" and spontaneous qualities—has become the most common and convenient way for prospective students to learn about a college or university. Although very few colleges have chosen to completely eliminate printed materials, the Internet has become the source of information of first resort, for obvious reasons: it reaches large numbers of prospective students, anywhere in the world, instantaneously and inexpensively. Additionally, the Internet is easy to update, especially as compared to print materials.

Given these benefits, Internet marketing efforts should be one of the highest priorities in the recruitment plans of colleges and universities. Schools that do not make use of this medium will almost certainly be left behind. Following are several avenues to consider for taking advantage of this powerful medium.

### Institution Web Pages

Because of the public's reliance upon the Internet, colleges and universities should dedicate an appropriately high level of resources to developing their Web sites. The campus Web site should be kept up-to-date and be easily navigated by its visitors. Additionally, the print materials that are produced and distributed should complement the school's Web site. All of the printed materials should drive the prospective students and parents toward the institution's Web locations, where additional updated information can be provided.

The main college Web site should be created and maintained with the prospective students' and parents' needs at the fore. Currently enrolled students and faculty will bookmark specific pages and can become quite adept at finding a page they did not readily locate from the homepage. However, first-time visitors—such as prospective students—should not have to possess advanced search skills to be able to find the information they are most likely to need. A link for prospective students *on the homepage* is one of the most common links college and university Web sites offer, and is a part of good practice for efficient Web navigation.

Market research shows that students choose institutions because of the academic programs offered, the geographic location of the institution, and the costs. Therefore, logically, the "prospective student page" should include links to those kinds of concerns—as well as links relating to online applications, transfer students, financial aid, and scholarships, and a list of frequently asked questions (FAQs). Any link, as appropriate, can be supplemented with links to additional locations.

### Online Applications

Online application pages come in two formats: those in which the student completes the application directly in a form that is offered online, and those applications that are intended to be downloaded and printed for completion, and returned by postal mail. Some institutions offer only one of the two formats for submitting applications, while others will offer incentives to students who submit one or the other.

There are benefits to either approach. Applications that are completed using an online form, submitted via the Internet, allow the user to create an account online. By creating such an account, the user can work on the application while being logged in. Such applications usually permit the student to work on portions of the application, and return later if they need to complete sections.

An added benefit for the institution is that the presence of an incomplete application in the system allows the college or university to identify strong applicant leads, and to follow up on any incomplete applications in the system. The online application also helps the admissions office in efficiency of processing, by not requiring staff to reenter data that the student has already typed. Rather, the data can be loaded directly into a student information system, after review, with little other intervention. Since online applications are already typed, they also eliminate the need to struggle to read poor handwriting on applications. Because of the efficiencies involved in processing online applications, some institutions have waived or reduced the application fees for submission of applications online.

The alternative is an application that is downloaded, printed, and submitted in hard copy to the admissions office. Such an application is frequently submitted in the form of a portable document file (PDF). PDF applications allow users to print a hard copy and complete it later by typing or printing in the data. This alternative may be helpful to students who do not have a computer easily accessible, or to students who, having downloaded the application off the Web, wish to take it home with them in order to ponder it. The PDF document does require that the processors enter the data into a student information system; therefore, additional time and resources are associated with PDF applications.

### Common Applications

The Common Application has also become available online. The Common Application is a document in which general information—that is, information which tends to appear across various applications—is collected by an agency or vendor, and colleges and universities can then accept the application as if it were their own. Online Common Applications allow students to complete one form online and then to submit the data to several schools. Since students frequently apply to multiple schools, the Common Application can assist them in not having to enter the same information repeatedly. By working closely with the entity that administers the Common Application, schools can develop or take advantage of already existing bridges to move the data from the application to their student information system.

Online applications have become increasingly commonplace, and many students are very comfortable applying online. However, institutions should be aware that some students may not have Internet access sufficient to complete an online application. Without sufficient alternatives, those students may be overlooked in the recruitment process.

### Viral Marketing

Online inquiries can be targeted for follow-up e-mail marketing messages. If text e-mails are particularly useful or "fun,"[113] they may be shared by the recipients with their friends—and thus may be considered to have achieved a "viral marketing" effect. Viral marketing occurs when a marketing message is transmitted from one intended audience to one or more additional audiences. Such marketing can be encouraged by the institution's providing a link for the receiver to "share with a friend." An institution's Web site can also be passed on from one student to another as a link in an e-mail, thus (it is hoped) also producing a viral marketing effect.

Viral marketing, when made use of in a positive spirit, is a highly desirable outcome of a marketing message. In some circumstances, however, viral marketing can have a negative result when students pass on messages that have typographical errors or convey a message which in any other way is not complimentary to the school.

### Hi-Tech Tours: Online and On-Campus

Touring the university campus has long been an important component of the marketing of colleges and universities. Online Web locations now provide an outstanding opportunity for institutions to showcase a robust view of the institution's campus and facilities for students who live too far away to visit.

[113] E-mails that link to Adobe® Flash® technology were once considered desirable because they integrated multimedia, including sound, into the messages that were sent. However, flash content when included in an e-mail will usually be filtered out, because it is so often perceived as "spam," and providers have generally anticipated the wishes of recipients not to receive e-mails with such technology. (Web sites, on the other hand, can and do make use of Flash® technology.)

Campus Web sites provide virtual tours in several forms. In some, virtual campus tours provide a Web site image that is image-mapped. The maps are linked to pages with photos and explanations of the images. Other virtual tours offer a sequence of photos of the campus in a "slide show" format. The user can click through the images and view different scenes or photos from the campus.

There are more robust virtual tour strategies than slide shows. Some campus virtual tours permit the visitor to view the campus live online via a camera or cameras mounted in strategic locations on campus. These "Webcams" give the visitor the ability to see activities that are occurring on the campus at any time of the day or night. Virtual tours have also have been given the ability to allow visitors to "fly though" campus locations or to rotate three hundred and sixty degrees and to zoom in and out on interesting scenes such as pedestrian malls or student centers.

Campus tours have also incorporated technology into the experience that onsite visitors have. Campus visitors who are not escorted by tour guides can navigate the campus using MP3 players and hard-copy maps outlining a tour route. The guests can listen to a narrated tour of the campus while maintaining their own pace. Handheld computers with global positioning satellite (GPS) capability can also be issued to guests, to assist them as they navigate the campus. As the campus visitors traverse the campus, a handheld computer can indicate where the visitor is located on an electronic campus map. In wireless Internet hot spots, audio and video presentations can be activated to inform the guest of the features of that particular location.

Using the GPS-enabled handheld computers, guests can also be encouraged to share their thoughts and comments, via the device, in particular locations. As the guests record their thoughts, the comments can be added to an online database. Those comments can then be reviewed by the tour administrators and can also be made available to other guests using handheld computers. The "tour blogs" can also be loaded to the Web for Internet visitors to view.

Handheld devices also allow tour administrators to administer surveys at the end of tours. The data from the surveys can be downloaded by synchronizing the handheld computers with a computer. If a survey is not administered at the end of the campus tour, a follow-up e-mail can be sent to students, asking them to complete a survey via a link provided to an online tour evaluation form. Analysis of tour data can be helpful in assessing the effectiveness and quality of the tour experience.

### Search Engines

Internet users make use of search engines to locate the information in which they are interested. Search engines such as Google, Altavista.com, Yahoo, and AOL are some of the best known. However, there are many Internet Web search engines and campus Web administrators should be cognizant of how to register their pages with several of them. Additionally, Web crawlers—programs that search or "crawl" through Web pages collecting keywords from Web pages—can be helpful in publicizing college and university Web content.

Internet pages can also be registered for a fee with some vendors and in other Web locations. Paying to advertise institutional Web pages in banners and in "pop up ads" can be beneficial in generating "hits" or visits to a particular institutional Web page. Typically, the fees for these services are based upon either a flat charge or upon the number of "clicks" or "hits" the advertisement receives.

### Frequently Asked Questions

College and university Web pages provide very large amounts of information to visitors. However, there always seem to be a set of commonly asked questions for which visitors either call or e-mail campus officials for answers. In order to minimize the need for human interaction, institutions often provide online responses to such frequently asked questions (FAQs).

FAQ lists can be delivered in various formats. The most straightforward way is to set out a list of questions on a Web page. Users can then search through the list of questions for the information they are seeking. Or, users can also be guided to the "find" feature in the browser's search bar, to access the information which would be helpful to them. In some pages keywords are hyperlinked from the text on the page.

In more robust FAQ engines, an interactive text box can be presented on every Web page, allowing the user to type in questions or keywords. Frequently, questions can be typed in as if the user were asking a question. The questions, or keywords from the questions, are associated by an administrator to questions in a database. The matched questions and answers are then posted to a Web page for the user to review. In cases where multiple matches are made, all of the questions would be posted, thus allowing the user to select the answer most appropriate to their question.

FAQ engines can be built in-house or can be purchased as annual subscriptions through third-party vendors. The benefit of providing FAQs is two-fold: the prospective student can obtain information at any time of the day or night; and the amount of staff time dedicated to answering routine questions by telephone or e-mail can be significantly reduced.

### Personalized Web Pages

Colleges and universities have allowed both current and prospective students to create their own customized interactive Web pages linked to the institution's Web page. Students are able to insert their own photos, select colors, and even determine what content material will be displayed onto their Web pages. Those Web pages or Web portals allow the students to customize a homepage to which it is hoped that others will repeatedly return. Students who take the time to create their own Web pages or portals at an institution have presumably made a significant emotional investment in the institution, and are thus assumed to have a higher interest in either attending, or conveying a positive portrayal, of the institution.

Schools can enhance the branding of their school by encouraging prospective students to make use of the school's Internet portals. Schools can make available study guides, individualized learning plans, and college preparation tools to prospective students who create such portals. The students may adopt an e-mail account through the school portal, which allows the institution to communicate directly with the student. Subtle messages may be offered to such students to encourage them to attend recruitment events or to participate in open houses and similar events. Links to the institution's online application, financial or scholarship applications, and housing applications can be introduced to such students at appropriate stages in their recruitment experience.

Web portals can be created by the institution, and the data maintained on a local server at the school—data which can be integrated, in turn, with the institution's student information system. Portals can also be outsourced to third-party vendors. Portals created by third-party entities may carry with them a requirement that the data submitted by the student be stored on the vendor's server. That data is shared with the school, but may also be shared with other companies or schools which may make contact with the student. Schools should explore the privacy implications of such an arrangement.

### Podcasts

With the popularity of iPods has come the increased opportunity for podcasting in student recruitment. Podcasting allows small and relatively short multimedia files to be delivered to prospective students and their parents via the Internet for review later on their iPods. Short presentations on topics such as college search processes, financial aid workshops, and completing applications, intermixed with campus recruitment messages, can be downloaded to the students' iPods. The podcasts can include both audio and video presentations and the podcasts can be shared among users, thereby achieving the viral marketing effect discussed earlier. For all these reasons, the use of podcasting in recruitment is increasing rapidly.

## Current Students in Recruitment

Current students can make a very important contribution to the success of an institution's recruitment strategies. Prospective students and parents value and trust the opinions of current students who are not paid to "sell" the school. Current students can provide information in usable forms to prospective students by meeting with them electronically.

### Online Video

Today's students report spending more time on the Internet than time spent watching television (Experience, Inc. 2006). Taking advantage of that trend, recruitment strategies enlist current students to share their experiences in college via online diaries. Prospective students can read about what college life is "really like" from the diaries posted by these students. On some campuses, the current students also record life on campus via video and then upload the video to the Internet. The popularity of YouTube, MySpace, and Facebook has allowed college students to share their experiences with prospective students via these popular media (or their successors). College administrators can either turn their backs on the popularity of these media or embrace them. By encouraging students to post positive diary commentary and videos, resourceful admissions officers can elicit recruitment messages which can be beneficial to the institution,

### Blogs

Students enjoy participating in public discussions on practically any topic via Web logs (blogs) and, more recently, video logs (vlogs). Schools can use currently enrolled students to write or post videos on topics of interest about the campus; tour coordinators may encourage campus visitors to blog about their experiences regarding the campus visit, or to video record their campus visit and then post to the Internet for other students to view; and prospective students can see a slice of what a campus visit or living on campus is like.

The concept of blogs and vlogs about campus life can be scary to university officials, and some may be reluctant to encourage this activity. However, the reality is that blog and vlog entries are available about institutions, even without their cooperation, through sites like TheU.com or LiveJournal.com.

On those sites, current students can post their college experiences for any prospective student or parent to review; and they do. One recent study found that 38 percent of students who used the Internet to investigate colleges read blogs (Joly 2006). Colleges and universities may choose to offer their own blogs and vlogs, so they can encourage responsible perspectives.

## Telecommunications

### Phonathons

In the last ten years, colleges and universities have begun using the telephone to market to the prospective student. Earlier, admissions counselors worked telephone lists for their respective territories, and made that "personal contact" with the students within their territories. The value of representatives calling prospective students and that "one on one" contact was recognized, and phonathons as a recruitment tool became popular.

Those early phonathons were conducted using a set of telephones in an office; volunteers, often students, alumni, or faculty, would call students from a hard-copy listing of prospective students. Such a phonathon might be an event that occurred only once or twice per year, per school. Volunteers might have been given a brief overview of the purpose of the call, and then be asked to begin calling prospective students on a list. Generally such phonathons were characterized as sporadic events that occurred only infrequently during the recruitment cycle.

### Telecounseling Units

Today, permanent "telecounseling units" call prospective students via calling campaigns with specific objectives. Such telecounseling units are manned by well-trained callers who may be professional staff or paid student employees. The calling systems make use of computerized software programs that may automatically dial the number of a prospective student, and connect the caller to a particular type of prospective student to match the calling campaign. Callers then proceed through scripts that are displayed on the computer screen. Answers are recorded by the caller for later analysis. The script may guide the caller in different directions depending upon the respondent's answers. Should a parent answer the call and respond that the prospective student is unavailable, the telecounselor would begin a scripted conversation with the parent.

In a robust calling center the specific calling purpose can be switched quickly by the supervisor to address forthcoming occasions or events on the campus. For example, a caller may be calling prospective students regarding applying to the institution. When an open house event is scheduled to occur relatively soon, the calling campaign may be switched to begin to invite students to attend that open house.

Specific audiences may also be targeted and scheduled for calls based upon gender, race, or even a specific academic major or geographic region. Targeted audiences may be invited to specific programs that address the known interests of that population. Calling campaigns may cover topics such as invitations to an open house, an honors program, or a follow-up to an incomplete application. Calls can be made to prospective students as well as their parents, who often contribute substantially to the student's decision as to which institution to attend.

### Outsourcing Pros and Cons

Campuses can outsource their telephone campaigns to a third party for nominal fees per call. In such arrangements, professional callers, who are usually unrelated to the campus, are informed about the institution's attributes. The third party is provided data on the prospective student pool, and information about the specific purpose or purposes of the calls. The callers then make the calls on behalf of the institution.

The advantages to outsourcing telecounseling initiatives are that many investments are eliminated: no investments in software and calling equipment, no staff training, no office space requirements, or use of internal paid staff. On the other hand, the benefits of having current staff or students calling include the fact that the callers are more likely to be able to establish relationships, and to share their experiences on the campus with prospective students.

### Cell Phone Text Messaging

In the past few years, some cell phone users have embraced text messaging with their peers over cell phones. Marketing initiatives have recently explored using such text messaging to communicate with target audiences. Colleges have also explored contacting prospective students by collecting their cell phone numbers and then contracting with outside agencies to send brief text messages. A brief message can be sent to prospective students reminding them of an important event or date that is approaching. The text message could be sent as a follow-up to a more informative brochure that was earlier sent to the student.

However, the short length of messages that are sent to student cell phones limits the usefulness of text messaging for all but very brief messages. In addition, Farrell (2004) notes: "In any case, survey data on high school students shows that most of them regard text messages as intrusive, because teenagers often exceed their text-messaging limits and run up huge cell phone bills."

## CD-ROMs and DVDs

Colleges and universities have also adopted interactive CD-ROMs and DVDs to deliver information about the campus to the prospective student. The multimedia disks provide images, video, audio messages, and interactive experiences to the students without requiring the student to be connected to the Internet. Students simply insert the media into their computers and explore the materials on the disks. In many cases, the interactive media will function using third party software such as Adobe® Flash® to view the multimedia presentations. Representatives from the colleges may be presented in video welcoming the student and encouraging them to further explore the disk and even visit the institution's Web site or arrange a campus visit.

The benefit to delivering information on a CD or DVD is that a complete set of information is delivered to the student on a disk. Students can explore the disk at their own pace on almost any computer, whether it is networked to the Internet or not. Many CDs or DVDs also allow the student to link to the Internet for even more information if the computer is networked.

This fact also allows the student to submit inquiry forms or to complete applications that may initially be started on disk but are eventually transmitted via the Internet to the institution. If the student's computer is networked, a program can be activated—sending information to the institution indicating that the CD or DVD was activated and from what IP address. In some cases, the program may ask the student to log on and provide some basic information, which can then be transmitted to the institution. This may be useful marketing information in that the student has indicated an interest in the institution by invoking the CD.

Institutions can either create their own CD or DVDs to be mailed to students or they can be outsourced. Some companies will offer templates in which the institution will select colors, provide text to be entered into text boxes, and insert photos and videos onto the disk. Narrations are also provided by actors who "guide" the prospective student through the CD or DVD. Generally, the more options that are selected, and the greater the number of CD or DVDs generated, the higher the cost to the institution.

## Summary

The use of technology in the recruitment of college students has become pervasive. The old college recruitment strategies, starting with the glossy printed brochures of our youth, have been supplemented by multimedia DVDs and CD-ROMs, the Internet, online applications, and inquiry forms. In addition telecounseling initiatives, student-generated blogs and vlogs, and online diaries of currently enrolled students are all being explored by adventurous admissions offices in their outreach to prospective students. That old staple, the campus tour, has become more than a well-choreographed stroll with a tour guide through a beautiful campus. Rather, tours have become interactive experiences for prospective students bearing handheld computers and walking through wireless Internet hot spots located strategically throughout the campus. This technology both delivers multimedia presentations and collects important marketing data.

The contemporary enrollment manager must keep abreast of the constantly evolving technology being used by competitors within the higher education marketplace. Although new mutations will occur constantly, the major theme is constant: one-to-one marketing and relationship building have placed exponential demands on the recruitment divisions in our colleges and institutions.

As a result admissions and enrollment managers must shrewdly assess the strengths and weaknesses of their institution in relation to comparable institutions, and must then make creative use of the technology available to them. Only with this combination of shrewd benchmarking and astute use of ongoing technology can admissions offices be maximally effective and efficient in their recruitment efforts.

/ CHAPTER TEN /

*by Joe F. Head, M.Ed.*
*Dean of University Admissions and Enrollment Services*
*Kennesaw State University*
*Thomas M. Hughes, Ph.D.*
*Special Assistant to the Dean*
*Kennesaw State University*

10

# Interactive Services:
## Staying in Tune with a Web-Savvy Generation

With 24x7 interactive services increasing in popularity, college admissions officers can make use of powerful interactive online marketing tools, and can—as an added benefit—ease their workload by channeling students to use these self-help tools.

This chapter presents an overview of six interactive services for prospects, applicants, and high school counselors, with an emphasis on how such services interact with each other at Kennesaw State University (KSU):

- Virtual Advisor
- Apply Online
- Application Status Check
- Freshman Admissions Predictor (FAP)
- E-Brochures
- High School Guidance Counselor Service Center

These interactive tools are powerful labor saving devices for admissions officers. Given the Web-savvy culture of today's high school student, it behooves admissions professionals to know what efficient and effective tools exist.

The operational philosophy pursued by the KSU office of admissions is one of traditional admissions functions overlaid with an array of 24x7 electronic tools. In the fall of 2003, the Board of Regents of the University System of Georgia recognized KSU's office of admissions with the 2003 Best Practices Benchmarking Award.[114] As we will discuss below, traditional recruiting and processing efforts are supplemented by a suite of interactive Web pages at every stage of an applicant's interaction with the school. Such interactive Web pages provide answers to queries (Virtual Advisor); enable online applications (Apply-Online); and (through a password-protected login) allow a student secure access to his/her records (Application Status Check) and requests for materials (E-Brochure). In addition, a Freshman Admissions Predictor (FAP) allows prospective students and transfer students to determine, unofficially, if their credentials meet or exceed admissions standards. Finally, the High School Guidance Counselor Service Center (HSGCSC) allows high school guidance counselors access to real-time information on all applicants from their respective high schools. This service is especially useful for counselors from high-volume feeder high schools.

## Student Responses to Electronic Communication

Since processes in our office increasingly depend on round-the-clock web-based interaction, we felt it would be useful to know how students view the use of electronic communications. A survey of 595 students attending orientation revealed diverse opinions concerning being contacted via electronic media. Table 10.1 (on page 167) summarizes the responses to a question concerning how students prefer to be contacted.[115]

Since personalized communications are widely desired, predictably Live Telephone was a favorite, with 48 percent indicating primary choice and 24 percent indicating secondary choice. It is important to note that a large, growing number of students prefer a Web-Internet option, with 18 percent indicating primary choice and 15 percent indicating secondary choice. This is especially good news for admissions officers, since budgetary constraints often limit front-line telephone response to inquiries. The intended impact of 24x7 Web-savvy tools is to provide alternative channels of response for inquires that would otherwise be directed to besieged office personnel during traditional office hours. Electronic interaction with students both *expands staff accessibility* and *limits costs*. When electronic media can deliver services on a round-the-clock basis, it is not necessary to bear the expense of additional admissions counselors and customer service and data entry personnel.

[114] This best practices award focused on Apply Online, Freshman Admissions Predictor, and the High School Counselor Web Service Center, as mentioned above; it also honored a document imaging system, used not only for archival purposes, but for front-counter handling of student inquiries; and a Registration "TRIED" Report—a report which identifies students who fail in an attempt to register for one or more courses. The Report captures the names and titles/times of dropped or attempted courses of non-registered students. Often the courses which are closed are those given at the most "desirable" times. With this report a case can be made to higher administration for adding additional sections at optimum times.

[115] Since the survey was conducted in 2003, it is likely that now an even larger percentage of students would prefer contact via e-mail or the Web.

Another survey conducted among freshman found a high level of satisfaction with e-mail notices. Table 10.2 indicates that 86 percent expressed either "satisfied" or "very satisfied" attitudes. Only 1 percent indicated dissatisfaction.

Even though Web-Internet is not the current primary or secondary choice of communication media of many, the findings summarized in this chapter indicate that a multitude of prospects, applicants, and current students are availing themselves of these electronic and interactive tools. Indeed, as more students become Web-oriented at ever-earlier ages, these tools will become even more popular and versatile. Today, students find it easier to transact business via an interactive Web site than the possible alternatives: a five- or ten-minute wait on the telephone or a drive to campus and then a wait in line for an admissions representative.

To encourage use, the six interactive services we discuss below—including the high school guidance counselors function—are all accessed from the main admissions page. (*See* Figure 10.1, on page 168.)

TABLE 10.1: **Preferred Contact Medium**

| | Primary Choice | | Secondary Choice | |
|---|---|---|---|---|
| Electronic Medium | n | % | n | % |
| **When using electronic media, how do you like for offices of admission to contact you with important, personal, enrollment information?** | | | | |
| Web Internet | 106 | 18 | 89 | 15 |
| E-mail | 211 | 35 | 302 | 51 |
| Live Phone | 288 | 48 | 144 | 24 |
| Automated Phone | 6 | 1 | 17 | 3 |
| Videos | 0 | 0 | 11 | 2 |
| Radio | 6 | 1 | 4 | 1 |
| TV | 3 | 1 | 6 | 1 |
| CD ROM | 2 | 1 | 4 | 1 |
| Kiosk | 0 | 0 | 3 | 1 |
| Other | 21 | 4 | 10 | 2 |

TABLE 10.2: **E-mail Reception**

| | n | % |
|---|---|---|
| **Did you receive e-mail notices from KSU?** | | |
| Yes | 239 | 80 |
| No | 60 | 20 |
| Total | 299 | 100 |
| **If yes, how would you rate your satisfaction?** | | |
| Very Satisfied | 83 | 35 |
| Satisfied | 121 | 51 |
| Neutral | 33 | 14 |
| Dissatisfied | 2 | 1 |
| Very Dissatisfied | 0 | 0 |
| Total | 239 | 100 |

## Interactive Services

### Virtual Advisor

Found at the top of every page in the Admissions section of KSU's Web site, "Ask Our Virtual Advisor" provides an electronic service that contains more information than the usual frequently asked questions (*See* Figure 10.1, on page 168). The value of Virtual Advisor is that it quickly provides targeted answers to questions. The Virtual Advisor is a vendor product from Hobson's and provides custom answers to basic enrollment questions such as "How do I apply," "Do you have housing," "Do you honor AP credit," "What are the fees," or "Do you offer online courses?" As new questions emerge, new answers are programmed into this interactive service. If a satisfactory answer is not received, an opportunity exists to e-mail the question to an admissions counselor. The Admissions Virtual Advisor was found to be extremely useful, and thus a link was placed on the main KSU Web page as well as on admissions-focused Web pages. The Virtual Advisor tool has been updated to answer a full range

FIGURE 10.1

Office of Admissions Home Page, Kennesaw State University

of 500 questions—academic programs, athletics, alumni relations, giving, etc. With the placement of Virtual Advisor on the main Web page as well as on the main page of admissions and other offices or departments, the average number of monthly inquiries has risen from 3,200 to over 15,000. Since its inception in August 2002, Virtual Advisor has had over 500,000 inquiries.

Figure 10.2, on page 169, illustrates the response to the question, "How do I apply?" This screenshot shows admissions requirements and fees for New Freshman, Transfer, Home-Schooled Students, and the Joint Enrollment Honors Program. Information for Nontraditional students and Non-degree seeking applicants is found by scrolling down the Web page.

A survey conducted among freshmen found a high level of satisfaction with the Virtual Advisor. Table 10.3 indicates that 84 percent expressed either "satisfied" or "very satisfied" attitudes. Some responses were neutral; this may be a result of the fact that such a tool does not provide an answer for every question, particularly personal questions. Some respondents indicated their preference to talk to a "real" advisor.

TABLE 10.3: **Use of Virtual Advisor**

| | n | % |
|---|---|---|
| **Did you use the Virtual Advisor to ask questions?** | | |
| Yes | 73 | 24 |
| No | 226 | 76 |
| Total | 299 | 100 |
| **If yes, how would you rate your satisfaction with this web service?** | | |
| Very Satisfied | 27 | 37 |
| Satisfied | 34 | 47 |
| Neutral | 11 | 15 |
| Dissatisfied | 0 | 0 |
| Very Dissatisfied | 1 | 1 |
| Total | 73 | 100 |

## Apply Online

The traditional hard-copy application is no longer in vogue. Apply Online has diminished the use of paper applications (*See* Figure 10.3). For fall 2005, 85 percent of applications came in via Apply Online. The application fee policy was changed to encourage a choice of application method; to apply online costs ten dollars less than submitting a paper application.

The electronic data push to Apply Online applications has been a tremendous boost to data entry production. Student records can now be created with an automated download. Now that we have the ability to scan paper applications, a data file is created in the same format as the online applications and is pushed into student records. (Note: Test scores are also downloaded. Testing services send a data file that is batched and pushed into Banner records.)

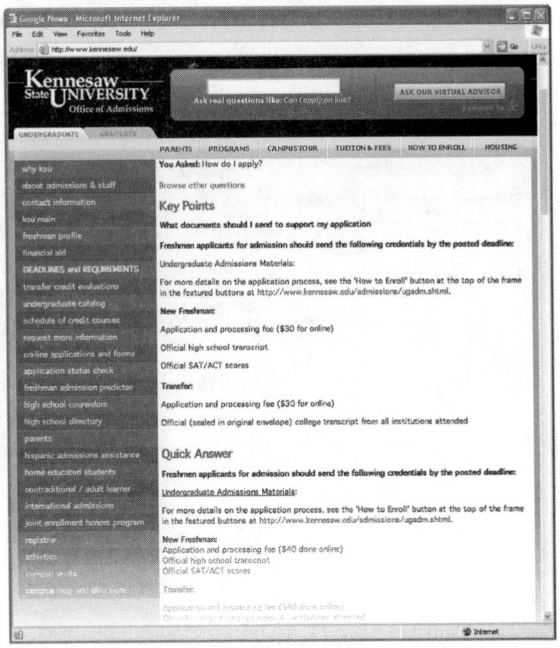


FIGURE 10.2

Virtual Advisor Answers: How Do I Apply?

With Apply Online applications and scanned applications being pushed into Banner, only 9 percent of applications are manually entered.

To support Apply Online, outbound e-mail systems provide maintenance notifications. College Net sends a bounceback e-mail upon completion of the application. The KSU office of admissions sends an e-mail acknowledging the receipt of the application from College Net and the entry into university records. This e-mail informs the applicant of financial aid, counseling, and housing services, among other items. Hot-links in this e-mail drive applicants to other key transactional services. Mail merge broadcasts provide all applicants with information concerning their Application Status Check (Figure 10.4). Freshman applicants also receive a mail merge inserted notification concerning the Freshman Admissions Predictor (see page 171).

FIGURE 10.3

Admission Applications and Forms Web Page

## Application Status Check

The first interactive 24x7 transactional Web service implemented by the office of admissions was the application status check, in 1988. Initially this service was provided by an automated telephone status check and was successful in diverting applicant inquiries from the front office or the telecenter. The

FIGURE 10.4

Application Status Check Information and Required Documentation

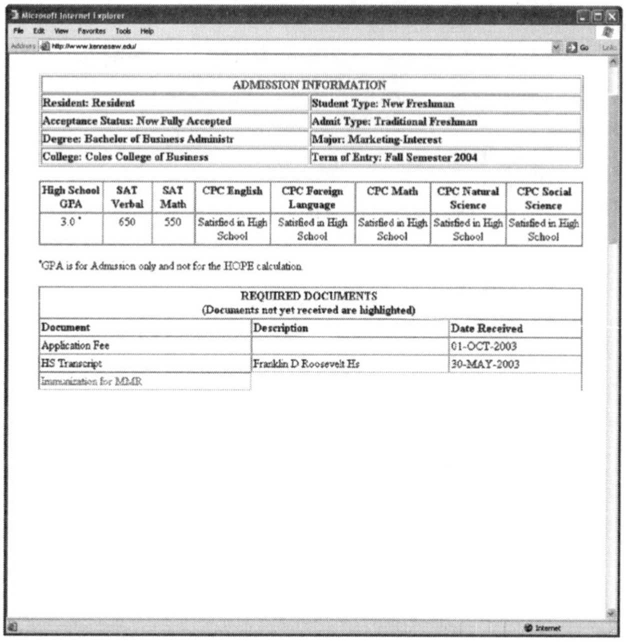
Microsoft Internet Explorer

File Edit View Favorites Tools Help

Address http://www.kennesaw.edu/

| ADMISSION INFORMATION | |
|---|---|
| Resident: Resident | Student Type: New Freshman |
| Acceptance Status: Now Fully Accepted | Admit Type: Traditional Freshman |
| Degree: Bachelor of Business Administr | Major: Marketing-Interest |
| College: Coles College of Business | Term of Entry: Fall Semester 2004 |

| High School GPA | SAT Verbal | SAT Math | CPC English | CPC Foreign Language | CPC Math | CPC Natural Science | CPC Social Science |
|---|---|---|---|---|---|---|---|
| 3.0 * | 650 | 550 | Satisfied in High School | Satisfied in High School | Satisfied in High School | Satisfied in High School | Satisfied in High School |

*GPA is for Admission only and not for the HOPE calculation

| REQUIRED DOCUMENTS (Documents not yet received are highlighted) | | |
|---|---|---|
| Document | Description | Date Received |
| Application Fee | | 01-OCT-2003 |
| HS Transcript | Franklin D Roosevelt Hs | 30-MAY-2003 |
| Immunization for MMR | | |

Internet

telephone option for an automated admission status check was a huge help whenever the telephone lines to the front office and telecenter became overloaded.

The web-based admission status check was implemented to ease the load on the front office, the telecenter, and the automated telephone system. Through password protected Web access, prospects, applicants, and enrolled students have access to their Banner records. This self-help service provides up-to-date record information such as received or unfulfilled documentation, SAT and ACT scores, transcripts, placement testing requirements, and the status of the admission decision.

Figure 10.4 illustrates the Admissions Information and Required Documents portion of the Application Status Check. Content displayed here provides essential information. Most important is the section called "Required Documents," indicating the current status of the documentation for the application. If the application has incomplete documentation, such documentation requirements are highlighted in red (visible online).

The High School Guidance Counselor Service Center (more fully described at the end of this chapter), another array of interactive Web pages, extends to those professionals the advantage of status check access to student application records at KSU. By having the ability to check electronically, on their own, the admissions status of their students, high school counselors can provide for their students a higher quality of counseling service than was possible through traditional advising methods.

Other vital information can be seen by scrolling down, as illustrated in Figure 10.5. In the Communications Log, all documents sent through conventional mail or electronic mail are listed. The Registration/Hold section informs of holds placed upon registration. Other sections concern testing requirements and learning support requirements. High school counselors as well as the applicants get to see the same information in Figure 10.4 and Figure 10.5.

Of all the interactive Web services, the online application status check has the highest rate of use. A recent survey revealed that 91 percent of new freshman respondents used this Web service to review the progress of their application.

## Freshman Admissions Predictor

As a result of raising the entry bar in early 2003, Admissions was faced with a challenge involving public dismay regarding the increased standards. This public outcry and the demand for appeals and informal reconsiderations reached an all- time high in the Office of Admissions at that time. Due to the growing volume of requests for personal appointments by denied applicants questioning their rejection, the professional admissions staff developed the Freshman Admissions Predictor to help prospects, guidance counselors, and parents pre-evaluate an applicant's eligibility. The Freshman Admissions Predictor (FAP)[116] is a timely advisement tool that promises to increase the percentage of eligible applicants and decrease the number of less prepared applicants.

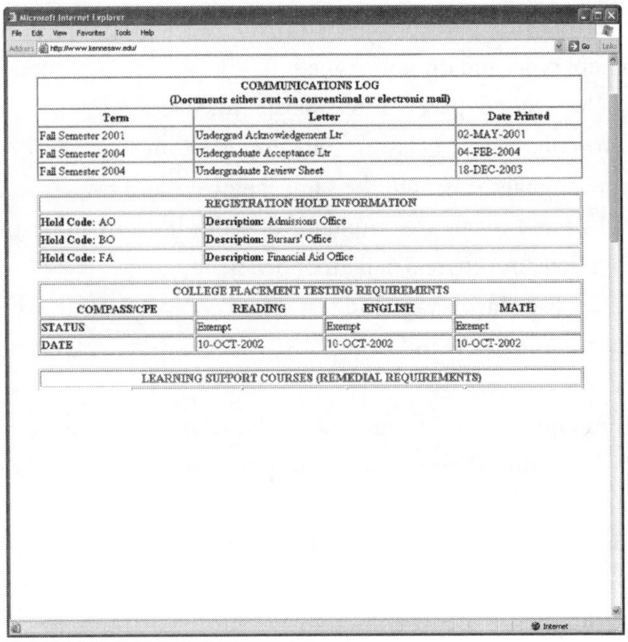


| COMMUNICATIONS LOG (Documents either sent via conventional or electronic mail) | | |
|---|---|---|
| Term | Letter | Date Printed |
| Fall Semester 2001 | Undergrad Acknowledgement Ltr | 02-MAY-2001 |
| Fall Semester 2004 | Undergraduate Acceptance Ltr | 04-FEB-2004 |
| Fall Semester 2004 | Undergraduate Review Sheet | 18-DEC-2003 |

| REGISTRATION HOLD INFORMATION | |
|---|---|
| **Hold Code:** AO | **Description:** Admissions Office |
| **Hold Code:** BO | **Description:** Bursars' Office |
| **Hold Code:** FA | **Description:** Financial Aid Office |

| COLLEGE PLACEMENT TESTING REQUIREMENTS | | | |
|---|---|---|---|
| COMPASS/CPE | READING | ENGLISH | MATH |
| STATUS | Exempt | Exempt | Exempt |
| DATE | 10-OCT-2002 | 10-OCT-2002 | 10-OCT-2002 |

LEARNING SUPPORT COURSES (REMEDIAL REQUIREMENTS)

FIGURE 10.5

Application Status Check: Vital Information

The FAP has two desirable purposes:

- First, it provides an interactive tool enabling parents, prospective freshmen, and transfer students with less than thirty credit hours to determine, unofficially, if credentials meet or exceed admissions standards.
- The second purpose is to improve communication concerning the new admissions standards. This desirable result occurs when prospects are electronically advised of their likelihood of admission. Thus, unnecessary fees/expenses, lost time, credential collections, and disappointment are prevented, and the need for personal contact with office staff is reduced. The volume, both in data entry and appointments with counselors, is better managed if ineligible prospects are redirected early in the process. This reduces the need to collect documents, build folders, and review files for ineligible applicants.

The structure of the FAP tool is relatively simple and requires less than ninety seconds to complete. An illustration of a completed form is provided in Figure 10.6.

[116] Addtional information of FAP can be found in Head and Hughes' (200x) article entitled "Freshman Admissions Predictor: An Interactive Self-Help Web Counseling Service."

In the first part, prospects provide demographic information such as name, state, high school type, and diploma type.

The second part addresses the completion of the following Collegiate Preparatory Curriculum (CPC) classes: four English, four mathematics, three natural sciences, two foreign language classes in the same language, and three social sciences. For each course, applicants must toggle the sequence of radio buttons indicating one of the following options: complete, in-progress, failed, or deficient.

Grade point average and test scores comprise the third part. To determine GPA, prospects choose one of the following: A+, A-, B+, B-, C+, C-, or D. Test scores are entered as indicated.

An advisory notification is displayed after the information is entered when the prospect clicks on the "Process Student Inquiry" hot link bar at the bottom of the Web form. One of three probabilities is indicated: strong, marginal, and ineligible. Strong prospects exceed admission standards, perhaps lacking only CPC courses in progress. Marginal prospects meet minimum standards for GPA and test scores. Ineligible prospects do not meet one or all of the admission standards in terms of GPA, test scores, or CPC requirements.

Ineligible prospects receive an explanation of deficiencies. They are also redirected to other institutions. Strong or marginal prospects receive specific information according to data entered in the form regarding classes that must be completed, possible placement testing, and other appropriate notations that will influence a final decision.

The FAP used in the illustration is from a hypothetical prospect, Joe Smith. Joe attends public school in Georgia, pursues a college preparatory curriculum, has a B-GPA, and scored 1090 on his SAT (560 in Verbal and 530 in Math).

Figure 10.7 depicts the Electronic Advisory Notice or "result page" generated as a result of the criteria Joe Smith entered in the example of Figure 10.6. Even though an indication of "Strong" probability was given, several sentences in this Electronic Advisory Notice clearly indicate that this is not an official decision and that it is subject to changing conditions. Similar language is used for "marginal" and "ineligible" probability. "Ineligible" advisory notices present probable reasons in bold for that advisory.

Survey research findings by KSU indicate that prospective freshman are aware of the FAP, but that much still needs to be done in marketing this tool. Table 10.4 (on page 174) indicates that about half of freshman prospects (299 freshman attending orientation completed questionnaires) know of this Web service, but half are still unaware of it. Survey results show that most came upon the Web site by surfing the Internet, but guidance counselors were also instrumental in pointing the way.

Table 10.5 (on page 174) reveals that 97 percent of freshman prospects believed the FAP to be either useful or very useful. Of some concern, however, 3 percent believed the FAP was not useful; this figure is higher than admission administrators want. A portion of those students probably knew they were accepted, making such a tool either perfunctory or unnecessary.

However, this issue merits further investigation.

The FAP tool is equipped with a "behind the scenes" counter that collects all transactions and that logs entered data. Reports reveal percentages of in-state and out-of-state inquiries, total number of transactions, and more. The reputation of FAP has spread among students, parents, and secondary counselors. During its first six months, a tracking study of FAP usage revealed that 5,302 submitted the form. Of this total, 64 percent resulted in a strong possibility of a positive admission decision. Unfortunately this study was not able to track those who applied with reference to strong, marginal, or ineligible probabilities. During the second year, an average daily user rate of 68 transactions produced over 2,000 hits per month and over 24,000 annually.

The expanded success of this ninety-second interactive Web service caught the attention of The Georgia Board of Regents. With some modifications, the Board has made plans to adopt the KSU FAP for optional use by 31 of the 34 public institutions in the state.

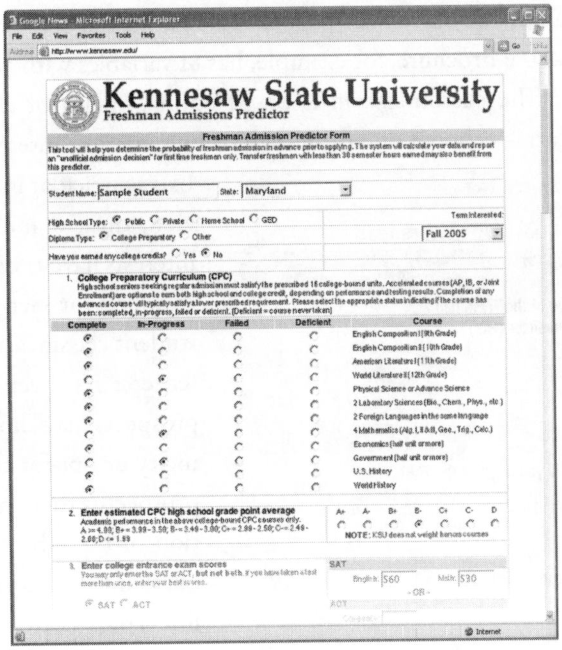


FIGURE 10.6

Freshman Admissions Predictor: Sample Prospect with Strong Admissions Probability

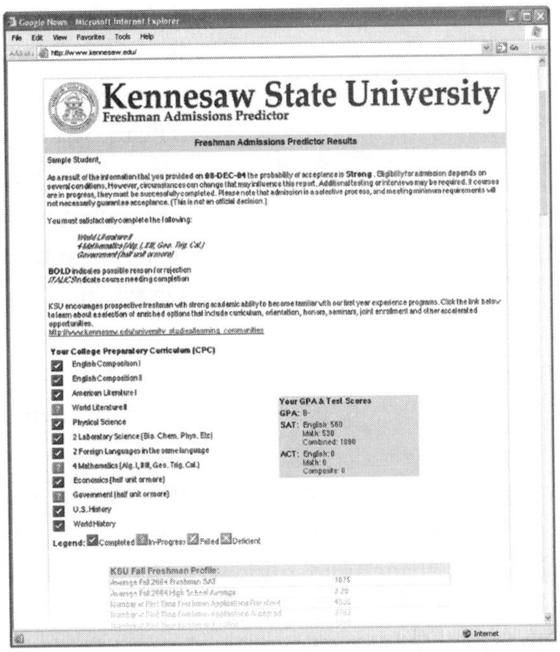


FIGURE 10.7

Electronic Advisory Notice for Figure 10.6 Example

## E-Brochures and Customized Web Pages

The e-brochure and personalized Web page is an interactive Web service that can provide a complementary boost to the communication media of many institutions. The e-brochure is a variable-based Web page that is customized according to the interests of the applicant. The KSU e-brochure, for example, has 81 variables with 388,000 possible combinations.[117]

The customization is based upon a menu of choices. First, prospects—using a Web form—choose one from each of four areas of interest. Academic interests have 49 choices. Extracurricular interests offer four choices—general overview, theatre, music, or fraternity/sorority life. Athletic interests have 11 options, either general overview or one of 10 sports for men and women. Six choices are offered for student classification types such as freshman, adult, transfer, etc. As diversity is a matter of institutional policy, prospects may chose one of the usual classifications of ethnicity or opt for the choice of international student. The prospect is then immediatedly sent a hot-link to the location of the e-brochure and personalized Web page. An outsourced company prints and mails to the prospect a four-color copy of the e-brochure within seven to ten days. The e-brochure may also be printed out by the applicant, and the personalized Web page may be accessed by the prospect for one year. Providing a personalized Web page is one way of conferring VIP status on a prospect.

TABLE 10.4: **FAP Awareness**

| | n | % |
|---|---|---|
| **Are you aware of the Freshman Admissions Predictor (FAP)?** | | |
| Yes | 152 | 51 |
| No | 147 | 49 |
| Total | 299 | 100 |
| **If yes, how did you learn of the FAP?** | | |
| Surfing the Internet | 126 | 83 |
| Referred | 12 | 8 |
| Guidance Counselors | 11 | 7 |
| Other | 2 | 1 |
| Total | 151 | 100 |

TABLE 10.5: **FAP Usage**

| | n | % |
|---|---|---|
| **Did you use the Freshman Admissions Predictor (FAP)?** | | |
| Yes | 111 | 73 |
| No | 41 | 27 |
| Total | 152 | 100 |
| **If yes, please rate its usefulness** | | |
| Useful | 53 | 48 |
| Somewhat Useful | 55 | 49 |
| Not Useful | 3 | 3 |
| Total | 111 | 100 |

Figure 10.8 and Figure 10.9 (on pages 175–176) illustrate parts of an e-brochure for a hypothetical prospect. Customized written copy and photos are presented here for John Smith, a freshman with an interest in information systems. Other than the departmental program overview, a profile of a successful alumnus is provided according to the prospect's academic major interest. John Smith indicated a desire for information concerning men's basketball and a general overview of campus activities rather than information concerning fraternity/sorority life, music, or theatre program. Information concerning housing, admission requirements for freshmen, and application deadlines for enrollment, financial aid, tuition, and fees are found on pages not illustrated here.

## High School Guidance Counselor Service Center

Finally, Kennesaw State Admissions has built on the concept of interactive services for students to develop a secure tool for high school guidance counselors—the High School Guidance

[117] To take a test drive of the e-brochure, visit <www.kennesaw.edu/admissions/ugadm.shtml>. Please type "Admission Professional" in the form's address field. This will remove your request from the prospect database.

FIGURE 10.8

E-Brochure: Third Page

Counselor Service Center (HSGCSC). This web-based service center, begun by KSU in 2002, provides access to real-time information on all applicants (*e.g.*, received or unfulfilled documentation, SAT and ACT scores, transcripts, placement testing requirements, and the status of the admission decision)—enhancing the counselor's ability to accurately ad-vise students and parents. (*See* Figure 10.4 and Figure 10.5 [on pages 170–171].)

In previous years, high school guidance counselors were provided hard-copy lists periodically. These hard-copy lists became outdated instantly. Providing hard-copy lists is also a slow-moving and labor-intensive process. The HSGCSC, on the other hand, enables high school counselors, on a password protected basis, to obtain this information directly. This saves hundreds of staff hours and also provides better and more tailored service.

Even though most high school counselors work within the time frame of traditional office hours, the HSCGSC operates under the same philosophy that delivers 24x7 transactional web technologies to applicants and admitted students beyond normal office hours.

The potential of this tool is that it offers the greatest assistance to counselors from high-volume feeder high schools with large counseling loads—counselors who thrive in a high touch, high tech environment.

The HSGCSC is not limited to providing information concerning student records. Anyone may access the main Web page of the HSGCSC and access certain links of general interest to high school guidance counselors and others. Examples of these links include the Counseling Resources, SDU (Staff Development Unit) Workshop, High School Guidance Counselor Directory, Virtual Advisor, and the Freshman Admissions Predictor.

## Information Systems Department

**Joe**, the Computer Science and Information Systems (CSIS) in the College of Science and Mathematics at Kennesaw State University is a leading provider of IT specialists in the Southeast. The CSIS Department and Information Systems (CSIS) at Kennesaw State University is a center of excellence in undergraduate and graduate education, scholarship, and service to the Georgia economy.

Housed in the Ann and John Clendenin Computer Science building with state-of-the-art electronic classrooms and computer labs, our twenty-two full-time faculty bring a wealth of academic preparation and industry know-how to the classroom. CSIS offers two undergraduate programs: The Bachelor of Science in Computer Science and The Bachelor of Science in Information Systems, as well as undergraduate certificates in Information Technology, e-business and Information Security. All undergraduate programs are based on a strong technical foundation including programming principles, systems analysis, systems architecture, data communications and database design and management. The department has an active co-op/internship program that employs students in organizations such as IBM, Hewlett-Packard, AT&T, Lockheed Aeronautical Systems, Coca Cola Enterprises, and the Center for Disease Control and serves traditional as well as non-traditional students by providing necessary classes during the day and evening. The department offers a unique NSF-sponsored scholarship program to qualified students. With outstanding student groups (Women in Technology, Association for Computer Machinery, and Information Systems Security Association) KSU provides opportunities for students to became engaged with working professionals and explore career opportunities as early as their freshman year. Kennesaw State University CS and IS graduates are experiencing highly successful careers throughout the world. The CSIS department at Kennesaw State University provides not only an exceptional education that is practical and technical, but an education that brings you to the front in Computer Science or Information Systems.

KSU's Information Systems degree program is one of the most technologically focused in the state of Georgia. The IS majors learn the core technologies that drive modern organizations, as well as strategic applications of Information Technology (IT) to contemporary business models. The degree not only provides a sound foundation in IT principles and practice, but also emphasizes practical applications to business problems. Core technology areas include object-oriented programming, computer architecture, operating systems, data communication, systems analysis and design, data base applications, and project management. The program of study also includes practical statistics, accounting, financial systems, and information security. KSU's IS majors are sought after by business from across the Southeast. Their strong technical, hands-on preparation with contemporary IT tools, makes them winners in any job market.

### ALUMNI SPOTLIGHT

*Susan Cardillo, Information Systems Outstanding Student 2004*

I am a senior Information Systems major at Kennesaw State University. I am currently Vice President of Women in Technology and also web master for the group. I have maintained a 3.94 GPA. I am a member of the Phi Kappa Phi and Golden Key Honor Society at KSU. My honors and awards at KSU include: Presidents and Deans list, Hope Scholarship, Women in Electronics Scholarship, Who's Who among American University and College students, STARs program, and Information Systems Student of the year. I have been very pleased with the Information Systems degree program. I feel that through the class-work, group-work and outside activities such as my directed study on web site usability, my involvement with the information security group and my work with the STARs program that I am very prepared for my career in the field of Information Technology. Because of my wonderful experience and quality of education I have plans to pursue my Masters of Information Systems degree at KSU.

FIGURE 10.9
E-Brochure:
Fourth Page

"Counseling Resources" provides a link to the Georgia School Counseling Institute Web page, as well as to Web sites maintained by the Board of Regents of the University System of Georgia. "SDU Workshop" provides a schedule and registration forms for this annual meeting hosted by KSU Admissions (counselors receive state department of education credit necessary for re-certification). In addition, for twenty-plus years, KSU has published the highly popular *Georgia High School Guidance Counselor Directory* (available online and in print). The Virtual Advisor and Freshman Admissions Predictor have already been discussed (*see* pages 167 and 171).

Certain services designated as premium are limited to counselors registering on an annual basis. Premium services can be accessed only through a membership login that is restricted to a single high school. Figure 10.10 illustrates the premium services, which include, applicant status check monitoring; a list of confidential office telephone numbers; a Web form enabling letters of reference to be submitted; a high school directory update form; and enrolled aggregate high school student summary information.

## Conclusions

This chapter has presented an overview of six interactive services for prospects and applicants, as these tools function at Kennesaw State University: Virtual Advisor, Apply Online, Application Status Check, Freshman Admissions Predictor, E-Brochure, and the High School Guidance Counselor Service Center.

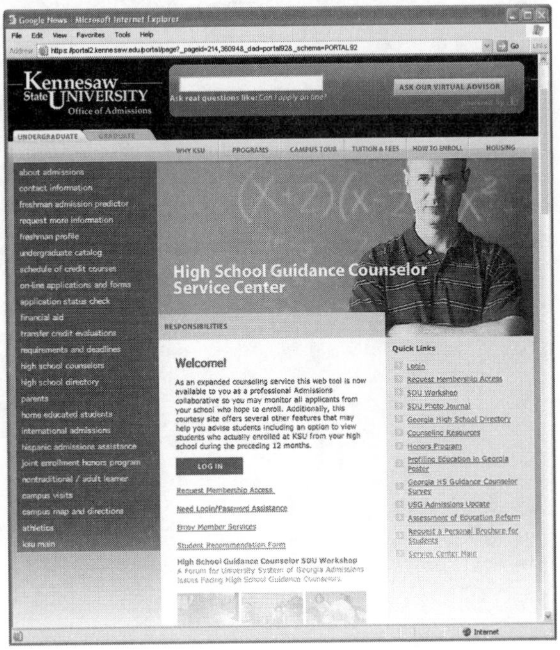


FIGURE 10.10

High School Guidance Counselors Service Center, Premium Membership Services

College admissions officers can increase the power of their recruiting or marketing tools and ease their workload by channeling students to use these self-help tools. A familiarity with these always-available interactive tools allows enterprising admissions officers to communicate both more efficiently and more interactively with today's web-oriented high school students.

/ CHAPTER ELEVEN /

*by Kevin Pollock, Ph.D.*
*Vice President of Student Services*
*West Shore Community College*

11

# Faculty's Role in Recruitment

In today's competitive environment, admissions officers and enrollment managers need to make use of all recruiting assistance available on their campuses in their efforts to fulfill enrollment goals. To do so, many such administrators are now asking faculty members to assist in recruiting undergraduate students to their institutions. This project can put pressure on faculty members, whose traditional responsibilities are usually defined as teaching, research, and other service activities. It also raises a number of questions concerning what factors might influence faculty participation in student recruitment, and what can be done to develop a strong working relationship between faculty participants and admissions officers.

This chapter will provide evidence that faculty indeed assist admissions offices in recruiting undergraduate students, and will provide information on the types of admissions-related tasks in which faculty can be productively involved. In addition, the chapter will address such issues as: What factors motivate faculty to assist in admission- and recruitment-related activities? What types of conflicts can be anticipated? And, what types of incentives are most appreciated by faculty?

## Advantages of Faculty Involvement

Why use faculty to assist in the recruitment of undergraduate students? As noted by Frank Kemerer (1985), "It is essential that the faculty be involved with enrollment management for success over the long haul. There can be no substitute for faculty involvement because it is the faculty that develops programs, establishes articulation agreements with feeder institutions, publicizes departmental programs, and is directly involved with students daily through teaching and advising." Nobody can provide more insight and evidence specific to classes and programs than faculty. Once classes begin, faculty are in more direct contact with students than any other office or department and, as such, are natural contributors to any enrollment management plan. If faculty members participate in recruiting activities, they will have already developed a rapport with many of the students who will enter their classrooms.

Institutional leaders have legitimate reasons for asking or, in some cases, requiring faculty members to support recruiting activities. The obvious reason is to help admissions offices reach targeted enrollment goals as one's own institution competes with others for the same pool of students. For institutions studied for this project, high enrollment goals were sometimes set to help offset reductions from other sources of funding, such as state funding. In some cases, institutions also had specific enrollment goals for some departments, or had mandated the reaching of certain recruitment targets for under-served or other categories of students. In addition, some recruitment targets reflect the fact that yields can decline, when students apply to more institutions than their predecessors did.

In what types of recruiting activities should faculty members be involved on campuses? Faculty can visit high schools and community colleges, call prospective students, organize and attend open houses and receptions, meet with prospective students visiting the campus, write letters to students, serve on enrollment or retention committees, and provide departmental information for inclusion in admissions literature (Dennis 1998; Green 1990; Hossler 2000; Ihlanfdeldt 1980; Keller 1997; Kemerer 1985; Kreutner and Godfrey 1980; Kuh and Wallman 1986; Smith, J.E. 1998).

Can faculty members be effective in drawing students to their campuses? The answer is yes; however, they can be just as effective in deflecting potential students if there is not a strong working relationship between the admissions office and the faculty. Critical to this collaboration are faculty who are enthusiastic about their college's programs, and who are willing to take the time to meet and work with potential students. Just as critical are programs and processes developed by admissions officers that enable faculty to recognize why their contributions are so crucial and how to participate effectively. This includes training for everyone involved.

Although we all strive to implement "best practices," sometimes failure is our best teacher. An example of what can go wrong appeared in Professor Stephen Winzenburg's (2006) article in which he recounted his daughter's six college admissions visits and her experiences meeting with faculty in her chosen major at each institution. Of their six campus visits, "four were failures and two were positive experiences," he concluded. Reasons for the failures included broken appointments, and faculty members who were "brusque and standoffish" or ill-prepared. In contrast, the two positive appointments were with faculty members who were personable, took time to answer questions, were knowledgeable about their programs, and acknowledged the importance of the visiting student. In Winzenburg's words, "meeting a professor can make or break a student's decision to attend."

## Michigan Case Study

In 2001, in the course of writing his Ph.D. dissertation on the subject, the author of this chapter studied the role of faculty in recruiting students at public four-year institutions in Michigan. The results provide useful recommendations for enrollment managers and admissions directors thinking about engaging faculty to assist in recruiting undergraduate students. These recommendations can be immediately applied by admissions officers to bolster working relationships with faculty recruiters.

### Recommendations

The Michigan study suggests that enrollment managers and admissions directors can improve the effectiveness of faculty as recruiters by better understanding what influences and motivates faculty members to participate in recruiting activities. Among the recommendations and observations are:

- *Faculty members are too often asked to assist in recruiting activities but are never told how enrollment goals have been created and why their assistance, as faculty, is important.* Thus, it is advisable to discuss how enrollment goals have been arrived at, as well as what they are. By informing faculty about how their involvement as recruiters can favorably affect enrollment, admissions officers can help to reduce or even eliminate misconceptions about the role of faculty in the recruiting process.
- *Faculty members are more motivated to recruit students into their own departments than into the institution as a whole.* The findings of the study revealed that faculty are most interested, and most effective, in recruiting students whose interests are aligned with the faculty member's department. Make every effort, therefore, to link faculty participation to potential enrollment increases in the faculty member's own department. Information provided by faculty members to potential students should be limited to their own department, and thus their area of expertise. Presenting the *overall* picture of the institution is the responsibility of the admissions office, not the faculty.
- *Faculty members are too often asked to assist in recruiting events without enough advance notice.* Develop well-organized recruiting plans that provide faculty members with advance notice of recruiting events, open-ended requests for participation, and an opportunity to pick and choose activities. Faculty members cite lack of planning, disorganized activities, and last-minute requests for recruiting assistance as sources of a less

than effective encounter with prospective students. Remember that faculty can participate in a variety of ways. Suggest innovative recruiting activities such as utilizing videotapes of lectures[118] or e-mail contact with prospective students.

- *Most admissions officers do not know what motivates faculty members to participate in recruiting activities.* Faculty members want to influence their own department's enrollment rather than the institution's overall enrollment. Accordingly, the desire to draw high- quality students to their own departments can often stimulate faculty into increasing their recruitment activities.
- *Most admissions officers do not know what rewards are most valued by faculty members.* Be a vocal advocate for meaningful rewards for faculty members who participate in recruiting activities. Trinkets and symbolic tokens of appreciation are nice, but incentives such as release time for time spent on recruiting activities, or even counting their time engaged in recruiting toward tenure decisions, promotions, or raises are far more meaningful rewards for faculty time and effort spent on student recruitment.

## Project Model

In shaping his dissertation, the author of this chapter created a "project model," which addressed two issues: First, to what extent were faculty in fact involved in undergraduate student recruiting? And second, for faculty who were involved, what was the time involved, and what were the motivating factors, conflicts, and rewards for participants?

The conclusions were based on two surveys: one of faculty and the other of admissions directors. The faculty survey involved faculty from selected Michigan institutions who were queried about their involvement in undergraduate student recruiting. At the same time, admissions officers from the same institutions were surveyed by telephone to provide information about enrollment situations from their perspective as admissions professionals, and about faculty involvement in recruiting activities.

The Michigan institutions studied were four-year public universities with undergraduate populations between 3,400 and 17,529 students, and with full-time faculty headcounts of between 114 and 707. These universities were selected because they faced similar enrollment challenges, including pressure from legislators and increased competition from distance-education and for-profit institutions even as their own costs rose (Gilmour 2000). The institutions studied tended to lack large endowments, and had little flexibility to retrench or create new programs due to their population of tenured faculty (Selingo 2000). They also faced a shifting population with somewhat hard-to-predict enrollment goals, while also competing with local community colleges where lower tuitions attracted students.

[118] Note that if videotapes of classes are "maintained" by the institution, they could be considered "education records," and if "class videotapes" are not listed by the institution as directory information, they would be subject to the requirements of the Family Educational Rights and Privacy Act (FERPA).

Michigan has 15 public four-year institution of higher learning. Using the Carnegie Classification system (2000 revision) in effect at the time of the study, ten of the institutions were classified as Master's Colleges and Universities I[119] or Master's Colleges and Universities II.[120] All the institutions studied were deemed to be predominantly teaching-oriented as opposed to research-based.

Due to time and budget constraints, the combined number of full-time faculty at these institutions created a sample size that was too large for convenient study. Therefore, a subset of departments was selected, according to a method devised by Andrew Biglan (Biglan 1973). This subset resulted in surveys of faculty and admissions directors from 10 of the 15 public four-year institutions of higher learning in Michigan. This research choice created a population with 1,431 members. Of this population, a manageable sample size of 575 faculty members (40%) was selected. Surveys were mailed to the sample and 312 surveys were returned, resulting in a response rate of 54 percent. The sample responses also resulted in a 22 percent representation of the larger 1,431 population of faculty members.

Three research questions guided the data collection and analysis:

- Do faculty members assist admissions offices in the recruitment of undergraduate students?
- Do enrollment concerns motivate faculty members to assist in recruiting students?
- Besides enrollment concerns, what influences faculty participation in recruiting undergraduate students?

Definitions of terms were culled from available research and were used for the study. These terms included "faculty workload," "historical faculty responsibilities," "faculty motivation" (Blackburn and Lawrence 1995), "faculty rewards," and "faculty participation in recruiting" (Dennis 1998; Green 1990; Hossler 2000; Ihlanfeldt 1980; Keller 1997; Kemerer 1985; Kreunter and Godfrey 1980; Kuh and Wallman 1986; Smith 1998).

Results of the faculty survey were compiled in an Microsoft Excel™ spreadsheet and were analyzed using an SPSS (statistical package for social sciences)™ software program for regression analysis.

## Survey Results

### ADMISSIONS DIRECTORS' SURVEY

The admissions directors from all ten universities studied reported that faculty members were assisting them in recruiting undergraduate students and that faculty involvement was increasing.

[119] "These institutions typically offer a wide variety of baccalaureate programs, and...award 40 or more master's degrees per year across three or more academic disciplines" (Carnegie Foundation 2001).

[120] "These institutions typically offer a wide variety of baccalaureate programs, and...award 20 or more master's degrees per year" (Carnegie Foundation 2001).

The directors also confirmed the types of activities in which faculty members participated. All of the institutions had faculty members visiting community colleges and attending open houses. Nine institutions had faculty members attending admissions receptions for prospective students, as well as reviewing and providing input on admissions literature. Half or more of the institutions had faculty members visiting high schools, calling prospective students, and serving on enrollment or admissions committees. (*See* Table 11.1, on page 185.)

### FACULTY SURVEY

Background information regarding faculty members' tenure, rank, and time spent on teaching, research, service, and other areas is reported in Table 11.2 and Table 11.3 (on page 185).

Overall, more than 90 percent of the faculty members surveyed described their institution's enrollment rate as increasing or stable, although 18 percent felt that their department's enrollment was declining. The responses from faculty also verified that they were very much involved in recruiting undergraduate students. The top five recruiting activities involving faculty were the following: Attending open houses; meeting with parents and students taking campus tours; hosting prospective student events on campus; serving on enrollment or admissions committees; and developing or providing information for admissions literature such as fact sheets, brochures, or newsletters.

The findings of the survey of faculty identified issues concerning motivation, conflicts with pre-existing duties, and the reward or incentive structure for faculty participation as recruiters. We discuss each issue briefly in turn.

### MOTIVATION

The main motivating factor for faculty participation in student recruitment emerged as concern about enrollment, both department- and institution-wide. Many faculty respondents also noted the desire to enroll quality students as a reason for participation.

The second most-cited motivating factor was service to the college. Other motivating factors included assisting colleagues, wanting to work with students, and general enjoyment of participation in the activities.

The perception that enrollment in the faculty member's particular department might decline, although not the strongest predictor of faculty participation, was nevertheless a significant factor for many faculty members.

### CONFLICTS

Nearly 60 percent of faculty respondents reported that their participation in recruiting activities led to conflicts with other duties. Often the conflict arose from the timing of the event, while others reported a dislike for the particular activity, such as calling prospective students. Also cited was the lack of advance notice of activities—a problem which could often result in a conflict between assisting in recruiting and performing other, more traditional, faculty duties.

### REWARDS AND INCENTIVES

A majority of the faculty members involved in the survey (78.3%) indicated that they received no conventional (tangible or monetary) "reward" for their role in recruiting activities. Those who did, received nominal incentives such a free lunches, gift certificates, or snacks during calling sessions to prospective students. The most common non-tangible reward was a letter of recognition from a chair, dean, or president that could be placed in a professional file. Notably absent were significant incentives such as release time, or any system of applying the time spent working with admissions toward tenure or promotion.

However, many faculty mentioned intrinsic rewards such as the "satisfaction of a job well done." In addition, others used such phrases as "warm and fuzzy," or "feeling good about helping out."

## Summary

Based on the findings of the study, admissions officers should focus on several important factors when asking faculty members to assist in recruiting undergraduate students. First, admissions personnel need to better communicate to faculty information about enrollment challenges and goals in an attempt to eliminate misconceptions about the recruiting process. Second, admissions personnel should work to minimize conflict with other faculty responsibilities, by providing faculty members with adequate advance notice of recruiting activities, as well as allowing faculty to pick and choose among selected recruiting activities.

In addition, admissions officers should make faculty members aware that their assistance in recruiting activities can also benefit their departments. In short, better organization of recruiting activities, and a shift to using faculty members to recruit students *departmentally* rather

TABLE 11.1: **Admissions Directors Reporting Faculty Participation in Institutional Events**

| Event | Participation Rate (%) |
|---|---|
| Visiting high schools | 50 |
| Visiting community colleges | 100 |
| Placing calls to prospective students | 60 |
| Attending open houses | 100 |
| Attending admissions receptions for prospective students | 90 |
| Serving on enrollment committees | 60 |
| Serving on retention committees | 70 |
| Being involved in the admissions decision process for new students | 50 |
| Reviewing and providing input on admissions literature pieces | 90 |

TABLE 11.2: **Faculty Charateristics**

| Characteristic | Respondents with Characteristic (%) |
|---|---|
| Tenured | 78.0 |
| Achieved rank of professor | 42.0 |
| Achieved rank of associate or assistant professor | 55.1 |
| Been at current institution for 10 years or less | 43.0 |
| Were teaching three classes | 44.6 |
| Were in department that had started a new program in the past three years | 67.0 |

TABLE 11.3: **Use of Faculty Time**

| Function | Time Spent on Function (%) |
|---|---|
| Teaching | 52.45 |
| Research | 15.84 |
| Service | 13.71 |
| Administration | 11.96 |
| Professional growth | 4.17 |
| Outside consulting or freelance work | 1.37 |
| Other duties | 0.41 |

than *institutionally* can all help increase enrollment and build a better working relationship with faculty.

Finally, admissions officers need to call for the recognition of faculty who assist in recruiting activities. Depending on the campus climate, the admissions office could initiate discussions with senior administrators concerning the implementation of more meaningful rewards for faculty participation—incentives such as offering release time to faculty, or even applying time spent on recruiting activities toward the service component involved in making tenure decisions, or allocating promotions and raises.

With an understanding of faculty motivation and strengths, admissions officers can work together with faculty members to achieve a common goal: increasing enrollments while building better working relationships for the benefit of students and the institution.

/ CHAPTER TWELVE /

*by Luke Schultheis, Ed.M.*
*Dean and former Director of Admissions*
*Monroe College*

12

# Low-Income Students:
## Outreach and Retention

The National Center for Education Statistics (NCES) defines "low-income" students as those whose family income was below 125 percent of the federally established poverty level for those of their family size (Choy 2000, p. 2). Students of low-income or low socio-economic status (SES) composed more than a quarter (26.4%) of the overall college enrollment in the United States in 1995–1996 (pp. 5–6). Low-income students are at greater risk than other students of not completing a degree or certificate (p. 52).

Such students often receive their secondary school education in areas which do not have the school or family resources—the social and cultural capital—enjoyed by wealthier school districts. With college graduates expected to earn nearly one million dollars more over their lifetime than those with just a high school education,[121] it is a moral calling for higher education to address the plight of the poor.

The purposes of this chapter are to illuminate some of the academic and cultural barriers to college entry for this cohort; to discuss some of the pitfalls of financial aid in the choice

[121] "According to the Census Bureau, over an adult's working life, high school graduates earn an average of $1.2 million; associate's degree holders earn about $1.6 million; and bachelor's degree holders earn about $2.1 million" (Porter 2002).

process; and to propose some recommendations on increasing retention so that a greater number are able to graduate.

Although it is well established that there are lower college enrollment rates for African-Americans and Hispanics relative to those of whites and Asians (Perna 2000), this chapter focuses on first-time or working-class students, regardless of race or ethnicity.[122]

We will first establish a threshold level of facts about what level of income constitutes SES; what the percentage is of college students who are from low-income families; where these prospective college students live; and what is the educational level of their parents, before we move on to discuss academic and cultural barriers to their performance; predictors of college persistence; and some practical steps which colleges can take to increase persistence and success.

## Definition of Low SES

The definition of "low SES" in 2007 ranges from an income of $13,110 for a family size of one to $48,719 for a family of nine or more (Choy 2000)(*See* Table 12.1). As we have already established, these low SES incomes are defined as being below 125 percent of the federally established poverty level for a given family size.

TABLE 12.1: **Comparison of 1994 and 2006 Incomes Qualifying Students as Low SES, Used for Financial Aid Calculations in 1996 and 2007**

| Family Size | 1994 | 2006 |
|---|---|---|
| 1 | $9,638 | $13,110 |
| 2 | $12,470 | $17,370 |
| 3 | $14,776 | $20,803 |
| 4 | $18,926 | $25,645 |
| 5 | $22,375 | $29,614 |
| 6 | $25,294 | $33,043 |
| 7 | $28,654 | $36,231 |
| 8 | $31,784 | $41,113 |
| 9+ | $37,875 | $48,719 |

**SOURCES:** Choy (2000, p.3); US Census Bureau, Housing and Household Economic Statistics Division.

## Percentage of Students from Low-Income Families

In 2004–05, more than 2.6 million undergraduates enrolled for the first time in postsecondary education in degree-granting institutions (*i.e.*, public and private four- and two-year, and private, for-profit institutions) (Snyder, Tan, and Hoffman 2007, p. 281). In the previous decade (1995–96), as we have noted, 26 percent of first-time undergraduates were low SES, as defined by the U.S. Department of Education (the Department).[123] (*See* Table 12.2, on page 189.)

[122] We note that the current IPEDS scheme for race and ethnicity reporting entails a two-tier format. First, the individual respondent is asked to indicate whether he or she is Hispanic/Latino. Then, respondents will be asked to identify themselves under one of five racial categories: American Indian/Alaska Native; Asian; Black or African American; Native Hawaiian or Other Pacific Islander; or White. Educational institutions will then report aggregated data on race and ethnicity in seven categories: the five listed above, Hispanic of any race, and "two or more races." A respondent who selected Hispanic in response to the first question and, for example, Black or African American in response to the second question would be reported to IPEDS only as "Hispanic of any race." However, an individual who selects "Asian" and "White" would be reported as "Two or more races." This classification scheme makes it difficult to draw distinctions among groups which might consider themselves culturally quite distinct. For example, black Americans,West Indians, and African immigrants may all be recorded as "black" if that is the identification they choose for IPEDS purposes, but there may be many social and cultural factors which differ greatly.

[123] See Choy (2000, p. 3) for a summary of the data relied on by NCES in creating its analysis. This study divides the low-income college student population into three types: dependent (traditional college-aged students who are financially dependent on their parents); financially independent students with no dependents of their own; and financially independent students with their own dependents (p. 4).

# Demographics

Great concentrations of ethnic minorities and the poor live in urban areas. In 2003, there were nearly 15 million youth living in large and mid-sized cities in the United States (Snyder, Tan, and Hoffman 2006). The results of an NCES study by Lippman, Burns, and MacArthur (1996) indicated that the urban poverty rate was 30 percent compared with 20 percent

TABLE 12.2: **Percentage of Undergraduates Who Were from Low-Income Families, by Dependency Status and Selected Student Characteristics, 1995–96**

| Characterisitic | | Dependent | Independent | | Total |
|---|---|---|---|---|---|
| | | | w/o dependents | w/ dependents | |
| **Gender** | Male | 16.5 | 35.4 | 31.1 | 24.4 |
| | Female | 17.1 | 28.3 | 44.9 | 28.0 |
| **Age** | Less than 24 years | 16.8 | 58.6 | 78.6 | 22.2 |
| | 24-29 years | — | 37.4 | 46.2 | 40.4 |
| | 30 years or older | — | 20.8 | 29.3 | 25.4 |
| **Race/Ethnicity** | White | 10.2 | 28.5 | 34.7 | 20.7 |
| | Black | 35.1 | 39.9 | 52.1 | 42.7 |
| | Hispanic | 35.8 | 38.3 | 48.2 | 40.1 |
| | Asian | 29.7 | 38.9 | 42.2 | 34.0 |
| **Marital Status** | Separated or not married | 16.8 | 40.0 | 56.7 | 28.2 |
| | Married | n/a | 14.3 | 23.6 | 19.7 |
| **Single Parent Status** | Not a single parent | 16.8 | 31.4 | 27.9 | 22.8 |
| | Single parent | — | — | 55.5 | 55.5 |
| **Parents' Education** | Less than high school | 55.0 | 25.0 | 37.8 | 37.6 |
| | High school | 23.2 | 32.4 | 38.8 | 30.5 |
| | At least some college | 12.0 | 35.0 | 45.3 | 22.1 |
| **Delay In College Enrollment** | No delay | 14.5 | 27.0 | 34.6 | 19.8 |
| | 1 year | 21.6 | 31.1 | 46.6 | 31.7 |
| | 2 years or more | 22.9 | 25.1 | 37.9 | 31.2 |
| **Attendance pattern** | Full-time | 15.6 | 51.3 | 55.1 | 25.3 |
| | Part-time | 17.7 | 23.4 | 33.5 | 24.7 |
| **Housing status** | On-campus | 14.2 | 64.3 | 59.8 | 18.3 |
| | Off-campus | 15.4 | 28.0 | 37.4 | 27.9 |
| | With parents or relatives | 19.7 | 47.9 | 67.2 | 27.2 |
| **Primary Role While Enrolled** | Not working | 17.9 | 35.5 | 51.3 | 30.4 |
| | Student working to meet expenses | 13.0 | 39.0 | 53.9 | 23.7 |
| | Employee enrolled in classes | 13.3 | 12.9 | 19.5 | 15.8 |
| **Institution Type** | Public 4-year | 15.3 | 38.9 | 39.5 | 24.1 |
| | Private, not-for-profit 4-year | 15.7 | 32.9 | 30.2 | 21.3 |
| | Public 2-year | 17.1 | 23.8 | 37.8 | 25.7 |
| | Private, for profit | 31.9 | 46.6 | 59.3 | 47.9 |
| **Total** | | 16.8 | 31.4 | 40.3 | 26.4 |

**SOURCE:** Choy 2000, pp.6–7, Table 1.

nationwide, with the very lowest SES quartile concentrated at 32.6 percent in urban areas (p. 5–6). There was also a greater concentration of minorities in the poor urban areas (50% white, 30% black, 14.8% Latino, and 4.5% other) compared with the suburbs (80% white) and the rural areas (83.5% white) (p. 10). Overall, 79 percent of urban school students were black and Latino, and 69 percent of the high poverty group were racial/ethnic minorities, with 42 percent of them receiving subsidized meals (p. 11).

Another factor, which complicates (or intensifies) a purely racial or ethnic analysis, involves the level of education of the parents. An NCES study from 2001 found that "those whose parents have no education beyond high school are considerably less likely to succeed [in higher education] than those whose parents have completed a bachelor's degree" (Choy 2001, p. 29). The study adds: "Students who are *nonwhite* or from *low-income families* tend to be disproportionately represesented among those whose parents have low education" [Emphasis added] (p. 29).

We now move on to academic and cultural barriers to college entry and success in that environment.

## Academic Barriers in High School

There are several kinds of academic challenges facing low SES youth in their high school years.

### Class Size

Urban high school class enrollments are larger than those in rural areas (1,313 vs. 577), and fewer than half of the ninth graders entering large city systems graduate in four years (Lippman, Burns, and MacArthur 1996, p. viii, 5; Anyon 1997, p. 6).

### Teachers and Counselors

Teachers and counselors have a significant impact, not only on the quality of schooling but on the students' decisions to pursue postsecondary education. These schools face a number of teacher and counselor problems.

One issue is that it is difficult to attract faculty and staff due to the belief that urban schools are dangerous or "difficult." For example, consider the number of teacher education programs which offer tuition assistance/forgiveness to those who will serve in urban high schools upon graduation. The faculty and staff serving these high schools often work at lower pay scales than teachers in non-urban settings (Lippman, Burns, and MacArthur 1996, p. 86).

In addition, nearly a quarter (24%) of urban high school administrators throughout the nation reported significant difficulties in hiring teachers, compared with 16 percent in non-urban districts (p. 88).

Teacher performance is also a problem. Teachers in poor areas can exhibit greater levels of absenteeism (p. viii), which sets a poor example for students and interrupts continuity of instruction.

### Academics

Instruction in poor urban schools is too often at a low level, relying on unchallenging and rote material (Anyon 1997, p. 7). Teacher expectations of students are especially low with black males, leading to a self-fulfilling prophecy of low academic achievement (Hubbard 1999, p. 365).

A rigorous high school curriculum helps mitigate the disadvantage of first-generation status (Choy 2001, p. 23; Adelman 1999). Students who take less advanced math in high school reduce their chance of entering four-year colleges, and since there is less advanced math offered in urban high schools, low-income urban students are at a disadvantage (Gandara and Moreno 2002). A correlation is that there is a decrease in the average level of mathematic achievement of 0.06 points with each one point increase in the percentage of students receiving free or reduced lunch (Rosigno 1998, p. 1046).

Only 20 percent of whites, 16 percent of Hispanics and 8 percent of blacks reported completing rigorous high school curricula. On every outcome measured, those high school students in areas of high poverty consistently performed at the lowest academic levels (Lippman, Burns, and MacArthur 1996, p. 20). The Lippman study describes students who attended public schools in the 1980s and examines their outcomes through 1990 (p. vi).

### Leadership and Extracurricular Activities

In high school, students who participate in school-sponsored sports activities (and academic clubs) "seem to have better grades, spend more time on homework, and have higher school aspirations" (p. 67). Approximately 56 percent of students in low-poverty high schools were involved in sports-related activities, compared with 44 percent of students in high-poverty schools (p. 70). In addition, black and Latino students are less likely to participate in leadership roles at high schools (Nora 2002, p. 72).

## Cultural Barriers

### Family Structure

Whether a child lives with one parent or two has been found to be related to a child's success in school (Lippman, Burns, and MacArthur 1996, p. 20). Approximately 80 percent of suburban and rural students lived with two parents, compared with only 68 percent of urban students (p. 20). "All other things being equal, with only one parent in the household, that parent is likely to have less time to spend with the child than parents in two-parent households. Also, in one-parent households, household income is generally lower than it is in two-parent households, which may produce more economic stress in the household and, in turn, affect a student's school performance" (p. 20).

In addition, Rosigno has found that reading test scores of students in single-parent or step-parent governed families are depressed by 0.6 points on average, compared to scores of students who live with both natural parents (Rosigno 1998, p. 1048).

### Homework and Home Life

Nearly half (43%) of the low SES cohort watched three or more hours of television per day, compared with 26 percent in schools with lower poverty concentrations. Students in the low SES cohort also felt less safe at school and neglected to complete as much homework as those less poor (Lippman, Burns, and MacArthur 1996, p. 110). The urban poor reported doing six and a half hours of homework per week compared with eight hours for other groups (p. 106).

In addition, low-SES youth were more likely to work (18%) than those in the suburbs (14%) or rural areas (12%), thus making the youth involved more tired, delinquent, and alienated from school. (pp. 72–73). Many multi-generational families may decide that work for the child represents a greater contribution to the household than can be made by pursuing a college education.

### Poor Behavioral Patterns

There are greater levels of student behavioral problems including possession and use of weapons, high absenteeism from school, and high teen pregnancy in low SES urban areas (pp. 4, 108–109). Black males are more often suspended in high school and for longer periods of time than other groups (Cokely 2001, p. 484). Some of these suspensions may be attributed to a greater number of violent activities, while others may reflect a greater willingness to impose more stringent punitive measures against this population.

### Culture and Language

When there is limited acculturation, the likelihood of college entrance immediately after high school decreases. There can be numerous problems associated with minimal use of English in the household, including lessened parental involvement with schooling; inability to assist with homework; and the inability, down the line, to understand college marketing materials and processes. These issues compound, and students are less likely to aspire to attend college.

## How Low-Income Prospects Approach College Choice

### Hossler's Choice Model

It is useful to utilize Hossler's *Choice Model*, because it is particularly pertinent to low-SES students. Hossler sets out three phases of college choice: predisposition, search, and choice (Hossler and Gallager 1987).

Hossler notes that of the three phases that are discussed, the predisposition stage has received the least attention (p. 210). At this stage, when students *first* crystallize whether they want to apply to college, "one of the most important background characteristics is that of socioeconomic status" (p. 210).

Choy (2001) emphasizes that high school graduates whose parents did not go to college tend to report lower educational expectations than their peers as early as eighth grade (p. 10).

For those would-be students who have developed a predisposition to attend, the college search process—the second phase in the choice model—then ensues. Students seek more information from various sources. Then students embark on the third, or choice phase, in which they evaluate the information they have, and submit applications for admissions and financial aid.

One of Hossler's goals was to affect policymaking interventions, especially in the first two phases. Specifically, he recommended that, "with the rising costs of higher education, information regarding financial aid and the net price of attending private and public institutions should be directed at students and their parents during the predisposition and search phases" (Hossler and Gallager 1987, p. 219).

In the late 1990s, the federal government acted to do just that. Working with information generated from the Integrated Postsecondary Education Data Surveys (IPEDS),[124] the Department of Education created "College Opportunities Online (COOL)," now called "CollegeNavigator."[125] For any student with access to a computer, if not at home then in a public library, it is possible to log on without special passwords and to find out a great deal of information about any college in the country included in the federal student financial aid program. Such information includes:

- General information, including the availability of special programs (ROTC, study abroad);
- Student services (on-campus daycare for students' children, for example); admissions data (number of applicants; percent admitted; percent admitted who are enrolled—full-time, part-time); SAT and ACT scores (numbers and percentiles), etc.;
- Estimated student expenses;
- Financial aid (percentage of students receiving aid—federal, state/local, or institutional aid; grants versus loans; average amount of aid received per student);
- Enrollment by race/ethnicity, using the IPEDS categories;
- Retention/graduation rates;
- Awards/degrees (by level of degree and by program).

Such a tool can be especially valuable for low SES students, who often do not have college-educated parents able to help them navigate the college-admission process.

The mere presence of information, however, cannot overcome all hurdles. Many low-SES high school students do not even take the SAT or ACT. Hurtado notes that 40 percent of the

[124] Chapter 40, "Accessing IPEDS Data to Shape Marketing," discusses how admissions officers can make use of publicly available information from the IPEDS surveys to present their schools in a favorable light, based on government data which parents can view for themselves, as well.

[125] CollegeNavigator is available at <http://nces.ed.gov/collegenavigator>.

black high school seniors who had good academic records had no plan to take the SAT at all, or planned on delaying it (Hurtado, Inkelas, and Rhee 1997, p. 52; based on the National Education Longitudinal Study of 1988 [NELS:88]). And 98 percent of the NELS:88 cohort of Latinos scored beneath the highest quartile on a four-subject cognitive test in the eighth grade, and they became academically predispositioned not to attend college (p. 50).

### Financial Aid Considerations

Though the factors above contributed significantly to the *concept* of attending college, none had as much bearing on college choice as affordability. At the choice stage, 90 percent of the students and parents felt that they understood financial aid, and students felt their parents would play a significant role in securing aid and paying for the balance. Overall, financial aid, or the perception of it, was one of the most critical factors affecting the choice of which college, if any, to attend (Hossler, Schmit, and Vesper 1999, p. 97).

Paulsen and St. John (2002) found that nearly two-thirds (64%) of low-SES students had chosen a college because of low tuition, large grants, or a combination, and more than half (54%) chose a college close to home and work (p. 205).

There is an important and unfortunate consequence which often follows, however. Low-income students who chose a college because of low tuition and not upon financial aid were less likely to persist once aid and fixed costs were calculated and found by the student to be inadequate—thus demonstrating that there is a very high sensitivity among students to tuition and financial aid awards which they find do not meet their needs. In essence, the low tuition they found was not low enough (p. 219). Additionally those who chose a college because of low living costs persisted only if those low costs were realized.

We will explore the impact of financial aid on persistence shortly, in the section on various factors making for persistence among low-SES students.

## Retention Variables for First-Generation Students

Thirty-one percent of college students are estimated to be first-generation college goers (Somers, Woodhouse, and Cofer 2004, p. 19).

### Financial Variables

As we have already discussed, first-generation students are extremely sensitive to cost. For every $1,000 increase in tuition, they are .00004 percent less likely to persist. A $1,000 increase in grants raises their persistence likelihood by five percentage points, current year loans by 5.03 percent and work-study by 6.08 percent (p. 427). However, first-generation students are much more loan-averse than other students (p. 430).

In addition, the study by Paulsen and St. John (2002) shows the importance of covering living expenses, as well as the traditional tuition, room, and board. Their study shows that although more of the low SES cohort attended lower cost colleges and received more aid, even exceeding tuition, than non-SES students, the aid often did not cover living expenses, and this negatively affected persistence (p. 207).

On the other hand, those who chose colleges because they were close to work or because of the low living costs coupled with close proximity to work were more likely to persist (p. 220).

### Residency Variables

Those who lived on campus were 5.43 percent more likely to persist. Those in full-time status were 15.26 percent points more likely to persist, but those who worked full-time (-9.39%) or had low GPAs (-18.24%) were less likely to persist (Somers, Woodhouse, and Cofer 2004, pp. 426–427).

### Grade Variables

In the Paulsen and St. John study, students with C averages were more likely to persist, possibly because they could maintain academic progress standards with the C average and, in addition, they had fewer options to exit (*i.e.*, transfer) with the seemingly low GPA. Understandably, those with As persisted at greater levels than those with Bs—possibly because of greater satisfaction and integration at the college, as well as academic achievement per se (2002, pp. 221–222).

### Aspiration Variables

Those with lofty long-term aspirations (of which poor blacks have the highest) (p. 223), had the worst persistence. These aspirations were often not logical outgrowths of the student's field, but rather, were unrealistic ones which were not necessarily congruent with the field of study. An outlier type of example would be the aspirations of those students who aspired to earn master's or doctorate degrees in fields which do not offer them. In addition, those with a concerted interest in earning very high salaries immediately following school also had persistence problems (Leppel 2005, p. 226, 230). Another contributing factor is that many students who choose their major in order to generate significant incomes may find they do not enjoy the course of study, and thus drop out of college (p. 230).

### Employment Variables

In all settings, students who worked many hours while in college had a greater likelihood of leaving within three years. In private not-for-profits, 38 percent of those who worked full-time and 19 percent of those who worked part-time left college in three years. At the community college level, 59 percent of those who worked full-time did not earn their associate's degree.

### Family Variables

Students who were married or had dependents had a more difficult time completing their degrees. Overall, 47 percent (58% in private and 60% in community colleges) who had ever been married or had dependents departed within three years (Bradburn 2002, pp. 13–15).

### Standardized Test Variables

Students who scored lower on the SAT or ACT had less likelihood of completing a four-year degree. (*See* Table 12.3, on page 197.)

### Academic and Social Integration

It is not surprising that SES students are also less likely to integrate socially until they are academically comfortable (Somers, Woodhouse, and Cofer 2004, p. 430). A study of 3,244 freshmen at private four-year colleges found that students with higher GPAs in high school had the greatest likelihood of persistence in college, and that negative high school academic attitudes (*e.g.*, not caring about academic achievement) signaled the greatest likelihood of dropping out (Glynn, Sauer, and Miller 2003, p. 56).

Students who had low grades (31.1%) and low social integration (28.1%) at public four-year institutions left within three years (Bradburn 2002, p. 29). At private colleges, 33.3 percent and 34.7 percent respectively left within three years (p. 31), and at community colleges, 49.1 percent and 48.6 percent percent did not complete their studies (p. 32).

### Causes for Dropping Out

Of the 1995–96 Beginning Postsecondary Students (BPS) leaving by 1998, reasons self-reported are shown in Table 12.4, on page 198.

## Increasing Retention: Practical Steps

### Anticipating Low-Income Students' Needs

Many institutions have various offices which are designed to aid students who experience problems. However, all too often these reactive measures may only trigger retention efforts which are too little, too late.

It is important, instead, that proactive early measures be implemented. For first-generation students as for transfer students, "student retention begins before matriculation" (Bell 2004). Advising for first-generation students, as for transfer students, should be both prescriptive (telling them what needs to be done) and developmental (recognizing other academic and personal concerns).[126]

[126] Lynne Williams Bell (2004), an academic counselor at the School of Community Service at the University of North Texas, has observed: "When asked what they most wanted an advisor to do, a group of transfer students replied emphatically, 'Listen!' " (p. 82).

## Co-Curricular Programs

In a study of what state boards of higher education can do to influence retention of minorities (including many first-generation students) in higher education, Sheehan has compiled a useful list of techniques: early awareness and outreach programs, and a range of support services that address areas of student anxiety, including academic skills deficiencies, lack of focus as to career plans, and difficulty in adjusting to campus life and academic expectations (Sheehan 1988, pp. 23–24).

In "Admissions' Evolving Role: From Gatekeeper to Strategic Partner," the opening chapter of this volume, Henderson describes in detail an ambitious statewide concept in South Carolina, known as The College Foundation of North Carolina (CFNC). This concept is a suite of services for parents, and for students as young as middle school, all now available online at www.cfnc.org. As Henderson notes at the end of the chapter, market research has shown that 80 percent of high school and middle school parents in North Carolina are aware of cfnc.org, and that 84 percent anticipate using its various modules—including modules on career planning, paying for college, a college fair online, and online applications for all in-state colleges and universities.

TABLE 12.3: **1995–96 Beginning Postsecondary Students According to Outcome of First Spell of Continuous Enrollment at First Institution as of Spring 1998, by SAT/ACT Composite and First-Generation Status**

| Characteristic/ SAT/ACT Composite | Still Enrolled/ Degree Attained at Institution | Transferred | Left Postsecondary Education |
|---|---|---|---|
| **Total** | 66.9 | 20.3 | 12.8 |
| 790 or lower | 55.2 | 27.1 | 17.7 |
| 800–1090 | 69.1 | 21.4 | 9.6 |
| 1100 or higher | 80.4 | 13.6 | 6.0 |
| **First Generation** | | | |
| Total | 60.1 | 20.7 | 19.3 |
| 790 or lower | 52.3 | 27.2 | 20.5 |
| 800–1090 | 66.3 | 22.7 | 11.0 |
| 1100 or higher | 81.1 | 10.6 | 8.3 |
| **Parent Had Bachelor's or Advanced Degree** | | | |
| Total | 72.8 | 19.4 | 7.8 |
| 790 or lower | 60.5 | 27.5 | 12.0 |
| 800–1090 | 72.2 | 20.6 | 7.2 |
| 1100 or higher | 80.6 | 13.4 | 6.0 |
| **Parent Had Some College** | | | |
| Total | 60.9 | 23.1 | 16.1 |
| 790 or lower | 48.9 | 30.5 | 20.6 |
| 800–1090 | 64.9 | 21.0 | 14.2 |
| 1100 or higher | 77.2 | 16.5 | 6.3 |

**SOURCE:** Warburton, Bugarin, and Nunez 2001, p. 32.

There is a strong correlation between poor high school academic progress and retention in college. To address this stiutation, some colleges introduce a bridge program during the summer for the most recent high school graduates. The goal is a strong curricular component, to develop basic skills and to improve academic performance. Such programs may include remedial or developmental coursework and aim to make students more comfortable in college through advising, social events, and other activities (Muraskin *et al.* 2004, pp. 17–18). In Muraskin's study, which analyzed the practices of 10 low-graduation rate colleges, several institutions or systems were cited as being especially effective with students in bridge programs: Georgia State University, University of California-San Diego, University of Maryland College Park, and UCLA (p. 18). UCLA's program was six weeks long.

TABLE 12.4: **1995–96 Beginning Postsecondary Students leaving by 1998**

| Characteristics | Academic Problems | Done Taking Desired Classes | Not Satisfied | Taking Time Off | Changes in Family Status | Conflicts at Home | Conflicts With Job | Needed to Work | Other Financial Reasons |
|---|---|---|---|---|---|---|---|---|---|
| **Gender** | | | | | | | | | |
| Male | 6.1 | 10.0 | 7.9 | 7.6 | 3.9 | 6.2 | 7.3 | 31.3 | 13.0 |
| Female | 2.1 | 9.9 | 4.8 | 6.9 | 10.9 | 12.8 | 5.1 | 20.5 | 17.9 |
| **Race/Ethnicity** | | | | | | | | | |
| White | 4.1 | 10.2 | 5.6 | 7.8 | 8.2 | 7.6 | 5.4 | 26.7 | 13.1 |
| Black | 1.9 | 4.8 | 10.3 | 2.6 | 6.1 | 15.0 | 9.8 | 18.2 | 28.7 |
| Hispanic | 5.1 | 10.1 | 6.7 | 10.3 | 6.3 | 14.9 | 8.4 | 25.3 | 14.0 |
| Asian/Pacific Islander | 8.3 | 25.2 | 2.1 | 6.9 | 9.1 | 13.6 | 0.1 | 36.1 | 5.2 |
| **1994 Income Quartile** | | | | | | | | | |
| Lowest | 3.2 | 7.3 | 7.3 | 7.5 | 11.8 | 10.0 | 5.7 | 25.3 | 14.7 |
| Middle Two Quartiles | 3.7 | 10.0 | 6.1 | 6.6 | 6.9 | 8.1 | 5.3 | 30.3 | 16.9 |
| Highest | 6.8 | 15.8 | 5.2 | 9.2 | 2.3 | 15.0 | 10.6 | 12.8 | 14.2 |
| **First Generation Status** | | | | | | | | | |
| First Generation College Student | 2.7 | 12.1 | 7.1 | 4.9 | 9.1 | 12.2 | 8.5 | 26.6 | 14.4 |
| Not First Generation | 5.4 | 4.9 | 7.4 | 6.3 | 7.8 | 8.2 | 5.9 | 24.1 | 16.1 |
| **Total** | 4.0 | 10.0 | 6.3 | 7.2 | 7.6 | 9.7 | 6.2 | 25.6 | 15.6 |

**SOURCE:** Bradburn (2002, p. 54).

Programs with block classes, which include several core classes taken together, along with a range of support services, can be of great benefit (p.21).

Freshmen Interest Groups which bring together students who share interests, and are often located in dormitories, can help to build a sense of community (p.21). Such interest groups can be sponsored by offices other than the academic departments. The more the activities are constructed to relate in some manner to the reason why the students are at the college (*i.e.*, to gain employment in a field or become expert in a topic) the better. Such co-curricular activities can help build more interest in academic fields in general, as well as in individual courses; may contribute to a student's resume; and may build relationships with faculty and others, which can be of great benefit. To develop this kind of program fully, it may be prudent to invest in staff development and reward those who are effective (Tinto 2004, pp. 8–9). Measuring effectiveness may be done in a number of ways, including overall department retention, number of students who participate, correlating grades to participation in such related activities, and so on.

## Academic Advising

Students need clear academic advising that prepares them for entry into the career they desire. Here are some ways of introducing first-generation students early to information which they can use as they test which lines of work are most compatible with their interests and aptitudes.

- Computerized access to schedules and curriculum so they can plan their courses of study (Muraskin *et al.* 2004, p. 35)
- Making use of faculty as advisors and keeping their advising load at 30 or fewer students, preferably having them advise students within their major or at least within the academic division (p. 36)
- Consider integrating one or more counselor positions within the academic departments. This individual would have access to faculty when necessary and would be available over longer periods of time. Academic advisement could take place in the academic offices, so that the academic counselor meets with the students in an academic setting, rather than in an office of people who know little about the various field of study or the nuances of appropriate coursework to be taken.
- Arrange internships, whenever possible, for students. At best, the student will discover a career. At worst, he or she will discover that he does not like a certain line of work, before he has made a commitment to a major or even to a first job in the field.

### Freshman Support and Living Arrangements

In freshman year, you have a rare occasion to capture students' attention. Try in many ways to build a program in the freshman year around college success, starting with study skills, but moving on to embodying what your school has to offer, via speakers, study groups, and interest groups.

First, of course, students need to be assisted with study skills, managing their time, and coping with academic stress. Make use of student services administrators, upper class students, and a core of selected faculty, if appropriate, to present a series of sessions on these topics. It may be a good idea to hold the session on *study skills* early in the semester, but to hold the session on *exam-taking skills* later in the semester. Students have so many things coming at them early in the semester that it is better to wait. After all, no one can absorb everything at once!

In addition, it may be a good idea to visit your dormitories and to look at the focal point in each. Is it just a room with televisions, pool tables, and couches? See if you can establish at least some open public spaces in the dormitory that provide appropriate settings for stimulating intellectual lectures or debates.

Consider holding some dorm-wide or even college-wide presentations in the dorms. Inviting faculty and outside speakers to speak within the dorm can create the feel of a residential college, even without an elaborate system of housemasters and resident faculty. For example, holding organized study groups led by graduate students (or even juniors or seniors), in math, chemistry, or languages can help to *integrate* living and learning.[127]

[127] You do not need a $200 million dollar Campus Initiative, as at Cornell, or a $150-million campus-within-a-campus, as at Vanderbilt, to give students the sense that their dorms can be sources of planned and interesting events that make their dorm more than just a hotel to sleep or lounge in (Weber 2007).

Another idea involves organizing dorms or at least floors of students who have classes together, share a major, or have some other academic interests in common; this may help students build relationships around those interests, which may lead later on to useful professional networking.

### Student Employment

We have seen that many low SES students have a challenge in balancing the ability to pay for college and their need to find adequate time to study. Student employment at the college has often been provided as a form of financial aid, but it is not generally always available to students at the beginning of their academic careers. Nonetheless, when it is available, it should be structured so that those who do participate gain more than a just a paycheck. Shelving books in libraries or watching the weight room may be appropriate for some majors, but not most.

These jobs should be interesting, engaging, and should offer a level of compensation that is better than the draw of competing opportunities in the neighborhood which may offer no academic development. It may also help temper some unrealistic aspirations students may have incorrectly developed about their field of interest, and help them better understand the infrastructure of the field.

### Goal Setting and Accountability

Whichever strategies one uses to build retention, it is integral that specific departments and individuals become accountable. It is of no real benefit to have an institution-wide initiative to help build retention, but with no one doing the work of measuring the effort, communicating what has succeeded, and redirecting the efforts which have not been as productive as expected.

It may take several departments and even committees to focus upon the retention problems. Relationships will need to be built with academic departments, financial aid and admissions, student support offices, and the variety of learning support entities including libraries, the IT department, and residence life. When a set of initiatives has been agreed upon, a means by which efforts and results can be measured must be implemented. Some possible measurements may include the number of contacts various offices have had with at-risk students; what was discussed and resolved during those contacts; the number of students who participate in activities designed to build community or provide academic focus; attendance patterns—by major, dormitory, and any other variable which may be relevant; what classes students don't perform well in and if they are related directly to the student's major; and what the percentage of students is who return each semester and graduate.

After time, if you ask the right questions and require the tracking of pertinent data, it may become evident what the institution is doing well and where it needs to redirect its energy.

## Conclusion

The low SES student who enrolls in college has a great many challenges. Ultimately, some of these cannot be addressed by the institution alone; students must motivate themselves to overcome deficits, both academic and social. However, when a variety of support services are offered, such students will have a much greater opportunity to succeed.

Institutions fail themselves, the students, and society when any of the three turn a blind eye to the issues affecting this group. For these students to have battled through their challenges prior to enrolling in college demonstrates a considerable amount of resolve, flexibility, and determination. With proper guidance, communication, and college involvement, these students have the ability to help break the pattern, and to provide opportunities for those who come after them.

/ CHAPTER THIRTEEN /

*by Rudolph Clay Jr., M.A., M.A.L.S.*
*Head of Reference, Olin Library*
*Washington University in St. Louis*
*James McLeod*
*Dean of the College of Arts and Sciences*
*Vice Chancellor for Students*
*Washington University in St. Louis*

13

# African-American Students:
## Recruitment and Retention

Ever since the Supreme Court decisions in *Bakke*[128] and *Grutter*, college admissions offices have been allowed to recruit a diverse student body as long as race or ethnicity were not the sole criteria for admission.

However, implementing this principle poses real challenges. This chapter focuses on the recruitment and retention of African-American (AA) college students. Specifically, it addresses itself to the following considerations: the numbers and primary locations of the African-American high school student pool; the issue of scores—both SAT/ACT and Advanced Placement; the role of high school guidance counselors; the process of college choice for AA students; characteristics of first-time AA college freshmen, AA college students, and AA college males; transfer rates of AA students from community colleges to four-year colleges; the role of financial aid; and some suggestions as to retention. Finally, we summarize various means, which should be pursued together, of reaching out and expanding the pool of black students.

[128] *Regents of Univ. of Cal. v. Bakke* (438 U.S. 265 [1978])

## Demographics

In 2003 the Western Interstate Commission for Higher Education (WICHE) published the sixth edition of "Knocking at the College Door: Projections of High School Graduates by State, Income, and Race/Ethnicity, 1988–2018," in collaboration with ACT and the College Board. The report provides updated projections of high school graduates for each year and each state (plus the District of Columbia) through 2018. The projections are based on U.S. Census Bureau data such as internal migration and birth patterns. The 2003 edition also provides projections by family income. State statistical projections are provided for national and regional high school (public and non public) enrollments and graduates by race/ethnicity and family income level. The report identifies a number of trends regarding African-American students:

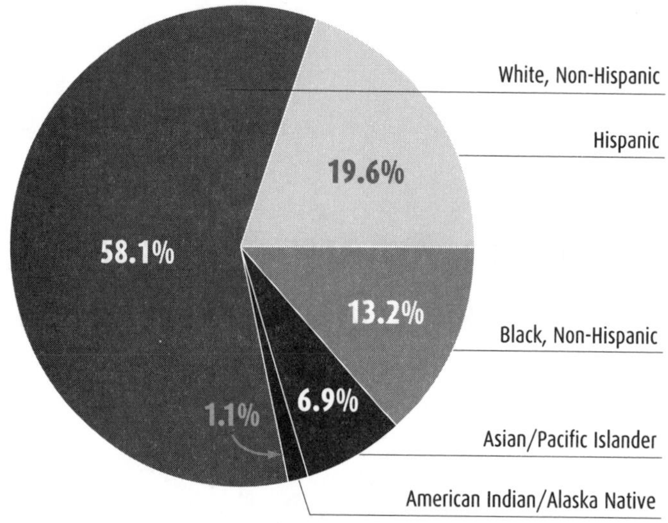


FIGURE 13.1

Distribution of Public High School Graduates by Race/Ethnicity, U.S., 2013–14 (projected)

+ *The number of black, non-Hispanic public high school graduates is not expected to increase as rapidly as those of other racial/ethnic minorities; the group of AA high school graduates is projected to increase from 350,000 in 2003–04 to 365,000 graduating in 2013–14.*
+ *The South has been graduating over one-half of all black, non-Hispanic students from public high schools, and that level is expected to continue.*
+ *The number of black, non-Hispanic graduates will fluctuate in most regions over the next decade; the West and the Midwest will each gain about one percentage point of the total share of all black, non-Hispanics graduating annually.* (*See* Figure 13.2, on page 205.)
+ *Nearly 25 percent of states nationally are projected to see fewer black, non-Hispanic public high school graduates in 2014 than they did in 2002. New Mexico, Hawaii, and Louisiana are expected to graduate between 12 and 19 percent fewer black, non-Hispanic graduates.*
+ *Nearly one-half of the states will see increases in black, non-Hispanic high school graduates that range from one percent to 23 percent. A handful of states—New Hampshire, Maine, Minnesota, South Dakota, and Utah—may see growth spanning from 110 to 269 percent, but the numbers in those states are very small to begin with* (WICHE 2003).

According to WICHE's analysis, the number of black, non-Hispanic public high school graduates will grow steadily, peak in the 2009–10 school year, and then begin to decline (*see* Figure 13.3).

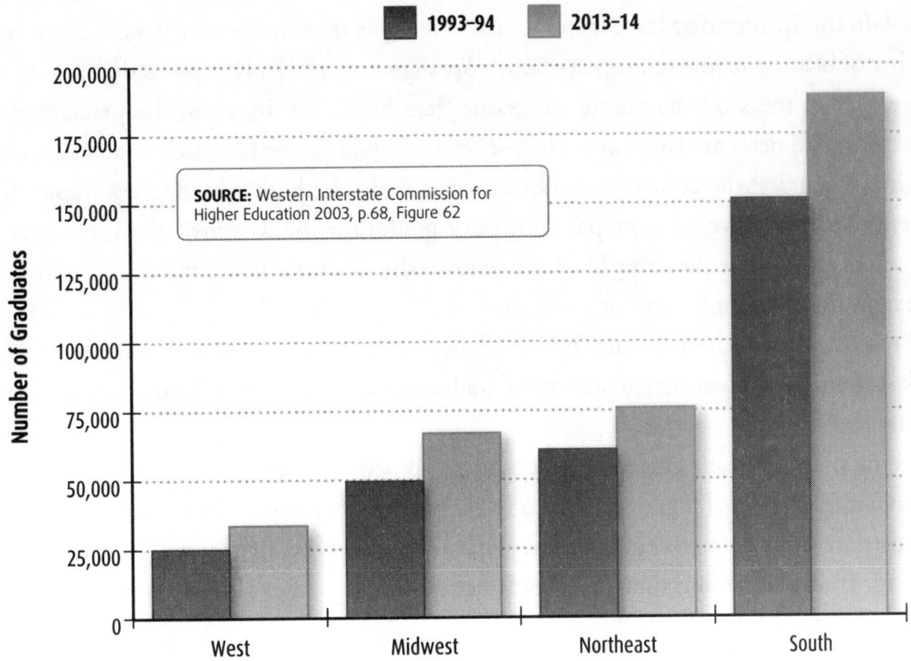


FIGURE 13.2

Number of Black, non-Hispanic Public High School Graduates by Region, 1993–94 (actual) and 2013–15 (projected)

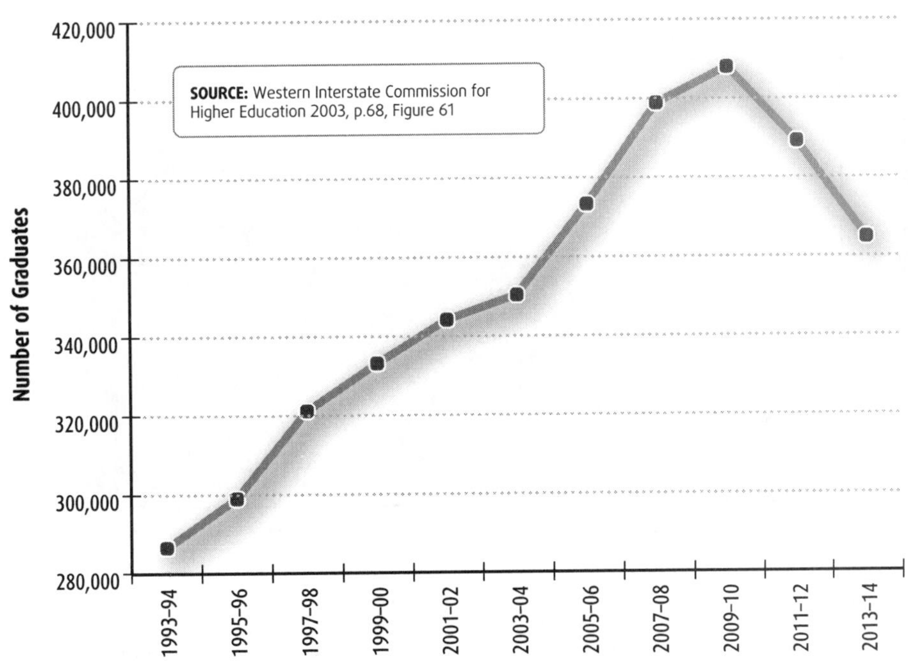


FIGURE 13.3

Black, Non-Hispanic Public High School Graduates, U.S., 1993–94 (actual) through 2013–14 (projected)

## The Gap in Scores

### Advanced Placement

Using College Board data, the *Journal of Blacks in Higher Education* (JBHE 2007a) tracks the number of black students who take challenging Advanced Placement (AP) courses in high school. In the Spring 2007 issue it shows that since 1985 there has been a large increase in the number of black students taking AP exams. (*See* Figure 13.4). JBHE reports that in 1985 only 1.4 percent of the students taking AP exams were black, but by 2006 the percentage had increased to 5.6 percent. The *Journal* lists several possible barriers to black student participation in AP courses: the courses may not be available in the high schools they attend; black students may not have been prepared in prior grades for the AP curriculum; teachers and counselors may not be directing black students to the AP curriculum; and the cost for taking the exams may be prohibitive for some students.[129]

The most recent data provided by the College Board shows that in 2006, about 45,958 black students, representing 6.9 percent of graduating seniors, took AP exams (*see* Figure 13.6, on page 208).

The median AP exam grade for blacks in 2006 was 1.96 and the median grade for the national total was 2.85 (JBHE 2007a, p. 87). A score of five is equivalent to receiving an A in a college level course, four is equivalent to a B, and three is equivalent to a C. Thus the median grade for blacks in 2006 is one letter grade below the median grade for the national total.

FIGURE 13.4

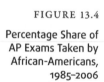

Percentage Share of AP Exams Taken by African-Americans, 1985–2006

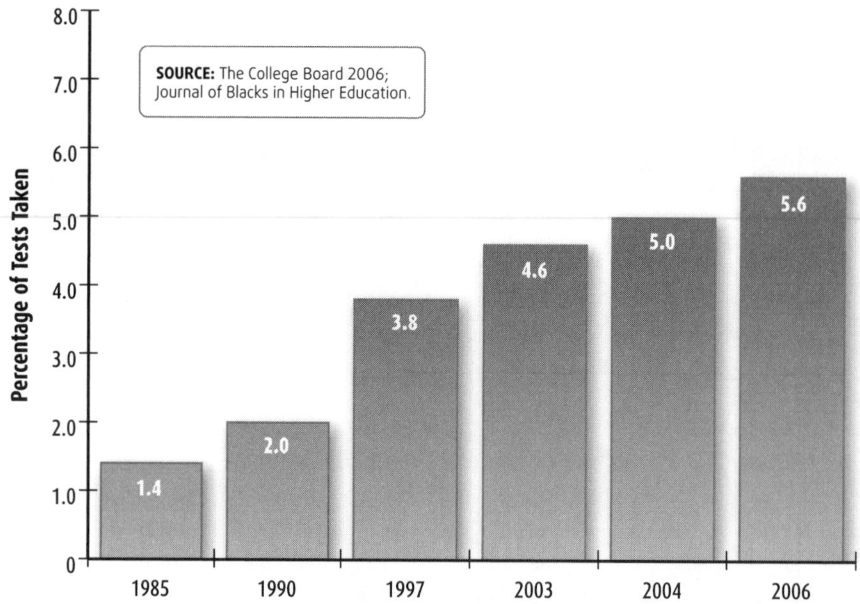


[129] As the chapter on the Advanced Placement exams points out, there is no cost to the student or the high school to take or offer the Advanced Placement courses; there is a charge ($84.00 in 2008) to take the optional, end-of-course AP exams. There are some mechanisms for eliminating the exam fee for students from low-income families. See Chapter 31, "Advanced Placement Program: Its Influence on Academics and Admissions Decisionmaking."

## SAT and ACT Scores

In its most recent annual analysis of racial differences on college admission tests, the *Journal of Blacks in Higher Education* (2006a) reported that the 2006 average score for blacks on the combined math and verbal portions of the SAT test was 863 (out of 1,200), the lowest of all other major ethnic groups in the United States (p. 9). (*See* Figure 13.7, on page 208.)

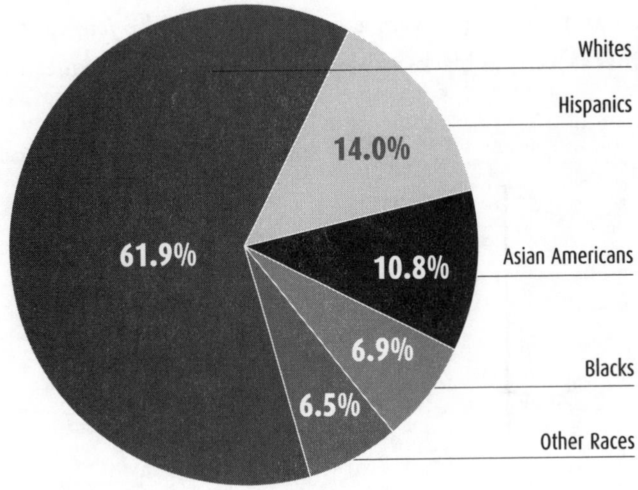


**Note:** Blacks are 6.9 percent of all students participating in the AP program. But because many students take more than one AP course and whites are more likely than blacks to take multiple AP courses, blacks took only 5.6 percent of all AP examinations administered in 2006.

**SOURCE:** The College Board 2006; Journal of Blacks in Higher Education.

FIGURE 13.5

Racial Breakdown of AP Program Participants

The *Journal* reports a number of possible reasons for the gap:

- Differences in quality and level of secondary education—Blacks having taken less rigorous courses in higher level mathematics (trigonometry and calculus) and English (American literature, composition, and grammar); fewer honor courses in science and social studies;
- Placing black students at an early age into vocational training and curriculum that is not college-preparatory;
- The possibility that black schoolchildren are taught by white teachers who have a low opinion of the scholastic abilities of black students and do not challenge them sufficiently to perform well on standardized tests;
- The effects of racial minorities living in segregated environments and adapting to oppression and lack of opportunity; and
- Black students may experience higher degrees of peer pressure to shun academic pursuits.

In a separate article in the same issue, JBHE (2006b) discuses a similar black-white gap in ACT scores. It reports that the 2006 median ACT score for blacks was 17.1 and the median score for whites was 22.0. It also reports that the gap remains slightly larger than it was a decade ago in 1997, when the median score for blacks was 17.1 and the median score for whites was 21.7. The *Journal* offers an analysis of the ACT gap by focusing on the top ACT scores. It reports that in 2006, 1.1 percent of black students (1,544) scored 28 or above, and that the highest ranked colleges and universities seek to recruit students who have ACT scores that are 28 or above. The same study indicates that of white students, 12.65 percent (995,391) had ACT scores that were above 28 in 2006. The *Journal* concludes that whites were eleven times as likely as blacks to score at a level equal to the mean score of students admitted to the

FIGURE 13.6

Race/Ethnicity of AP Examinees vs. Graduating Seniors in U.S. Public Schools, Class of 2006

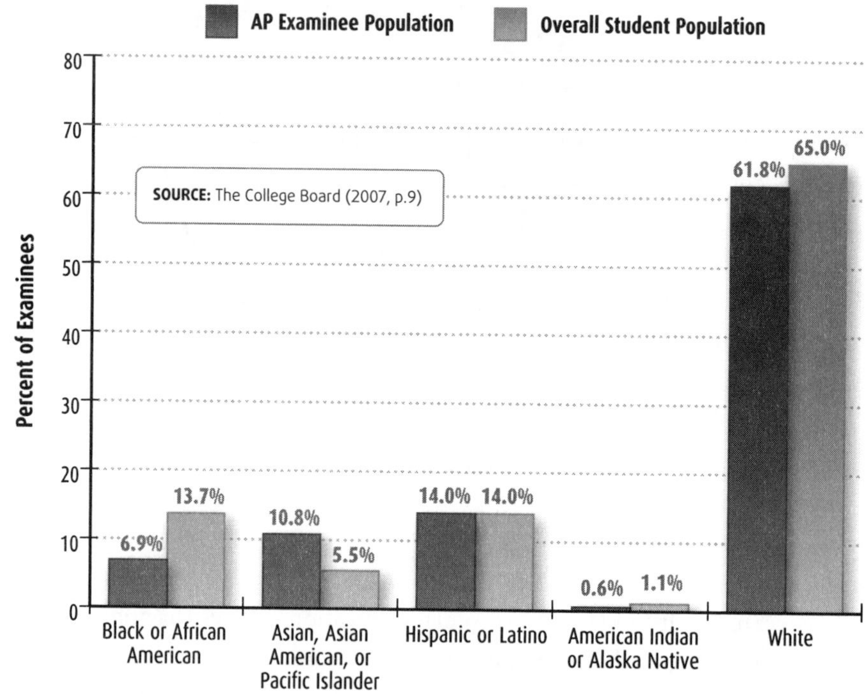


FIGURE 13.7

Mean Combined Math and Verbal SAT Score, by Ethnicity (2006)

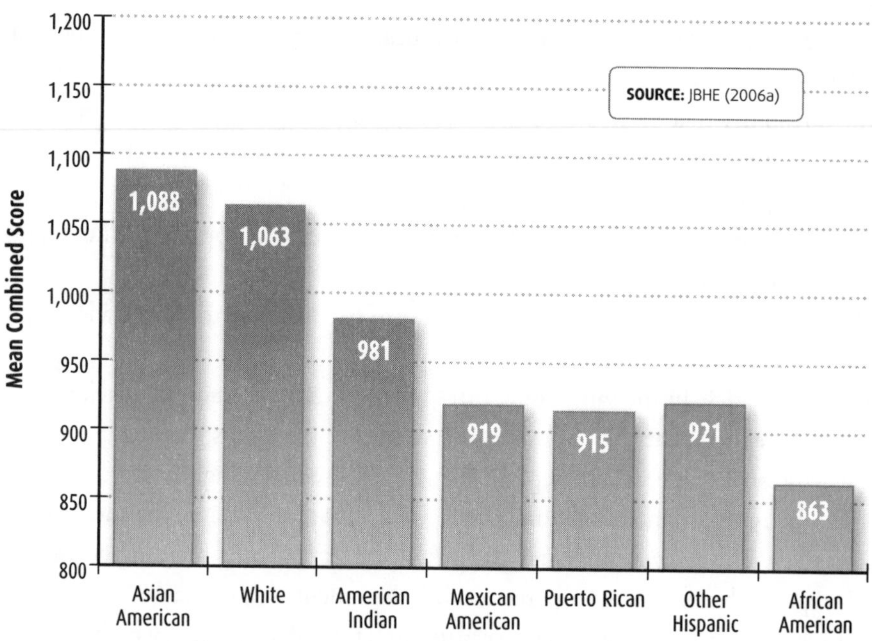

nation's most prestigious colleges and universities. The analysis of both SAT and ACT scores indicates that if colleges make admission decisions based primarily on either of these test scores, the effect on admission of black students would be devastating.

## Role of High School Guidance Counselors

In an article called "Social Capital and College Preparation," Farmer-Hinton and Adams (2006) review the recent literature on the counseling services received by minority students in predominantly poor high schools. They highlight the challenges faced by these high school counselors, including: high student-counselor ratios, fewer college planning resources, and an environment with "limited school-wide emphasis on college access." Farmer-Hinton and Adams conclude: "When Black students are provided with consistent exposure to the viability of college access and greater personalized support from their counselors, they can better navigate the college preparation process" (p. 114). The authors also include a review of Gonzalez's (2003) work which found that students in community colleges had minimal access to guidance counselors. This may affect their ability to later transfer to a four-year institution.

## Characteristics of First-Time Black Freshmen

In 2005 the Higher Education Research Institute at UCLA's Graduate School of Education and Information Studies released a new study that reported on trends in black college freshmen enrollment, based on national data collected from 1971 to 2004 by the Cooperative Institutional Research Program. The study, "Black Undergraduates From *Bakke* to *Grutter*," includes the responses of over a half million black college freshmen attending more than 600 baccalaureate-granting colleges and universities, surveyed over the 33-year period. The lead author of the study, Walter R. Allen, is professor of education and of sociology at UCLA. The data have been statistically weighted to represent the responses for the 3.6 million black first-time, full-time freshmen students attending institutions of higher learning during that period. The study is considered to be the most comprehensive look at black first-time college freshmen students at both historically black (HBCUs) and predominantly white four-year institutions (PWIs). Data was collected on a number of topics, including demographic background, family socioeconomic status, academic background, career aspirations, college choice, financial aid, political and civic engagement, student attitudes, beliefs, values, behaviors, and future aspirations. Some of the major findings detailed in the study are listed below.

### Enrollment and Gender Differences

Though enrollment tripled since 1965 to 1.8 million African-Americans enrolled in college in 2004, they represented only 10 percent of students on college campuses. Allen (1992) reported that by 1990, more than three quarters of African-American college students attended predominantly white institutions. In 2004, black women comprised 59.3 percent of all first-time, full-time black students attending four-year institutions, compared to 54.5 percent in 1971—an ongoing gender gap among black students.

### Parents' Educational Attainment

In 2004, the parents of black freshmen had a significantly higher educational attainment than the parents of black freshmen in 1971. In 1971, 8 percent of fathers and 11 percent of mothers had earned college degrees. By 2004, 20 percent of fathers and 25 percent of mothers were college graduates. Fifty-three percent of fathers of the general freshmen population in 2004 and 52 percent of mothers had a least a college degree in 2004.

### Financial Concerns

In 1971, 26 percent of black freshmen had major concerns about financing their college education. Twenty-three percent had major concerns in 2004. Thirteen percent of all freshmen had major concerns about financing their college education in 2004.

### Academic Preparation

Eight percent of black freshmen in 1971 reported high school grade averages of A- or better, as compared to 20 percent of all freshmen. In 2004, 28 percent of black freshmen reported high school grade averages of A- or better, as compared to 48 percent of all freshmen.

### Educational Aspirations

Twenty-four percent of black freshmen intended to obtain doctoral degrees in 2004, compared to 17 percent of the general population of freshmen.

There was a significant gender difference in black female freshmen aspiring toward medical degrees (16%), compared to black male freshmen (8%). In the general freshmen population, 11 percent of female freshmen and 7 percent of male freshmen aspire toward medical degrees.

### College Choice

In a national survey of African-American high school juniors, Sevier (1992) sought to learn more about how and why such students choose a college, and what special services/activities they expect college to provide. Of the 1,127 students who returned the survey, it was found that the four most important college choice items were:

- Reputation of the college
- Availability of a specific major
- Total cost of attending
- Availability of financial aid

Table 13.1, on page 211, illustrates other important findings involved the value of high school guidance counselors, parents' role, and campus visits.

Allen (2005) found that between 1971 and 2004, the most compelling reasons for black freshmen to attend college have been upward mobility and a desire to acquire a greater knowledge base. Fifty percent of the black freshmen in 2004 reported that their parents were influential in the development of their college aspirations.

Table 13.2 reveals the top ranked factors influencing black freshmen in choosing a particular college in 2004.

The report suggests that black high school students may not acquire useful knowledge about colleges from school agents. It was found that high school teachers impacted college choice by only 5 percent, and high school counselors by 7 percent. In 2004, black college freshmen reported using the information sources for choice of college shown in Table 13.3.

Proximity was reported as a factor for black students in choosing a PWI over a HBCU. In either case, black freshmen reported considering distance from home as an important reason for choosing their particular college. Seventeen percent of black freshmen at an HBCU and 21 percent of black freshmen at a PWI rated staying close to home as an important reason for choosing their particular college.

TABLE 13.1: **Selected Results of Sevier Survey (2002)**

| Response | % |
|---|---|
| **Talked to a High School Guidance Counselor** | |
| Yes | 44.3 |
| No | 14.5 |
| No, but I intend to | 39.2 |
| Don't know | 2.0 |
| **Parents' Role in the College Decision** | |
| Provided guidance | 56.3 |
| Helped narrow the field | 7.7 |
| Did not help | 32.1 |
| Recommended specific colleges | 3.9 |
| **Value of the Campus Visit** | |
| Very important | 45.6 |
| Have not visited a campus but plan to | 29.2 |
| Important | 20.8 |
| Not very important | 3.3 |
| Very unimportant | 1.1 |

TABLE 13.2: **Top-Ranked College Choice Factors (2004)**

| | %[1] |
|---|---|
| Academic Reputation | 59 |
| Job Opportunities for Typical Graduates (job market success of college's graduates) | 54 |
| Offered Financial Assistance | 45–50 |
| Graduate School Prospects | 37 |
| Social Activities | 30 |

[1] Figures add up to more than 100 percent because students could name more than one factor.

TABLE 13.3: **Sources Informing College Choice (2004)**

| | Students at HBCUs (%) | Students at PWIs (%) |
|---|---|---|
| College Ranking Magazines | 22 | 17 |
| Relatives | 17 | 12 |
| Friends | 10 | 9 |

## Persistence Rates

Another report which profiles African-American college students (among others) is the *Minorities in Higher Education Annual Status Report* from the American Council on Education (ACE). It uses data from the U.S. Department of Education's National Center for Education Statistics (NCES) and the U.S. Census Bureau to provide a comprehensive statistical compendium on students of color—African-Americans, American Indians, Asian Americans, and Hispanics. The annual report focuses on four major areas: high school completion, college participation and enrollment, degrees conferred, and the number of minorities employed as full-time faculty in U.S. colleges and universities. The report does not include data on high school completion and college participation rates for Asian Americans or American Indians. Beginning with the twenty-first annual report (2005), persistence rates are shown through five years among students who entered postsecondary education in 1989–90, and are contrasted with with persistence among students who entered in 1995–96. The report explains that looking only at institutional six-year graduation rates, as had been done previously, does not provide a complete picture of college student persistence because the large number of part-time students in the college population is increasing the average time to complete a degree. The report states that in 2001, nearly 40 percent of undergraduates were enrolled part-time. Another reason given for utilizing the five-year persistence rate is that one-third of all bachelor's degree recipients had transferred from their first institution, so institutional graduation rates would not reflect the persistence and attainment of transfer students.

The twenty-second annual report (2006) provides data for 1992 to 2004 and a focus on the most recent data, 2002–2004. Some of the major findings of the *Status Report* are outlined in the following sections.

### High School Completion Rate

- The high school completion rate for eighteen- to twenty-four-year-old African-American students increased two percentage points from 75.6 percent in 1992–94 to 77.8 percent in 2002–04. During this period the rate for Hispanics increased from 56.6 percent in 1992–94 to 64.4 percent in 2002–04. The rate for white students increased from 85.6 percent in 1992–94 to 87.6 percent in 2002–04 (Cook and Cordova 2006, p.1).
- There was a high school completion gender gap during this period. The high school completion rate for African-American males increased 0.8 percentage points between 1992–94 (73.0%) and 2002–04 (73.8%). The rate for African-American women increased 3.3 percentage points between 1992–94 (78.0%) and 2002–04 (81.3%). (p. 2).

### College Participation

- The percentage of African-American eighteen- to twenty-four-year-old high school graduates who were enrolled in college increased by 7 percentage points from 34.1 percent (1992–94) to 41.1 percent (2002–04). The rate for whites increased during this period by 4.5 percentage points, from 42.8 to 47.3 (Cook and Cordova 2006, p. 3).
- The gender gap for African-American college participation was 8.0 percentage points. The college participation rate for African-American males increased 2 percentage points from 34.5 (1992–94) to 36.5 (2002–04). The college participation rate for African-American women increased 7 percentage points from 37.5 (1992–94) to 44.5 (2002–04) (p. 39).

### College Enrollment

African-American enrollment in higher education rose by 42.7 percent to total more than 1.9 million students between 1993 and 2003. The African-American share of enrollment increased from 10.0 percent in 1993 to 12.0 percent in 2003. African-American women's enrollment increased by 50.4 percent (or more than 424,000 students). African-American men's enrollment increased by 30.4 percent (p. 7).

### College Graduation Rates

- Among students who began in 1995–96, the rate of obtaining a bachelor's degree within five years was 36.4 percent for African-Americans, 42 percent for Hispanics, 58 percent for whites, and 62.3 percent for Asian Americans (pp. 14–15).
- 25.6 percent of African-Americans who began in 1995–96 were still enrolled after five years but did not have a degree. Another 30.1 percent left without a degree. The percent still enrolled but without a degree for Hispanics was 23.6, for Whites 17.8, and for Asian-Americans, 19.2 (p. 14).

In "Comparing Black and White College Enrollment Rates of the High School Class of 2005," the *Journal of Blacks in Higher Education* (JBHE 2007b) reports U.S. Department of Education statistics which show the following for the Spring of 2005:

- 354,000 African-Americans between the ages of 16 and 24 graduated from high school.
- Of these, 201,000, or 56.8 percent, had enrolled in either a two-year or four-year college by October of 2005.
- 1,799,000 white high school students graduated in the spring of 2005.
- Of these, 1,317,000, or 73.2 percent, had enrolled in either a two-year or four-year college by the fall of 2005.

The *Journal* lists several possible reasons for the racial differences in college enrollment immediately after high school:

- Black high school graduates as a group are less prepared academically for college and therefore may choose not to enroll or may have difficulty in gaining admission to the college of their choice.
- The cost of college, the unavailability of adequate financial aid, and the need to get a job to fulfill family financial obligations are all economic factors that might disproportionately reduce the black enrollment rate.
- Blacks, more often than whites, may take a year or two off after completing high school in order to earn money for college. When necessary, whites have been more inclined than blacks to assume debt to pay for their college education and therefore do not delay enrollment.

- High school guidance counselors, parents, and other advisors may steer young blacks away from college.
- Many blacks may continue to believe that because of race discrimination (and social barriers disproportionately affecting blacks), there is no employment opportunity payoff in going to college, particularly a four-year college (p. 43).

To summarize: Academic preparation, college costs, and lack of information as to the benefits of a college education may all be barriers which affect black high school students' decision to go to college.

## African-American Male College Students[130]

In two major works, Michael J. Cuyjet explores the issues related to the retention and graduation of African-American men. The first, *Helping African-American Men Succeed in College*, focuses on the unique difficulties encountered by African-American male college students. The sequel, *African-American Men in College*, continues the discussion and provides specific examples of programs and activities which have been launched on various campuses.

Cuyjet (2006) explores, among other issues, the impact of the skewed African-American male/female ratio on college campuses. His analysis of college enrollment statistics from the *2005 Chronicle of Higher Education Almanac* shows that in 2002 African-American men were outnumbered by African-American women by almost two to one (35.8% men versus 64.2% women). Not only does this create an out-of-balance environment for social dating, but Cuyjet identifies other possible cultural impacts related to the lower number of African-American men on college campuses. He views the absence of African-American men as a missed opportunity to counter often negative stereotypes of African-American men by the dominant culture. Thus students, faculty, staff, and administrators from other racial/ethnic cultures may not have the opportunity to have positive face-to-face interactions with African-American men.

Cuyjet also points out that if a larger percentage of African-American college students on predominately white campuses are athletes, it may be more difficult to promote the perception of African-American men as not only sportsmen but also as scholars, intellectuals, or campus leaders. He suggests that campuses should try to recruit and retain African-American men for academic and leadership reasons, and not just for sports.

Cuyjet identifies a number of possible interventions for the successful recruitment and graduation of African-American men. As an additional comment on the sports issue, Cuyjet suggests that if some African-American male students have internalized perceptions of them-

[130] For insight into issues concerning female African-American students, see Mary F. Howard-Hamilton's (2006) *Meeting the Needs of African-American Women*, and Hrabowski, Maton, Greene, and Greif's (2002) *Overcoming the Odds: Raising Academically Successful African-American Young Women.*

selves as being part of a permanently marginalized population, this may distract energy from their academics as they pursue alternate status-enhancing pursuits, such as sports.

The majority of the chapters in *African-American Men in College* are devoted to strategies aimed at successfully retaining and graduating African-American men. Other chapters explore the circumstances of African-American men at historically black colleges and universities (HBCUs) and at community colleges. The second part of the book profiles a range of programs at large and small institutions to support African-American men on campuses.

## Male Athletes

As previously discussed, 36.4 percent of African-American students who began college in 1995–96 completed a bachelor's degree within five years (Cook and Cordova 2006, pp. 14–15). In her review of African-American male college athletes, Messer (2006) explores the National Collegiate Athletic Association's (NCAA) *2004 Graduation-Rates Report,* which calculates a 48 percent graduation rate for African-American male athletes in 2003. Messer states that even though this rate is higher than the overall graduation rate for African-American college students, it is still a serious problem. Messer provides a comprehensive review of the literature on African-American male student athletes and identifies factors which may inhibit their progress toward degree completion:

- Recruiting students with athletic abilities who may be academically underprepared for college; and/or
- Negative stereotypes and perceptions about college athletes which may diminish African-American student athletes' self-confidence if they are already performing below average in the classroom (p. 168).

Messer identifies academic and social support services which may aid students' progress toward degree completion, such as orientation programs, tutoring, mentoring, and financial support. She adds that these programs must be consistent and continuous throughout all of the college years. More specifically she suggests the following:

- In the recruiting stage, verbally outline the academic obligations and responsibilities of a college student.
- Maintain a continued collaboration between the athletic department and faculty to ensure that students receive the necessary advising and resources from both the athletic and academic departments.
- Employ African-American coaches, faculty, administrators, and staff of color who can serve as role models and potential mentors for African-American students.
- Draw on African-American alumni (and former student athletes) as guest speakers, mentors, and for career connections.

- Require that male athletes get involved in the life of the campus outside of the athletic arena, perhaps in the off-season of their sport (Messer describes a volunteer program which assists the community, under the auspices of the University of Louisville).
- Provide career education for sports-related careers and occupations that use sports expertise such as entertainment law, physical therapy, journalism, or sports writing (p. 169).

Messer points out that in the process of examining factors that help African-American male student *athletes* to be successful in college and graduate, colleges can modify and apply these factors to assist *non-athletes* among African-American students. Messer lists several successful programs at Georgetown University, Fairfield University in Connecticut, the University of Louisville, and Florida State University, as well as successful programs at several historically black colleges and universities (HBCUs).

## Transfer Rates from Community Colleges to Four-Year Colleges

According to the *Digest of Education Statistics*, the 2005 fall enrollment in degree-granting institutions of black students was 2,214,600. Of those, 59.3 percent (1,313,400) were enrolled in four-year institutions and 40.6 percent (901,100) were enrolled in two-year institutions (Snyder, Dillow, and Hoffman 2007, p. 310).

As noted above, these community college students often do not receive services from guidance counselors to help prepare them to transfer to a four-year institution. Henriksen (1995) reported on a study by the Center for the Study of Community Colleges, which surveyed 4,695 community college students. The study found that only 12 to 24 percent of Hispanic and black students later transferred to a four-year college or university, compared to 23 to 32 percent of white students. This study indicates that there is an unmet need to increase the number of black and Hispanic students to transfer to four-year institutions after their initial study at community colleges after high school.

## Financial Aid

As we have already noted, only 18 percent of the black freshmen reported no concerns about financing their college education in 1971, but that figure had increased to 26 percent by 2004. In that same year, only 13 percent of all freshmen in the study had no major concerns about financing their college education (Allen 2005). Thus though college costs were of concern to most students, they were of greater concern to black students.

In the 2003–04 school year, 75.8 percent of black (non-Hispanic) undergraduates and 63.2 percent of all undergraduates received some type of financial aid (Snyder, Tan, and Hoffman 2006, p. 516). It goes without saying that lower family income is more likely to make students dependent on receiving financial aid to begin, and complete, a college education. Marc H. Morial (2007), president and CEO of The National Urban League, has stated that "with a median income of $30,858 and net worth of roughly $6,000, African-American households are at a substantial disadvantage in affording college compared with whites, whose median income is at least $20,000 more a year and whose net worth is 10 times that of blacks."

The College Board (2003) conducted a year-long study on college financial aid, "Challenging Times, Clear Choices." In January of that year, it made the following recommendations which favored a shift from merit-based financial aid to need-based aid:

- Substantially increase Pell Grant funding;
- Improve loan terms for students;
- Assure that growth in merit programs is not at the expense of need-based funding;
- Reaffirm commitment to need-based student aid;
- Improve the design of and increase the funding for federal matching programs for need-based subsidies;
- Simplify the federal financial aid application process;
- Link increases in tuition to increases in need-based aid;
- Increase support for programs providing college success skills;
- Support federal student support services; and
- Support and expand the role of clearinghouses that monitor and report on the success of students (pp. 6–10).

Holsendolph (2005) notes that several Ivy League institutions with large endowments (Yale and Harvard) have eliminated the parent contribution for some lower-income parents of promising students. The authors suggest that experts agree that the increases in enrollments of low-income students will result in larger number of graduates only if new kinds of assistance are found.

TABLE 13.4: **Six-Year Graduation Rate for Students Entering College in Fall 1994**

| Ethnicity | % |
|---|---|
| Asians | 61.1 |
| Whites | 56.9 |
| Blacks | 41.7 |
| Hispanics | 41.7 |
| American Indians | 35.8 |

**SOURCE:** Seidman 2005, p.8

## Retention

The number of African-American students entering college has continued to climb over the years, but their retention rate has remained low. Seidman (2005) provides a comprehensive review of research on minority retention and graduation, including the Consortium for Student Retention Data Exchange's findings for six-year graduation rates of students who began college in Fall 1994 (*see* Table 13.4).

Seidman lists some of the negative consequences of such statistics: lower lifetime earnings, greater health problems, greater involvement with the criminal justice system (as a defendant), and a shorter life expectancy, as compared to college graduates (p. 8).

Vincent Tinto introduced a sociological model for college students who leave college before graduating or "institutional departure" in his article, "Dropouts from Higher Education: A Theoretical Synthesis of the Recent Literature," and later in his book, *Leaving College: Rethinking the Causes and Cures of Student Attrition*. In Tinto's model, the student's personal variables (family background, skill and ability, prior schooling, goals and commitments) interact with institutional experiences (the degree of academic and social involvement and investment) to predict if students will persist in an institution until they complete their degree (Flowers 2004, p. 24). Jones (2001) has identified the following institutional factors that can influence African-American student's decisions not to persist until graduation: a non-inclusive campus culture, perceived racism, low expectations of African-American students by white faculty, lack of African-American staff and administrators, and lack of such faculty to serve as role models. Flowers (2004) provides a review of the research literature on factors that influence African-American college retention using the Tinto model as the overarching theoretical template. He concludes his article with a proposed practitioner model of African-American student retention:

1. ***Assess African-American Students' Pre-enrollment Characteristics, Dispositions, Degree, Intentions, and Aspirations.*** *This initial data collection should occur at least two weeks before the first day of classes. In addition, the following data should be collected: a) student's demographics; b) student's perceptions and expectations of the university environment; and c) student's commitment to the university.*
2. ***Utilize the data.*** *Utilize the assessment data in two ways: a) to make recommendations to student affairs professionals regarding which services are needed to help African-American students with their transitions; and b) to make recommendations to African-American students regarding which existing services and programs are in their best interest.*
3. ***Reassess African-American Students' Pre-enrollment Characteristics, Dispositions, Degree, Intentions, and Aspirations.*** *After the first semester, a follow-up study, similar to the precollege assessment, should be conducted to determine the extent to which students' expectations matched their experiences.*
4. ***Advise African-American Students as to Appropriate Support Services.*** *After the follow-up study, African- American students who are experiencing academic and social problems on campus should be advised to attend relevant support services.*
5. ***Advise African-American Students to Participate in Annual Service and Program Evaluation Studies to Assess their Level of Integration and Involvement on Campus.*** *Given the existing data collected on each student and the great expenditure of human, as well as physical resources, at this time in the process it is important to evaluate the programs and services utilizing multiple methodologies to explore the total benefit of the programmatic effort for each African-American student.*

6. ***Provide Additional Support to Meet African-American Students Needed Academic and Social Goals.*** *At this point in the student's college career, academic support services should continue to meet the needs of each individual student. As such, additional support should be provided to all African-American students who are still experiencing academic and social problems on campus.* (p. 31–33)

The ACT survey report, *What Works in Student Retention?*[131] summarizes the current state of affairs in retention practices and concerns among over 1,000 colleges and universities (Alberts 2006). The report contains a five-page review, "Programs with Greatest Impact on Retention" and eighty-two retention interventions which have been used and are rated by the institutions surveyed. Advising program strategies were the most highly rated. Alberts (2006) advises, "If you are looking for a short cut to the starting point of a long and potentially fruitful journey to improved student retention, begin with *What Works in Student Retention?*"

## Summary

There is no doubt that black students are attending college in greater numbers than ever before. But lower scores on standardized tests and the Advanced Placement exams—for whatever reason—indicate that there is more work to be done.

There needs to be more, and earlier, outreach to black students (and minority students generally) to provide the motivation to consider going to college; to explain that financial aid is available; and to bring them to campus to introduce them to the culture of the higher education community. Using minority students as recruiters or as "ambassadors" in school visits is also a technique which has proven its value.

Since studies, referred to above, have shown that fewer black and Hispanic students transfer from community colleges to four-year schools, there also needs to be a greater effort to improve articulation between community colleges and four-year institutions.

Chapters 5 and 6 discuss efforts by various institutions to develop holistic methods of assessment, so that students who do not "test well" can prove their value in other ways.

Finally, admissions officers must work in concert with student affairs officers and with upper levels of the administration to further all the above initiatives. These efforts are necessary both in order to further the education of the students involved and to ensure, as Justice O'Connor hoped in *Grutter v. Bollinger*, that people of talent, without regard to race or ethnicity, will be able to participate in the civic life of the nation.

[131] See <www.act.org/path/policy/reports/retain.html>.

/ CHAPTER FOURTEEN /

*by Esther B. Hugo, Ed.D.*
*Coordinator of Student Outreach*
*Santa Monica College*

*Alicia Ortega, M.S.*
*Assistant Director of Admissions*
*Oregon State University*

14

# Hispanic Students: Recruitment and Retention

The Hispanic population of the United States is a large and growing as well as challenging and multi-faceted one. Devising effective outreach, recruitment, and retention strategies for such a demographic requires an understanding of Hispanic students and their cultures.

## Demographics

The U.S. Census Bureau (2006b) uses the terms "Hispanic" and "Latino" interchangeably to refer to persons of any race who are of Mexican, Puerto Rican, Cuban, Central or South American, Dominican, Spanish, or other Hispanic descent. A 2002 survey by the Pew Hispanic Center (2004) indicates that more than half of Latino immigrants surveyed have no preference as to which term is used to describe their ethnicity (p. 3), and accordingly, the terms "Hispanic" and "Latino" will be used interchangeably throughout this chapter.

In 2005, the Latino population on the U.S. mainland was composed primarily of Mexican Americans (64%), Puerto Ricans (10%), Cubans (3%), Salvadorans (3%), and Dominicans (3%). The remainder are of some other Central American, South American, or Hispanic origin (17%) (U.S. Census Bureau 2006a). With this broad array of backgrounds, it is difficult to generalize about the customs and needs of all Hispanics with regard to higher education.

However, it is unquestioned that the Hispanic population is the largest and fastest-growing ethnic group in the United States, and that the pace of growth shows no signs of slowing. In 2005, U.S. Census Bureau (2005a) data reports estimated that the total Hispanic population in the U.S. was 42.7 million self-identifying Hispanics, constituting 14 percent of the nation's total population.[132]

Between 1990 and 2000, the Hispanic population increased 57.9 percent, compared to a nationwide rate of growth of 13.2 percent (U.S. Census Bureau 2001). The most recent population projections predict that by 2050 the Latino population will total roughly 102.6 million people, or 24 percent, of the entire U.S. population (U.S. Census Bureau 2004a). These statistics have major implications for the nation's 4,321 degree-granting colleges and universities.[133]

The fact that the Hispanic population has a higher proportion of people under 18 than other U.S. sub-populations is particularly significant for the higher education community. Recent census data show that more than one-third of the Hispanic population is younger than 18 years of age, compared to approximately one-fourth of the total population (U.S. Census Bureau 2002). Because of the growing numbers of Hispanic students, recruitment of this population for higher education is poised to become one of the most important public policy initiatives in the 21st century.

## Recruitment Challenges

There are many challenges in developing a successful recruitment plan targeting Hispanic students. One major obstacle is the comparatively low level of Hispanic student persistence in K–12 programs, at least as of this writing. In the United States, Hispanic students have the highest drop-out rate of all ethnic groups, with only 57.0 percent of all Hispanics graduating from high school in 2002 compared to 84.4 percent for whites (U.S. Census Bureau 2003). Thus, although the overall population numbers indicate booming growth in the Hispanic population, the Hispanic *college bound* population is not following suit. According to a 2004 Pew Hispanic Center report, only 53 percent of Hispanics are considered "minimally qualified" for admission to a four-year college, and as of 2002 only 24.9 percent of Hispanic high school graduates ages 18 to 21 were in fact enrolled in college, as opposed to a rate of 45.9 percent for whites (Swail, Cabrera, and Lee 2004; U.S. Census Bureau 2004b). In terms of sheer numbers then, Hispanic enrollment in postsecondary education has increased, but Hispanics remain underrepresented in higher education (Fry 2003).

132 In the fall of 2006, the U.S. Department of Education announced new categories of racial and ethnic reporting to be used for data collecting across various federal agencies and for various purposes, including completion of the Integrated Postsecondary Education Data System surveys. See Chapter 12, "Low-Income Students: Outreach and Retention," footnote 122 (on page 188), for an explanation of the full classification scheme. Here it suffices to note that Hispanic/Latino is a category which can include many races, and is not further broken down into "black Hispanic," "white Hispanic," or any other composite category of Hispanic.

133 As reported by June (2006b), the 2006 version of the Carnegie classifications includes 4,321 colleges and universities, up from 3,856 in 2000. "An additional 60 institutions were not classified in the revision because their degree data were incomplete, or the institution was too new to have produced any graduates...."

These statistics raise the question: Why is recruiting Hispanic students important and why should enrollment managers care? The first and most obvious answer is that there is a growing pool of prospective students for colleges to draw from. But there is also the larger ethical and cultural perspective to consider. As the U.S. Hispanic population continues to grow, that growth will inevitably have an impact on campus climate, and on society at large. Enrollment managers who have a proactive strategy in place now will help to establish their institutions as welcoming and culturally sensitive. However, the strategy must be realistic; it must clearly take into account both the objectives and the resources necessary to recruit and retain Hispanic students.

An effective enrollment management strategy involves several components: understanding the student body, analyzing marketing messages, identifying recruitment populations and enrollment patterns, and researching the best use of campus facilities.

The recruitment strategies begin with *outreach*, a concept which involves both reaching students and families in their community and demystifying the college admission process. An effective outreach program requires significant institutional support in the form of both finances and staff, since prospective students, particularly Hispanic students, prefer and respond best to direct, personalized outreach contacts—a shoe-leather approach that makes an unfamiliar and complex college admission process more personal and less scary (The College Board 1999).

### Outreach Strategies

This personalized approach involves reaching students and families in their schools and communities. A successful model developed at Santa Monica College involves the use of a team of counselors who dedicate regularly scheduled admissions counseling services to feeder high schools to accomplish various related goals: helping students establish an early connection to college; facilitating the students' transition to college; providing exposure to test preparation and course selection, thereby ensuring proper placement; and disseminating feedback to the schools on student achievement. In addition, counselors assist students with completion of financial aid forms, as well as with the selection of course schedules aligned with student goals. The entire prospect-to-applicant-to-first-time-student process is broken down into a series of tasks, thereby helping to create a seamless transition.

Some institutions have found success in outreach programs by partnering with other campus departments or community organizations. The Office of Admissions at Oregon State University, a suburban land-grant institution, has partnered with the federally-funded College Assistance Migrant Program (CAMP) as a way to reach students in more rural or agriculturally based communities throughout the state.[134] CAMP and admissions staff mem-

[134] The College Assistance Migrant Program (CAMP) is a program of the U.S. Department of Education (ED 2007b) which "assists students who are migratory or seasonal farmworkers (or children of such workers) enrolled in their first year of undergraduate studies at an IHE [institution of higher education]. The funding supports completion of the first year of studies.... The program serves approximately 2,400 CAMP participants

bers coordinate joint visitations to high schools and community centers to promote the benefits of college attendance, and to explain financial aid in English and Spanish. Many of these visits take place in the evening with the assistance of local migrant education or TRIO program coordinators.[135]

## Middle School Programs

It is important to begin the college choice process early, and one successful program features exposure to the college admission process through an experiential program called *Camp College*, in which a consortium of schools representing all segments of higher education sponsors day-long campus visits on Saturdays for Hispanic middle school students and their families.

In furtherance of this program, community colleges, state schools, and private universities collaborated to develop a curriculum of college information, complete with bilingual support and cultural experiences, so that students can experience college life for a day. Links to career opportunities and courses of study are emphasized, and students maintain a written journal of their experiences. The visits culminate in a campus tour with a hosted lunch. At the community college, students earned a unit of credit for their study of higher education options. The program has been funded through grants from local education agencies and associations.

It is vital to involve students and families in recruitment of Hispanic students, as family is a critical part of the college decision-making process. Effective outreach strategies have included forming alliances with local churches, which attract large numbers of Hispanic families. To boost Hispanic recruitment, churches publish college announcements in their bulletins and provide space for colleges to conduct information sessions and application workshops (in the church hall, for example). A bilingual counselor, armed with bilingual publications, can easily respond to concerns from students and their families. The message is clear: We are sensitive to your culture and we want your student to enroll. Community colleges, with their open enrollment status, may also encourage parents to return to school for a degree, or to take classes for job enhancement and English language development.

## High School Programs

The high school coursework completed by Hispanic students tends to be less rigorous than the coursework completed by their peers. Within the discipline of mathematics, for example, over 58 percent of Hispanic students ended their math education with geometry, as compared to 41 percent of white students and 44 percent of all students (Swail, Cabrera, and Lee 2004). The importance of a strong high school curriculum is validated by recent research

annually." Services include financial aid stipends, skills workshops, health services, tutoring, counseling, and housing assistance for eligible students during their first year of college. "Limited follow-up services are provided to participants after their first year."

135 "The Federal TRIO Programs are educational opportunity outreach programs designed to motivate and support students from disadvantaged backgrounds. TRIO includes six outreach and support programs targeted to serve and assist low-income, first-generation college students, and students with disabilities to progress through the academic pipeline from middle school to postbaccalaureate programs. TRIO also includes a training program for directors and staff of TRIO projects..." (ED 2007c).

that says that the intensity and quality of a student's high school curriculum is the strongest influence in terms of bachelor's degree completion (Adelman 1999). The research also says that Hispanic students who complete a high school mathematics course beyond Algebra 2 increase their bachelor's degree attainment rate from 61 percent to 79 percent. The rigor and successful completion of an academic program has significant ramifications for Hispanic students (Adelman 2006).

Santa Monica College, a public community college located in Southern California, includes several academic offerings along with its extensive outreach services. In several majority-Hispanic high schools, the college offers college-level classes in an after-school format for students. The courses are offered at no cost to the students, and students gain exposure to college-level work in a convenient, familiar setting. Students are able to start their college careers while they are still in high school, thereby demonstrating to four-year colleges that, as high school students, they are capable of college-level work. The world of college becomes less threatening, and students enhance their academic profile by earning both high school and college credit.

Popular courses of study include speech, psychology, dance, and other visual and performing arts classes. For students in schools where elective and supplemental academic opportunities are often meager, such as inner-city schools, the program provides substance and academic capital (Hugo 2001). The more quickly students gain access to challenging courses, the more likely they are to complete a degree program (The Education Trust 1999). Academic offerings combined with counseling support services provide a strong network for Hispanic students new to college.

Another example of a successful high school program is the Oregon Leadership Institute (OLI). OLI is a cooperative program funded by the Oregon Council for Hispanic Advancement (OCHA) in the Portland metropolitan area. OLI serves Hispanic high school students, grades 9–12. Students apply for the opportunity to participate in a six-month program with a neighboring college one Saturday each month. Students are placed into small groups where they work with college student mentors. The focus of OLI is on overall leadership development, with special emphasis placed on higher education and cultural identity. Each monthly workshop provides students with the academic skills, coping mechanisms, and social support necessary to complete high school and plan for the future.

### High School Recruitment

In the first decade of the 21st century, Hispanic students in high school represent 14 percent of the current school population in grades 9–12. By the year 2010, Hispanics will constitute about 20 percent of the high school population—and almost 50 percent of Hispanic high school students are enrolled in urban schools (U.S. Census Bureau 2000, Table 5). Consequently urban schools serve as excellent sites for Hispanic high school recruitment. Outreach personnel can offer personalized attention to students by first establishing a relationship with local school site personnel. The relationship-building leads to the development of prospects who are moved through the recruitment and enrollment processes. Pool development begins with application workshops, which can be conducted at high schools, in churches, and at local community centers.

Effective outreach programs take students through all stages of the process: applying, testing, and enrolling. These steps are referred to in the literature as the "pipeline steps." Research conducted by Alexander, Pallas, and Holupka (1987) revealed that academic preparation for college was more important than socio-economic status in achieving college enrollment. The researchers found that completion of what is referred to as the "pipeline steps" played a key role in eliminating the disparity in college preparation rates between low socio-economic status (SES) high school graduates and their middle- and upper-SES counterparts—an important consideration since many Hispanic students come from low-income families.

Strategic activities that have proven effective in getting Hispanic students into the college pipeline include application workshops, assessment administration (administering the required entry-level placement tests in mathematics and English), financial aid workshops, and classroom visitations. Classroom presentations are particularly effective in recruiting Hispanic students in urban schools, since students hear the college "message" in a familiar setting in which they are comfortable asking questions, and the message may be subsequently validated and reinforced by the classroom teacher.

Another strategy involves the identification of prospects through use of the Preliminary Scholastic Aptitude Test (PSAT) or through ACT's College Readiness Test for 10th graders, known as PLAN. (Either test can also be used by the high school as a springboard for discussions about career preparation, generally.) Hispanic students, who have a traditionally low college-going rate, might take the PSAT or PLAN as a part of a district-wide or school-wide initiative. For a variety of reasons, Hispanic students might not consider themselves college-eligible. Identifying students through their exam scores is one method to reach students early in the process, and to enroll them in challenging coursework that will better prepare them for college. Outreach programs that have established relationships with counselors in schools with Hispanic students can work together to identify college-eligible students.

## Marketing

A comprehensive communication plan developed in connection with the college's marketing department maintains regular contact between the college and the student through all stages of the admission process—from the initial point of contact to after an application has been submitted. Messages to students should be crafted to be appropriate to the student's level in school and to the stage of the admission process.

Although many first-generation Hispanic students of high school age are native English speakers, many of their family members or influencers may not be. For many American Hispanics, the Spanish language stands as a symbol of difference for them, regardless of their country of origin or generational status. Spanish is a key to their individual and collective pasts (Sonderup 2006). As a result, many students have the additional responsibility of assisting their families in understanding any English language information that comes into the home, including college recruitment materials.

From a marketing perspective, there is an increasing emphasis by retail and consumer groups (ranging from Ford Motor Company to *People Magazine*, with its Spanish-language edition) on Spanish language marketing; and higher education is no different. Many colleges are now segmenting their marketing efforts with this fact in mind: that in order to successfully recruit Latino students, they must also recruit Latino families. Research shows that while Hispanics consume every type of media, they do seem to have a special attraction to television and radio (Sonderup 2006). When asked about general advertising effectiveness, 38 percent of Hispanics surveyed found English language ads less effective than Spanish ads in terms of recall, and 70 percent less effective than Spanish ads in terms of persuasion. Many younger and acculturated Latinos mix languages into a form of "Spanglish," in which they speak English peppered with Spanish words. But when it comes to selling, 56 percent of Latino adults respond best to advertising when it is presented in Spanish (Sonderup 2006).

This dual language concept poses a challenge for many colleges and universities in terms of marketing their institution. The decision to provide culturally appropriate translations and selecting what (if any) publications or services will be provided bilingually can become a major resource issue. However, publications that are translated into Spanish send a clear message of welcome and support. For example, colleges can use mass phone communication systems to recruit applicants; messages are delivered in both English and Spanish, thereby informing and involving the parents in the college admission process.

## Families and Student Decision Making

Family and parental support are critical in the college attendance decision-making process, as is the student's own initiative in exploring and deciding on college options. Research indicates that the home is an important source of information for students involved in the college choice process (McDonough 1997). Chapman (1981) found that among all college-bound students of traditional age, the most important factors influencing college choice were socioeconomic status, "influential people" (parents, counselors, friends), and fixed variables such as campus location and cost.

The impact of "influential people" holds especially true in the recruitment of Hispanic students, as Hispanic parents tend to be less knowledgeable concerning the higher education process (Zarate and Pachon 2006). Consequently many Hispanic students might benefit from a more proactive outreach approach, in which the complex college admission process is broken down into a series of manageable tasks facilitated by the outreach counselor. Colleges might consider hosting evening events in such already familiar settings as community centers or schools to help make the "ivory tower" idea of college seem more accessible, and to provide an opportunity for college recruitment personnel to share information in a setting which is comfortable for the students and their families.

Another key recruitment strategy might include staffing information tables at community fairs and centers, adult schools and centers, youth centers, and job skill development centers.

## Community Outreach

Hispanic young adults have a high labor force participation rate and many attend community colleges on a part-time basis (Saenz 2002), which suggests that it is critical to explore the recruitment potential of this non-traditional student group. Community-centered college and career fairs are a viable outreach option; locations and institutions for such recruitment can be as diverse as adult schools, youth centers, housing projects, and community agencies. The community's needs in key areas such as job retraining, part-time college participation, financial assistance, and adult education can be met through the college's ability to offer affordable, flexible, and short-term programs.

Recruitment strategies in this area could include presentations that specifically target vocational education students, presentations at church youth/adult groups, and coordination with existing workforce and economic development programs.

## Technology and Access

The development of online application processes and the implementation of computerized testing should be balanced by a commitment to minimize any potential negative impact on Hispanic student applications and enrollment—especially, those negative impacts which can arise from a student's lack of Internet access in the home.[136] The "digital divide" is thus a real challenge which institutions must consider when implementing technological changes (Tornatsky, Macias, and Jones 2002).

In particular, Hispanic students with limited access to technology need adequate and equitable alternative sources of college information and services.

One area of concern raised by the increasing use of technology-based shortcuts is that of unintentional bias, especially in relation to online submission of applications. At Oregon State University, nearly 90 percent of the 2005 applicant pool submitted applications online (Oregon State University 2006), and as a result the production of paper applications has all but ceased. The OSU online application (like the online applications at many schools) requires that students have ready access to a computer, and also have a credit card for payment of the application fee. Students needing to use a fee waiver or deferral have no choice but to submit a paper application. The message this sends to students can be discouraging. Colleges must make sure they take all necessary precautions to ensure that they are not creating additional

[136] In a study exploring how Hispanics can benefit from the expansion of information technology, Tornatzky, Macias, and Jones (2002) determined that while national computer ownership rates had increased, significant disparities persist across ethnic and socioeconomic lines. In particular, the same study found, Hispanics tend to have less Internet access at home, as opposed to in school and library settings.

barriers for students wishing to apply to their institution, but who may have limited access to technology.

Finally, in using technology in recruitment, admissions, orientation, and testing, it is important to remain appropriately sensitive to language barriers. As an example, it is helpful not only to emphasize campus strengths in key areas relevant to prospective Hispanic students, but to provide Spanish-language alternatives in relation to key pages and procedures.

## Financial Aid Processes

A survey conducted by Zarate and Pachon (2006) indicates that awareness of financial aid options is often lacking in the Hispanic community, and this lack of awareness has an impact on college attendance. The survey findings reveal that knowledge about financial aid is a key predictor in determining the likelihood of college attendance among various ethnic groups.

The results of the survey indicated that many Hispanic families are not planning for college prior to the end of high school, and that more than two-thirds of Hispanic parents did not receive financial aid information while their child was in high school. The results of this survey further indicated that nearly 65 percent of Hispanic families prefer to learn about financial aid from face-to-face interactions, such as workshops or meetings with high school or college personnel.

The implications of this study are clear. It is not sufficient for college recruitment personnel to provide admissions information without any connection to financial aid information. Rather, financial aid processes and procedures must be presented as part of every interaction with students and their families. The most effective strategy is to offer personalized assistance to students and families as they complete the complex financial aid forms. One college had success in its recruitment efforts when it hosted weekend financial aid workshops and invited parents via bilingual invitations. Schools and colleges worked together, and schools provided address labels with "to the Parents of" in the student address.

College recruitment personnel should also be responsible for dispelling some myths regarding college scholarships and financial aid programs. For example, many students have "heard" from a young age that simply because they are Hispanic, they will automatically receive some type of special assistance. With increased scrutiny of race-based programs becoming an emerging trend (Schmidt 2006), however, scholarship administration has changed at many universities nationwide. Thus, it is important that institutions be open about the types and amounts of aid available. Just because someone in the family fifteen years ago earned a "minority student scholarship" does not mean that program exists in the same form today.

## Case Study: Benefits of Gaining Title V Status

Colleges with growing populations of Hispanic students may be eligible for federal funding by becoming a Hispanic-Serving Institution (HSI) under the provisions of federal law, specifically Title V of the *Higher Education Act of 1965*, as amended. An HSI is defined as an institution that has an Hispanic enrollment constituting at least 25 percent of its undergraduate full-time equivalent student enrollment, and that "provides assurances that not less than 50 percent of [its] Hispanic students are low-income individuals" (House 1998, p. 187). This federally-funded program assists institutions of higher education in expanding their capacity to serve Hispanic and low-income students.[137] Title V funds may be used for renovation of instructional facilities, faculty development, laboratory or other scientific equipment, administrative management, development of academic programs, counseling, student support, and tutoring (HACU 2002).

Effective strategies to maximize service to Hispanic students according to Title V criteria have included additional counseling, parent education workshops, dual enrollment classes, a designated financial aid counselor, community outreach, and bilingual publications.

In order to achieve HSI funding status, Santa Monica College—a public community college of 32,000 students in Southern California—developed a strategic plan to communicate the college-going process to Hispanic students and parents, remaining sensitive to differences in language, culture, and college-going familiarity. The operating principle was to achieve a balance between high-quality mass communication and high-quality personal communication. Students needed (and received) information about college in a variety of pre-existing formats—flyers, brochures, podcasts, phone calls, and mailers. But they also needed a personalized connection with a college admission officer with knowledge of the culture and community to customize the interaction (McDonough 1997).

At Santa Monica College, the Hispanic student population stood at about 22 percent for several years, when administrators decided to provide resources to position Santa Monica College as an advocate and resource for Hispanic students. The decision to make Santa Monica College a Hispanic-Serving Institution resulted in the hiring of bilingual outreach personnel, and in the placement of outreach counselors in schools with high concentrations of Hispanic student enrollment.

Counselors made presentations to English as a Second Language classes, conducted group presentations, participated in college fairs, and established a regular presence in the school counseling offices. Counselors staffed information tables in community centers and churches and conducted application workshops for undocumented students. Counselors also encouraged student interaction by working as cyber counselors and frequently communicated via e-mail. One counselor reflected, "The students that I kept in contact with, stayed on. It helped them maintain their link to the college." In addition, a financial aid counselor assisted students and families in completing financial aid forms. Overall, counselors worked to create

[137] The Hispanic Association of Colleges and Universities (HACU) is a national educational association with 450 non-profit, accredited institutional members, located in the United States and Puerto Rico (plus Latin America and Spain). See <www.hacu.net>. HACU includes more institutional members than are defined by the U.S. Department of Education as HSIs. HACU states that "Listing as an 'HSI' by HACU does not 'certify' an institution as an HSI for Title V or other Federal grant purposes" (HACU 2007).

a sense of urgency about the college admission process, and a record number of Hispanic students enrolled in the college.

At the conclusion of the 18-month program of recruitment, Santa Monica College achieved its Title V designation and was awarded a multi-million dollar grant. Monies from the grant have been used to establish a "Welcome Center" on campus—a one-stop center for new students to access admissions, counseling, financial aid, extended opportunity programs and services, and cashier services all in one location. Outreach counselors assisted students in building a 12-unit schedule consistent with student achievement level. Student concerns were addressed in a one-stop model that was completely student-centered and personalized.

In addition to counselors, the Welcome Center features Student Ambassadors who are extremely effective and efficient in directing new students to the different stations, offering assistance with college online services, conducting campus tours, answering basic questions, and phoning students about upcoming deadlines.

Moreover, learning communities and summer bridge programs provided an academic component to the student services. The program resulted in more students receiving financial aid, the creation of academic communities for new students, increased faculty collaboration, and higher number of full-time equivalent students among first-time students. Although the Hispanic-Serving Institution grant was written for Hispanic students, all students at Santa Monica College have benefited from the Title V status of the college.

## Case Study: Increasing Latino Enrollment on a Mostly-Caucasian Campus

While reports show that almost half of all college-bound Hispanic students enroll in Hispanic Serving Institutions (HACU 1997), reaching out to the Hispanic population has become a priority at many other institutions across the country. Oregon State University (OSU) is one example of a campus that is trying to gain a presence in the Hispanic community. OSU is a predominantly white, land-grant research university in suburban Oregon. The number of Latino students enrolling has nearly doubled in the past decade, but has yet to reach the institution's goal of reflecting the state's overall Hispanic population. Current data shows that 9.9 percent of Oregonians are Hispanic, while OSU's Hispanic population is 3.8 percent of the total student body (Oregon State University 2006).

In 2001, the university's enrollment management unit brought together key stakeholders from both the campus and the outside Hispanic community to discuss what institutional investments needed to be made in order to effectively recruit, retain, and graduate Hispanic students. This workgroup, named the Hispanic Initiative Group, began by establishing monthly meetings to discuss key areas of community concern and student recruitment. Representatives from the Latino student cultural center (the Centro Cultural Cesar Chavez), the newly established College Assistance Migrant Program, the Casa Educational Minority Education Office, the Educational Opportunity Program, prominent Hispanic leaders, and student affairs staff from areas such as Admissions and Financial Aid formed the initial work group. Slowly, other units like University Marketing and OSU Orientation were brought in to serve in an advisory capacity, since they were also preparing to launch a Spanish-language marketing campaign and a bilingual parent orientation program, respectively. The university had many things working in its favor, primarily a committed leadership in the administration, existing grass-roots efforts, and an open line of communication with the Hispanic community.

Growth in the Hispanic student population from approximately 400 students in 1996 to 732 in 2006 is a result of significant work and careful planning (Oregon State University 2006). Prior preparation is essential: "If you build it, they will come." Not vice versa (*i.e.*, waiting until after they've come, to build it!) Many institutions fail to effectively recruit Hispanic students if they do not have the student support services and campus infrastructure necessary to help Hispanic students in their transition before they even set foot on campus. Institutions must invest and prioritize resources if they want to be successful in the Hispanic market. It is not simply enough to have a general multicultural center; it is also about having a diverse and/or culturally competent faculty, dedicated support services, and a welcoming campus climate. Losing a student for the wrong reasons can derail an expensive ad campaign immediately, and the damage to reputation in communities can take years to repair. On the other hand, a handful of happy and successful students can effectively recruit and promote an institution for years to come. Family and neighborhood ties are invaluable.

One key area of success for Hispanic students at Oregon State University is the cultural support resource center or Centro Cultural Cesar Chavez ("The 4 Cs"). Like many student cultural centers across the nation, it has a few key components: it is a place to study and reconnect with other students, and it is a home for resources which include a cultural reference library, pertinent art, and visible and active faculty and staff members to serve as role models and mentors. The 4 C's also has space to cook and prepare meals (critical since kitchens and food are key in Hispanic culture as a way of bringing people together), a television/radio to watch Spanish-language programming (which may not be openly available or accepted in community areas of residence halls), and computers for academic work. The overwhelming theme is that here, students can still "be who they are" on a predominantly Caucasian/English-speaking campus.

## Recommendations

For most institutions there is much work to be done to develop or improve their strategies to recruit Hispanic students. Here are just a few items that enrollment managers should consider:

- *Assess your current campus climate.* Is your institution ready (and willing?) to support Hispanic students? Work with your institution's marketing department to survey current Hispanic students in focus groups. Enrollment managers can utilize that information to fine-tune recruitment messages and identify areas on campus (programming, facilities) that may need improvement prior to implementation of a Hispanic recruitment initiative.

- *Determine what resources are currently allocated or available to use for the recruitment of Hispanic students.* Many successful initiatives begin by developing a partnership with other departments which work with early outreach or retention. For example, Oregon State University's University Housing and Dining Services created Multicultural Intern positions (MCI) for bilingual first-year students as a stepping stone into the Resident Advisor positions for second-year students. This program served as a positive and double-sided recruitment tool: it offered students a stipend and it encouraged a more diverse population to choose on-campus housing. Working with your institutional leadership to identify and develop support programs and services for Hispanic students across campus ensures larger buy-in and success.
- *Encourage the development of cultural competence among staff.* As part of a full-campus partnership and Hispanic recruitment initiative, develop culturally competent staff members who can address the issues and needs of Hispanic students and families. At traditional campuses, staff may not fully understand the additional issues Hispanic students face, such as the pressure to work, have children, and provide for their family back home. In many Hispanic families, college is seen as a luxury or not a priority, and there is often pressure to stay close to home or live at the family home and serve as a caregiver. These additional priorities may interfere with the student's academic work. Holding ongoing staff trainings, sharing the results of student focus groups, and engaging successful Hispanic students in your outreach and recruitment efforts (panels, visits, etc.) promotes shared success. Stay connected with the families of current Hispanic students and be aware of how their students are doing on your campus. They hold you and therefore the institution responsible for the success of their student.

The nation's success lies in evoking the full potential of all its citizens. This chapter offers suggestions for good practice for any institution wishing to serve all its students—Hispanic and non-Hispanic—effectively.

/ CHAPTER FIFTEEN /

*by Mark Mitsui, M.Ed.*
*Vice President of Student Services*
*South Seattle Community College*
*Stephen Bischoff, M.B.A.*
*Retention Counselor*
*Asian American and Pacific Islander Student Center*
*Washington State University*

15

# Asian Pacific American Students:
## Recruitment and Retention

Asian Americans and Pacific Americans (collectively, APAs) are two of the fastest growing populations in the United States.[138] This diverse population encompasses people with roots of origin in locations as diverse as India, Hawaii, Korea, Samoa, China, and Pakistan. Many languages, cultures, and levels of prior family engagement with higher education are represented within this population.

Unfortunately, the "model minority" stereotype, which developed in the 1960s as a political wedge against African-Americans, continues to affect APA students adversely. On the one hand, this stereotype sometimes works to hold successful Asian Pacific American students to higher levels of academic achievement than white students, and on the other hand, it denies targeted support to APA students who may be struggling financially or educationally. Acknowledging the presence and impact of the "Model Minority" myth is critical to understanding and developing effective polices for recruiting and retaining Asian Pacific American students at both ends of the socioeconomic spectrum.

[138] Although the next section of this chapter will draw a distinction between "Asian Americans" and "Americans from the Pacific Islands," in order to pinpoint the far-flung origins of these groups, we will otherwise generally refer in this chapter—other than in the next section and in the tables referring to "Educational Attainment"—to "Asian-Pacific Americans," or APAs, as a term encompassing both groups.

## A Diverse Community

The Asian Pacific American (APA) population in the United States is diverse, dynamic, and growing. Understanding the diversity of this population is one important key to effectively recruiting and retaining APA students.

### Origins and Cultures

According to Reeves and Bennett (2003), "'Asian' refers to those having origins in any of the original peoples of the Far East, Southeast Asia, or the Indian subcontinent including, for example, Cambodia, China, India, Japan, Korea, Malaysia, Pakistan, the Philippine Islands, Thailand, and Vietnam. 'Pacific Islander' refers to those having origins in any of the original peoples of Hawaii, Guam, Samoa, or other Pacific islands" (p. 1).[139]

The Asian American population in the United States is largely concentrated among five groups: Asian Indian, Chinese, Filipino, Korean, and Vietnamese. These five groups account for 10 million Asians in the U.S., or about 80 percent of the American Asian population (Reeves and Bennett 2004, p. 4).

The Pacific Islander population is of Polynesian, Micronesian, and/or Melanesian origin.[140] The native populations of Hawaii, Samoa, and Guam account for approximately three-quarters of the total Pacific Islander population in the United States.

### Size of Population

The Asian and Pacific Islander populations in the United States are two of the fastest growing populations in the United States today. There are approximately 13.5 million U.S. residents identified as "Asian" and nearly 960,000 identified as "Native Hawaiian and Other Pacific Islanders." From 2000 to 2003, the Asian population grew 12.5 percent, and the Native Hawaiians and Other Pacific Islanders grew 5.8 percent. By comparison, the growth rate of the total U.S. population was 3.3 percent (U.S. Census Bureau 2004).

### Recency of Immigration

The length of residence of the various groups varies significantly within the APA population. There are Japanese and Chinese American families which have been in the United States for multiple generations. Other groups, such as Laotian Americans or the Hmong, arrived more recently. Of course, Native Hawaiians and other Pacific Islanders are, for the most part, the original peoples of Hawaii and the other Pacific Islands.

[139] Reeves and Bennett (2004) identify eleven Asian groups that comprise at least one percent each of the total Asian population in the United States: Asian Indian, Cambodian, Chinese, Filipino, Hmong, Japanese, Korean, Laotian, Pakistani, Thai, and Vietnamese (p. 2).

[140] Groups comprising the Pacific Islander population include those from Fiji, Guam (including its indigenous inhabitants, the Chomorros), the Marshall Islands, Native Hawaiians, Samoans, Tongans, and Other Pacific Islanders.

### Geographic Distribution within the United States

Reeves and Bennett (2003) point to a high concentration of APAs in the West and in metropolitan areas. About 50 percent of the Asian Pacific American population live in the West, 19 percent in the South, 12 percent in the Midwest, and 19 percent in the Northeast. Ninety-five percent live in metropolitan areas (p. 2).

### Level of Education, by Sub-Group

In addition to geographic variation, there is also a wide variation in educational attainment (*see* Figure 15.1, on page 238). Asian Americans (representing the first component of the two-part APA population) are almost twice as likely as the total population to hold a bachelor's degree (44% as opposed to 24%).

At the same time, many other Asian Americans have less than a high school education. That is true of nearly 60 percent of Hmong, 53 percent of Cambodians, and nearly half of the Laotian population in the United States (Reeves and Bennett 2004, p. 12).

American students of Pacific Island extraction have a high school graduation rate comparable to that of non-APAs (78% as opposed to 80% for the population at large), but they have a lower level of bachelor degree attainment than the total population (13.8% as opposed to 24.4%) (Harris and Jones 2005, p. 12).

### Socioeconomic Diversity

The diversity within the APA population also extends to economic status. While APAs are more likely than non-Hispanic whites to have incomes of seventy-five thousand dollars or more, others in the APA category are more likely than whites to have incomes of less than twenty-five thousand dollars (Reeves and Bennett 2003, p. 6). The median family income for Pacific Islanders ($45,500 in 1999) is slightly below the national average for all families ($50,000 in 1999) (Harris and Jones 2005, p. 16). And the poverty rate (17.7%) is higher among Pacific Islander families than for all families (12.4%) (p. 17).

### Language Spoken at Home

The APA population is culturally and linguistically dynamic, due to factors such as immigration. According to Reeves and Bennett, 69 percent of all APAs were born outside the U.S. However, there is considerable variation among Asian American sub-groups: only 40 percent of Japanese Americans are foreign born, as opposed to 75 percent of those of Thai, Pakistani, Korean, Vietnamese, or Asian Indian origin (p. 9). Moreover, the majority of Asian Americans who were born outside the U.S. came to this country within the past twenty years (p. 10). By contrast, 80 percent of the Pacific Islander population are U.S. natives, while of those who were foreign-born, 44 percent came to the U.S. in the 1990s (Harris and Jones 2005, pp. 9–10).

FIGURE 15.1

Educational Attainment of APA Population, Age 25 or Older

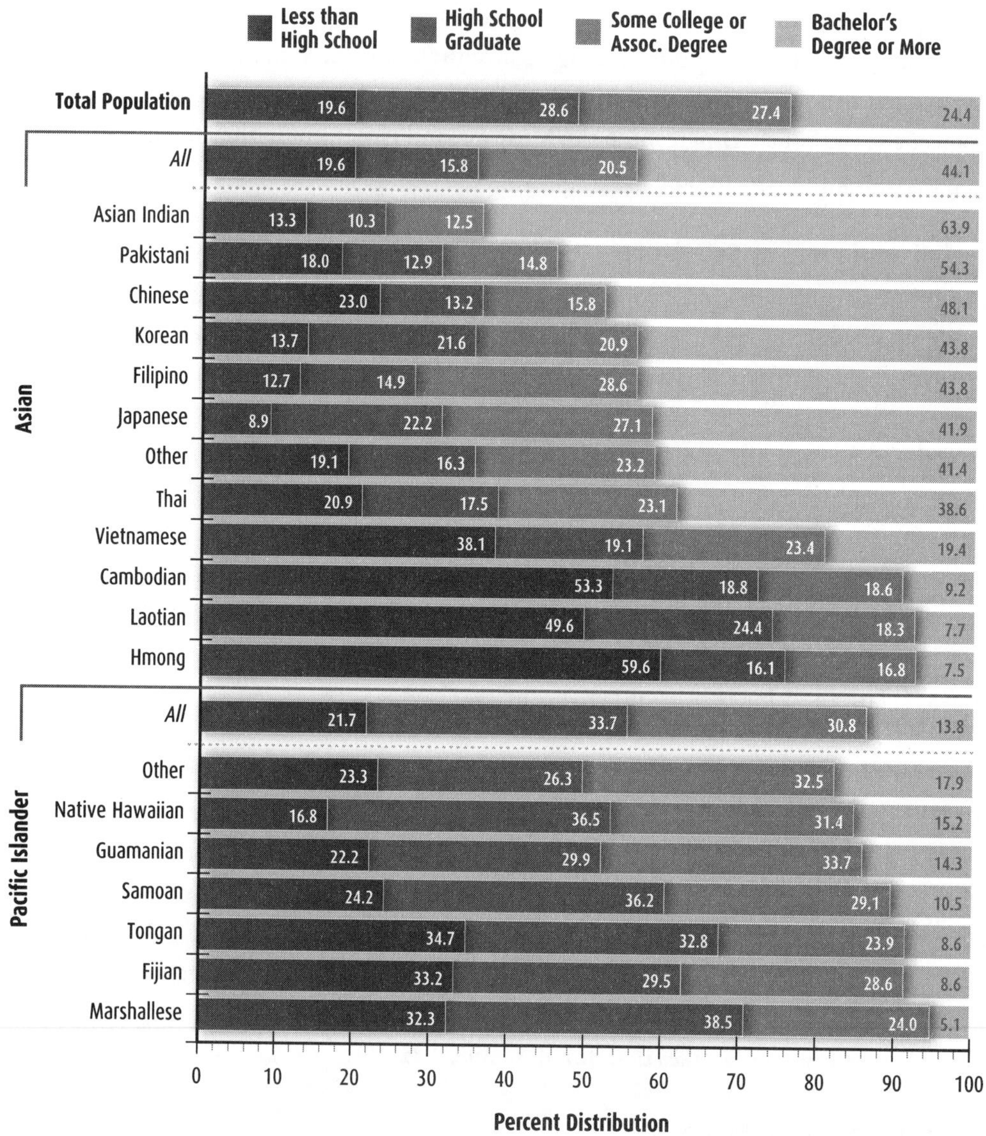


**SOURCE:** U.S. Census Bureau, Census 2000 (special tabulation)

APAs speak a language other than English at home at a much higher rate than the population at large. Almost 80 percent of APAs speak a language other than English at home, compared to 17.9 percent of the total population. Again, there are considerable variations among the APA categories. For example, over 90 percent of Laotians, Cambodians, Hmong, Pakistanis, and Vietnamese speak a language other than English at home, compared to only 47 percent for Japanese Americans (Reeves and Bennett 2004, p. 11) and 44 percent for the Pacific Islander population (Harris and Jones 2005, p. 11).

Language is a particularly important factor for many APAs. Lee and Kumashiro (2005) point to the barriers and challenges that APA students from immigrant families face in our educational system: "Like other immigrant students, they must learn to negotiate their parents' ethnic culture, the school culture, and their peer culture. Not insignificantly, these different cultures may clash, thereby creating conflict and confusion for the youth" (p.4).

## The "Model Minority" Myth and Other Stereotypes

The seemingly flattering "Model Minority" myth and the countervailing image of Asian Pacific Americans as perpetual foreigners, are two of the most common and harmful stereotypes affecting this student population.

Lee and Kumashiro (2005) outline the negative effects of this seemingly benign stereotype:

> *According to the model minority stereotype, Asian Americans have achieved academic, social, and economic success through hard work and adherence to Asian cultural norms. Asian American students are depicted as valedictorians, violin prodigies, and computer geniuses. Unlike many racial stereotypes, the model minority designation seems at first to be flattering and even positive. A closer examination, however, reveals its damaging effects for both Asian American and Pacific Islander students and for other students of color. The model minority stereotype hides the diverse and complex experiences of Asian American and Pacific Islander students.*
>
> *It erases significant differences related to ethnicity, social class, language, generation, history, gender, sexual orientation, disability, religion, immigration status, and region* (p. xi).

Helen Zia (2000) traces the emergence of the "Model Minority" stereotype to the political context of the 1960s.

> *In the 1960s, a new stereotype emerged on the American scene. As urban ghettoes from Newark, New Jersey, to Watts in Los Angeles erupted into riots and civil unrest, Asian Americans suddenly became the object of "flattering" media stories. After more than a century of invisibility, alternating with virulent headlines and radio broadcasts that advocated eliminating or imprisoning America's Asians, a rash of stories began to extol our virtues* (p. 46).

The "Model Minority" myth may also play out in the process of admission to elite universities. Golden (2006) describes a study by Espenshade, Chung, and Walling that indicates that Asian American students must score fifty points higher on the SAT than other students in order to receive an equal chance of admission to elite universities (p. 203).

In fact, the "Model Minority" stereotype disserves both segments of the APA population. In many instances high-achieving APA students are held to a higher admission standard than other students. At the same time, APA student populations with significant needs, whether cultural or economic, are often not assisted, because affirmative action seemingly does not apply to them.[141]

To address both issues selective colleges and universities need to disaggregate APA data in order to develop recruitment and retention initiatives that are targeted both to the highly prepared Asian American applicant, and to the APA student who may be foreign-born, or the first in the family to attend college.

## Recruitment

### Community Outreach

The term "community" summarizes a theme which is important to APA populations. Word of mouth is a very potent form of recruitment for prospective students from these groups, and it is equally important that the "voice" of the community be heard by the college. An APA community advisory group, composed of community leaders from the local APA populations, represents one approach to developing a relationship with APA students and parents. Such a group can inform the policy development process regarding recruitment and retention of students from those various populations. Another way of incorporating the APA voice in the college environment is to invite key leaders to sit on existing college committees.

In short, when the voice of the community is heard by the institution, the institution is more likely to be heard by the community. In addition, trusted representatives of the institution are more likely to be able to access the informal networks of the community (*e.g.*, churches, mosques, temples, community organizations, etc.).

### Using APA Students in Recruitment Efforts

It is also very important for both current and prospective students to see themselves reflected in the representatives of the college. When the institution includes APAs in recruitment efforts, prospective students can engage with people who are not that far removed from their own situations. Current students are more aware of commonly-occurring obstacles, and can communicate relevant information. The role model effect that APA college students have on APA high school students can be very powerful. For example, the co-author from Washington State University has found that APA high school students who interact with APA university students experience an important and positive change in their outlook on higher education.

To produce this type of effect through student-to-student recruitment, it is important to attempt to counter the sometimes intimidating effect of the "model minority" myth. Rosie Rimando, Director of Student Outreach and Retention at South Seattle Community College, has stated: "At South [Seattle Community College], we have found it valuable and

[141] It is interesting that in the *Bakke* case in 1978, "Asians" were considered to be a minority group (along with "blacks, Chicanos, and American Indians."). See *University of California Regents v. Bakke* (438 U.S. 265 [1978]). In both cases emanating from the University of Michigan in 2003, however—*Gratz* from the undergraduate school and *Grutter* from the law school—Asians were not considered to be an "under-represented minority." Instead, the list included only "African-Americans, Hispanics and American Indians." See *Gratz v. Bollinger* (539 U.S. 244 [2003]) and *Grutter v. Bollinger* (539 U.S. 306 [2003]).

## Resources—Organizations Devoted to APA Concerns

| Organization | Description | URL |
|---|---|---|
| Asian Pacific Americans in Higher Education | A national organization formed to address issues related to student admissions, faculty tenure, under-representation in hiring and promotion, affirmative action, and Asian American Studies. | www.apahe.net |
| The Association for Asian American Studies | From a press release on their Web site: "[The Association] was founded in 1971 for the purpose of advancing the highest professional standard of excellence in teaching and research in the field of Asian American Studies." | http://aaastudies.org |
| Center for Asian American Media | Its Web site states that the "Center is a non-profit organization dedicated to presenting stories that convey the richness and diversity of Asian American experiences to the broadest audience possible. We do this by funding, producing, distributing and exhibiting works in film, television and digital media." | http://asianamericanmedia.org |
| Commission on Asian Pacific American Affairs | Specializes in legislative bill tracking. | www.capaa.wa.gov |
| Japanese American Citizens League | The Japanese American Citizens League is a national organization whose ongoing mission is to secure and maintain the civil rights of Japanese Americans and all others who are victimized by injustice and prejudice. The leaders and members of JACL also work to promote cultural values and preserve the heritage and legacy of the Japanese American community. | www.jacl.org |
| The Model Minority | This site addresses social justice and civil rights issues that pertain to Asian Americans. | www.modelminority.com |
| National Asian Pacific American Women's Forum | Describes itself as "the only national, APA women's organization in the country." It has published the second edition of Asian American Women: Issues, Concerns and Responsive Human and Civil Rights Advocacy (2007), by Lora Jo Foo. | www.napawf.org |
| The National Coalition for Asian Pacific American Community Development (CAPACD) | National CAPACD is a membership-based network of local community-based agencies which have been and are active players in various social and economic empowerment movements that came together after the Civil Rights era and developed through the War on Poverty initiatives. The work of CAPACD member organizations range in experience, approach, and technique to encompass community building, planning, and empowerment. Member organizations, whether they were founded five or thirty-five years ago, serve a diverse community base including Asian Americans, Pacific Islander, Native, refugee, immigrant, and low-income communities nationwide. Such organizations work to promote community empowerment through service, housing and economic development, and organizing impacted constituencies. | www.nationalcapacd.org |
| National Council of Asian Pacific Americans | The National Council of Asian Pacific Americans, founded in 1996, is a coalition of twenty-one Asian Pacific American organizations nationwide. Based in Washington D.C., NCAPA serves to represent the interests of the greater APA community and to provide a national voice for APA issues. | www.ncapaonline.org |
| Organization of Chinese Americans (OCA) | OCA is a national organization dedicated to advancing the social, political, and economic well-being of Asian Pacific Americans in the United States. | www.ocanatl.org |
| South Asian Network (SAN) | SAN is a grassroots, community-based organization dedicated to advancing the health, empowerment, and solidarity of persons of South Asian origin in Southern California. | www.southasiannetwork.org |

important to *counter* the model minority myth in our talks with prospective students by involving college students in the outreach process who may not fit this stereotype. Be aware that the model minority myth affects us within our communities, and may force some students to feel alienated from college based on their perceived failures or shortcomings in college preparation" (e-mail correspondence with author Mitsui, 2007).

Parents are another key element in the recruitment of Asian Pacific American students. However, the role of the parents may vary depending on the socioeconomic status of the family. According to Rimando, "For more 'established' groups, the parents may be as involved as the student in college selection, so communicating with them is just as important [as communicating with the would-be student]. However, for more recent immigrant groups, often the children are the translators and communicators, and parents leave the college selection largely in their hands." For the latter group, the fact that the institution is close to home may be very important.

### Special Considerations for Community Colleges

"Like many students of color, children of Asian American or Pacific Islander families must weigh their college decision against more immediate family support needs. From the community college perspective, it is important to share the message that attending the community college near your home may allow you to still meet home responsibilities and further your own education" (Rimando, personal communication with author Mitsui, 2007).

## From Recruitment to Retention: "The Handoff"

"The handoff" refers to the transition of a student from the recruitment process to the retention process. The act of smoothly integrating recruitment and retention can have a positive effect on how prospective APA students and their families feel about a particular college or university. At Washington State University, for example, an APA-specific recruiter and an APA-specific retention counselor work closely together. This organizational design allows for close collaboration between the two in providing resource information to students. The benefits of a having a well-implemented "handoff" are two-fold: students and family feel supported, and access to holistic advising is easier. When students are given early knowledge of campus resources, the recruitment process can provide a "head start" on the retention process.

### Involvement of Student Organizations

Setting up a college campus to be a place where APA students feel comfortable can be aided by cultural-interest student organizations. Such groups can help new students in navigating the campus system and making social connections that can assist in developing their persistence, achievement, and leadership. Cultural-interest student organizations should be encouraged to reach out to new students as much as possible, without detracting from their members' own success.

### Mentor Programs

Peer mentor programs, not necessarily tied to a cultural or ethnic student organization, offer another way for students to have a point of contact on campus that can give them insight and tips for a successful first year. Students can be matched with peer mentors according to various identifications, whether by ethnicity, experience as a freshman/transfer student, gender, or major. Proper training of peer mentors is needed to provide them with the tools to work with new students in an advisory capacity, as well as being their friend.

### Faculty and Staff Diversity

The presence of a diverse staff and faculty is an important element in retaining and recruiting APA students. It is helpful for students to be able to see themselves reflected in the people who interact with them. However, students will quickly sense whether a college is really attuned to them or not. If the college represents itself as having a diverse or empathetic staff, and faculty and students then find out otherwise, disappointment can ensue, which will then be conveyed to the student's family or to the student's larger community.

What role does faculty and staff cultural diversity play in effectively reaching out to APA students? A diverse faculty and staff can push for a campus climate that encourages students of color to succeed in whatever field they choose. This is not to say that white faculty and staff do not or cannot provide this support. But many faculty and staff of color can serve as formal and informal mentors to students, even though such a role adds an additional responsibility to an already busy faculty workload.

Culturally knowledgeable faculty and staff also play a role in helping the various APA populations work through identity development issues. There has been a positive impact on students who have the opportunity to take classes that deals with their histories and experiences as APAs. Departments of Ethnic Studies, or similar opportunities offered through other departments or settings, have consistently been helpful to students both in developing a cultural understanding of their own community and in applying that knowledge to their surroundings before and after graduation. A co-author of this chapter has seen such positive results firsthand at Washington State University. Equally positive results have been observed among Hmong students at Oregon State University (OSU), according to Dr. Janet Nishihara, the Academic and Counseling Coordinator for OSU's Educational Opportunities Program. Such classes help APA students to validate their experience in the college venue.

## Summary

Asian Americans are a varied, talented and growing population. Whether they come from families which have long pursued higher education or whether they are first-generation college students, they have much to add to the campus climate and to the nation's intellectual and cultural resources.

/ CHAPTER SIXTEEN /

*by Odie Brant Porter, M.B.A.*
*Assistant Provost*
*Syracuse University*
*Stephanie Waterman, Ph.D.*
*Faculty Associate, Native Student Program*
*Syracuse University*

16

# Indigenous Students: Recruitment and Retention

When the Haudenosaunee (Iroquois Nations) first came into contact with the European nations, treaties of peace and friendship were made. Each was symbolized by the Gus-Wen-Tah, or Two Row Wampum. There are two rows of purple wampum, and those two rows have the spirit of your ancestors and mine. There are three beads of wampum separating the two rows and they symbolize peace, friendship, and respect.

These two rows will symbolize two paths or two vessels, traveling down the same river together. One, a birch bark canoe, will be for the Indian people, their laws, their customs, and their ways. The other, a ship, will be for the White people and their laws, their customs, and their ways. We shall each travel the river together, side by side, but in our own boat. Neither of us will try to steer the other's vessel.[142]

The path of the Iroquois symbolizes the mutually productive relationship which Indigenous or Native American students seek in higher education.

[142] The Guswenta, or the Two Row Wampum Treaty Belt, reflects an agreement between the Haudenosaunee Nations and the Dutch, French, and British (1613).

America's public commitment to provide access to Indigenous people who seek postsecondary education has improved in recent years. Enrollment of Indigenous students in colleges and universities has more than doubled in the past 25 years[143] to include more than 100,000 students (Henig 2007). In 1994, for the first time, more Indigenous students enrolled in four-year than in two-year postsecondary institutions.

However, when one scratches beneath the surface, one finds that Indigenous student enrollment and retention trail that of other populations. Only 18 percent of Indigenous 18- to 24-year-olds are enrolled in a college or university, compared with 42 percent of whites, 60 percent of Asian/Pacific Islanders, and 32 percent of blacks. Between 1990 and 2003, the Indigenous high school dropout rate fluctuated between 10.2 percent and 17.5 percent, showing no consistent trend, compared with 6.3 percent for whites, 3.9 percent for Asian/Pacific Islanders, and 10.9 percent for blacks (Pavel *et al.* 1998). Given these statistics, one might inquire why this situation has come about, and secondly, what can be done to increase enrollment, persistence rates, and degree-completion rates for Indigenous students in postsecondary institutions.

The purpose of this chapter, after providing a brief discussion of terminology, is to 1) provide an abbreviated history of Indigenous education from the early 19th century, when the education offered to Indigenous peoples often disconnected them from their tribal identities (Pewewardy 2005); 2) describe how postsecondary institutions can recruit Indigenous students, and 3) offer strategies to promote retention and improve graduation rates and academic success of these students.

## Terminology

There are over 500 federally recognized Indigenous Nations and 50 state-recognized Indigenous tribes (Wilkins 2003) located within the United States. The diversity of each Nation elicits an ongoing debate as to the appropriate terms to apply to these distinct peoples. What should Indigenous people be called? There is no term that is suitable for everyone, since within these Nations, there are incompatible preferences.

The term "Indian" was imposed upon the Indigenous population by Christopher Columbus who was seeking India over 500 years ago. When he mistakenly reached the Caribbean Islands instead, he referred to the land as Indian and its inhabitants as Indians—a label that continues to be used today. In addition to "Indian," other terms have emerged, including: Native American, American Indian, Indigenous, or as in Canada, First Nations Peoples. Depending on region, generation, or ideologies, each native person identifies himself differently. In some regions, native peoples identify themselves exclusively as a citizen of their own Indigenous Nation, rather than by a term that was assigned by outsiders.

[143] Based on data from 2002.

Terminology can be a sensitive issue, so addressing it at the outset demonstrates respect in forming new relationships. Researchers note "the tendency of many Native Americans in the company of fellow in-group members to refer to each other as 'Indian,' whereas in the company of 'outsiders' there is a tendency to refer to themselves as 'Native American' and to expect non-Indians to do the same out of respect" (Garrett and Pichette 2000, p. 4). For the non-Indian or non-native person, we recommend asking what name is preferred, and, if necessary, requesting proper pronunciations. The authors will use "Native," "American Indian," "Indigenous," and "Native American" interchangeably throughout this chapter.

## Historical Context

To provide greater opportunities for educating Indigenous peoples, educators should take time to better understand the underlying tensions often associated with the Indigenous education process, and what may sometimes appear to be a subconscious resistance to it.

Historically, education policies for Indigenous peoples have been rooted in "promoting civilization;" but Indigenous peoples have often experienced it as "social engineering." Given the bleak history of often forced education, briefly described below, it is not surprising that statistics reflect higher high school dropout rates, lower college enrollment rates, and lower graduation rates for Indigenous students than for others. Our role here is to help the reader develop strategies to improve educational opportunities for Indigenous peoples, by better understanding the population's history.

### Early European Contact and Christianization

Prior to European contact, Indigenous nations maintained their own diverse educational systems that were responsive to their own cultures and languages. These systems were designed to provide education informally through parents, extended families, elder members of the tribe, and religious and social groups. Indigenous perspectives were and continue to be rooted in Indigenous experiences, both cultural and political (Pewewardy 2005).

Early colonial settlements, such as the Virginia Settlement, adopted strategies to mold Indigenous peoples' minds according to "Christian" values—all in efforts to civilize the Indian and (according to some scholars) to appropriate Indian land and resources (Adams 1988).

Some Indigenous peoples were trained in trades and exposed to "European" or non-tribal attitudes so that they, too, could become productive members of the settlements. In 1618, the Jamestown settlement planned to develop a classical style college, Henrico, to formally educate Indigenous boys (Carney 1999). Before its completion, however, the Indigenous peoples demolished Henrico in the massacre of 1622, thus symbolizing their discontent with the European style of life being imposed on them.

In other new settlements outside Virginia, education continued to be part of a strategy to civilize and assimilate Indigenous peoples. In 1650 Harvard University's charter stated that it was dedicated "to the education of English and Indian youth of this Country in knowledge and godliness." In 1655, Harvard Indian College was established to teach English language and Protestantism to local Indigenous peoples, but it lasted only 43 years before being torn down after a period of neglect.

Treaties between the colonial governments and the Indigenous nations often included provisions to provide European-style educational opportunities for Indigenous youths in exchange for land and other resources. At that time, however, the primary purpose of formal education was to educate men for the ministry, so few native youths were, in fact, educated (Carney 1999; Rudolph 1990).

### Residential Schools for Natives: A Mixed Legacy

After the Revolutionary War, the newly independent colonies were ready for expansion, but the Indians possessed the land—and the colonists needed land to fuel the country's growth. To move westward, white settlers worked toward removing Indians from their territories, either by force or by assimilation efforts. Assimilation, or Christianizing and civilizing, was viewed as the humane way for Europeans to address the Indian problem, and education and vocational training were tools to effectuate this strategy.

Eventually educating native youth became a formal federal policy, which launched the boarding school era. By 1880 the federal government established day and residential schools for native youth, for the primary purpose of creating citizens (Carney 1999). Since most land was now occupied by non-Indians, reformers concluded that Indians were capable of being assimilated into mainstream America and could fit into the social order without disruption.

However, in the late nineteenth century, creating citizens still meant severing children's cultural and psychological connections to their native heritage. Children were sent to residential schools as early as age three and given new European surnames. None of them were permitted to speak their language or practice traditional ceremonies. Their hair would be cut and their traditional clothing would be replaced with uniforms. Daily life was conducted in a regimented, militaristic style, which included living in barracks (Lindsey 1995).

For some students, the abuse and mistreatment proved to be intolerable; some ran away, while others died at the schools from neglect and disease. Boarding school survivors report physical and sexual abuse, as well as near starvation. Not knowing the conditions which prevailed in many of these schools, many native parents sent their children to them, since the parents had experienced such destructive changes—disease, war, and forced removal from their aboriginal homelands—that they thought this type of education might better prepare their children for the future. In other cases they simply did not have the means to care for their children. Finally, in many instances, if native parents did not voluntarily send their children to the government schools for native children, they saw their children forcibly removed from home.

Today's Indigenous college student is too young to remember the boarding school era, but many have grandparents who attended residential schools. That era's legacy continues to negatively impact Indigenous peoples today—despite efforts by Indigenous nations working to recover their lost languages and traditions. The social problems that accompany loss of traditional knowledge at times resulted in alcohol and drug use as survivors struggled with their Indigenous roots and identities. When native elders denounce formal education, this is the type of education they remember and discourage. However, others recognize how education can facilitate the recovery of traditions that have been driven nearly to extinction.

### Self-Determination Policies

In 1932, the Bureau of Indian Affairs identified only 385 Native American college graduates. As late as 1958, higher education programs for native people were still primarily vocationally oriented (Carney 1999).

The 1960s marked a philosophical shift in Indian Education policy. Along with economic development incentives (such as job training programs), native people were now better able to control and develop their own programs (Wright and Tierney 1991). The Rough Rock Demonstration School was founded in 1966, and the Navajo Community College (now called Diné Community College) in 1968. Congress passed laws supporting native education, such as the Indian Education Act of 1972, the Indian Self-Determination and Educational Assistance Act of 1975, and the Tribally Controlled Community College Act of 1978; the latter provided additional funds for tribal colleges. These laws provided financial aid for students and some support for native studies programs, as well. In their monograph on *Serving Native American Students*, Fox, Lowe, and McClellan (2005) consider this the true beginning of the self-determination period for native peoples.

Despite increased funding and the emergence of more native-directed programs, however, these initiatives were unable to effectuate widespread and significant changes in native education. Most native children continue to be educated in public school environments, which tend to operate under a "deficit ideology" (Deyhle and Swisher 1997). This ideology asserts that native children need to be "'enriched' in Eurocentric experiences" (p. 123).

In addition, such schools generally lack optimal funding levels and often are not academically competitive. That is not to suggest there are no high-achieving schools that serve native students, but rather that the majority of them are not well-funded or academically intensive.

## Educating Staff and Committees

Because native communities often operate with different governments and spiritual systems, and many are located in remote rural areas, interacting with such communities may seem like entering a different country. Thus it is vital that university personnel learn more about the communities they wish to work with. Discovering who and where the Nations are—the Nations from which you wish to recruit—and investigating their history, are critical to the process.

The first step in recruiting native students from their territories is to make a personal connection and establish a relationship with Nation leaders and their neighboring school counselors. Find at least one person who will "sponsor" and host your visit. There may be certain events or times of the year when visiting is productive, like during festivals, and other times in which it is inappropriate, like during traditional ceremonies. Let your contact people guide your visitation schedule so that you are welcomed by the community, as opposed to being perceived as an intrusion.

Secondly, you should consider inviting representatives from area native communities to provide cultural training to your staff. This will prepare your recruiting staff to be respectful in their communications and overtures, and ultimately optimize their recruiting efforts.

Since the 1970s, several universities and colleges have implemented successful programs for Indigenous peoples. In 1970, Dartmouth College President John Kemeny created the Native American Program, motivated by the institution's desire to redress the historical lack of opportunities for Native Americans in higher education. Since its implementation, the program has graduated over 500 Native Americans, more than all of the Ivy League schools combined; it now has a graduation rate of 72 percent (Dartmouth College 2006).

The University of Nebraska-Lincoln (UNL) offers a summer course for new faculty and others at UNL "to help [them] predict, recognize and avoid potential cultural conflicts" (Associated Press 2006). Administrators at UNL have found this course to be beneficial to college recruiters, their education program and students, and the native community.

In fall 2005, Syracuse University (SU) announced its unprecedented Haudenosaunee Promise Scholarship program, which, in fall 2006 welcomed SU's largest Native American class in its 135-year history. Recognizing that Syracuse's geographic location was situated in the center of the historic Haudenosaunee confederacy (also known as Iroquois or League of Six Nations), Chancellor Nancy Cantor was motivated to express Syracuse University's gratitude and appreciation for the historical, political, and cultural legacies of the Haudenosaunee. This appreciation translated into full scholarships for Haudenosaunee members residing in one of their Nation's territories. In addition to scholarships, Syracuse University sponsors Indigenous cultural, political, and academic events to raise awareness and sensitivity. The faculty associate hired with the program educates the SU community at-large regarding the Haudenosaunee culture.

## Recruitment Strategies

- **Make use of community venues and specialized organizations:** When developing a recruiting plan, we suggest that it include an initial section for process objectives, in addition to standard enrollment targets. These process objectives could include strategies for building relationships with students and their families, tribal leaders and counselors, and the institution's different schools and programs.

  College admissions officers who wish to increase their native student population should be open to alternative venues in their recruiting efforts. Besides traditional college recruiting fairs, we recommend seeking out Indigenous events, such as community festivals, conferences, and pow wows. These present your institution as accessible, flexible, and interested.

There are several organizations—including the American Indian Science and Engineering Society, the American Indian Higher Education Consortium (tribal colleges), and the American Indian College Horizons program—which host conferences that support Indigenous postsecondary education. These and other native organizations, like the National Congress of American Indians (tribal governments), invite sponsors to participate as conference vendors. (*See* Table 16.1.)

Recruiting Indigenous peoples takes a genuine commitment from institutions—it requires more than sending a glossy publication to an empty mailbox. Community and family relationships are a high priority for Indigenous people; therefore relationship building is a necessary component for recruitment and retention. If these overtures to the communities are sincere, the results can be very productive.

**TABLE 16.1: Native American Support Organizations**

| Organization | Description | URL |
|---|---|---|
| American Indian Science and Engineering Society (AISES) | AISES's mission is "to increase substantially the representation of American Indian and Alaskan Natives in engineering, science and other related technology disciplines." | www.aises.org |
| American Indian Higher Education Consortium (AIHEC) | AIHEC's mission is to be the voice of the more than thirty tribal colleges and universities. | www.aihec.org |
| College Horizons | A program which introduces American Indian youth as young teenagers to college admissions. For a sample program, see the Harvard Gazette Archives at <www.hno.harvard.edu/gazette/2005/07.21/29-native.html>. | www.collegehorizons.org |
| National Congress of American Indians (NCAI) | A forum for the more than 250 tribal governments from around the country. | www.ncai.org |

- **Host annual campus visits for Native students:** This should be a focused recruiting event that addresses the specific issues common to Native students. More than just a campus tour, it should have the visible involvement of everyone from leading college administrators to the more predictable particpants, such as faculty and staff. All should be on hand to describe the institution from their perspective, and to explain the financial aid and enrollment processes. Finally, the staff hosting the event should be accessible for ongoing communication with participants, before and after the visit. This is an opportunity to build relationships and communicate that the institution values Indigenous students and is committed to supporting them.

- **Develop relationships with high school guidance counselors or Native home-school liaisons:** High school counselors have direct access to student recruits, and they are your partners in this process. They mentor and guide students through many life decisions, and it is important to view this partnership as mutually beneficial. You may advise your high school counterparts on higher education opportunities and strategies, while they assist you with the recruitment process.

- **Develop relationships with tribal officials and education directors, and tribal (Nation) postsecondary counselors:** Working with both the in-school counselor and the tribal officials is a productive way to recruit Native students who reside on their territories. Your efforts will demonstrate that you are not only concerned with recruiting students but are also interested in establishing an ongoing relationship with the community. When meeting with tribal officials, it is advisable and appreciated to send a senior level representative to convey this commitment.

- **Offer scholarships and waive application fees:** Since many Native people come from economically disadvantaged backgrounds, financial support is a key element for students to consider applying and eventually enrolling in an institution.

- **Invite students to sporting, theater, or other campus events:** The earlier high school students attend your campus, the more comfortable they are with envisioning themselves going to college—and possibly attending your institution. Giving students access without "selling" them on your campus will put them at ease and allow them to enjoy the campus. (Keep in mind, there is a healthy dose of skepticism shared among Indigenous peoples resulting from their history, so any sense of selling may raise red flags among this population.)

## Retention Strategies

With the exception of those students who attend one of the 34 tribal colleges, most native students enroll in predominantly white institutions. Because indigenous peoples comprise less than one percent of the United States population (U.S. Census Bureau 2007), and they attend postsecondary institutions at the lowest rate of any group, achieving a critical mass of native students is a difficult task. This creates significant challenges for empirical research; thus, qualitative studies have been pursued to gain a meaningful understanding of Indigenous student persistence.

Past research indicates that culture and language are barriers to degree attainment (Ledlow 1992; and Pottinger 1989). Because research has typically relied on Tinto's (1993) theory of attrition, which is based on an individual's ability to integrate into the college campus, much of the failure was blamed on the individual student (although Tinto surely did not intend to lead to this conclusion in relation to native students specifically). Reyhner (1992), however, disputed Tinto's theory by arguing that native students are "pushed out" of college (p. 38) due to "uncaring teachers, passive teaching methods, inappropriate curriculum, inappropriate testing/student retention, tracked classes, and lack of parent involvement" (p. 39). This theory suggests that the burden should not be on native students to adapt to the institution; rather, the initiative should be to encourage staff to be proactive and pursue various means of encouraging student persistence. Before enacting any native student retention programs, it would be helpful to assess whether your campus is generally welcoming to students of color.

Like other distinct students, indigenous students maintain their own cultural capital. Deyhle (1995) and Jorgenson (1993) found that many students continue to resist assimilation, and struggle to maintain their native identity within sometimes hostile college environments. Furthermore, researchers have found that students of color need not break away from their communities in order to achieve academic success; on the contrary, their community connections can be a significant source of support in college (Davis 2004; Guiffrida 2005; Rendón, Jalomo, & Nora 2000; Waterman 2007; and Tierney 1999). Brayboy (1999), and others such as Castillo (1982), have found that native people who are firmly grounded in their traditions can experience success in school and work.

Noted scholar William Tierney (1992) examined the interaction between the culture of the university and the native students who attend those institutions, and how cultures change over time. He notes:

> *...anyone who enters an organization needs to learn its cultural mores and symbols. However with regard to Native American students, virtually all of higher education's efforts have gone toward integrating Indian students into the system.*
>
> *Institutions geographically close to reservations might speak with tribal leaders about how best someone new to the institution could learn about tribal ways. Repeated and consistent interaction with tribal elders, students, and their families offers opportunities for Anglo faculty and staff to learn about a culture uniquely different from their own, and in turn teach individuals how best to interact with Indian students* (pp 152–153).

Native studies programs can be an integral component to native student retention. These programs may combine academics, student life, community service opportunities, and student support services, such as tutoring, counseling, and career development. They can be viewed as a catalyst to building vibrant native communities within higher education institutions, as they can be places where native people congregate for activities or events. Dedicated program space is vital to its success, as it creates campus awareness and provides a "home base" for students to feel comfortable. Native studies programs are not purely student support programs, however; they are also interdisciplinary centers of scholarly activity addressing a wide variety of issues facing native communities (Champagne and Stauss 2002).

## Supporting Student Persistence

Admitting and enrolling students is only one step in the process toward earning a college degree. Many native students are first-generation college students, from low-income families, and often from low-performing schools. Students with these characteristics have lower graduation rates (Adelman 2006); thus, they may need additional support and advising to improve their opportunities for success.

First-generation families are not as familiar with higher education structures and hierarchies as those families in which some members have attained postsecondary degrees. We recommend that you provide an orientation for both students and families, and present information in basic yet respectful terms. Academic and financial deadlines should be explicitly stated, and the *process* of applying for financial aid and programs should be made clear. The procedures for enrolling in courses, earning good grades, and making use of a syllabus are elements that we recommend be included in this discussion. Once orientation is complete, academic advising sessions should be incorporated into the schedule. With this process, families are given the opportunity to develop an understanding of what their child will encounter, and it will provide the family with the tools to support the students. Finally, families should also be given a summary of native-focused events, so they may schedule times to return and visit campus.

Native student support programs and native studies departments are places where the student can meet with other students, staff, and faculty who are native or interested in native issues. If a native program exists on your campus, be sure to discuss this during the recruiting stages. Students should be made aware of those services at the outset, so they know there is a safety net during their college transition. We recommend your becoming familiar with any such staff and services, since this will help you expand your information base and keep you informed on current events. Native recruits and their families will often want to know about such programs and events, and by regularly communicating with the native issues program, you will be prepared to respond appropriately.

In addition to becoming familiar with the staff and services, it is also critical to recognize that some native students participate in their traditional religious ceremonies. These ceremonies may not necessarily track with the academic calendar, so it is important for the institution to respect students' needs to attend these events (within reason) without penalty. An office of native student programs might be a good source—of information for non-native students, and of support for Indigenous students in their religious and cultural observances.

When working with Indigenous students, it is to your advantage to assess the institution's attitude toward people of color. Unfortunately for Indigenous peoples, Native American history and culture is glossed over and insufficiently portrayed in mainstream education, resulting in a generally ignorant society as it relates to Indigenous issues. This can result in stereotyping and misconceptions on the part of faculty, staff, and classmates. Campuses do not necessarily have to be overtly hostile to Indigenous people or people of color to be considered unwelcoming. Statements like "You mean there are still Indians left?" and "You're Indian, then you must have a casino. Otherwise, how you could you afford this school?" represent stereotypes that are conveyed in the media. This can be a rude shock for the Indigenous student who is just trying to survive his or her first year in college, and it provides yet another reason to offer a cultural education for university staff.

For the native student who may be the victim of stereotyping, the student needs to know that there are people on campus who are supportive. The native student may not be comfortable fighting this battle, so multicultural or native support offices can assist him or her by providing a safe haven, and can advise the student on how best to handle such occurrences.

## False Claims of Ethnicity

Now that college admission has become increasingly competitive, some students resort to "gaming the system" by choosing an ethnic identity which they think may provide them with a competitive advantage. So, what are admissions officers to do when given the charge to increase Indigenous student enrollment when they are presented with applicants who are all too eager to fit the profile just to gain access as "box-checkers?"

In his article, "You Think You Hired an 'Indian' Faculty Member?" Dr. Cornel Pewewardy (2004) describes what he calls "ethnic fraud" (that is, deliberately inaccurate self-identification as to race or ethnicity to gain an advantage), and he suggests some proposed hiring policies for faculty—policies which can easily be modified in relation to student applicants:

+ *Provide a space on the employment (or enrollment) application for self-identifying individuals to list their tribal affiliation(s).*[144]
+ *Construct a heritage sheet that would accompany the application which self-identifies as "Native American," "American Indian," or "Alaska Native." This will allow applicants an opportunity to provide verification of their enrollment in a tribe.*
+ *The policy should be enforced at the office of admissions level. There should be an administrator who is specifically assigned to handle the verifications of those self-identified as American Indian, and who should be granted the authority to remove any from the list who do not comply with the policy.*
+ *Pewewardy and Runningwater recommend that the verification policy should be formally announced and enforced by the institution* (Pewewardy 2004, p. 212).

These recommendations offer a mechanism for preventing ethnic fraud. They also honor tribal sovereignty and the right of tribes to determine their own membership criteria.

## Conclusion

The Two-Row Wampum is as relevant today as it has ever been. It symbolizes how, in many cases, traditional Indigenous students perceive a college education—as an enhancement that lives side-by-side with the traditions in their lives. It neither replaces their traditional religion, nor does their traditional teaching interfere with their openness to learning Western ways of inquiry. The two shall live side-by-side—coexisting peacefully through the river of life.

Native students are increasingly represented in American higher education, both in the tribal colleges and in general (non-tribal) institutions. Such students often face distinct challenges, but none that cannot be overcome by tailored methods of recruiting and retention.

[144] A listing of federally recognized tribes can be found at <www.ncai.org/Tribal_Directory.3.0.html>.

/ CHAPTER SEVENTEEN /

*by Julie Martin Trenor, Ph.D.*
*Director of Undergraduate Student Recruitment and Retention*
*Cullen College of Engineering*
*University of Houston*

*Chidiogo Madubike, Ph.D.*
*Electrical Design Engineer*
*Schlumberger, Inc.*

17

# Women in Engineering: Recruitment and Retention

Our nation is facing an impending shortage of scientists and engineers, since one quarter of the workforce in those sectors is expected to retire by 2010 (Jackson 2002). To further complicate matters, the number of engineering graduates produced by the United States has declined in recent years, while comparable numbers have increased abroad. American pre-eminence is being threatened by countries such as China, Japan, and Russia, which are far out-producing the U.S. in numbers of engineers entering the workforce each year (CAWMSET 2000; Jackson, 2002). The threat of economic ramifications represents one major incentive for building a stronger technical workforce; another motivation is national security, since engineers contribute significantly to our country's defense, homeland security, intelligence, and bioterrorism efforts (WEPAN 2006). In order for the United States to remain competitive in our interconnected, global economy, we must increase the number of engineering graduates our country produces. This task will require drawing from all available talent pools, including under-represented minorities and women (WEPAN 2006).

While women represent more than half of all undergraduates enrolled in college, fewer than 18 percent of engineering students are women.[145] Female representation in the engineering workforce is a mere 10 percent. Contrast this to other professional fields, where, for example, women make up 30 percent of lawyers and 32 percent of physicians and surgeons (WEPAN 2006).

Increasing the representation of women in engineering is not simply a social or moral issue; a diverse workforce will ensure our country's ability to create innovative products that meet the demands of an evolving marketplace. While this is true of many fields, diversity is particularly important in engineering because engineers work in team environments, and wide-ranging viewpoints are necessary to achieve innovative solutions to today's complex problems (Chubin, May, and Babco 2006). Dr. William Wulf, President of the National Academy of Engineering, asserts that the issue of increasing diversity in engineering "...is not an equity issue, it's a workforce issue. As a creative field, without diversity, engineering cannot take advantage of life experiences that bear directly on good engineering design."

## The Engineering "Pipeline"

The "pipeline" metaphor is often used when discussing the "flow" of potential engineering students through an engineering curriculum and into the workforce. The creation of a diverse, technical workforce necessitates proactive recruitment and retention practices to ensure both that more young women enter the pipeline, and that fewer are lost as "leaks" along the way. This chapter will discuss best practices for recruiting and retaining women in undergraduate engineering programs, along with some of the barriers to doing so.

### Recognizing Traits of Potential Engineers

In order for high school teachers, counselors, parents, and university personnel to help solve the problem of gender inequity in engineering, they must, at the outset, have a clear understanding of what kind of student might be well suited for the field. The first characteristic that comes to mind might be someone who likes to "tinker" or build things, or someone who enjoys using technology, such as computers. These characteristics are certainly understandable choices, but are they are not necessarily requirements for entering engineering. An aptitude for science and math may seem like other obvious identifiers, but what about the young person who wants to help make the world a better place? The student who is creative or enjoys collaboration? The youngster who is innovative, an independent thinker, an adept problem solver? These are all legitimate and important traits for a future engineer to possess.

---

[145] In comparison, women were awarded more than 60 percent of the undergraduate degrees in biology in 2003 (WEPAN 2006).

## Reasons Women Enter the Field

Studies of female undergraduates enrolled in engineering indicate several primary motivations for entering the field: confidence in math/science abilities, having an engineer as a family member or family friend, and parental encouragement (Goodman and Cunningham 2002). Additionally, one study of female engineering undergraduates from over 50 universities across the country showed that 90 percent of the young women polled cited the altruistic nature of the field as well as the value of social contributions made by engineers as reasons for entering engineering (Goodman and Cunningham 2002; Seymour and Hewitt 1997).[146] This fact is echoed in engineering enrollments across the country; engineering disciplines with obvious societal contributions boast much higher percentages of women than other disciplines where the connection is less obvious. For example, 42 percent of biomedical engineering and 43 percent of environmental engineering undergraduates in 2004–2005 were female, while only 11 percent of computer engineering and 13 percent of mechanical engineering undergraduates were women (Grose 2006). Understanding the motivations of females for entering engineering has important and potentially revolutionary implications for recruitment of young women to the field. The future of recruiting young women to engineering rests on the ability of the field to market itself as a socially-conscious, application-driven, and team-based profession.

Engineering summer camps or weekend outreach activities are one mechanism for marketing the field to young women across the nation. Girls Reaching and Demonstrating Excellence in Engineering (GRADE) Camp at the University of Houston (Glover *et al.* 2005) is one such camp that emphasizes the teamwork and problem-solving aspects of engineering. Funded by a Texas Workforce Development Grant, the primary objective of GRADE Camp is to introduce high school girls to engineering as a college and career option. Young women in middle and high school who participate in similar activities across the country gain a better understanding of what the field entails, the contributions engineers make to society, and the math and science background needed to be successful in the field.

**What Young Women Should Know About Engineering**

- Engineers need a strong math and science background to solve engineering problems, but science, math, and computers are *tools* engineers use, not the *goal* of engineering.
- Engineers are problem solvers, and the problems they solve contribute to the betterment of society, from designing tissue-engineered skin for burn victims, to creating portable water filters to ensure safe drinking water in under-developed countries, to developing cleaner and cheaper fuel alternatives to decrease our dependency on fossil fuels.
- Engineers are not just "builders" or "operators;" they are creative and inventive (Engineers Dedicated to a Better Tomorrow 2006).
- Engineers do not work in isolation; the complexity of today's engineering problems necessitates teamwork and diverse points of view.
- Engineers do not sit in front of a computer screen all day; instead, a variety of work environments are available. Furthermore, opportunities for travel are available in many engineering positions.

[146] Smith College (Northampton, MA) offers an engineering program, the first at a women's college, and describes it as follows: "Smith College's Picker Engineering Program emphasizes unity of knowledge across disciplines and promotes engineering as a liberal art and a profession in service to humanity." The College goes on to state: "Rather than offering an array of specialized engineering degree programs, Smith offers a single degree, a B.S. in engineering science, which focuses on the fundamentals of all the engineering disciplines," in particular mechanics, electrical systems, and thermochemical processes. "Students will complete a four-year curriculum that culminates in a final design project that unites engineering science and practice with broad-based societal issues." One year after the first class graduated, engineering had become the third-most popular major among incoming Smith students. See <www.science.smith.edu/departments/Engin/>.

### Barriers to Recruitment

In order to enter an undergraduate engineering curriculum, students generally must be on track to enroll in, or have already completed, calculus in their first semester of college. In most cases, students must make decisions as early as seventh or eighth grade about their mathematics course selection—decisions that will determine whether or not they will be able to graduate with the requisite math courses to enter engineering. In addition, some states do not require students to take four years of mathematics in high school, and thus some students all too often opt out of taking a math course in their senior year—a distinct disadvantage in college preparation for a student who generally must complete four semesters of college math in an engineering curriculum.

While math ability and preparation can be major barriers to entering an undergraduate engineering curriculum, there are other, non-academic barriers that may hinder participation from an early age. Gender-biased attitudes, which often affect young women's perceptions of the field, are one major barrier. Females are often socialized against participating in math and science activities, and "tinkering" may be discouraged as gender-inappropriate play (Goodman and Cunningham 2002). A girl who assimilates the gender-biased attitudes of the general public, her family members, or teachers regarding engineering may not even consider the field as a career option, or may avoid participating in math and science activities from an early age (CAWMSET 2000).

**What Admissions Personnel Can Do to Market the Profession**

- Help students understand what is required for admission from an early stage, so they can enroll in appropriate high school courses.
- Avoid perpetuating stereotypes found in the popular media (*e.g.*, using only male pronouns when referring to engineering students and professors).
- Utilize your school's engineering alumnae base, female faculty, and students in the recruitment and admissions process.

Gender bias is further perpetuated and complicated by the profession's public image problem. While doctors and lawyers are portrayed in a positive and glamorous light on prime-time television, scientists and engineers (when they are portrayed at all) are almost always stereotypically nerdy, socially inept, *men* (CAWMSET 2000). Who are arguably the most recognizable engineer characters? Dilbert and Star Trek's Scotty (Engineers Dedicated to a Better Tomorrow 2006)! A United States Department of Commerce study examined scientist and engineer characters in prime time television, finding that 75 percent of the time, they were portrayed as white males. When women were portrayed in these roles, they usually were relegated to subordinate roles, such as lab assistants (CAWMSET 2000). For young women who do not have family or friend role models, there are few available in the public eye.

Peer pressure and isolation can also play a role in discouraging young women from entering technical fields. One student's description of the reason she decided to drop her high school's programming class illuminates this point. On the first day of class, she approached the door of the classroom and saw that it was filled with only male students. Without entering the classroom, she turned around and went directly to her counselor's office to drop the course!

# Retention

## Barriers to Retention

Nationwide, undergraduate engineering retention rates for men and women are widely disparate: 62 percent for men vs. 42 percent for women (Adelman 1998). At the University of Houston, for example, historical enrollment data for the Department of Electrical and Computer Engineering (ECE) reveal that approximately 60 percent of the female students who started a degree in ECE dropped out of engineering entirely, and nearly 65 percent of the "leavers" did so within their first two semesters. These trends are consistent with other published reports (Jackson 2002; Adelman 1998). Those familiar with engineering curricula will recognize that this trend reveals a disturbing fact: many, if not most, women who drop out of engineering majors do so before they even take a technical engineering course. For those who do make it to their first technical course, we risk losing them if their expectations for their chosen particular discipline are not met. Women who leave engineering majors tend to change their major to another field entirely rather than switching between engineering departments.

The factors influencing attrition of female students in undergraduate engineering programs are complex, and it is important to understand that academic preparation and classroom performance issues comprise only a small part of the problem. In fact, studies have shown that women who leave undergraduate programs are equally as strong academically as those who remain (Goodman and Cunningham 2002). In some cases, the women who leave engineering have been shown to have higher grade point averages than many men who stay (Meade 1991). So, if attrition is not primarily an academic issue, then what other barriers to retention exist? The interested reader will find a plethora of papers discussing these topics in the engineering education and educational psychology literature. This discussion is based on the work of Goodman and Cunningham (2002) and Seymour and Hewitt (1998); additional information about these topics can be found in those two excellent works.

First, the gender bias that plagues recruitment efforts also affects female students once they have chosen to enter the engineering pipeline. Messages heard at home, at school, or from society in general, whether implied or overt, can make female students doubt their ability or place in the field. Another related factor is self-confidence and engineering self-efficacy. Self-efficacy is similar to self-confidence, and "engineering self-efficacy" is defined as an engineering student's belief that she is capable of succeeding in an engineering program. Female college students generally show lower levels of self-confidence than male students, and to complicate matters, studies have shown that female students' self-confidence often drops once they are in college, whereas male students' self-confidence does not. Low self-confidence or engineering self-efficacy contributes to female students' attrition. Indeed, even students who have a strong sense of self-efficacy prior to enrollment show a dramatic drop in the first year of college. A related issue is the manner in which women tend to internalize failure while externalizing success (Felder *et al.* 1994). They may blame themselves for setbacks or failures (such as doing poorly on an engineering exam) and interpret the setback as personal incompetence, while they attribute their successes (making an A, for example) to good luck or other external forces. Male students, on the other hand, tend to *externalize* failures and *internalize* successes.

Classroom climate and curricular focus have also been implicated as a barrier to retention of female engineering students. The competitive atmosphere of traditional engineering classrooms, the promotion of the idea that engineering is an "exclusive" major that requires complete devotion and no outside interests, the "weed out" philosophy of many professors, and the traditional focus on individual performance rather than group work have all contributed to the "chilly climate." In one author's own experiences as an undergraduate, a male engineering professor routinely addressed the class as "gentlemen." In an effort to move toward more inclusive pedagogy, many schools have begun to emphasize collaborative learning environments and have placed increased emphasis on the context or societal implications of engineering.

TABLE 17.1: **Advocacy for Women Engineering Students**

| Organization | Description | URL |
|---|---|---|
| **Women in Engineering Programs and Advocates Network (WEPAN)** | The mission of WEPAN is to be a "catalyst, advocate, and leading resource for institutional and national change that will result in the full participation of women in engineering." | www.wepan.org |
| **Society of Women Engineers (SWE)** | The mission of SWE is to "stimulate women to achieve full potential in careers as engineers and leaders, expand the image of the engineering profession as a positive force in improving the quality of life, and demonstrate the value of diversity." | www.swe.org |

The "chilly" classroom climate experienced by some female students is compounded by a lack of female peers and role models, which can lead to feelings of isolation. A female student who never has a female professor for an undergraduate engineering course (the experience of both authors), and who looks around a classroom, seeing only a few other women, may easily internalize her feelings of isolation as a sign that she does not belong in the field.

The experiences of one author in recruiting students and teaching freshmen courses reveal another barrier to retention: uninformed choices. When pressed about the reasons behind their selection of a particular engineering department for their undergraduate career, many prospective students and engineering freshmen confess, "I knew I wanted to be an engineer, but I didn't know what kind. I just checked a box on the application." Students who fail to make an informed choice about their specific discipline often get to their first technical course and, when it is not what they expected, leave the field entirely instead of simply making a more informed choice in favor of another engineering discipline.

In addition to the reasons already discussed, many students simply try to take on too much. This may be especially true of students with a financial need to work, or students who are expected to contribute to their family's income. Because of the rigor associated with the engineering curriculum, engineering students often find that their job interferes with their ability to perform academically.

## Using Support Activities to Increase Retention

Studies have shown that persistence in engineering is linked to participation in support activities (Goodman and Cunningham 2002). The more involved a student is in campus life, and the more support she feels, the more likely she is to persist in the face of obstacles. Many engineering schools have women-in-engineering (WIE) programs to help provide an inclusive, supportive campus climate for female engineering students.

### WOMEN-IN-ENGINEERING PROGRAMS

Many colleges and universities across the county offer women-in-engineering (WIE) programs as a way to enhance engineering self-efficacy, improve classroom climate, decrease feelings of isolation, and promote informed choices among female engineering students in efforts to improve retention. The scope of the programs differs from institution to institution; in many cases, the activities offered by the program are dependent on factors such as funding and staffing. WIE programs may also contribute to recruitment efforts, inspiring girls and young women to pursue the unlimited opportunities within the world of engineering and empowering them to become engineers who benefit society.

Many programs include professional and academic development components, connecting current students with information about careers and companies and working to create and maintain an environment conducive to the successful completion of their studies. In the Cullen College of Engineering at the University of Houston, the primary goal of the Women in Engineering Learning Community for Maximizing Excellence (WELCOME) program is to establish a sense of community among female students, giving them the opportunity to meet fellow classmates, while interacting with women currently working in the field of engineering, both in industry and academia (Trenor, Madubike, and Claydon 2006). The WELCOME program offers two main initiatives: an "Engineering Your Success" seminar series, and an electronic-based mentoring program, which pairs incoming students with upper-division female students in their major, and links upper-division students with women working in industry or academia. In addition, WELCOME hosts retreats and social events to foster a stronger sense of community among the female engineering students.

### LEARNING COMMUNITIES

Many universities with residential campuses cluster female students in the same section of a designated dormitory to increase feelings of community among female students and reduce the potential for isolation. Many schools also use class clustering to achieve the same goal. In some programs, the female engineering students are encouraged to enroll in classes which explore critical issues surrounding women's roles in predominantly male fields.

#### SEMINARS AND WORKSHOPS

Many WIE programs offer seminars or workshops that relate to the professional, personal and academic development of female engineering students. Topics discussed at the University of Houston's WIE Engineering Your Success seminar series cover a wide range, including "Stress Management," "How to Get the Most Out of Your Professors," "Opportunities and Challenges for Women in the Corporate Workplace," "Financial Planning for the Newly Hired Professional," "How to Communicate with Men," "Work-Life Balance," and "Undergraduate and Graduate Research Opportunities," among others. Professional women with experience relating to the topic at hand are often invited to lead the seminars and subsequent discussion.

#### OUTREACH AND CORPORATE RECRUITING ACTIVITIES

Many WIE programs incorporate outreach activities to help recruit more young women to the field. Current engineering students are often given the opportunity to visit with K–12 students to talk about engineering and act as role models for younger girls. Some programs also address the pipeline issue by providing undergraduate students with access to corporate recruiters or other industry representatives for networking and job recruitment.

#### MENTORING PROGRAMS

Two kinds of mentoring programs are common in WIE programs around the county: peer mentoring and professional mentoring. Peer mentoring or "big sister" programs allow new students to "learn the ropes" from junior- and senior-level students in the engineering program. They have guidance throughout the first year, and obtain insight into the programs and support from upper-division students when they have concerns, doubts, or questions. For upper division students preparing to make the transition to the working world, a WIE program may connect them with a mentor who is a working professional, allowing the protégé to gain insight into the field of engineering and network with successful professionals. Both types of mentoring programs are usually geared towards helping female engineering students build a support network.

#### ADVISING, PROFESSIONAL DEVELOPMENT, AND CAREER GUIDANCE

Many Women-in-Engineering programs support informed choices in both academic and professional matters by offering advising for courses, professional development opportunities, and career guidance. Alumnae as well as university personnel may participate in these activities in order to provide guidance and support.

### Admissions' Role in Retention Efforts

Admissions personnel can help retention efforts in a number of ways. First of all, admissions staff, academic advisors from engineering colleges or departments, and instructors of freshman level courses would be well advised to work together to support incoming students in making an *informed choice*. Universities differ in their requirements for first-year students pursuing degrees in engineering: some require students to select a specific engineering degree path prior to entering the university, while some allow or even require students to take a common set of engineering courses before matriculating into a specific engineering department. Knowledge of the engineering curriculum and policies, and pointers as to where students can find information about various degree plans offered, will help guide students in making intelligent choices in the first place and, in the process, help to reduce attrition. In many instances, helping students make an educated choice about an engineering major also means educating their parents about career opportunities, dispelling misconceptions, and addressing their concerns about their daughter working in a "man's field."

A good working relationship between admissions officers on the one hand and engineering faculty and academic advisors on the other can be crucial in helping to facilitate parental education about these misconceptions. Additionally, admissions personnel can also serve as a valuable liaison with financial aid personnel. The engineering curriculum is rigorous, and students who have a financial need to work may face severe strains on their time, with their academic work suffering accordingly.

Finally, female students need to be made aware, as early as possible in the admissions process, of any science-oriented support systems that would be available to them once they are students at your institution.

In conclusion, here is a handy summary of ways that admissions personnel can help to recruit and retain female students in engineering programs:

- Assist students in making informed choices about their major; connect them with engineering faculty during and after the admissions process.
- Educate parents to dispel misconceptions and combat gender bias.
- Serve as a liaison with financial aid personnel to ensure that students are aware of all options for support; this may relieve the burden some students have of working to pay for their education, thus allowing them more time to devote to their studies.
- Serve as a liaison with WIE programs or other student support systems.

/ CHAPTER EIGHTEEN /

*by Christie M. Kangas, M.A.*
*Director of Undergraduate Admission*
*Texas State University—San Marcos*

18

# Recruitment of Transfer Students

National discussions of transfer tend to focus on U.S. Department of Education statistics that show that a majority of college graduates are transfer students; they have attended more than one college or university.[147] Bearing this in mind, the inclusion of transfer students in your admissions cohort, should be a product of care and thought, rather than happenstance. Why recruit transfer students? That is a question each institution needs to ask itself.

Whether an institution's service area is regional, statewide, or national, admissions directors should study the demographics in thier area. Is the traditional 18-year-old college-going population growing or shrinking? Is the economic environment causing older people to enter higher education? Are people seeking to change careers? Are you near large military installations with military personnel or families who wish to complete degrees? Are there large segments of first-generation students ready for college? Asking questions like these will assist you in answering the initial question: Why recruit transfer students?

[147] The data show that, among college students who graduated in 2001, nearly 60 percent had attended more than one college or university (Peter and Cataldi 2005, p. 37).

In Texas, community colleges are experiencing faster growth than the four-year institutions. While the potential population of high school graduates is continuing to grow, the Anglo population is declining and the Hispanic population is increasing. The strong sense of family may be one reason many Hispanics in Texas are choosing to start higher education at a two-year institution near their homes. Another factor is that an institution closer to home—whether a two- or four-year institution—saves a student related costs, such as housing and transportation.

The author's institution, a four-year university whose highest offering is the doctorate, has developed a commitment to serving the needs of transfer students. The fall entering transfer class is similar in size to the fall entering freshman class (3,010 new freshmen vs. 2,977 new transfers); over the full academic year transfers compose 59 percent of new students. When you add in those freshmen who bring with them transfer work as a result of opportunities for enrollment while in high school or those native students who take classes at institutions near their homes in the summers, the proportion of students with transfer credit within a student body grows. In 2006, 63 percent of the graduating class started at Texas State as transfer students. Numbers speak. We must be attentive to the transfer population.

This attentiveness entails making decisions about such topics as staffing, types of outreach, course articulation, transfer advisory councils and other means of understanding one's transfer market, the uses of joint and concurrent enrollment options, transfer orientations, and various means of assessing one's transfer operation. The transfer student is a moving target; thus, even successful initiatives need to be evaluated on an ongoing basis for continuing usefulness.

## Staffing Issues

Institutional commitment to recruitment of transfer students should include a commitment to appropriate staffing. Recruitment responsibility can be assigned to specific staff members, or there can be a philosophy of shared responsibility. At the author's institution, there is a blend of the two approaches. While selected staff have been assigned primary recruitment responsibility for various targeted feeder institutions, all recruitment staff have received training to work with transfers, and meet with transfers who visit campus. In addition, most staff, although some more frequently than others, recruit at two-year colleges. An Assistant Director oversees the recruitment planning and monitors progress toward goals.

Institutional decisions must also be made regarding which office will prepare evaluations of transfer work. This generally occurs in either the admissions or registrar office, although some universities are creating separate "transfer credit centers" which are devoted completely to that function. At the author's institution, transcript evaluators are part of the admissions staff. This staff, wherever it is located within the administrative offices, should be keenly aware of the need for timely evaluations within the application cycle and of the close relationship between timely evaluations and successful recruitment of transfer students.

Institutional commitment should also embody embracing best practices from around the nation. One avenue to achieve this is by providing staff the opportunity to learn how other universities are addressing transfer recruitment and related issues. The AACRAO Annual Meetings, and many of the state and regional conferences, often have significant portions of their programs devoted to transfer topics. Some presentations inform the members of initiatives mandated in one state that may provide good ideas to those in other states; others focus on specific issues involving articulation, orientation, advising, or such trends as learning communities and other support systems for transfer students.

TABLE 18.1: **Selected Transfer-Oriented Events, Organizations, and Resources**

| Resource | Description | URL |
|---|---|---|
| **Institute for the Study of Transfer Students** | Through an annual event held at the University of North Texas, the Institue offers professional development opportunities for those working with the transfer population | www.unt.edu/transferinstitute |
| **Biennial Conference on Transfer and Articulation** | Started in 2001, this gathering seeks research-based presentations that can be generalized to the larger transfer community | http://bcta.asu.edu |
| **National Orientation Directors Association** | An organization that "encourages excellence in orientation, retention and transition programming" | www.nodaweb.org |
| **National Resource Center for the First-Year Experience and Students in Transition** | An organization whose mission is "to support and advance efforts to improve student learning and transitions into and through higher education" | www.sc.edu/fye/center/ |
| **National Academic and Advising Association** | Publishes a monograph entitled "Advising Transfer Students: Issues and Strategies" | www.nacada.ksu.edu |

## Recruitment Tools

In planning for recruitment of transfer students, institutions need to provide the recruitment staff with tools to be effective. Take a focused look at what you are already doing.

### Publications

Do your publications speak to the potential transfer student, or are they focused primarily or exclusively on the entering freshman? In either case, decide whether a separate transfer publication would be advisable, or whether including a section on transfer in existing publications would be more appropriate. The decision will vary by institution. You may wish to consider a full viewbook specifically for transfer students if your prospective transfer student pool is significant. The author's institution currently uses a multi-page transfer brochure as a supplement to other general publications which contain basic transfer information.

### Web Sites

Today, Web sites are generally recognized as one of the most important marketing tools for higher education. Students routinely use the Web for basic research in their daily lives, and they are encountering our institutions early in their K–12 educational experience. Once again, step back and ask yourself some basic questions. Is your Web site already transfer-friendly? Do you have messages for transfer students which convey useful information? If not, promote necessary changes to include this population. First, inform transfers of what requirements they will need to enter your institution, and provide links to application forms. Also, provide links to key information like course equivalencies and transfer planning guides.

Let prospective transfer students know how to reach your transfer specialists. Not sure where to start? Perform a Web search using "transfer students" as your key words, and you will find links to a variety of different Web site approaches.

### Newsletters

Print publications and Web sites are only part of the arsenal of recruitment tools. Do you have prospective student newsletters? Is there a version for transfer students? Or do you include transfer topics in the general newsletter? At Texas State, an electronic newsletter is sent twice each semester to academic advisors at primary feeder institutions. Information about such time-sensitive matters as deadlines is included, along with updates on academic programs, information on transfer visit opportunities, links to specific parts of the Web site, and key contact information. This effort assists our allies at the community colleges as they work with students who are considering transfer.

### Visits

Just as it is important to visit feeder high schools and meet with the potential freshman student, it is essential to visit feeder two-year institutions to meet with the potential transfer student. How often visits are made will be dependent on the market area. Decisions may be made to visit weekly, monthly, or each semester.

Generally, staff at two-year institutions take seriously their role to assist with transfer, and they have a primary contact designated for making visit arrangements. One model is a "browse," in which a college representative sets up an information table in a student traffic area and speaks with students as they drop by. Another model operates via appointments that are set up in advance in a quieter location—an available office, conference room, or corner of a library. This appointment model has the advantage of allowing for one-on-one attention to prospective transfer students and their specific questions, needs, and goals. A third model involves a presentation to a class or a student organization. This works especially well when recruiting for specialized majors.

### Transfer Day

A more elaborate recruitment model is a "transfer day." In addition to a transfer recruitment counselor from an undergraduate admissions office, key faculty and/or advisors from the university's academic departments travel to the community college for a half or full day. Each academic area sets up an information table for prospective students. A portion of time may be devoted to individual student appointments with an advisor/faculty member in the academic area of interest. Community college staff assist by providing transcripts for the individual advising sessions. A portion of the time may also provide an opportunity for faculty to meet with their counterparts at the other institution. Transfer days are a means of bringing the university to the student. Such events introduce the students to key individuals at the university, and allow for specific advising designed to provide a smooth transition to the university when the student is ready.

Universities might also choose to host a transfer visit day on the campus. This event may be limited to transfers, especially to those students interested in specific colleges or departments. Another format involves including transfer sessions within a general campus open house event. However, welcome sessions, even at general events, should recognize the transfers in the audience and speak to their concerns, within the presentation. In addition, representatives at department information tables at a browse session should be alerted in advance to respond to the transfer student who comes by. If the program includes a variety of concurrent sessions, some of those sessions should address specific topics like the transfer of credit and transfer admissions processes. Remember that some of those freshmen at your campus open houses may eventually come to you as transfers, so your audience is broader than the subset of acknowledged transfer students.

### Long-Term Relationship-Building

One of the givens of working with transfer students is that they need information specific to their situation and goals. This often means that a transfer specialist or other admissions staff person must personally attend to their needs, guiding them through course selections at their current institution, helping fine-tune academic goals, and possibly assisting them through the application/admission process. This may be a long-term relationship. An admission counselor may recruit a high school senior who makes a decision to start college at a two-year institution near his or her home, but who intends to attend the university after the first or second year. That admission counselor might be called upon to build on the initial recruitment relationship to provide a smooth transition two years later to the university.

## Articulation

Articulation is at the forefront of institutional initiatives to assist the transfer of students. As DiPaolo (2006) states: "Having a permanent record of the transferability of a course, not only for the student immediately involved but for future students, means that the course is articulated, not merely evaluated" (p. 259). Con and Hardy (1978) define articulation as not only a process, but also an attitude and a goal:

+ *As a process, it is a coordination of policies and practices among sectors of the educational system to produce a smooth flow of students from one sector to another.*
+ *As an attitude, it is exemplified by the willingness of educators in all sectors to work together to transcend the individual and institutional self-interest that impedes the maximum development of the student.*
+ *As a goal, it is the creation of an educational system without artificial divisions, so that the whole educational period becomes one unbroken flow, which varies in speed for each individual, and which eliminates loss of credit, delays and unnecessary duplication of effort.*

Process, attitude, and goal all come together in efforts to establish articulation at the institutional and state levels. Common course numbering, common core/general education designations, transfer planning guides, course equivalencies, and 2+2 agreements are some of the articulation vehicles in use across the country. At Texas State we review the catalogs of the Texas two-year schools each year and enter the equivalencies in a database. Prospective students may access the listing for their respective community college via the Texas State Web site. Many other institutions have a similar approach.

In addition, Texas State has an ongoing effort to establish transfer planning guides for the primary feeder institutions for each of our undergraduate majors. These guides, known informally as 2+2 agreements at some institutions, help the students plan their enrollments at the two-year school so their work will fit well with their intended major at Texas State.

Development and maintenance of transfer planning guides is human resource-intensive, since curriculum can be a moving target: new courses are introduced at both four- and two-year campuses, and degree programs are added, deleted, or revised. Some institutions are beginning to move away from transfer planning guides, since technology enhancements provide a means to marry degree audit systems with transfer credit databases. One excellent example was developed at the University of Northern Iowa (UNI 2007) called "Transfer Plan-It"—a web-based service "designed to assist [students] in determining which UNI requirements [they] may have satisfied at an Iowa community college." Once a prospect is admitted, they receive a "personalized Degree Audit and Advisement Report."[148]

Across the United States, articulation is addressed in varying degrees at the state level, via grassroots efforts and via legislation. Texas has a common course numbering system that facilitates transfer of lower-division coursework, as well as a common core curriculum that facilitates applicability of appropriate general education work. Efforts are ongoing in the state to create articulation of fields of study. These are a form of 2+2 that can be followed for any of the state's public universities that offer a particular field of study, such as elementary education. For a comprehensive reference to statewide efforts, visit AACRAO's "Transfer and State Articulation Web Sites" page (www.aacrao.org/pro_development/transfer.cfm). It is a great reference point if discussion is taking place in your area.

## Transfer Advisory Councils

Whether your institution is just beginning to consider transfer recruitment or has been committed to transfers for decades, a transfer advisory council can provide a means to understand your transfer market and identify strategies to improve your efforts. Texas State has had a Transfer Advisory Council in place since 1984. It meets annually in the fall. Membership consists of a representative from each of our largest feeder institutions, along with rotating memberships from other feeder institutions. The day-long meeting includes reports about

[148] See <https://access.uni.edu/cgi-bin/transfer/transferPlanIt.cgi>.

the transfer population at Texas State, reports from each two-year institution, and discussion of selected topics. Through a dialogue, representatives can gain a better understanding of issues at the two-year colleges that may enhance or affect recruitment efforts; listen to recommendations for new or enhanced strategies; and get feedback as to changes the university may be considering.

## Joint/Concurrent Enrollments

Various joint or concurrent admission programs exist around the country. These may take the format of the Blinn TEAM program, a collaborative effort between Texas A&M University and Blinn College (a two-year state college in Brenham, TX), where students selected for the program take courses *simultaneously* on both campuses. When the student reaches an identified threshold and meets specific requirements, he or she may enroll full time in the university without a further application process.[149]

Another format has students fully enrolled at the two-year institution for their coursework while being allowed to access *some* of the resources of the university. An example is the Gateway Program[150] between Texas Tech University and South Plains College (a two-year state college in Levelland, TX). Students may live in a Texas Tech residence hall and purchase an activity package that permits them to make use of resources at Texas Tech University, even though all classes are taken at South Plains.

A third example is Texas State's Guaranteed Admission Program (GAP), a one-year step-into-Texas State program. In this program, students who apply to Texas State and do not meet admission requirements, but do meet requirements of a four-year sister institution in our university system, are offered the opportunity to attend Angelo State University (a four-year state university in San Angelo, TX) for one year. If students meet certain criteria at the end of the year, they may enroll in Texas State without further application. Each of these types of joint or concurrent admission programs provides students seeking a four-year degree an alternative pathway to become eligible to attend an institution of choice.

## Transfer Credit Evaluations

Transfer credit evaluations serve to move students' coursework from their previous institutions into the new one. Whether these evaluations are made and stored manually or electronically, the purpose is the same: to develop a database of decisions so that any decisions made may be applied to multiple students, rather than being reinvented one by one.

As mentioned earlier, at Texas State we review the catalogs of the Texas two-year schools each year and enter the equivalencies in a database. We also develop equivalencies for certain

[149] See <http://blinnteam.tamu.edu> for more details.

[150] Details of this program are found at <www2.southplainscollege.edu/programs-of-study/gateway/>.

Texas four-year institutions from which we receive more than minimal numbers of students. Thus, we have fewer students for whom we need to evaluate courses on a case-by-case basis.

An established database assists in many ways in speeding up the transcript evaluation when a student applies. First, the transcript(s) require minimal data entry. Taken a step further, if an institution receives college transcripts electronically (*i.e.*, via SPEEDE), technology can match that electronic transcript against the database and can produce an evaluated transcript quickly. An automated process such as this permits an institution with a high volume of transfer students to prepare evaluations in a timely manner.

Whether an institution is using technology for evaluations or manually preparing each evaluation, the key point to remember is that the evaluation is information the student needs to make the decision on whether to enroll at an institution. Some institutions provide unofficial evaluations prior to application as a courtesy, seeing the evaluation as an important recruitment tool. Other institutions provide the evaluation only following an application for admission, either enclosed with the notice of admission or available prior to advising and registration. Others are providing a self-service vehicle for the student (*e.g.*, the University of Northern Iowa's Transfer Plan-It program [*see* page 272]). Staffing, technology, and institutional philosophy all play roles in the timing.

## Transfer Orientation and Transition

Do not overlook the need for transfers to transition to your institution. Give serious consideration to some form or level of transfer orientation program. Yes, transfers have already attended college, but they have not attended *your* college. Transfer students are likely to find that academic advising and course registration procedures are different in the new environment. At the two-year school they may have completed the whole process in one sitting in the advisor's office. At the university, they might be advised in one location and then need to go to a central computer lab to register via the Web. The internal university lingo may throw them off. They might be used to paying at the cashier, but you now tell them to go to the Bursar.

A transfer orientation program may be organized as a one-day event. Students arrive in the morning and receive packets of needed information (*i.e.*, copy of transcript evaluation, degree audit, university catalog, schedule of classes, advising worksheets, student handbook, campus map). An introductory session outlines the day and introduces the student to key university staff. Students are then escorted to advising locations based on their degree interests. Students emerge from advising with a plan for their schedule which they take to a computer lab to access the web registration process. The web registration may also provide a way for the student to request a parking permit and/or meal plan and make an initial payment on their bill.

Sometime during the day, the student might be provided information on getting involved in campus life. Consider having a browse session, while students are arriving in the morning or near the computer lab, with information tables about student organizations, wellness/recreation centers, support services (tutoring, writing labs, mentoring, counseling), student health center, commuter services, and housing opportunities on- and off-campus, to give a few examples.

Remember that incoming transfer students will come from a variety of backgrounds and have a variety of needs. An on-campus orientation program on a weekday may not be convenient for a working adult. Online orientations provide an alternative means of conveying critical information, and guiding students through processes they need to know in order to navigate. However, if an institution requires orientation but allows an online option, the institution should make use of technological tools to ensure that students who choose the online option are, in fact, logging in and participating.

## Assessment

### Internal Uses

As with any recruitment efforts, consideration should be given to assessment of those efforts. Monthly trend reports that show comparisons from year to year by each feeder institution—including indications of number of applicants, admitted, denied, incomplete, committed and enrolled—help those with oversight of transfer recruitment to monitor progress throughout the recruitment cycle. Weekly summary reports of application activity provide information to university administrators responsible for budgetary decisions about number of course sections and faculty assignments. Individual program and travel reports can be reviewed in planning for future recruitment efforts. Are the programs or travel efforts producing the desired results? Are they cost-effective? Should efforts be repeated, revised, or dropped? The answers will vary with the institution and situation. The important point is having the data available for decision making.

### Feedback to Feeder Institutions

Feedback reports to primary feeder institutions are important to planners at those institutions. Summary reports on how many students transferred from Institution A to Institution B, average number of hours enrolled, average grade point average, distribution by major, proportion on probation or suspension, number who graduate in a given term/year, how many persist each year, etc. can be invaluable to both the sending and receiving institution. Feeder institutions gain a sense of how well they are preparing students academically for transfer. Receiving institutions might review the same data for confirmation that admission standards are appropriate.

### Transfer Student Surveys

Another assessment tool would involve a survey of transfer students at a given institution. An institution may want to learn more about how students gathered information to make their transfer decision; whether they judge the institution's admission and transcript evaluation processes to be useful and timely, or not; or to learn of any other customer service issues which arise as students transition to the university. An institution may want to identify which support services are most needed by new transfers as part of an initiative to improve retention. At the author's institution, staff in the Division of Student Affairs developed a "Transfer Student Survey" that was first administered in fall 2004. The results reinforced some beliefs of staff, and provided insight as to ways to improve aspects of services.

For a more comprehensive look at transfer students, consider reading Bonita Jacobs' (2004) book entitled *The College Transfer Student in America: The Forgotten Student*. A collaboration between AACRAO and the Institute for the Study of Transfer Students, it provides a comprehensive perspective for anyone considering working with transfer students.

/ CHAPTER NINETEEN /

*by Angela J. Evans, Ed.D.*
*Assistant Director of Admissions*
*Kennesaw State University*
*David Wallace, M.S.*
*Director of Admissions*
*The University of Memphis*

19

# Homeschooled Students:
## Background and Challenges

There is no doubt that the population of homeschooled students is increasing. The National Center for Education Statistics (NCES) states that both the number and the proportion of students in the United States who were being homeschooled increased between 1999 and 2003. Approximately 1.1 million such students (1,096,000) were counted as of the spring of 2003, an increase from the estimated 850,000 in the spring of 1999 (Princiotta and Bielick 2006, p. 1). In addition, the percentage of the entire student population, ages 5 through 17, who were being homeschooled increased from 1.7 percent in 1999 to 2.2 percent in 2003 (p. 1). NCES plans to collect and report data about homeschooled students with future Parent and Family Involvement in Education Surveys (PFI), scheduled to occur on a four-year cycle (p. 22).

This chapter will briefly discuss the characteristics of homeschooled students, and will present a succinct overview of the range of regulation of homeschooling in the fifty states. It will then discuss, as a jumping-off point, both the requirements in the state of Georgia and the "Admissions Package for Home Educated Applicants" of an institution in Georgia (Kennesaw State University). It will note that homeschoolers (in Georgia) are now eligible, as they had not been previously, for HOPE (merit-based) scholarships; will refer to three suggestive studies of the first-year performance of the homeschooled college student; and will make some recommendations as to next steps in assessing and guiding homeschooled students.

The variety implicit in homeschooling and the sheer numbers of students participating in home-based education at the high school level will present college admissions offices with unique challenges (Head and Evans 2000).

## Motivating Factors and Impact of Homeschooling

Data from the Parent Survey of the National Household Education Surveys Program (NHES) of 1999, which was conducted along with NCES's first comprehensive survey of homeschoolers nationwide, in that same year, show that, "compared to non-homeschooled students, homeschooled students were more likely to be white, to have families with three or more children in the household, to have two parents (especially when only one parent was in the labor force), and to have parents whose highest level of educational attainment was a bachelor's degree or higher" (Princiotta and Bielick 2006, p. 8).

Even more interesting were the reasons reported by parents in the NHES survey of 1999 for choosing to school their children at home. (Percentages add up to more than 100 percent because respondents were allowed to name more than one reason.) The top three reasons were: Concern about the environment of the child's original school (including safety, drugs, or negative peer pressure), 85.4 percent; desire for religious or moral instruction in the school, 72.3 percent; and dissatisfaction with academic instruction available at other schools, 68.2 percent. The next three reasons were as follows: the child has special needs, 28.9 percent; the child has a physical or mental health problem, 15.9 percent; and "other reasons," 20.1 percent (Table 4, p. 13).

Although all these considerations are weighty ones, critics have contended that when more than a million students remove themselves from the public schools, there is a substantial negative impact on the public schools, in two ways: first, the loss of student enrollment means the loss of per capita funding provided by state governments to the local school districts; and second, the public schools are also losing the time, talents, and resources of some of their most involved parents.

In any event, as homeschooled children reach college age, more than 69 percent of them are seeking to pursue a college education (Ray 1998). As a growing number of students and families choose what is in effect a self-constructed alternative form of secondary education, college and university administrators, and also the state legislatures, are facing difficult questions about how to regulate homeschooling—and how to evaluate the students who present themselves to college in the admissions process.

## Regulations and Requirements

According to the Home School Legal Defense Association (HSLDA 2007a), an advocate of home schooling, homeschooling is legal in all 50 states—but it is subject to varying degrees of regulation.

Ten states, Guam, and Puerto Rico require no notice at all, from the parent to the state government, that the parent intends to teach the child entirely at home.

Another fourteen states, the District of Columbia, and the U.S. Virgin Islands require only a low (minimal) level of notice that the parents intend to home school the child.

Twenty states require a "moderate" level of notice—that is, parents are required to send a notification of intent to homeschool, as well as ongoing test scores and/or professional evaluations of student progress.

Six states, American Somoa, and the Northern Mariana Islands require a "high" level of notification. Such states require, beyond a notification of intent and the sending of achievement test scores and/or professional evaluations, submission of such additional items as one or more of the following: curriculum approval; qualification of the parent(s) as teachers; or home visits by state officials.

TABLE 19.1: Level of Notification Required by U.S. States and Territories

| None | Low/Minimal | Moderate | High |
|---|---|---|---|
| **Mainland** | | | |
| Alaska, Connecticut, Idaho, Illinois, Indiana, Michigan, Missouri, New Jersey, Oklahoma, and Texas | Alabama, Arizona, California, Delaware, District of Columbia, Kansas, Kentucky, Mississippi, Montana, Nebraska, Nevada, New Mexico, Utah, Wisconsin, and Wyoming | Arkansas, Colorado, Florida, Georgia, Hawaii, Iowa, Louisiana, Maine, Maryland, Minnesota, North Carolina, New Hampshire, Ohio, Oregon, South Carolina, South Dakota, Tennessee, Virginia, Washington, and West Virginia | Massachusetts, North Dakota, New York, Pennsylvania, Rhode Island, and Vermont |
| **Territories** | | | |
| Guam and Puerto Rico | U.S. Virgin Islands | American Samoa and Northern Mariana Islands | — |

Source: HSLDA 2007b

### Case Study: The Georgia Homeschooling Statute

Georgia is an example of a state with a compulsory school attendance law. See Official Code of Georgia Annotated, O.C.G.A. sec. 20–2–690.[142]

The Georgia Home Education Association (GHEA 2007) has provided a plain-language version of the Georgia home-study statute.[143] Here are the main features of what is required:

- DECLARATION OF INTENT TO HOME STUDY—Parents must submit such a Declaration to the superintendent of the school system the child would have attended; such a submission must be made within 30 days after the establishment of the home

[142] Georgia's compulsory attendance law applies between the 6th and 16th birthdays. However, if a child is under six and has attended more than twenty days in a public school, he or she is then subject to the compulsory attendance laws. Official Code of Georgia Annotated sec. 20-2-690(c)(5). Required subjects include, but are not limited to: reading, language arts, math, social studies, and science. O.C.G.A. sec. 20-2-690(c)(4).

[143] See <www.ghea.org/pages/resources/stateLaw.php>.

study program, and by September 1 every year thereafter. This Declaration must include the names and ages of students, the location of the home school, and the time the parents designate as their school year.

- BASIC ACADEMIC EDUCATIONAL PROGRAM—Homeschooling parents must provide a description of the educational program being pursued.
- LENGTH OF SCHOOL DAY—Four-and-one-half hours per day, minimum.
- ATTENDANCE RECORDS—Parents must keep and submit such records to the superintendent each month.
- ANNUAL PROGRESS REPORT—Parents must write one and retain it for three years.
- WHO MAY TEACH? The "teaching parent" must have at least a high school diploma or a GED. Or the parents may employ a private tutor who has at least those qualifications. "Parents or guardians may teach only their own children in the home study program," but they may employ a tutor with at least the qualifications just set forth.
- STANDARDIZED TESTS—Homeschooled children are required to take a national standardized achievement test every three years beginning with the third grade. "Test scores are not required to be submitted to public school authorities." However, as noted above, the parents are required to write an annual progress report and retain it for three years.
- PROOF OF CONTINUING COMPLIANCE—The local superintendent has the authority only to request, not to require, the parents to produce evidence of their continuing compliance. 1986 Opinion of the [Georgia] Attorney General, No. U86–19.

## Case Study: Kennesaw State University's Requirements

The influx of home-educated students into the college admissions process has raised many issues, both of process and of substance. In relation to process, homeschooled students do not have traditional grade-point averages or high school graduation honors to show (Head and Evans 2000, p. 28). In terms of substance, in addition to the submission of a current Declaration of Intent to Homeschool, as filed with the local Board of Education, Kennesaw State University (KSU 2007) requires the following items, so as to make possible a meaningful assessment, for admissions purposes, of homeschooled students:

- Submission of SAT or ACT scores
- A national standardized high school summation exam taken during the twelfth grade year (examples: Iowa Achievement Test Series, SAT II, California Achievement Test, Stanford Achievement Test)
- Form showing curriculum completed, with supporting documentation
- Portfolio of extracurricular activities and academic achievements during high school that support academic preparedness for college. "This portfolio should include awards received, academic accomplishments, and activities you participate in—church, civic, volunteer, and athletic, etc."

- Two letters of recommendation from non-family members (examples: employers, clergy, civic leaders, tutors)
- Affidavit from primary teacher and from the student, certifying completion of high school and date of high school graduation, and a copy of your diploma if you have already graduated (a notary public attests to the signatures)

## State Certification[144]

Issues of teacher certification, curriculum rigor, and certification or accreditation[145] of the home school itself have complicated the admissions process for many homeschool graduates. Public institutions of higher education in the state of Georgia have posed particular difficulties for homeschoolers.

In 1997, the Georgia Board of Regents adopted a policy that required home-educated applicants to the state's 34 public colleges and universities to submit numerous SAT II subject exam scores in lieu of a diploma from an accredited high school.[146] Georgia is still grappling with issues of equity and accountability for home-educated applicants and is a good state to look at concerning issues of state certification of homeschool preparation, both because of the popularity of homeschooling in the state[147] and because the state created an accreditation agency designed specifically to develop credible measures for home education. This is the Accrediting Commission for Independent Study—an accrediting commission designed specifically to evaluate home-based programs of study.[148]

The development of such an accrediting commission would prove to be imperative for Georgia to establish a truce between concerned homeschool supporters and the state's institutions of higher education. As of 1997, the University of Georgia system required homeschooled students—or other students who had not graduated from a recognized (accredited or approved) high school—to take and pass eight SAT II subject matter tests in order to demonstrate proficiency with the college preparatory curriculum (Evans 2005, p. 8). Homeschoolers argued that the additional testing requirements added financial burdens to them that were not being imposed on traditionally-educated students.

---

[144] Called "accreditation" in Georgia.

[145] Georgia's use of the term "accreditation" is not to be confused with the process of recognition by the U.S. Department of Education of regional, specialized, and faith-based and/or vocationally-oriented accrediting organizations. "Federal recognition is currently required for accrediting organizations that certify institutional eligibility for participation in federal student financial aid programs under Title IV of the 1965 Higher Education Act or certain other federal funding" (CHEA 2005, p. 10).

[146] In May 1996, the Board of Regents for the University System of Georgia (USG) approved a report by a USG Admissions Task Force (of senior administrators, faculty, and admissions personnel representing all 34 public colleges and universities in Georgia) which contained a series of recommendations focused on "raising the bar" for admissions to USG institutions. The problem was aggravated by the fact that there was, at the time, no professionally recognized accreditation or review process for homeschool programs of study as there is in the public and private secondary school sectors.

[147] In 1996, 15,353 students were reported as being enrolled in home-study programs in Georgia; in 2005, that number had risen to 36,413. See Georgia Public and Non-Public School Enrollment Reports, 1996 and 2005, respectively.

[148] Beginning in August of 2005, the Georgia Accrediting Commission assumed jurisdiction of Non-Traditional Educational Centers (including homeschooling). The centers were formally members of the Accrediting Commission for Independent Study. See <www.coe.uga.edu/gac/about/history.html>.

By 2001, the University System of Georgia had repealed some of the SAT II requirements that had been objected to, but steadily upheld the premise that accreditation of high school course work was essential. A compromise emerged. As an alternative to submitting the SAT II exams (or other subject matter tests), homeschooled students could submit an "academic portfolio," so that their pre-college preparation could be evaluated by colleges or the state university system. The use of the portfolio was widely accepted by homeschooling families, but it still posed a problem in that the state Board of Regents did not clearly define what constituted an acceptable portfolio. Institutions were left to grapple with the portfolio review with little guidance from the governing agency.

The Accrediting Commission for Independent Study (ACIS) was instituted by a group of concerned educators and lawmakers in 1997 as a solution for homeschoolers in Georgia, and for colleges and universities as well, all of whom needed a validating agency to act as an intermediary. ACIS was a nonprofit commission that was established to give professional recognition and professional approval to the study that students pursue while in independent and home study in the state of Georgia. Dr. W. Starr Miller, president emeritus of Brewton Parker College, was instrumental in establishing the ACIS organization through his role as an advisor to the Georgia Accrediting Commission (a century-old accrediting group for pre-college accreditation in the state.)

Georgia is currently the only state to have initiated an accrediting agency for homeschooling and independent study programs that is not regulated by any state or federal agency. As previously noted, ACIS has now been made a part of the Georgia Accrediting Commission (GAC).

To date, however, no published research has attempted to evaluate the usefulness of ACIS, GAC, or any other "accreditation" as a tool for college admissions officers to evaluate home-educated candidates in the college admissions process. Thus an important question remains unanswered: Is ACIS/GAC a valuable tool for colleges and universities and homeschooling families, or is it merely a political tool used to quiet a disgruntled populace?

## HOPE Scholarship Eligibility

Although the existence of ACIS is only a first step in clarifying the preparedness of homeschooled students for college, the fact of ACIS/GAC accreditation is helpful to homeschooled students in obtaining a HOPE (Helping Outstanding People Educationally) scholarship. The HOPE scholarships began in 1993.[149] Under a Georgia law passed in 2007, homeschool students who graduate from an institution accredited by the ACIS/GAC can receive a HOPE scholarship at the beginning of their freshman year in college if they scored in the ninetieth percentile or higher on the ACT or SAT. Before the passage of that law, homeschool students

[149] For a history of the evolution of the HOPE scholarship program, see "HOPE Scholarship" in The New Georgia Encyclopedia, at <www.georgiaencyclopedia.org/nge/Article.jsp?id=h-1483>.

were eligible for a HOPE scholarship for the freshman year only after earning 30 semester or 45 quarter hours with a 3.0 GPA. The change is that homeschooled students with the right academic qualifications can now receive the scholarship at the beginning of their freshman year.

## Recommendations

A 1997 study concluded that admissions personnel do not have objective criteria for measuring a homeschool applicant's potential for success at their institution (Prue 1997).

Research has just begun on the performance of homeschooled students once they reach college. Three empirical studies in the mid and late 1990s focused specifically on the academic performance of homeschooled students in their first year of college.[150] The results are encouraging, but the samples were small.

Kennesaw State University has considerable experience with homeschooled students; between 1995 and 2007, over 200 home-educated students have applied, been accepted to, and enrolled at KSU. We rely on the concept of *portfolio assessment* and, based on our use of it, recommend it in a generic sense, in that each institution will need to tweak the concept to suit its own campus culture.

As Evans (2003) explains,

> *"The concept of portfolio assessment applies when a student is a graduate of a non-accredited high school, or is a homeschool graduate. Admissions personnel can use the portfolio to help determine a student's eligibility for admission by assessing his [or] her academic preparedness as demonstrated through the materials submitted in the admissions portfolio. Typically, the portfolio would include a qualifying SAT I and demonstration of a completed college preparatory curriculum (CPC). To be a qualifying SAT I, an applicant's results would [have to] equal the previous year's freshman SAT average for the institution. A completed CPC is demonstrated through a thorough explanation of curriculum used, and supporting documentation including, but not limited to, textbooks used, sample assignments, and methods of evaluation"* (p. 29).

In addition the portfolio for Georgia would comprise the other items already enumerated above, including extracurricular activities, two letters of recommendation from non-family members, and so forth.

> *"The completed portfolio is evaluated by an admissions professional who must use his or her experience and professional discretion to determine if the applicant meets the admissions criteria established by the institution"* (p. 29).

[150] Jones and Gloeckner (2004) reported that "Galloway (1995) found that home school graduates outperformed their conventional private school peers on the ACT English subtest. Jenkins (1998) found that full- and part-time community college home school students' average first-year grade point averages were higher than non-home school [students]. ...Finally, Gray (1998) found no significant differences between homeschool and traditional students at three institutions in Georgia (including a public university, a private university, and a private college) on SAT scores, English grades, or cumulative grade point averages" (p. 18).

To better serve this emerging population, the Director of Admissions at KSU dedicated an admissions counselor to work with the home-educated applicants. This specialization allowed for relationship development with the homeschooling community; that the results have been very positive is evident in the hundreds of applications from home-educated students.

KSU has introduced and hosted a Home School Student Union that serves as an aid to students in transitioning from the homeschool environment to that of a large public university. The Home School Student Union serves as a springboard for students into participation in other activities, and it encourages students to get involved in a variety of student organizations, including seeking positions in campus leadership. Former homeschoolers have held the position of student government president for four out of five years, editor of the student newspaper for three years, and have served in a variety of other positions in numerous clubs and organizations. In addition, two KSU homeschoolers have served as student advisors to the University System Chancellor, and their advice was instrumental in the system's adoption of the Portfolio Assessment model.

In an informal 1997 study conducted by the Admissions Office at Kennesaw State University, researchers compared home-educated college freshmen to their traditionally-educated counterparts and discovered that the homeschoolers outperformed other students by almost a full grade point. Future studies are needed to help establish support for our argument that homeschoolers are definitely a pool of students worth attracting to our institution.

A 2000 study by Davis concludes that "admissions officials should begin tracking homeschool applicants after enrollment to evaluate admissions decisions, gather data regarding the academic success of these applicants at the postsecondary level, and help in the development of future policies or procedures for other special population groups" (p. 146). A more systematic program of tracking our admitted homeschooled students will help those of us involved in working with this particular population to better gauge our success, both in terms of the student and the institution.

/ CHAPTER TWENTY /

*by Meredyth A. Leahy, Ed.D.*
*Susan Smith Nash, Ph.D.*
*Susan Dewan, M.B.A.*
*All from the School of Liberal Arts at Excelsior College*

20

# Recruiting Military Students

To successfully recruit students who are also military professionals, the institution of higher learning must have an in-depth understanding of this unique population. The rewards to the education provider can be worth the investment of time, effort, technology, infrastructure, and personnel, since there are literally tens of thousands of prospective students. It is very satisfying to realize that we are helping the Department of Defense Voluntary Education Program provide valuable educational opportunities to service members while they serve their country, and afterwards. Military students may enroll in associate, bachelor, and graduate-level programs, as well as certificate programs, on institutional campuses, military installations, and armories within the United States and overseas.

The Department of Defense (2003) states that its voluntary education programs "constitute one of the largest continuing education programs in the world. Each year about 300,000 service members enroll in postsecondary courses leading to associate, bachelors, masters and doctorate degrees." Blumenstyk (2006) reports that "the military is now spending nearly half a billion dollars a year in tuition assistance for the members of its active-duty force, more than double the amount it spent in the 2002 fiscal year." Many individuals joined the all-volunteer military to fund a college education, among other motivations. But Blumenstyk

(2006) also reports that college degrees are increasingly becoming a prerequisite for promotion *within* the military. "Last August [2006], for instance, the Navy put in place a rule that, beginning in 2011, will require all sailors to hold at least an associate degree to qualify for promotion to senior enlisted ranks."

Despite the existence of a large market, however, being a provider of high-quality support services and admissions counseling is not as easy as it might appear. There are numerous challenges. First, the average military student has special needs and requirements due to the conditions of work, which may include deployment, frequent travel, and erratic work schedules. Despite such logistical challenges, the military student is often highly motivated to take courses because he or she has access to a unique array of benefits, programs, and equipment. While this support system is definitely a boon for the military professional, it presents a challenge for institutional providers because they must conform to very exacting, specific requirements. Further complicating the task for the educational institution is the fact that the military has its own training and educational programs, as well as transcripting and reporting methods it has devised. Finally, military students, like their civilian counterparts, are becoming better informed through access to the Internet and other electronic sources, and can thus target their search to a college or university that readily meets their needs.

## Case Study: A Typical Military Professional

It is useful to follow the steps of a typical military professional—Staff Sergeant (SSgt) Maria Lopez. As a nine-year veteran of the Army, she is very excited that she has finally made it to a job location and a rank that will allow her to have time and Internet access sufficient to take a few courses. Before this point, even though she was eligible for DOD voluntary education programs, she did not have time to take courses. She did, however, take exams (CLEP, DANTES, and Excelsior College Exams), through which she earned college credit. She has been waiting for this moment for years.

When SSgt Lopez first enlisted, she knew participating in a DOD voluntary education program was the only way that she would be able to pay for college and, although she did not have a clear picture of what her goals were at the time, she had completed a few college courses from different schools during her first assignment, stateside. Little did she know that she would have to go through two tours of duty in Iraq and be separated for a total of thirty-six months from her young children and her husband. The separation and the hardship have made her more determined than ever to obtain a college degree.

SSgt Lopez's first step is to go to the education office on base, where she meets with a military education counselor, who has a checklist of items that students are encouraged to consider when selecting a college and degree program. To her relief, she finds that some of the questions she wanted to ask are on that list, as are some she hadn't thought of yet. SSgt Lopez is surprised to learn that she has a number of options and decides to check out several before beginning her studies. She wants to find a college to serve as her "home school" that appears best suited to meet her needs and offers the program she thinks she wants.

She learns that eArmyU, which is an online option within GoArmyEd, offers a number of programs, undergraduate and graduate, from multiple colleges and universities. From the GoArmyEd Web site, at www.goarmyed.com, she can learn of additional degree programs from well over 145 colleges with approved Letters of Instruction (LOI). Many such programs are offered in both online and CD-ROM formats. GoArmyEd is an online portal for soldiers that enables them to request online Tuition Assistance for classroom, distance learning, and eArmyU online courses. Courses offered through eArmyU are delivered exclusively online and currently include the following benefits: free textbooks and free Internet Service Provider access. In addition, all course fees are included in the eArmyU tuition price.

Through the GoArmyEd portal, Tuition Assistance (TA) is approved and monitored, so that SSgt Lopez does not have to pay for her courses out of pocket and wait to be reimbursed if she takes courses from an LOI school—and she will know when she has used her TA allocation for the current year.[142] Finally, there are several colleges which are represented on the base. Some of them offer onsite classes, which she finds appealing, and others are distance institutions providing academic advising and other services to soldier students on site.

SSgt Lopez likes the portal concept because it saves her time and money. Instead of having to go to the education center in person each time she wants to find out what classes are available or check degree requirements, she can log in, and the information she needs is there. The portal gives her access to online registration, her records, and even her grades.

## Specialized Services Available to Military Personnel

Let's take a look at some criteria for the military student to consider when selecting a college or program. In the course of doing so, we can describe many of the specialized services available to the military student with which admissions officers will want to be somewhat familiar. Along the way we will also discuss some of the unique circumstances facing military students, so we can develop in the reader a better understanding and appreciation of what they bring to the table.

SSgt Lopez was concerned about those courses she had taken several years ago and wondered if they could be applied towards a degree. She wanted to make sure that the college she chose was a legitimate college, one recognized by others. She had also heard that some of her training might be worth college credit and wondered how she could get a record of her training, beyond that big binder of certificates and other documents she had collected over the years.

142 The National Defense Authorization Act of 2000 raised the percentage of tuition assistance that the services could pay from 75 percent to 100 percent. The individual service member should check to see how the Act applies to the four services (Army, Navy, Marines, and Air Force), the Coast Guard, the National Guard, and the Reserve Component. There can be a cap on the amount of the semester-hour charge which will be reimbursed, the total number of credits which can be taken per semester, and the total allowed payment per student.

The Education Counselor assured her that every college available to her through GoArmyEd, eArmyU, or on base was a member of SOC (Servicemembers Opportunity College).

## Servicemembers Opportunity College

Just what is the Servicemembers Opportunity College (SOC)? SOC is a consortium of more than 1,800 colleges and universities which, within each degree level and curriculum, agree to accept each other's credits in transfer, thus making it easier for service members to complete their degrees or certificates. SOC is funded by the Department of Defense (DoD) through a contract with the American Association of State Colleges and Universities (AASCU). The DoD also works with the four Military Services (plus the National Guard and the Coast Guard); the American Association of Community Colleges (AACC); and with other higher education associations to facilitate the exchange of credit for military personnel between member institutions.

Because of the pervasiveness of the required mobility faced by service members, SOC has established criteria to ensure that institutional policies and practices are fair, equitable, and effective in recognizing the special and often limiting conditions faced by the military student. Institutions should be familiar with the *Servicemembers Opportunity Colleges SOC Principles and Criteria 2007–2009*.[143] In addition to other requirements delineated in this publication, SOC institutions are expected to:

- Limit academic residency requirements for active-duty members to no more than 25 percent of the undergraduate degree program;
- Work to minimize loss of credit transfer and avoid duplication of course work;
- Award credit for at least one of the nationally recognized testing programs including the College Level Examination Program, DSST (DANTES subject specialized tests), and Excelsior College Examinations; and,
- Award credit for military training and experience.

SOC helps to coordinate associate and bachelor's degree work in a variety of curriculum areas for the Army (SOC Army Degrees, or SOCAD), Navy (SOCNAV), Marine Corps (SOCMAR), and Coast Guard (SOCCOAST). These degree programs are offered by colleges and universities which are on or accessible to Army, Navy, Marine Corps, and Coast Guard installations worldwide, and credits earned will be accepted within the consortium.

## Accreditation

SSgt Lopez's second question was about a college's "legitimacy"—its recognition related to accreditation. Is the college accredited by a regional or national accrediting body recognized by the U.S. Department of Education, and why is this important?

[143] *See* <www.soc.aascu.org/socgen/Criteria.html>.

Accreditation is critical to military students who, because they rotate from location to location, typically take courses from a number of institutions over the course of their military career. They need to make sure that all the colleges they attend are accredited, so that when the time comes to consolidate all that college course work and apply it towards a single degree program, the student can be confident that all or at least a large majority of the credits earned will be accepted in transfer. In addition, it is not uncommon for less than credible institutions and diploma mills to actively target the military community, and so a knowledge of the various types of accreditation becomes especially important to the student.

Overly aggressive marketing has become a serious issue in this context, and is just one concern being addressed by a DoD task force charged with developing standards for the provision of distance learning. Currently in draft form, the *Principles of Good Practice for Higher Education Institutions Providing Voluntary Distance Education Programs to Members of the U.S. Armed Forces & their Families* should be available soon and should be consulted by any institution intending to serve the military. This document addresses everything from institutional mission, goals, and objectives to responsiveness and flexibility toward service members; from faculty qualifications, to training in facilitating distance learning, to student engagement, and course and faculty evaluation.

### Guide to the Evaluation of Educational Experiences in the Armed Forces

The third item on the list speaks to SSgt Lopez's concerns about whether or not the training she has completed during her nine years of service is applicable to her degree. She learns that there is a publication, the *Guide to the Evaluation to Educational Experiences in the Armed Services*, which serves to guide colleges in their review of military training in relation to credit for degrees. Published in hard copy for a number of years, the *Guide* is now available at the American Council on Education (ACE) Web site.[144]

The guide is the result of many years of experience. Since 1942 ACE has collaborated with the U.S. Department of Defense, and the Military Services including the National Guard and the Coast Guard, to conduct in-depth reviews of military education and training programs to determine if such programs are comparable to college-level courses. The *Guide* is the result of those efforts.

This guide is similar in nature to ACE's *National Guide to Educational Credit for Training Programs*[145] in civilian life, which followed some 30 years later, and was based upon the success of ACE's publications related to training within the military. Both the military and civilian guides make use of teams of qualified faculty and content specialists to conduct the assessments, and determine the appropriate credit recommendation. ACE periodically offers valuable training workshops on how to best use the *Guide to the Evaluation of Educational*

144 *See* <www.militaryguides.acenet.edu>.

145 Available online at <www.acenet.edu/nationalguide/>.

*Experiences in the Armed Services*, and every institution should have at least one staff member who is familiar with it and trained in its use.

## The Military Transcript System

To her delight, Staff Sergeant Lopez learns that the Army had already been keeping close track of the various training programs she had completed over the course of her career in the Army, and that she would find it all carefully documented on something called an AARTS transcript. The education counselor mentions that all the services provide similar transcripts for their members, so her husband, who is in the Army National Guard, may request a copy of his records as well. These documents are available electronically. The SOC includes National Guard members among the people who can benefit from its services.

The various military transcript services typically include a record of the military-sponsored education and training which the service member has successfully completed. Information listed on the transcript is specific to the service and typically includes:

- Military Service School Courses
- Army Enlisted and Warrant Officer Military Occupational Specialties
- Marine Corps Military Occupational Specialties
- Navy Enlisted, Limited Duty, and Warrant Officer Ratings
- Navy Enlisted Classifications and Navy Certifications
- Coast Guard Correspondence Courses
- Coast Guard Enlisted, Warrant Officer, and Aviator Ratings
- Additional skill identifiers and skill qualification identifiers
- College Proficiency Examination Programs to include College Level Examination Program (CLEP), DANTES Subject Standardized Tests (DSST), and Excelsior College Examinations (ECE)[146]
- Defense Language Proficiency Tests (DLPT)

### AARTS: Army/ACE Registry Transcript System

AARTS is a computerized transcript system that produces official transcripts for eligible soldiers, and provides college credit recommendations for military education and training as endorsed by the American Council on Education (ACE). All ACE recommendations are advisory, *not* mandatory. The official AARTS transcript may be requested at http://aarts.army.mil.

[146] The Defense Activity for Nontraditional Educational Support (DANTES), described in the next section, funds most Excelsior College Exams taken at authorized DANTES test centers for all active duty military, National Guard, and Reserve Component personnel. (The Excelsior College Writing Exam is *not* funded by DANTES and is therefore not free for military personnel.) *See* "Excelsior College Examinations," at <www.excelsior.edu/portal/page?_pageid=57,83281&_dad=portal&_schema=PORTAL>.

### SMART: Sailor/Marine ACE Registry Transcript

SMART provides college credit recommendations for military education and training as endorsed by ACE. The official Web site for SMART is https://www.navycollege.navy.mil.

### Coast Guard Transcript

The Coast Guard Transcript provides college credit recommendations for military education and training as endorsed by ACE. The Coast Guard Transcript also documents college credit recommendations for the following: Coast Guard Correspondence Courses, Coast Guard Enlisted Ratings, Coast Guard Warrant Officer Ratings, and Coast Guard Aviator Ratings. The official Web site for the Coast Guard Institute is www.uscg.mil/hq/cgi/.

### Army National Guard Transcript

The Army National Guard (ARNG) Transcript provides college credit recommendations for military education and training as endorsed by ACE. To order an official Army National Guard Transcript, students must complete the ARNG Transcript Request Form. To validate information for the transcript, the member must have an education assessment on file with the Army National Guard Education Support Center. Transcripts can be requested through the Army National Guard Education Support Center at www.virtualarmory.com.

### Community College of the Air Force

Community College of the Air Force (CCAF) is a college which is accredited through Air University by the regional accreditor Southern Association of Colleges and Schools (SACS) for the awarding of associate degrees. CCAF transcripts include credits awarded for military service school courses and for Air Force Specialty Codes (AFSCs). Air Force personnel may order their free transcript online through the Air Force Portal at www.my.af.mil. Or, written transcript requests can be sent to CCAF/DFRS, 130 West Maxwell Blvd, Maxwell AFB, AL 36112–6613.

### DD Form 214—Report of Separation

The DD Form 214 may be submitted if one of the above documents is not available to the student. The National Personnel Records Center (NPRC) has provided the following Web site for veterans to submit requests for their DD-214 online: vetrecs.archives.gov. After a request is submitted online, a signature page must then be faxed or sent by mail to activate the request.

## Testing Programs and Credit by Examination

### Testing

The education counselor was pleased to see that SSgt Lopez had been successful in her earlier efforts at college study. She had a strong GPA, and it was apparent that she had the basic skills necessary to continue her studies. She had also taken courses that could be applied toward a degree program and was advised to make sure that any course she registers for is also applicable towards her degree program or certificate, or else Tuition Assistance (TA) would not be approved.[147] While studying all the information that was included on her AARTS transcript, SSgt Lopez asked about the various testing programs and whether or not she could earn credits through that process. If so, she wanted to make certain that the college she chose accepts the examinations, and also accepts the passing score recommended by ACE.

She learned that the three testing programs that focus on college-level learning—DSST (DANTES Subject Specialized Tests), CLEP (College Level Examination Program), and ECE (Excelsior College Examinations)—are all offered free of charge to service members through the credit-by-examination program of a DoD organization commonly referred to as DANTES (Defense Activity for Nontraditional Educational Support). In addition to examinations leading to college credit, DANTES provides several other examination programs through which students may earn a high school credential, satisfy college admission requirements, and gain professional certification.

### DANTES: Defense Activity for Nontraditional Educational Support

In addition to offering credit by examination, free of charge, as just referred to above, DANTES also provides a number of information resources that help service members research, select, and pursue their educational goals.

- The DANTES Distance Learning Program maintains three online catalogs that list distance learning courses and programs:
  - DANTES Independent Study Catalog,
  - DANTES External Degree Catalog, and
  - DANTES Catalog of Nationally Accredited Distance Learning Programs.
- The DANTES Military Evaluations Program collaborates with ACE to provide academic credit recommendations for training completed while in the service. The results of these credit recommendations are published in the *Guide to the Evaluation of Educational Experiences in the Armed Services*, also known as the *ACE Guide*, as discussed above.

DANTES also distributes a number of guidance materials and inventories that education centers and family support center personnel use in counseling service members and family members. These materials include:

- INTEREST AND APTITUDE INVENTORIES (QUESTIONNAIRES)—These provide measures for assessing interest in career fields and aptitudes for a number of areas of studies.
- DANTES CERTIFICATION PROGRAM—This program offers service members an opportunity to participate in an assortment of credentialing examinations for such areas

[147] In some cases students may need remedial or developmental work, particularly in math and writing, before they are ready to begin college level work. Others may experience difficulties because English may not be their native language. Military Tuition Assistance is approved for college preparatory/remedial courses when students are working toward an undergraduate degree.

as information technology, federal communications, human resources management, automotive services, and emergency medical technology. These are tests of achievement.

- TROOPS TO TEACHERS PROGRAM (TTT)—The purpose of this program is to assist eligible military personnel to transition to a new career as public school teachers in targeted schools. The program has a national reach, and a network of State TTT Offices has been established to provide participants with counseling and assistance regarding certification requirements, routes to state certification, and employment leads.

## Ingredients of a Military-Friendly Institution

SSgt Lopez asked the education counselor what would happen to her efforts to earn a college degree if she is deployed again. She knew some individuals who had been able to continue their studies while deployed to Iraq, although others had run into serious difficulty in getting their courses to transfer.

The education counselor suggested to SSgt Lopez that, once she has narrowed her search to three or four colleges, she research their Web sites for information which might indicate whether these institutions are military-friendly. A few such indications include:

- WITHDRAWAL POLICIES—Some colleges readily assure military students that if they accompany their request for withdrawal with a copy of their orders, they will be withdrawn without academic or financial penalty, and will be welcomed back when they return from their new duty assignment. Others are not as flexible and pose difficulties for students.
- Offering of courses in both flexible schedules and multiple formats. One example: Courses available on CD-ROM, which can be especially convenient for students who are deployed at sea or in other areas where Internet access is unreliable.
- Along those same lines, the counselor suggested that SSgt Lopez look into the level of academic advising that is provided by the colleges of her choice. Does the college provide information on its Web site specific to the military? Are academic advisors readily available evenings, even 24x7, via phone, mail, or fax? Is student satisfaction important to the college?

It became apparent to SSgt Lopez that not only was there was a lot of information to gather, but that she really could become an informed consumer.

## Financial Assistance

Affordable tuition is critical to military personnel, and many institutions offer special rates to them. Current undergraduate and graduate Tuition Assistance (TA) for soldier students is limited to $250 per credit hour (as of 2006).[148]

[148] The Army will pay 100 percent of the tuition and authorized fees charged by a college, up to the established semester hour cap and annual ceiling. *See* "GoArmyEd," Tuition Assistance, at <https://www.earmyu.com/public/public_tuition_assistance_policies.aspx>.

Unless directly related to course tuition, miscellaneous fees are not covered, and thus any costs over the TA amount are out-of-pocket costs to the student. Most students are highly motivated; they are, or should be, aware that if they fail a course or withdraw after the withdrawal period has ended, they will be required to reimburse the military's tuition assistance.

Currently students have a maximum TA of $4,500 per year, and while the GoArmyEd portal manages students' TA, those dollars are limited and, on occasion, are spent before the end of the fiscal year. In that case, a hold is placed on all course registrations until funds are available. Students should make sure, if the college of their choice is located in a state other than their current location, that they do not have to be concerned with being charged *out-of-state rates*.

Just as so many of us do not think about retirement early enough, military students are not apt to think about how they will continue their studies if their degree is not completed before they decide to leave the service. Thus students should look into whether or not the college of their choice serves the veteran community and how well it does so.

Veterans benefits may be used by students while on active duty or after separation from active duty with a fully honorable discharge. With some exceptions for disability and other circumstances, eligibility expires ten years after separation.

A number of different types of education and training are covered under the Montgomery G.I. Bill, for courses at colleges that lead to associate or bachelor or graduate degrees, including accredited independent study for a certificate or degree through distance education; courses leading to a certificate or degree from a business, technical, or vocational school; apprenticeships or on-the-job training for those no longer on active duty; correspondence courses under certain conditions; flight training if the veteran holds a pilot's license upon beginning the program and meets medical requirements; state-approved teacher certification programs; prep courses necessary for admission to a college or graduate school; and license and certification tests approved for veterans, such as Microsoft certification examinations.

Guidelines for veterans benefits[149] are complex, and unfortunately too many veterans do not make use of their benefits, even though most contribute to an education fund set aside specifically for that purpose while on active duty.

## Military Partnerships

### Navy

This chapter would not be complete without information regarding the many partnerships established between the various services and higher education institutions. We have already discussed the Army's contribution to ongoing education leading to degrees for its soldiers, via GoArmyEd and eArmyU.

[149] Detailed and up-to-date information can be found at <www.va.gov>. See also Krecek (2006, pp. 241–243) for a listing/description of the various types of educational programs and services administered by the Department of Veterans Affairs.

The Navy has established the Navy College Program Distance Learning Partnership (NCPDLP), which supports partnerships with a number of colleges and universities to offer degrees via distance learning to sailors everywhere. These partnerships provide associate and bachelor's degree programs and establish connections between academic studies and most ratings in the Navy, thereby making maximum use of military professional training and experience to fulfill degree requirements. Courses are offered in a variety of formats.

The Navy College Program for Afloat College Education (NCPACE) is designed specifically to serve sailors while they are on sea duty assignments, and it allows military personnel to take courses while at sea. There are two types of course delivery methods through the NCPACE Program: instructor-based and CD-ROM. NCPACE is a part of the Navy College Program, and all undergraduate courses are from institutions with a Servicemembers Opportunity College-Navy (SOCNAV) affiliation, thus ensuring sailors the opportunity to pursue a degree or certificate.

### Coast Guard

The Coast Guard Institute provides educational guidance and support services to members of the Coast Guard. "SOCCOAST Afloat," the Coast Guard's partnership, includes SOCCOAST institutions which by definition have degree programs where the requirements can be fulfilled by stand-alone CD-ROM or PDA courses. As already discussed, such delivery systems are necessary aboard ships and cutters where there is limited Internet connectivity. Currently SOCCOAST Afloat is composed of six institutions that have that capacity: Coastline Community College (associate level), Excelsior College (associate and bachelor's levels), Florida Community College at Jacksonville (associate level), Fort Hays State University (bachelor's and master's levels), Governors State University (bachelor's level) and the University of Oklahoma (bachelor's level with some lower division courses). Other SOCCOAST institutions may join SOCCOAST Afloat as the concept is further developed and implemented. Specific information about courses being offered through CD-ROM or PDA by SOCCOAST Afloat institutions, and other pertinent information, can be found in the SOCCOAST Afloat catalog located at www.uscg.mil/hq/cgi.

### Air Force

The Air Force has established through its Air University a new approach to the delivery of an Air Force enlisted bachelor's degree. This program helps enlisted personnel who possess a Community College of the Air Force (CCAF) associate's degree to obtain a baccalaureate degree related to their Air Force specialty. Further, The Air University Associate-to-Baccalaureate Cooperative (AU-ABC) Program is an initiative between Air University and civilian higher education institutions to offer baccalaureate degree opportunities to every Air Force enlisted member.

AU-ABC directs airmen who have completed their associate degrees to a collection of accredited "Air Force friendly" colleges and universities.

The Air Force intends to build on the degree programs offered through the Community College of the Air Force (CCAF), which is accredited through Air University by the Commission on Colleges of the Southern Association of Colleges and Schools to award the associate degree.

### Army National Guard

The Army National Guard Education Support Center (ARNG ESC) serves as a centralized education support activity for all 50 states and four territories. The Center provides Army National Guard soldiers, their spouses, and employees of the ARNG with direct assistance in accomplishing their educational goals. Located at the Professional Education Center at Camp Robinson (Little Rock, AR), its services include over 500 degree plans, plus educational counseling and professional guidance to assist soldiers in pursuit of their educational goals from associate degrees to bachelor's, master's, and doctoral degrees. A number of colleges and universities across the country readily accept ARNG students referred to them. Additional information can be found at www.virtualarmory.com/education.

### Marine Corps

The Marine Corps' Academic Explorer (AeX) is a web-based tool that will enable students and education counselors to explore and identify higher education options. AeX is designed to be a powerful, unbiased search engine with various selection parameters to enable students to locate academic programs and institutions that best meet their individual needs. Students will be able to obtain comprehensive information on course and degree programs of accredited academic institutions approved by the Marine Corps—searchable by location, degree level, degree discipline, delivery method, accreditation status, and membership in the SOC networks.

## Outreach Strategies

As we have seen in the case of SSgt Lopez, a combination of online information, convenient, personalized advising, and up-to-date information can make a great deal of difference for military students. In addition, the actions which a college or university take can make a great deal of difference in attracting such students.

As we noted at the beginning of this chapter, when military professionals begin their quest for a college education, they often start by going to the Internet. A positive action plan for institutions that should flow out of this fact should start with the college's Web site: educational institutions that have a *strong web presence*, particularly with the military-friendly features we have suggested, often succeed in attracting military students. Further, those institutions that have joined one of the partnerships we have discussed are often better able to meet students' needs for *flexible delivery* of course material.

In addition, military students are especially interested in courses and curriculum that help them with critical thinking and strategic problem-solving skills—factors that are especially critical in today's high-tech military. Consortia can provide additional depths of resources for such resourceful students.

Moreover, although it was once commonplace to see large education centers on base, budget constraints and structural realignments have resulted in different, more distance-oriented methods of providing advising and support services, starting with online registration.

## Future Challenges

As troops are deployed to increasingly remote locations for longer periods of time, the need to offer courses and educational support services in a wide variety of formats, delivery modes, and technologies is continuing to expand. Furthermore, in their deployments as professionals, the military in all the services have come to expect remote training, the use of portable devices, and "anytime, anywhere" access to information. They now expect it of their higher education experience as well.

While multiple delivery modes are becoming the norm in distance education, the lack of appropriate flexibility by some schools can lessen the appeal to military students of otherwise attractive programs. As in all distance education programs, successful institutions are able to provide multiple pathways to obtain college credit at an affordable price. When distance education is targeted to serve military students, in particular, institutions must add to their repertory the ability to offer delivery models that can work in often harsh conditions.

Thus it is important to continue to offer credit for ACE-approved military training, credit by examination, and innovative distance learning using technologies and equipment that military professionals are likely to have at their disposal.

/ CHAPTER TWENTY-ONE /

*by Luke Schultheis, Ed.M.*
*Dean and former Director of Admissions*
*The School of Hospitality Management*
*and the Culinary Arts*
*Monroe College*

21

# Reaching the Adult Market

From the viewpoint of admissions officers, it would be hard to find a more elusive category of prospective students than adult students. Many work, raise families, travel, and relocate; as a result it is often difficult to reach such a broad group. In addition, rather than being funnelled directly into college as high school students are, the adults are often set in their life commitments, and college represents an addition to an already busy schedule. Thus this chapter will focus on five topics: identifying the types of adults who are prospective students; outlining the factors which contribute to their decision to return to school; highlighting some of their needs and wants in a school; proposing vehicles to reach them with a message; and crafting a message which will call them to action.

## Characteristics of Adult Students

Adult students are classified as being at least 25 years of age, financially independent, and responsible for costs incurred (Kasworm 2003, p. 3). In other words, they usually cannot rely on direct financial support from other family members. They may earn wages or salaries, or rely on other types of income including Social Security income or public assistance/welfare.

Whatever the case, and regardless of the amount of income, they are usually earning it, or receiving it, directly rather than through parental resources.

## Share of Total Undergraduate Enrollment

In the thirty-four years starting in 1971, the percentage of adult students aged twenty-five to twenty-nine years who had completed some college increased from 34 percent in 1971 to 57 percent in 2005. The percentage of the entire population, of the same age range, who completed a bachelor's degree or higher increased from 17 percent in 1971 to 29 percent in 2005 (Rooney *et al.* 2006, p. 68). The National Center for Education Statistics (NCES) projects a rise in enrollments of 15 percent from 2005–2014 for this group, as illustrated in Table 21.1 (Snyder, Tan, and Hoffman 2006, p. 277).

TABLE 21.1: **Projected Fall Enrollments in Degree Granting Institutions**

| Year | Age | | |
|---|---|---|---|
| | 25-29 | 30-34 | 35+ |
| 2005 | 2,374,000 | 1,290,000 | 3,181,000 |
| 2010 | 2,724,000 | 1,399,000 | 3,178,000 |
| 2014 | 2,913,000 | 1,573,000 | 3,287,000 |

By 2010, according to a projection by NCES, it is estimated that college students aged twenty-one and under will represent less than half of the undergraduate population—46.3 percent. Students aged twenty-five and older will account for 38.2 percent. And students aged twenty-two to twenty-four will account for the remaining 15.5 percent (Kasworm 2003, p. 4; Gerald and Hussar 2002, Table 10, p. 41).

## Gender Distribution

The differences in percentage increases by gender are of particular note: Between 1970 and 2000 there was an increase in the adult male enrollment population of 40.8 percent, and an increase of 59.2 percent in women students—with an even more substantial growth, amounting to 500 percent, in the number of women students aged thirty-five and older (Kasworm 2003, p. 5).

## Postsecondary Education Level

The 1996 U.S. Census listed 159 million people in the U.S. as twenty-five years or older, with 117 million of them holding no tertiary (postsecondary) degree, and ten million of them without any formal education past an associates degree (Hadfield 2003, p. 17).

Of all adult students, 58.7 percent are enrolled in two-year schools; 22 percent in four-year public colleges; 9.4 percent in four-year private and non-profit colleges; and 8.3 percent in for-profit settings (Kasworm 2003, p. 7). As for minority students, nearly 60 percent of those twenty-five and older are enrolled in two-year or under institutions—community colleges, technical institutes, or for-profit entities (p. 7). A final consideration: By 2025, 70 percent of the international demand for higher education (of an estimated 7.2 million students at that time) will be from Asia (Pappas and Jerman, p. 92). Those able to attract and serve adults, who will likely comprise a large part of that demand, will be well positioned.

### Employment Level

The unemployed participate in credential programs (degree or vocational certification) at the highest rate of all groups, accounting for 19 percent of those enrolled in degree or vocational certification programs. Part-time workers participate in such programs at 15 percent, and full time workers at 14 percent, followed by those not in the labor force at 7 percent and the retired at 2 percent (Creighton and Hudson 2002, p. 72).

As to type of work pursued, of those who are employed, 18 percent work in professional and managerial roles, 13 percent in sales and support services, and 10 percent in the trades (Kasworm 2003, p. 8; Creighton and Hudson, pp. 28–29). There are many other areas of employment, which represent smaller percentages.

### Annual Income

More than a quarter—28 percent—of adult students report less than $10,000 in annual income, compared with 58 percent of traditional students reporting the same. An additional 43 percent reported income between $10,001 and $29,999, and 29 percent reported income of $30,000 or more. (Kasworm 2003, p. 8). Compared with those who enter college directly after graduating from high school, the adult cohort is more likely to come from low-income families, to be single parents (including the younger members of this cohort), and to be black (Horn, Cataldi, and Sikora 2006).

### Attendance

Attendance for adults who enroll in college is 39 percent full-time; 12 percent mixed full-time/part-time; 23 percent half-time; and 26 percent less than half-time (Horn, Cataldi, and Sikora 2006, Figure D, p. vi).

### Summary of Data

These data sets illuminate some important issues. The number of adult students has been increasing rapidly, and most of them work (although they are not earning significant incomes). There are gender and ethnic variants which warrant further research, especially as schools try to tailor programs to attract these cohorts. Notably, community colleges are currently enrolling the bulk of adult learners as well as ethnic minorities, and a considerable rise in adult enrollment from Asia is expected in the not-too-distant future. Latinos have surpassed blacks in the 25-to-29 age group in having completed some college, and in the number of those who have earned associate degrees, as noted in Table 21.2, on page 302.

### Academic Preparedness

Of additional note, adults would appear to be substantially less academically qualified for post-secondary studies than are students of traditional age (*i.e.*, those younger than 24 years of age who generally enroll immediately after completing high school). While the adult students were in high school, their math classes were less rigorous, their high school programs were less focused upon core academic subjects, and 59 percent of the 1992 high school graduates who enrolled in college late (that is, at least one full year after high school), were not academically prepared for undergraduate work at a four-year college (Horn, Cataldi, and Sikora 2006, Figure H, p. x).

TABLE 21.2: **2005 Educational Attainment by Age, Gender, and Ethnicity**

| Characteristic/Age | High School Graduates | Some College Completed | Associate Degree Earned |
|---|---|---|---|
| **Males** | | | |
| 25–29 | 3,223,000 | 1,853,000 | 781,000 |
| 30–34 | 3,013,000 | 1,731,000 | 839,000 |
| 35–39 | 3,397,000 | 1,624,000 | 838,000 |
| 40–49 | 7,722,000 | 3,597,000 | 1,911,000 |
| **Females** | | | |
| 25–29 | 2,510,000 | 1,961,000 | 885,000 |
| 30–34 | 2,556,000 | 1,819,000 | 1,019,000 |
| 35–39 | 2,977,000 | 1,827,000 | 1,126,000 |
| 40–49 | 7,011,000 | 4,162,000 | 2,692,000 |
| **Whites** | | | |
| 25–29 | 3,309,000 | 2,404,000 | 1,097,000 |
| 30–34 | 3,351,000 | 2,227,000 | 1,284,000 |
| 35–39 | 4,143,000 | 2,291,000 | 1,431,000 |
| 40–49 | 10,360,000 | 5,557,000 | 3,591,000 |
| **Blacks** | | | |
| 25–29 | 940,000 | 558,000 | 224,000 |
| 30–34 | 859,000 | 596,000 | 223,000 |
| 35–39 | 1,016,000 | 460,000 | 212,000 |
| 40–49 | 2,128,000 | 1,054,000 | 436,000 |
| **Latinos** | | | |
| 25–29 | 1,205,000 | 608,000 | 244,000 |
| 30–34 | 1,064,000 | 507,000 | 223,000 |
| 35–39 | 928,000 | 476,000 | 179,000 |
| 40–49 | 1,473,000 | 735,000 | 335,000 |

**SOURCE:** Snyder, Tan, and Hoffman (2006, Table 9, pp. 24–25)

## Motivation Factors Affecting Adult Enrollees

It appears that what is often assumed about enrollment is true. Adults return to school for employment reasons, or because they have a powerful personal drive to satisfy something that was not completed. A 2001 study of 858 inquiries into Indiana University found that the greatest number were interested in enrolling at the college to develop their careers, followed by those who wanted to "keep up with a changing work environment" or to acquire personal fulfillment (Brown 2004, p. 54). In other studies, 85 percent of adult students similarly reported career-related reasons as affecting their decision to (re)enroll in college (Kasworm 2003, p. 5). Other reasons include personal transitions/changes such as divorce, having children in school, unemployment, or denial of a promotion. There were also many who took a proactive life-planning stance which posited higher education as fundamental to achieving certain goals. Finally, there were many who had mixed motivators which would include two or more of the aforementioned reasons (p. 6).

Studies focusing on adult enrollment in community colleges show the same mix of motivations: personal development, professional growth in job-related areas, remediation in English, mathematics and technology (often at the request of their employers) and access to four-year schools (Palazesi and Bower 2006, p. 45; Hagedorn 2005, p. 24).

### Impact of Time Elapsed Since High School Graduation

An individual's likelihood of enrolling in a bachelor's degree program declines with each successive year following high school graduation—from 30 percent of individuals enrolling one year after high school graduation to 8 percent of those who graduated ten or more years ago. Additionally, this long-delay group is much more likely to focus upon attaining a vocational certificate. The percentage of students aiming at such a certificate increased from 23 percent of those who graduated from high school only one year earlier to 45 percent of those who had a ten-year or greater delay (Horn, Cataldi, and Sikora 2006, p. xi).

In short, two trends become apparent: first, that the longer adults delay entering higher education, the less likely they are to aspire to earn a bachelor's degree. Second, as the delay gets longer, so does the likelihood of entering a vocational certificate program (p. xi–xiii).

TABLE 21.3: **Comparison of 1992 High School Graduates Enrolling in College, by Timing and Type of College**

| Type of College | 1+ years of delay (%) | No delay (%) |
|---|---|---|
| Public 2-Year College | 56 | 34 |
| 4-Year Private College | 29 | 55 |
| For-Profit College | 11 | 5 |
| Other | 4 | 6 |

**SOURCE:** Horn et al. (2006).

### Studying While Working

There is also information on the 1999–2000 enrollment of adults comparing those who were studying while working (*i.e.*, work is the primary activity, and studying is something done in addition to the work) with those who were working while studying (*i.e.*, attending school is the primary activity, and working is something supplemental).

Of those who were studying while working, 87 percent worked fulltime, 76 percent attended college part-time, and 68 percent did both concurrently (Berker and Horn 2003, p. iv). When comparing the type of institution at which they enrolled, those who studied while working were more likely to attend community colleges (61% vs. 39%); were less likely to attend four-year colleges (17% vs. 34%); and were more likely to attend for-profit institutions (14% vs. 10%) (p. vii). They were also more likely to take courses which were not leading to a degree (10% vs. 2%) when compared with those who were working while studying (p. vii).

## College Choice

In theory, it is easy to suggest that people make economic-based decisions. If they are considering making an investment in time, money, and opportunity costs, they will weigh the expected returns and make a decision as to whether the investment is worthwhile.

However, it is easy to see that people in general, and adult students in particular, do not make decisions which fit so neatly into concepts of "investments and returns" which are the same for all. Rather, each adult student has a different set—or more specifically, different subsets—of competing factors to weigh when considering enrollment into higher education.

The Hossler-Gallagher model[150] suggests that people proceed through three distinct stages in their decision making process: predisposition, search, and choice. This model may be of assistance when considering how to market to adults.

During the predisposition stage, students are influenced by family and peers (Hossler, Schimdt, and Vesper 1999, p. 23). Peers who have never attended college—many of whom may work with the adult, who is considering entering college in order to be eligible for a promotion—often know little about admissions, financing, studying, and other aspects of navigating the system.

If family members have been enrolled in college, they are better sources of primary information about the process. For adults, the category of "family" may include not only parents, but their spouse, siblings, and children. Parents who graduate from college have a greater likelihood of having their children attend college (Cabrera and LaNasa 2000b, p. 8), which suggests that since these adults are not in college, the majority of them may likewise not have college-educated parents, who are in turn less likely to promote college. That leaves spouse, siblings, and children as those more likely to know about college and to provide good information to the adults. It is not uncommon to hear adults entering college speak of their children as motivators for their entry. Indeed, it often occurs that the children did more than motivate; they also encouraged.

Once a predisposition to enroll in college has occurred, the search process ensues. For high school students, this search would include reading publications from colleges, speaking with guidance counselors, and being the recipient of many other options not readily available, if at all, to adults. Colleges buy mailing lists of those in high school who are at various stages in their studies, have particular grade point averages, and so forth—SAT mailing lists would be an example. Adults do not participate in activities which are likely to place them on mailing lists to colleges, so they will probably gain most of their information from the Internet or from the college directly. In short, they are likely to be seeking out this information, rather than merely receiving it as traditional students do.

Once the search has concluded, the adults will choose an institution and apply. Nontraditional students typically look at only two institutions (Pappas and Jerman 2004, pp. 92–93; Brown 2004, p. 54). For the two institutions chosen, this fact is a positive one, since the competition is thus reduced. However, there is a third choice which the prospective student may make if neither college seems to fit the adult's needs, and that is to delay enrollment altogether. So, it is important to recognize that the application is still just part of the beginning of the process for adults.

[150] See Hossler, Schimdt, and Vesper (1999) for more information on the Hossler-Gallagher model.

## Preferences of Adult Prospects

### Convenience

Adults appear to want both convenience and quality. Traditional college students often have the luxury of having their college experience as their primary commitment. In many cases, they can live on campus, away from home, and need not commute to class. Most of all, many students of traditional age are the beneficiaries of the financial support of their parents. For adults, on the other hand, work and home are their primary commitments, and college (although very important to them) must take second place. For these reasons, studying needs to present as minimal a disruption to their daily lives as possible.

It is thus not surprising that, in the study by Brown (2004), 82 percent preferred classes during the week as opposed to the weekend. And in a poll of day versus evening preference, 57 percent preferred evenings to days. Many were also responsive to the Internet as a vehicle for learning. Nearly three-quarters (73%) indicated a preference for studying part-time, although only 58 percent actually enrolled in part-time status.

Potential adult learners also hoped for access to tutoring, and advice on adjusting to study. Many were concerned about young people's reaction to sharing class space with them (p. 54); they had spent several years considering reentry into higher education.

While some of what they desire/need is out of the admissions officer's purview, it nevertheless makes sense, from a marketing perspective, that any support services which are offered by your institution should be highlighted in outreach to such students.

The response to the all-important convenience factor thus starts with the admissions office. Adults desire concise and easily accessible information, much of which will be discussed later in the next section.

In addition to easy-to-access information, adults look for a course of study which is focused and direct, getting them through the educational system as quickly as possible. Accelerated degree programs are the vernacular of the day (Husson and Kennedy 2003, p. 51). It is not known how thoroughly adults really comprehend what an accelerated degree entails (*i.e.*, an intense commitment of time). Today, many colleges offer night, weekend, and online classes to all comers, but the adult seems to desire a program branded specifically for "adult learners," even if there is no difference between these offerings and the regular course offerings/schedules.

### Services

Adult students also have concerns about the services they will receive, such as access to the library and computer labs, administrative office assistance, and even when and where classes are offered (Hadfield 2003, p. 20; Brown 2004, p. 57; Maehl 2004, p. 8). Colleges which schedule their support services around the traditional student schedule (normal business hours) are not providing adequately for adults. They expect access and service into the night and on weekends. They also desire a sense of community which night advisors could provide (Brown

2004, p. 59). In short, adults seem to be much less interested in the spectacle of rolling scenery than in access to classrooms and resources in times and places that are convenient for them.

### A Variety of Delivery Options

Satellite campuses (physical space off campus) are a real asset, provided they are well maintained (Maehl 2004, p. 8). Offering a variety of delivery options (Husson and Kennedy 2003, p. 53), which includes distance learning, is helpful in recruiting to the adult market. Whatever the learning platform, adults express a strong interest in interactive pedagogy—participatory, rather than lecture-based (p. 51).

### Instructors with Practical Experience

Finally, adult students appreciate industry professionals (adjuncts) as instructors (Husson and Kennedy 2003, p. 56; Hadfield 2003, p. 22); indeed, they demand excellent professors. Learning centers exclusive to their program, typically including spacious classrooms with tables and chairs in seminar style, breakout areas, computer lab facilities, and a range of personal reception areas (Husson and Kennedy 2003, p. 53) make adults feel comfortable, possibly since such a style looks like a workplace, rather than a classroom.

## Outreach Strategies

Much of what the adult student desires may already be present on campus. The issue at hand is communicating your assets to them. Admissions offices vary in structure. However, when target marketing to a group such as adults, specific vehicles need to be utilized to reach them.

### Staffing Considerations

One essential vehicle is a dedicated staff. A core of sales reps (admissions officers) needs to be well versed in communicating the programs to the adults. Many adults may desire to visit the campus to get a feel for it before they make the many sacrifices necessary to begin their studies. This core should be complemented by an admissions call center which does not route questions to different offices, but rather is a complete resource for the adult. Finally, a corporate outreach group should be established for the purpose of visiting large businesses and promoting the program (Husson and Kennedy 2003, p. 57).

The admissions office hours need to reflect the times during which adult students are likely to appear as walk-ins. As discussed above, they are much less likely to be familiar with the college admissions process and, rather than completing inquiry fields on a Web site and waiting for information to be mailed, they would like to stop into the office, ask personal questions which address their anxieties, and even get a tour of the facilities so they see they are not the only adults on campus (Brown 2004, p. 54).

These leads are "gold" in that such potential students have come to your campus of their own volition. In general, admissions offices work very diligently to get the very few campus visitors they receive. It is essential that the admissions officers extend every courtesy to the applicant—courtesies which may include making food and beverages available, and providing a comfortable, private, sophisticated area in which to speak. It may not be ideal to have a recent college graduate manning the office during these hours because of possible generational concerns on the applicant's side, and staff members may perform better if they can relate to the challenges of handling multiple responsibilities including profession, family, and the like. Some of the issues the applicants will need to discuss include financing their education, transferring in previously earned college credit (if any), credit for life and professional experience, and—highly important—a concise outline of the timeline for the admissions process.

The call center should be available both to receive incoming calls and to generate outgoing calls. Adults need to be kept on communication lists for up to two years (pp. 54–55). The decision to enroll in college takes a long time, and such prospective students need to be *touched* by the institution regularly in order to keep it fresh in their minds and plans. Calls to their workplace or home during business hours, however, are not appropriate. They need time to sit on the phone and ask personal questions without concern for their work or other responsibilities. The weekend call is often a good time to reach adults. They are better able to contextualize college while away from work. The call center would thus need to be in operation on Saturdays and Sundays and again, the staff should be able to speak knowledgeably about the aforementioned issues.

### Targeting Businesses

Outreach teams may target larger businesses having many levels of staff. It is conceivable that many of the staff could be promoted if they complete their college degrees. The larger businesses often have some form of tuition assistance program—but often, employees are unaware of its availability. Meeting with the administrators of the tuition assistance program would both make them aware of your programs and provide your office with a contact person through whom you can gain insights into the needs of the company's staff. One may be able to schedule informal lunches, with food provided by the college, to allow for general presentations of the college programs (Husson and Kennedy 2003, pp. 58–59). It is important that follow-up be provided to those who express interest from this group. The call center is a likely candidate to begin a campaign, which should be supplemented by print materials. Adults require more sophisticated materials and regular frequency of contact, to solidify an image of the program (p. 59).

### Crafting Web Sites Geared Toward Older Students

Many adults are Web-savvy. However, the more savvy one is, the more one is able to see e-noise. From the point of view of an older student, "noise" would consist of graphics, clubs, mascots, and even financial aid-related pages, online catalogs, or e-campus newspapers which may "skew young" (Hagedorn 2005, p. 24).

Remembering that adults are less likely to be familiar with the enrollment process, it is important to integrate aspects of the site which allow adults to quickly see what needs to be done to enroll, when deadlines are, and to anticipate questions which adult students are likely to have (and provide specific and concise answers).

It may also be useful to provide additional e-services such as pages which allow applicants to get a feel for how much aid they will receive, through an interactive page; and how many credits will transfer, both through tables referencing policy on life experience credit and perhaps tables showing possibilities for course-by-course articulation from feeder schools the adult students may once have attended.

### Other Marketing Vehicles

Other vehicles for reaching adults may include traditional media such as rush hour radio, banner ads in the appropriate newspapers, and direct mail—preferably in postcard form—to target markets. Again, a sophisticated message is in order which addresses the needs and desires of adult students. One will need to be careful that this marketing does not interfere or conflict with other campaigns attracting traditional students.

## Customizing Your Message

### Tailored Service

The cumulative effect of marketing to adult students often emerges only after a couple of years of marketing effort (Brown 2004, p. 56). With this fact in mind, the admissions director should accept that the message may not act as a time-sensitive call to immediate action, but rather as one which helps adult prospects build higher education into their life plan.

It is also likely that the working adult knows what field he or she intends to enroll in, and has done adequate research to identify two colleges which offer those programs. Therefore, the focus should be made upon the points of tailored service, and quality service.

The campaigns should be planned to run in long rotating intervals so that messages are constantly fresh, yet reinforcing. Such messages should also allow entry into the campaign at any point by a prospect. In other words, the messages should not rely upon previously highlighted points, but should act independently, but in a targeted manner.

In addition, quality messages aimed at adult students need to be centered upon the expertise of the faculty. As previously mentioned, adult students respond best to up-to-date professionals who can speak in the current jargon of the field as it is practiced. Granted, there will be many classes they will take with full-time professors, but unless such faculty are perceived to be at the cutting edge of relevant research, the marketing should focus on adjuncts from the working world—people who are brought in especially to teach the expertise which they practice daily.

Highlighting access to interactive facilities—such as a library, electronic reserves, computer labs, and tutoring services, which will help the adult actively learn and flourish—is a paramount consideration in marketing to adults (Pappas and Jerman 2004, p. 93). Any other information which speaks to the institution's commitment to adults as a population with specific needs of its own is useful in your marketing to that population. Messages which address the concerns of adult students in relation to child care, financial aid, taxes, and other issues of special interest to them (Hatfield 2003, p. 31) will also position your institution well.

### Quality Service

Quality service may determine if the adult will actually enroll in your institution or at the competing one. Therefore, the marketing message must coincide with actual services delivered; otherwise the prospect may feel misled. Promoting the ease of enrolling, financing, and matriculating will likely attract prospects to your institution. Highlight issues such as immediate transfer credit evaluation, immediate financial aid estimates, same-day acceptance, and so on.

Adults are looking for a painless way to enroll in college. Provided that you inform them of the necessary documentation they should bring to the admissions office, you should be able to institute a one-stop shopping concept. Another means of offering streamlined access is to offer many services via the Web. The application itself is one example. Not all prospects will want to visit the campus, or get all of their documents together in order to submit a mailed application. The Web provides a convenient way for them to work through the process and submit their completed application when it is ready. This service should be included in your promotional materials.

The adult market is one which requires focused efforts and likely a different recruitment model from the ones used for traditional students. Identifying the current adults who perform well at your institution may provide insights into feeder organizations which supply you with good applicants and good students. A custom-crafted message complemented with superior customer service and constant support will increase the number of adults who enroll in colleges.

## Conclusion

Reaching out to adult students is a challenging process, but it is one of the most rewarding ones in higher education. It opens minds to new knowledge, and doors to new careers. It is not a myth that Abe Lincoln studied law by candlelight—and that he became a very good lawyer. With the additional resources available to us today, we can do no less for ambitious students in our own time.

/ CHAPTER TWENTY-TWO /

*by Carl F. Einhaus, M.A.*
*Colorado State University*
*Wanda L.E. Viento, Ph.D.*
*Boise State University*
*James M. Croteau, Ph.D.*
*Western Michigan University*

22

# Recruiting LBGT Students

This chapter addresses issues involving recruitment and outreach to lesbian, bisexual, gay, and transgender students and uses the acronym "LBGT" when referring to all four of these sexual/gender orientation groupings. At times, however, we will refer to only lesbian or gay students, or only lesbian, bisexual, and gay (LBG) students when we are discussing a particular source that does not include bisexual and/or transgender students.

LBGT students have largely been ignored in diversity-oriented admission practices. A key to advancing LBGT recruitment on college campuses involves an effort to increase admissions professionals' awareness of the practical potential for increasing admissions numbers, of the educational significance of having a diverse student body that includes sexual orientation diversity, and of the issues of social justice in responding specifically to the unique needs of potential LGBT students.

This chapter describes the range of recruitment strategies that the authors first employed at Western Michigan University (WMU). Our discussion of recruitment initiatives encompasses two general strategies: instituting specialized LBGT recruitment, and incorporating LBGT-specific marketing initiatives into existing general recruitment. These strategies, of course, will have to be critically evaluated and adapted to fit the realities of each particular college or university climate.

## Diversity Issues in a New Context

A rich representation of diversity on college campuses has become an objective for many institutions. As the Carnegie Foundation for the Advancement of Teaching (1990) stated, "...a college or university is a just community, a place where the sacredness of each person is honored and where diversity is aggressively pursued" (p. 25). Bryant (1996) maintained that "a diverse student population is just as important as a first-class curriculum or a faculty made up of Nobel Prize winners" (p. 51). The interweaving of diversity on campuses has been asserted as being a key factor in quality education, as well as an essential element in preparing students for a pluralistic future (Dungy 1996; Bryant 1996). In fact, Blimling (2001) reviews research from the last 20 years that clearly indicates that students' learning is improved by diverse campus environments, essentially arguing convincingly that "diversity makes you smarter" (p. 517).

Pascarella *et al.* (2001) wrote that "the efforts of admissions offices and international programs to recruit a diverse student body are important not only for the social environment that a diverse student population creates, but also as a means to encourage the development of critical thinking in college students" (p. 270). In addition to the campus diversification advantages of an admissions program that is sensitive to racial and ethnic differences, among other factors, admissions numbers can be increased by marketing and recruiting sizeable diverse population segments that colleges might otherwise miss by limiting themselves to a single marketing strategy (Sevier 1996). To achieve these benefits and more, targeting specific diverse student groups in recruitment is a standard practice in most admission departments. LBGT students, however, have largely been ignored in diversity-oriented admissions practices.

More and more lesbian and gay people are becoming aware of and acknowledging their sexual orientation while they are still in high school (Ryan and Futterman 1998; Troiden 1998; Herdt and Boxer 1996). This increasing consciousness about sexual orientation among high school students has resulted in the formation of over 1,800 high school gay-straight alliances (GSAs). Information about GSAs is made available through organizations such as the Gay, Lesbian, and Straight Education Network (GLSEN).[151] LBGT high school students will undoubtedly be assessing colleges on their LBGT-affirmative environments, policies, and available services (Lucozzi 1998). A study that surveyed LBG college student organizations reported that nearly 30 percent of LBG students considered their sexual orientation as a factor in making their college choice and 40 percent reported that their college choice would have been different if they had had information regarding the campus climate toward LBG individuals (Sherrill

[151] Notable GLSEN resources include: (1) "Finding an LGBT-Friendly Campus: A Guide for LGBT Students Pursuing Higher Education" at <www.glsen.org/binary-data/GLSEN_ATTACHMENTS/file/200-1.pdf>; (2) "Finding an LGBT-Friendly Campus: A Guide for Counselors Advising LGBT Students Pursuing Higher Education" at <www.glsen.org/binary-data/GLSEN_ATTACHMENTS/file/199-1.pdf>; and (3) "Common Questions and Answers About Gay-Straight Alliances" at <www.glsen.org/binary-data/GLSEN_ATTACHMENTS/file/170-1.pdf>.

and Hardesty 1994). Recognizing that students are increasingly considering sexual orientation in their college choices, GLSEN (2002a; 2002b) published a guide for students in "Finding an LGBT Friendly Campus," just referred to above, and three recent publications also addressed the issue of helping students in their search for such campuses (Cook 2002; Mitchell 2000; Sherrill and Hardesty 1994). Given these realities, we assert that it is the responsibility of college or university admission officers to represent the LBGT-affirmative aspects of their institutions and actively seek LBGT high school students as potential candidates for enrollment.

Though there has been some informal information sharing through the caucus of the American Association of Collegiate Registrars and Admissions Officers (AACRAO) that focuses on LBGT issues and through the conference programs presented by the caucus, we found that the admission recruitment-related professional literature has given almost no attention to LBGT recruitment. The only published article was one that offered colleges a few broad suggestions in attracting LBGT students: addressing LBGT college services in recruitment brochures and Web sites, clear visibility of LBGT—affirmative information in admissions office environments (*e.g.*, LBGT event announcements, books etc.), networking with other campus professionals involved in LBGT affirmative work, and sponsoring LBGT related campus events (Hrabe 2002). The only other source we found about LBGT admissions was a higher education weekly magazine's coverage of the budding efforts of colleges recruiting LBGT students, particularly the Boston Gay/Straight Youth Pride College Fair (Cavanaugh 2002).[152]

In 2000 we began to focus on Western Michigan University's LBGT affirmative admissions practices. Given the lack of professional literature for guidance, we began by gathering information ourselves about such practices through a national survey of college and university recruitment departments. We then designed and implemented our own outreach recruitment program. The purpose of this chapter is to assist admissions and recruitment professionals by presenting some of the information we collected regarding LBGT student recruitment and then by describing our own LBGT outreach recruitment initiatives.

# LBGT Enrollment Survey

### Procedures and Data Analysis

A short survey was sent in September 2002 to the heads of admission/recruitment departments at four-year public higher education institutions in the United States from a list provided by AACRAO. Of the 571 potential participants who received surveys, 147 (26%)

[152] See Windmeyer's (2006) *The Advocate College Guide for LGBT Students,* a book containing chapters of special interest, including: "Top 10 Criteria LGBT Students Look for in a Campus;" "100 Best Campuses for LGBT Students;" "Your LGBT Campus Choice Index" (by state, region, type of institution, tuition in-state and out-of-state, etc.); "Advice for Incoming LGBT Students;" and "Advice for Campus Officials to Improve LGBT Efforts."

In addition, in the fall of 2007 the Princeton Review published a guide called *The Gay and Lesbian Guide to College Life.* According to the Princeton Review, the Guide features "advice from students and administrators at more than seventy of the nations' top colleges," and "lets you know how to thrive on campus."

Finally, FinAid's Web site contains a section entitled "Financial Aid for Lesbian, Gay, Bisexual, and Transgendered Students." See <www.finaid.org/otheraid/gay.phtml>.

completed either the paper or online version of the survey. Tables 22.1A–22.1D report descriptive data that the participants provided about their institutions' size, LBGT services and policies, and targeted recruitment market segments.

An overwhelming majority of participants (95+%) did not engage in any recruitment activities that specifically targeted LBGT students. These participants answered open-ended questions about why they had not recruited LBGT students or about what had prevented them from doing such recruitment. The data were analyzed initially by the first and second authors, revised for clarity and meaningfulness based on feedback from presentations (*e.g.*, Einhaus 2003) and finally examined critically by all three authors. The analysis identified barriers to LBGT student recruitment. Most barriers were easy to identify because they were *explicitly* stated by participants; such barriers are described in the first section that follows. In the next section we describe an *implicit* perspective apparent in some participant responses that we believe could constitute a significant barrier to LBGT recruitment. Only six participants (4%) reported specifically targeting LBGT in recruitment, and their efforts are briefly described in the final section about the survey.

## Explicit Recruitment Barriers

We organized participant responses into six general barriers, presented in the bolded text below in order from most to least cited. The barrier most frequently mentioned by participants was that LBGT students were not part of their department's or college's recruitment goals. For example, one participant stated that LBGT students are not an "under-represented population identified within the university's goals for diversity." Some participants clarified that their recruitment initiatives were based on such factors as academics, ethnicity, income levels, and proximity, not sexual orientation. Some participants reported that no "specific market segment" was targeted at their institution.

Participants cited the next three barriers less frequently, though still in substantial numbers. Some participants stated that they did not recruit LBGT students because it was an idea that had not occurred to them, *e.g.*, "it has never come up." One participant admitted, "I'm glad that you are doing this study. You have certainly jogged my attention regarding this issue." Some participants stated that a barrier involved a non LBGT-affirmative campus climate due to factors such as location in a conservative geographical area, *e.g.*, "rural," "southern," "bible belt," or a politically conservative university leadership among boards of regents/visitors or university administrators. Some participants also saw the LBGT population as "relatively difficult to identify and access," thus difficult to recruit. For example, some reported ignorance of venues for reaching LBGT students or lack of a "way to collect information from high school students pertaining to LBGT orientations."

The last two barriers were cited by a few participants. Limited time, economic, and people resources were identified as barriers in recruiting LBGT students (*e.g.*, no "time to target this specific group" or "extremely scarce advertising dollars and marketing materials [make it] not feasible"). A few participants thought that no recruitment efforts were necessary because of the LBGT-friendly communities in which their campuses were located. They maintained that their location "naturally brings diversity to the campus," therefore, no recruitment efforts were needed.

**Descriptive Data of Institutions, Including LBGT Services (Valid Responses = 147)**

TABLE 22.1A: **How many students are enrolled at your institution?**

| | N | % |
|---|---|---|
| Under10,000 | 80 | 54.4 |
| 10,000–20,000 | 32 | 21.8 |
| 20,000–30,000 | 21 | 14.3 |
| 30,000–40,000 | 7 | 4.8 |
| Over 40,000 | 7 | 4.8 |
| Total | 147 | 100.0 |

TABLE 22.1B: **Does your institution have...**

| | Yes | | No | | Don't Know | |
|---|---|---|---|---|---|---|
| | N | % | N | % | N | % |
| LBGT office? | 33 | 22.3 | 99 | 66.9 | 8 | 5.4 |
| LBGT student group? | 114 | 77.0 | 24 | 16.2 | 7 | 4.7 |
| LBGT alumni group? | 10 | 6.8 | 75 | 50.7 | 53 | 35.8 |
| LBGT employee group? | 25 | 16.9 | 75 | 50.7 | 38 | 25.7 |
| Domestic partner benefits? | 31 | 20.9 | 72 | 48.6 | 43 | 29.1 |
| Non-discrimination clause which Includes sexual orientation? | 111 | 75.0 | 21 | 14.2 | 14 | 9.5 |

TABLE 22.1C: **Do you have any openly LBGT professional staff in your admissions department?**

| | N | % |
|---|---|---|
| Yes | 30 | 20.3 |
| No | 88 | 59.5 |
| Don't Know | 30 | 20.3 |

TABLE 22.1D: **What market segment does your institution actively recruit?**

| | N | % |
|---|---|---|
| African American | 128 | 94.1 |
| Asian American | 81 | 59.6 |
| Hispanic | 112 | 82.4 |
| Native American | 92 | 67.6 |
| People with Disabilities | 48 | 35.3 |
| Honors | 45 | 33.1 |
| International Students | 90 | 66.2 |

### The "Inclusion Illusion:" An Implicit Recruitment Barrier

The barrier to recruiting LBGT students that we saw as implicit in some participants' responses involved a notion we first heard described by Jesse Jackson in his speech at the 2000 National Democratic Convention. He used the term "inclusion illusion" to refer to organizations' claims that they were inclusive to diversity, when he adamantly believed they were not. Some participants claimed adequate service to LBGT students in their recruitment practices, but we saw their claim of adequate service as illusory when participants reported no specific attention to the needs of LBGT students in recruitment. For example, one participant responded that his or her institution did not recruit LBGT students because "...we have a non-discrimination clause. It applies to those students too so we don't have to target them." Another participant thought an open recruitment policy made specifically targeting LBGT students unnecessary. Other participants believed that since they already had LBGT students on their campus, it was not necessary to target them with specific recruitment initiatives. The illusion of inclusion seemed to involve the notion that non-discriminatory, non-targeted enrollment of everyone, or the simple presence of LBGT students, somehow equated to LBGT-affirmative recruitment initiatives.

### LBGT Recruitment Initiatives

The initiatives that six of the respondents had implemented included participating in college fairs that were explicitly for LBGT students, attending and supplying recruitment materials at LBGT events (community LBGT pride festivals, LBGT campus programming attended by high school students), and making a recruitment visit at a high school for LBGT youth. A few other initiatives were mentioned as well: campus information about LBGT resources in recruitment publications, mailing recruitment materials with LBGT-specific information to high schools and high school counselors, and maintaining a web-based e-mail program that allows prospective students to ask questions of a diverse group of current students including those who identify as LBGT.

### Discussion of Survey Results

The low average response rate and limited mailing—only to four-year public colleges and universities—make it impossible to draw any firm conclusions about the nature and extent of LBGT recruitment efforts that are occurring on United States college campuses. However, the fact that very few of the admissions directors who responded to the survey stated that recruitment efforts were occurring on their campus does give some indication that such efforts are very infrequent. The lack of recruitment efforts that were reported mirrors the lack of discussion of LBGT issues in the admission literature.

As indicated previously, participants also mentioned practical obstacles to LBGT student recruitment including lack of resources, the challenges of identifying LBGT students, and conservative leadership, as well as the lack of awareness or education about LBGT issues and the illusion that a non-discrimination policy or the presence of a few openly LBGT students makes targeted recruitment unnecessary. Thus, admissions professionals may often fail to see the need for, and significance of, recruiting LBGT students. A key to advancing LBGT recruitment on college campuses will be increasing admissions professionals' awareness of the practical potential for increasing admission numbers, of the educational significance of having a diverse student body that includes sexual orientation diversity, and of the issues of social justice in responding specifically to the unique needs of potential LBGT students.

In addition to this increased awareness, admissions professionals will also need information on LBGT-specific recruitment strategies in order to be successful in LBGT admissions work. The brief discussion of recruitment strategies by Hrabe (2002) along with the few LBGT recruitment efforts mentioned by survey participants provides some possibilities for LBGT student recruitment. A systematic and detailed articulation of recruitment strategies in the admissions literature is needed to adequately assist admissions professionals in recruiting LBGT students.

## An LBGT Recruitment Framework

In the following section, we offer the first detailed exploration of LBGT college recruitment illustrated with our own work. We begin by discussing the assessment of campus climate on LBGT issues and garnering support for LBGT recruitment. We then discuss recruitment initiatives specific to LBGT students, followed by LBGT-specific marketing initiatives within existing general recruitment.

### Assessing the Campus Climate for the LBGT Community

The first logical step in developing a LBGT recruitment plan suited to a particular campus is to assess the campus climate regarding LBGT issues and the support services available. Most colleges and universities do not have an ideal environment for LBGT students, and the results of such an evaluation on most campuses will be mixed in terms of degree of LBGT support and affirmation. LBGT students are most often making choices among such "mixed climate" institutions, as well as considering many other factors related to educational and social needs. Openly LBGT students will be savvy in their consideration of institutions, and admissions professionals will need to be able to thoroughly and honestly communicate to these students, and sometimes their parents, what it might be like to be a LBGT student on their campus. Evaluating the campus climate at our institution allowed us to better provide an accurate portrayal of the campus environment and existing services for, or friendly to, LBGT students.

Western Michigan University is a mid-western public four-year institution with an enrollment of nearly 30,000 students. The university is located in a community with a mixed conservative and liberal population. In assessing our campus climate for the LBGT community, the first consideration was the "LBGT appeal" of the surrounding area. While not ideal, both the city and university are increasingly making the atmosphere for the LBGT community more inclusive and attractive. The city, for example, has extended health care benefits to employees with same-sex partners, and the community LBGT organization has seen much growth and now has multiple paid staff.

The Web site of the National Consortium of Directors of LGBT Resources in Higher Education lists colleges that have done formal self-assessments to determine campus climate, and the reports from these colleges and universities can provide much guidance for formal assessment.[153] These examples of formal assessment can be very useful to colleges and universities that have the resources and institutional commitment for a formal assessment process. While a formal assessment is ideal, an informal assessment can provide adequate information for successful LBGT recruitment initiatives. In completing an informal assessment of our campus climate, two resources were particularly helpful in identifying factors to consider in assessing the LBGT climate. The National Consortium (2003) and GLSEN (2002a) provide material on their Web sites that identify questions that can be used in assessing climate. Questions from these sources include:

- "Do the college's equal opportunity policy and non-discrimination statements include sexual orientation?"
- "Are courses offered in LGBT/queer studies?"
- "Is there an active LGBT student group?"

Our assessment resulted in identifying our campus as a mixed climate for LBGT students. Many LBGT-positive elements were revealed: for example, sexual orientation is included in the university's non-discrimination statement, an Office of LBGT Student Services is present on campus, the student affairs division seems quite LBGT-affirmative, and there is an active undergraduate student group. However, many areas for growth were also identified: for instance, the university does not supply domestic partner benefits for its employees, and the Office of LBGT Student Services is not staffed by a full-time employee. Further, there is a strong religiously conservative element on campus that is not LBGT-affirmative, and many LBGT students do not feel safe being open. Upon completing our assessment process, we began pursuing ways within the university setting in which we could garner support for our efforts to reach LBGT students.

### Garnering Support

Garnering campus support is necessary to gain access to resources and is particularly needed should such efforts come under scrutiny or receive criticism from administrators and political or religious groups that oppose LBGT inclusion and civil rights. As such, we were extremely fortunate to have the dean and associate directors as well as the staff of the admissions office supportive and encouraging from the start of our process. Unfortunately, not all colleges will

[153] See "Bibliography: 'Campus Climate Reports'" at <www.lgbtcampus.org/resources/campus_climate.html>.

have the same level of support for recruiting LBGT students. Admissions professionals may have to begin their work by building support for LBGT outreach recruitment. Other admissions professionals may find that some key administrators need basic education on LBGT issues before recruitment can even be considered, and these admissions professionals may have to approach such efforts with patience and political savvy.

One way to build support within the admissions area and across campus is by collaborating with other departments and organizations that would have an investment in the quality of life for LBGT students on campus. Our Office of LBGT Student Services, our Student Activities and Leadership Programs department, as well as our undergraduate LBGT student group all supported and contributed to recruitment efforts. LBGT-friendly staff, faculty, and alumni, as well as off-campus LBGT organizations like local chapters of Parents and Friends of Lesbians and Gays (PFLAG) and GLSEN or a local LBGT resource center can provide much assistance in actual LBGT student recruitment initiatives and in efforts to garner internal political support.

## Recruitment Strategies

In this section, we describe the range of recruitment strategies that we employed on our own campus. These strategies, of course, will have to be critically evaluated and adapted to fit the realities of each particular college or university climate. Our discussion of recruitment initiatives encompasses two general strategies: instituting specialized LBGT recruitment, and incorporating LBGT-specific marketing initiatives into existing general recruitment.

### SPECIALIZED INITIATIVES FOR LBGT STUDENTS

While recruitment efforts that target other specific populations such as students of color or honors students provided some ideas, we found that such methods could not always be directly applied to recruiting LBGT students. For example, a student's sexual orientation is not requested on our admissions applications or inquirer cards, unlike other targeted student group descriptors, so we had to discover other less traditional avenues to identify and contact prospective LBGT students.

- LBGT INFORMATION FLYERS. We first had to create the information that we wanted to disseminate to potential LBGT students. We developed a flyer, entitled "Q&As for LBGTAs at Western Michigan University" ("A" is for heterosexual allies) that specifically focused on campus climate and resources, including information on student groups, LBGT services, LBGT campus events and policies, and brief information on the local community (Einhaus 2000). We also developed a flyer titled "Searching for a Gay-Friendly College: Measuring the Campus Climate for LBGTA Students" (Einhaus 2001). This flyer included questions for students to consider in assessing a college's LBGT climate, avenues for finding information related to the questions, references to books on the LBGT college experience, local LBGT organization contact information, and advice on how to engage in a successful college search as it relates to being LBGT. While the flyer utilized and cited some information from the previously mentioned GLSEN material, it was written for, and labeled explicitly from, our admissions office.

- MAILINGS TO GAY/STRAIGHT ALLIANCES. To reach LBGT students, we mailed general information regarding our university and the two flyers described previously to the high schools with Gay/Straight Alliances (GSAs) in our state.

  We located GSAs through newspaper articles that reported their existence and by visiting the GLSEN Web site. In the mailing, we also extended an offer for an outreach presentation at a GSA meeting regarding the college search process for LBGT students.
- GAY/STRAIGHT ALLIANCE VISITS. In the outreach presentation to GSAs, we always brought current LBGT college students so they could provide the high school students with a direct and personal account of campus life. We began by introducing ourselves and explaining the purpose of the visit to assist LBGT students in the college search process. We then initiated an open discussion with the GSA students to learn about their experiences in high school. Our questions centered on the history of the GSA, what activities and programs they were involved in, and what type of experiences they had being LBGT or a heterosexual ally student in high school. The LBGT college students then shared their personal experiences being LBGT in college. The high school students seemed to appreciate this part of the presentation the most. The "Searching for a Gay-Friendly College" flyers, along with "Q&A for LBGTAs at WMU" flyers, were then distributed and discussed. We closed the presentation with open discussion and a request for feedback regarding the visit.
- LBGT PRIDE FESTIVALS/EVENTS. Staffing a table at local LBGT pride events is an excellent way to show a college's support for the LBGT community and reach potential students. At an LBGT pride festival, staff from the admissions office and student activities office answered questions regarding our college's LBGT services and distributed the aforementioned informational flyers. Potential students also completed inquirer cards. While the pride festival did not result in many direct recruitment leads, we believe our participation will contribute to our college's image of being LBGT-inclusive, especially if done consistently over time. Many alumni from our college and other colleges, as well as LBGT parents of potential college students, approached our table, impressed that a college would send a recruiter to an LBGT event.
- COLLABORATION WITH COLLEGE AND LOCAL LBGT SERVICES. Admissions departments can receive great assistance from the college LBGT student services office and/or local LBGT community organizations in recruitment and outreach to LBGT students. Potential LBGT students and their parents do contact the college's LBGT student services office to ask questions regarding services and the campus climate. When we in the admissions office collaborate with the LBGT student services office, we can more effectively convey information regarding the college. In addition, local LBGT community organizations work with youth frequently. These organizations may be very willing to display or

distribute college recruitment materials and further develop and communicate the college's support of the LBGT community.

### INCORPORATING LBGT INITIATIVES INTO EXISTING RECRUITMENT TRAINING AND STRATEGIES

In order for our general recruitment efforts to be more inclusive of LBGT students, it was essential to train all admissions officers as to the campus's LBGT climate and services, as well as potential issues LBGT students may be facing regarding the college search process. During our annual staff training, we presented information on what LBGT services our institution offers, general issues surrounding the LBGT community, and answers to questions that may be posed by LBGT students and their parents. The flyers developed for LBGT students discussed earlier were distributed, discussed, and made available to the staff. We encouraged admission officers to include LBGT issues in the diversity portion of their admissions presentations and whenever it was relevant in discussing the university at college fairs. We conveyed that LBGT students commonly will not self-identify and ask outright about such services, underscoring the importance of including LBGT information in our general presentations.

With the growing number of students coming out in high school, both students and their parents will increasingly and actively seek information on LBGT services and climate. Many LBGT students may want to find this information anonymously. College recruitment publications and Web sites can offer a safe avenue for LBGT students to assess campus services and climate. The absence of LBGT-related information in publications will leave LBGT students guessing at the causes of such omissions, and they may well assume that the college does not offer an inviting atmosphere for LBGT students.

Our admissions Web site offers a direct link to diversity services on campus, including our LBGT office. Further, we advocated successfully for the mention of sexual orientation in the diversity section of our recruitment resources guide for prospective students. These were modest but significant steps in providing another avenue of information for LBGT students, and also were part of the overall effort in communicating that our college values and desires a diverse student body including LBGT students.

While the LBGT recruitment initiatives specific to LBGT students discussed in the previous section do require additional staff time, the initiatives that incorporate LBGT issues in existing recruitment are very cost efficient, often simply involving the inclusion of LBGT issues alongside the issues of other targeted diverse populations in written recruitment materials and presentations. Whatever the cost efficiency of particular LBGT recruitment strategies, assessing their relative success cannot rely on concrete measures of increased enrollment.

In contrast to racially and ethnically diverse students and even honors students, universities generally do not track data on the sexual orientation of their students. Thus, assessment of recruitment initiatives must include such indicators as increased interest and participation in LBGT student groups, increased requests from GSAs or LBGT-oriented community groups for presentations or information, and positive changes in the campus climate for LBGT students, staff, and faculty. These indicators can be assessed both formally through the collection of longitudinal quantitative data, or informally through the perceptions of key faculty, staff, and student leaders. Such assessment must occur over the course of a number of years to yield any visible or readily measurable results.

At our university, LBGT recruitment efforts began around 2001, and our efforts seem to be gaining some momentum. Key LBGT student leaders have been recruited successfully, LBGT community groups and GSAs in the state have requested visits and information more frequently, and the national media has taken notice of our recruitment efforts (Marklein 2004).

## Conclusion

LBGT issues are becoming more visible in our society as the media have become more inclusive of sexual orientation, and major LBGT legal and civil rights issues have increasingly gained public attention. This visibility is clearly alive in the nation's high schools, with increased student activism and organization among LBGT high school students and their heterosexual counterparts who care about LBGT people and issues. These students are increasingly concerned about the climate around sexual orientation in their search for colleges. Admissions professionals need to rise to the challenge of being inclusive of LBGT issues in their recruitment work. As Mitchell (2000) argued, this challenge must be met "because we believe in America's young people. Each and every one of them" (p. 19).

/ CHAPTER TWENTY-THREE /

*by Mary E. Baxton, M.S.*
*Director of Admissions, The Tseng College of Extended Learning*
*California State University-Northridge*

23

# International Students: Marketing and Recruitment

International students have an important role on U.S. campuses, as institutions have come to recognize that these students expand the global dimension of the campus, contribute almost $13.5 billion to the U.S. economy, enrich the academic experience of U.S. students, become future alumni, and promote interchange of values in an interactive global world (Koh and Bhandari 2007, p. 15). According to *Open Doors 2006*, the annual report of the Institute of International Education, 564,766 students from abroad studied in the U.S (p. 3). Approximately one in five international students are attending two-year institutions in the United States.[150]

## Vision and Commitment

A strong recruitment plan will flow from a well-thought-out vision as to how international students will fit into your particular institution.

Although American colleges and universities are aware of the benefits of incorporating international students into our cohorts, we have only begun to be aware of the many ramifi-

[150] In 2002–03, over 96,000 international students attended two-year colleges in the U.S. (Koh 2007). Ashburn (2006) reports that, in an effort to bring students from developing countries to American community colleges, the U.S. Department of State announced a three-million dollar initiative that "would concentrate specifically on students who want to earn associate degrees and return to their home countries."

cations of competing to attract international students to the United States—competition from institutions in other countries; complications arising out of large educational initiatives such as the Bologna Process in Europe;[151] and implications of country dynamics such as the rapid development of China and India, among other nations.

The days of having a tried and true marketing strategy and expecting international students simply to arrive at the door of the institution are gone. Although such organizations as NAFSA: Association of International Educators have advocated that "America needs an international education policy,"[152] the fact remains that the U.S. does not as yet have such a policy, or even a concerted strategy for attracting international students.[153] Thus U.S. institutions must rely on their own policies and initiatives.

Finally, there is a growing trend in some countries to increase the capacity and quality of higher education institutions within the student's own country.

Developing an international community and building upon it takes time. Institutions cannot enter into the process and expect it to grow overnight. Thus, as we have already emphasized, each institution must assess for itself how a population of international students will fit into the mission and strategic enrollment management plan on its own campus. Goals can range from merely adding numbers to the student body as a whole, to recruiting students with interests in specific academic disciplines, to targeting students from a specific part of the world. Whatever the goal in recruiting students from abroad, your institution must be prepared to muster the resources and the support services necessary to address the special needs of international students.

## Preliminary Considerations

A primary factor must first involve gaining the support of key players and policy makers on campus—and in particular, their commitment to provide necessary funds for the recruitment plan for a few years before expecting huge results.

Second, the plan should be flexible enough to be able to respond to ever-changing world events, including changes in demographic and economic factors overseas.

Thirdly, you should be aware that you must differentiate your school as purposefully for students from abroad as you do for students from the United States. When a prospective international student contacts you, whether at a distance or in person, you should be prepared to set forth "what makes your institution different." Your recruiters should have given thought in advance to such a question—and as to how they would respond, or how they

[151] The Bologna Process can shorten the length of time to receive a bachelor's degree from signatory nations from four to three years. See Chapter 38, "Examining The Bologna Process."

[152] NAFSA (2007) recommends a three-pronged approach: Promoting international-oriented, foreign-language, and area studies; establishing study abroad as "an integral component of international education;" and "creating a comprehensive strategy to restore America's status as a magnet for international students and scholars."

[153] As of 2000, only one hundred American institutions of higher education educated half of all foreign exchange students (Riley 2000, pp. 13–14).

would initiate such a conversation. In short, consider the importance of differentiation and marketing strategy, and identify your key attributes.

## Recruitment Principles

The previous discussion establishes that it is critical to adopt or devise good recruitment principles before implementing or expanding an international recruitment program. Various organizations have developed statements of good principles over the years. AACRAO's "Bill of Rights and Responsibilities for International Students and Institutions"[154] is particularly helpful in setting out eleven services which you should be prepared to provide to your international students. Additional resources are *The AACRAO International Guide: A Resource for International Education Professionals* and NAFSA's "Principles of Good Practice for the Recruitment and Admissions of International Students."[155] The following broad principles are compiled from these resources:

- Admissions goals, and policies relating to international students, should be directly related to overall institutional goals and policies.
- Admissions materials should be sensitive to candidates' unfamiliarity with the U.S. education system and lack of fluency in English. You should make clear what the admissions process entails—what documentation is necessary, and under what timelines.
- It is highly advisable to assess the language abilities of international students, to determine if their skills are sufficient to enable them to benefit from the host institution's academic course offerings.
- Information should be presented in a manner in which students can make informed academic judgments. You should make available a clear and complete description of the academic offerings—and the approximate time normally required to complete an academic program.
- Application for admission and transcripts/documents should be evaluated by international admissions evaluators or credential evaluation agencies skilled in evaluating international credentials.
- Materials should provide a clear and accurate account of all costs for the academic year. This explanation should be included along with the response to an application.[156]
- Clear and complete information should be provided as to all legal requirements governing the enrollment of international students, including how to maintain their student status.

[154] *See* <www.aacrao.org/international/rights/bill.cfm>.

[155] *See* <www.nafsa.org/about.sec/governance_leadership/ethics_standards/nafsa_s_principles_of>. (Note: Though it seems truncated, the referenced URL is correct.)

[156] See also, NAFSA's "Financial Aid for Undergraduate International Students" at <www.nafsa.org/students.sec/financial_aid_for_undergraduate>. NAFSA (2008) states: "The Institute for International Education (IIE) reports in *Open Doors 2005* that of the paid tuition and fees to attend a U.S. undergraduate institution in the 2004–05 academic year, 80.9 percent of payments came from personal and family sources." NAFSA continues: "Minimal scholarship aid is available to international students, and most of it is reserved for graduate study. Generally, U.S. institutions offer little, if any, discount on tuition, although both private and public institutions may waive application fees in some situations."

- A Visa is not just a credit card! International students must obtain a visa—a requirement, of course, which is not necessary for domestic students. You must become familiar with a whole different vocabulary. Provide visa information in general terms and then link international students to the immigration Web site for more information.[157]
- International students have the right to know what personal information is collected about them, why it is being collected, and how they may review their files and correct any errors.

## Optimizing Recruitment Efforts

Those responsible for the development, implementation, and assessment of international enrollment strategy should locate and make use of resources that tell them where international students come from, what they study, and why they wish to come. *Open Doors* is a good source for such information.

Once you have decided which segments of the international market you wish to target, you need to determine what strategies will be most effective in reaching those populations. A good place to start is with the international population on your own campus or attending local colleges. Why did they select that institution? The information they provide can be valuable in designing effective outreach. Find out what they have heard about U.S. institutions, how they heard it, why they came, and how well their expectations have been met.

In order to be effective in countries you want to target, you must become knowledgeable about the educational systems in these countries. There are a number of excellent resources that provide a wealth of information on educational systems, both specific countries and world regions, published by AACRAO, such as the *World Education Series*, the *Country Guide* series, and the AACRAO *Electronic Database for Global Education* (EDGE).

By doing some initial fact-finding you will be better able to anticipate the questions and concerns your target population might have. Also know your own campus and how to sell it. State straightforwardly your location, size, accreditation, reputation, admission requirements, strong majors that will be of interest to international students, costs, housing, campus organizations, sports programs, and ethnic diversity, for example. Anticipate questions about such topics, then formulate marketing messages and materials that will attract your target population.

## Recruitment Abroad

Effective marketing and recruitment takes place in a variety of ways, starting in the office and expanding to the countries and areas that are being targeted. Remember that it is wise to maximize the institution's reach from the office before expanding to recruitment in the targeted locations. Only then should the discussion move on to the steps necessary for trav-

[157] See the listing of contacts and resources provided by the ICE Student Exchange and Visitor Information System at <www.ice.gov/sevis/contact.htm>.

eling outside the U.S., and the opportunities as well as the occasional pitfalls in recruiting in other countries.

Expansion beyond "armchair recruiting" can take place by having a recruiter contact local colleges in the area/state where there is an international population. To staff such a move, you might consider a combination of admissions and outreach staff skilled in international admissions matters. Then you can consider the possible move to overseas travel.

Once you decide to send recruiters overseas (or work with locals who are already abroad), one often-used technique is to research and identify the best college fairs that are located in countries of interest to you, and initiate potential relationships with agencies, agents, or other organizations.

## Effective Communication

Effective recruitment means you have a communication plan. And that plan can be as simple as a list of what letters, brochures, and e-mails are being sent to students and when they are being sent, or it can be a massive multi-media database that segments out the applicant pool and tracks multiple streams of communications to different types of prospects and applicants. Whatever your mode and level of tracking, be mindful that school budgets can head up or down, and that the numbers and origin of international students coming to the U.S. from various countries or regions can shift. Thus communications planning, documentation, and assessment of effectiveness is essential.

Start with the development of an informative and effective Web site. Both domestic and international students rely heavily on the information they can access on the Web. Establish a Web site that is easy to find and uses clear terminology, contains the information in one location, and includes the following topics:

- Contact information for the admissions and/or recruitment office, with links to other key areas such as housing, major departments, and immigration information
- Application deadlines, detailed information about documents required, and what is considered an official transcript
- Exact information about admission requirements at each entry level: first-time-freshman, undergraduate transfer, graduate level
- English proficiency requirements and/or other entry test requirements
- Costs of attendance and what financial documentation is required
- International student financial aid policy
- Web-housed forms for inquiries to build a prospect file, financial verification forms, and other necessary information
- Easy links to the application for admission
- Easy links to SEVIS

It is important, also, to have an international student link on the homepage or on the second screen of the Web site. Remember that in some countries downloading large images can take time. In terms of type of language used, avoid slang. It may lead to confusion. But do not go overboard with highly official language, either. Too wordy a presentation, or even a complicated sentence structure, can be a problem.

As to e-mail, it is two-thirds blessing (allowing for personalization) and one-third curse (requiring promptness to be most effective). Communication by e-mail is by far the best way to maintain contact and stay in touch with international prospects and applicants—gone are (or should be) the days of using the postal system as the only means of communication. Be sure to give out as much detailed contact information as you can to applicants. It is amazing what you can accomplish in several e-mails to clarify requirements, and verify that documents have been received. E-mail also allows for personalized—and, as already noted, prompt—responses to student needs, and even anticipation of them.

Prospect information can be kept at a more general level, with all the current message delivery methods available, along with a well-designed Web site. Various other multimedia methods, such as videotapes, CDs, printed publications, and advertising in magazines and journals are also available. Newer techniques such as instant messaging, text messaging, telecounseling, and blogs can also be used. Some colleges are integrating documents or presentations in other languages into their communication plan.

Do not forget the power of your already-enrolled international students to dialogue with international student prospects. Some schools are using interactive orientation and registration for out-of-country international students. Coming full circle, do send your paper admission materials and I-20 visa paperwork by express mail if at all possible. The cost will fade away compared to the speed of your admission information reaching the student quickly and increasing the odds of the student's selecting your school.

Use dual marketing to speak to the students and to the parents in your outreach and promotional communication. These are two distinctly different audiences, often with very different values, aims, and stakes in the process. In addition, there can be strength in partnering, such as occurs in conditional admissions, where an admissions office can partner with a strong on-campus or local ESL (English as a Second Language) program.

International alumni are students who attended your school and have returned to their home country. Contact them. They are a necessity if you attend college fairs in the field.

Last, streamline any admissions processes you can. Accept faxed financial documents and application forms. Consider providing pre-admission advisement. It will not only help the prospective students to understand how their credit might transfer, but it will buy you an immeasurable amount of good will if you establish such a relationship through advisors at local community colleges, for example. If possible, establish an international transfer articulation database. Transfer is one of the most popular topics in higher education these days, because—especially in relation to international admissions—there are still so many gaps in the mapping of one course or program to another. One solution to the issue of international transfer credit is to develop a database of your articulations to ensure that course X from university A will always map to course Y at your institution. Such an international transfer articulation database allows for transparency and consistency.

AACRAO's Electronic Database for Global Education[158] does not provide course-to-course articulations, but it is a web-based resource which provides country profiles, including grading systems, sample credentials, glossaries, and other means of decoding the educational system of more than 100 countries, with regular expansions and updates provided to subscribers electronically.

## Retention

Successfully recruiting and enrolling students is but the first step of the process. Retaining them is the second and equally important step. Establishing or enhancing services will be necessary for an institution planning to increase its international student population. As part of the planning process, an assessment should be made of existing resources on campus. Consider what will be an adequate number of personnel available for student services and academic advisement, and for addressing immigration regulations; the need for an English language placement or bridge program; and personal counseling, housing, and dietary considerations for students from different cultures who may not be leaving the campus for holiday breaks.

## Recommendations

It has often been observed in recruitment and admissions that staff who work in international education do so because of a passion for the field. Sometimes, however, the admissions process can seem overwhelming. Overall there are some basic steps that can be learned and cultivated for the benefit of staff and for the overall recruitment process:

- Review all the application data you have in sight, including the paper application or a database, the educational history of where the applicant attended school, and his/her date of birth. Now you are getting a feel for the educational level of the student—first-time freshman, undergraduate transfer, or graduate.
- Verify that you have all the required documents and that they are authentic. Research the accreditation of the school, and the educational level. Is the school recognized by the country's Ministry of Education?
- Make sure you have the required financial documents and that there are enough funds available to meet your estimate of expenses.
- Determine that English proficiency has been met. This may be through an appropriate TOEFL score or through an alternative test or coursework. (*See* Chapter 24, "The New TOEFL.")

[158] See <www.aacraoedge.aacrao.org>.

- Determine the actual class level of the applicant, eligibility, and award transfer credit.
- Issue the notice of admission and visa documents by express mail.

## Conclusion

In recruiting international students, decide which countries or what type of subject areas you want to recruit in. Then determine the various needs of international students as set out in AACRAO's "Bill of Rights and Responsibilities for International Students and Institutions." Finally, make sure you will have the resources, in terms of both money and personnel, to meet and to anticipate those needs.

After you have made all these preparations, be sure to communicate with the applicant along the way. The United States and its higher education system is still a highly attractive magnet to international students, even though we have more competition than ever before. All it takes to succeed with international students is a bit of practice, careful preparation, knowing how to find helpful resources, and a genuine desire to see international students on your campus.

/ CHAPTER TWENTY-FOUR /

*by Robert Watkins, M.A.*
*Assistant Director of Admissions,*
*Graduate and International Admissions Center*
*University of Texas–Austin*

24

# The New TOEFL

"Why can't they just leave things alone instead of changing them all the time?" Sound familiar? Perhaps *you* have been guilty of muttering that same line on occasion. I know I have. This time the thing "they" have tampered with is the TOEFL® (Test of English as a Foreign Language). *Again*! It was bad enough that we had to endure the change to the computer-based test (CBT) with its new scoring scheme, which differed from the original pencil-and-paper version, but now we have this new TOEFL that is completely different even from the CBT version—it is scored in a way totally unlike the previous two incarnations of that English proficiency test we all know and love/hate. But the good news is that it is not as daunting as you might think, and it is *definitely* better!

## Role of Testing

First, we need to explore again the reasons why English proficiency exams are important to the International Admissions Officer who rarely, if ever, has a background in English as a Second Language (ESL), let alone psychometrics. In order to determine the suitability of an international applicant in a holistic sense, we must ascertain his or her English language ability. Grade point averages, other standardized test scores (SAT, ACT, GRE, GMAT, etc.), letters of recommendation, essays, resumes, or lists of personal achievements are all important and should be factored into the admissions calculus. But English proficiency is a vital element, and should be accorded as much care and concern as the other factors mentioned.

If a student is coming to *your* campus where he or she is expected to participate in discussion sections, understand all of the information flowing from a large lecture section of 300 or more, or submit coherent responses to essay exams in history or government or other required non-major subjects, then success in some form of standardized test that provides information as to English language ability is of critical importance. And it is *your* responsibility to decipher that ability. At the undergraduate level, the international admissions office is the *only* place making that determination. At the graduate level, it is the international admissions office that makes a recommendation to the graduate departments, which render the final decision on admission with regard to English language proficiency.

## Available Measurements

"Which test should I use?" There are various ways of determining English language ability, but the easiest for the international admissions officer is a standardized test readily available throughout the world and that measures the four essential skills students need in order to perform satisfactorily in the classroom: listening, speaking, writing, and reading. TOEFL did not include all four skills as mandatory for much of its existence, though schools could require the applicant to take the optional Test of Spoken English, for example, in order to be considered for admission. But all too often most of us simply instructed the student to take the standard TOEFL, whether paper-and-pencil or computer-based version, and tried to draw a conclusion based on the overall final score.

### International English Language Testing System

The International English Language Testing System (IELTS), available worldwide through the British Council, includes as mandatory all four skills, and is rapidly becoming an option for many international applicants as U.S. schools become more aware of that test. The four skills are graded on a series of bands (levels), with an overall band score supplied to show the test-taker's comprehensive ability. The bands progress from 1 to 9, with a 6.5 band representing roughly a TOEFL paper-and-pencil score of 570 out of 677. (Bear in mind that the top score for the CBT version is *300*, and for the new internet-based test [TOEFL® iBT] is *120*.) Because the British Council maintains offices in so many areas of the world, IELTS may be available in places where other tests are not.

### Internet-Based TOEFL

It has been TOEFL that has been the standard test of choice among most international admissions officers. For some time, there were rumors of a new test that would be better than ever—even better than the CBT. Originally called TOEFL 2000, with the debut to coincide with a new century, the complexity of revamping the test resulted in delays. In the Fall of 2005, the new TOEFL iBT (internet-based test) began roll-out in the United States and selected parts of the world. Uniform and total implementation turned out to be a bit ambitious, given the need to upgrade overseas sites with all the technical support required for delivery of the new test. As TOEFL moves toward full implementation in the next year or so, those geographic areas not yet geared for the new test will be using the paper-based version (the CBT computer version began total phase-out in 2007), until the remaining centers needing upgrades can be brought online as well.

### SECTIONAL SCORING

So what does this new internet-based TOEFL have that the previous versions did not? It has *all four skills* as mandatory aspects of the test. This means a scoring scheme that is totally different from the two previous scoring methods, used in the paper-and-pencil and computer-based editions, respectively. The CBT came out with a concordance to illustrate how the paper-and-pencil version intersected with the CBT grading scheme, so that one could quickly glance at the table to see that a 213 CBT was the same as a 550 TOEFL that had often been the minimum required at Big State U. TOEFL iBT will be scored in an entirely different fashion. That may appear to be "the bad news." But the *good news* is that now the four sections (skills) will play a cumulative role in the overall grading scheme. The speaking score plus the listening score plus the reading score plus the writing score will add up to the final score. The sections are graded on a scale of 0–30, so that a score of 120 represents a perfect score overall.

The most important single point to remember about the new TOEFL iBT is the necessity of using *sectional* scores in the admissions process. Now one needs to learn the importance of the reading section or the listening section, rather than simply looking for a certain single overall score. Graduate departments may now select their admittees based on skills that are more important for *that* department, rather than for the department in the next building where a different skills emphasis altogether may be appropriate. To give one important and frequently-occurring example: A *higher* score on the Speaking skill may be expected of the prospective teaching assistant from abroad, than would be the case for a regular (non-teaching) applicant to that same department.

### DELIVERY MECHANISMS

Another interesting new feature is the delivery mechanism. Instead of receiving a paper test with ovals to mark, or a computer with the special disc and a series of questions, the test-taker now merely logs on to an Internet-capable computer and, once the security system is satisfied, takes a test that is not hierarchical in nature (*i.e.*, moving from levels of complexity based on the answer to the prior question along a node) but instead consists of answering a series of questions based on information received during the testing process. For example, students will be required to integrate skills such as listening to a lecture and then answering a series of questions. Or, they may be required to speak about a given topic, with only a brief period of preparation time. In other words, it is overall communicative competence which is stressed in the new TOEFL iBT.

### ASSISTANCE IN SETTING CAMPUS STANDARDS

"How do we know *what* score is good or average among selective institutions, or is embraced by colleagues in the field who have been doing this for years and to whom we have always looked for guidance?" I am glad you asked that question! TOEFL has instituted a series of standards-setting exercises, of various types, for institutions across the country. What happens is that a group of TOEFL experts involved with the new test arrives on campus and, over a period of two days, works with a panel of faculty and administrators of various offices to peg the right combination of scores—sectional and overall—for *that* institution. The exercise involves the experts on the panel taking the exam themselves, to understand what it is and how it is formulated. At the conclusion, as the panel is made familiar with the scoring rubric, a decision is made for that institution, and is ultimately transmitted to TOEFL for inclusion on the TOEFL pages of the Educational Testing Service Web site (www.toefl.org).

Information is also disseminated by means of numerous presentations by senior TOEFL staff, along with university-based admissions officers familiar with the new test and the standard-setting exercise, at various conferences such as AACRAO, NAFSA, and the state and regional partners of each. Once prospective users of the TOEFL iBT see what other institutions are requiring in this new scoring scheme, they can begin to set their own score requirements based on comparison with those other institutions. If preferred, TOEFL will also make available the tools for a standard-setting exercise for those institutions wishing to make their own analysis.

My own institution, The University of Texas at Austin, decided to have 21 be the average required score on all sections and to establish 79 as the overall required minimum score for applicants not applying for teaching assistantships. True, four multiplied by 21 does not equal 79. But this overall score gives our departments the flexibility to look carefully at those skill areas of most concern or value to them. If it is the Speaking skill, then a 21 is definitely what the applicant should make on that section. If, for example, the applicant scores a 19 in writing, but a 21 or better on the Speaking section, then the applicant has performed satisfactorily according to the needs of the department. An overall score of 79 is still required, but the individual scores may vary so long as that overall score is achieved, and the most highly valued skills set is present based on the recommended sectional scores.

## Adapting to Improvements

Change is often challenging. One reason so many of us enjoy international admissions is that it is a dynamic field. Countries change educational systems, add new schools, alter the grading system, or replace degree systems altogether. In such an atmosphere of ever-changing elements, we long to embrace those aspects that seem unchanging. TOEFL has been one of those elements for so long, for those of us who have been in the field for more than twenty-five years. Now TOEFL too has changed, and changed radically. But, in my opinion, it has radically changed for the better!

/ CHAPTER TWENTY-FIVE /

*by Michael A. Olivas, J.D. Ph.D.*
*William B. Bates, Distinguished Chair in Law and Director of the Institute for Higher Education Law and Governance*
*University of Houston Law Center*

25

# The DREAM Act and In-State Tuition for Undocumented Students

In 1982, the U.S. Supreme Court struck down an attempt by Texas to deny free public education to alien children. In *Plyler v. Doe* (457 U.S. 202), the Court ruled that undocumented children—children whose parents effected illegal entry into the country—had a right to attend *public elementary and secondary* schools. However, the Court was silent on the issue of whether the protections extended to the college setting.

The next move of interest to college admissions officers occurred in 1996. In that year Congress passed the Illegal Immigration Reform and Immigrant Responsibility Act of 1996 (IIRIRA). Section 505 of that Act contained a convoluted statement which some states interpreted as *forbidding* a state to grant in-state resident levels of tuition to undocumented students at public institutions of higher education, but which other states interpreted as *permitting* the practice, via the following paraphrase: "State A cannot give more consideration to an undocumented student from in its own state than it gives to a non-resident student from State B."[159] In other words, a state could not allow undocumented students to be

[159] The actual wording of the section in question is as follows: "Notwithstanding any other provision of law, an alien who is not lawfully present in the United States shall not be eligible on the basis of residence within a State (or a political subdivision) for any postsecondary education benefit unless a citizen or national of the United States is eligible for such benefit (in no less amount, duration and scope) without regard to whether the citizen or national is such a resident" (8 U.S.C. 1623).

eligible for in-state resident status for college tuition after a mere twelve months, if it requires other out-of-state students to wait eighteen months.

In the face of this ambiguity, ten states,[160] by state law, now allow undocumented students to gain resident tuition status, while several others have moved to deny such eligibility. A number of other states are formally considering pertinent legislation. (*See* Figure 25.1, on page 339.)

The third development, which is of great interest to admissions officers, is that Congress has repeatedly considered enacting a law which would repeal section 505 of IIRIRA, and making that repeal retroactive, as if Section 505 had never existed. That proposed law—The Development, Relief, and Education for Alien Minors (DREAM) Act of 2007—would allow eligible undocumented students (those who entered the United States before they were sixteen years old) to begin the path toward legalization. It would also remove an ostensible federal barrier—Section 505, as just discussed—to allowing undocumented students to establish residency for the purposes of in-state tuition. The DREAM Act would *not require* states to allow undocumented students to establish in-state residency, but it would *allow* states to do so.[161]

## Framing the Issues

Unauthorized aliens are neither entitled to nor prohibited from admission to postsecondary educational institutions in the United States. As Bruno (2007) notes: "Even if they gain admission, however, unauthorized alien students often find it difficult, if not impossible, to pay for higher education. Under the Higher Education Act of 1965, as amended, they are ineligible for federal financial aid" (p. CRS-2). In most states, they are also ineligible for state

[160] The ten states that offer in-state tuition to undocumented students are: California, Illinois, Kansas, Nebraska, New Mexico, New York, Oklahoma, Texas, Utah, and Washington. Those states offer the in-state rate to undocumented students who have attended high school in the state for anywhere between two and four years; complete a high school diploma or GED in the state; and file an affidavit stating intent to become a permanent U.S. citizen (Krueger 2006). Note that although the California law passed in 2001 makes undocumented students eligible for in-state tuition at state community colleges and California State University campuses, it does not apply to the University of California system (Bruno 2007, p. CRS-3).

Three of the states in question—Texas, New Mexico, and Oklahoma—allow undocumented students to apply for state financial aid. In 2007, Oklahoma enacted legislation that rendered such aid uncertain.

As to Oklahoma, note that although there had been reports of the new Oklahoma Taxpayer and Citizen Protection Act of 2007 (HB 1804) repealing the 2003 provision for according residency tuition to eligible undocumented students, the actual language of the bill, signed into law in May, 2007, does no such thing. It does throw down more documentation requirements and will likely scare off some students, but it is still possible for those students who have met other eligibility and admissions requirements to become in-state students in the state's public institutions.

Moreover, if the student is a U.S. citizen but one or more parents are undocumented, the student is eligible for federal student aid (Kantrowitz 2008). Kantrowitz goes on to explain: "However, if the parents supply a fake or stolen social security number (SSN) on the form, the student's FAFSA will be rejected when the parent's social security number fails to match. The FAFSA may also be rejected when the parents submit a SSN or Taxpayer Identification Number (TIN) that is valid for work purposes only. If the parents do not have a social security number or the social security number fails the match, they should use 000-00-0000 as their social security number on the FAFSA form."

[161] The DREAM Act was caught up in the failure of comprehensive immigration reform in the summer of 2007, and it was pulled from the Senate floor as an amendment to the Department of Defense authorization bill in June. On October 24, 2007, the Senate voted down a cloture motion which would have allowed a stand-alone DREAM Act to reach the Senate floor. However, the issue is obviously alive and will inevitably be revisited at the federal level.

FIGURE 25.1

Table of State Legislative Action Concerning Undocumented College Students (Fall 2007)

**States that Allow Undocumented Students to Gain Resident Tuition Status (by state statute)**

- 2001—Texas, H.B. 1403, 77th Leg., Reg. Sess. (Tex. 2001), amended by S.B.
- 1528 (Tex. 2005)
- 2001—California, A.B. 540, 2001-02 Cal. Sess. (Cal. 2001)
- 2002—Utah, H.B. 144, 54th Leg., Gen. Sess. (Utah 2002)
- 2002—New York, S.B. 7784, 22 5th Leg., 2001 NY Sess. (NY 2002)
- 2003—Washington State, H.B. 1079, 58th Leg., Reg. Sess. (Wash. 2003)
- 2003—Oklahoma, S.B. 596, 49th Leg., 1st Sess. (OK 2003)
- 2003—Illinois, H.B. 60, 93rd Leg., Reg. Sess. (Ill. 2003)
- 2004—Kansas, K.S.A. 76-731a (KS 2004)
- 2005—New Mexico, N.M.S.A. 1978, Ch. 348, Sec. 21-1-1.2 [47th Leg. Sess. (2005)]
- 2006—Nebraska, LB 239 (enacted over veto, April 13, 2006)

**States that Do NOT Allow Undocumented Students to Gain Resident Tuition Status (by state statute)**

- Arizona
- Georgia
- Mississippi

**States That Have Formally Considered Legislation Concerning Undocumented Students and Residency Tuition Status (Statutes Introduced by Fall 2007)**

- Alaska
- California (eligibility for state aid)
- Colorado
- Connecticut[1]
- Delaware[2]
- Florida
- Hawaii
- Kansas[3]
- Maryland[1]
- Massachusetts[1]
- Michigan
- Minnesota[4]
- Missouri[5]
- New Jersey
- North Carolina
- Oregon
- Rhode Island
- Virginia[6]
- Wisconsin
- Wyoming[7]

[1] Pro-immigrant bill vetoed by the governor
[2] Public institutions in Delaware have agreed to allow undocumented students to establish residency status, in lieu of legislation that had been introduced
[3] Bill introduced to repeal existing residency statute.
[4] Legislation enacted that eliminated non-resident tuition, irrespective of immigration status)
[5] Bill introduced to preclude undocumented attendance.
[6] Anti-immigrant bill vetoed by the governor. (In addition, a bill in 2006 (SB 542) affected refugee tuition.)
[7] W.S. 21-16-1303 enacted, limiting state scholarships to LPR and citizens

financial aid. (In footnote 160, we have already noted the few exceptions.) Finally, the difference in in-state versus out-of-state tuition often makes it prohibitive for such students to attend, if the state in question does not consider them to be "residents" for purposes of in-state tuition.[162]

The DREAM Act, as it was re-proposed in 2007, does not mandate that states offer in-state tuition to undocumented students (as has often been charged). What it does propose to do is to restore the state option to determine residency for purposes of higher education benefits (S. 774, Sec. 3).

The DREAM Act, if enacted, would provide for a two-stage process. In the first stage, eligible students must show that they entered the United States five years prior to the passage of the legislation, and were under the age of sixteen at the time of entry. Moreover, they must show that they graduated from high school in the United States, or obtained a GED. Fulfilling

[162] As noted above, Texas allows undocumented students to enroll at the in-state rate. (It was the first state to do so, in 2001). In 2005, when the Washington Legal Foundation challenged that action, it cost an in-state student only $588 per semester to enroll at the Houston Community College—but $1,476 per semester (two and a half times as much) to enroll as an out-of-state student (Mittelstadt 2005).

these conditions would be enough to grant them conditional permanent resident status. In the next six years, they would have to complete either an associate degree (or two years toward a bachelor's degree), or complete two years of military service (with an honorable discharge, if discharged). At that time, and upon completion of additional conditions, they could become legal permanent residents (LPRs), with green cards.

Bruno (2007) summarizes with efficiency both the broad policy arguments in favor of repealing the restrictive (or ostensibly restrictive) provision of the 1996 law, and arguments against, as follows: "Those in favor of repealing the 1996 provision and granting LPR status to unauthorized alien students argue that many of these students were brought into the United States at a very young age and should not be held responsible for the decision to enter the country illegally. Those who oppose making these students eligible for in-state tuition or legal status emphasize that they and their families are in the United States illegally and should be removed from the country, not granted benefits" (p. CRS-1).

The DREAM Act, if enacted, could affect an estimated 65,000 high school graduates per year (NCLR 2007).

A final framing consideration is the oft-repeated argument that American taxpayers are subsidizing undocumented persons through government expenditures. New Mexico Voices for Children (NM Voices 2006), a group which believes that "much of the government's approach to immigration is unnecessarily punitive," has conducted a study of the cost of services provided to, and the tax contribution of, New Mexico's relatively small undocumented population—about 40,000 (2%) as of 2006 (p. 2).[163] "Contrary to popular belief," the study concludes, "undocumented immigrants pay taxes and are not able to receive public benefits, except for K–12 education for their children and emergency health care" (p. 6) The study notes that the public services which undocumented aliens are restricted from receiving include Social Security, Medicare, Medicaid, food stamps, child care subsidies, housing assistance, and Temporary Assistance to Needy Families (TANF). The study contends that the taxes that these families pay through unavoidable sales and property taxes cover the state and local share of the public education costs.

The study goes on to state: "In addition to paying their own way for education, undocumented immigrants often pay for Social Security and Medicare when those taxes are deducted from their paychecks. Neither of those social programs is available to them as they age, so in effect, they contribute to the costs of caring for the elderly who are citizens of this country" (p. 6).

The study concludes: "...to assume that [the undocumented] get a free ride in New Mexico is a mistake: they pay for the services they receive, and then some" (p. 6).

[163] See also "Undocumented Immigrants in Texas: A Financial Analysis of the Impact to the State Budget and Economy." This 2006 study, conducted by State Comptroller Carole Strayhorn, highlights the financial impact of undocumented immigrants in the state of Texas. The study is available at <www.window.state.tx.us/specialrpt/undocumented/undocumented.pdf>.

Since Olivas' (2004) article on the subject of in-state tuition for undocumented students, a number of developments have kept the DREAM Act and the issue of undocumented college students in the news and on legislative agendas. The following treatment updates the developments from that time, and is current through mid-October, 2007.

## Federal Litigation

### Challenge of the Texas and New York Statutes

In 2005, the Washington Legal Foundation filed a complaint with the Department of Homeland Security (DHS) to challenge the Texas and New York statutes, although it is not entirely clear why the DHS would have jurisdiction over the pertinent sections of IRRIRA. However, as of fall 2007, no action had been taken on this matter by DHS, and discussions with attorneys and officials involved indicated that there would be no action forthcoming.[164]

### Challenge of the Kansas Statute

In *Day v. Sibelius* (376 F. Supp. 2d 1022 [D. Kan. 2005]), lawyers challenged the Kansas statute which, like those in California and New York, allowed in-state tuition for undocumented college students who could establish in-state residency status. The judge of the United States District Court for the District of Kansas dismissed that lawsuit without ruling on the merits, finding that the out-of-state student plaintiffs did not have standing to sue, because whether the objected-to law was in place or not, they would have been charged the same higher, out-of-state tuition rates.

The Federation for American Immigration Reform (FAIR), a group opposed to the DREAM Act, filed an appeal to the United States Court of Appeals for the Tenth Circuit.[165] The appeals court, like the district court, ruled against the plaintiffs, on two grounds: both that the plaintiffs lacked standing and that they lacked a private right of action to sue to enforce pre-emption by 8 U.S.C. 1623.

In the fall of 2005, state data showed that 221 students had used this state law to enroll in Kansas public colleges since 2002. In January 2006, a Kansas representative filed a bill to eliminate the law allowing in-state tuition for undocumented students who met residence requirements, but as of 2007, no hearings had been scheduled.

### Challenge of the California Statute

In December 2005, the same groups that filed the Kansas matter filed in a California state court. In October 2006, the attempt by FAIR to bring the same issues from the Kansas federal

164 To follow this story, see the Washington Legal Foundation documents at <www.wlf.org/Litigating/casedetail.asp?detail=366>. See also Fischer (2005).

165 Since the Kansas governor, Kathleen Sibelius, had been dismissed from the lawsuit, the case was titled on appeal as *Day v Bond*.

case to litigation in a California state court was also rejected, when the California judge ruled against them.[166]

In the fall of 2007, another case was brought against the California state residency statute. This case is *Martinez et al. v Regents of the University of California*, CV-05–2064. The appeal in this case is pending.[167]

In contrast to the previous cases discussed, which were brought by challengers of in-state tuition for the undocumented, the most recent higher education immigration/residency case in California—*Student Advocates for Higher Education et al. v Trustees, California State University et al.*—was brought by a number of immigrant organizations. They were challenging one facet of the California Education Code (Section 68040; 5 CCR 41904), and the State Constitution (postsecondary residency and financial aid provisions). In this lawsuit, California students who were U.S. citizens, but with undocumented parents, were asserting that they were being prevented from receiving the tuition and financial aid benefits due them, at least in part because the California statute is not precisely drawn (or else, imperfectly administered).

In addition, there was a confusing interaction among several overlapping features of the system: immigration, financial aid independence/dependence upon parents, and age of majority/domicile. The State agreed to enter into a consent decree,[168] so the matter was resolved *in favor* of the plaintiffs. The resulting order overturned the odd take, by the California State University System, on undocumented college student residency—that if a *documented college student*, in-state and of the age of majority, had *undocumented parents*, he or she was not able to take advantage of the California statute in question, even if the student were otherwise eligible.

## State Legislation

### Texas

In 2005, the State of Texas enacted several modifications to its postsecondary residency statutes (S.B. 1528), and the implementing Texas Coordinating Board regulations, some of which affect undocumented students. The changes make it slightly easier for such students to avail themselves of in-state tuition, and put an end to the anomalous situation in which international students (required to maintain foreign domiciles in F-1 visa status) were taking advantage of the original statute and regulations.

Note that, as of 2007, Texas state legislators have filed at least four bills to repeal the 2005 law, "which grants lower, in-state tuition to undocumented students who have lived in Texas at least three years, have graduated from a Texas high school, and plan to become citizens"

---

[166] See Hebel (2006).

[167] See <www.law.uh.edu/ihelg/undocumented/regentsorder_10062006_033944pm.pdf>.

[168] The consent decree has been entered in the official San Francisco, California Superior Court site at: <www.sftc.org/Scripts/Magic94/mgrqispi94.dll?APPNAME=IJS&PRGNAME=ROA&ARGUMENTS=-ACPF06506755>.

(Robison and Ratcliffe 2007). In response to these efforts to repeal the Texas law, HB 1403, Governor Rick Perry said he would not accept or sign any changes to it. In 2001, Perry had signed the original legislation.

### New York State

New York State also enacted changes to its statute. Undocumented aliens who attend a New York State high school for two years (and graduate from same) may be eligible for the in-state tuition rate.[169]

### New Mexico

In January 2005, New Mexico extended resident tuition to the undocumented, and also altered its residency statutes for some American Indians and for Texans from border counties. In doing so, it became the ninth state to enact such legislation, and it is among the most generous, extending financial aid and lottery scholarship eligibility as well as resident tuition.

### Massachusetts

In January 2006, the Massachusetts legislature voted down a measure that would have accorded in-state tuition to the undocumented. However, as a counterpoint, in 2007, Governor Deval L. Patrick proposed to abolish tuition at the state's fifteen community colleges—a proposal which, if enacted, would moot the residency issue.

"The Massachusetts Board of Higher Education estimated that such a change would cost about $180-million a year in a state where the total higher education budget is about one billion dollars" (Smith 2007).

### Minnesota

Early in 2007, legislation pertinent to in-state tuition for the undocumented was introduced, both to accord residency status and to restrict it (Hopfensperger 2007, p. 5B).[170]

At the end of a complicated session, on May 30, 2007, Governor Tim Pawlenty signed into law an interesting partial victory for in-state/residency tuition advocates. Under the Minnesota bill[171] a number of the state college system institutions will eliminate nonresident rates altogether, allowing anyone, apparently regardless of state of residence or immigration status, to qualify for the flat (formerly in-district) rate.[172] The press coverage on this has not yet fully canvassed the entire legislation, which was complex and which originally had a specific DREAM Act provision that was stripped.

---

169 See <www.suny.edu/Student/paying_residence.cfm>.

170 Hopfensperger's article also includes a discussion of DREAM Act proposals in Minnesota.

171 See H.F. 1083 (85th Leg. Sess. 2007).

172 The analysis of the bill is at <www.house.leg.state.mn.us/hinfo/sessiondaily.asp?yearid=2007&storyid=1098>.The entire bill history is at <www.house.leg.state.mn.us/bills/billnum.asp?Billnumber=1063&lsyear=85&session_year=2007&session_number=0&Go.x=17&go.y=6>.

The Minnesota legislation has a 2009 sunset clause, and somewhat finesses the larger issue, which goes beyond the immigration dimension. Many DREAM Act kids are likely to attend two-year colleges. (In Texas, for example, even before HB 1403 passed, some community college districts had moved to this practice of not charging non-resident tuition, led by the Houston Community College System, which was the real precursor of this practice in Texas.) Many of these students enroll in transfer curricula, but partly due to the costs and their inability to work for pay in the country, they never end up transferring to senior colleges.

### Nebraska

On April 14, 2006, Nebraska became the tenth state to provide in-state tuition to undocumented immigrant students who have attended and graduated from its high schools. It did so in dramatic fashion, overriding Governor Dave Heineman's veto. The bill (LB 239)[173] had passed by a 26 to 19 margin, but needed 30 votes for an override of the veto; supporters managed to change exactly four votes to get the necessary 30.[174]

### California

On September 30, 2006, Governor Arnold Schwarzenegger declined to sign S.B. 160, a bill that would have allowed undocumented students in California, already eligible for in-state tuition, to participate in the state's financial aid grant programs.[175] In October 2007, Governor Schwarzenegger again vetoed the measure (state financial aid for undocumented students). For insight into the rationalle behind the vetos, see Scott Jaschik's (2007) article entitled "Schwarzenegger Vetoes DREAM Bill for Immigrant Students."[176]

### Connecticut

In 2007, Connecticut's legislature passed and sent a bill (H.B. 5656) to Governor Jodi Rell for her signature, which would have granted alien students who graduated from the state's high schools the opportunity to qualify for resident tuition. She vetoed the bill on June 26, 2007, saying: "I understand these students are not responsible for their undocumented status, having come to the United States with their parents.... The fact remains, however, that these students and their parents are here illegally and neither sympathy nor good intentions can ameliorate that fact" (Stowe 2007).

### Georgia

In fall 2007, there are still uncertainties over what the restrictionist Georgia and Arizona state statutes mean for this issue, and the situation is in flux in these two states. Georgia held

173 The final copy is available at <http://uniweb.legislature.ne.gov/FloorDocs/Current/PDF/Final/LB239.pdf>.

174 In an article entitled "Immigration's Scrambled Politics," Ruth Marcus (2006) provides an interesting perspective on the issue.

175 Schwarzenegger's veto message is available at <http://gov.ca.gov/pdf/press/sb_160_veto.pdf>.

176 Available at <www.insidehighered.com/news/2007/10/15/calif>.

public hearings in April 2007 to get public input on how state officials should proceed, but the behind-the-scenes waiver system that allows each public college to use waivers for up to 2 percent of their headcount may change. The statute took effect on July 1, 2007.

### Arizona

At the start of the Spring 2007 semester, Wingett (2007) reported that Arizona officials were confused about what they were to do with requirements enacted in Proposition 300—a new statute approved late in 2006.

Nonetheless, state officials decided to discontinue enrollment of undocumented students. As a result, by Summer 2007, "[n]early 5,000 people in Arizona [had] been denied in-state college tuition, financial aid, and adult education classes..." (Wingett and Benson 2007).

Wingett and Ruelas (2007) later reported that Arizona State University (ASU) had sought to assist 150 to 200 undocumented students in the fall semester of 2007, using "private money already in the university's coffers to help bridge the gap.... The authors further noted that "[t]he gap between in-state and out-of-state tuition for full-time students at ASU's Tempe campus is about $12,000."

According to a report of the Joint Legislative Budget Committee, 1,500 students from ASU and the University of Arizona were denied financial aid or in-state tuition status, and an additional 1,790 community college students were affected (Wingett and Ruelas 2007).

### Missouri and Virginia

Following the lead of Missouri, which in 2007 saw the introduction of a "death-penalty" provision that would have banned undocumented students from enrolling in any fashion in its public colleges, Virginia legislators introduced a similar bill in the legislature in August 2007.[177]

The Missouri Senate Committee on Pensions, Veterans' Affairs, and General Laws heard testimony on March 14, 2007 on five proposed bills, including the "Missouri Omnibus Immigration Act" (SB 348) and a bill to ban undocumented students from public institutions (HB 269). The legislation was not enacted.

As of this writing, no states have banned undocumented aliens from enrolling (aside from the issue of level of tuition charged), but this surely seems to be the route that some states will travel.

[177] See Craig (2007) for a description of the bill..

## Attorney General Opinions

### Colorado

On January 23, 2006 Colorado Attorney General John W. Suthers issued an Attorney General Opinion (AGO) on the subject of whether the Colorado Commission on Higher Education (CCHE) had the statutory authority to grant in-state residency status to undocumented aliens; he held that the CCHE lacked the authority to establish such a policy or regulation.

However, Attorney General Suthers (2007) later determined that state residency law *did* allow undocumented students to establish residency, if they otherwise met the durational requirements. In an AGO issued on August 14, 2007, he opined: "Because it is the student, rather than the parents, who is the legal beneficiary of in-state tuition status, the fact that the parents may be in the country illegally is not a bar to the student's receipt of that benefit" (p. 2).

### Utah

In January 2006, the Utah Assistant Attorney General Bill Evans issued an opinion, determining that the Utah statute granting *in-state* tuition status to the state's undocumented college students is constitutional (Bulkeley 2006). There has also been movement in Utah to repeal its residency statute allowing for in-state tuition for undocumented students, but, as of Fall 2007, that has not occurred. "Although a repeal would only affect a few hundred undocumented students and cost about $200,000 in tuition dollars, education leaders say that's nothing compared to the price of sending a negative message to minority students" (Stewart and Bulkeley 2007).

### Texas

In 2005, the Texas Attorney General issued an Opinion saying that a phrase in the state's Hazlewood Act (a military scholarship program) referring to a "citizen of Texas" should be interpreted as a person who lives in the state and is a U.S. citizen. Prior to this AGO, Texas public colleges and universities gave the Hazlewood benefit to all qualifying military veterans regardless of whether they were U.S. citizens or legal permanent residents when they entered the military. In 2007, two Mexican American permanent resident veterans (eligible except for the timing) were rendered ineligible under this revised criterion, and they brought suit, which remains unresolved as of Fall 2007 (Garay 2007).

## The DREAM Act in Congress

Of course, against the backdrop of considerable state activity, the federal sector has also been active. On November 21, 2005, the DREAM Act[178] was reintroduced in Congress. The DREAM Act languished until comprehensive immigration reform efforts failed in June 2007.

[178] For an index of several resources on the Act, see <www.nilc.org/immlawpolicy/DREAM/>.

Then, in July 2007, the Senate tried a different legislative approach, and developed plans to attach the legislation to the Department of Defense authorization bill. In the end, Senator Harry Reid pulled it from the floor when an Iraq timetable amendment failed and the Senate never got to the DREAM vote. Redden (2007) noted that "[s]till, the attempt to connect a critical defense bill with the DREAM Act...may represent a shift in strategy for advocates who have watched the bill long languish amidst contentious and inconclusive immigration reform battles."

The DoD Authorization bill was scheduled to return to the Senate floor in September, 2007, but—as already noted—on October 24, 2007, the Senate could not muster the 60 votes required to allow the DREAM Act to reach the Senate floor on a standalone basis for a vote.[179] The White House issued a statement as to its view of the Senate bill in question (S. 2205), in which the Administration stated: "By creating a special path to citizenship that is unavailable to other prospective immigrants—including young people whose parents respected the Nation's immigration laws—S. 2205 falls short. The Administration therefore opposes the bill."

The House Judiciary Committee held a DREAM Act of 2007 hearing on May 18, 2007 ("Hearings on Comprehensive Immigration Reform: The Future of Undocumented Immigrant Students"), and the testimony and written statements are online.[180]

## Studies Available on the Internet

- The *National Association of College Admissions Counselors* (NACAC) has made the DREAM Act an organizational priority; materials providing background information from NACAC are made available online.[181]
- In February 2005, the *National Immigration Law Center* produced a two-page report called "The Economic Benefits of the DREAM Act and the Student Adjustment Act."[182] Among its conclusions: "...based on estimates in a 1999 RAND study, an average 30-year-old Mexican immigrant woman who has graduated from college will pay $5,300 more in taxes and cost $3,900 less in criminal justice and welfare expenses each year than if she had dropped out of high school. This amounts to a total annual increased fiscal contribution of more than $9,000 per person."
- As mentioned earlier in the text, *FinAid* contains a page about financial aid and scholarships for "undocumented students" and "illegal aliens" (the two terms being used inten-

[179] For the roll call on that vote, see <http://senate.gov/legislative/LIS/roll_call_lists/roll_call_vote_cfm.cfm?congress=110&session=1&vote=00394>.

[180] See <http://judiciary.house.gov/oversight.aspx?ID=321>.

[181] See <www.nacacnet.org/NR/rdonlyres/659C54BA-566D-4440-B9BA-3B56A644D6C9/0/PressAttachments_July06.pdf>.

[182] Available at <www.nilc.org/immlawpolicy/DREAM/Econ_Bens_DREAM&Stdnt_Adjst_0205.pdf>.

tionally and interchangeably on that Web page to reach the maximum number of students searching for information).[183]

- The *Mexican-American Legal Defense Fund* has a document available on its Web site listing "Scholarships/Becas for All Students Regardless of Immigration Status." It is available, in paragraphs which alternate between English and Spanish.[184]
- The *National Conference of State Legislatures* issued a report, entitled "2006 State Legislation Related to Immigration: Enacted, Vetoes, and Pending Gubernatorial Action," detailing the 57 state statutes enacted in 2006 in 27 states, related to various aspects of immigration.[185] A total of 570 bills had been introduced (Morse, Blott, and Speasmaker 2006). A more recent "Overview of State Legislation Related to Immigration and Immigrants in 2007" shows a spike in activity, counting 1,169 bills across all 50 states proposed between January and April (Hegen 2007).
- The *Heritage Foundation* featured an article by Kris Kobach (2006) entitled "The Senate Immigration Bill Rewards Lawbreaking: Why the DREAM Act Is a Nightmare," that followed activites surrounding the proposed legislation and outlined why the Act is problematic and tends toward "shockingly bad policy."[186]
- The *Congressional Research Service* (CRS) produced two recent reports: Jody Feder's (2006) "Unauthorized Alien Students, Higher Education, and In-State Tuition Rates: A Legal Analysis;"[187] and Andorra Bruno's (2007) "Unauthorized Alien Students: Issues and 'DREAM Act' Legislation."[188]
- The *School of Education at the University of Southern California* produced "The College & Financial Aid Guide for: A540 Undocumented Immigrant Students," a useful booklet containing information about AB 540—the statute enabling undocumented students to qualify for resident status.[189]
- The *Migration Policy Institute's* "New Estimates of Unauthorized Youth Eligible for Legal Status under the DREAM Act" is ten-page report on students who would benefit from the DREAM Act.[190]

[183] See <www.finaid.org/otheraid/undocumented.phtml> (English); <www.finaid.org/otheraid/spanish.phtml> (Spanish).

[184] Downloadable from <www.maldef.org/pdf/Scholarships_072003.pdf>.

[185] See <www.ncsl.org/programs/immig/06ImmigEnactedLegis2.htm>. NCSL offers regular updates on immigration policies at <www.ncsl.org/programs/immig/>.

[186] See <www.heritage.org/research/immigration/bg1960.cfm>.

[187] Downloadable from <www.ilw.com/immigdaily/news/2007,0910-crs.pdf>.

[188] Downloadable from <www.opencrs.com/rpts/RL33863_20070130.pdf>.

[189] Downloadable from <www.law.uh.edu/ihelg/undocumented/CollegeFinancialAidGuidAB540Students.pdf>.

[190] Downloadable from <www.migrationpolicy.org/pubs/Backgrounder1_Dream_Act.pdf>.

/ CHAPTER TWENTY-SIX /

*by C. Michael Cook, M.S.*
*(Operations and Systems Management)*
*Senior Associate Director*
*Office of Admissions*
*Michigan State University*

26

# Delivering Outstanding Service in Admissions Processing

The role of admissions operation and technology is to facilitate the process of transforming applicants to enrollees. This chapter will focus on methods and processes appropriate to meet the needs of the conventional first-time applicant (*i.e.*, a prospective student of high school age or close to it). Chapter 21, "Reaching the Adult Market," focuses on techniques appropriate to recruiting and processing adult students.

## A Customer-Focused Mission

Simply stated, colleges and universities want to enroll qualified applicants. Billions of dollars are spent each year as institutions allocate valuable marketing and administrative resources in an attempt to bring in the desired class. The mission and vision statements of higher education institutions proudly display a commitment to serving the educational needs of the community. In turn, desirable applicants research their options and apply primarily to institutions best meeting those educational needs. Thus the admissions process is nothing if not a customer-oriented business.

Although some applicants will be willing to enroll despite an unpleasant admissions experience, the admissions office is the first to represent the institution, and as such it must establish a goal of providing excellent customer service to *all* prospects, applicants, and parents.

The heart of admissions customer service, however, extends beyond a pleasant experience with an admissions officer or a telephone conversation with a nice admissions representative. Virtually every admissions activity and internal process affects the satisfaction of prospective students and their parents.

High levels of customer satisfaction can be achieved by, first, establishing customer satisfaction as a priority; second, establishing a culture of continuous improvement; and third, adopting proven "quality methods," such as such as Total Quality Management (TQM)[191] or the Six Sigma approach.[192]

Although TQM was first introduced to American companies in the 1980s, and has been both widely adopted and (by reaction) widely disparaged since, the principles and technique still produce results, when applied carefully.[193]

In addition to adopting a focus on customer satisfaction, establishing a continuous improvement culture, and adopting a quality method suitable to the needs of the institution, the proactive admissions office will carefully but creatively employ technology. Admissions-related technology can introduce innovative leaps in customer service, redefining how admissions work is accomplished.

Ultimately, to create and sustain positive change, the leader in the admissions office must demand—and make possible—an enduring quest for quality from all admissions employees.

## Knowing Your Customers

### The Applicant

The college admissions process is always an important event in a teenager's life, and both the process and the outcome can be a stressful one. For many students, the process did not start with the tedious task of submitting a pile of college applications to targeted institutions of higher education. Instead, it began with a purpose, a carefully detailed academic plan, and a commitment to be well prepared for college.

These educational roadmaps and associated experiences are very personal journeys for students. Students are intently focused on the opportunities provided by colleges. They are, for the most part, blind to the other ten or twenty thousand applications moving through

[191] Total Quality Management is a management strategy "aimed at embedding awareness of quality in all organizational processes. ...[It] provides an umbrella under which everyone in the organization can...create customer satisfaction at continually lower real costs" (Wikipedia 2008a).

[192] "Six Sigma is a business improvement methodology...originally defined as a metric for measuring defects and improving quality.... [It is] a methodology of controlling a process to the point of plus or minus six sigma (standard deviations) from a centerline (for a total span of twelve sigma). Six Sigma has now grown beyond defect control. It is now commonly used to obtain detailed information regarding customer, employee and shareholder demands and then using this information to improve process and product design" (Wikipedia 2008b).

[193] Some previous failures of quality efforts in admissions offices have often been due to a lack of commitment by the upper levels of leadership to the new program, leaving the staff with the attitude of "we tried it once, but it didn't work."

the application decision process. They have purely personal concerns that inspire many questions: Have their required application documents reached the admissions office? Will they be admitted? When will they be notified of the admissions committee's decision?

### The Parents

The parents of these college-bound students are also on a personal and emotional roller coaster. They face the overwhelming task of preparing their offspring for adulthood. Although some parents are referred to as "helicopter parents" because of what seems an over- involvement in their child's activity, most parents have one thing in common—a concern for the well-being of their children.

Parents share a similar perspective to their children, with one notable exception: they are even more likely to expect the same quality of customer service provided by the bank, automobile mechanic, and cable TV provider. With urgency, parents ask questions: We applied months ago—why is my child's decision taking so long when the neighbor heard from the university three weeks ago? What do the student's ACT or SAT scores really mean? The student next door was admitted and they took the same courses—is my child getting a fair assessment of his (her) academic preparedness? Does the university truly understand the rigor of my son's or daughter's high school? Why is it so hard to actually speak to a real person in the admissions office?

## Creating Excellence in Customer Service

### Overcoming Institutional Processes

The challenge for admissions professionals is to provide each prospect, applicant, and parent with a commitment to quality customer service: a service that reflects an awareness of the personal journey throughout the admissions process, regardless of the institution's size, application process, or admissions standards.

However, admissions processes tend to be inherently unfriendly to customers for many reasons. Institutions often make the majority of applicants wait for a decision delayed by the process. For example, required documents must be received and processed before a decision can be rendered. The seasonal volume of incoming material may have temporarily exceeded the capabilities of the current staffing level. Some decisions may be withheld for the receipt of senior grades, or the shaping of a desired class. The student information system and the imaging system do not always operate flawlessly. In some cases, the application processing may have stalled or is not satisfying the demands of the workload. Yet admissions officers must implement procedures and practices that will mask these processing issues from the customer, while at the same time, providing a level of customer service congruent with the personal experience and expectations of the customer.

## Opening Multiple Lines of Communication

Admissions offices can enhance the applicant's personal experience throughout the admissions process by maintaining quality customer service programs for the direct lines of communication: office visits, telephone calls, the admissions Web site, and e-mail service. While admissions offices may not always be able to provide information that will *please* the applicant, we can create procedures designed to offer caring and personalized quality service.

## Responding with Hi-Tech, Personalized Messages

One of the fundamental factors in improving organizational performance involves the assessment and understanding of what your customers value; what satisfies their needs, wants, and aspirations (Drucker 1998). In 2006, the University System of Georgia implemented a Customer Service Plan setting standards for its 34 institutions of higher education. This benchmark requires member institutions to solicit customer service feedback, and to provide metrics to measure employee performance in relation to the following standards:

- Own the customer's issues.
- Greet customers promptly and courteously.
- Listen to customers with respect. Be polite. Focus on their perspective.
- Honor your commitments in a timely manner.

There are many tech-savvy ways admissions officers can offer improved customer service. For example, catering to a preferred mode of communication with today's students, Michigan State University admissions expanded customer service in 2003 by offering online chat sessions with prospects and applicants. In addition, a well-designed admissions Web site can provide a variety of general information to prospects, applicants, and parents, thus reducing the volume, time, and cost of office visits and telephone calls. Many admissions Web sites offer intelligent search engines. Not only do these search engines return specific admissions information, they can also be used to establish e-mail communication with an admissions professional.[194]

For more personalized web service, a secure password-protected Web site can assist in customer service. This student Web portal can provide personalized student information and specific application status updates, such as the receipt of the application, transcripts, and standardized test scores.

Finally, a series of automatically triggered e-mail campaigns can provide detailed applicant status information and inform the applicant about the next step in the admissions process.

[194] See Chapter 10, "Interactive Services: Staying in Tune with a Web-Savvy Generation."

### Addressing Disappointment with Sensitivity

The conclusion of the application process sometimes ends in disappointing news for applicants and parents. An established customer-focused program will pay dividends when communicating with denied applicants or parents. It is also critical to develop standardized procedures and staff training in preparation for these often-stressful discussions. Although more intense, these conversations must be handled with the same commitment to customer service that is evident throughout the application process. This is a most important time to listen, remain polite, and focus on the student's perspective, regardless of the emotional response of the rejected family. In conclusion, this sensitivity demonstrates that the institution understands the applicant's disappointment, values their interest in the institution, and has carefully considered every detail of their application.

A large number of denial conversations occur with a parent of the applicant, and typically end in one of three ways.

In the first scenario, good customer-focused skills will help earn a dismayed parent's respect and guide the conversation toward the most positive outcome possible. Since admissions decisions are primarily based on academic preparedness, many institutions may conclude the conversation by inviting the applicant to apply again later as a transfer student based on subsequent collegiate performance, rather than on the previous credentials that resulted in rejection.

The second scenario often occurs with the helicopter parent(s), who swoop down in defense of their child. Despite the unpleasant tone these parents can convey, the best course of action for the admissions professional is to remain calm and focus intently on employing the best listening skills possible. If your institution has an appeal process, this may be the appropriate time to explain the appeal procedure. The conversation may ultimately end with the parent(s) summarizing their dissatisfaction with you and your institution, but the situation has been contained with tact and sensitivity.

In the final scenario, the parent insists on taking the conversation to a higher level. When the parent is referred to the subsequent official, a consistent message, along with the same customer service skills, is the best that can be offered. Typically the intensity of the parents' tone will diminish as they perceive that their concerns are being addressed by a higher authority. They may focus on what they may begin to perceive as the student's best interest, rather than on their own disappointment.

## Operations and Processing Staff

While the timing of admissions decisions may depend, to some degree, on the admissions goals of the institution, the leaders of the admissions office must nevertheless continually attempt to improve application processing, especially by decreasing the amount of time required to allow the institution to offer an admissions decision.

## Turning Applicants Into Enrollees

The legendary pioneer of the TQM movement, W. Edwards Deming, stated that the first principle of good management is to create "a constancy of purpose" for improvement of products and services (Walton 1986). Another management adviser, R. M. Kanter, author of *The Change Masters*, emphasized that organizations which survive and thrive "encourage and listen to new ideas from within the organization" (Kanter, p. 65).

Directors of admissions offices should make use of various quality tools that are particularly suited to the admissions setting in order to reliably analyze problems and data:

- KEY PERFORMANCE INDICATORS—Identify and monitor them.
- FLOWCHARTS—These show how the whole process works, and help identify the critical stages of a process.
- RUN CHARTS—Show changes in a process over time, thus helping one to recognize improvements and/or abnormalities along the way.
- BENCHMARKING—Comparing a process as it works at your school, with that at schools which are comparable to yours.

Beginning in the 1980s, community colleges, private colleges, and large public universities began adopting continuous improvement methods which had first been seen in industry and government settings. Today, embracing continuous improvement is critical to long-term success in higher education (Dew and Nearing 2004).

## Motivating Change

A primary goal of continuous improvement is to drive organizational change toward a more productive and efficient outcome for a product or service. Of course, change can be particularly challenging for any organization. For many admissions offices, age-old and patched-up processes are typically serviced by experienced employees naturally resistant to change.

In his book *Leading Change*, John P. Kotter provides a multi-stage process for creating and sustaining an organizational culture of change. The first step is to ask questions which will combat complacency, starting by questioning the timing of various stages of application processing. Does the current system produce acceptable and timely service to the customers? If not, the head of the office should move to make changes, after consultation with appropriate other offices in the institution.

Less than one percent of leaders' communication with employees addresses a change vision (Kotter 1996). The volume of applications and multiple activities involved in routine admissions work will overshadow the need for change unless a perpetual message of the need for beneficial improvement is communicated passionately by the office leadership. The recurring themes of the change message should focus on the *need* for the change, the expected positive *result* of the change, and how employees will *benefit* from the change.

## A Primer to Continuous Process Improvement

Admissions offices have traditionally developed a series of different processes designed to assist in recruiting, admitting, and enrolling students. At most institutions, these processes have been in place for a very long time and are periodically modified to accommodate the growing needs of the institution. Over time, these processes acquire layers upon layers of modifications, with a band-aid approach to addressing the concerns of the day. As a result, such processes tend to lose their original purpose and instead take on a life of their own.

Indeed, some of these mutated processes fall short of adequately satisfying the originally intended purpose, thus allowing the *process* to dictate the service provided to the potential students. Such processes are often defended by an employee mantra of "But that's the way we've always done it!" However, these broken processes do not provide adequate customer service. Often, in fact, they result in an unfortunate shift of resources as the system's failure to keep pace with current needs leads to an increased volume of calls from concerned students and parents. Sometimes even higher-level resources are wasted, if parents choose to call the provost or the president.

The TQM approach of continuous improvement can help the admissions office not only improve performance and customer service, but also establish a systematic approach to change management, ready to handle future needs.

## Encouraging Employee Input

In any case, admissions leaders, like the leaders of other process-centered organizations, should concentrate on improving the process, not blaming the employees for sub-par production (Deming 1986). It is important, Deming emphasizes, to "drive out fear" in the organization. Experienced employees are intimately familiar with the process and thus are the primary candidates for inclusion in process improvement teams. In addition, such involvement leads to a sense of ownership in the resulting product, and pride in service. In general, admissions directors should maintain a work culture that encourages employees to have the freedom to openly identify and correct problems with the system.

## Generating "Short-Term Wins"

Admissions leaders should plan a change agenda that will foster motivation and inspire staff persistence. In his eight-stage process of creating major organizational change, Kotter (1996) stresses the importance of generating short-term wins to motivate employees in the implementation of change. Establishing and achieving periodic milestones helps sustain change momentum as employees make sequential progress toward reaching goals. Recognizing progress toward goals, both office wide and individually, is highly motivating.

## Applying the Continuous Improvement Cycle

Deming (1986) broke down the elements of the continuous improvement cycle, commonly referred to as the *Plan, Do, Check, Act* model (PDCA):

*Plan a change to the process;*
*Implement the planned change;*
*Measure and analyze the result of the change; and*
*Act on the results accordingly before repeating the cycle.*

Since the purpose of the continuous improvement cycle is to improve the overall outcome of the process, all four processes highlighted above should be followed in order to achieve the hoped-for outcome.

Application processing is an example of a situation which occurs in every admissions office and has many components:

- The daily mail is opened, sorted, identified, and imaged.
- Electronic applications are downloaded in the student information system (SIS).
- Paper applications are manually keyed into SIS.
- The applications are prepared and delivered to the counseling staff or committee for review.
- Admissions decisions are rendered.
- Decisions are keyed into SIS.
- Decision letters are generated for the applicants.

Each of these processes can be further broken down into sub-processes where metrics are measured over time and analyzed as to their contributions to the process, thus leading to fact-based actions to improve the process.

For example, one possible metric might arise from the following situation: the time it takes to assign an application packet to a review committee after all required application documents have arrived. Using the PDCA cycle, the employees responsible for this area will attempt to achieve metrics gains by planning and implementing changes to the process. If it appears that the changes required would be fundamental, the process could be considered for total reengineering.

## Adopting Technological Solutions

During the past 20 years, admissions-applied technology has revolutionized many aspects of admissions processing, thus leading to innovative leaps in levels of customer service.

### Fixing Inefficient Processes

The ability of technology to leverage effort is already well-established. The following are some of the most common examples. Admissions Web sites allow students to find customized answers for admissions criteria, apply online, check their admissions status, sign up for admissions events, and securely pay deposits. Computer code flawlessly tackles complicated tasks in the blink of the eye, eliminating days, weeks, and even months of manual work. Data-driven enrollment management decisions are facilitated by accurate information management and reporting systems. Customer Relationship Management (CRM) database systems track student communications, enhancing recruitment and yield activity. Tons of paper documents are stored and accessed on electronic imaging systems, freeing up valuable floor space and employees. The future evolution of technology will likely continue to conserve already limited resources and provide opportunities for efficiency, process improvement, and better customer service.

In his study of "Good-to-Great" companies, Jim Collins found that great companies were compelled to utilize existing technologies to creatively accelerate growth, while the technological advancement of less established companies was driven by competition and the fear of being left behind (Collins 2001). For admissions officers who are operating in either a growth or a "catch-up" scenario, the challenge is to get the "biggest bang for the buck" from technological resources.

## Setting Priorities

A methodical and shared approach to setting priorities can best assist in the allocation of valuable technical resources. This structured approach allows admissions leaders to work together as a team in formulating unit goals, and defining what technical direction will be needed.

In addition, institutions with limited technical resources must be prepared to advocate for their needs, and to present well-organized justification and impact statements to acquire technical assistance from the institution's Information System department.

Even if an admissions office is fortunate enough to have several full-time programmers dedicated specifically to the office, the wish-list of technical requests can become quite overwhelming. In selecting the technical priorities, whether the programmers are "yours" or shared with another unit, the most important consideration is the impact the project will have on customer service.

## Strategies for Maximizing Customer Service

A few other factors should be considered within the context of extending customer service.

- *Tackle the low- hanging fruit first.* Look for opportunities to develop simple technical solutions that will result in significant decreases in staff work. For example, students call to request major and/or term changes. In a low-tech office the following scenario plays out: After taking the call, an employee documents the request and sends it to be electronically imaged. The request sits in a work queue until another employee can key the change into SIS. Alternatively, however, with the help of an appropriate program, a secure Web service can allow applicants to make the change themselves. Once the change is submitted, computer code easily stores it in SIS. In this example, the solution saves countless hours of staff time, is relatively easy to produce, and delivers an Internet option for the applicant.

- *Select projects that will set your staff free to perform other important duties.* Perhaps the best example is the online application. This Web service allows applicants to enter their personal information and ship it virtually to SIS. Online application services have revolutionized the college admissions process by allowing institutions to receive 75 to 90 percent of the applications electronically. When you consider that it may take an employee up to twenty minutes to enter information from a handwritten paper application and that not all information may be keyed correctly, significant progress has been made by moving to online applications. National testing agencies allow the same type of automated opportunity by sending scores to institutions electronically. Now programming code can send the data directly to SIS. Although these are obvious examples, many of them already widely implemented, various similar opportunities can be adopted in admissions work.
- *Carefully examine the associated resource requirements and plan the timing of complicated projects.* In admissions work, the operational mode exists at only three levels: busy, very busy, and extremely busy. A more-than-basic tech project will require the assistance of your programmers, but it will also require the input of your processing staff, in the design, development, and testing stages of your project. Because participation from both types of experts is essential, start these projects when it makes the most sense in the admissions cycle. Once the project enters the development stage, programmers will have time available for other projects, while the users test and evaluate the progress of the program in its current stage.
- *Beware of using technology to bandage broken processes.* Although throwing a technological solution at the problem may address immediate needs, it is ultimately not a good use of resources, and it further deflects the process from its original purpose. As a result, the ability to provide excellent customer service continues to diminish as processes become burdensome and technical resources are consumed. Instead, admissions leadership should determine the cost and risk of reengineering the entire process, with a customer focus on the current needs. If a decision is made to reengineer, the process slate will be wiped clean and the possibility of an all technical or semi-technical approach to the process should be considered.

## The Tech-Admissions Liaison

Given the nature of the process-driven work of an admissions office, there tends to be an overwhelming demand for technical solutions. As this chapter has already suggested, technical "fixes" are omnipresent, whether they merely assist or completely replace current, low-tech processes.

Given the fact that various levels of technology are now inextricably a part of admissions processing, it is particularly important to have at least one employee in the office who can "speak both languages"—admissions work and techspeak. Employees can, of course, provide general descriptions of their technical needs, but often their perception and understanding of technical capabilities are limited. On the other hand, programmers are knowledgeable in their own field, but usually have only a limited knowledge of the demands made on an admissions office, and how best to adapt technical wizardry to those demands. Thus, the development of the resulting computer code will only be as good as the staff's informed communication with the programming staff.

Therefore, for the most effective utilization of technology, it is critical for admissions offices to have at least one individual with a combination of admissions process experience and a solid understanding of technological techniques and capabilities, so as to break through these communication barriers. The presence of this liaison function is vital from project design to delivering the optimum solution.

## Conclusion

Selective institutions compete for a finite group of highly qualified students. Public and private universities and community colleges also compete in their own peer markets. In all these settings, admissions offices lead the charge in recruiting and enrolling students, and in shaping the class according to the goals of the institution.

Thus, all admissions functions should perform at the most efficient levels possible, so as to optimize the effort and cost involved in these processes. This reality underlies the need—indeed, the necessity—for an admissions culture to be driven at all times to the delivery of excellent customer service.

Admissions offices that apply continuous improvement methods to admissions processing can provide better service to applicants and parents. In addition, the careful planning and allocation of technology can serve two supportive functions: supplementing continuous improvement efforts and providing opportunities, if necessary, for process reengineering.

Accordingly, admissions leaders must strive to create a sense of organizational urgency for change, and must make the case for it, both to the upper levels of the administration and to their colleagues. In addition to higher levels of customer satisfaction, employee dedication and morale will improve, as admissions work becomes more personal and meaningful.

/ CHAPTER TWENTY-SEVEN /

*by Adriana Farella, B.A.*
*Executive Director, Strategy & Analytics, Enrollment*
*The College Board*

*John T. "Tom" Stewart, M.S.*
*Retired College Registrar*
*Miami Dade College*

27

# Developing a New XML Standard

The AACRAO Committee on the Standardization of Postsecondary Education Electronic Data Exchange (SPEEDE) began working on a national standard format for the electronic exchange of postsecondary student records in 1989. Initially the work of the committee was funded by AACRAO. At about the same time, the U.S. Department of Education's National Center for Education Statistics (NCES) began developing a national standard format for the electronic exchange of student records for kindergarten through high school students. The K–12 community was primarily represented by the Council of Chief State School Officers (CCSSO).

To gain more credibility in the creation and widespread adoption of the standards, the two groups (AACRAO and NCES) approached the American National Standards Institute (ANSI) and its Accredited Standards Committee (ASC) X12 for assistance in developing and approving the two standard formats.

ANSI ASC X12 reviewed the two proposals and insisted that only one standard be developed and approved. That standard would be the Kindergarten through Postsecondary Education Student Record. At that time, NCES decided to fund the work of the AACRAO SPEEDE Committee as well as those working on the K–12 standard. The standard was approved in the early 1990s as ANSI ASC X12 Transaction Set (TS) 130 for the Student

Educational Record (Transcript). This was a standard in the Electronic Data Interchange or EDI format.

During this time period (before the Internet was widely available), an emphasis in the format was to send as much data as possible, using the fewest characters. This was because transmission costs were based on the number of characters or bytes being sent over the Value Added Electronic Networks.

The TS130 standard is now in use by a significant number of postsecondary institutions in the United States and Canada. Over 600,000 postsecondary transcripts are exchanged electronically in this EDI format through the University of Texas at Austin Internet Server in the ASC X12 EDI format each year.

After the Student Transcript (TS130) was approved, the AACRAO SPEEDE Committee began work on the electronic version of the Application for Admission.

It was approved by ANSI ASC X12 as Transaction Set 189. It was intended for use by vendors who collected applications from applicants and then distributed them to many postsecondary institutions. Then each of the schools receiving electronic applications from several vendors would receive them all in one standard format. This process is currently in use by schools in Texas, and in several other areas throughout the U.S.

The Postsecondary Electronic Standards Council (PESC), of which AACRAO is a founding member, created the XML Forum to determine if an eXtensible Markup Language (XML) standard format might be feasible and might result in significantly increased use of the electronic exchange of student educational records, since the XML format is newer and is perceived to be easier to implement and use than the EDI format.

It was felt that the perceived complexity of the process of implementation of the EDI standards was one of the reasons that the EDI format was not being used by more schools. The wide availability of relatively inexpensive XML software tools and the already existing and pervasive use of XML by the information technology staffs of many institutions made the XML process appear to have an excellent chance of rapid acceptance and implementation at the postsecondary level.

The early efforts of the PESC XML Forum (now known as the PESC Standards Forum) emphasized the creation of standard core components. Once this work was significantly accomplished, PESC agreed to develop an XML Standard Format for the College Transcript to demonstrate that this could be done.

Bruce Marton from the University of Texas at Austin headed this effort and was largely supported by the AACRAO SPEEDE Committee that had developed the earlier EDI standard. PESC approved the XML Standard for the College Transcript in the summer of 2004.

PESC then created a workgroup to explore the development of an XML Standard for the Application for Admission. Adriana Farella, then from Xap Corporation, was appointed chair and Tom Stewart, retired college registrar from Miami Dade College in Florida, volunteered to assist her as co-chair. The workgroup has been holding weekly conference calls since June of 2006.

Participants on these calls represent The College Board, the College Foundation of North Carolina, Oracle Corporation, SunGard Higher Education, Xap Corporation and postsecondary institutions in the U.S. and Canada.

It is anticipated that the workgroup will complete its work and PESC will approve the schema as a PESC standard by late fall of 2007 or possibly early 2008.

## Business Case and Guiding Principles

As noted earlier, there are various entities which serve as centralized "portals" for students to submit their college applications. These organizations and vendors provide a service to students by allowing them to enter the application data and designate which colleges and universities should receive it.

The purpose of the XML Standard for the Application for Admission is to provide interoperability between all of the entities that must use these data. These entities include the application vendors and central organizations, such as the Texas Common Application and the Florida Academic Counseling and Tracking for Students (FACTS), who provide these data directly to the institutions, with each institution being able to import those data into their student information systems. It could also facilitate the internal exchange of admissions data among various databases on campus, thus allowing for easier analysis of the data for research purposes.

The following guidelines have been developed by the workgroup to ensure that valid decisions are being made as to what should be included in the standard:

- COMPREHENSIVE DATA SET: The different needs of all the entities which use application data should be accommodated, such as undergraduate, graduate, professional, international, transfer, etc.
- SELF-REPORTED DATA: The data within the standard is assumed to be the self-reported data of the applicant. This means that additional data collected by the institutions in support of the student application, such as transcripts, official test scores, and letters of recommendation, are outside the scope of this standard.
- USER INTERFACE: The standard is assumed to be the data that are collected, and the data elements within the schema are labeled according to the standards that have been established by PESC. The way that the data entry is presented to the applicant can be determined by the entities providing the application access as far as labels, edits, code values, etc. It can then be mapped to the standard through the import/export process that will be used.

## Proposed XML Schema for the PESC Application for Admission

The XML Schema is composed of four primary parts. (*See* Figure 27.1.)

For this presentation, data elements or groups of data elements contained in boxes with solid borders are *required* for the schema; those in boxes with dashed borders are optional. And data element boxes with a + at the right side indicate that this complex data element may be further expanded.

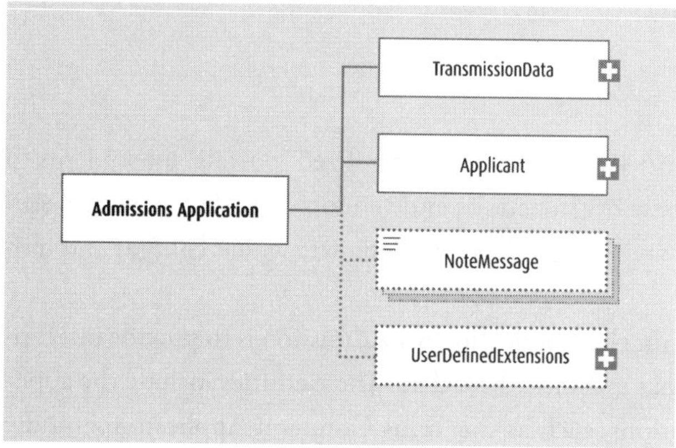


FIGURE 27.1

Primary Schema Elements

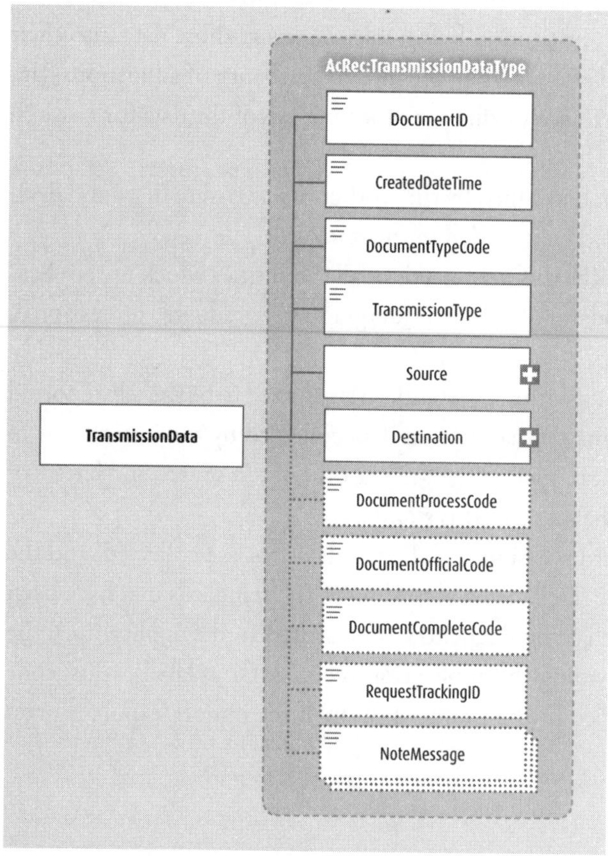


FIGURE 27.2

TransmissionData Element

*NoteMessage* is an optional data element which can be repeated as many times as is needed. The use of the NoteMessage is discouraged, since it cannot normally be automatically processed by the receiving school's computer. It can be used to include information that does not have a specific place or format in the schema, but which the sender feels is important to include.

*UserDefinedExtensions* are actually mini schemas. They are included in the schema so that states or other groups of schools can include specific information used by that group of schools in a previously agreed upon format. Other schools not in that group can ignore the UserDefinedExtensions.

An expansion of the first required data element group, Transmission Data, is shown in Figure 27.2.

The required transmission data are composed of four required data elements (Document ID, Created Date and Time, Document Type Code, and Transmission Type), two required data element groups (Source of the Transmission, e.g., the Sending Vendor or Agency, and Destination for the Transmission or Receiving School), and five optional data elements.

The second major (and required) portion of the XML Schema is information about the *applicant*. This portion is shown in Figure 27.3.

The two required portions of data in Figure 27.3 are as follows:[195]

- PERSON: This expandable (complex) data element is required and includes those data items that identify the applicant as a person. Included in the *Person* complex data element are
  - Name (and Alternate or Former Names, as well as the Preferred Name)
  - Contact Information (address, phone, email, IM and Text Messaging addresses)
  - Birth information (date and place)
  - Gender
  - Ethnicity and Race
  - Citizenship
  - Social Security Number
  - School Assigned Person ID
  - SIN and NSN (Canadian ID numbers)[196]
  - Agency and Recipient Assigned Person ID
  - Religious Affiliation
  - Immigration Status and Information
  - Marital Status

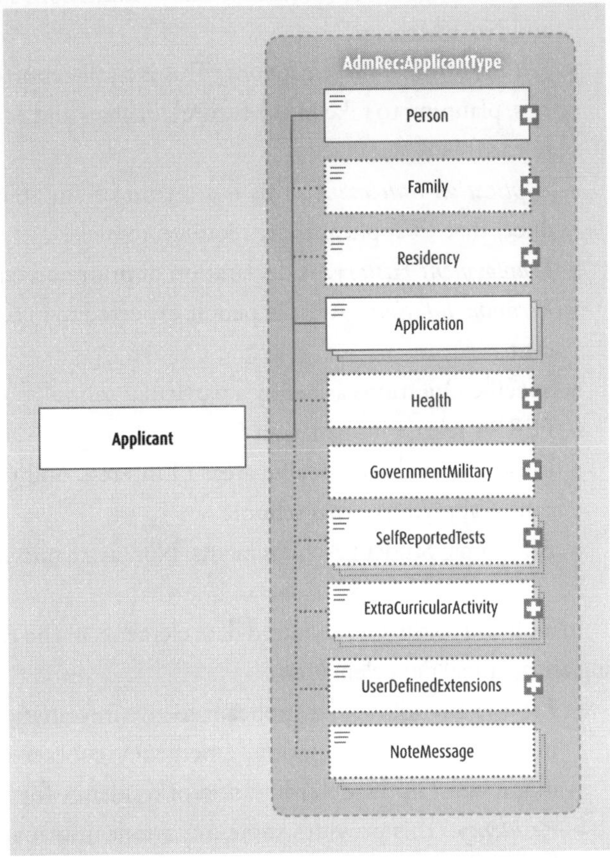


FIGURE 27.3

Applicant Element

[195] The main difference between the UserDefinedExtensions and NoteMessage is that the UserDefinedExtensions are really mini schemas, so they can be automatically interpreted and processed by the receiving school's computer. They must be formatted using the same rules as the overall schema for the Application for Admission. And, of course, since they are extensions to the regular schema, they can be ignored by the schools that don't care about them.

The NoteMessage, on the other hand, can be just text. Unless there is a prior agreement on how the text is formatted, it cannot be processed automatically by the receiving school's computer. However, it can be printed out and read by a person, such as an admissions counselor.

[196] SIN is the Canadian Social Insurance Number; NSN is the National Student Number, which is meant to replace the SIN for educational use.

- First Spoken Language in the home
- Note Message

- **APPLICATION**: This complex data element is also required and includes the following:
  - *Application Detail* (Required Complex Data Element): Six pieces of information that assist in processing an application for admission (Term or session; Campus; Degree and/or Program; Indicator for Early Admission; Priority of this particular application; and Note Message)
  - *Self Reported Academic Record:* This is a self-reported record of courses (taken, in progress, planning to take in the future), degrees and academic awards (earned or scheduled to earn)
  - *Application Statement*: This is a record of any statement (that can include prior conduct) that all applicants are required to make
  - *Employment History:* A declaration of prior and current employment of the applicant
  - *Recommendations:* A list of people expected to make recommendations about the applicant
  - Specific Questions asked by a particular school
  - FERPA release information
  - Information about specific areas of interest, additional info requested, why the applicant is applying to this school
  - Additional Student Achievements: Non-academic achievements earned by the applicant

In addition to the two required data elements in the Applicant diagram above, the following are optional data elements:

- *Family:* This allows the applicant to give information about family members that might include legacy information, emergency contact information, and information that might assist in the determination of residency for fee purposes.
- *Residency:* This provides some important information needed to make an initial, preliminary determination of the applicant's residency status for fee purposes.
- *Health:* This allows the applicant to describe any health conditions that the applicant might consider to be of interest to the school.
- *Government and Military:* Information that the applicant might wish to provide about current or prior government or military service.
- *Self Reported Tests:* Self reported information about tests already taken with results of those tests as well as tests that the applicant plans to take in the near future.
- *Extra Curricular Activity:* Activities other than academic in which the applicant participated.
- *UserDefinedExtensions* and *NoteMessage*

## Information Available through PESC

Among its many resources, PESC hosts an Admission Application Workgroup, which provides the following items of interest for those following the organization's XML proposed standard for the application:[197]

- Latest version of the Draft Implementation Guide for the Application for Admission
- Most of the notes from workgroup conference calls held since June of 2006
- List of the participants in the workgroup

## Other XML Schemas

- Approved by PESC:
  - College Transcript
  - High School Transcript
  - Acknowledgment of Receipt of a Student Transcript
  - Batch Submission of Multiple XML Instance Documents
- Under development by PESC:
  - Request for Transcript
  - Response to a Request for Transcript
  - Education Test Score Reporting
  - Education Course Inventory

[197] See <www.pesc.org> to download the resources listed and to view the final standard, once it is approved.

/ CHAPTER TWENTY-EIGHT /

*by Dan D. Garcia, M.A.*
*Vice President for Enrollment Management*
*West Texas A&M University*

28

# Predicting Enrollments and Yields

The demand for access to higher education is greater now than at any previous time in history, with projections that the so-called "baby boom echo" will result in a 2008 high school graduating class exceeding 3.1 million students, or seven percent more than graduated at the peak of the post-war baby boom in 1979 (Layzell 1997).

However, enrollment managers have more work to do than simply wait for the masses to arrive: If the institution enrolls too many students, the quality of education and the ability to provide adequate resources and services may decline; but if too few students enroll, funding from tuition, fees, and perhaps state support, may diminish.

Add the need to meet institutional goals and priorities, such as type and mix of student body, and the significance of managing enrollments effectively becomes even more apparent. Thus, the hard work to recruit and retain students must result in a balanced enrollment. For most institutions this cannot be left to chance, so planning must begin long before the first class day.

Projecting enrollments through the use of yield prediction is a major component of these efforts. While yields at all stages of enrollment are important, those at the pre-enrollment period—the recruitment and admission stages—will be the focus of this chapter.

## Definition of Yield

Yield may be defined as a measurable output or result. In terms of student enrollment, yield may be considered, in general terms, the number or percentage of students who move from one stage of enrollment to another. This movement from stage to stage may occur at all periods of enrollment, with perhaps three broad categories of movement:

- PRE-ENROLLMENT. The recruitment and admission stages prior to and up to initial enrollment.
- ENROLLMENT. Initial enrollment through persistence from one term (quarter or semester) to another.
- GRADUATION. Completion of degree or certification requirements.

In terms of pre-enrollment, the *recruitment funnel model* provides perhaps the best-known depiction of associated yields for this period; the funnel visually describes how students progress from one stage to another toward their initial enrollment. The recruitment funnel as described below typically consists of the following stages: prospect, inquiry, applicant, completed applicant, accepted, confirmed, and enrolled (*see* Figure 28.1, on page 371).

- PROSPECT STAGE: This consists of students who have been contacted by the institution and not yet responded. These students have characteristics desirable to the institution and/or are deemed apt to apply and enroll. The prospect stage generally consists of purchased or rented names, based on variables identified by the institution—such as geography, gender, GPA, test scores—obtained from organizations like the College Board, the American College Testing (ACT) program, and the National Research Center for College and University Admissions (NRCCUA).
- INQUIRY STAGE: This includes students who have expressed interest in the institution through direct contact and have provided information about themselves. This may be through means such as a phone call, e-mail, table visit at a college fair, or completion of an online inquiry request form; it may also be in response to an unsolicited search mailing sent by the institution. Test scores and transcripts that were sent by the student to the institution should be considered an inquiry because they represent an expression of interest.
- APPLICANT STAGE: This consists of students who have submitted the institution's application for admission. Most institutions will track application yields for both incomplete (form only) and complete versions (form and all other required documents, such as transcripts, personal statements, letters of recommendation, etc.)
- COMPLETED APPLICANT STAGE: When an applicant has submitted all required items for consideration, the file is considered complete. These items may include transcripts, test scores, and application fees.
- ACCEPTED STAGE: This encompasses students who have received an offer of admission from the institution, been denied admission, or are wait-listed.

- **CONFIRMED STAGE:** This refers to students who have demonstrated some commitment to attend, such as an enrollment deposit, fee, or signed letter of intent, as required by the institution. Not all institutions require a confirmation.
- **ENROLL STAGE:** Students who have matriculated at the institution.

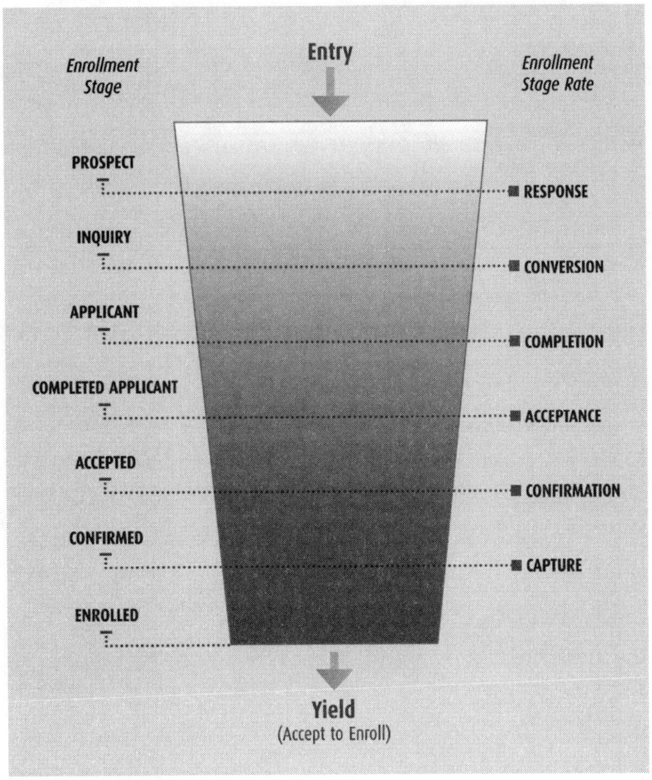


FIGURE 28.1

Recruitment Funnel Model Stages

## Yield Progression

Just as each stage is identified (prospect, inquiry, applicant, etc.), the progressions from one stage to another in the recruitment funnel and the resulting yields have descriptors. These progression rates are usually defined as follows:

- Prospect to inquiry is referred to as "response;"
- Inquiry to application is referred to as "conversion;"
- Application to complete application is referred to as "completion;"
- Application to admit is referred to as "acceptance;"
- Admit to confirm is referred to as "confirmation;"
- Confirm to enroll is referred to as "capture;" and
- Admit to enroll is simply referred to as the "yield."

Each successive stage generally results in a smaller or decreased number as students opt out of the progression toward enrollment or are not offered admission—hence the "funnel" metaphor of an initial, broad flow of students tapering down to a narrow stream. For example, some but not all students who make an inquiry about admission to the institution will later apply; the number of students who do apply for admission divided by the original number who made inquiry is the resulting yield, and is often expressed as both a number and a percentage. If 100 students made inquiry and 87 applied for admission, the rate would be 87 percent.

While there is a progressive decrease in the total number of students from one stage of enrollment to another, this fact is not unexpected, given that student decision-making varies.

FIGURE 28.2

Recruitment Funnel Model Stages

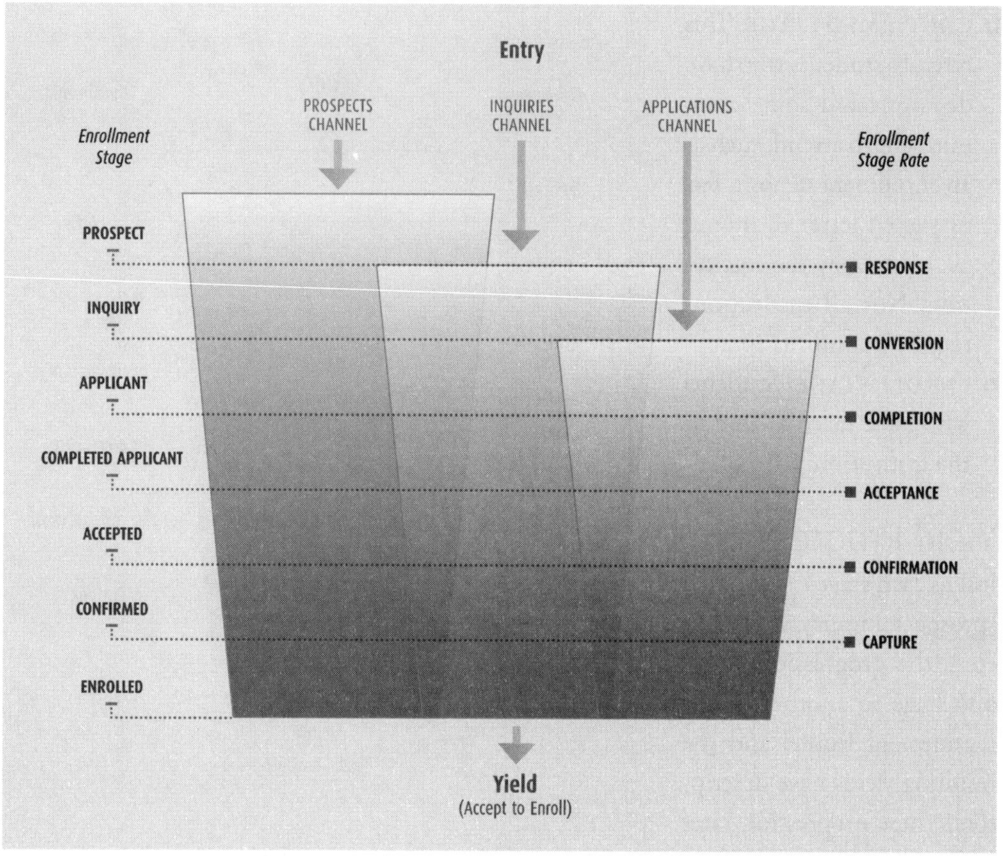


Some students will choose not to move to the next stage or may not receive an offer of admission from the institution, which will result in an output that is less than the figure from the preceding stage. It is important to recognize that at each stage of the recruitment funnel, students move to subsequent stages on the basis of choice—save those who are denied admission or wait-listed—and thus institutions have great opportunities to influence student decisions throughout those stages of the funnel.

It is equally important to note that the enrollment funnel model described above and in Figure 28.1 (on page 371) indicates that students in a particular stage had all progressed from the previous stage(s). For example, it would be equivalent to assuming that all applicants had earlier been in the inquiry pool. It is, however, known that students may enter the funnel at different points—some make an inquiry without having been contacted as a prospect, and some make application without having made an inquiry. Therefore, true funnel rates and yields should be calculated based upon the stage in which the student entered. Figure 28.2 illustrates these differences.

## Importance of Yield

We often tend to think of and report recruitment, admissions, enrollment, and graduation figures in terms of "how many." For instance, the number of applications that have been submitted, the number of deposits received, and the number of new students enrolled are common data points of interest. Of course these are important data, but it is yield that progressively results in each successive stage of the recruitment funnel. And that yield largely quantifies student decision-making outcomes.

## Projecting Yield

Making a projection of the yields in the recruitment funnel—the percentage of student inquiries who will apply for admission, offers who will deposit, deposits who will enroll, and so forth—is possible through one or more common methods; we will next discuss two methods.

### Using National Figures as a Basic Guide

A basic guide for yield rates consists of national and/or regional figures. These are in aggregate and may not be reflective of—or even close to—a particular institution's actual yields. The yields may be used by an institution as a general yardstick for projections, usually if there are no available sets of historical data for the institution or for rough comparisons to average rates at like institutions. National figures are often grouped according to institution type (public or private, two- or four-year), size (large, medium, small), and target populations (transfer, freshman, graduate).

Below are data derived from the Noel-Levitz National Enrollment Management Survey of 142 non-profit, four-year institutions' fall 2006 and 2005 admissions funnels, and perhaps the best guide available for national figures. (*See* Table 28.1 and Table 28.2, on page 374.)

The yield figures represent the midpoint, or median, of all reporting institutions, above which half of the scores occurred and below which half of the scores occurred. Not all institutions require a deposit or confirmation of intent to enroll; thus these data are not reported in the table yields. For institutions that require a deposit or confirmation it is important to calculate yield rates because a higher percentage of students who make the commitment in some form—either a written commitment or deposit in amounts that may range from $100 to $400—will ultimately enroll.

### Historical Data

Projecting yields based on historical figures is possible if stability and consistency are observed from the data, or if increasing or decreasing patterns (trends) over time are apparent and can be factored into future outcomes. National figures in the previous section make clear that yields from one year to the next vary slightly, and thus it is useful to identify such trends and make projections accordingly. Often yields change in correlation with activities or events

TABLE 28.1: **Recruitment Funnel Yields, Four-year Public Institutions**

| | Freshman (%) | | Transfer (%) | |
|---|---|---|---|---|
| | Fall 2006 | Fall 2005 | Fall 2006 | Fall 2005 |
| **Funnel Stage** | | | | |
| Inquiry to Application | 28.0 | 25.4 | 71.1 | 61.2 |
| Application to Admit | 70.2 | 72.5 | 66.3 | 72.3 |
| Complete Application to Admit | 82.8 | 83.1 | 91.4 | 87.3 |
| Admit to Enroll | 42.1 | 42.6 | 68.2 | 69.0 |
| **Additional Applicant Activities** | | | | |
| Melt Rate from Deposit/ Confirmed to Enrollment | 7.8 | 7.8 | 11.1 | 13.0 |
| Applicants not completing the application process | 9.5 | 11.9 | 22.1 | 19.9 |
| Applicants for whom it was the first recorded contact with the institution | 29.9 | 26.4 | 49.1 | 46.5 |

**SOURCE:** Noel-Levitz (2006b)

TABLE 28.2: **Recruitment Funnel Yields, Four-year Private Institutions**

| | Freshman (%) | | Transfer (%) | |
|---|---|---|---|---|
| | Fall 2006 | Fall 2005 | Fall 2006 | Fall 2005 |
| **Funnel Stage** | | | | |
| Inquiry to Application | 13.8 | 12.7 | 47.2 | 40.4 |
| Application to Admit | 69.6 | 71.7 | 59.0 | 59.5 |
| Complete Application to Admit | 86.0 | 86.5 | 90.7 | 90.4 |
| Admit to Enroll | 34.6 | 35.1 | 57.1 | 57.0 |
| **Additional Applicant Activities** | | | | |
| Melt Rate from Deposit/ Confirmed to Enrollment | 9.9 | 11.0 | 11.5 | 11.5 |
| Applicants not completing the application process | 16.8 | 17.4 | 30.5 | 30.3 |
| Applicants for whom it was the first recorded contact with the institution | 22.1 | 19.8 | 41.5 | 42.5 |

**SOURCE:** Noel-Levitz (2006b)

(such as the addition of a new academic program or increased marketing initiatives); when historical yields are inconsistent, however, or occur with wide variations from year to year, the basic data are not sufficient for yield projection.

But in the case of consistent historical yields within the recruitment funnel—or if there is a percentage movement from one stage to another that has occurred in the past at an even rate for multiple, consecutive years—it may be anticipated, if all other variables remain constant, that the same yields will persist. Collecting data over time is critical for establishment of stability or trends that may be used in the development of a useful enrollment projection model.

An example of this projection method would be assigning one figure for an upcoming term, such as the number of student inquiries anticipated, as well as the historical yields at each stage of the funnel; this information could be used in a projection of likely outcomes for the numbers of applications, admits, deposits, and enrollments. Table 28.3 (on page 375) illustrates a fictitious sample of this progression.

This projection method is perhaps most useful for enrollment planning purposes such as setting goals and assessment of ongoing performance. In the case of goal-setting activities, historical figures can help establish future recruitment goals: that the number of inquiries, applications, and other recruitment stage figures are based on reasonable expectations and institution-driven improvements.

For performance assessment purposes, the institution can make some limited assessments regarding how well a particular recruitment cycle is producing figures at each stage of the recruitment funnel—particularly toward its established goals—by making comparison to past performance at similar year-to-date points, rather than waiting for final figures to be known.

TABLE 28.3: **Historical Funnel Figures with Next Term Projection**

| Stage | Fall 2008 Projected | Fall 2007 | Fall 2006 | Fall 2005 | Fall 2004 |
|---|---|---|---|---|---|
| Prospects | 35,000 | 35,000 | 25,000 | 20,000 | 20,000 |
| Inquiries | 9,500 | 8,456 | 7,867 | 5,890 | 6,008 |
| Response Rate (%) | 23.0 | 23 | 23 | 24 | 20 |
| Applicants | 2,200 | 1,945 | 1,789 | 1,420 | 1,203 |
| Conversion Rate (%) | 23.2 | 23.0 | 22.7 | 24.1 | 20.0 |
| Admits | 1,615 | 1,421 | 1,318 | 1,078 | 984 |
| Acceptance Rate (%) | 73.4 | 73.1 | 73.7 | 75.9 | 81.8 |
| Confirms | 940 | 827 | 770 | 637 | 561 |
| Capture Rate (%) | 58.2 | 58.2 | 58.4 | 59.1 | 57.0 |
| Enrolled | 875 | 770 | 712 | 589 | 500 |
| Yield Rate (%) | 93.1 | 93.1 | 92.5 | 92.5 | 89.1 |

When used for other enrollment management efforts, it is important to remember that this type of basic projection not only relies upon historical yields remaining constant at all stages of recruitment funnel for a future term—which, again, is not an unreasonable assumption if these figures have been stable—but also relies upon *all other variables* remaining constant, which is not a certainty. These variables may include such factors as changes to the strategies and tactics used to recruit students; the economy (local, regional, or national); the number of available students; competitor activity, etc. The more such variables emerge and need to be factored in, the less useful this type of basic historical projection becomes.

Therefore, institutions should be aware that introduced variables can and will affect yields. This is not always a negative consideration, since some of these variables are in the control of the institution—such as marketing, communications, and degree offerings—and can result in an increase of students or in improved yields at one or more stages of the recruitment funnel. Other variables, however, are not within the control of the institution, such as in the cases noted immediately above.

Enrollment managers should be working to manage that which is within the institution's control, while remaining aware of and responsive to variables outside of the institution. The key to successful prediction of yield is to gather pertinent data, and then conduct reasonable assessments that weigh multiple factors—for many variables (and combinations of variables) may influence yield differently at each stage of the recruitment funnel. Indeed, enrollment managers should continuously be seeking to implement adjustments to recruitment and admission activities and practices to improve yields.

## Variables Influencing Yield

It is important to recognize that yields may be affected by different variables. These variables fall into one of three categories:

- Characteristics of or actions taken by students;
- Characteristics of or actions taken by the institution; and
- Outside variables that are not controlled by either students or the institution.

### Student Variables

Consider that each stage of the recruitment funnel is filled with diverse populations of students. Characteristics like gender, race, ethnicity, geographic location, and intended major vary, and these variations, of course, may result in different expectations of and behaviors by students.

Geography is a good example of how a characteristic among students at a particular recruitment stage may influence behaviors (and thus, the yield rate) for later stages of the funnel. Table 28.4 shows Texas Tech University's admit-to-enroll yield rate of students for the Fall 2001 term based on distance from campus at the time of application. As the distance from the campus increased for students admitted to Texas Tech University for fall 2001, the yield rate, or percent of students who accepted the offer, decreased.

TABLE 28.4: **Yield Rate for Accepted Freshmen by Distance from Lubbock—Texas Tech University, 2001**

| Counties within | Admitted | Enrolled | Yield (%) |
|---|---|---|---|
| 100 miles | 969 | 668 | 68.94 |
| 200 miles | 857 | 486 | 56.71 |
| 300 miles | 2,275 | 1,026 | 45.1 |
| 400 miles | 1,893 | 689 | 36.4 |
| 500 miles | 1,793 | 649 | 36.2 |
| Over 500 miles | 119 | 26 | 21.85 |
| Unknown | 555 | 83 | 14.95 |
| Total | 8,461 | 3,627 | 42.87 |

**SOURCE:** Texas Tech University (2008, Table 2-4).

In fact the correlation between distance and yield is not unusual, or even unexpected, for most institutions, since greater distances often mean increased costs (housing, travel, tuition) for students, as well as fewer connections (family, friendships, familiarity with area).

Furthermore, the Texas Tech example helps illustrate how such information might provide the enrollment manager with a clearer picture of what might result in future admission cycles: If the historical trend and most other variables remain constant the following year, every 100 offers to applicants within 100 miles will result in approximately 68 enrollments, while the same number of offers to applicants who live more than 500 miles from campus will result in only approximately 21 enrollments.

While there is less ability to control student variables than institution-related ones, understanding student tendencies based on identifiable and measurable values is important. Geography is, of course, a student-based characteristic and is but one student variable affecting yield. An institution that wishes to increase accuracy and ability to predict yield, and therefore to project enrollments, must collect and evaluate historical data for *multiple* student characteristics and behaviors at *each stage* of the funnel.

So while it makes sense that geography, in general, should be a single, reasonably good measurement of student interest—we might conclude that students have a general yield rate in the recruitment funnel based on where they live—those probabilities and yields are likely to change when further variables are considered.

For example, the student who lives out-of-state and makes an inquiry during his junior year may seem less likely to apply for admission than a student who also makes an inquiry and lives within thirty minutes from campus. However, consider the result if the second, close-in student makes no further contacts, while the first student who is out-of-state initiates four more contacts with the institution, sends his SAT scores, and visits campus for a tour: it would not be surprising if the student from out-of-state is the only one of these two students to apply and enroll. This example illustrates why the collection of data and assessment of yields in relation to *multiple* variables is so important. Some additional student variables that affect yield include, but are not limited to, the following:

- GEOGRAPHY. As described earlier, this may be measured by in- and out-of-state residency, distance from campus, location of high school, community college, or zip code, or any other means by which students may be identified geographically.
- APPLICATION TYPE. Differences in application completion rates are often significant between online and paper applications, and between the institution's own applications and common applications. While yields tend to be lower with online and common applications, the ease of application may increase the total numbers received. It is thus important to consider the *type* of application when projecting yields, because statistics from the past may be weighted with more or less of one type (Noel-Levitz 2006b).
- ABILITY TO PAY. This is the student's self-reported family income or ISIR data (from FAFSA)[198] received by the institution. The ability to pay, as well as the eligibility or entitlement for grants, scholarships, and other aid, affects students' post-secondary enrollment options and college choice.
- STUDENT ACADEMIC PROFILE. Standardized test scores, GPA, rigor of curriculum. In general, the higher the achiever, the more likely it is that the student will be applying to multiple institutions and receiving competitive offers from those institutions.
- INTERESTS AND PREFERENCES. This classification covers a wide and varied range of topics, but the most common interests include potential major (the academic program[s] of study the student wishes to pursue); college size, type, and distance from home; social interests (clubs, sports, community environments); and campus climate (student body demographics, safety, housing options, etc.).

### Institutional Variables

Institutional variables, like student variables, are either characteristics that are unchangeable by the institution or are actions taken that are within the control of the institution. Some include:

[198] ISIR is the Institutional Student Information Record; FAFSA is the Free Application for Federal Student Aid.

- **LOCATION.** Is the institution located in a metropolitan or an urban area? Within the prospective student's state, or elsewhere? In a high-, stagnant-, or decreasing-growth area? Warm, cold, or mild climate throughout the year?
- **TYPE OF INSTITUTION.** Public or private, two- or four-year, level of instruction (associate, bachelor, master, doctorate).
- **INSTITUTIONAL RESOURCES AND OFFERINGS.** Colleges, schools, and majors within the institution; campus housing; services and activities.
- **COST OF ATTENDANCE.** The tuition, fees, board, books, and other costs set by the institution.
- **SCHOLARSHIP AND/OR FINANCIAL AID OFFER.** The amount of aid a student is offered by the institution to offset the cost of attendance. These are offers of aid made based on need, merit or a combination of the two.
- **RECRUITMENT EFFORTS.** The communications, activities, and messages that the institution delivers to prospective students.

## Outside Variables

- **EFFECTS OF NATURAL DISASTERS.** Natural disasters like hurricanes, earthquakes, and tornadoes can have unforeseen affects upon enrollments. As examples, it is well known that institutions in and around New Orleans experienced unforeseen damage from hurricanes in 2005 that resulted in fewer or no enrollments for a period of time.[199] Similarly, California State University, Northridge was damaged from a major earthquake and aftershocks, resulting in fewer applications in subsequent years.
- **ECONOMIC CONDITIONS.** Increases in fuel costs, declines in state support of public institutions, and high unemployment rates are examples of economic conditions that may affect enrollments negatively.
- **COMPETITION.** The presence and activity of competing institutions may draw enrollments away, beyond the control of those affected institutions. And with increasing accessibility by students to post-secondary education via distance learning options, competition can be a factor without the presence of traditional brick and mortar institutions.
- **DEMOGRAPHICS.** Just as competition from other institutions may affect enrollments, the supply of eligible students is also an important consideration despite being beyond an institution's control. Most notable are national, state, and local high school graduating class sizes, which may grow or diminish from year to year. Fortunately there are ample sources for projections, such as the U.S. Census, and such factors should be factored into institutions' enrollment planning activities.

[199] Mangan (2007) reported that, according to Louisiana's higher education commissioner E. Joseph Savoie, most New Orleans colleges were doing significantly better in 2007, two years after Hurricane Katrina, but were "still expected to be below their Katrina numbers this fall." Mangan points out that in the fall of 2005 (the last fall enrollment before Katrina), Tulane University had 1,679 entering freshmen. In the fall of 2007, that number had been cut nearly in half—prompting the university to develop a "restructuring plan...[to] permanently become a smaller institution, with a goal of 1,400 new freshmen each year."

## Measuring Yields

An overview of how yields are calculated in terms of progression from one stage of the recruitment funnel to the next is found earlier in this chapter. But because yields are affected by many variables, some of which are more influential than others, it is important to measure yields in terms of subgroups or segments of the pool within each stage.

It is critical that the *appropriate* student data is being collected for yields to be measured by segment, and calculated accurately. This is particularly important at the inquiry stage, which is often an overlooked data-collection point within the recruitment funnel: Tracking "where" and "when" the initial inquiry originated, or "which" recruitment effort was responded to, is important because it can help identify those students more apt to inquire, apply, deposit, and enroll, as well as the institutional activities that are most successful (and least successful).

For example, by associating inquiry information and/or student characteristics with subsequent yield results the manager can answer the question, "What are the best indicators of student interest?" After all, a student will select and enroll in an institution that can best meet his or her needs and interests. When these multiple variables are joined, a student profile emerges that helps identify students with greatest potential for progression to subsequent stages of the recruitment funnel, and thus, higher yields. The following are additional data points that are important to consider:

### Inquiry Source

Measuring the yields of inquiries received from various sources is critical because it provides an indication of when and how the student chose to contact the institution:

- STUDENT-INITIATED. From the student, directly, through incoming letters, phone calls, e-mails, standardized text scores (SAT, ACT) sent, campus visits, etc.
- TRAVEL-INITIATED. By institution representatives—staff, students, faculty, or alumni—during high school visits, college fairs, special site visits.
- REFERRAL-INITIATED. Examples may include referrals from high school counselors, alumni, faculty/staff, or athletic personnel. It is important to note that referrals should be considered inquiries if the source is passing along an expression of interest from a student; otherwise, the student should be counted as a prospect.
- SOLICITED. Through response to advertising, direct mail programs (purchased or rented from College Board, NRCCUA, American College Testing, etc.)

### Inquiry Response

In addition to assessing yields based on source of initial inquiry, measuring the historical outcomes of yield based upon the number of contacts made by the student can often assist with projection of future yields. Table 28.5, on page 380, illustrates the stage progression outcomes of students who make multiple contacts with the institution.

As an example, assessment of data may indicate how the yield averages increase as the number of student-initiated contacts with the institution increase. Measurements may also be made based on type of contacts. For example, this might mean measuring outcomes of students who attend admission-advising sessions, take a campus tour, or come to an open house—one particular activity or multiples of activities for students may correlate to higher yields.

TABLE 28.5: **Conversion and Yield Rates, by Number of Student Initiated Contacts**

| | Number of Contacts | | | | | | | |
|---|---|---|---|---|---|---|---|---|
| | 1 | 2 | 3 | 4 | 5 | 6 | 7 | 8 |
| Inquiries | 27,395 | 8,495 | 3,886 | 2,116 | 1,198 | 684 | 407 | 241 |
| Applicants | 1,585 | 1,274 | 1,036 | 790 | 587 | 405 | 273 | 176 |
| Confirms | 429 | 404 | 362 | 317 | 251 | 190 | 146 | 102 |
| Inquiries/Apps (%) | 6 | 15 | 27 | 37 | 49 | 59 | 67 | 73 |
| Inquiries/Confirm (%) | 2 | 5 | 9 | 15 | 21 | 28 | 36 | 42 |
| Apps/Deposits (%) | 27 | 32 | 35 | 40 | 43 | 47 | 54 | 58 |

## Qualifying Students—<br>Self-Reported Level of Interest

"Qualifying" means literally asking students to self-report their level of interest in attending the institution, and generally occurs at the inquiry and acceptance stages of the recruitment funnel. It's likely that students in an institution's inquiry pool are also investigating other institutions—making comparisons, developing opinions, and perhaps making decisions about where to attend; as a result, these students may become less or more interested in your institution. It's also possible that the inquiry isn't a serious attempt to learn more about your institution, but rather more of a curiosity than an expression of serious interest to enroll.

Gathering self-reported levels of interest from students in the inquiry pool can help identify students who have a strong interest in attending, thus allowing the institution to dedicate limited resources to their recruitment, while also identifying students who are less serious about attending. Moreover, the qualifying of students also provides enrollment managers with an indication of how strong the inquiry pool is generally—and, if compared to historical data, how many and which students are likely to progress to the next stage.

The "qualifying" of students may occur at the time of inquiry (on the request card, for example), or at some point(s) after the initial inquiry has been made or an offer of admission has been made. Providing students with the opportunity to indicate a range of interest levels at different time intervals, then collecting that information and assessing self-reported interest can provide important information for subsequent recruitment cycles.

A common qualifying activity is for the admissions office to call students who have made inquiries, shortly after recruitment materials have been sent to the student. The caller confirms that the materials have been received, allows the student to ask questions, and then asks the student to assess his or her level of interest on a scale provided. Consider the sample results shown in Table 28.6.

The results assessed at the end of the recruitment cycle show that students in this example who responded as being "very interested" accounted for more than 25 percent of the inquiry pool, yet applied at a much higher rate than other respondents and accounted for 60 percent of all applications received (1,589 out of 2,661 received). While all inquiries may receive the same information and communications from the institution as part of its recruitment efforts, those students who indicated early on a greater degree of interest did, indeed, apply for admission at a higher rate.

TABLE 28.6: **Yields from Qualifying with Self-Reported Interest Level**

| Interest | Inquiries (n) | Applications (n) | Conversion (%) |
|---|---|---|---|
| Very Interested | 5,809 | 1,589 | 27 |
| Somewhat | 8,941 | 801 | 9 |
| Uncertain | 7,899 | 266 | 3 |
| No Longer Interested | 412 | 5 | 1 |
| Total | 23,061 | 2,661 | |

Qualifying can also take place with students who have been in the inquiry pool for a longer period of time. At that point, the interest level scale regarding the institution may show gradations as follows: "Top Choice," "Will Apply," "May Apply," and "Not Sure." Furthermore, students who have been offered admission and are in admit stage may be qualified using the following scale: "Will Deposit/Enroll," "May Deposit/Enroll," and "Probably will not Deposit/Enroll."

## Supplemental Recruitment Efforts Affecting Yield Outcomes

There are many institutional variables that figure as factors in student decisions to apply and enroll at a particular college or university. While features like a winning football team, a state-of-the-art exercise facility, or an award-winning student newspaper are examples that may not have a high degree of influence but still affect student decisions, it's the active recruitment efforts made by the institution and its representatives that ultimately serve as the most important variables.

As mentioned earlier, research to assess the effects of recruitment efforts on student decisions makes it possible for the institution to know which are successful and should be continued, and which are not successful and should be discontinued or improved. Results such as response and conversion rates by demographic, inquiry source and institution-initiated activities and contacts, to name a few, have been discussed in this chapter, as well as qualification methods to determine student interest. The following are other commonly used techniques to further assess recruitment efforts as related to yield outcomes:

- SURVEYS. Written responses from students can provide both qualitative and quantitative data needed to assess recruitment efforts in an organized and consistent fashion. Surveys may seek information concerning "influencers" (publications, peers, counselors, parents, competitors, etc.), interests, and relative effects of specific recruitment and marketing efforts. Questions may allow for open-end response, provide a scaled response, use multiple choice, or a combination of all three. Furthermore, surveys may be launched at any point in the recruitment process, but should include questions linked to efforts made at a particular stage of the recruitment process. For example, it should be considered why students who inquired did not take the next step to apply for admission.

Surveys don't need to be administered at one time to all students in a particular pool, either. Collection of data can be ongoing, such as asking students at the time of application what prompted the activity, or one-time only, seeking assessment of a particular activity (for example, a short-survey feedback mechanism to learn about satisfaction with an admissions advising session or campus tour).

- FOCUS GROUPS. Such a technique gathers information in ways that are similar to written surveys, but focus group results provide less anonymity and less quantitative data. However, the facilitator may receive more detailed responses and a better sense of student emotion and thought processes from a focus group, while being able to delve deeper into subjects and issues that emerge as having greater importance.
- CONTROL GROUPS. Control groups divide the subjects and provide varied services or resources to each. For example, half of the number of purchased names will get a search publication that is different from the other half—in each publication there will be different pictures, messages, call to action, and/or focus. Tracking the response rate of each group may reveal that one publication has a greater impact than the other in prompting the students to make an inquiry.

With information gained from an assessment of yields based on demonstrated and measurable student behaviors, the qualitative information that emerges from activities like focus groups, control groups, and surveys can help institutions direct resources toward activities and students who are most likely to progress in the recruitment funnel.

## Predicting Yield

### Basic Predictive Modeling

As noted earlier, predicting yield may be accomplished by relying first on known historical patterns. This technique involves application of past yields to current and/or anticipated figures. We have also discussed the fact that basic predictive modeling can take the process of yield projection further, by adding to the mix known patterns of student behaviors and known effects of institutional influence in order to predict students' future behaviors.

Thus, basic predictive modeling simply looks at the historical figures and/or trends, and also common institutional and student variables, and makes an assessment by applying those yield formulas to produce anticipated figures. An even more sophisticated enrollment projection may add the persistence rates of continuing students, including graduation rates, to the mix, in an exercise to anticipate total student enrollment numbers for a future term.

## Advanced Predictive Modeling

It goes without saying that the purpose of enrollment-related research, at least for enrollment managers, is to identify variables that truly influence yields that are critical for any institution. Advanced predictive modeling can identify students who are most likely to enroll, based upon the use of *multiple regression analysis*. Conducting a multiple regression analysis of the variables representing student characteristics may be used to identify the impact of each variable (or of combinations of any number of variables) on yield outcome. In simple terms, multiple regression analysis is a way to decide if a relationship exists between one variable of interest (response, such as application for admission or enrollment) and a set of other variables (predictors or explanatory variables, such as geography, test scores, GPA, etc.).

While multiple regression models are commonly used and provide important information, the equations are based on the assumption that the response and predictors are continuous in nature—an assumption which inevitably limits the accuracy of any derived model as a predictor of future outcomes. Therefore, once these relationships have been established, predictive models using *discriminant analysis*[200] of the variables may be developed. Use of this type of analysis can provide insights into how each variable individually and in combination predicted (or affected) the actual outcome. Once the best predictive model is identified, it may then be put to use to project future outcomes, and to suggest best allocation of resources.

## Software Packages for Statistical Analysis

Most enrollment managers possess the ability to collect, review, and utilize the information gathered. However, working with the college or university's institutional research staff is generally important in each of these measurement activities, and will help ensure that the analysis is done properly, especially if using general statistical analysis software. Popular software packages for statistical analysis like SPSS and SAS are generally needed for development of complex enrollment projection models. These software packages can help admissions and enrollment officers to develop enrollment projection models, and also to develop profiles of students who are most likely to progress from one stage of the enrollment funnel to the next. The development of profiles allows for the ability to target these students and improve yields.

## Specialized Software Services

Specialized software applications and services for enrollment management do exist and should be considered for possible use. Products which compare the characteristics of prospective students to the characteristics of students who have enrolled, and customized research from various providers offer comprehensive assistance with enrollment projection modeling.

---

[200] "Discriminant function analysis is used to determine which variables discriminate between two or more naturally occurring groups. For example, an educational researcher may want to investigate which variables discriminate between high school graduates who decide (1) to go to college, (2) to attend a trade or professional school, or (3) to seek no further training or education.... Discriminant Analysis could then be used [after gathering data on numerous variables] to determine which variable(s) are the best predictors of students' subsequent educational choice" (StatSoft 2008).

In the case of new student enrollments, a model may identify students who are most likely to progress from one stage of the recruitment funnel to the next by using institution-specific statistical models. These models use multiple variables, including historical student data (academic profile, high school code, initial inquiry source, qualification scores). Successful models incorporate those variables that have historically and independently proven to be the best predictors of student behavior.

Just as each variable is selected based on a demonstrated history of indicating subsequent yield, each variable is also assigned a relative strength in the model. This strength is relational to the frequency or degree of how predictive the variable has been in regard to historical yield outcomes, and plays an important role within the model. Figure 28.3 illustrates how variables may have different strengths in terms of predicting yield.

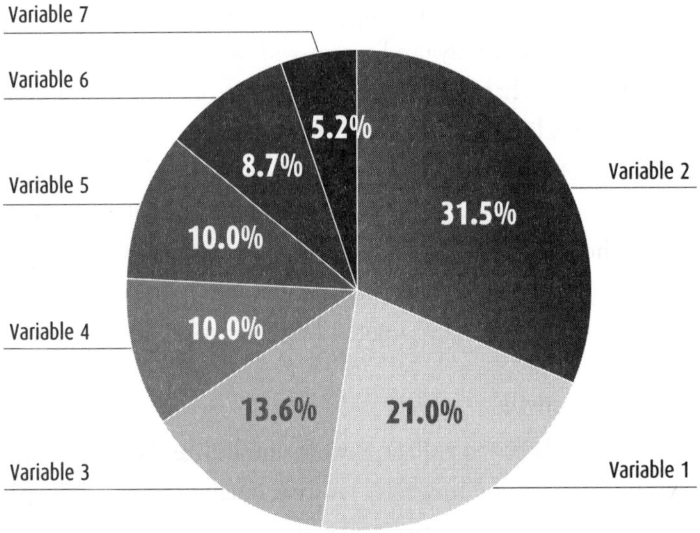


FIGURE 28.3
Relative Strength Model Example

Past recruitment funnel data can be entered into the developed models in order to test efficiencies. The development of a model proceeds as follows: data is collected, a statistical model is formulated, predictions are made using the model, and then the model is validated or revised. Once the enrollment manager is confident of the model, future funnel data (student variables) may then be entered and the results used to target students who are projected to produce higher yield rates. Some products that track inquiries and applications—such as Recruitment Plus, a College Board product—have built-in capabilities that utilize selected variables and weights captured in the database and based upon developed models to rank individual students according to likelihood to apply, enroll, etc.

Development of effective enrollment projection models relies on the collection of accurate and complete data, the application of the information learned, and finally, the regular assessment of outcomes. And such models can be much more reliable than simply applying basic historical yields to future outcomes.

## Influencing Yield

It should be emphasized that institutions may use information gained from assessment of yields based on student variables, including the relative strength of each variable, not only to understand future student behaviors, but also to target those students most likely to enroll.

In other words, predictive enrollment models can and *should* influence active recruitment efforts by the institution, which is to say the efforts to identify and direct resources and activities toward those students who are most likely to progress in the recruitment funnel. It is when institutions develop recruitment goals with research-based strategies and tactics, articulated in the form of a comprehensive and documented plan that includes tools for assessment, that an enrollment projection model is most useful. These plans should be tied to desired academic and demographic profiles, and supported by dedicated and appropriate resources.

Finally, it is important to remember that yields may also be measured in terms of continuing students, most notably the number persisting from one enrollment term to the next or graduating. Understanding yields relative to current students, and utilizing that information to affect their persistence toward graduation, should be considered as part of a larger enrollment management plan, since new, continuing, and graduating students—as well as those lost to attrition—all affect institutions' total enrollments.

/ CHAPTER TWENTY-NINE /

*by Robert J. Sternberg, Ph.D.*
*Dean, School of Arts and Sciences*
*and Professor of Psychology*
*Tufts University*

29

# Enhancing Academic Excellence and Diversity

Many colleges simultaneously seek to accomplish two goals: To increase academic excellence and to enhance diversity. Often, these two goals are seen as being in opposition to each other. Tests such as the SAT and the ACT show group differences in scores. If one were to seek to increase only academic excellence through maximization of conventional test scores, certain groups—those that score well—would be much more strongly represented than others in entering college classes. And if one were to seek to increase only diversity across these groups, conventional test scores would go down because groups with lower scores, on average, would have a higher representation in entering classes.

Might it be possible to maximize both academic excellence and diversity such that they work synergistically rather than in opposition to each other? I declare "yes," such a goal can be realized. The path to achieving this goal is to create a new kind of entrance assessment—one broader in scope than the traditional SAT and ACT—which measures abilities that are relevant to college success and that are found at higher levels in groups that typically do not score as well on conventional tests.

## Traditional Closed Systems in Education

The essence of the problem in using merit-based approaches has been that certain groups consistently perform more poorly on traditional admission tests than do other groups. The traditional response has been to throw up one's hands and conclude that a merit-based system will not work because it always will disfavor members of groups that do not score well.

The argument presented here is based on the author's psychological theory of abilities: the theory of successful intelligence (Sternberg 1997, 1999). The theory has three key postulates.

- (Successful) intelligence is the ability to succeed in life, according to one's own conception of success, within one's own cultural milieu. People have different conceptions of success (*e.g.*, to be a successful scientist, athlete, actor, musician, writer, accountant, plumber, secretary, business executive), and a conception of intelligence needs to take into account people's working toward diverse goals.
- People succeed by capitalizing on strengths and by compensating for or correcting their weaknesses. There is no one formula for success. Rather, everyone has to find his own formula according to his unique pattern of strengths and weaknesses. This postulate implies that abilities are modifiable—that people can indeed correct their weaknesses if they set their sights on doing so.
- They succeed by variously blending creative, analytical, and practical skills and attitudes. Creative skills and attitudes are needed to formulate ideas; analytical skills and attitudes are needed to determine which are their good ideas; and practical skills and attitudes are needed to successfully implement the good ideas and to convince others of their value.

This framework suggests that conventional tests of abilities are not fully adequate, either in design or in implementation. They are less than adequate in design because they so heavily emphasize analytical (as well as memory-based) abilities, to the exclusion of creative and practical abilities. And they are less than adequate in implementation because too often they are used in a way that assumes that abilities are fixed rather than flexible—that a score represents what a person is capable of doing overall rather than a rough estimate of what a person does at a given time and place.

Some students enter the school and college sweepstakes with an enormous advantage conveyed by the match between the abilities socialized in their environment and the abilities required for success in traditional ability testing, instruction, and achievement testing. Schools emphasize analytical and memory-based skills—precisely the abilities that enable some students to excel. Although many students with diverse patterns of abilities grow up in low socioeconomic strata, many others grow up elsewhere. Upper-middle-class children demonstrate a wide variety of challenges and patterns of abilities. Thus, the story here is not just about children of lower SES but about *all* children—children with diverse patterns of abilities.

## Hidden Talents

If my view is correct—that children may have substantial hidden talents that are relevant for success in postsecondary education—then how can one show it?

Our belief that we can show it dates back at least to a study in which my collaborators and I administered a test to more than 300 high school students across the United States in order to identify students as intelligent on the basis of their analytical, creative, and practical abilities (Sternberg *et al.*, 1996). This identification was prior to their being placed into sections to take a college-level summer psychology course. When the students were divided into such groups, we noticed something that, at the time, was unexpected: Students in the high analytical group, who excelled in the abilities measured by conventional tests, were, for the most part, White and middle-class. Many had been identified previously as gifted. Students in the high creative and high practical groups were ethnically diverse, and many had never before been identified as gifted or talented.

The question, of course, is whether those identified as bright in the alternative ways (*i.e.*, creatively or practically) actually performed as expected. The answer was clear: When students were taught at least some of the time in a way that matched their patterns of abilities, they excelled. In other words, the creatively and practically gifted students did excel, so long as the way they were taught matched, at least some of the time, the way they learned. Good teachers use a variety of teaching methods to meet the diverse learning styles of their students, so that any student taught in a way that is responsive to his or her pattern of abilities can excel. But traditional assessments of college readiness tend to emphasize the memory-analytical mode of learning, to the exclusion of other modes.

After this study, my colleagues and I went on to show that teaching to all styles of learning does indeed improve achievement relative to teaching that emphasizes only traditional memory-analytical patterns of learning and thinking (Sternberg, Torff, and Grigorenko 1998). But the seeds of a further question were planted: Is it possible that many students who are not now being identified as having impressive credentials for college or graduate work might in fact be so identified if they were assessed in a way that focused on creative and practical, as well as analytical, forms of skills? The Rainbow Project[201] sought to answer this question.

## The Rainbow Project

The Rainbow Project (Sternberg and the Rainbow Project Collaborators 2006) comprises measures that supplement the SAT-I.

Existing data suggest reasonable predictive validity for the SAT in regard to college performance. Indeed, traditional intelligence or aptitude tests have been shown to predict perfor-

[201] Participating institutions in the Rainbow Project included Brigham Young University; Florida State University; James Madison University; California State University, San Bernardino; University of California, Santa Barbara; Southern Connecticut State University; Stevens Institute of Technology; Yale University; Mesa Community College; Coastline Community College; Irvine Valley Community College; Orange Coast Community College; Saddleback Community College; Mepham High School; and Northview High School.

mance across a wide variety of settings. But as is always the case for a single test or type of test, there is room for improvement. The theory of successful intelligence provides one basis for improving prediction and, possibly, for establishing greater equity and diversity. It suggests that broadening the range of skills tested beyond analytic skills, to include practical and creative skills, as well, might significantly expand the prediction of college performance beyond current levels. Thus, the theory does not suggest *replacing*, but rather *augmenting*, the SAT in the college admissions process. A collaborative team of investigators sought to study how successful such an augmentation could be.

## Methodological Considerations

In the Rainbow Project, data were collected at 15 schools across the United States, including 8 four-year colleges, 5 community colleges, and 2 high schools. Most of the data were collected from mid-April through June 2001, although some institutions extended their data collection into the summer.

Participants—1,013 students in either their first year of college or their final year of high school—received either course credit or money. In this report, we discuss analyses only for college students (they were the only ones for whom college performance data were available). The final number of participants included in our analyses was 777.

Baseline measures of standardized test scores and high-school grade-point average were collected to evaluate the predictive validity of current college admissions criteria and to provide a contrast for our current measures. Students' scores on standardized college entrance exams were obtained from the College Board.

### MEASURING ANALYTICAL SKILLS

The measure of analytical skills was provided by the SAT plus analytical items of the Sternberg Triarchic Abilities Test (STAT). The items included:

- *Analytical-Verbal*: Figuring out meanings of neologisms (artificial words) from natural contexts. Students see a novel word embedded in a paragraph and have to infer its meaning from the context.
- *Analytical-Quantitative*: Number series. Students have to identify what number should come next in a series.
- *Analytical-Figural*: Matrices. Students see a figural matrix with the lower right entry missing. They have to identify which of the options fits into the missing space.

### MEASURING CREATIVE SKILLS

Creative skills were measured by STAT multiple-choice items and by performance-based items. The multiple-choice items were of the following forms:

- *Creative-Verbal*: Novel analogies. Students are presented with verbal analogies preceded by counterfactual premises (*e.g.*, money falls off trees). They have to solve the analogies as though the counterfactual premises were true.
- *Creative-Quantitative*: Novel number operations. Students are presented with rules for novel number operations, for example, "flix," which involves numerical manipulations that differ as a function of whether the first of two operands is greater than, equal to, or less than the second. Participants have to use the novel number operations to solve presented math problems.
- *Creative-Figural*: In each item, participants are first presented with a figural series that involves one or more transformations; they then have to apply the rule of the series to a new figure with a different appearance and complete the new series.

Creative skills also were assessed using open-ended measures. One measure required writing two short stories with a selection from among unusual titles, such as "The Octopus's Sneakers;" one required orally telling two stories based upon choices of picture collages; and the third required captioning cartoons from among various options. Open-ended performance-based answers were rated by trained raters for novelty, quality, and task appropriateness. Multiple judges were used for each task, and satisfactory reliability was achieved.[202]

### MEASURING PRACTICAL SKILLS

Multiple-choice measures of practical skills were obtained from the STAT:

- *Practical-Verbal*: Everyday reasoning. Students are presented with a set of everyday problems in the life of an adolescent and are asked to select the option that best solves each problem.
- *Practical-Quantitative*: Everyday math. Students are presented with scenarios requiring the use of math in everyday life (*e.g.*, buying tickets for a ballgame) and have to solve math problems based on the scenarios.
- *Practical-Figural*: Route planning. Students are presented with a map of an area (*e.g.*, an entertainment park) and have to answer questions about navigating effectively through the area depicted by the map.

Practical skills also were assessed using three situational-judgment inventories: the Everyday Situational Judgment Inventory (movies), the Common Sense Questionnaire, and the College Life Questionnaire, each of which measures a different type of tacit knowledge. The general format of tacit-knowledge inventories has been described elsewhere (Sternberg *et al.* 2000), so only the content of the inventories used in the current study will be described here. The movies presented everyday situations that confront college students, such as asking

202 Details in Sternberg and the Rainbow Project Collaborators 2006; Sternberg, The Rainbow Project Collaborators, and University of Michigan Business School Project Collaborators 2004.

for a letter of recommendation from a professor who shows, through nonverbal cues, that he does not recognize you very well. The student taking the test then has to rate various options for how well the options would work in response to each situation. The Common Sense Questionnaire provided everyday business problems, such as being assigned to work with a coworker one dislikes to the extreme, and the College Life Questionnaire provided everyday college situations for which a solution was required.

Unlike the creativity performance tasks, the practical performance tasks do not provide participants with a choice of situations to rate. Rather, for each task, participants were told that there was no "right" answer and that the options described in each situation represented various ways in which different people approach different situations.

All materials were administered either in paper-and-pencil format (41% of the college students) or on the computer via the World Wide Web (59% of the college students). Participants were tested either individually or in small groups. During the oral stories section, participants who were tested in the group situation either wore headphones or were directed into a separate room so as not to disturb the other participants during the story dictation.

Each student participated in two discrete sessions conducted one immediately after the other. The first session included the informed-consent procedure, demographics information, the movies, the STAT batteries, and the cartoons, followed by a debriefing period. The second session included obtaining consent (again), followed by the rest of the demographics and "additional measures" described earlier, the Common Sense or College Life Test (depending on the condition), the Written or Oral Stories (depending on the condition), and ending with the final debriefing. The order was the same for all participants. No strict time limits were set for completing the tests, although the instructors were given rough guidelines of approximately 70 minutes per session. Time taken to complete the battery of tests ranged from two to four hours.

Given the lengthy nature of the complete battery of assessments, participants were administered parts of the battery using an intentional incomplete overlapping design, as described in McArdle and Hamagami (1992; McArdle 1994). Participants were randomly assigned to the test sections they were to complete.

### WHAT WE FOUND

What we found depends on how the data are analyzed (*see* Sternberg and the Rainbow Project Collaborators 2006, for details). However, the conservative analysis described below does not correct for differences in the selectivity of the colleges at which the study took place. In a study across so many colleges differing in selectivity, validity coefficients will seem lower than is typical, because an "A" at a less selective college counts the same as an "A" at a more selective college. When we corrected for college selectivity, the results described below appeared stronger. But correcting for selectivity has its own problems (*e.g.*, on what basis does one evaluate selectivity?), and so we use uncorrected data in this report.

### BASIC STATISTICS

When examining college students alone, it becomes evident that this sample shows a slightly higher mean level of SAT than that found in colleges across the country. Our sample means on the SATs were, for two-year college students, 490 verbal and 508 math, and for four-year college students, 555 verbal and 575 math. These means, although slightly higher than typical, are within the range of average college students.

There is always concern about restriction of range in SAT scores when considering students from a select sample of universities; such concern is heightened when the means run a bit high. However, our sample was taken from a wide range in selectivity of institutions, from community colleges to highly selective four-year institutions. In addition, the standard deviation of the SAT scores (for the total college sample, $SD_{SAT\ Verbal} = 118.2$, and $SD_{SAT\ Math} = 117.5$) was comparable to the standard deviation of SAT scores in the broader population. If anything, an analysis of variance test suggests that the variance for the sample for these items is statistically larger than for the typical population of SAT examinees. For these reasons, the concern of restriction of range of SAT scores across the whole sample actually is reduced.

### FACTOR STRUCTURE OF THE RAINBOW MEASURES

Factor analysis reveals the structure that underlies observable scores on a test. A factor analysis therefore was conducted to explore the factor structure underlying the Rainbow measures. The results are shown in Table 29.1 (on page 394).

Three meaningful correlated factors were extracted: One represented practical performance tests; a second, weaker factor represented the creative performance tests; a third factor represented the multiple-choice tests (including analytical, creative, and practical). Thus, method variance proved important. The results show the importance of measuring skills using multiple formats, precisely because method is so important in determining factorial structure.

### PREDICTING COLLEGE GPA

In order to test the incremental validity provided by Rainbow measures above and beyond the SAT in predicting freshman GPA, a series of hierarchical regressions was conducted that included the items analyzed above in the analytical, creative, and practical assessments. (Hierarchical regression tells us how much a new assessment contributes over and above old assessments.) Table 29.2, on page 395, shows the results.

The Rainbow measures increased explained variation in college freshman GPA beyond SAT and high school GPA combined by about 50 percent (from 0.156 to 0.248); it increased prediction versus the SAT alone by close to 100 percent (from 0.098 to 0.199). That is, relative to the SATs, it roughly doubled prediction. Absolute values of coefficients are lower than in many studies because we did not correct for differences in grading across colleges. Thus, an "A" at a nonselective school counted the same as an "A" at a highly selective institution. This form of analysis was used because it was the most conservative.

TABLE 29.1: **Exploratory Factor Analysis of Rainbow Measures (2001)**

| | Test | Estimated correlations[1] 1 | 2 | 3 | 4 | 5 | 6 | 7 | 8 | F1 | F2 | F3 |
|---|---|---|---|---|---|---|---|---|---|---|---|---|
| 1 | Oral Stories | 1.00 | | | | | | | | 0.57[2] | -0.06 | -0.06 |
| 2 | Written Stories | 0.07 | 1.00 | | | | | | | 0.79[2] | 0.01 | -0.02 |
| 3 | Cartoons | 0.14 | 0.24 | 1.00 | | | | | | 0.20[2] | 0.28[2] | -0.08 |
| 4 | STAT-Creative | 0.11 | 0.27 | 0.29 | 1.00 | | | | | 0.00 | 0.73[2] | 0.09 |
| 5 | STAT-Analytical | 0.14 | 0.24 | 0.21 | 0.58 | 1.00 | | | | -0.06 | 0.80[2] | -0.04 |
| 6 | STAT-Practical | 0.14 | 0.31 | 0.29 | 0.61 | 0.63 | 1.00 | | | 0.03 | 0.81[2] | -0.02 |
| 7 | Movies | 0.02 | 0.22 | 0.14 | 0.29 | 0.17 | 0.26 | 1.00 | | 0.12 | 0.05 | 0.52[2] |
| 8 | College Life | 0.01 | 0.13 | 0.12 | 0.38 | 0.24 | 0.30 | 0.59 | 1.00 | -0.13 | 0.01 | 1.00[2] |
| 9 | Common Sense | 0.03 | 0.30 | 0.05 | 0.38 | 0.38 | 0.33 | 0.55 | 0.33 | 0.12 | -0.01 | 0.92[2] |
| Factor Intercorrelations | | | | | | | | | | | | |
| | F1 | | | | | | | | | 1.00 | | |
| | F2 | | | | | | | | | 0.45 | 1.00 | |
| | F3 | | | | | | | | | 0.30 | 0.40 | 1.00 |

[1] Correlations estimated using FIML
[2] Salient loadings of tests on factors

**NOTE:** 62.4% of variation explained; Nominal N = 776

## GROUP DIFFERENCES

Although one important goal of the present study was to predict success in college, another important goal involved developing measures that reduce racial and ethnic group differences in mean levels. One can test for group differences in these measures in a number of ways, each of which involves a test of the size of the effect of race. We chose two: omega square ($\omega^2$) and Cohen's d.

We first considered the omega squared coefficients, essentially, a measure of the strength of relation between two variables. These results are shown in Table 29.3 (on page 396). This procedure involves conducting a series of one-way analyses of variance (ANOVA) considering differences in mean performance levels among the six ethnic and racial groups reported, including White, Asian, Pacific Islander, Latino, Black, and Native American, for the following measures: the baseline measures (SAT-V and SAT-M), the STAT ability scales, the creativity performance tasks, and the practical-ability performance tasks. The omega-squared coefficient indicates the proportion of variance in the variables that is accounted for by the self-reported ethnicity of the participant. The Rainbow measures showed reduced values relative to the SAT, as can be seen in the table.

The test of effect sizes using the Cohen's d statistic allows one to consider more specifically a standardized representation of specific group differences. For the test of ethnic group differences, each entry represents how far away from the mean for Whites each group performs in terms of standard deviations. For the test of gender differences, the entries represent how far away women perform from men in terms of standard deviations.

TABLE 29.2: **Incremental Prediction of College GPA Using the Rainbow Measured Abilities (2001)**

| | Above and Beyond the SAT and High School GPA (HSGPA) | | | | Above and Beyond the SAT | | | |
|---|---|---|---|---|---|---|---|---|
| | **Step 1** | **Step 2** | **Step 3** | **Step 4** | **Step 1** | **Step 2** | **Step 3** | **Step 4** |
| **SAT/HSGPA**[1] | | | | | | | | |
| Verbal | 0.098 | 0.084 | 0.066 | 0.005 | 0.145* | 0.125 | 0.098 | 0.039 |
| Math | 0.070 | 0.011 | –0.008 | –0.069 | 0.188* | 0.114 | 0.082 | 0.021 |
| High School GPA | 0.285[2] | 0.276[2] | 0.267[2] | 0.270[2] | — | — | — | — |
| **Analytical** | | | | | | | | |
| Analytical STAT | | 0.096 | 0.054 | 0.012 | | 0.122[2] | 0.068 | 0.021 |
| **Practical** | | | | | | | | |
| Performance Latent | | | 0.119[2] | 0.049 | | | 0.133[2] | 0.058 |
| Practical STAT | | | 0.025 | –0.033 | | | 0.055 | –0.015 |
| **Creative** | | | | | | | | |
| Written | | | | 0.003 | | | | –0.003 |
| Oral | | | | 0.273[2] | | | | 0.252[2] |
| Cartoons | | | | –0.072[2] | | | | –0.068 |
| Creative STAT | | | | 0.258[2] | | | | 0.290[2] |
| **R square** | 0.156 | 0.152 | 0.159 | 0.248 | 0.098 | 0.099 | 0.110 | 0.199 |

[1] Z-score transformation applied
[2] $p < 0.05$; N = 777

**NOTE:** Entries are standardized beta coefficients

These results indicate two general findings: First, in terms of overall differences represented by omega squared, the Rainbow tests appear to reduce race and ethnicity differences relative to traditional assessments of abilities such as the SAT. Second, in terms of specific differences represented by Cohen's d, it appears that Latino students benefit most from the reduction of group differences. Black students, too, seemed to show a reduction in difference from the White mean for most of the Rainbow tests, although a substantial difference appears to be maintained with the practical performance measures. Important reductions in differences also can be seen for the Native American relative to White students. Indeed, their median was higher for the creative tests. However, the very small sample size suggests that any conclusions about Native American performance should be made only tentatively.

Although the group differences are not perfectly reduced, these findings suggest that measures can be designed that reduce ethnic and racial group differences on standardized tests, particularly for historically disadvantaged groups such as Black and Latino students. These findings have important implications for diminishing adverse impact in college admissions.

## Follow-up at Tufts University

We have followed up on the Rainbow Project at Tufts University. With my assistance, the Tufts University Admissions Office has developed Rainbow-based measures and has piloted them on an experimental basis. The office has found that lower SES students may have low

SAT scores but high scores on measures of creative and/or practical skills. These encouraging data have led us to plan to use Rainbow-like assessments not as a separate test but rather as an integral part of the assessment process. We are including, on an experimental basis, items such as creative story-writing, cartoon-captioning, and practical problem solving as an integral part of the Tufts application.

TABLE 29.3: **Amount of Variance in Each Assessment Accounted for by Ethnicity, Using the Omega Square Effect Size Statistic**

| Measure | F | P | N | Omega squared ($\omega^2$) |
|---|---|---|---|---|
| **SAT** | | | | |
| Verbal | 35.8 | <0.001 | 341 | 0.09 |
| Math | 15.2 | <0.001 | 341 | 0.04 |
| Total (combined) | 28.2 | <0.001 | 340 | 0.07 |
| **STAT** | | | | |
| Analytical | 0.5 | ns | 370 | 0.00 |
| Practical | 12.8 | <0.001 | 374 | 0.03 |
| Creative | 6.7 | <0.010 | 369 | 0.02 |
| **Practical Performance** | | | | |
| EDSJ (Movies) | 5.9 | <0.050 | 493 | 0.01 |
| Common Sense | 2.6 | ns | 273 | 0.01 |
| College Life | 8.4 | <0.010 | 298 | 0.02 |
| **Creative Performance** | | | | |
| Cartoon Captions | 14.0 | <0.001 | 569 | 0.02 |
| Oral Stories | 6.0 | <0.050 | 152 | 0.03 |
| Written Stories | 3.1 | ns | 329 | 0.01 |

Items such as these will not radically change admissions. Students who perform poorly in school and who had little chance of being admitted before, whether because of low grades, a weak record of extracurricular accomplishments, or very low test scores, still will not be admitted. Students with outstanding records of accomplishment will still be accepted. Where these tests will prove most useful is in the broad middle—among the students whose records do not dictate an admissions decision one way or another. Rainbow-based measures can help make distinctions between whom to admit and whom not to. At Tufts, we will follow up on students admitted through these assessments by comparing them to students who are from the same admissions band but for whom the decision to admit was based on factors other than Rainbow-like measures.

## Conclusion

Based as it is on a conventional psychometric notion of cognitive skills, the SAT has had substantial success in predicting college performance. But the time may have come to move beyond conventional theories of cognitive skills. Based on multiple regression analyses, the Rainbow measures alone nearly double the predictive power of college GPA when compared to the SAT alone (comparing $R^2$ of 0.199 to 0.098, respectively). In addition, the Rainbow measures predict an additional 9.2 percent of college GPA beyond the initial 15.6 percent contributed by the SAT and high school GPA. These findings, combined with encouraging results regarding the reduction of between-ethnicity differences, make a compelling case for furthering the study of the measurement of analytic, creative, and practical skills for predicting success in college.

Although this first study presents a promising start for the investigation of an equitable yet powerful predictor of success in college, it is not without its share of methodological problems. Better tests and scoring methods, larger samples, and more representative samples all are needed. Future development of these tests will help resolve some of the problems borne out of the present findings.

In sum, the theory of successful intelligence appears to provide a strong theoretical basis for augmented assessment of the skills needed for college success. Evidence indicates that it has good incremental predictive power and serves to increase equity. As teaching improves and as college teachers emphasize more the creative and practical skills needed for success in school and life, the predictive power of the test may increase. Cosmetic changes in testing over the last century have made relatively little difference to the construct validity of assessment procedures. The theory of successful intelligence could provide a new opportunity to increase construct validity even as it reduces differences in test performance between groups. It may indeed be possible to accomplish the goals of affirmative action through tests such as the Rainbow assessments, either as supplements to traditional affirmative-action programs or as substitutes for them.

/ CHAPTER THIRTY /

*by Jonathan Gayles, Ph.D.*
*Assistant Professor of African American Studies, Georgia State University*

30

# Predicting Graduating Performance:
## Georgia State University's Freshman Index

The Freshman Index (FI), a combination of SAT score and high school grade point average, is the primary mechanism facilitating admissions decisions at Georgia State University (GSU). This chapter examines the relationships between these three admissions criteria and the graduating grade point averages of Asian, Black, and White six-year graduates.

In addition, this chapter examines the impact of limiting the analysis to graduates with "strong" (75th percentile) admissions criteria. This research indicates that the Freshman Index explains more variation in graduating grade point averages than either SAT score alone or high school grade point average alone for all graduates.

However, caution is warranted as high school grade point average alone explains a comparable amount of variation in graduating grade point average and more variation. Further, no admissions criterion consistently explains variation in graduating grade point average for each racial group.

## Background

Georgia State University's (GSU) freshman index (FI) is the primary admissions mechanism for its admissions decisions.

GSU's formula for computing the FI is as follows:

*(High school grade point average [HSA] x 500) + SAT Math + SAT Verbal = Freshman Index*

By including SAT scores in the calculation of the FI, admissions decisions at GSU are based, to some degree, on a mechanism that has a long and contentious history. The precursor to the SAT and tests like it is the intelligence, or aptitude, test. Carl Brigham, one of the individuals intimately involved in developing what was to become the SAT, cautioned against the possibility of devolving into "pseudo-phrenology" (Lemann 1999, p. 33) and in a later communication asserted that "test scores very definitely are a composite including schooling, family background, familiarity with English, and everything else, relevant and irrelevant. The 'native intelligence' hypothesis is dead" (Lemann 1999, p. 34). In fact, the "native intelligence" hypothesis is not dead (Brigham 1929; Herrnstein and Murray 1994), but to be fair, the College Board no longer describes the SAT as either an aptitude or an intelligence test. "SAT" is now an empty acronym.

The College Board asserts that the SAT provides the means to make objective, merit-based decisions as to which students should earn access to limited postsecondary opportunities. The College Board offers a response to the persistent problem of deciding on what basis opportunity should be distributed. For the College Board (2004b), the SAT is a solution to this problem because it provides "a common and objective scale for comparison;" for others, the SAT poses a continuing problem of being on the "wrong side" of the distribution decision of a system that "has artificially decided on selection rules that ultimately determine which traits win out" (Sacks 2001, p. 219).

It is folly to ignore the fact that the SAT has "a historical tie to the concept of innate mental abilities and that such abilities can be defined and meaningfully measured" (Atkinson 2001/2002, p. 31). While it is important to acknowledge the evolution of the SAT from a mechanism driven by biogenetic concerns (Scholastic Aptitude Test) to its present iteration as the SAT, it also is important to consider the degree to which the SAT and the debate around its use continue to possess "the residue of the Census of Abilities" (Lemann 1999, p. 4).

Despite the national reliance on the SAT in admissions decisions, criticism of the test is abundant. The College Board (2006c) indicates that "each institution has a unique mission and institutional goals and must develop and implement admissions policies and procedures that are not only consistent with, but also serve to advance those goals." However, if an institution is truly interested in ethnic and socioeconomic diversity, the SAT can prove to be a problematic mechanism. The College Board's own data reveal that the SAT is persistently and highly correlated with family income (2004a) and parental education (2004b). In addition, the persistent "racial gap" in SAT scores is a source of great debate and contention (College Board 2004a). Persistent disparities in scores (among other issues) prompt some scholars to question the fairness of the continued use of the SAT (Bracey 1980, 2002a, 2002b; Burdman

2001; Crouse 1985; Crouse and Trusheim 1988, 1991; Jencks and Crouse 1982; Slack and Porter 1980; Zwick 2002).

In examining patterns of disparity, many researchers place testing outcomes in a broader context that requires a more critical perspective of what the SAT actually measures, or fails to measure—especially as it relates to the ability of the SAT to predict college performance. Steele's research on the stereotype threat is but one example (1997; Steele and Aronson 1995). His thesis asserts that tests are subjectively experienced even though they are objectively administered. Steele defines stereotype threat as "the social-psychological threat that arises when one is in a situation or doing something for which a negative stereotype about one's group applies...for those who identify with the domain to which the stereotype is relevant, this predicament can be self-threatening" (Steele 1997, p. 614).

Parallel to the research reported here, some scholarship challenges the ability of the SAT to accurately predict student performance at colleges and universities. The work of Crouse and Trusheim (Crouse 1985; Crouse and Trusheim 1988, 1991, 1982) is particularly prominent in this area. This work directly challenges the utility of the SAT as an admissions tool. When compared to high school performance, Crouse and Trusheim assert that the SAT is redundant at best and, at worst, unfairly restricts access for minority applicants. To offset such potential restriction, some researchers have proposed mechanisms that supplement (Hunter and Samter 2000) or adjust (Freedle 2003) SAT scores in a manner that best reflects the capacity of all students who take the test. Not surprisingly, this research has prompted rebuttals from scholars associated with the College Board (Camara and Sathy 2004, Dorans 2004; Willingham and Ramist 1982).

In addition to the claims of the College Board, some research indicates that the SAT independently predicts college performance (Stricker 1996; Weitzman 1982). Consistent with the College Board's (2005c) assertion that "the most important factor for college admission is your child's high school transcript...SAT scores are intended to supplement your child's record," most of the research supporting the predictive value of the SAT pairs performance on the SAT with other admissions data—high school performance, in particular. Burton and Ramist (2001) present a thorough review of the predictive value of the SAT for nearly twenty years of high school graduating classes and find that a combination of SAT score and high school performance serves as a stronger predictor for college performance than either measure alone.

A number of studies have examined the ability of standardized admissions tests to predict college performance in comparison to HSGPA. The majority of these studies focus on the first year of college. Beyond the work of Crouse, some research indicates that standardized admissions tests offer only minimal predictive value (Baron and Norman 1992). Additional research suggests that students' high school academic records predict postsecondary performance as well as, if not better than, standardized test performance (Boyd 1980; Wolfe and Johnson 1995; Deberard *et al.* 2004).

Ultimately, race is a central reference point for the research presented here. Fleming and Garcia provide an excellent summary of numerous studies that examine the predictive validity of the SAT at Black and White institutions (1998). The results indicate great variation in the degree to which the SAT predicts first-year grades for Black students at White colleges (.01 percent to 23 percent of the variation in first-year grades, with an average of 9.9%) as compared to Black students at Black colleges (11.6 percent to 31.9 percent, with an average of 21.3%). Of all the studies included in Fleming and Garcia's analysis, SAT explained an average of 14.7 percent of the variation in college grades.

Other research offers a focus on the performance of minority students and suggests that the predictive value of admissions criteria differs from that of white students (Lunneborg and Lunneborg 1986; Ting 2000; Ting 2003; Fleming and Garcia 1998). A comprehensive treatment of the differential validity and prediction of the admissions tests is offered by Young (2001). Young reviews more than 25 years of research examining differential validity and prediction of college admission testing. In total, 49 studies are included in this comprehensive treatment of the research.

Within Young's research, I focus on those studies that use cumulative graduating GPA (CGPA) as the criterion given that this is the outcome criterion (or dependent variable) used in the research reported here. Of the six such studies referenced in Young's report, five reveal lower correlations between some combination of SAT and HSGPA for Black students as compared to White students (Baggaley 1974; Farver *et al.*1975, Hand and Prather 1985; Moffatt 1993; Young 1994). Only Elliott and Strenta (1988) obtained results inconsistent with this trend. In terms of prediction, fewer studies use CGPA as the criterion. However, both of the studies employing CGPA in this manner report overprediction of Black CGPA as compared to White CGPA (Nettles *et al.* 1986; Young 1994).

Other examinations of the use of the SAT consider issues of power implicit in establishing a norm to which all students will be compared—this despite the fact that the United States of America is an increasingly diverse country. GSU's own Asa Hilliard challenges the manner in which the concept of intelligence is socially constructed and the way in which this undermines the legitimacy of the assessment of African American students (1990).

Despite challenges to the use of the SAT in admissions decisions, the College Board (2005c) asserts that the test is "the best independent, standardized measure of a student's college readiness. It is standardized across all students, schools, and states, providing a common and objective scale for comparison." As an indication of college readiness, the primary purpose of the SAT is to predict first-year grades. This places great weight on the first year and ignores the relationship between the SAT and student performance beyond the first year.

As the most diverse public four-year institution of higher education in Georgia, GSU must critically consider the use of the SAT in admissions decisions. GSU is the most diverse public four-year institution of higher education in Georgia. In fact, GSU graduates more Black students than many historically Black colleges and universities. This is a point of particular

TABLE 30.1: **Descriptive Summary of GSU Analysis (1998–2004)**

| Ethnicity | | SAT | Freshman Index | GPA | HSA |
|---|---|---|---|---|---|
| Asian (n = 207) | Mean | 1026.08700 | 2705.5070 | 3.164251 | 3.361353 |
| | Std. Deviation | 111.37120 | 268.5318 | 0.383869 | 0.434053 |
| Black (n = 437) | Mean | 1000.17800 | 2646.6770 | 2.992586 | 3.292906 |
| | Std. Deviation | 94.92283 | 212.0888 | 0.398425 | 0.366636 |
| White (n = 721) | Mean | 1094.11800 | 2745.8240 | 3.271456 | 3.303745 |
| | Std. Deviation | 114.40250 | 267.6814 | 0.401246 | 0.427622 |

pride for GSU: We are living proof that it is possible to have diversity and excellence. Not only do we continue to recruit a highly ethnically diverse student body while significantly increasing our admission requirements, we also are in the top ten universities nationally for numbers of black students who graduate in non-HBCUS (Fritz 2001).

Black students at GSU consistently account for approximately 30 percent of students. With such a diverse student body, it would seem that GSU's admissions mechanism should not disproportionately penalize one group of students while disproportionately benefiting another, as some critics of the SAT assert.

## Method

All Asian, Black, and White students entering GSU in August 1998 and graduating by May 2004 are included in this analysis.[191] (*See* Table 30.1.)

The percentage of students graduating in six years is an increasingly important reference for judging the efficiency and quality of colleges. The high-profile annual ranking presented by *U.S. News and World Report* partially reflects these data. Indeed, 80 percent of the total retention score is represented by "the average proportion of a graduating class who earn a degree in six years or less" (Morse and Flannigan 2005). As GSU transitions into a more traditional university with younger first-year students and more full-time students, its performance on national reference points such as six-year graduation rate becomes increasingly important.

As indicated in the literature review, differential outcomes on the SAT and the limited ability of the SAT to predict college grades remain a lightning rod for criticism of the SAT, some of which is ill informed (Jacobs 1995). While this research offers a critical examination of the utility of the SAT that is potentially consistent with this criticism, it extends the dialogue regarding the use of the SAT in two ways: First, research presented here is consistent with Lawlor *et al.* (1997) as it focuses on those students who have graduated in no more than six years and therefore provides "data reflective of a student's ultimate college success that goes beyond typical studies that attempt to measure short-range success" (p. 4). Second, this research offers a focus on students with particularly strong (scores at the 75th percentile or

[191] The number of graduates reporting other ethnic groupings or not reporting a race were excluded because they represented a minuscule percentage of graduates. Cases including missing data also were excluded.

above) FI, HSGPA, and SAT scores. In doing so, we are able to consider the relationship between admissions criteria and CGPAs of students with "the best scores." There are two central goals of this research:

- Determine the comparative utility of each admissions criterion in relation to Georgia State University cumulative graduating grade point average (CGPA).
- Determine the degree to which limiting the analysis to graduates with "strong" (75th percentile) scores in each of the three admissions criteria affects the utility of each admission criterion.

Four types of analyses are reported: (1) Separate simple linear regressions were computed to respond to the goals of the research so that comparisons may be made between all graduates and those with strong admissions criteria; (2) Kruskall-Wallis;[192] and (3) Mann-Whitney U[193] tests were administered to determine whether significant differences are apparent between the CGPAs of students with strong admissions criteria within each racial group. Finally, (4) statistically significant differences were determined between slopes using the unpaired t-test.[194]

# Results[195]

## Initial Regression: All Graduates

### THE FRESHMAN INDEX AND CGPA

Although the results of the linear regression are significant, a poor model fit is apparent for prediction of CGPA across each of the racial groupings included in this analysis. Only a maximum of approximately 29 percent of the CGPA is explained (Adjusted $R^2 \leq 0.287$). Further, the increase in CGPA per increase in FI is nominal for each group (slope = 0.001).

### HIGH SCHOOL GPA AND CGPA

The results of the linear regression are significant for HSGPA while an even poorer model fit is clear ($R^2 \leq 0.241$) across each group. However, the increase in CGPA per increase in HSGPA is, comparatively speaking, much greater than the similar increase in FI (slope = 0.408 to 0.461).

### SAT AND CGPA

Of the three admissions criteria included in this analysis, SAT yields the poorest fit of the three models ($R^2 \leq 0.111$). Although the results are significant, like FI, the increase in GPA per increase in FI is nominal for each group (slope = 0.001).

[192] Kruskal-Wallis tests are a nonparametric alternative to one-way analysis of variance. This is an appropriate choice because the data in each condition are not consistently distributed normally.

[193] The Mann-Whitney U test is a nonparametric alternative to the students' t-test.

[194] The unpaired t-test was used here: $t = b1 - b2 \div \sqrt{SE^2_{b1} + SE^2_{b2}}$ on (N−4) degrees of freedom.

[195] See Table 31.2, on page 405.

TABLE 30.2: **Linear Regression: All Graduates**

| Ethnicity | | F value[1] | Degrees of Freedom | Adjusted $R^2$ | Slope | Constant | t statistic[1] |
|---|---|---|---|---|---|---|---|
| Asian (n=201) | FI | 72.873 | 1, 205 | 0.259 | 0.001 | 1.184 | 8.537 |
| | HSGPA | 55.314 | 1, 205 | 0.209 | 0.408 | 1.794 | 7.437 |
| | SAT | 23.571 | 1, 205 | 0.099 | 0.001 | 2.029 | 4.855 |
| Black (n=437) | FI | 117.458 | 1, 435 | 0.211 | 0.001 | 0.700 | 10.838 |
| | HSGPA | 78.933 | 1, 435 | 0.152 | 0.426 | 1.590 | 8.884 |
| | SAT | 34.965 | 1, 435 | 0.072 | 0.001 | 1.848 | 5.913 |
| White (n=721) | FI | 289.498 | 1, 719 | 0.287 | 0.001 | 1.066 | 17.015 |
| | HSGPA | 229.250 | 1, 719 | 0.241 | 0.461 | 1.747 | 15.141 |
| | SAT | 90.887 | 1, 719 | 0.111 | 0.001 | 1.986 | 9.533 |

[1] $p < 0.001$

### INITIAL REGRESSION SUMMARY

Comparatively speaking, the FI appears to be a more promising admission mechanism than either HSGPA or SAT. This is consistent across each of the three groups. Four specific outcomes relevant to the research questions are important:

- SAT is the weakest admission criterion, explaining the least amount of variation in each group and yielding a nominal direct relationship with CGPA;
- While FI explains the most variation in CGPA, HSGPA explains nearly as much variation in CGPA as does FI. The mean difference between the amount of variation explained by FI and the amount explained by HSGPA is 5.2 percent;
- HSGPA consistently explains more than twice the variation in CGPA that SAT explains; and
- Considering the slope, the increase in CGPA per HSGPA clearly exceeds that of the two other admissions criteria. (*See* Table 30.3, on page 406.)

## Graduates with Admissions Criteria at the 75th Percentile

### THE FRESHMAN INDEX AND CGPA

Limiting the analysis to graduates with strong admissions criteria reveals one particularly prominent change: no significant relationship is apparent between FI and CGPA for Asian graduates with strong FIs. In addition to the poor model fit for Black and White graduates, FI now explains less variation in CGPA for Black and White graduates. For Black graduates, the decrease is 4.9 percent (21.1 percent to 16.2%) while the decrease for White graduates is much more pronounced, at 21 percent (28.7 percent to 7.7%). As in the initial regression, the increase in CGPA per increase in FI is nominal (slope = 0.001).

TABLE 30.3: **Linear Regression: Graduates with Admissions Criteria at 75th Percentile**

| Ethnicity | | | F value | Degrees of Freedom | Adjusted $R^2$ | Slope | Constant | t statistic |
|---|---|---|---|---|---|---|---|---|
| Asian | FI | (n=53) | 0.760[1] | — | — | — | — | — |
| | HSGPA | (n=55) | 5.356[2] | 1, 53 | 0.075 | 0.663 | 0.800 | 2.314[2] |
| | SAT | (n=56) | 4.990[2] | 1, 54 | 0.085 | 0.002 | 1.049 | 2.234[2] |
| Black | FI | (n=114) | 22.867[3] | 1, 112 | 0.162 | 0.001 | -0.866 | 4.782[3] |
| | HSGPA | (n=112) | 28.117[3] | 1, 110 | 0.196 | 0.716 | 0.196 | 5.303[3] |
| | SAT | (n=121) | 4.925[2] | 1, 119 | 0.032 | 0.001 | 1.560 | 2.219[2] |
| White | FI | (n=183) | 16.157[2] | 1, 181 | 0.077 | 0.001 | 1.917 | 4.020[3] |
| | HSGPA | (n=226) | 20.731[3] | 1, 225 | 0.081 | 0.488 | 1.664 | 4.553[3] |
| | SAT | (n=198) | 10.332[2] | 1, 186 | 0.048 | 0.001 | 2.075 | 3.214[2] |

[1] $p = 0.387$ (not sig.)
[2] $p < 0.050$
[3] $p < 0.001$

### HIGH SCHOOL GPA AND CGPA

Unlike the relationship between FI and CGPA, significant relationships persist across racial groupings for graduates with strong HSGPAs, although poor model fits are apparent here, as well (adjusted $R^2 \leq 0.196$). Further:

- The amount of variation explained in CGPA by HSGPA decreased for Asian (from 20.9 percent to 7.5%) and White graduates (from 24.1 percent to 8.1%) while *increasing* for Black graduates (from 15.2 percent to 19.6%); and
- The increase in CGPA per increase in HSGPA increased for each group, with a considerable increase for Black graduates (slope increase from 0.426 to 0.716). This is the only increase in slope.

### SAT AND CGPA

As with the initial regression, the poorest model fits are apparent with SAT ($R^2 \leq 0.085$). While the results remain significant across racial groups, the amount of variation in CGPA explained by SAT decreased across racial groups.

### SUMMARY OF REGRESSION OF GRADUATES WITH "STRONG" ADMISSIONS CRITERIA

Limiting the analysis in this manner reveals a number of outcomes that differ from the initial regression:

- Less variation is explained in CGPA across groups and across admissions criteria, with the *exception* of HSGPA for Black graduates;
- SAT continues to explain the least amount of variation in CGPA across groups;
- Comparatively, HSGPA consistently explains more variation in CGPA than does FI for Black and White graduates (no significant relationship was apparent for Asian graduates). This is a reversal of the initial regression; and

TABLE 30.4: **Comparison of Slopes**

| | Group | HSGPA/FI | Unpaired t value | HSGPA/SAT | Unpaired t value |
|---|---|---|---|---|---|
| 75th Percentile | Asian | * | * | 0.663/0.002 | 2.311175[3] |
| | Black | 0.716/0.001 | -5.07092[1] | 0.716/0.001 | 5.070794[1] |
| | White | 0.488/0.001 | -4.55140[2] | 0.488/0.001 | 4.551203[1] |
| All Graduates | Asian | 0.408/0.001 | -7.40000[1] | 0.408/0.001 | 7.400000[1] |
| | Black | 0.426/0.001 | -8.85417[1] | 0.426/0.001 | 8.854167[1] |
| | White | 0.461/0.001 | -15.33300[1] | 0.461/0.001 | 15.333000[1] |

* FI was not a significant predictor.
[1] $p < 0.0001$
[2] $p < 0.0010$
[3] $p < 0.0500$

- Consistent with the initial regression, HSGPA explains more variation in CGPA than does SAT for Black and White graduates. However, SAT explains more variation than HSGPA for Asian graduates, a reversal of the initial regression.

*Comparison of Slopes*

Considering the prominent difference between the slopes of regressions including HSGPA and those including FI and SAT, t values[196] were computed to determine whether the slopes associated with regression formulas including HSGPA were significantly higher. As Table 30.4 indicates, the slopes were, in fact, significantly higher.

## Discussion

### COMPARATIVE WEAKNESS OF THE SAT

The SAT is, without exception, the weakest of the three admissions criteria. It explained no more than 11.1 percent of the variation in CGPA for any of the three groups in either condition. While all of the models reported here are poor, the purpose of this analysis is comparative in nature. As a result, we must acknowledge that the SAT is the weakest independent criterion. The fact that strong SAT scores explain no more than 8.5 percent (Asian graduates) and as little as 3.2 percent (Black graduates) of the variation in CGPA further weakens its utility as an independent admission mechanism. That the amount of variation explained in CGPA *decreased* across groups when the analysis was limited to graduates with strong SAT scores is further cause for concern about the SAT's utility as an independent admission mechanism. Considering this, we shift our focus to HSGPA and FI.

### USING HSGPA OR THE FRESHMAN INDEX

As an independent admissions mechanism, HSGPA shows much promise. Across racial groupings, each regression yielded significant results with CGPA. While this is also true for SAT, it is

[196] The unpaired t-test was used here: $t = b1 - b2 \div \sqrt{SE^2_{b1} + SE^2_{b2}}$ on (N−4) degrees of freedom.

not true for FI (Strongest Asian applicants). The most pronounced difference between HSGPA and the other two criteria can be found in the slope of the regression equation. In both regressions and across groups, the slope of regression equations with HSGPA as a regressor predicts significantly greater increases in CGPA than those using FI and SAT as predictors. Furthermore, limiting the analysis to graduates with strong HSGPAs yields an *increase* in the slope's value. This is *only* the case with HSGPA. Finally, the only increase in the amount of variation in CGPA explained in the second regression is found with HSGPA (Black graduates). FI and SAT both evidenced decreases in the amount of variation in CGPA explained in the second regression.

The utility of the FI is clear in the first regression. It explains the most variation in CGPA across racial groups. The second regression qualifies the comparative utility of the FI in three primary ways:

- The regression analysis is no longer significant for the strongest Asian applicants;
- The slope of regression equations including HSA is significantly higher that those including FI; and
- For graduates with strong admissions criteria, FI is second best (after HSGPA) at explaining the variation in CGPA, which represents a reversal for White and Black graduates.

The results of this analysis generally support the use of the FI and HSGPA even as they provide little support for the use of the SAT as an independent admissions measure. Still, the utility of the FI is qualified, as indicated in the preceding discussion. Consider first the fact that the FI and HSGPA explain comparable amounts of variation across each of the racial groups in the initial regression. (*See* Figure 30.1, on page 409.)

Across racial groups, FI explains, at most, only 5.9 percent more variation in CGPA than HSGPA (Black Graduates). In conjunction with the fact that increases in HSGPA predict much greater increases in CGPA, it becomes more difficult to frame the FI as the best admission mechanism without qualification. The results of the second regression qualify the utility of the FI further and offer direct support for the independent use of the HSGPA. For six-year graduates with strong admissions criteria, HSGPA explains more variation than does FI for Black and White graduates; note that the results of the linear regression were not significant for Asian graduates when FI was used as the predictor. (*See* Figure 30.2, on page 409.)

As in the initial regression, increases in HSGPA predict much greater increases in CGPA. Further support of HSGPA alone is found in the increase in the value of the slopes of regression equations across groups in the second regression, as indicated in Table 30.4 (on page 407). An additional outcome that weakens the degree to which the FI distinguishes itself from HSGPA is the comparable mean CGPAs across each of the three admissions criteria within each racial group when limited to strong scores. This is consistent across racial groups. (*See* Figure 30.3.)

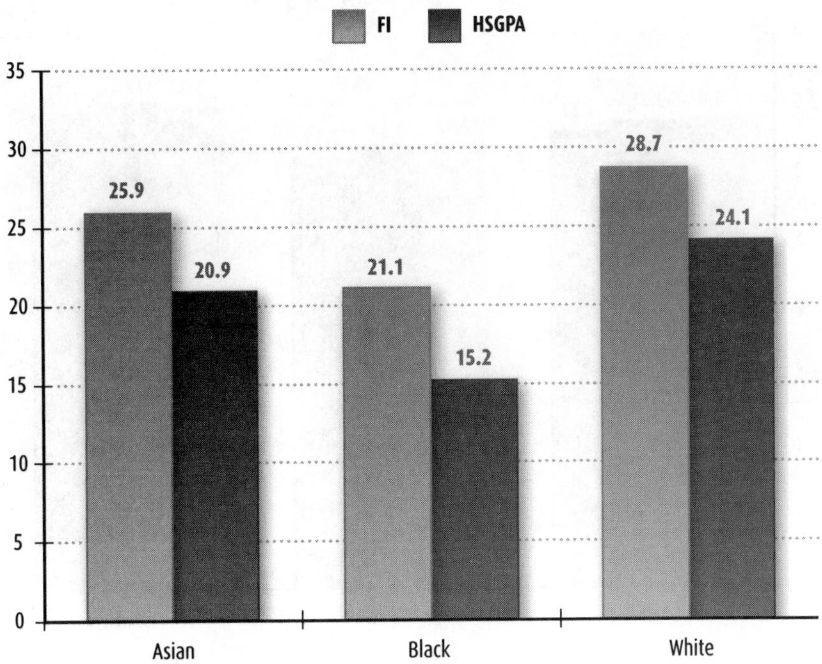


FIGURE 30.1

Amount of Variation in CGPA Explained (All Graduates)

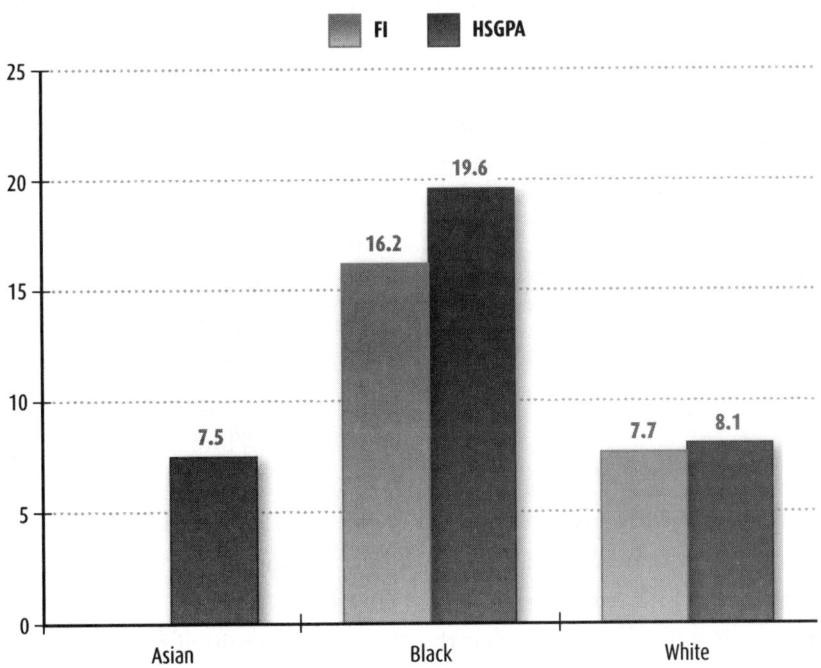


FIGURE 30.2

Amount of Variation in CGPA Explained ("Strong" Graduates)

FIGURE 30.3

Mean CGPAs of "Strong" Graduates

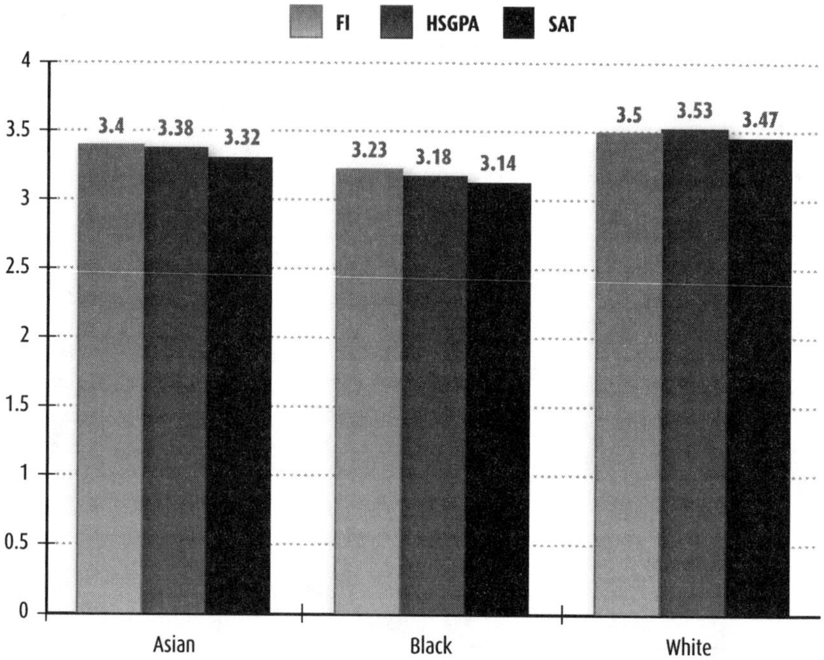


Kruskal-Wallis tests were administered to determine whether there are significant differences between the CGPAs of strong students. No significant differences were found between the three admissions criteria for Asian graduates ($H(2) = 3.076$, $p > 0.05$) and Black graduates ($H(2) = 3.025$, $p > 0.05$). However, a significant difference was found between the three admission criteria for White graduates ($H(2) = 7.926$, $p < 0.05$). To further examine this significant difference, Mann-Whitney U tests were administered for the three potential pairings of the three admissions criteria. (*See* Table 30.5.)

TABLE 30.5: **Mann-Whitney U Results**

| Pairing | Mann-Whitney U Value[1] |
|---|---|
| FI and HSGPA | 18584 |
| FI and SAT | 14368 |
| HSGPA and SAT | 19707 |

[1] $p > 0.05$

Only the pairing between FI and SAT was significant, indicating that the CGPAs of White graduates with SATs at the 75th percentile were significantly lower than those with FIs at the 75th percentile. More important, no significant differences exist between the CGPAs of White graduates with strong FIs and HSGPAs.

The fact that no statistical difference exists between the CGPAs of graduates with strong HSGPAs and FIs is an indication that the FI cannot statistically distinguish itself from the HSGPA for graduates with strong scores in each criterion.

Ultimately, it is difficult to argue that the FI distinguishes itself from the HSGPA as an admission mechanism for the six-year graduates included in this study. Six outcomes are relevant to this claim:

- HSGPA explains nearly as much variation as does FI;
- The slopes of regression equations including HSGPA are much greater than those including FI;
- For graduates with strong HSGPAs and FIs, HSGPA explains more variation in CGPA;
- Comparing graduates with strong HSGPAs and FIs to all graduates, the slopes of regression equations including HSGPA evidence an increase in value while those including FI do not;
- HSGPA maintains a significant relationship with CGPA across race in both regressions while FI does not; and
- The CGPAs of graduates with strong HSGPAs and FIs are not statistically different.

## Limitations of Research

The results of the research reported above should be considered in conjunction with some limitations. While the six-year graduation rate is increasingly important to four-year university "profiles," limiting this analysis to those students who met this mark yields results that may not be consistent with a larger sample. In addition, while HSGPA provides a common point of reference for this analysis, no data regarding the difficulty of the graduates' curriculum were available. Therefore, HSGPA likely represents a wide range of courses and curricula. Finally, most of the students included in this research graduated from Georgia high schools, so that the results reported here may not be representative of national trends.

## Conclusion

The FI is a combination of SAT score and HSGPA. When considered alone, the SAT is clearly the weakest of the three admissions criteria included in this analysis. Consistent with the claims of the College Board, FI explains more variation in CGPA than either HSGPA or SAT alone—even when the analysis is extended beyond the first year to graduating GPA. This is consistent across each of the racial groups included in this analysis. However, the fact that the FI explains, on average, less than 6 percent more variation in CGPA than does HSGPA for all graduates challenges the exclusive utility of the FI in GSU admissions. Furthermore, the strength of HSGPA as a predictor increases when analysis is limited to "strong" graduates while the predictive value of FI decreases. What is the threshold for determining whether an admission mechanism is or is not appropriate? The results of this research suggest that caution is warranted in the continued use of the FI—especially for Black students and, in particular, for Black students with "strong" HSGPAs. Identifying and providing a reasonable justification for a particular threshold for including the SAT in admissions decisions at GSU is beyond the scope of this research. However, it would appear that FI should explain considerably more variation in CGPA than HSGPA alone in order to justify its use. Exactly what this amount should be is a question that must be critically examined in further scholarship and critically considered by admissions officers.

/ CHAPTER THIRTY-ONE /

*by Trevor Packer, M.A.*
*Vice President, Advanced Placement Program*
*The College Board*

31

# Advanced Placement Program: Its Influence on Academics and Admissions Decisionmaking

In the mid-1950s, a number of *New York Times* articles reported a brand new opportunity in American education: "Even though they have never spent a day on any college campus," a "small number of selected students" were earning "advance [sic] credit for courses that they have taken in high school" (Fine 1956, p. E9). The initial journalistic coverage was fascinated with the possibility, wondering whether any high school students were actually "capable of doing college work while still attending their secondary schools" and then reporting that "the answer appears to be 'yes'" (p. E9). The reason for this "unorthodox program" was distilled as follows:

> *Each examination was comparable to those now given in most colleges to students who have completed one of these twelve courses. And the assumption is clear: If a high-school student can pass an examination in English literature, for example, which a college freshman or sophomore takes, then the student knows the subject.*
>
> *He might profit more educationally by taking other courses, or more difficult and challenging subjects* (Fine 1956).
>
> *The program attempts 1) to avoid the repetition of work already covered in secondary schools; 2) to give students the opportunity for more advanced, freer, and more demanding*

*work, and 3) in some cases, to permit them to earn a degree in less than the usually required four years' time* (n.a. 1957).

Fifty years after the first awarding of college credit via Advanced Placement (AP) exams in 1956, 406,000 or 14.8 percent of the 2.7 million students who graduated from U.S. public schools in 2006 earned an AP exam grade of 3 or higher on one or more AP exams they took while in high school (College Board 2007).

## Origins of the AP Program

What led to the establishment of the Advanced Placement Program in 1955? In the early 1950s, a number of groups across American education rallied around the need for colleges and high schools to work together to promote the best possible use of the last two years of high school and the first two years of college. Three elite prep schools (Andover, Exeter, and Lawrenceville) and three higher education institutions (Harvard, Princeton, and Yale) met at Andover in May 1951, and published through Harvard University Press a final report of their work, entitled *General Education in School and College*, which called for schools and colleges to see themselves as "two halves of a common enterprise."

This eagerness of colleges and high schools to partner in improving the educational experience of students at the advanced high school and beginning college levels spurred the development of college-level examinations that universities would find rigorous enough to use as the basis for determining placement and granting credit in eleven subject areas.

A project to create such examinations was undertaken by representatives of twelve colleges (Bowdoin, Brown, Carleton, Haverford, Kenyon, MIT, Middlebury, Oberlin, Swarthmore, Wabash, Wesleyan, and Williams) and twelve secondary schools. These advocates of this new credit-by-examination program asked the College Board, a not-for-profit membership organization founded in 1900 and composed of thousands of U.S. colleges, universities, and secondary schools, to assume management of this program, using exam fees to fund ongoing development, printing, shipping, and scoring of the exams.

This groundswell of collaboration between colleges and high schools produced the first set of AP courses and exams, which were offered during the 1955–56 academic year in 104 high schools to 1,229 students who then received college credit and advanced placement at 130 colleges and universities in the fall of 1956.

More than fifty years later, the Advanced Placement Program annually provides more than 1.4 million motivated students, primarily in grades eleven and twelve, the opportunity to take more rigorous courses than would traditionally be offered in high school. By being able to experience the intensity of a college course in the familiar environment of their high schools, students can hone their preparation for the full slate of college courses they will experience as freshmen.

How can a program that was deemed highly unusual, even "unorthodox," fifty years ago become in just five decades a national standard for high school rigor and college readiness?

While it is possible to explain some of AP's expansion by looking at the passion and commitment of the AP teacher community, or the influence of federal and state funding,[197] recent research (described later in this chapter) identifies an even more powerful influence: a mutually reinforcing effort by colleges and high schools to increase the quality and rigor of the high school curriculum. What began as an attempt among just three high schools and three colleges in 1951 for joint effort between higher and secondary education to advance the quality of student learning has evolved into a unique partnership in which thousands of colleges, universities, and high schools see themselves as "two halves of a common enterprise."

The rest of this chapter will address the overall question: How can the admissions process make best use of Advanced Placement courses and exams?

Along the way, however, we will first briefly summarize how AP courses and exams are created, and what AP exam scores are intended to represent. Then we will address the question: What kinds of success do AP courses and exams predict? Next, we will discuss how AP exams are being used in placement and credit decisions.

Finally, the chapter will culminate by addressing not only the usefulness of Advanced Placement courses and exams in college admissions, but also some limits and caveats as to their use.

## How Courses and Exams Are Created

The role the College Board plays in its management of AP is to bring together representatives from higher and secondary education to determine the standards that should be required of high school students in order for them to be deemed worthy of receiving credit, placement, or other recognition based on their performance in the AP Program.

Accordingly, the College Board convenes committees of college faculty and experienced high school AP teachers to review the current state of the introductory college curricula in the various subject areas tested by AP: biology, calculus, English, physics, and so on. These panelists, nominated by disciplinary associations and professional organizations such as the National Science Foundation (NSF), the Organization of American Historians (OAH), the American Association of Physics Teachers (AAPT), and other disciplinary groups, review hundreds of syllabi and exams from colleges and universities nationwide, and identify by consensus the elements represented in high quality introductory college courses. Using this curricular research, the committee identifies the skills and knowledge that must be measured on an AP exam to ensure that the high school AP student has developed the same level of mastery as students who take the course in college. In essence, this research enables the committees to produce:

[197] Although there is no cost, either to the student or the high school, to take or offer an AP course, there is a charge ($84.00 in 2008) to take the optional, end-of-course AP exam, of which $8.00 is retained by the school to pay proctors or cover other expenses related to the AP exam administration. Currently 74 percent of students enrolled in AP courses opted to take the AP exam, a percentage that increases by 1 to 2 percent each year. A combination of College Board fee reductions and federal/state funding eliminates the exam fee in most states for students from low-income families (College Board 2008a).

- A "Course Description" booklet that provides participating high schools with an overview of the knowledge, skills, and abilities that must be developed among students in AP courses in order for those courses to be true parallels to the introductory college course; and
- Exam specifications that provide schools with an understanding of both the breadth and the depth at which the student will be assessed.

Each AP exam question is written by one or more college professors, and then is reviewed by an entire committee of professors in that field. The exam questions are pre-tested at colleges and universities to ensure appropriateness and fairness, and each AP exam question also undergoes a rigorous analysis (differential item function) to ensure that it does not contain any bias in favor of a particular subgroup of students (ethnicity, gender, geographical region).

Each AP exam, with one exception, contains two sections: a multiple-choice section that contains embedded, re-used questions that allow psychometricians to compare quality of student achievement from year to year, and then a free-response section that consists of some combination of essay questions, document analysis, problems to solve, experiments, translations, speech recordings (for the world languages exams), and sight-singing recordings (for AP Music Theory). The exam that is an exception to this two-section format is AP Studio Art, which instead consists of a structured portfolio.

Following the AP exam administration, which takes place each May on set dates and times at 16,000 schools worldwide, the free-response booklets are shipped to college campuses and convention centers throughout the United States, where more than 10,000 college professors and AP teachers gather for the AP Reading each June. The AP Reading is yet another opportunity provided within the AP Program for colleges and high schools to partner as two halves of a common rigorous enterprise. All too rarely does American education provide opportunities for high school and college educators to work side by side to ensure rigor and quality and readiness for college, but both groups of educators who attend the AP Reading come away freshly committed to the improvements they are helping to make. Statements such as the following from professors who attend the AP Reading (97 percent of whom report that it was a rewarding experience) convey well the power of this model in American education:

> *As soon as I became involved as an AP English Language reader in 1992, I realized that the AP Reading was the very best professional development activity I engaged in every year. To have the opportunity to sit at a table with seven or eight other readers—three or four excellent high school teachers and three or four excellent university faculty members—and to read, discuss, and evaluate student work together for a week—what a marvelous opportunity to learn about ways of promoting excellence in our profession. In my first years as a reader, I directed the first-year writing program at two large universities, one public and one private, in Chicago. I can't overstate how valuable the reading was to helping me in these positions that focus specifically on the students' high school-to-college transition* (Jolliffe 2007).

## AP Exam Scores Explained

By the time the AP Reading ends each June, millions of AP exams have each received a raw score reflecting the number of points the student earned on the AP exam. But, to be meaningful to colleges and universities, this raw score must be converted to a five-point scale representing equivalence to college grades. The five-point scale is designed to provide the following information for colleges and universities:

- 5: The student has earned at least the same number of points on the AP exam as actual college students whose professors assigned them an A grade.
- 4: The student has earned the same number of points on the AP exam as actual college students whose professors assigned them an A-, B+, or B grade.
- 3: The student has earned the same number of points on the AP exam as actual college students whose professors assigned them a B-, C+, or C grade.
- 2: The student has earned the same number of points on the AP exam as actual college students whose professors assigned them a C-, D+, or D grade.
- 1: The student earned fewer points on the AP exam than actual college students whose professors assigned them a D.

In other words, the number of points AP students are required to earn in order to receive an AP exam grade of 5, 4, 3, 2, or 1 is determined by identifying the equivalent knowledge and skills which college professors would require their own students to demonstrate, at the end of the introductory college course, and then asking the college professors to identify how many points on the AP exam they would require of their own students to confirm that they had developed such knowledge and skills.

To determine these standards, the AP Program works with colleges and universities nationwide to administer the AP exam to college students at the completion of the introductory college course, and each year dozens of prominent higher education institutions participate in this exercise to help ensure that AP's standards reflect the standards of participating colleges and universities. *See* Table 31.1 for examples of the colleges and universities that administered AP exams to their college students in spring 2007.

TABLE 31.1: **Examples of Colleges and Universities that Helped Establish The AP Scoring Standards in 2007 by Administering and Scoring the AP Exam Among Their Own College Students**

| | |
|---|---|
| ▸ Baylor University | ▸ UCLA |
| ▸ Brigham Young University | ▸ UC-Berkeley |
| ▸ Duke University | ▸ University of Colorado-Boulder |
| ▸ Grinnell College | ▸ University of Maryland-College Park |
| ▸ Harvard University | ▸ UNC-Chapel Hill |
| ▸ Michigan State University | ▸ University of Pennsylvania |
| ▸ Middlebury College | ▸ University of Southern California |
| ▸ Princeton University | ▸ University of Virginia |
| ▸ Purdue University | ▸ University of Washington |
| ▸ Smith College | ▸ University of Wisconsin-Madison |
| ▸ Stanford University | ▸ Washington University |
| ▸ Tufts University | ▸ Yale University |

# College Successes Predicted by AP

### Performance in Upper-Level College Courses

AP students exempted from introductory college courses, including mathematics and science courses, earned higher course grades than students who took the introductory course on the college campus (Morgan and Ramist 1998; Dodd *et al.* 2002).

### Likelihood of Deeper College Studies in a Discipline

Students who took AP exams were more likely to take at least one additional course in the discipline of their AP exam while in college, compared to their peers who did not take AP exams in those disciplines (Morgan and Mancekshana 2000).

### College Graduation

Students who earned a 3 or higher on one or more AP exams in the areas of English, mathematics, science or social studies were more likely to graduate from college in five years or less compared to non-AP students (Dougherty, Mellor, and Jiana 2006).

### College Grades in Math and Science

AP exam grades were a strong predictor of second-year undergraduate GPA in biological sciences, mathematics, and physical sciences, second in strength only to high school grade point average (Geiser and Santelices 2004).

# Placement and Credit Considerations

Currently more than 90 percent of four-year colleges and universities in the United States use AP exam grades to make placement and/or credit decisions. While the traditional AP score required for credit or placement is a 3, there are a number of issues that higher education institutions should consider before determining the most appropriate AP score for awarding credit or placement.

The most important consideration among universities seems to be an analysis of how well AP students at each of the AP score points will do when allowed to skip the introductory college course and move directly into the sequent college course. The American Council on Education, which regularly reviews the AP exams and makes recommendations to colleges regarding credit-by-examination programs, recommends that college credit and/or placement be provided for AP exam scores of 3 or higher, and recurring studies over the past three decades have confirmed the validity of AP exam scores in predicting student readiness for placement, each finding generally that students who score 3 or higher on the AP exam and then place directly into the subsequent college course do better in that subsequent course than those students who took the introductory college course first.[198]

---

[198] See, for example: Burnham and Hewitt (1971); Morgan and Crone (1993); Morgan and Ramist (1998); and Dodd *et al.* (2002).

As Maureen Ewing (2006), who has conducted the most comprehensive review of AP research studies to date, has stated, "It is important to note that these studies were not attempts to demonstrate that the experience of taking the AP course itself caused or impacted a student's college success, but instead, these studies were designed to investigate whether AP Examination grades were valid indicators of a student's readiness for placement into a course beyond the introductory college course" (Ewing 2006, p. 2).

Randall (2007) reported that, in 2007, several more sophisticated studies were released by the University of Texas at Austin in the "most comprehensive, data-rich examination of AP in the past decade, ...the largest-ever study of the effects of AP on college success." Jointly conducted by the Texas Higher Education Coordinating Board and the College of Education at the University of Texas at Austin, this study examined 222,289 students at several Texas universities, finding that "students who successfully participated in one or more AP tests and courses 'significantly outperformed' their non-AP peers. These comparisons were made among peers with similar levels of academic ability and family economic status. Students who took one or more AP tests and courses had higher college GPAs, earned more credit hours and were likely to graduate in four years or fewer." Lead researcher Linda Hargrove summarizes the findings as follows: "The findings indicate that even if an AP student who took the course and exam scores two out of a possible five points on an AP test—and most universities require at least a score of three—they still tend to do better in college than students who don't take AP courses or who skip the AP exam" (Randall 2007).

In addition, other University of Texas researchers undertook a parallel study which compared AP students who qualified for college credit to non-AP students with the same SAT/ACT score and same high school class rank. That study found a statistically significant difference between the higher GPA the AP students achieved in subsequent college courses and the lower GPA of the matched, non-AP students who took the introductory college course without benefit of an AP course in the subject (Keng and Dodd [in press]). *See* Figure 31.1, on page 421, for a summary of these findings.

While no research findings call into question the general appropriateness of granting credit or placement for an AP exam grade of 3 or better, it is important to recognize that other factors play into the determination of an appropriate AP credit policy at each higher education institution. The College Board does not advocate a "one size fits all" approach to determination of AP credit policies, and has declined to support state legislative initiatives that have argued for a blanket AP and IB policy across public higher education institutions in the state, believing instead that each higher education institution should set an AP policy that jointly

- serves its own institutional needs; and
- fosters a higher level of preparation for college by providing incentives (credit, placement, or admissions benefits) that encourage high school administrators, teachers, and students to create or participate in a more rigorous high school course of study.

While only 13 percent of four-year colleges and universities have raised the minimum AP score required to receive placement/credit, a slightly greater percentage of colleges and universities have imposed other types of restrictions on AP credit/placement that might better serve their institutional needs (CRUX 2007).

For example, some highly selective colleges and universities are now receiving applicants who present an average of five or six AP exam grades, and so a number of different AP policies have been introduced at such institutions to ensure that students are not using their AP grades in ways that would prevent them from having the richest possible undergraduate experience. Some of these institutions cap the total number of AP credits that will be provided by the institution. Other institutions award the student placement, but not credit, thus ensuring that the student will stay for the full four years, while yet other institutions have the opposite policy: credit will be granted, enabling students to fulfill elective or graduation requirements, but placement is not granted, so the student must take the introductory college course. A summary of the percentage of four-year colleges and universities that have adopted these types of AP credit/placement restrictions appears in Table 31.2 (CRUX 2007).

TABLE 31.2: **Restrictions on AP Credit/Placement at Four-Year Colleges and Universities**

| Does your institution/department... | % |
|---|---|
| Cap the total number of AP credits a student can apply at your institution | 28 |
| Not allow students to use AP to satisfy requirements in their major | 15 |
| Allow students to use AP credits for placement, but not to reduce their course load in college | 16 |
| Require a student to take at least one course in a department in order to use AP credit | 8 |

These recent changes in the AP credit policies of institutions do not appear to be driven by concerns in higher education about losing revenue by granting AP credit—virtually no admissions officers report this being a concern in a 2007 survey of admissions officers. However, some of the changes in AP policies may be driven by a common myth about AP credit: that providing a student with AP credit will deplete the pool of students choosing to take courses within that academic department or subject area. Instead, studies consistently show the opposite result: that students who qualify for AP credit are taking many more additional courses in that academic department than students who did not qualify for AP credit. (*See* Figure 31.2, on page 421, for an overview of the difference.)

Finally, 14 percent of admissions officers at four-year colleges and universities report that they would like to make their AP credit policies more generous, ostensibly as a means of encouraging and recruiting highly qualified applicants (CRUX 2007).

## The Effect of AP Exams on Admissions

While credit and placement benefits certainly motivate high school students to challenge themselves in AP courses, the messages students are hearing from chief enrollment officers and admissions offices are even more powerful influencers of the coursework these high school students are choosing to take: 83 percent of high school seniors in a recent study indicated that they took AP courses to improve their chances of getting into college, while

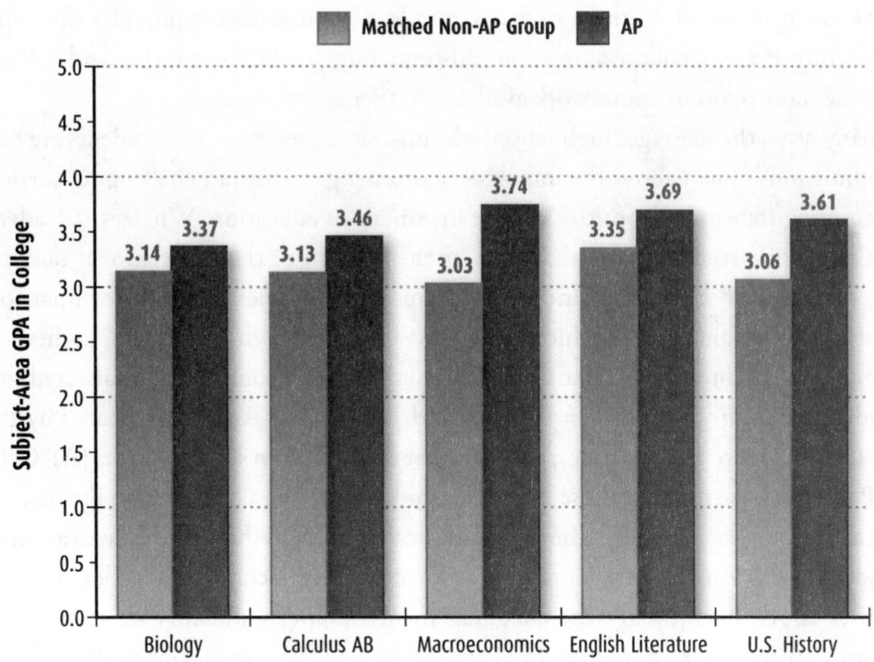


FIGURE 31.1

Subject-Area GPA in Subsequent College Courses: AP and Non-AP Students

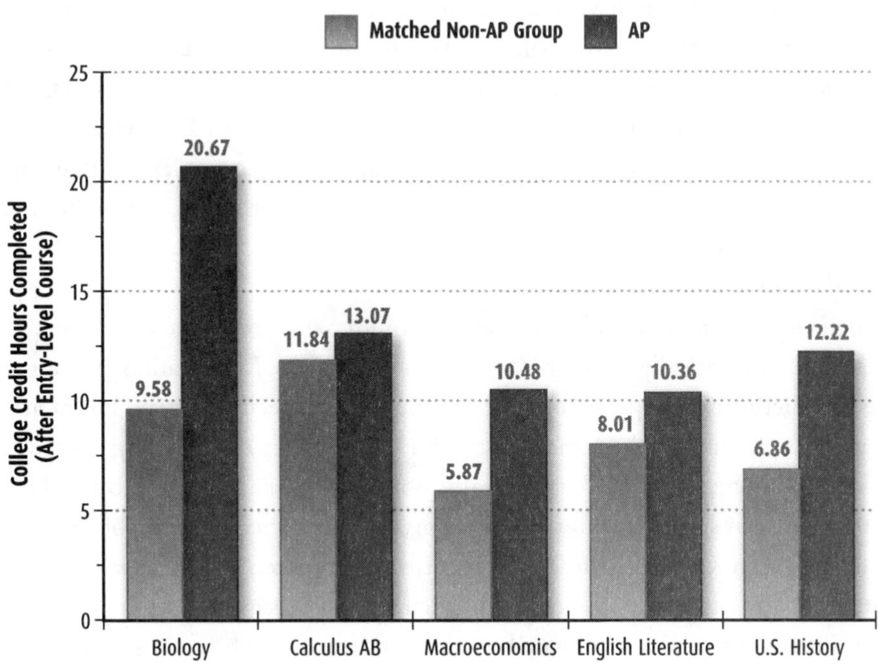


FIGURE 31.2

College Course Work Completed in a Subject Area beyond the Introductory College Course

Keng and Dodd (in press)

just over two-thirds reported that their decision was based on the desire to receive placement benefits (Morgan 2002). In these students' minds, AP course-taking provides the opportunity to demonstrate to college admissions officers a high level of motivation and willingness to take the most rigorous coursework available to them.

In many ways, the messages high school administrators, teachers, and students are hearing from admissions offices about the importance of taking a rigorous, challenging curriculum are promoting tremendous positive change in American education. Whereas U.S. advanced math and physics students ranked at or near the bottom of the international rankings in recent TIMSS (Trends in International Mathematics and Science Study) comparisons of international math and science achievement, U.S. AP students who scored 3 or higher were at the very top of the international rankings. In this study, many countries administered to their most advanced high school students a math and/or a physics assessment created by TIMSS. Figure 31.3 and Figure 31.4 (on page 423) show that the American students taking AP Calculus and AP Physics—particularly those American students scoring 3 or higher on the AP exam—earned a much higher average on these TIMSS assessments than the rest of American students (who jockey with Austrian students for the lowest average scores) (Gonzalez, O'Connor, and Miles 2001). Accordingly, the encouragement American students are receiving from admissions offices to take more rigorous courses like AP is heartening, given the wide difference the TIMSS study found between AP students' and other American students' math and science knowledge, skills, and abilities.

Simple correlation studies have long shown that AP students have much higher four-year bachelor's degree attainment rates than non-AP students, but a recent spate of studies from the National Center for Educational Accountability (NCEA) and the University of California at Berkeley have moved beyond simple correlations (Camara 2003). They have shown much higher graduation rates among students who take and do well on AP exams than among a control group of students with similar college admissions test scores, high school grades, socioeconomic backgrounds, and other such matches (Dougherty, Mellor, and Jiana 2006; Geiser and Santelices 2004).

The Berkeley researchers, Saul Geiser and Veronica Santelices, conclude by stating that their research "emphatically supports the conclusion that AP Examinations are among the very best predictors of college performance.... The subject-specific, curriculum-intensive AP exams are the epitome of 'achievement tests,' and their validity in predicting college performance should not be surprising." Importantly, however, Geiser and Santelices make a clear distinction between students who take AP exams, and an aggregate group of students who claim to have taken AP *courses* without necessarily having taken an AP *exam*—and this distinction points to a possible problem with placing official weight on AP in an admissions decision. Because the caution provided by the Berkeley research is so important, we will return to it briefly at the close of this chapter.

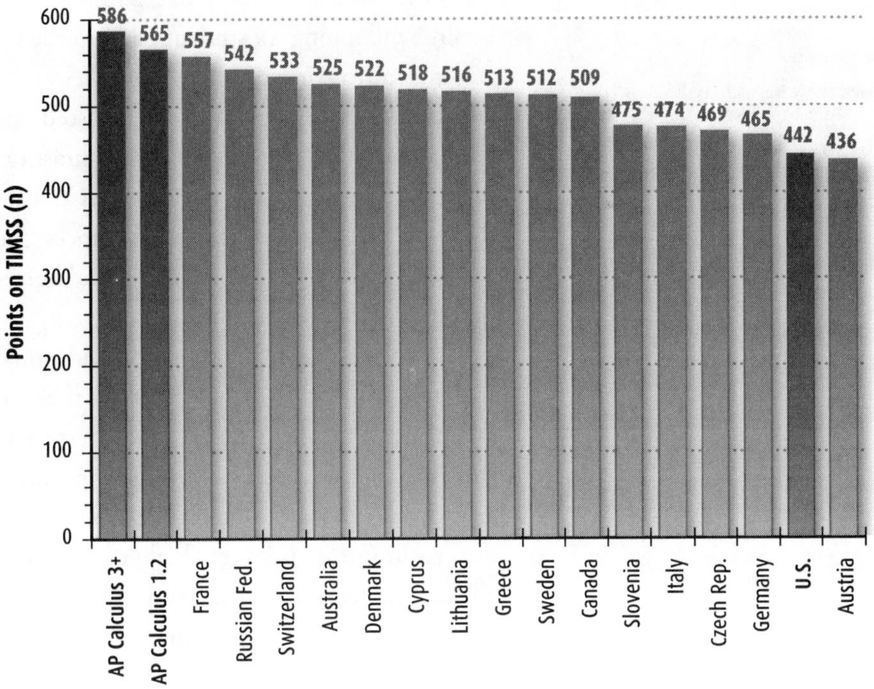


FIGURE 31.3

International Comparison of High School Achievement in Mathematics
TIMMS (2001)

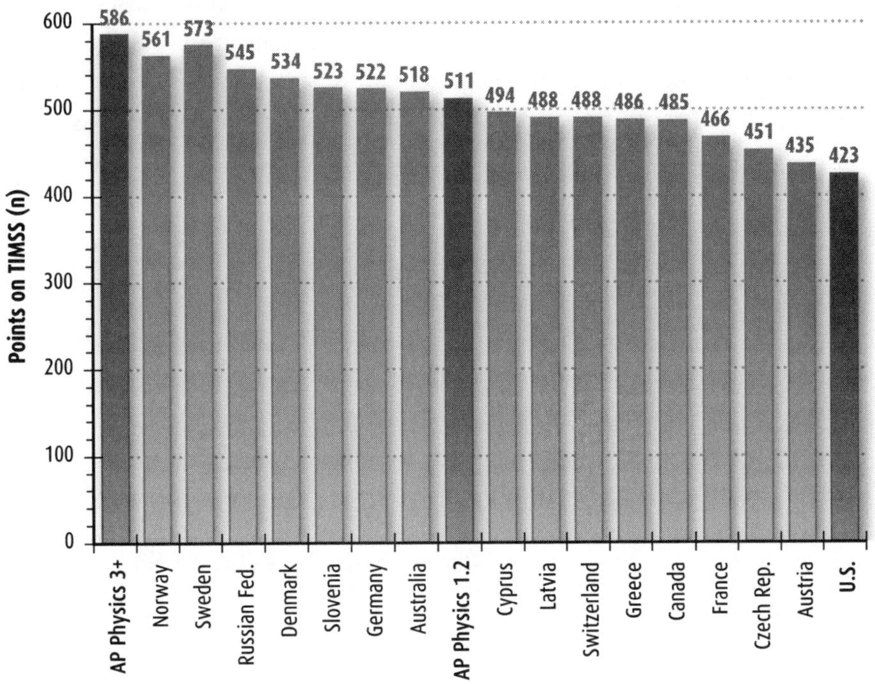


FIGURE 31.4

International Comparison of High School Achievement in Physics

**TABLE 31.3: Uses of AP by Admissions Offices**

| Uses of AP to Support Admissions Decisions | % |
|---|---|
| Determining how prepared a student is for the rigor of college academics | 83 |
| An indicator of a student's motivation/willingness to challenge him/herself | 83 |
| Placing students in appropriate courses | 74 |
| Evaluating candidates from a range of high schools | 58 |
| Secondary criterion for admissions | 37 |
| Secondary criterion for awarding scholarships | 31 |
| Sorting applicants into evaluation groupings | 27 |
| Guarding against grade inflation | 20 |
| Making loan decisions | 2 |

**TABLE 31.4: Use of AP in Admissions Decisions, Change Expected in Five Years**

| Change in Use | % |
|---|---|
| No Change | 58 |
| More than Now[1] | 41 |
| Less than Now | 2 |

[1] The result is higher among *selective* institutions (47%)

Admissions officers have long recognized the higher motivation levels and likelihood of degree attainment among AP students, and in the College Board's 2007 review of admissions offices' use of AP, enrollment officers nationwide attested to their consideration of AP coursework in admissions and related decisions. Table 31.3 summarizes the most frequent uses of AP by admissions offices, showing the percentage of four-year colleges and universities that use AP for specific purposes.

The charts that follow provide additional perspectives from admissions offices on their current and planned future uses of AP, and attest to the fact that higher education's call for rigor in the secondary school curriculum has created a highly symbiotic relationship between higher and secondary education, centered on AP and other challenging courses. (*See* Figure 31.5, Figure 31.6 [on page 425], and Table 31.4 [on this page].)

Higher education sends messages to teachers, administrators, counselors, and students about the importance of providing and taking the most challenging courses available; and powerful credit, placement, and admissions incentives reinforce this message. In turn, secondary schools send their teachers to colleges and universities each summer to receive training as AP teachers, build vertically-aligned curricula that increase the rigor across grade levels, and sequentially prepare a greater array and diversity of students for AP courses and subsequent college coursework.

The result is that a greater percentage of U.S. high school graduates than ever before, and many more minority and low-income students than a decade ago, are earning an AP exam grade of 3 or higher before leaving high school.[199]

[199] There has been increased diversity in AP classrooms, especially for Latino students. The good news is that the growth in participation in AP courses is much higher among traditionally under-represented minorities than among white and Asian students: from 2002 to 2006, the compound annual growth rate among African American students was 15.03 percent, and among Latino students was 13.88 percent, as compared to 9.79 percent among Asian students and 7.63 percent among white students. However, African American and American Indian/Alaska Native students remain significantly underrepresented in AP classrooms. In public schools nationwide, African American students make up 13.7 percent of the student population, but only 6.9 percent of AP exam takers, and American Indian/Alaska Native make up 1.1 percent of the student population but only 9.6 percent of the AP examinee population. Latino students are well represented in AP classrooms nationally in public schools—they represent 14 percent of the student population and 14 percent of AP examinees. "However, Latino students remain underrepresented in AP programs in many states" (College Board 2007).

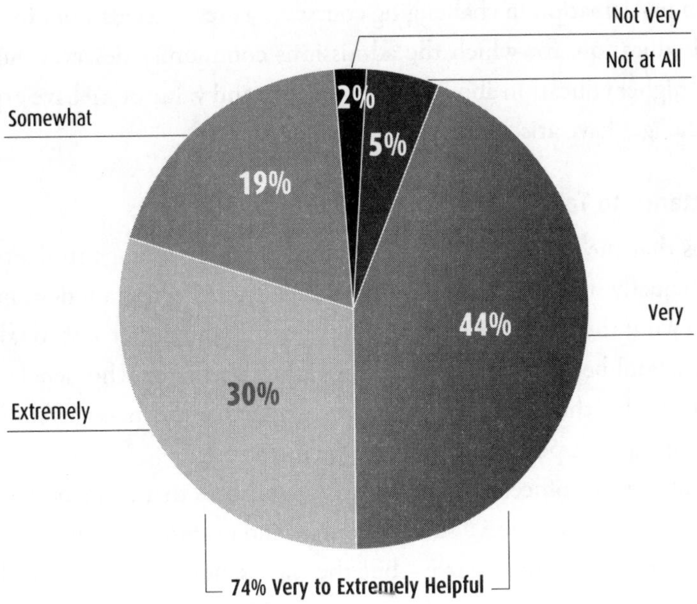


FIGURE 31.5

Helpfulness of AP Course Experience in Evaluating Candidates for Admission

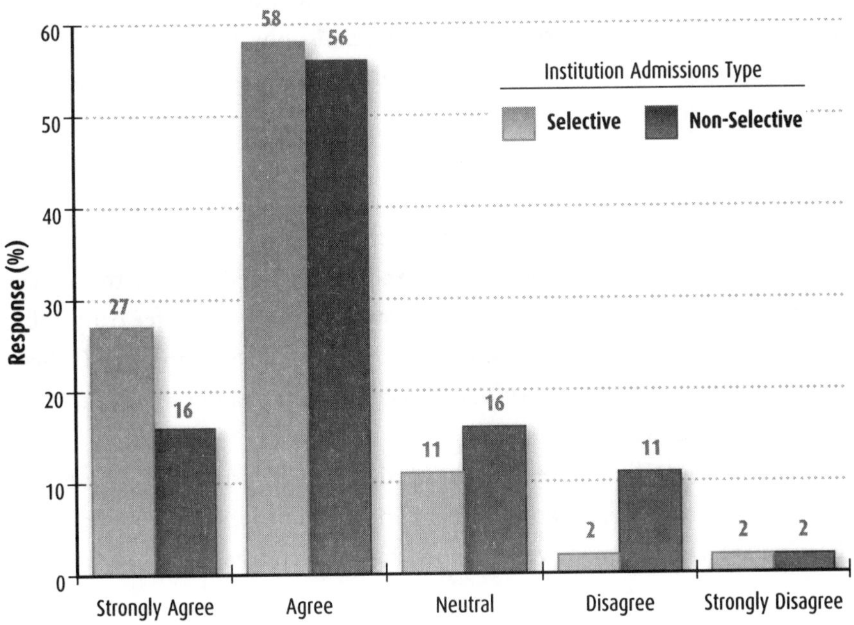


FIGURE 31.6

AP Course Experience Favorably Impacts Admissions Decisions

## AP Exams: Issues and Challenges

This increase in participation in challenging courses is a great success story in American secondary school education, for which the admissions community deserves much credit. As messages from higher education about the importance and value of AP have expanded, however, some challenges have arisen that should also be noted.

### Student Reluctance to Take Courses in Non AP-Tested Subjects

One concern is that the value ascribed to AP courses can discourage students from taking other, perhaps equally stimulating, courses for which the AP Program does not provide an offering. When we at the College Board hear of students who decide not to take a sociology course in high school because there's no AP Sociology exam, or who decide not to take a course in dance because there is no AP Dance, we worry that the messages students are hearing about the value and importance of AP may be too strong.

Concerned admissions officers state repeatedly to schools that if the high school offers a great course that falls outside the AP suite of courses and exams, the admissions office is very willing to consider it a rigorous course—but the high school does then need to make the effort to inform the admissions office about that course.

This seems to be a reasonable response from the admissions community, one that fairly places the burden of proof on the secondary school if it wants to make the case without an externally-scored assessment like the AP exam that it is nonetheless offering a college-level course of its own devising. But this is also a reminder of why it is probably best that colleges and universities resist formalizing the use of AP in admissions decisions, instead continuing to use AP and other rigorous courses as an informal yet meaningful consideration within the holistic admissions decision.

### AP Course Audit Requirement[200]

Another challenge that has arisen is that some schools have recognized the value that AP courses have in the eyes of admissions offices and have rushed to seek to implement AP courses without having invested the time or effort to develop and offer truly college-level courses. In 2004, representatives from admissions offices requested that the College Board restrict the use of the trademarked "AP" label to courses that had been *validated* by college and university faculty as AP.

This "AP Course Audit," the largest review of high school curricula ever undertaken on a national or international level, began in January 2007, and by June 2007 more than 120,000 AP teachers' syllabi had been reviewed by more than 800 college professors, a truly stagger-

[200] High schools will still develop their own curricula, but the College Board will evaluate the courses to make sure they meet AP standards (*e.g.*, science courses must have a laboratory component)

ing operational and educational collaboration between secondary and higher education.[201] In this audit, 71 percent of the courses submitted to college professors were deemed equivalent or superior to the introductory college course and accordingly, these courses received legal authorization to be labeled "AP." The remaining 29 percent of courses submitted will undergo further work with college professors and providers of teacher professional development until such time as they also qualify to be labeled "AP."

The result of the AP Course Audit is that, beginning with the 2007–08 academic year, no school will be authorized to label a course "AP" without having succeeded in the audit and received legal authorization to present the course as "AP" on students' high school transcripts. The results of the audit are made available to the public, and the College Board is currently working with several large state university systems to provide tailored, state-specific reports that will enable these states to make use of the data to understand the array of AP opportunities provided by each specific school.

### Presentation of an AP Course Without an AP Exam

It appears that the AP Course Audit will help address the concerns raised by the Berkeley researchers Geiser and Santelices, who noted that students who took AP exams were much more likely to succeed in college than matched students who did not take AP exams. In addition, Geiser and Santelices also found that simply having "AP" or "honors" listed on a high school transcript "has little, if any, validity with respect to the prediction of college outcomes" if an AP exam grade is not attached.

Some institutions have considered formal AP policies that would include AP, in a specific and defined way, within the admissions decision, particularly through assigning AP course grades a higher weight in the calculation of high school students' GPAs, based merely on the taking of an AP course. One set of researchers supports this practice. A study by Philip M. Sadler and Robert H. Tai (2007) favors adding bonus points for AP and honors courses taken in high school. They add:

> *Those students taking these more advanced courses perform better in their college science courses. There is a large difference between AP and honors in their predicted impact on college grades, with honors courses valued at about half the level of AP courses. Thus, we find no support for these courses to be valued equally. We find strong support for high schools to calculate weighted grade point average and assign RIC (rank in class) and honors based on these measures.*

However, there are factors which weigh against this conclusion. Specifically, it must be noted that the Sadler and Tai research was based upon a *very small sample size* and also relied

[201] It is useful to emphasize here that the AP Course Audit is a curriculum certification process, *not* a teacher certification process. The College Board does not mandate any one set of educational or professional background requirements as to who can serve as an AP teacher. The AP Program recognizes that there are many paths to becoming an effective AP teacher (College Board 2008b).

upon students' *self-reported* AP scores rather than official AP exam grades—a methodology that has been proven to be highly problematic in the past. So we are reluctant to encourage secondary or higher education to weight AP grades solely upon the basis of the Sadler and Tai findings.

In summary, there appears to be consensus across research studies that students who have not just taken AP courses, but who have persisted and taken the end-of-course AP exam, have experienced a quality of educational experience that is predictive of greater college success than will be attained, on average, by students with comparable SAT/ACT scores and high school grades but who did not take an AP course *and* exam.

But much less can be said with confidence about students who merely take AP courses without an accompanying exam result. The AP Course Audit will promote greater consistency in quality across courses labeled "AP," but until research findings consistently demonstrate that simply taking an AP course, regardless of exam performance, positively impacts college success, we encourage admissions offices to continue what seems to be the current and common practice regarding AP and college admissions: encouraging high school students to take the most challenging courses available to them, but not specifying or mandating within admissions criteria specific quantities or types of AP, IB, or dual enrollment experiences.

## Conclusion

Admissions officers are proving able to affect secondary school preparation of students in very positive ways by continuing to regard the presence of an AP course, with exam, as an indicator of students' willingness to challenge themselves by participating in a rigorous course of study. Indeed, both secondary and higher education benefit greatly from advocating rigorous coursework, without transforming such advocacy into formal admissions policy or requirements.

/ CHAPTER THIRTY-TWO /

*by Sandra Wade Pauly, M.A.*
*University & Government Liaison*
*IB North America*

32

# The International Baccalaureate:
## Part I—A Program Primer

"Over the past 30 years, the International Baccalaureate (IB) Diploma programme has quietly matured into one of the most widely available, and arguably one of the best, advanced academic programs available at secondary schools today. It is clearly time for admissions officers and faculties to step back and take a long academic look at the IB as a reliable indicator of promise, perseverance, and social commitment" (Sjogren and Campbell 2003).

The objective of the article quoted above, written as a product of the IB North America College and University Recognition Task Force (CURT),[202] was to examine the potential of the IB Diploma as an instrument to assess an applicant's readiness for a challenging university experience. It reflects the group's conclusion that because of the breadth and depth of the IB Diploma Program, including its "extended essay" Theory of Knowledge and CAS (Creativity, Action, Service) requirements and an assessment by an international board of examiners,[203] the holder of an IB diploma will have demonstrated the academic strength and readiness for a rigorous university experience.

[202] The IB North America College and University Recognition Task Force (CURT) is composed of admissions personnel from leading colleges and universities in the United States and Canada.

[203] See "How students are assessed: principles and practice" (IBO 2006b, pp. 5–6).

The article concludes with the following comment:

*Students comment that their primary reason for choosing an IB program is to better prepare themselves for an academically demanding college or university, and to receive credit or waivers for freshman and sophomore level courses. U.S. and Canadian colleges and universities are increasingly recognizing the academic strength of the IB Diploma and are demonstrating an eagerness to attract those students who are completing this world class diploma program* (Sjogren and Campbell 2003, p. 58).

## IB Overview

### Purpose

The International Baccalaureate was established in 1970 in Geneva, Switzerland to provide a respected high school education credential that would transfer across borders. The IB Diploma Program is aimed at students in the final two years of secondary school (roughly, ages sixteen through nineteen).

The IB also offers newer programs for the Middle Years (established 1992, for ages thirteen through fifteen) and for the Primary Years (established 1997, for ages three through twelve). This chapter, however, will focus exclusively on the high school program.

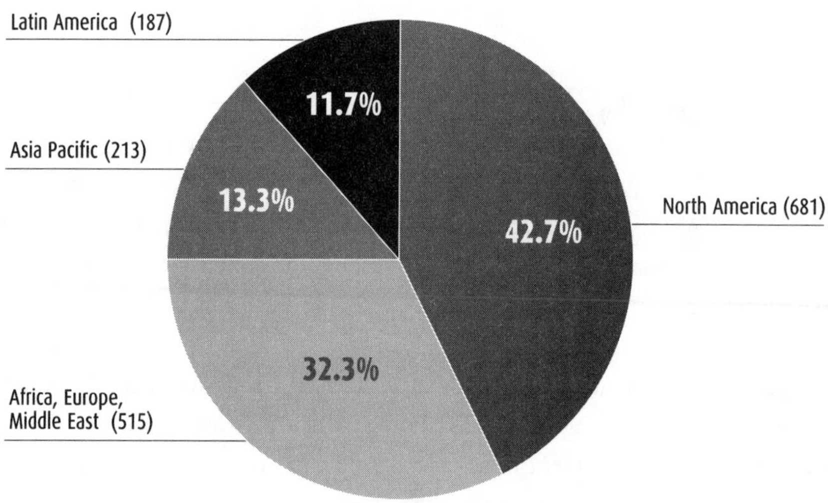


FIGURE 32.1
IB Diploma Program Schools, by Region (July 2007)

### World-Wide Reach

Sjogren and Campbell have commented that "while the IB is still often thought of as a 'foreign' credential, the two largest IB countries are the United States (406 IB schools) and Canada (89 schools) (p. 55). In addition, over 85 percent of the schools offering the IB Diploma in the U.S. and Canada are in the public sector (p. 57). Today there are 119 IB-offering schools in Canada and 555 in the United States, of which 89 percent are in the public sector.

Schools authorized to offer IB programs (as part of or in addition to their regular curricula) currently serve over half a million students in more than 2,000 high schools representing 125 countries around the world.[204]

The IB Diploma program is offered in four regions: North America (which comprises Canada, the Caribbean, and the United States); Asia Pacific; Latin America; and Africa, Europe, and the Middle East).

As can be seen in Figure 32.1 (on page 430), 682 or 42.7 percent of 1,597 IB World schools offering the IB Diploma are in North America. Of those 682, 555 are in the United States, 119 in Canada, and 8 in the Caribbean.

The states and provinces with the largest number of exam entries in the May 2006 examination session are noted in Table 32.1.

## IB Diploma Curriculum

The IB Diploma Program is a rigorous two-year pre-university course of study that leads to examinations. It is for highly motivated secondary school students. Candidates for the IB Diploma are students who take six subjects from different groups that represent the traditional academic disciplines. These groups are reflected in the hexagon below. In addition, they must complete three core elements at the center of the hexagon—the Extended Essay (EE), Theory of Knowledge (TOK), and Creativity, Action, Service (CAS)—that are compulsory and central to the philosophy of the program. The candidate who has successfully completed all requirements of the Diploma Program is awarded the IB Diploma.

Alternatively, a student may opt to take one or more individual subjects, if the school permits this option. The candidate who does not satisfy all requirements of the Diploma Program, or who has elected to take fewer than six subjects, is awarded a certificate for the examinations completed. Additionally, Diploma candidates who successfully complete more than six subjects receive an extra certificate for the additional subjects.

**TABLE 32.1: U.S. (Top Ten) and Canadian Examination Entries, May 2007**

| Location | Candidates (n) | Exams (n) |
|---|---|---|
| **U.S. State** | | |
| Florida | 6,693 | 22,111 |
| California | 6,130 | 14,646 |
| Virginia | 4,600 | 11,543 |
| New York | 3,611 | 9,007 |
| Texas | 2,108 | 5,711 |
| Colorado | 1,917 | 5,623 |
| Minnesota | 1,642 | 3,410 |
| North Carolina | 1,713 | 4,812 |
| Maryland | 1,596 | 4,082 |
| Oregon | 1,458 | 3,163 |
| **Canadian Province** | | |
| Ontario | 2,540 | 7,718 |
| Alberta | 2,218 | 5,335 |
| British Columbia | 1,118 | 3,837 |
| Manitoba | 390 | 971 |
| Nova Scotia | 311 | 885 |
| Quebec | 292 | 1,361 |
| Saskatchewan | 220 | 457 |
| New Brunswick | 163 | 339 |
| Newfoundland | 18 | 89 |

**SOURCE:** IBO (2007, p. 29, 36).

[204] A high school that wishes to offer the IB Program must apply to the IB, be visited by a delegation from the organization, and be subject to re-evaluation by the IB every five years.

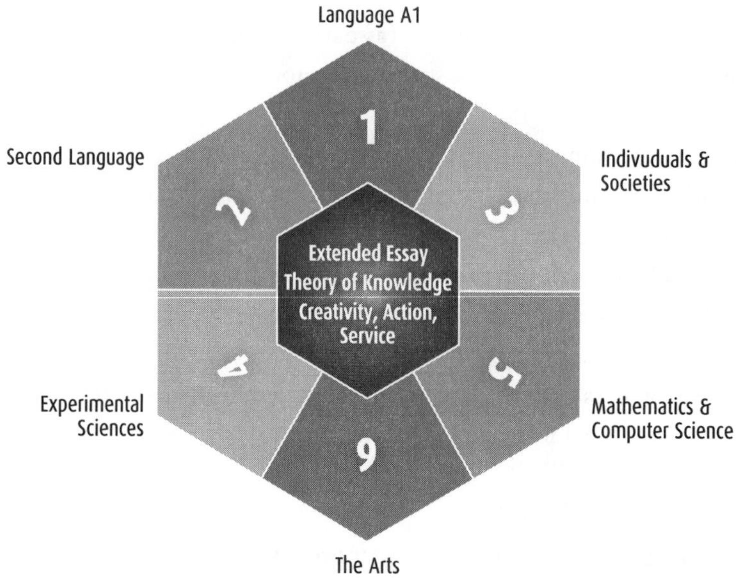


FIGURE 32.2
The Diploma Hexagon
(IBO 2006b, p. 4)

## The Diploma Hexagon

The Diploma hexagon provides graphic representation of the curriculum (*see* Figure 32.2). An IB Diploma student must choose one subject from each of Groups One to Five, thus ensuring breadth of experience in literature, a foreign language, the social sciences, the experimental sciences, and mathematics and computing. The sixth subject may be either an arts subject from Group Six; a second subject from Groups One to Four; further mathematics standard level (SL); computer science; or a school-based syllabus approved by the IB. Subject offerings within each group are provided in Table 32.2, on page 433.

At least three and not more than four courses must be taken at higher level (HL), with the remaining taken at standard level (SL). Higher level courses represent a recommended 240 teaching hours; standard level courses a recommended 150 teaching hours.

In general, student selection of the higher level subjects may be seen as a reflection of their academic strength or interests, or as requirements expected for admission to postsecondary programs they wish to pursue.

HL courses go beyond the core content of a subject, allowing depth of study within the discipline. SL courses cover the core content knowledge of a subject and ensure exposure to the breadth of a traditional and broad curriculum.

The center of the hexagon includes the compulsory core for the IB Diploma student: Theory of Knowledge (TOK); Creativity, Action, Service (CAS); and Extended Essay (EE).

Theory of Knowledge is an interdisciplinary requirement intended to stimulate critical reflection on knowledge and experience gained inside and outside the classroom. The 100-hour course challenges students to reflect critically on the bases of knowledge within their academic disciplines as well as on their own experiences, and to see the interaction and common goals between the academic disciplines, as they reflect upon what they are learning from their six subjects. They learn to be aware of subjective and ideological biases and to develop rational argument for an opinion, idea, or perception—arguments that are grounded in rigorous analysis of evidence.

CAS involves compulsory participation in community service so as to serve others and develop the ability to work collaboratively and cooperatively with other people.

The Extended Essay (EE) of some 4,000 words provides a first experience in preparing an independent research paper, its standard being university writing expectations.

TABLE 32.2: **IB Diploma Curriculum, Six Subject Groups**

| Group | Subject | Description |
|---|---|---|
| 1 | Language A1 | First language, including the study of selections from world literature |
| 2 | Language A2 | A language and literature course for fluent or bilingual students |
| | Language B | A foreign language course for students with two to four years previous experience with the language |
| | Language ab initio | A foreign language course for beginners |
| | Classical Languages | Classical Greek, Latin |
| 3 | Individuals and Societies | Business and management, economics, geography, history, Islamic history, information technology in a global society, philosophy, psychology, social and cultural anthropology, environmental systems and societies |
| 4 | Experimental Sciences | Biology, chemistry, physics, design technology, environmental systems and societies |
| 5 | Mathematics and Computer Science | Mathematics HL, mathematics SL, mathematical studies SL, further mathematics SL, computer science (elective only) |
| 6 | The Arts | Film studies, music, theatre arts, visual arts |

## Understanding IB Transcripts

Each school determines which courses it will offer. Given this wide selection of subjects, students have flexibility of choice within the structure as set forth, and thus the admissions officer may encounter a variety of subjects in an IB diploma candidate's application transcript. Table 32.3 shows two examples of what you may find.

Student #1 has chosen HL subjects in the humanities. His choice of biology and mathematical studies at standard level may reflect his intention not to pursue them as part of his future education and/or work plans. However, adding Spanish as a learned language might facilitate his study of the visual arts at a university in Spain or Mexico. This student has chosen one subject from each of the six subject groups.

Student #2 is probably heading toward mathematics, physics, or engineering. Note that she has used the option to take a second science as her sixth subject choice. Adding Mandarin as a learned language, she is probably well aware of the growing importance of China and how facility in that language may increase her career opportunities.

TABLE 32.3: **Two Possible IB Programs**

| higher level | standard level |
|---|---|
| **Student #1** | |
| ▸ English A1<br>▸ History: Americas<br>▸ Visual Arts | ▸ Spanish B<br>▸ Biology<br>▸ Mathematical Studies |
| **Student #2** | |
| ▸ Economics<br>▸ Physics<br>▸ Mathematics | ▸ English A1<br>▸ Mandarin B<br>▸ Chemistry |

At the end of the two-year program, if the student has earned a minimum of twenty-four points in the exams, *i.e.*, an average grade of four, and completed the three compulsory core components, the diploma will be awarded.

## Theory of Knowledge and the Extended Essay

An IB Diploma candidate can earn points beyond the minimum twenty-four required in the subject examinations. The Extended Essay and Theory of Knowledge (TOK) are assessed according to the application of the IB Diploma Program assessment criteria, as follows:

- A = Work of an excellent standard
- B = Work of a good standard
- C = Work of a satisfactory standard
- D = Work of a mediocre standard
- E = Work of an elementary standard

Using these performance levels for TOK and the Extended Essay and the Diploma Point Matrix, a maximum of three diploma points can be conferred for this combined performance (*see* Table 32.4, on page 435).[205]

For example, the student who writes a satisfactory Extended Essay and whose performance in TOK is judged to be good will be awarded one point, while a student who writes a mediocre Extended Essay and whose performance in TOK is judged to be excellent will be awarded two points.

Likewise, when performance in both TOK and the Extended Essay is of an elementary standard, this is a failing condition for the award of the diploma. In such a case, a certificate would be issued indicating the examination results earned in the individual subject examinations.

Approximately 80 percent of students who enroll in the IB program are awarded the diploma (as opposed to the subjects certificate). These students have completed an externally examined, pre-university course of study that qualifies them for matriculation at universities around the world. Based on a report to staff worldwide by the Director General in February 2006, there has been a less than 3 percent variation over seven years, an indicator of the strength of the assessment model (*see* Figure 32.3, on page 436).[206]

## Grading and Assessment within the Diploma Program

The assessment of the Diploma Program is high-stakes, criterion-related assessment.[207] According to Pook (2004),

> *...the principal distinguishing features of a criterion-referenced test are that: 1) criterion-referenced test items are selected to represent discrete units of student learning; and 2) the*

[205] See also IBO's *Theory of Knowledge Course Guide—For First Examinations 2008.*

[206] There are two main qualities which testers look for in a test: validity (the test's ability to predict a certain outcome) and consistency or reliability (similarity of results over different administrations of a test). The definitions that Pook (2004) provides, in his IB-oriented monograph on assessment, are: "According to the standard definition, the validity of an assessment is the extent to which it *actually* measures what it is stated to measure. The term reliability is used to define the accuracy of measurement resulting from an assessment, and how likely it is that the same result would be produced in slightly different circumstances. An assessment is reliable if a student would gain the same result were he/she to repeat the assessment on difference occasions, and also give the same result if the assessment were marked by different markers" (p. 8).

[207] In other words the criterion-based IB assessment system means that results are determined by performance against set standards, rather than on a curve.

TABLE 32.4: **The Diploma Points Matrix**

| Extended Essay | Theory of Knowledge: Excellent A | Good B | Satisfactory C | Mediocre D | Elementary E | Not Submitted |
|---|---|---|---|---|---|---|
| Excellent A | 3 | 3 | 2 | 2 | 1 | N |
| Good B | 3 | 2 | 1 | 1 | 0 | N |
| Satisfactory C | 2 | 1 | 1 | 0 | 0 | N |
| Mediocre D | 2 | 1 | 0 | 0 | 0 | N |
| Elementary E | 1 | 0 | 0 | 0 | Failing Condition | N |
| Not Submitted | N | N | N | N | N | N |

*outcome of the test depends on whether the student has reached a theoretically pre-determined cut-off score rather than how the student's score compares to a pre-determined distribution of performance* (p. 7).

That is to say, in the criterion-referenced test, mastery of the relevant information is shown (or not shown). The grade earned indicates the skill level a student has achieved within the particular domain of learning. What is perhaps more important is the fact that this information is included in the subject guide for each subject as what skills must be demonstrated in order to achieve the range of performance levels possible from Very Poor (one) to Excellent (seven).

The award of the diploma requires students to meet defined standards and conditions. In each examination, the student is graded on a scale of one (minimum) to seven (maximum). There are separate criteria for the Extended Essay and the Theory of Knowledge. IB courses are graded by the IB teachers at the local school, which usually accounts for about 20 percent of the grade in a subject, and then by three levels of international examiners trained by IBO (IBO 2006b, p. 5). There are written examinations at the end of each course, which encompass a variety of examination techniques, and which may consist of two or three separate examination papers (p. 6). There are also final examinations at the end of the two-year teaching period.

An underlying philosophy of the process is to give students ample opportunity to demonstrate what they know and what they can do. This is accomplished through the following strategies:

FIGURE 32.3

Consistency, Reliability of Exam Results

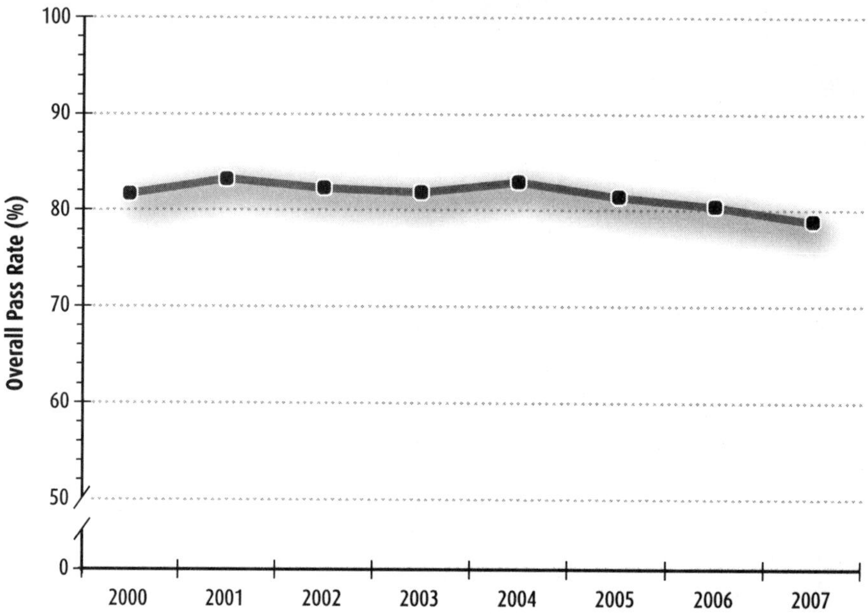


- *Transparency.* Assessment is criterion-referenced. Each student knows what knowledge and skills must be demonstrated in their work to earn a score from one to seven.
- *Both internal and external assessment using established grading criteria.* In each subject there is an internally assessed component. This is work prescribed in the syllabus to be carried out by all students and assessed by the teacher based upon criteria and guidelines provided. Upon completion of the teacher evaluation, all student work is collected. A sample (based on clear guidelines) of student work is sent for moderation by an examiner, whose responsibility is to ensure that the students have been assessed appropriately based upon the grading criteria. This component makes up approximately 20 percent of the total assessment.

  External examiners assess the written external examination papers in the sessions in May for the Northern Hemisphere and in November for the Southern Hemisphere. The external component makes up the remaining percent of the total assessment.
- *Multiple methods of assessment used for each course.* For example, an assessment task may take the form of multiple-choice questions, a short-response question, an extended-response question, an essay, a project, a single piece of work from a portfolio, and/or a research assignment. These tasks overlap with an assessment instrument or component, which is made up of one or more tasks collected together, for the sake of thematic or content continuity.

- *Varied skills tested across disciplines, within disciplines.* For example, the writing skill is tested in all disciplines within the context of the specific discipline. In the experimental sciences, the student will learn to write a laboratory report as expected in the scientific world. In an English course, students learn to write a précis or commentary. In a history course, students learn to write a response based upon document analysis. In mathematics work, students are not only expected to do computation to solve a problem, they are also asked to explain why and what they have done and must also present a written portfolio of work.
- *Balance between independent and teacher-supervised work.* Within the context of general performance requirements, students usually have a choice of presentation style—for example, extended essays, research papers, portfolio work, etc.

## Interpreting IB Transcripts

### Examination Performance

A student's examination performance for individual subjects is graded on a scale of one to seven, where:

- 7 = Excellent performance
- 6 = Very good performance
- 5 = Good performance
- 4 = Satisfactory performance
- 3 = Mediocre performance
- 2 = Poor performance
- 1 = Very Poor performance
- N = No grade, indicating that the student has not provided all components of the assessment required by the subject

Each subject group has a set of written grade descriptors. These descriptors have been formulated with the assessment criteria in each subject guide. They indicate what skills are demonstrated at each grade level from one to seven.

### Theory of Knowledge and Extended Essay

The Theory of Knowledge (TOK) and Extended Essay (EE) are graded according to the following scale:

- A = Work of an Excellent standard
- B = Work of a Good standard
- C = Work of a Satisfactory standard
- D = Work of a Mediocre standard
- E = Work of an Elementary standard
- N = Failure to submit work—No grade

### Maximum Possible Score: 45

Diploma Program subjects can yield up to 42 points, that is, achieving a grade of seven in each examination. Because a maximum of three diploma points can be awarded for the combination of the EE and the TOK, the maximum possible score is 42 points. Achievement of less than 24 points will result in a certificate for subjects successfully completed, but a full diploma is not awarded.

### Diploma or Certificate Awarded

IB examination results are available in mid-July for May session candidates, and in mid-January for November session candidates. If requested, an official transcript of results will be sent electronically to universities. The transcript will indicate the level of each subject, the grade awarded in each, the total points scored, and the completion of the additional components. It is typically marked *diploma awarded* or *certificate awarded.*

A transcript indicating *bilingual diploma awarded* means that the candidate has either studied two A1 language courses, or has studied one A1 language course and an A2 language course, or has taken an examination in at least one subject from Group Three or Group Four in a language other than his or her A1 language.

Approximately 76 percent of candidates in the United States are awarded a full diploma. In Canada, 92 percent of candidates receive a full diploma. Throughout the world the average is 83 percent.

## Accessing Curriculum

IB scores are criterion-referenced rather than norm-referenced. Criteria are set out in course guides by subject and level, and are available for download through the IB secure site for those with valid accounts. University access to IB course guides, which contain detailed syllabus outlines and assessment criteria, is also available through a secure site. A thorough review of this material is necessary for faculty to evaluate content and skills development within an IB subject and to determine appropriate placement of a student into a department course sequence.

You may register for access at www.ibo.org/universities/. Also available at this site are examination papers and markschemes. Brief descriptions of course content, by group, are available by clicking on the link to the *Guide to the IB Diploma Programme for Universities & Colleges,* to which we have already referred in several footnotes.

All curriculum documents are reviewed on a seven-year cycle. This cycle is fixed, but if significant change occurs in a body of knowledge (for example, computer science), then changes will be introduced more quickly. Likewise, if any other improvement to an existing Course Guide were deemed necessary, a revised or interim document would be provided. Updated curricula are available on the secure site.

## Becoming an IB World School

A school cannot just decide to offer IB courses. Authorization entails an intensive process that begins with an application to become a candidate school. During this time the school does a thorough self-study to determine the feasibility of implementing the program. This includes assessment of current curriculum and its alignment with Diploma subject "résuméd knowledge" for students entering the two year program in grade eleven. Following successful review of the formal application documents and the site visit, the school can be authorized. At this point teaching can begin. The entire process can take up to two years.

An evaluation of the school's IB Program takes place every five years after authorization and can conceivably lead to loss of authorization. So, as a recruiter you already have a good sense of the quality of a school that is offering the program.

A significant requirement for authorization is the training of IB teachers in their subject areas. IB teachers and schools are challenged to constantly reflect upon and improve their practice. To that end, an extensive professional development program exists to keep both new and experienced IB teachers current in course content, assessment criteria, and teaching strategies through workshops and seminars offered around the world.

TABLE 32.5: **Web-Based Resources**

| Resource | URL |
|---|---|
| Guide to the IB diploma program for universities and colleges | www.ibo.org/universities/ |
| The learner profile | www.ibo.org/programmes/profile/ |
| Link to North America pages with information focusing on North American universities and colleges | www.ibo.org/ibna/ |
| One stop access to documents and publications about North America including the annual Examination Review and Data Summary: 1998-2006 | www.ibo.org/ibna/elibrary/ |
| IB North America research PowerPoint | www.ibo.org/ibna/research/ |
| Resources for universities and applicants | www.ibo.org/ibna/recognition/ |
| How to find an IB World Diploma program school | www.ibo.org/school/ |
| IB World statistics | www.ibo.org/facts/schoolstats/ |
| Twenty-one things you should know about the IBO: Key information about the International Baccalaureate Organization | www.ibo.org/facts/21things/ |

While the syllabus outline is well structured for each subject and level, as are the assessment criteria, teachers have great flexibility and choice in how they teach a syllabus. For example, in Language A1 English there are four parts to the syllabus. Teachers may select from a wide range of authors, works, genres, periods, and places in putting together their course. Additionally, part four of the syllabus is called "Schools' Free Choice," allowing schools to meet local, state, and/or provincial requirements. In the experimental sciences, for example, the teacher may select the experiments a student must carry out to demonstrate a particular topic. This flexibility applies in each curricular area.

## Admitting IB Students

Universities want students who understand their responsibility in the learning process, who are fluent in the concepts of the major academic disciplines, and who come with the critical thinking, content, and knowledge skills that are needed to move them into a demanding university learning experience.

In making a decision to actively recruit IB Diploma students, you will attract students of the highest academic preparation, who have been challenged to think while they learn. You will eliminate concerns about grade inflation. You will know that state and/or provincial standards are being met and exceeded through effective teaching and learning. Your institution will benefit from the richness of experience and perspective that the IB Diploma student will bring to your campus.

The IB Diploma student will come to you with fluency in languages, self-confidence with university texts and materials, the capacity for independent and/or collaborative group work, and a broad perspective.

Your challenge is to acknowledge the good fit between your desire to view candidates holistically and the goals, skills, knowledge, and personal growth espoused by the IB curriculum and gained by IB Diploma students.

Once this is done, you can work to develop a recognition policy that acknowledges the preparation the IB Diploma student brings to postsecondary learning.

/ CHAPTER THIRTY-THREE /

*by Michele Sandlin, M.S.*
*Director of Admissions*
*Oregon State University*

33

# The International Baccalaureate:
## Part II—An Institutional Perspective

If your institution has not looked at pursuing and attracting students who are in the International Baccalaureate (IB) academic program, but you have a recognition policy for students who have completed Advanced Placement (administered by the College Board), then your campus is missing a major recruitment opportunity to bring students to your campus who are of high academic ability, are well rounded, are community-minded, and are well prepared for the total college experience.

IB encourages lifelong learning. The IB (2008) mission statement states:

> *The International Baccalaureate aims to develop inquiring, knowledgeable and caring young people who help to create a better and more peaceful world through intercultural understanding and respect.*
>
> *To this end the organization works with schools, governments and international organizations to develop challenging programmes of international education and rigorous assessment.*
>
> *These programmes encourage students across the world to become active, compassionate and lifelong learners who understand that other people, with their differences, can also be right.*

As is apparent to many admissions officers, the full academic experience of the IB Diploma Program (comprising the junior and senior years of high school) prepares students to move directly into the university experience and to manage the academic demands of college life successfully. The core compulsory areas of the Diploma Program, with the addition of interdisciplinary work, the requirement of an extended essay, and participation in community service work, combine to develop independent thinking, research skills, ability to work productively in groups, write major papers, and speak publicly with confidence.

IB's College and University Recognition (CURT) Board is beginning extensive research across the country to measure the success of IB students at the college level. In addition, some colleges across the country are beginning to monitor the success of their IB students. At Oregon State University, the author's institution, we have been tracking IB students since the inception of our innovative IB recruitment policy about seven years ago. What is most significant about Oregon State's IB students is their retention rate. The retention rate of IB students from year to year is approximately 95 percent. This speaks to the academic preparedness they bring to the classroom, and their capacity for social adjustment once on campus.

These are high-achieving students academically, and the numbers of IB students are only going to increase in the US. In fact in 2005, of the top 100 high schools in America, 39 were IB World Schools, and of the top ten high schools in the country, seven were IB schools (Newsweek 2005).[208] This growth in IB is further evidenced by a recent grant of $1,081,800 awarded to IB by the U.S. Department of Education, to grant access to the IB curriculum for low-income students (IBO 2006a).

Another strength of the IB program and the IB student is the international and diverse perspective that is an ingrained part of the curriculum. Having spent time with IB students over the past six years, in interviews, at programs, and at IB schools, I can attest to the fact that many IB students are searching for a college that has strong international programs and study abroad opportunities so they can continue their international education. They come to college with an instilled curiosity and a thirst to know more about the world beyond their own backyard, while still caring about their community. And with this desire to know more about their world, IB fosters acceptance and openness to those different from oneself. This is a refreshing perspective to see as part of an academic program that is globally available.

The International Baccalaureate has described its origins in a way which makes clear why the program is so attractive to students—and to admissions officers who seek good students.

> *Established in the late 1960s, with its first full year of operation in 1970, the Diploma Program was originally designed to cater to the educational needs of globally mobile students in international schools. It was developed as a deliberate compromise between the specialization required in some national systems and the breadth preferred in others, with-*

208 Newsweek's "Best [Public] High Schools" List is based on a ratio—the number of Advanced Placement (AP) and/or International Baccalaureate (B) tests taken by all students, divided by the number of graduating seniors.

*out bias toward any particular national system. The general objectives of the IB were to provide students with a balanced education, to facilitate geographic and cultural mobility, and to promote international understanding through a shared academic experience.*

*From its inception, the development of the Diploma Programme was based on three fundamental principles:*

- *The need for a broad general education, establishing the basic knowledge and critical thinking skills necessary for further study;*
- *The importance of developing international understanding and citizenship for a more peaceful, productive future;*
- *The need for flexibility of choice among the subjects to be studied, within a balanced framework, so that the students' options could correspond as far as possible to their particular interests and capacities* (IBO 2002a, p. 3).

Another helpful learned behavior of IB students involves their strong time management skills. Most IB students (according to IB coordinators) are students who are very involved in many diverse activities and groups. These are the students who are involved in student government, music/band, athletics, honor society, freshmen mentoring, community projects and service, girl/boy scouts, and school promotion; at a high rate they are often involved in more than two of these activities in addition to the demanding academic schedule of being an IB student. IB students are learning life skills that will help them handle the world around them—to multitask, balance, and survive not only in college, but in life. The IB student comes to your campus better equipped to be an engaged student, and an active and responsible participant in the campus community. So, the question is, why isn't your campus actively recruiting the IB student? Now that you know you need to attract the IB student, the next step is to develop an IB policy for your campus.

## Developing Your Institution's IB Policy

The first place to start is to do your homework! You need to research the IB program and have a general understanding of how the program works: what are the requirements, what is the difference between a certificate program and a diploma program, and how does the grading work? All these questions, plus a description of the IB "hexagon model," the concept of higher level and standard courses, and what is the minimum score (across the six subjects, plus the extended essay and the interdisciplinary "Theory of Knowledge" course) for earning an IB diploma, are covered in the preceding chapter, although we will recapitulate the most salient points briefly here in order to orient you as you begin to recruit IB students.

There are basically two results of IB study that a college official needs to be aware of–one resulting in a certificate and the other in a diploma–and two levels of courses: *standard level* and *higher level.* Let us build on some of the points made in the previous chapter and highlight issues which are of greatest interest to college admissions officers. The issue most under discussion among admissions officers concerns the kind of college credit that should be awarded to IB students.

A brief recapitulation is in order:

> *Each subject is graded on a scale from one point (the lowest) to seven points (the highest). Each diploma student takes six subjects, most taking three at higher level [with a recommended 240 hours of instruction] and three at a standard level [with a recommended 150 hours of instruction].*
>
> *In addition, there is a maximum of three points available for combined performance in the Extended Essay and Theory of Knowledge. Thus, the maximum score is 45 points.*
>
> *The minimum score needed to gain the Diploma is 24 points, provided that certain conditions are met* (IBO 2002a, p. 17).

As Sandra Wade Pauly of the International Baccalaureate organization has stated, in the previous chapter: "Achievement of less than 24 points will result in a certificate for subjects successfully completed, but a full diploma is not awarded." An IB student receives a transcript, showing all courses completed, with scores (no matter how low the score).

Thus, a student who presents with a certificate rather than a diploma may have performed less well in the courses and other requirements, as just set out, than a student who presents with a diploma. On the other hand, the student may have performed very well in the courses he or she did take, but for whatever reason did not pursue the full sequence. The transcript which you will receive from the IB organization should make clear what the situation is, by its notation of the grade (points awarded) for each course taken.

## Awarding Credit: IB versus AP Coursework

IB certificates typically result in the student's receiving credit similar to that awarded for Advanced Placement (AP) courses, by discipline.

For certificate earners, many institutions have followed an earlier practice—as established by early institutions' assessment of IB, or by analogy to their own existing policies for awarding AP credit—of awarding college credit for higher level IB courses presented that show grades of four or five and higher. When I began researching IB about eight years ago, the majority of colleges and universities had set the bar at a grade of "five," for a higher level course, as the minimum IB grade to be awarded college credit. But as more institutions have come to know, learn, and understand IB, a score of four is becoming more recognized as meeting the level and the outcomes expected of equivalent college freshman level courses.

It has also been a topic of discussion during IB presentations at national and regional conferences, and at IB coordinator meetings, that many institutions award the same credit for AP courses and for IB higher level courses. But some IB coordinators in the U.S. have pointed out that some AP students are sitting in the *same* classroom with IB *standard level* students and completing the exact same course requirements. This has led to heated discussions and comparisons of the curriculum of IB and AP, and has prompted many to ask why we do not award credit for standard level IB certificates—or even, to take the contrary tack, why we do award credit for students sitting in the same classrooms as standard level IB students but presenting their work for AP credit? Some U.S. institutions are in fact reviewing their policies, so as to award either partial credit for standard IB level, or to reduce AP credit awarded.

For the 80 percent of IB students who are awarded an IB diploma, a passing total score to be awarded an IB diploma, as we have already noted, is 24 (IBO 2006a, p. 4). However, institutions that award substantial credit for completion of the IB diploma typically set the minimum score above the 24 needed to receive an IB diploma. Many institutions have followed an earlier unofficial guideline, set by some of the first universities to recognize the IB diploma, requiring a minimum total score of 30 in order to receive any admission, "packaged" credit, placement, and/or scholarship based on IB work.

Nine years ago at Oregon State University, we conducted our own internal research on IB students who were choosing to attend OSU. OSU had a policy in place, similar to that which applied to the AP, that awarded credit for certificate programs, with courses taken at the higher level, if grades in those courses were five, six, or seven.

For two years we tracked the IB students coming to OSU, and found that not only were they persisting, and in good academic standing, from first to second year at a extremely high rate (approximately 95%), but they were also testing out of first-year courses successfully in the same discipline areas that they completed their higher level certificates in, or completed within a "diploma program." At the time we were not aware of what an IB diploma was, and we were starting to see a handful of students coming to OSU with an IB diploma from Oregon high schools. It was time to find out what the IB diploma was, what was this "diploma curriculum," and take action—time, in short, to be proactive in working to attract more IB diploma students to our campus.

It behooved us to ask ourselves why we were making it so difficult for such students to obtain credit for subjects they had already mastered and for which they had demonstrated competency. We had our faculty review the IB diploma programme and evaluate the work of the IB students in their challenging first-year courses at OSU. We quickly came to the conclusion that the IB diploma provided students with a solid foundation in general education at the university level, and that they were performing above the level of first-year coursework—both in terms of the challenging courses they chose and in terms of the success with which they completed such courses.

## IB Recognition Policies

Institutions typically develop recognition policies in relation to IB for:

- Admission
- Advanced standing credit

- Placement
- Scholarships

### Admission Considerations

Some institutions will offer admission as part of the recruitment package to attract an IB diploma candidate. As stated above, a minimum total score on the diploma is usually specified by the institution for any recognition. That score, at whatever the number the institution chooses to set, should be set forth as part of the institution's IB admissions policy.

Such a score may operate in lieu of a high school diploma, but in the U.S. that is a bit of a moot point. The IB diploma is usually posted on the high school transcript with a graduation date, but the IB diploma transcript is often not available until July of the final year, usually *after* regular U.S. high school graduation dates. However, the IB score and diploma can be an attractive option for an IB diploma student on a non-traditional high school track. To view other universities' IB admission policies, check the IB Web site according to the instructions in the Credit section, next.

### Credit Considerations

As before, start by researching other institutions' IB policies. That will give you the essence of many existing policies for awarding IB credit, and will also provide you with a baseline to begin creating your own school's policy. As we have noted above, IB recognition policies from quite a few institutions are listed on the IB Web site. To narrow down your research of comparables, search for the IB policies of institutions that are your primary competitors, as well as your qualified peer/comparable institutions. Your policy should be competitive with your peer group.

Most institutions start with the development of a certificate policy, because currently they may be receiving more individual certificate transcripts then diploma transcripts. Why? Certificate programs have been in existence longer, and also many students begin the diploma program but for whatever reason cannot complete, so they will finish individual certificates and submit them for credit to the universities to which they are applying.

However, more and more high schools in the U.S. are becoming IB diploma-awarding schools and are pursuing training and authorization to offer the IB diploma. In fact, the IB curriculum is one of the "most prestigious and rapidly growing brands in education today" (Shapira 2006). Thus, the IB diploma is becoming more widely available to U.S. high school students.

So developing a diploma policy along with your certificate policy is strongly advisable, and will help you to attract these well-prepared students.

In fact the IB has noted repeatedly that it hears from students, parents, IB coordinators, and school counselors that college and university recognition is of primary concern to IB students and their parents, and that students expect institutions to recognize and award their

> **The IB Web site: A Place to Jump-Start Your Policy Development**
>
> To start developing an IB policy for your institution, begin with the IB Web site at www.ibo.org. Click on the "Information for..." tab at the top of the page, and drop down to the Universities page to review other institutional IB policies by country. Currently there are 115 countries listed, and there are currently 1,016 (and counting) U.S. colleges and universities which recognize IB. There is a hotlink to a very useful Guide for assisting colleges and universities in understanding IB (IBO 2006a). This new IB Web page not only includes information about what the diploma is, how it is recognized around the world, and how students are assessed, but also discusses how to interpret and translate the IB transcript, its subject areas and grades into a policy for your institution.
>
> From time to time, IB will reference some of the best college recognition policies on its Web site. Be sure to bookmark the IB Web site and check it periodically, even after you have a policy in place, in order to stay current and competitive with your peers. The new, improved Web site contains a link to request assistance from IB with the development of your campus recognition policy. IB also provides a password-protected online site (hot linked) where you can find IB course syllabi for each subject with assessment information, sample exam questions, "markschemes," and sample transcripts. This is extremely helpful, especially for your campus faculty who are reviewing IB curricula to determine equivalent credit at your campus. When researching other institutions' policies, note that schools usually set out their policies separately as to IB work which resulted in a certificate, as opposed to a diploma.

achievement in this rigorous program; many are perplexed when a university faculty and administration are unfamiliar with the IB program.

Oregon State University, for example, has a policy of awarding credit to students who score five or above on higher level IB exams. And it offers guaranteed admission to those students who have an IB diploma score of 30 or higher (OSU 2008).

### GRANTING COURSE CLEARANCES OR EQUIVALENCIES

When developing your IB diploma policy, do not forget to build into your diploma recognition the awarding of equivalent credit *by subject matter*, so your diploma policy will not come under criticism for awarding empty credit through a lump sum of total hours.

For example, if you build a policy to award a blanket number of credits for an IB diploma with a minimum score, also build into your policy a mechanism so that the subject areas within the IB diploma that meet various distribution requirements in your school will in fact be awarded those course equivalencies or clearances. This policy of awarding course equivalencies for distribution requirements can also apply to certificates awarded to IB students, depending on your school's recognition scheme.

An example of a policy which is mindful of this factor is the statewide policy in California for the University of California system schools. The UC IB policy awards 30 quarter credits/20 semester credits to IB diploma students who have a diploma score of 30 or higher. Higher level exams with scores of five or higher receive general education requirements clearances.

### CHALLENGES TO YOUR CREDIT-AWARDING POLICY

When considering credit, be prepared in advance for IB students who will challenge your policy. As stated earlier, at Oregon State we experienced a high number of students who chose to test out of first-year courses because they already knew the material and wanted instead to receive the credit on their transcript. Most institutions have a policy or process in place that allows for a student to test out of a course or challenge the policy. This same process can be applied to an IB student wanting to appeal for credit or placement.

If your policy or process allows for a student to meet with a department chair, dean, or faculty member to demonstrate knowledge of the course, be sure—when counseling IB students about this process or when speaking with IB coordinators—to recommend that IB students *save* and be able to *show* a syllabus and/or their work from their IB program to the faculty member at the college or university. Documentation of the work the student completed in the IB program could be crucial for the college or university faculty member to assess the depth and breath of the subject matter that the student mastered in the IB program.

## Placement Considerations

Another possible recognition policy would involve considering awarding placement instead of, or in addition to, credit within individual subject areas. This approach can be used for individual subject area certificates and also for diplomas. For example, your faculty may recommend, based on the student's performance and competency in a subject area, that he or she be granted placement at a higher level within a discipline, or that a course be waived. This approach is more likely to be used in foreign language departments.

Those universities which have IB policies with a high minimum score requirement for the diploma may choose to provide sophomore standing at the institution.

## Scholarship Considerations

Very few U.S. universities have developed a scholarship specifically for IB students, but this result can be accomplished more easily than most schools realize. Of course, scholarship funding is a commodity in high demand, and many institutions have strict guidelines or donor instructions for making such awards. But think about approaching your scholarship office to make use of existing merit scholarship funds, and have some of them be directed specifically toward IB diploma students.

To begin with, run the data for the previous two years and identify IB students at your institution. This is easier of course if you already award IB credit at the certificate level, because you can run your query based on credit awarded upon admission. You may be pleasantly surprised to find how many IB students are already at your school.

From there you can research the transcripts of the IB students to get a sense of the number of possible full IB diploma earners who applied to your institution, who met the minimum diploma score you are considering setting for scholarship eligibility, and who are currently in residence or otherwise enrolled in your institution. As an example, at Oregon State, our two years of data revealed that we received annually five to seven IB diploma students who met a minimum score of 30 or higher on the full IB diploma. When we cross-referenced these diploma students with scholarships they received, we found that we were already honoring almost all of them with the award of merit scholarships. It didn't take long for our scholarship office to see the merit in setting aside existing merit-based scholarship funds specifically for IB diploma students.

Depending on the availability of funds, the scholarship office will determine whether or not this will be an entry scholarship only or can be an annual renewable scholarship. Any restriction on the scholarship regarding maintenance of a minimum grade point average and earned hours is typically targeted at renewal of merit-based scholarships.

## Recruiting the IB Student

Once you have developed an IB recognition policy for your campus, the next step is to get the word out to the IB organization, IB high schools, IB coordinators, and most importantly to IB students. The IB Web site can help you get started.

First, contact IB and get your new IB policy posted! From the IB homepage click on "Information for...," then click on the "universities" link and you will find the following information listed in the center column on the page about how to post your policy with IB, under the following rubric: "Your IB Recognition Policy."

Next, develop an IB recruitment/communication plan and map it directly into your annual master recruitment strategy/plan. Compare the strengths of your institution that would align with IB, and would be attractive to an IB student. First and foremost promote your IB recognition policy, but it is also important to market your institution to the strengths of IB.

For example:

- *IB has an international/global perspective or focus.* Such a rubric could promote study abroad opportunities, international research opportunities, international internships, international students on campus, international seminars and programming, and international course availability.
- *IB diploma earners complete an extended essay.* Such a rubric could promote undergraduate research opportunities, extensive writing courses, campus writing centers, undergraduate internships, capstone projects, and honors college thesis and orals requirements.
- *IB students complete a highly challenging, rigorous curriculum.* Such a rubric could promote honors college opportunities, advanced curriculum options, group participation opportunities, practicum experiences, faculty interaction and availability, undergraduate research, quality and rankings of strong undergraduate *and* graduate programs, and success data on graduates (*i.e.,* what percentage of your students go on to graduate and professional schools); also, professional exam results, job placement rates, named employers, success stories, etc.

- *IB has a community/civic responsibility component.* Such a rubric could promote student involvement opportunities on campus, student activities, student government, capstone projects, community-university opportunities, practicums, internships and partnerships, group learning, and Greek life.

Colleges and universities are marketing to IB students in various ways: brochures to targeted IB feeder high schools and IB coordinators, an IB policy and promotion page on your admissions Web site, hosting IB events or IB coordinators on your campus, presenting at IB events and activities, and visits to IB high schools.

One of the best ways to begin to build relationships with IB high schools is to plan fall recruitment travel visits to get to know the IB coordinators in your key travel areas. From the IB Web site you can identify IB high schools and coordinator contact information. Start by e-mailing an introductory greeting and offering to visit the school and meet with the IB coordinator. IB coordinators usually do double duty at their school and are incredibly busy people, so e-mail your request early in the fall term to be able to get on their calendar. Once you have identified the IB coordinators, made the first initial contact, and have a reply, be sure to set up a listserv so you will have their contact information handy. It is important to know your IB coordinators. Find out if they meet regularly within the region, and who is the current convener of the regional meetings.

Make a contact with the regional convener to see if you can get on their agenda at a quarterly meeting in order to present your institution's new IB policy and to promote those aspects of your institution that would be attractive to and supportive of the IB program.

There are many different avenues to promoting your IB policy and demonstrating how much your institution values and supports the IB program.

Other possible presentation and supportive opportunities for your institution are:

- Senior extended essay presentation ceremonies (typically held in the spring)
- Sophomore diploma information nights (typically occur in the late winter and spring)
- Eighth grade parent information nights (typically held in the early spring)
- IB classroom presentations

Senior extended essay presentations are amazing events. From the first one I attended, I was overwhelmed with the depth of the presentations, the passion the students demonstrated for their topics during their oral presentations, and the advanced public speaking skills of these students. At a senior essay presentation night, the opportunity to speak and promote your institution usually does not occur, but it is a wonderful opportunity to learn more about the IB program in general and its extended essay component in particular. You will be acknowledged for attending and supporting this event. This speaks volumes to an IB coordinator, the parents, and to the students themselves. Do not rule out the opportunity to attend if you receive an invitation. It is an honor. And be sure to have your IB promotional brochure available to be able to speak with students and parents.

Sophomore Diploma Information Night is another rare opportunity to present and reach these top students at the perfect time. Sophomore nights are attended by the students and their parents, and usually are conducted by the IB coordinator just before junior year registration in the spring. The IB coordinator will review the IB diploma program, requirements, benefits, costs, etc. Many IB coordinators value having a university admissions presenter on the agenda for these information nights to present the "beyond high school" value of the IB program. Be prepared; this is an event where college/university officials receive many questions from students and parents about their IB policy and the value of IB to colleges and universities.

An IB coordinator may also request that you attend an eighth grade parent informational night. The purpose of this event is to provide information to parents who have a child who will be entering high school the next school year. The focus of the evening is informational: what is IB, how does it work, what are the costs and benefits, and ultimately to demonstrate how IB (2002b) "educates the whole person and fosters a more compassionate and active citizenry" (p. 7). This is a very important promotional event for IB coordinators and a rare opportunity to cultivate early recruitment relationships.

An IB classroom presentation is another opportunity not only to promote your IB policy, but to learn more about IB from the classroom experience perspective. This is typically the least available IB presentation opportunity. Classroom hours are limited, and curriculum content coverage requirements are demanding, not only in the IB program but in all high school classes. So being invited to speak directly with an IB class about your IB policy is a very rare occurrence. If you are offered an opportunity to present, particularly if it is a primary feeder high school for your institution, or in a target area you are trying to cultivate, do not pass up the opportunity to have this direct, personal interaction with these students and their IB coordinator.

## Conclusion

The International Baccalaureate program is gaining momentum in the U.S. as many high schools are struggling to find a sustainable, rigorous academic curriculum that is engaging, challenging, global, and instills a culture of lifelong learning. More and more high schools in the U.S. are learning about IB and are working to become IB-approved high schools. Faculty and staff at colleges and universities need to get up to speed about what IB is, be able to address the increasing numbers of IB students coming to our campuses, and fully recognize the IB program at our institutions.

/ CHAPTER THIRTY-FOUR /

*by Anne M. Richard, J.D.*
*Associate Dean for Admissions and Financial Aid*
*The George Washington University*
*Law School*

# 34 Law Schools

There currently are 195 ABA-approved law schools in the United States,[209] with combined annual entering classes numbering in the range of 42,000 to 49,000 students (LSAC 2008, p. 5). In each of the past seven years, 72,000 to 100,600 individuals have applied for admission to law school Juris Doctor (J.D.) programs.[210] These figures reflect the fact that, in any given year, there are more law school applicants than seats available. Thus, in order to gain admission, prospective law students must navigate the extremely competitive law school admissions process.

This chapter is intended to provide guidance not only to the law school admissions officer, but also to the undergraduate admissions officer, who is often asked by students and parents, "What are law schools looking for? How can I choose the best law school which would be suited to my needs?"

[209] The District of Columbia, Puerto Rico, and every state in the U.S., except Alaska, are home to one or more of these institutions.

[210] The first law degree, the Juris Doctor or J.D., is the degree that one must earn in order to be qualified to sit for a bar exam and to obtain a license to practice law. The J.D. is a doctoral level degree. The vast majority of practicing attorneys in the United States have only the J.D. Some attorneys will go on to earn a post-doctoral level law degree, known as the L.L.M., generally in specialized areas of law. The discussion in this chapter focuses only on admission to J.D. programs. To review detailed applicant volume statistics, see <http://members.lsacnet.org>.

Accordingly, this chapter will discuss the issue of "right fit" in the context of what questions to ask about what a given law school offers—how to try to assess in advance whether a given law school will be a good fit for student applicants. The chapter will also address parent and student questions about what law schools are looking for. We will discuss the issue of rankings. And finally, the chapter will address itself to the financing of a legal education.

## Preparing Students for the Search and Application Process

### Preliminary Factors

In order to guide students through the demanding law school admissions process and bring about the best long-term outcome for the candidate, each individual must determine not only which law schools are likely to be within his or her reach in terms of gaining admission, but also which law school among those will be the best fit.

Many resources are available: pre-law counselors, law school admissions counselors, Web sites, chat rooms and blogs, printed material,[211] and pre-law events across the nation. Since most individuals have neither the time nor the inclination to apply to all available law schools (not to mention the funds to pay application fees to all of them), it is critical that prospective law students devote time to investigating the different law schools prior to beginning the application process.

Although all of the accredited law schools in the United States are alike in many respects and offer rigorous training for future lawyers, each law school is unique in many ways, and invests its resources differently.

The first-year curriculum in law schools is substantially standardized, but in upper-class courses, clinics, and other special programs, law schools can vary considerably in their emphasis. Some law schools have more faculty, courses, and extracurricular programs focused on the corporate/business areas; other schools make available a particularly wide range of clinical programs, legislative drafting, and public interest offerings. Some law schools are well-known for their specialized programs of study in environmental law, trial advocacy program, or law and economics. Other schools offer various combinations of dual-degree programs—J.D./M.B.A. and others. The availability and scope of these various special courses, clinics, and dual-degree programs are readily apparent on the Web sites of the various law schools.

Prospective students also should factor in the location of the school. If an individual ultimately hopes to practice law in a small town in Idaho, that person should certainly consider the University of Idaho. If she wishes to work in a large law firm in New York City, Washington, D.C., or Los Angeles, she should consider law schools in those metropolitan

[211] The American Bar Association (ABA) and the Law School Admission Council (LSAC) publish the annual *ABA-LSAT Official Guide to ABA-Approved Law Schools*—an excellent resource containing a wealth of information about ABA-approved law schools. This guide is the best resource for an individual interested in exploring law school, since it contains detailed information about each law school's programs, curriculum, physical plants, and student activities, as well as detailed statistics for each law school relating to applicants, student bodies, faculty, placement, etc. The *Guide* can be found in some bookstores or can be purchased by visiting LSAC's Web site at < www.lsac.org>. Selected information from the *Guide* is also freely available at <http://officialguide.lsac.org>.

areas, as well as national law schools that tend to place large percentages of their graduates in such firms.

Make prospective applicants aware of the substantial financial commitment and investment involved in pursuing a legal education. Counsel them to investigate both public law schools in their state of legal residence (which generally charge not only lower rates than private institutions, but which also, in almost all states, offer significantly lower tuition rates to residents) and private law schools. Prospective students should also research the sources and types of financial aid available at the different schools.

## General Requirements[212]

When applying to law schools, individuals must pay special attention to the application requirements and deadlines of each school. The following are the general requirements that an applicant must fulfill in order to be considered for admission to most law schools:

- BACHELOR'S DEGREE: One must have earned a bachelor's degree. Although individuals may apply to law school during the final year of a bachelor's degree program (law schools may offer admission to an applicant as long as he or she has successfully completed six semesters of a bachelor's degree program), admission to law school is conditioned upon applicants being awarded their bachelor's degrees prior to enrolling in law school classes.
- THE LSAT: In order to be considered for admission to law school, one must take the Law School Admission Test (LSAT), which is administered by the Law School Admission Council.[213]
- LSDAS: All applicants to law school must subscribe to the Law School Data Assembly Service (LSDAS). LSDAS serves as a clearinghouse and prepares a uniform law school report for each applicant: a report that includes an analysis of undergraduate transcripts, as well as copies of the actual transcripts and the LSAT writing sample. The LSDAS report also states the applicant's LSAT score. It is through LSDAS that applicants submit to all law schools to which they apply their undergraduate (and any graduate) transcripts, letters of recommendation, and LSAT score.[214]
- LAW SCHOOL APPLICATION FORM/RÉSUMÉ/APPLICATION FEES: Each law school has its own application form that must be completed. Most law schools also require or encourage applicants to submit résumés. Each law school will also charge an application fee, generally ranging from $25.00 to $90.00.

[212] Most of these requirements are discussed in greater detail later in this chapter.

[213] For information about the LSAT and to register to take it, prospective students should go to <www.lsac.org/LSAT/about-the-lsat.asp>.

[214] For information about and to subscribe to LSDAS, prospective students should go to <www.lsac.org/Applying/lsdas-general-information.asp>.

- **PERSONAL STATEMENT/OPTIONAL STATEMENT:** All law schools require that individuals provide a personal statement. Some law schools also allow applicants to submit optional statements, such as diversity statements.
- **LETTERS OR RECOMMENDATION:** Most law schools require either two or three letters of recommendation.

## Application Timing Considerations

Some students are admitted to and enter law school immediately upon completion of the bachelor's degree; others enter law school one or two years after completing the bachelor's degree; still others enter law school five, ten, twenty, or thirty years after college. There is not a "right" or "best" time to begin law school; nor is there a certain set or combination of academic credentials and/or professional accomplishments that makes a person the ideal candidate for law school admission. Individuals enter law from all different academic programs, with varied professional backgrounds, and at all different stages of life. The best time for one to apply to law school is when he or she has made an informed decision to pursue a career in law and feels prepared in terms of maturity, focus, and ability to make the financial commitment.

### Applying Within Two Years of Completing Undergraduate Degree

Prospective students often ask if they should take one or two years following college and work before applying to law school. This is something each individual has to decide. Some students are "burned out" and feel that they need to take a break from school before entering law school. Law school admissions committees certainly look favorably upon candidates who have had some professional experience. However, spending one or two years in the work force will not make an applicant stand out significantly—particularly when compared to applicants who have worked for many years and who have established careers. Law schools also look favorably on applicants who have outstanding college records, have had some internship/work experience in summers, and who are ready to enter law school right away. Therefore, each individual has to decide whether entering law school immediately following college or whether working for one or two years before starting law school is the best course for his or her own personal and professional development.

Prospective students who have weak academic records often ask if working in a law-related field or earning a master's degree prior to applying to law school will compensate for their poor college performance. The answer to these questions is usually "no." Working for one or two years in a law-related job following college, or earning a master's degree, will not inevitably or necessarily compensate for a poor undergraduate performance.

However, gaining some experience in a law-related job may be extremely valuable for the individual in providing exposure to what really goes on in a law practice, and may strengthen that person's commitment to pursue a legal career. This factor may be particularly true for individuals who think they want to be lawyers but who have never had the opportunity to observe practicing attorneys on a daily basis. Pursuing a graduate degree program prior to applying to law school can likewise be very valuable to those who have a sincere interest in pursuing that particular field of study.

### Applying Later in Life

Each year, law schools receive many applications from individuals who have been in the work force for a number of years, are established in their professions, and are seeking either to enhance or to change their careers. These applicants often express concern that they may not be strong law school candidates because they have been away from school for a lengthy period and/or their college records may not appear to be as strong as they should be because grade inflation was not as common when they were in college. However, for these individuals, their years of professional experience will in many cases significantly enhance their applications, and thus the grades they earned ten, fifteen, or twenty years ago will be less meaningful to admissions committees.

## Matching Applicants to the Right Schools

### Investigate a Broad Range of Schools

The goal of the prospective law student should be to gain admission to and matriculate at the law school that is the best "fit," with many factors involved in each individual's determination of what constitutes that best "fit." [215] Therefore, it is important that prospective applicants investigate a broad range of law schools before beginning the application process.

### Identify "Reach" and "Safety" Schools

First, there is no guarantee that an individual will gain admission to his or her first choice law school. Individuals should apply to their top choice or "reach" schools; they should also apply to a few schools to which it is possible they will gain admission based upon the objective standards (LSAT and GPA)[216]; and they should apply to at least one or two schools to which it is very likely they will gain admission based upon the objective standards ("safety" schools).

[215] Two of the best sources of information are the American Bar Association (ABA) and the Law School Admission Council (LSAC). The ABA Web site (www.abanet.org) provides a great deal of statistical information about the different law schools. LSAC (www.lsac.org) provides information about the LSAT, as well as access to online applications for most law schools. Both the ABA and LSAT Web sites also provide links to individual law school Web sites. Most law schools currently are posting a great deal more information on their Web sites than they are producing in print. There also are numerous commercial publications available at most bookstores that can help guide individuals through the law school admissions process. Finally, there are opportunities for prospective students to meet law school representatives at various events held throughout the country each year. LSAC hosts large law school forums in a number of major cities (go to <www.lsac.org/Choosing/law-school-recruitment-forums.asp> for details about these forums); individual schools and regional consortiums also host smaller recruiting events. (For example, Case Western University School of Law, in Cleveland, posts a list of its recruiting events held across the nation at http://law.case.edu/visiting/recruiting_schedule.asp?sec_id=58&cat_id=33 This listing is for 2007–08. For subsequent years' events, input "Case Western Reserve University School of Law, Recruitment Events in Your Area," for an updated list, and try the same search strategy for other law schools.

[216] These factors, which are two of the primary factors considered by admissions committees, are discussed in more detail later in this chapter.

### Find Programs Catering to Specific Interests

Different law schools have different strengths and weaknesses. If a student knows that she is definitely interested in pursuing a career in international law with a specific focus on Chinese law, she should apply to one or more law schools that offer multiple courses in international law and in Chinese law specifically. If a student is particularly interested in pursuing a career in public interest law, he should apply to schools that offer extensive clinical opportunities and the opportunity to network in the public interest arena while in law school.

Of course, many students entering law school are not sure about exactly what type of law they may ultimately wish to practice, and thus they approach law school open to several different areas of law.[217] Prospective students should review course descriptions, faculty biographies, and information related to special academic centers and clinical programs offered by the different law schools.[218]

### Take Geographic Location into Consideration

Geography is an important consideration for two reasons: work during law school, and job placement afterwards. If it is important to the student to be able to work during law school, both for income and for the career-focusing aspect of the experience, then he or she should probably focus more on law schools located in metropolitan than in rural areas.[219] If, on the other hand, the prospective student is looking for a setting that more resembles the college experience and where the main hub of activity will be the law school itself, he should focus on law schools located in more remote and rural settings.

Geography is also important in relation to job placement. Prospective law students should take into account where they think they want to begin their legal careers upon graduation, and with that factor in mind, they should investigate in what locations the different law schools tend to place their graduates. Some law schools have a more national reputation and place their graduates in firms and other organizations all across the country, while other schools have more regional or local reputations and tend to place the majority of their graduates with employers in the geographic region in which they are located.

Another aspect of location in relation to job placement is the law school's Career Development Office (CDO). All law schools have such offices. Most of them are staffed by attorneys or by non-attorney counselors with long experience in working with any entities which employ lawyers on a large scale—law firms, corporations, the public sector (including

[217] Law school is very different from college in terms of declaring a specialty; there is no point at which a law student must specialize or "declare a major." Many students spend their entire time in law school taking a broad range of courses, and it is only in their first job that they will become more focused on a specific area of practice (there is a great deal of on-the-job training for all lawyers—being a member of the legal profession is a continuing learning process). Students who have a clear view of exactly what area of the practice they wish to enter, whether based on a clinical experience or for other reasons, likely will take a number of elective courses in that specific area after the first year of study.

[218] Students' experience in clinics, and their summer jobs as law students, are often a great influence on what particular practice area they will choose to specialize in.

[219] The issue with work or internships for law students in a rural area is not that there are no such opportunities, but that there are not as many of them—and such opportunities are probably not as varied as what could be found in a metropolitan area.

the courts), and public interest organizations. The career development officers work closely with students to help them gain both summer and permanent employment.

The career offices sponsor many programs for students such as résumé writing workshops, mock interviews, and panel discussions—discussions at which students can hear from practicing attorneys and judges, many of whom also are prospective employers. In addition, such offices provide individual counseling to students and host recruiting programs on campus. Prospective students should review material available from career development offices to get a sense of how many employers participate in a law school's recruiting programs and whether these employers are from across the country or tend to come from the local or regional area.

Finally, law school CDOs maintain employment statistics on their graduates—namely, where their graduates go to work immediately upon graduation (in what geographic locations, in what types of practices, in what sizes and types of firms or organizations, and at what average starting salaries, etc.). Prospective students should review this information as well. The information available from a law school career development office is invaluable in helping to determine if a school will provide varied and extensive professional opportunities, as well as a high level of assistance in helping the student to achieve his or her ultimate career goals.

### Assess the School's Alumni Network

Prospective students should also try to obtain information from law schools' alumni offices to determine the size and strength of each school's alumni network. Reviewing recent alumni magazines, either online or in print, can provide useful information. How active and involved does the alumni network appear to be? Prospective students should also inquire as to whether a law school offers an alumni program or any joint events at which current students and alumni can network and form relationships. In many instances, alumni can be invaluable resources for current law students through mentoring programs and, in other ways, helping students achieve their career goals.

### Choose Schools in which the Student can Compete

In choosing a law school, a prospective student should consider at which schools he or she will be competitive as a student. Prospective students should review the profile of each law school's current first-year class, paying specific attention to the median LSAT scores and median GPAs reported. Many law schools also publish grids, showing the number of applicants, the number of admitted applicants, and the number of enrolled students in different LSAT score and GPA ranges. These pieces of information will assist a prospective student in assessing not only the chances of gaining admission, but also in determining how many of his or her classmates will have similar profiles in terms of LSAT score and GPA.

### Encourage Campus Visits

It is critically important that prospective students, once admitted, visit each of the law schools they are considering. There is no substitute for spending time at a law school. Prospective students should take a tour, talk with admissions officers and students, sit in on classes, and attend any preview or "admitted student" events. How open and welcoming a law school is, as reflected in its admissions staff, faculty and students, can tell an individual a great deal about how he or she can expect to be treated once a student.

Prospective students should also make it a point to spend some time observing current students outside of formal tours and preview events to get a real sense of the outlook and mood among the students. Although all law schools have similar first-year curricula, each law school has a distinctive atmosphere, which is reflected in the spirit of its students. Only by observing the goings on, outside of formal programs, can one get a real feel for whether the student body tends to work as a team and exudes a genuine sense of camaraderie (notwithstanding the reality that students are inevitably competing with one another for grades and class rank), or whether the atmosphere seems to be dominated by an ultra-competitive spirit. Prospective students should keep in mind that their law school classmates will not only be their classmates for a few years, but also will be their colleagues for life.

### Cost Considerations

Prospective students must consider the costs and the financial aid available at the different law schools. Although the majority of law students take on substantial debt to fund their legal educations (primarily in the form of federal student loans), each person must determine what he or she reasonably is going to be able and/or willing to manage in terms of debt load. In the last major section of this chapter, we will discuss the student financial aid system, as it applies to law students, in more detail.

### Practical Use of Rankings

There are a number of different commercial rankings of law schools. Rankings can provide useful information; however, a prospective student should not allow any ranking, in and of itself, to determine which school he or she will attend. Unfortunately, some candidates place too much weight on the rankings and choose to attend the law school ranked the highest, without regard to whether that particular law school is really the best fit for them. Moreover, prospective students often have to contend with parents, friends, and pre-law advisors who view the rankings as gospel and who pressure them into selecting a law school based solely upon which school is ranked the highest.

In the past fifteen years, the annual law school rankings published by *U.S. News & World Report* seem to have become the most popular among prospective students. In generating its annual rankings, *U.S. News* uses a formula that includes factors for: (1) each law school's reputation as rated by a sample group of lawyers and judges throughout the country; (2) each law school's reputation as rated by a sample group of law professors and law school administrators throughout the country; (3) selectivity as measured by the median LSAT and median GPA of each law school's full-time entering class, as well as the percentage of applicants offered admission; (4) two different placement statistics, namely: (a) the percentage of graduates employed at graduation; and (b) the percentage of graduates employed nine months following graduation; (5) each law school's expenditure of funds per student; and (6) each law school's bar passage rate.[220]

Different individuals have different views about the usefulness of the *U.S. News* rankings. While these rankings certainly provide valuable statistical information, a student should not allow the *U.S. News* rankings, or indeed any other rankings, to substitute for his or her own judgment—made after careful research and visits to a number of law schools.

## Law School Expectations: Elements of a Desirable Candidate

After having discussed what *applicants* should be looking for (at least in terms of a preliminary scan in relation to their own interests and needs), we now turn more specifically to what *law schools* are looking for.

In the competitive law school admissions process, law schools seek to admit and recruit qualified individuals who will (1) excel in their legal studies; (2) add to the richness and diversity of their academic communities; (3) pass a bar exam and obtain a license to practice; (4) become successful attorneys in whatever setting and field they choose; and (5) become loyal and involved alumni. The admissions process is not only competitive among applicants; it likewise is competitive among law schools, as each strives to bring in the strongest classes possible each year.

Admissions committees will review, evaluate, and consider all of the information they request, with some factors playing greater roles than others. In general, the three most important factors considered by admissions committees are: (1) undergraduate record; (2) LSAT score; and (3) personal statement. The other factors—(a) extracurricular activities; (b) professional experience; (c) personal, academic, and professional accomplishments and honors; and (d) recommendations—are also very important, but significant weaknesses in the first three factors will pose significant hurdles for the applicant, notwithstanding great strengths in factors a-d.

The first and most important rule in applying to law school is:

Pay attention to the individual requirements and deadlines of each law school. Read each law school's application and instructions carefully, provide the information requested, and answer all questions completely and honestly.

[220] Details about the *U.S. News* rankings can be reviewed in the magazine itself. For more information about the *U.S. News* rankings, go to <www.usnews.com/education>.

### Academic Record and Undergraduate Cumulative GPA

Law school admissions committees seek to admit individuals who will be able to excel in their legal studies. Therefore, they are looking for an applicant's demonstrated ability to pursue a challenging curriculum and to perform at a very high level. Admissions committees review undergraduate transcripts (as well as transcripts of any graduate work) to see if the applicant has taken upper-level courses and seminars in which substantial research papers have been required.

The applicant's undergraduate cumulative grade point average is one of the objective factors upon which admissions committees place great weight. However, a very high GPA earned in a minimally challenging course of study will be viewed in a much less positive light than one earned in a course of study in which the individual has taken a number of intensive upper-level courses and shown continued development. Thus, prospective students should avoid taking "gut" courses in order to raise their GPAs.

Students entering college often ask whether there is a preferred major they should pursue. Some think that majoring in political science or government is necessary for a candidate to gain admission to law school. This is not true. Law schools admit students from all different majors—including English, foreign languages, the social sciences, the hard sciences, engineering, computer science, performing arts, and business.

Thus, college students should not choose any particular major solely because they believe it will help them gain admission to law school. Rather, they should focus their undergraduate studies in the areas that are of greatest interest to them. Individuals tend to perform better when they are studying topics about which they are passionate. Students should also keep in mind that many things can change during their college years. A student who enters college sure that he or she is going to law school at some point may completely lose interest in law. For that person, it is important that the focus of his or her college studies has been good preparation for an alternative career path.

### Undergraduate Performance Outweighs Graduate Work

Prospective students whose undergraduate records are weak often ask if admissions committees can put more weight on their graduate records. Unfortunately for this group of candidates, the answer is "no." The two objective factors that all candidates bring to law school admissions committees are LSAT score and undergraduate GPA—these are the two objective bases of comparison of all applicants.

In addition, the two numerical statistics that law admissions operations report to the ABA and that are also used by the different entities that produce law school rankings each year are median LSAT score and median GPA undergraduate. Therefore, in the admissions process, the most important number related to each applicant's academic record is the undergraduate cumulative GPA. Admissions committees will consider any graduate work that an applicant has completed, and that work can certainly enhance and strengthen an application on a subjective basis; however, the undergraduate GPA is the number that carries the weight.

Prospective students who may have had a rough start in their college careers and/or who floundered until they discovered the major about which they are passionate frequently ask if admissions committees can consider only the GPA earned in their major or only the GPA earned in their last two years of college. Again, the answer is "no." It is the undergraduate cumulative GPA that carries the weight.[221]

Prospective law school students, who are freshmen, sophomores, or juniors, must keep in mind that their primary mission in college is to focus on their studies—they should be counseled to take advantage of the multitude of course offerings available, to challenges themselves academically, to work hard, and to do very well. Prospective students who have excelled in their undergraduate studies will have the maximum number of opportunities available to them when they are ready for law school.

### The Law School Admission Test

All law schools require that applicants take the Law School Admission Test (LSAT),[222] administered by the Law School Admission Council. The LSAT is a test of skills, not a test of knowledge. A prospective student cannot memorize a volume of information and, by doing so, be guaranteed a high score on the LSAT. Rather, the LSAT tests one's ability to: (1) read and understand; (2) analyze and reason; and (3) work through logic problems. Hence, the three types of multiple choice questions on the LSAT are:

1. Reading Comprehension;
2. Analytical Reasoning; and
3. Logical Reasoning.

The LSAT also consists of a writing section in which test takers are required to prepare a short writing sample based upon a factual scenario. Although the LSAT writing sample is not graded and is in no way factored into one's LSAT score, copies of the writing sample are provided to the law schools to which an individual applies, and may be reviewed by admissions committees in their assessment of the applicant's writing ability.

The LSAT is a difficult test and each section is strictly timed. It is critical that prospective students prepare in some way for the LSAT. There is no one perfect method or preparation that will work for everyone. Each individual should spend some time reviewing sample LSAT questions and determining what the best method of preparation should be for him or her. Some students work best in a classroom setting and may want to take a commercial LSAT preparation course; others work better in a setting emphasizing individual and focused atten-

221 Of course, in reviewing transcripts, admissions committees take note of rough starts and upward trends.

222 Detailed information about the LSAT can be found at <www.lsac.org/Applying/lsdas-general-information.asp>. Prospective students may also register to take the LSAT on this site.

tion, and thus such students may choose to work one-on-one with an individual tutor; still other candidates may have the discipline to work on their own, using various LSAT preparatory materials that can be found at most bookstores and by practicing questions on past tests.[223] Pre-law advisors and law school admissions counselors can often guide students to a variety of LSAT preparation courses, tutors, and practice materials.[224]

The best way to begin LSAT preparation is by working through the sample questions provided in the LSAT/LSDAS Information Book that is available at most college counseling offices, at law school admissions offices, or from LSAC. Whatever method of preparation one chooses, it is critical that students test themselves and practice on the different sections under the time constraints. A common problem for test takers is that they are not able to complete one or more sections. Leaving sections incomplete makes it impossible to get a top score.

The LSAT is given four times a year—in June, September or October, December, and February. The LSAT continues to be given only on paper and only in a limited number of locations throughout the United States and the world. Some law schools require that applicants take the LSAT no later than December if they are applying for admission in the following fall; other law schools will accept scores from any of the four test administrations, including the one in February of the year in which the applicant is seeking admission. Prospective students should check to be sure that they do not take the LSAT too late for any of the law schools to which they intend to apply. Applicants may take the LSAT more than once, but students should strive to prepare well and take it once and only once. If an applicant has taken the LSAT more than once,[225] most law schools will consider the highest score in the admissions process.[226]

The LSAT is scored on a scale of 120 to 180. Typically, test takers who score in the top 10 percent on the LSAT achieve scores in the mid-160s and higher. The higher one's LSAT score, the stronger is one's law school application.

Each year, law school admissions counselors hear from a number of prospective students that they simply do not do well on standardized tests; they ask that their LSAT scores be disregarded. Unfortunately for those who have difficulty with standardized tests, the LSAT is given great weight in the admissions process. It is the only completely standard measure by which law school admissions committees are able to compare all applicants. Law school applicants come from hundreds of different academic programs and professional backgrounds and have widely diverse personal histories. It is impossible for law schools to assign

223 Students may purchase past LSATs from LSAC at <www.lsac.org>.

224 Searching the Internet for the key words "LSAT Preparation" also locates a multitude of LSAT preparatory options.

225 In addition to the significant amount of time and energy involved, taking the LSAT also requires payment of a fee to LSAC. Therefore, for physical and emotional—as well as financial—reasons, one should strive to prepare as well as possible, take the test when he or she feels best prepared, and take the test only once.

226 Notwithstanding the text leading to this footnote, if an individual has a bad test day or if something happens to adversely affect his or her performance, that person should take the LSAT a second time to try to raise his or her score. It is generally recommended that prospective students take the LSAT in June or September/October in the year prior to the year in which they intend to begin law school. Taking the test earlier rather than later will allow for retaking of the test in December or February, if necessary.

any sort of numerical values to students' varied backgrounds and to plug them into a formula that will determine who will be admitted. The LSAT allows students' skills to be compared.

Moreover, the LSAT is deemed to test skills that are important skills for law students to have mastered. Thus, prospective students should be cautioned about emphasizing in their applications or to admissions counselors that they "have never done well on standardized tests" and never will. Prospective law students should also keep in mind that a significant portion of the bar exam (the Multistate Bar Exam) which law graduates must pass in order to obtain their licenses to practice law is a standardized test. No law school is seeking to admit individuals who will never be able to obtain a license to practice.

### The Personal Statement

All law schools require applicants to submit a personal statement. Some law schools also allow submission of optional diversity statements or statements on specific prescribed topics. Any writing that an applicant submits as part of a law school application will be reviewed and evaluated for: (1) the content and message being conveyed; and (2) the applicant's writing ability.

The personal statement is the applicant's opportunity to convey to admissions committees information that is not reflected elsewhere in the application. It is the applicant's chance to supplement the raw data (academic record, LSAT score, listing of work experience, and extracurricular activities, etc.) with information that will give the admissions committee greater insight into the applicant as a person—his or her values, character, and strengths. Law schools generally do not grant personal interviews as part of the admissions process. Therefore, applicants should view the personal statement as their only chance to have personal, one-on-one interaction with the admissions committee.

Applicants should keep in mind that law schools are committed to diversity (not only in terms of race and ethnicity, but also in terms of professional and personal backgrounds and experiences). Every law school wants its entering class to include individuals who have had a variety of academic, personal, and professional experiences; who are of various ages, races, and ethnicities; who come from around the country and the world; and who are from varying socioeconomic backgrounds. As students choose what to write in the personal statement, they should consider emphasizing how they will contribute positively to the diversity and strength of the student body, and to the legal profession.

Personal statements should be positive and engaging. They should focus on strengths. Personal statements should not be devoted to explaining or making excuses for weaknesses that may appear in other parts of the application. If an applicant wants to explain why his or her LSAT score is not as high as it should be or why his or her academic performance was very weak in a given semester, the applicant should do so in a short addendum, rather than using the personal statement for that purpose.

It is critical that the personal statement be well-written and that any guidelines set forth by the law school are followed (word limits, format, etc.). Writing skills and the ability to digest and explain complicated material are crucial for success in law school and in the practice of law. Being able to express oneself in a concise manner likewise is an important skill (hence, applicants should be sure to abide by any stated word limits). The stronger and more developed one's writing abilities, the stronger one's law school application. Applicants must take time drafting and perfecting their personal statements. And they must be careful never—ever—to submit statements that have typographical errors.

### Focused Involvement in Extracurricular Activities

Law school admissions committees like to see that applicants are well-rounded and have the ability to balance academic work with other activities and responsibilities. Students often ask if there are particular student organizations or activities in which they should become involved in order to impress admissions committees. Just as there is no required or perfect major for law school-bound individuals, there is no list of "best" organizations or activities.

Students should become involved in a limited number of extracurricular activities that interest them and that they are able to handle. Becoming involved in every activity under the sun just for the sake of being involved will not impress law school admissions committees (particularly if too much extracurricular involvement is at the expense of one's academic performance). A student's being involved in substantial or leadership roles in one or two activities while maintaining strong performance in coursework will be viewed in a much more positive light than his or her being a member of every group on campus.[227]

For students considering taking one or two years off between college and law school to enter public service organizations, admissions committees look favorably upon participation in organizations such as the Peace Corps, Teach for America, and AmeriCorps. In fact, a number of law schools have entered into partnerships with some of these organizations and offer special scholarships for their alumni. Information about such partnerships is generally available on the organizations' Web sites.

### Full Disclosure on Applications

Each law school has its own application form. In the past several years, most law schools have partnered with LSAC so that applicants can submit their applications (including recommendations and personal statements) electronically through LSAC.[228] This has streamlined the process

[227] Every law school admissions committee reads applications each year from individuals who have been officers in their fraternities, who have had internships while in school, and who have been heavily involved in several student organizations—but who have very weak academic records. A law applicant's plea that the admissions committee ignore his poor grades but focus on all the activities will not succeed. What such an applicant is showing an admissions committee is poor judgment—he overextended himself getting involved in too many extracurricular activities and allowed his grades to suffer. College students must keep in mind that college is primarily an academic experience and only secondarily a social experience.. One's primary mission while a college student is to excel in coursework.

[228] Go to <www.lsac.org/LSAC.asp?url=lsac/lsdas-general-information.asp> for information about LSAC's online services, and click on "LSDAS Electronic Applications Demo."

greatly, both for the law schools and for the applicants. Law schools also accept paper applications, but increasingly, the vast majority of law applicants are applying online through LSAC.

All law schools ask for similar information in their applications. However, some schools ask for more information; some for less. Some law schools require that applicants provide dean's certifications from their undergraduate institutions; some do not. Applicants must pay careful attention to the specific information sought by each law school. This is information that the admissions committee wants to have before it, as it evaluates and makes decisions on each file.

Practicing attorneys are placed in unique positions of trust. They are entrusted with confidences of their clients, and, in many situations, they are charged with safeguarding and directing to the appropriate payees the funds of their clients. In addition to passing very difficult bar examinations upon graduation from law school, law graduates must be determined to be "fit" for admission to the bar by state bar "character and fitness" committees. Therefore, at the law school admission phase, law schools want to be sure that the individuals they admit ultimately will be able to gain admission to the bar. As part of this process, law school applications include questions asking applicants to disclose any academic suspensions or probations, and/or disciplinary actions, as well as any criminal charges or convictions. In response to these questions, it is critically important that applicants disclose everything—completely and truthfully.

Many law school applicants (and many lawyers) have had past difficulties. An academic suspension or criminal conviction will not necessarily preclude one from gaining admission to law school or to the practice of law. [229] However, what will cause serious problems for a future lawyer is failure to disclose material information, or misrepresentation of material information, on his or her law school application.

If an applicant is found to have failed to disclose or to have misrepresented material information on a law school application, offers of admission may be withdrawn if the student has not yet matriculated. A current law student who is found to have been dishonest on his or her application may be suspended, or even dismissed from the law program. Moreover, when the time comes for law graduates to take bar examinations, the character and fitness committees of state bars usually check criminal records as well as law school records. Any inconsistencies that are found may have serious implications for an individual seeking to gain admission to the bar.

### Letters of Recommendation

Most law schools require two or three letters of recommendation, and most require or prefer that at least one be from a college or graduate school professor (the other letters can be from

[229] If an applicant has a lengthy criminal record or has been convicted of crimes involving moral turpitude or abuse of positions of trust, the applicant may face significant hurdles gaining admission to law school and/or to the practice of law. In such cases, the applicant should talk with law school admissions counselors and should also check with the state bar office to get a real sense of the magnitude of the hurdles.

work supervisors, colleagues, etc.). What is most important is that the letters be from individuals who really know the applicant and who have had the opportunity to work with, observe, and evaluate the applicant.[230]

Letters of recommendation are of great help to an admissions committee, since these letters provide first-hand evaluations and insights into the talents, work ethic, character, and personality of the applicant. Applicants must choose their recommenders carefully and be sure that their recommenders will provide positive and detailed letters.[231] When applicants approach individuals and ask if they will write letters of support, applicants should be prepared to provide information to assist those individuals in writing their letters. It may be particularly useful to the recommender to have copies of the applicant's transcript, résumé, and personal statement.[232]

## Financing Options[233]

When an individual decides to attend law school, he or she is making a very substantial commitment—not only of time and energy, but also of money. Legal education is expensive; each individual must figure out how to finance his or her legal education. Annual tuition rates currently range from approximately $3,000 to $40,000 per year.[234] Most law schools have some scholarship funds available to help their students. However, the vast majority of individuals will graduate from law school with significant debt. Students must determine how much they are willing to invest in their legal educations and how much debt they reasonably will be able to handle.

All law schools offer financial aid in different forms—which may include merit-based scholarships, need-based scholarships, and federal student loans.

Of course, some schools have much larger scholarship budgets than others; and some schools have much higher tuition rates than others. In recent years, many law schools have been committing more of their available funds to merit-based scholarships rather than to need-based scholarships. Other law schools continue to commit most or all of their funds to need-based aid, and very little or none to merit-based awards. Prospective students should investigate financial aid opportunities at each school in which they are interested. Students

[230] Applicants should not try to work through connections to get letters of recommendation from their U.S. Senators or other high-profile people the applicant does not know—that will not impress admissions committees and it likely will be evident from the blandness of the letter that the recommender has never met the applicant.

[231] Most recommendations read by admissions committees are positive. However, there are always some that are negative and those are the letters that may actually carry greater weight. A negative letter of recommendation raises a red flag to admissions committees and may significantly hurt the applicant's chances of gaining admission.

[232] A recommendation will not be viewed in a positive light if the author makes statements that are not true. For example, if a recommender states that student X had a stellar career at college Y, but in fact the student graduated with a 2.5 cumulative GPA, the admissions committee will not put great weight on that positive recommendation.

[233] This section provides a summary of the main sources of financial aid available at most law schools. It is intended as a very basic and general discussion. Prospective students should seek information from each law school about any special institutional funding (endowed scholarships, work-study funds, etc.) that may be available.

[234] For academic year 2006–2007.

should understand, up front, the financial aid processes and policies of the different law schools, and assess the likelihood of their being able to obtain the level of financial aid they feel they will need.

Working with their chosen law school's financial aid office, students may obtain funds—in the form of scholarships, grants, and loans—in an amount up to the total cost of attendance each year. The total cost of attendance is a budget figure established by each law school each year. Included in an institution's total cost of attendance are the year's tuition expense, plus the average cost of: (1) room and board; (2) books and supplies; (3) health insurance; (4) transportation; and (5) personal expenses.

## Scholarships and Grants

Prospective law students should investigate scholarship opportunities that may be available at different law schools and the criteria used by each school in making scholarship awards. Most law schools offer merit-based scholarships to a limited number of the most outstanding admitted students. These scholarships may range in amount from a several thousand dollars to an amount sufficient to cover full tuition plus a stipend for living expenses.

## Student Loans

There are numerous loans, both federal and commercial, available to law students. It is important, however, for students to do their best to minimize the amount of debt they will take on. Financial aid counselors frequently advise: *Law students should live like students (and not like lawyers) while in law school so that they can live like lawyers once they are lawyers.*

## Federal Student Loans[235]

There are a number of federal student loans available to law students who qualify.[236] The two federal student loans most frequently used by law students are the Stafford Loan and the Graduate PLUS Loan.

### FEDERAL STAFFORD LOAN

The Federal Stafford Loan is a fixed interest rate loan (presently 6.8%) available to all law students who are citizens or permanent residents of the United States. Law students may borrow up to $20,500 per year, regardless of credit history.

[235] Specific amounts related to the Federal student loans discussed in this chapter are those in effect for the 2007–2008 academic year. Interest rates, maximum loan amounts, and repayment terms may change in any given year.

[236] In order to qualify for federal student loans, one must be a U.S. citizen or permanent resident. Students who do not qualify for federal student loans will have to rely solely upon commercial loans and any scholarships they receive.

*Application Process*

The student (and, if married, the student's spouse) must complete the Free Application for Federal Student Aid (FAFSA) as soon as possible after January 1st in the calendar year in which he or she intends to enroll in law school. No parental information is required on the FAFSA for purposes of the student obtaining the Stafford Loan. However, individual law schools may require that the student's parents provide their financial information on the FAFSA if the student wishes to be considered for any of the school's institutional need-based aid.[237]

Students should file their FAFSA online at www.fafsa.ed.gov. Once a student submits the required information, his or her FAFSA data will be transmitted electronically to all law schools to which the student has requested that the FAFSA information be sent. The student's Stafford Loan will be certified by the law school and will flow through the student's law school or university account.

### SUBSIDIZED/UNSUBSIDIZED STAFFORD LOAN FUNDS

Up to $8,500 per year of the Federal Stafford Loan may be subsidized (no interest accrues on a subsidized Stafford Loan while students are in school, or during the six-month grace period following graduation or termination of at least half-time enrollment). Whether students qualify for the maximum subsidized amount of the Stafford Loan is based upon a calculation of financial need. The remaining portion of the Stafford Loan, up to the total annual amount of $20,500 (less any subsidized amount received) is unsubsidized; that is, interest begins to accrue immediately upon disbursement of the unsubsidized Stafford Loan funds.

### FEDERAL GRADUATE PLUS LOAN

The Federal Graduate PLUS (GradPLUS) Loan is a fixed interest rate (currently 8.5%) loan. Eligible students may borrow up to the annual cost of attendance through GradPLUS (less any other aid, including other loans such as the Stafford Loan, any merit or need-based scholarships, and any other outside aid).

*Application Process*

Eligibility for the GradPLUS is based upon the applicant's financial data (and, if married, that of the applicant's spouse) as submitted in the FAFSA. Whether the applicant is dependent upon parents or is independent, parental information is not required in the FAFSA for purposes of the student obtaining a GradPLUS Loan. In order to qualify for GradPLUS, the

[237] Although many law students are solely responsible for financing their legal educations, many law schools, as part of their financial aid process, will make a determination as to whether the student is to be deemed dependent or independent of his or her parents. Different law schools have different policies regarding what makes a student dependent versus independent. For example, if the student has been claimed as a dependent on parents' tax returns in either of the most recent two years, or if the parents have provided more than a certain percentage of financial support for the student in the past year, the student may be deemed dependent for financial aid purposes. If a student is deemed dependent, the parents' financial information will be factored into the needs analysis utilized to determine whether the student will be awarded a need-based scholarship. If the student is deemed to be independent, only the student's financial information is considered.

applicant must not have any adverse credit for the 90 days preceding the making of application for the GradPLUS loan. If an applicant does not meet the Federal credit standards for a GradPLUS Loan, he or she nevertheless may qualify for GradPLUS funds with a creditworthy endorser/cosigner.

### Private Commercial Loans

There also are numerous commercial educational loans available to law students from private lenders, separate and apart from federal student loans. Having good credit is critical for students who seek to borrow from private commercial lenders, since the student's eligibility and the specific terms of the loan will be based upon the student's creditworthiness.

### Loan Reimbursement Assistance Programs

A number of law schools have in place loan reimbursement assistance programs (LRAPs). These are programs that provide assistance to law graduates in repaying their student loans. Law graduates generally may participate in LRAPs if they work in public interest law upon graduation. Different law school LRAPs have different policies with respect to the specific public interest jobs that will qualify, the maximum income one may earn, and the maximum amount of assistance that is provided each year. Individuals who are positive that they want to work in public interest positions upon graduation should be sure to find out if the law schools they are considering have LRAPs.

### Outside Scholarships

There are numerous scholarships for law students sponsored by the American Bar Association, private firms, regional bar associations, and other public and private entities. Many law schools post on their Web sites information about any and every outside scholarship that comes to their attention. Students should continually investigate outside sources of scholarships funds that may be available to them.

## Conclusion

Gaining admission to law school is a competitive, challenging, and arduous process. It involves a substantial commitment of time and money. The more informed and knowledgeable a prospective student becomes about different law schools and about the admissions process prior to applying, the more likely that individual is to matriculate at the law school that is the right fit.

Law school admissions counselors and office staff (from the most senior dean of admissions to the receptionist) are there to help prospective students work their way through the process. Prospective students should never hesitate to call or e-mail law school admissions offices to ask for guidance and assistance. Finally, although the law school admissions process can be overwhelming and daunting, all prospective law students should keep in mind that the ultimate reward—becoming a lawyer licensed to practice—is worthy of all the effort. It allows one to choose to make one's mark from among a wide variety of fields of practice, in a great variety of settings.

/ CHAPTER THIRTY-FIVE /

*by Catherine Solow, M.A.*
*Assistant Dean of*
*Student Affairs and Curriculum and*
*Director of Admissions*
*Carver College of Medicine*
*University of Iowa–Iowa City*

35

# Medical Schools

The goal of a highly selective medical school admissions process is to choose students with the academic abilities, commitment to service, and personal characteristics to become successful medical students and practicing physicians. The process has a number of similarities across all medical schools, but some aspects can be as unique as the 125 medical schools found in the United States (and the 17 accredited Canadian medical schools which are also members of the Association of American Medical Colleges).

A three-pronged mission of education, research, and service guides the selection of students, but some medical schools have distinct programs and strategic goals that may also influence the selection process. For example, public medical schools have a duty to train physicians who will ultimately serve the people of that state; thus, such medical schools offer applicants who are in-state residents a distinct advantage in the application process.

While much of the information contained in this chapter can be generalized across all medical schools, this chapter is written from the perspective of an admissions officer at a public medical school. This chapter discusses the competitive applicant and what he or she needs to do to prepare for medical school; resources available to applicants; and information about the application and interview process. The chapter also provides some discussion of combined degree programs, criminal background checks, and financing a medical education. Table 35.1, on page 477, contains a sample timeline to guide applicants.

## The Competitive Medical School Applicant

The competitive applicant has an academic profile that points to potential success in a rigorous basic science curriculum of the type found in medical school. Components of this profile considered by admissions committees include performance in undergraduate, post-baccalaureate, and graduate courses, particularly science and math courses; scores on the Medical College Admissions Test (MCAT), a standardized entrance exam; the rigor of the undergraduate curriculum completed by the applicant; and the trend of the overall grade point average. In addition to this academic profile, it is hoped that a competitive applicant would have a service orientation, including experience working or volunteering with patients in a health care environment, and involvement in co-curricular activities that enhance preparation and readiness for medical school. Medical school admissions committees also look for superior communication skills, since future physicians will need to communicate with patients from a range of socioeconomic, racial, ethnic, and cultural backgrounds.

Many medical schools specifically note that an applicant's contribution to the diversity of the entering class is an important consideration when selecting students. Each applicant's unique strengths, experiences, and background enrich the learning environment and, as a result, provide support for training culturally competent physicians who can better serve the needs of a changing American population.[238]

Most important, each applicant should reflect on his or her experiences, activities, strengths, and differences and be able to respond with specificity and depth to the question, "Why medicine?"—the universal question asked of applicants to medical school.

## Preparing for Medical School

All medical schools expect prospective students to master content in basic science courses, and most will require specific courses in physics, chemistry, and biology prior to entering medical school (AAMC 2007a, p. 12). There may be school-specific policies related to courses completed on the Internet; AP and CLEP credit; and courses taken at international institutions. Applicants should check directly with the medical schools in question about how such courses and credit will be considered in the selection process. Some schools have recently revised premedical course requirements to include completion of coursework in the humanities and social and behavioral sciences, so as to encourage breadth in the undergraduate

[238] An emphasis on diversity reflects back to the attitudes of the medical school, as well in dealing with its variety of students. Note particularly the last sentence of the "Statement on Diversity" of the University of Iowa (2008) Carver College of Medicine: "Consistent with its academic mission and standards, the University of Iowa Carver College of Medicine is committed to achieving excellence through diversity. As a community of faculty, staff and students engaged in research, patient care, scholarship, teaching and learning, the College of Medicine fosters an environment that is diverse, humane and welcoming. Efforts are made to provide a supportive environment in which people from a wide variety of backgrounds and cultures may encounter each other in a spirit of cooperation, openness, and mutual respect."

curriculum. A discussion about the value of the current premedical requirements and undergraduate preparation is beginning at the national level among the membership of the Association of American Medical Colleges (AAMC).

A premedical advisor can be of significant assistance to students as they select appropriate courses and a major, determine the best path through college, and prepare for entrance into medical school. Students are strongly encouraged to take advantage of advising services early in their undergraduate years and to sustain this important relationship throughout college. The National Association of Advisors for the Health Professions has an excellent working relationship with medical schools, and the AAMC is also an outstanding resource for advisors assisting students interested in medical school.

The rigor of the basic science curriculum and the courses taken by an applicant to fulfill the premedical requirements are often a good predictor of success on the Medical College Admission Test (MCAT), the standardized exam required by most medical schools.[239] With a recent move to computerized testing, there are now 22 different administrations of the exam.[240]

As mentioned earlier, admissions committees will use the MCAT score in their decision-making, but it is only one of many selection criteria considered. There are commercial preparatory courses that many applicants feel are beneficial in preparing for the MCAT, although applicants can also expect to perform well on that examination if they have taken a disciplined approach to a review of their basic science courses, and have also taken one or more practice tests in a simulated test environment. An applicant may choose to retake the MCAT if he believes that the score received does not accurately reflect his abilities, and he believes he can improve his performance. Multiple scores are treated differently by schools; some may consider only the most recent score, others average the scores, and some schools may take the highest score from each of the sections. Before retaking the exam, the applicant should check the MCAT policy at medical schools of interest. The Medical School Admission Requirements (MSAR) guide is a good resource for information about the mean scores in each MCAT section for entering classes at individual medical schools.

## Application Process

Most medical schools require applicants to utilize the services of the American Medical College Application Service (AMCAS) to submit their primary application. However, the six public institutions in Texas require applicants to apply through the Texas Medical and Dental Schools Application Service, and there are two medical schools with their own application process (AAMC 2007a, p. 17).

[239] The Association of American Medical Colleges commissioned a report on the "Validity of the Medical College Admission Test for Predicting Medical School Performance." An abstract of the report, as well as a link to the full text, are available on the MCAT Web site, at <www.aamc.org/students/mcat>, under the section titled "For Admissions Officers and Pre-Health Advisors."

[240] See <www.aamc.org/students/mcat> for FAQs and more information on the MCAT schedule and registration.

Most schools also require submission of a secondary application, as well, which is requested of applicants who meet preliminary screening criteria. The secondary application asks applicants to provide responses to one or more short essay questions, in addition to some further demographic information. A file is considered complete when both primary and secondary applications, as well as letters of recommendation, have been received.

AMCAS provides a service to both the applicant and the participating medical schools. The applicant is able to send application materials to a central location, and AMCAS will then forward them to medical schools designated by the applicant. The primary function of AMCAS in support of the admissions process at medical schools is verification of all academic transcripts, with the exception of those from international institutions.[241]

Deadlines for primary and secondary applications will vary slightly by medical school, but it is to the applicant's advantage to apply in a timely manner, since review of a file may begin as soon as it is considered complete.

All medical schools have criteria—including but not limited to grade point average and MCAT scores—which they use to screen primary and secondary applications. Receipt of a secondary application and a subsequent interview invitation are dependent on meeting screening guidelines, although there are some schools which will send a secondary application to all applicants. Interviews are a mandatory component of the application process at most medical schools and provide an important opportunity for the admissions committee to gauge an applicant's communication skills and to gain additional information about the applicant's suitability for medicine.

The format of the interview varies across medical schools, but typically applicants meet with faculty, from both basic science and clinical teaching backgrounds; interact with current students; tour facilities; and receive important information about financial aid. Applicants may be interviewed one-on-one or as part of a group, and there is usually a defined time limit for the interaction. At some medical schools, the interviews are conducted by members of the admissions committee. At others, the interviewers may not have access to the applicant's file, so it is highly advisable for the applicant to consider which important pieces of information contained in her admissions file she would like to introduce or underscore in the interview. The results of the interview are considered in any appraisal of the application.[242]

Applicants are also required to submit letters of recommendation, and the number of letters required varies by medical school. At least one letter typically is written by someone who knows how the applicant performs in an academic setting, preferably a professor from a science course. Some undergraduate institutions have premedical committees, whose members interview all students interested in medical school and then write a composite letter for each applicant. Others have offices that serve as a central repository for letters of recommenda-

[241] See <www.aamc.org/audienceamcas.htm> for more information about AMCAS.

[242] See <www.studentdoctor.net> for more information about interview processes.

tion, and then send packets of letters to medical schools designated by the applicant. In any case, it is incumbent upon the applicant to determine how many letters are allowed and how composite letters and packets are considered by the medical schools.

It is very important that applicants designate letter writers who can comment on the candidate's abilities beyond a test score and a final grade in a given course. For example, information about and assessment of an applicant's communication skills, ability to work in a team environment, and those personal characteristics important to the practice of medicine are considered to be of considerable value to the selection process.

Applicants will apply either through the Early Decision Program (EDP) or the regular application process. Those applying through EDP should have outstanding credentials, and are allowed to apply to only one medical school during that process. The applicant is informed of the outcome of the review process by October 1st and, if admitted, she is considered to be obligated to attend that school. If an applicant is not admitted through EDP, her application will again be considered during the regular application process. At this time, she may submit additional applications to other medical schools.

TABLE 35.1: **Sample Timeline for an Applicant to the 2008 Entering Class**

| | |
|---|---|
| **2007** | |
| **Jan. 27–Sept. 8** | Medical College Admission Test (MCAT) dates. Refer to the AAMC Website for registration and test dates: www.aamc.org/mcat |
| **May 3** | AMCAS Application available for applicant data entry on the AAMC Web site: www.aamc.org |
| **June 5** | Completed and certified AMCAS applications may be submitted. |
| **June 15** | Last day for Early Decision Plan (EDP) applicants to sit for the MCAT |
| **Aug. 1** | Deadline for receipt of applications & transcripts by AMCAS for Early Decision Plan (EDP) |
| **Sept. 1** | Deadline for receipt of supplemental materials by the Carver College of Medicine for EDP applicants |
| **Sept. 8** | Last date for 2008 applicants to sit for the MCAT |
| **Oct. 1** | EDP applicants notified of decisions by this date |
| **Nov. 1** | Deadline for receipt of completed AMCAS applications (including MD/Ph.D.); Applicants are urged to send materials to AMCAS earlier and to keep in touch with AMCAS regarding receipt of transcripts. |
| **Dec. 15** | Absolute deadline for receipt of supplemental application materials by the Carver College of Medicine. We have a rolling admissions process; therefore, files becoming complete earlier will be reviewed for earlier interview positions. Applications with missing materials will be cancelled or rejected if not received by this date. |
| **2008** | |
| **January 1** | Submit the Free Application for Federal Student Aid FAFSA or renewal FAFSA designating the University of Iowa (001892) to Federal Student Aid Programs as soon as possible after this date. |
| **March 15** | Target date for all final admissions decisions to be announced |

The regular admissions process usually begins in the early fall, and admissions decisions—whether the student will be deemed an admit, an alternate, or a denied candidate—may be made on a rolling basis or in batches throughout the fall, winter, and early spring. Medical schools are committed to offering admission by March 30th to the number of applicants at least equal to the size of the entering class. Public medical schools reserve a greater number of seats in the class for residents of the state, and construct separate alternate lists for residents and nonresidents. Alternate lists are maintained until the first day of orientation, and slots in the class are filled by alternates as admission offers are declined. The MSAR provides information as to the percentage of residents and nonresidents applying to and accepted by individual public and private[243] medical schools.

## Appraisal Process

All admissions decisions are made by an admissions committee which is usually composed of clinical and basic science faculty, physicians practicing in the community, and current medical students. Admissions staff and financial aid personnel may also attend meetings as non-voting members to support the work of the committee. The size and organization of the admissions committee will vary, depending on the number of applications received and whether the committee also conducts interviews with applicants. When possible, the membership of the committee includes a broad representation by academic departments, and by gender, race, and ethnic background.

Applications are reviewed holistically; that is, AMCAS and secondary applications, letters of recommendation, the academic profile, and interviews are all considered in the review process. The applicant's potential to be successful in a rigorous basic science curriculum, previous healthcare experience, commitment to service, personal characteristics important to the practice of medicine, and enriching qualities are important factors taken into account by reviewers. The admissions committee review of files is guided by the medical school's mission, the annual charge by the dean, and faculty input. The university's Office of the General Counsel also acts as a valuable resource in ensuring fair and equitable treatment of all applicants.

In the unfortunate event that an applicant is denied admission, many admissions officers will provide feedback from those who reviewed the file and will discuss options available to the candidate to enhance future applications, if he or she chooses to submit one. It is to the applicant's advantage to solicit advice, since admissions committees will note, upon a subsequent re-submission of the application, how the applicant responded to the advice given.

## Combined Degree Programs

A number of medical schools now offer combined degree programs in a variety of disciplines that serve to better meet the professional interests of students. One advantage of a combined degree program is that the time necessary to complete both degrees is shortened. Most common is the M.D./Ph.D. program, which provides training for a career as a physician-scientist. There are approximately 40 programs across the country that are funded by the National Institutes of Health and are known as Medical Scientist Training Programs (MSTP). At schools with MSTPs, students most likely will receive full funding for both M.D. and Ph.D. training. There may be a separate admissions committee for the MSTP that considers an applicant's commitment to and potential for a research career, or an admissions decision may be made by the M.D. admissions committee. If an applicant is not admitted to the MSTP, it is

[243] For those private medical colleges which receive state funding.

possible to be considered for the M.D.-only program. At some schools it is possible to enter an MSTP or M.D./Ph.D. program after the first year of medical school.

Other combined degree programs most commonly found at medical schools are M.D./J.D., M.D./M.P.H., and M.D./M.B.A. programs. It is necessary for the applicant to meet all application, admission, and graduation requirements for the degree program combined with the M.D.

About 25 percent of medical schools offer a combined undergraduate college (B.A. or B.S.)/M.D. program to outstanding high school students (AAMC 2007a, p. 59). There are a number of advantages to entering this kind of combined degree program, although ultimate progression to medical school may be contingent on meeting the expected standard of performance in the undergraduate years of the combined program.

## Post-Admission

Once an applicant is accepted, all 125 U.S. medical schools that are members of the AAMC follow "traffic rules," which are a set of recommendations that assist in ensuring that communication to applicants about acceptance processes is clear and timely. Likewise, there is a set of recommendations for applicants to follow related to multiple acceptances and timely notification of a final decision.[244]

In addition to meeting admission requirements, medical schools have criteria known as technical standards that are essential for students to meet in order to fulfill the academic requirements of the program. Students, with or without disabilities, will all be expected to meet the same technical standards, although reasonable accommodations will be made to assist a student in learning, performing, and satisfying them. Candidates for the M.D. degree must have observation abilities, communication skills, motor skills, intellectual, conceptual, integrative, and quantitative abilities, and behavioral and social attributes as set out in the technical standards.[245] Each medical school has slightly different technical standards, so checking with the individual medical schools is advised. Reasonable accommodations may be made for some disabilities in certain areas, but students must be able to perform in a reasonably independent manner. Admitted students are encouraged to contact the admissions office or the designated office that serves students with disabilities soon after admission and well before matriculation if accommodations are necessary.

Criminal background checks are increasingly becoming a necessary step in the post-admission process and before a student matriculates. State laws and a compelling interest in guarding patient safety are leading medical schools to conduct checks on each admitted student. The AAMC has endorsed criminal background checks (AAMC 2005a). During the admissions process, applicants are advised to be forthcoming on AMCAS and secondary applications when addressing questions about misdemeanors and felonies. This allows admis-

[244] See <www.aamc.org/students/applying/policies/applicants.htm>.

[245] For the technical standards of the University of Iowa Carver College of Medicine, as an example, please see <www.medicine.uiowa.edu/osac/admissions/Apply/apply_reqs.htm>.

sions committees to make decisions based on all available information, including a criminal record, although the criminal background check itself is expected to be conducted only on accepted applicants. Applicants need to provide a release for the check to be done and may request a copy of the results. If a pilot program with the classes entering in fall 2008 at ten medical schools goes well, AMCAS will provide a CBC service for all applicants starting with medical school classes entering in fall 2009—an arrangement which is expected to significantly reduce redundancy of effort and expense to both applicants and schools.

For a number of reasons, an admitted student may choose to delay entrance to medical school. An opportunity to travel, continue with a research project, or follow through on a commitment to a service mission or fellowship offer are examples of occasions when an admitted student may request additional time before matriculating. Most schools have a policy which limits the time for a deferral to a year, although exceptions can be made for unusual opportunities. The school's policy may also limit the number of deferrals granted and may not allow the student to apply to other medical schools between the point of admission and matriculation. The admitted student is encouraged to contact the medical school as soon as he or she has determined interest in deferring, so that expectations and instructions can be clearly communicated.

## Financing a Medical Education

Tuition and fees at private medical schools in 2006–2007 ranged from just over $14,000 to over $48,000 per year, while tuition and fees at public medical schools ranged from about $9,300 to over $32,000 per year (AAMC 2007b; 2007c).

Medical school is expensive, but has long been considered a good investment, since it is expected that most graduates will be able to pay off their debt with relative ease. In recent years, however, there have been significant increases in medical school tuition and fees; more students are graduating from college with higher undergraduate debt; and thus the median indebtedness of medical school graduates has substantially increased (AAMC 2005b, p. 1).[246] In fact, the projected median educational indebtedness for 2007 graduates at public medical schools is close to $120,000, while projected indebtedness for graduates of private medical schools is about $160,000 (p. 4).

During the admissions process, medical schools are expected to fully disclose all costs associated with obtaining the M.D. degree, the average debt incurred by recent graduates, and the types of aid available to students (p. 9). Students complete the Free Application for Federal Student Aid as well as forms required by the individual medical school in order to determine eligibility and need for funds.

The overwhelming majority of medical students receive aid of some type to help finance their medical education. Merit- and need-based scholarships, grants, and loans are available

[246] See www.brynmawr.edu/healthpro/documents/MedSchoolDeg05.pdf.

although repayment programs like those funded by states, the Indian Health Service, the military, and the National Health Service Corps. Educational loans—federal subsidized or unsubsidized and private—are the most typical form of financial assistance received by students. It is highly unusual for medical students to receive funding through work-study programs. Financial aid officers work actively with students to help with budgeting and debt management throughout and beyond medical school. It is also common practice for exit interviews to be held with all students before they graduate to discuss repayment options and strategies to meet debt obligations.

## Support for Student Success

Most schools hold formal orientation programs just prior to the start of classes that serve to acquaint incoming students with the environment, culture, and expectations of the medical school. Equally important, orientation programs introduce new students to valuable personnel and resources that will help ensure their success. Academic, personal, and career counseling; writing program services; and free tutoring assistance are but a few ways students are supported outside the classroom throughout medical school.

A pre-matriculation program may be offered during the summer preceding the start of medical school to selected admitted students. Basic science course content, academic advancement techniques, and an introduction to the collegiate community are the goals of most such programs, to help ensure a successful transition to medical school.

## Conclusion

Choosing the next generation of physicians is a complex and highly selective process—but it serves to help ensure that future health care needs will be met by well-trained, service-oriented, and compassionate professionals.

/ CHAPTER THIRTY-SIX /

*by Carmen Fortin, M.A.*
*Assistant Dean/Director of Admission*
*Simmons College—School for Health Studies*

36

# Health Studies Programs

According to the Bureau of Labor Statistics (BLS 2008) of the U.S. Department of Labor, "more new wage and salary jobs—about 19 percent, or 3.6 million—created between 2004 and 2014 will be in health care than in any other industry." A population which is both growing and aging has precipitated a demand for increased health services; technological advances in patient care allow for a greater number of medical conditions to be treated; and the public's increased focus on healthy lifestyles is also a factor. Eight out of twenty occupations projected to grow the fastest are in health care (BLS 2008a).

Why are there so many positions to be filled in the health care professions? Because many of the retiring baby boomers comprise a large portion of these workers! Thus there will be an urgent need for highly skilled individuals in all clinical settings, from nurses to health care administrators, and from nutritionists to physical therapists. Moreover, experienced practitioners will also be needed to teach the next generation of professionals in health care.

The range of job opportunities in the spectrum of health care professions is broad, and thus the required education for different specialties is equally varied. Institutions of higher education have responded to the range of needs by creating a variety of pathways for future professionals to obtain the appropriate credentials and preparation. In certain health care specialties, master's or doctorate degrees have become the terminal degrees. However, employees can advance in many career paths without an advanced degree. Employers in some work settings offer tuition reimbursement, flexible work hours, and on-site opportunities to acquire appropriate academic and clinical foundations for further professional advancement.

What is the expected academic and experiential preparation needed to qualify for these future jobs? In addition, what academic options are available to those without prior academic backgrounds in health science, but who are nevertheless interested in such challenging careers?

This chapter will address four different health-related pathways at the graduate level:

- Health care administration
- Nursing
- Nutrition
- Physical therapy

All of the disciplines noted above, except for health care administration, are driven by professional licensing and certification requirements. As will be discussed later in this chapter, such requirements influence admission criteria, application processes, and curriculum content.

Most of these degree programs can be pursued on a part-time or a full-time basis—*if* the student is a U.S. citizen or permanent resident alien. For foreign students requiring an F-1 student visa to study in the United States, however, the path can only be full-time. Since almost all of these programs assume an undergraduate degree, foreign students who need prerequisite courses would not (as of this writing) be able to obtain such a visa to take prerequisite courses before applying for graduate-level work.[247]

This chapter will first discuss the application process generally, and then will address specific issues in applying to each of the four programs named above.

## Application Process

While each institution varies in its specific application requirements, all require an application (print or electronic), accompanied by supporting documents. These include but are not limited to official academic transcripts from all accredited institutions attended in the U.S. or abroad, whether or not a degree was conferred; recommendations; a current résumé; and a personal statement or essay. While all of these items are reviewed as a whole, certain aspects weigh more heavily in the admission decision process, depending upon the specific academic program and institutional policies and goals.

In most cases standardized test scores—such as the Graduate Record Exam (GRE), Graduate Management Admission Test (GMAT), and (for non-native speakers of English) the Test of English as a Foreign Language (TOEFL)—are required for admission. Institutions

[247] One subject of possible change in the immigration laws would allow foreign professionals who are highly skilled, such as nurses, but who do not have all the elements of a bachelor's degree (the normal prerequisite to pursuit of further education in the health professions in the U.S.) to apply for F-1 visas while needing to fill in parts of their U.S. education (such as a bachelor's degree).

may differ in their allowance of a waiver of any of these exams. Some universities exempt the GRE or GMAT for applicants who already hold a master's degree, while others will waive a standardized test score only if the student earned a master's degree in a certain discipline, or works in a setting which requires use of scientific knowledge. Also, if students have successfully completed certain foundation courses before they have formally applied to the program, some institutions will allow a waiver of one of the standardized exams. As to the format in which the scores can be reported, some institutions are equipped to accept electronic scores from the testing agency, while others require a paper record.

The GRE or GMAT should be taken within five years prior to application; the TOEFL should be taken within two years prior to application.[248] Each institution may or may not require certain subject or total scores. In addition, some institutions will create a new composite score by combining the highest individual score for multiple administrations of a test.

Admission committees (usually faculty) in graduate health care seek subjective qualities, as well—qualities which can be ascertained on the evidence of recommendations, the applicant's type of employment and work setting, and/or volunteer experience. These aspects of the application can demonstrate compassion for others, sensitivity to diverse populations and cultures, appreciation of social differences, and the requisite stamina needed in fast-paced environments made complex by limits in health insurance coverage and by statutory and administrative regulations.

Accreditation of the baccalaureate institution is also a factor of great importance. Since the majority of positions in the health care industry require licensing and/or certification, applicants must have earned postsecondary degrees at accredited institutions. Since accreditation is a process unique to the United States, it is thus very important that offices of admission verify that institutions abroad are legitimate.[249]

## Programs in Health Care Administration

### Commonly Offered Degrees

The most common master's degrees in the field of health care administration and management are:

- M.H.A.: Master of Health Administration or Master of Health Care Administration
- M.H.S.A.: Master of Health Services Administration
- M.P.H.: Master of Public Health
- M.B.A.: Master of Business Administration: various health tracks (international health policy, financial health management, etc.)

There are also variations of these degrees.

[248] The Educational Testing Service stores exam scores only for limited periods of time. Students and their advisors should thus check these time limits; then they can determine when such exams should be taken for admissions purposes.

[249] See also AACRAO's *Guide to Bogus Institutions and Documents* for more information on this complex topic.

At the end of this chapter, we will discuss the Certificate of Advanced Graduate Study (CAGS)—in this case, a CAGS in Health Care Administration.

### Accreditation

Graduate programs in health services management and administration can choose to submit themselves for accreditation by the Commission on Accreditation of Healthcare Management Education (CAHME), an accreditor recognized by the U.S. Department of Education.[250] CAMHE is also separately recognized by the Council for Higher Education Accreditation (CHEA).[251]

CAHME promotes and evaluates graduate healthcare management education in the United States and Canada. This voluntarily chosen peer review allows for the improvement of graduate education in this discipline. As such, for students, this accreditation is a benchmark for program content and quality of academic standards.

### Types of Courses

Courses in such programs often include finance, human resources management, ethics, health law, conflict resolution and negotiation, market principles, and quantitative analysis for health care administration. Most programs require two years of full-time study, including either a research project or thesis.

The management segment of the health care profession includes a myriad of employment options in various public or private agencies. The employment outlook for this segment is good: the U.S. Department of Labor predicts a 26 percent increase in job opportunities through 2014 (BLS 2008, Table 2). Many nurses, to take one example, have made a job transition by becoming nurse managers, with the aid of a business-oriented degree. Other settings in which these types of graduates can work include public health departments, law firms, research centers, hospitals, and pharmaceutical companies.

### Admission Criteria

An undergraduate degree from an accredited postsecondary institution in the United States, or from an institution abroad which is recognized by the Ministry of Education in that country, is required to apply to a graduate program with this focus. Although undergraduate degrees, certified by CAHME, do exist in health care administration and provide a specific, relevant foundation for a graduate program, a B.S. or B.A. degree in any academic discipline is acceptable. Two years of prior relevant work experience is expected, whether the health

[250] CAMHE is the accreditor recognized by the U.S. Department of Education with the following scope of recognition: "...accreditation throughout the United States of graduate programs in health services administration" (ED 2008, p. 8). See <www.ed.gov/admins/finaid/accred/accreditation_pg8.html#NationalInstitutional>. See also <www.cahmeweb.org>.

[251] "CHEA's standards are focused primarily on the accrediting organization's ability to promote academic quality and quality improvement" (CHEA 2005, p. 9).

care setting is a health insurance firm, a hospital, a veteran's facility, or a nursing home. In short a degree in health care administration is designed for the working professional.

As noted earlier in this chapter, in relation to standardized tests which need to be submitted, the GRE or GMAT is required, as is TOEFL, when applicable. A semester course in statistics is also generally required.

### Application Review and Evaluation

While all parts of the application are important and considered, the factors which are looked at most carefully for admission to such programs are a combination of the following: academic preparation and performance, related work experience, and the quality of the references. Faculty evaluators look for a solid aptitude in quantitative and analytical skills, leadership abilities, appreciation for diversity, and work experience in a health care setting or related administrative experience which would serve as a good basis for a transition to health care.

## Pathways in Nursing

According to the U.S. Department of Labor, nurses represent the largest segment of workers in the health care field (BLS 2008b). Employment in nursing is projected to grow "much faster than average," (*i.e.*, by 27 percent, between 2004 and 2014) (2008c). Indeed, "registered nurses are expected to create the second largest number of new jobs, in all occupations," through 2014 (2008b). As we have noted at the outset of this chapter, this trend reflects changes in the population (aging); changes in technology (more advances which allow more illnesses to be treated); and, imminently, an anticipated number of retirements in both the clinical and educational settings. None of these trends is expected to change any time soon.

There is a paradox in the field of nursing education. Candidates have applied in great numbers to nursing programs at all levels, but shortages of both faculty and facilities are restricting nursing program enrollments (AACN 2007).[252]

### Employment Options

Employment options for all nursing specialties vary by employment setting, but in hospitals a significant need exists in oncology, geriatrics, rehabilitation, and outpatient surgery. To fill the large number of nursing vacancies, hospitals are offering signing bonuses, flexible work schedules, child care, and tuition reimbursement for further education. Additionally, many healthcare facilities offer online bidding where nurses can sign up to fill open slots at premium wages. Other employment sites include hospices, community clinics, physician offices, public health departments, government agencies, the military, and acute care centers.

[252] "According to AACN's report on *2006–2007 Enrollment and Graduations in Baccalaureate and Graduate Programs in Nursing*, U.S. nursing schools *turned away* 42,866 qualified applicants from baccalaureate and graduate nursing programs in 2006 due to insufficient faculty, clinical sites, classroom space, clinical preceptors, and budget constraints" (AACN 2007). [Emphasis added.]

Two other healthcare settings will share in the increase in employment opportunities: nursing care facilities and home health care. A substantial increase is expected in employment in nursing homes, since an increasing number of elderly will require long-term care. Also, hospitals often discharge patients as soon as possible because of financial or business constraints, thus generating more admissions to nursing facilities. In particular, job growth is expected in units offering rehabilitation for patients with Alzheimer's, stroke, and heart problems. Nursing jobs in home health care will also increase rapidly in response to consumer and health provider preference for care in the home, and advances that make it possible to implement and monitor more sophisticated treatments in the home.

### Preparatory Undergraduate Programs

Educational preparation for nursing varies by the type of position desired, the nature of the specialty, and the health care setting. Nurse training (the former accepted term used in hospitals) was initially provided in hospitals, which awarded diplomas or certificates, before the profession transitioned to an educational pathway in colleges and universities. While hospitals still offer short-term seminars in certain areas germane to their setting, the most common pathway now for nurse preparation is the completion of a formal degree-granting program. The educational path to become a registered nurse (RN) is via an associate's or bachelor's degree and the successful passing of an examination developed by the National Council of Licensure Examination (NCLEX)—the NCLEX examination for Registered Nurses.[253]

For individuals who already have a bachelor's degree, in a discipline other than nursing, some institutions now offer such candidates the option of a second bachelor's degree, which is "fast-tracked" to grant that degree within twelve to eighteen months (depending on the individual's prior degree of preparation *and* the institution's general academic requirements—for example, having a liberal arts core). Such "fast-tracked" second-degree students can then become RNs if they pass the NCLEX-RN exam.

### Levels of Nursing Status

- LICENSED PRACTICAL NURSE (LPN): Academic preparation and clinical experience last about one year. Applicants can enter from high school, and take courses at technical or vocational schools, or in community colleges. Most LPNs provide basic bedside care. In states where the law allows, they may administer prescribed medicines or start intravenous fluids.[254] LPNs are required to take the NCLPX examination for Practical Nurses. That examination is then used by state boards of nursing to assist in making licensure decisions. This is an option which is less widely pursued than the others we will discuss, since this credential only allows for very basic responsibilities.

[253] This NCLEX examination, and another one for Practical Nurses, were both developed by the National Council of State Boards of Nursing (NCSBN).

[254] See U.S. Department of Labor, Bureau of Labor Statistics, *Occupational Outlook Handbook*, at <www.bls.gov/oco/ocos102.htm>.

- **REGISTERED NURSE (RN):** To become RNs, high school graduates can earn associate degrees in two-year nursing programs in community colleges; or they can earn diplomas in three-year programs offered by hospitals (in Massachusetts, there is only one hospital now which offers such a program) or in independent schools of nursing; or they can earn bachelor of science in nursing degrees (BSN). BSN programs usually take four to five years to complete and combine liberal arts courses with a scientific and technical track. All programs include practical experience. Those who have completed an approved program are eligible to take the national written licensing exam, which is administered by each state. All states require licensing.[255]
- **ADVANCED PRACTICE NURSE:** Some RNs choose to become Advanced Practice Nurses. There are four categories of such nurses: Nurse-Practitioners, Clinical Nurse Specialists, Certified Nurse Midwives, and Certified Registered Nurse-Anesthetists.[256]
- **NURSE PRACTITIONER (NP):** Nurse Practitioners hold a master's degree in advanced practical nursing. They have earned NP status by successfully passing the national NP exam. The NP provides extensive patient care, only referring patients to medical specialists if needed. NPs can prescribe medications just as Physician Assistants (PA) can. The primary difference between the role of the NP and the PA is one of independence and autonomy: the PA is under the supervision of a medical doctor who must approve all procedures which the PA wishes to implement, whereas NPs have complete authority to make final decisions about care and treatment.

## Pathways Between Levels

At the graduate level in nursing—master's degrees and post-master's certificates—there are several pathways, depending on a student's prior educational background; every college or university offers different programs and tracks (concentrations). Nearly all graduate nursing programs require a research project which demonstrates the student's ability to complete scholarly work of publishable quality.

This chapter addresses these programs, but not the numerous specific tracks, which could include adult primary health care (with additional focus on gerontology or occupational health), parent-child primary health care (with further concentrations such as special needs, school health), or family primary health care.

Common pathways include:

- RN to MS—For individuals who have diplomas or certificates from the former hospital system, or associate's degrees and an RN license.
- BSN to MS—For individuals with bachelor's degrees in nursing and an RN license.

[255] See <http://careers.stateuniversity.com/pages/496/Registered-Nurse.html>.

[256] See <http://careers.stateuniversity.com/pages/496/Registered-Nurse.html>.

- BA/BS to MS—For individuals with a bachelor's degree in a discipline other than nursing.
- CAGS (Certificate of Advanced Graduate Study)—For individuals who hold a master's degree.

Historically, holders of bachelor's degrees in nursing (BSN) decide after a few years of practical experience to pursue the next level of academic preparation, the master's degree in nursing. The current nursing shortage and the need for more advanced skills has motivated nurses with RN status with either certificate or associate degree qualifications to pursue a master's degree.

The most popular and fastest growing program to prepare for master's degreed nursing is designed for individuals with a bachelor's degree in a discipline other than nursing. This program has no common name; indeed, each university refers to it differently: *direct entry nursing, accelerated nursing,* or *generic master's nursing.* The first half of such a master's program prepares the student in basic nursing knowledge and skills in order to take the NCLEX (RN exam). Admission has become very competitive due to limitations in faculty size and clinical rotation sites. It is important to note that some institutions offer both the BSN and MS degrees upon completion of the requisite curriculum, while others only offer the MS. This variation in practice is determined by institutional policy.

## Admission Criteria

### RN TO MS

Candidates for this entryway must possess a current U.S. RN license in the state of the institution to which they wish to apply, plus work experience in a health care setting. Some universities and colleges in fact require a certain number of years of work experience in order to apply to a master's program. As noted earlier in this chapter, recent completion of courses in statistics and health assessment is often required, as well as standardized test scores (typically GREs are required but can be waived at some schools, such as ours, pending the completion of a foundation course with a grade of B or better); once again TOEFL is required for non-native speakers of English. Moreover, if the candidate earned an associate's degree in the U.S., the institution must have been accredited by an accreditor recognized by the U.S. Department of Education.

### BSN TO MS

Applicants must hold a bachelor's degree in nursing from an accredited U.S. college or university, and a current U.S. RN license in the state of the institution to which they wish to apply. As is true for the RN to MS route, a recent course in statistics and health assessment is required. (A BSN student would have taken statistics and health assessment, but those courses might need to be repeated, depending on how long ago the BSN was earned). Standardized exams (GRE and, for non-native speakers, TOEFL) are also required. Generally there is no requirement of any specific number of years of experience.

*Application Review and Evaluation*
For the above two programs, since most applicants have been working as RNs, the most important factors considered for admission are the candidate's prior academic preparation, his or her work experience, and the quality of the recommendations. However, the emphasis can vary by program and institution; some institutions place more emphasis on test scores and prior academic performance. A common expectation is that applicants have a 3.0 GPA in prior nursing courses as well as in the overall undergraduate record. In addition, institutions look for indications that the candidate can write and communicate clearly—including in shorthand, due to the pace of work environments!

### BA/BS TO MS (CROSS-DISCIPLINE)

*Admission Criteria*
Applicants must hold a bachelor's degree in any academic discipline other than nursing from an accredited U.S. institution or postsecondary institution abroad which is recognized by the Ministry of Education in the home country. While no specific undergraduate discipline is required, most students who apply have bachelor's degrees in biology or psychology. However, the beauty of this type of program is that students bring a wide variety of prior academic foundations, skill sets, and experiences, ranging from undergraduate degrees in business administration to theater, or Peace Corp experience, or work as a research technician. Standardized test scores are required: GRE and TOEFL, where applicable. In addition, institutions usually look for a 3.0 GPA in prerequisite courses and in the overall GPA.

A series of prerequisite courses is also required before the student applies (although some institutions offer the option to complete the prerequisites just prior to the start of the program). Required courses vary slightly by institution, but several are commonly required: one year of human anatomy and physiology with labs, one half-year of organic chemistry with a lab, one half-year of inorganic chemistry with a lab, one half-year of microbiology with a lab or one semester of biology with a lab, one half-year of statistics, and one half-year of either developmental psychology (birth to death content) or nutrition.

Typically such nursing programs require three years of full-time study, or longer if the student decides to reduce enrollment to part-time after taking the RN exam. Essentially, this type of program condenses the theoretical foundation and clinical experience achieved by individuals who followed a nursing curriculum (four years for a BSN and two years for the MS) into three years for someone with no prior nursing focus.

*Application Review and Evaluation*
Applications are closely reviewed for a variety of factors, since this pathway, from the non-nursing BA/BS, is the most competitive in terms of admission. Nursing programs in the Boston area have experienced a significant increase in applications over the past four years—in some cases, four hundred applications for thirty places.

A candidate's academic performance in the prerequisite courses, as well as the overall grade point average, test score results, and recommendations which speak to the candidate's ability to handle rigorous graduate work and the stamina/caring needed to assist individuals in medical need are the key components in the review process. The academic quality and rigor of the institution(s) the applicant previously attended can also be a factor.

Since leadership, critical thinking, and problem-solving skills are important elements in becoming an effective advanced primary care nurse, there should be evidence of such attributes in the application. While paid or volunteer experience in a health care setting and interviews are generally not required, students who have these would have an advantage in the admission process.

### The Future of Nursing Education

Major professional nursing associations—the National League for Nursing, the American Association of Colleges of Nursing, and the American Nurses Association—have expressed great concern about the lack of support for graduate-level nursing education. This failure to invest in master's and doctoral education for nurses has created a shortage of qualified nurse-educators to carry on nursing education at a high level for the next generation.

In 2004, the American Association of Colleges of Nursing (AACN) presented a road map for a new degree—a Doctor of Nursing Practice (DNP). The AACN adopted a goal that such a program should be in place by 2015. This new degree, the DNP, would be designed for people in clinical practice who will eventually transition to administration, organizational management, and policy development.

The program will prepare students with a blend of clinical, organizational, economic, and leadership skills. While the Ph.D. is research-intensive, the proposed DNP degree would be practice-focused. The DNP graduate would seek leadership roles in health care organizations, legislative staff, and policy institutes. The proposed new DNP degree, in short, is intended to have a focus all its own; it would not replace the Ph.D., Ed.D., DNSc, or the master's in nursing degree.

Rather, the DNP embodies a vision for the future of specialty nurse education; it represents a practice-focused doctoral education. The MS in nursing will probably change to being a degree for advanced generalists. The DNP will be similar to the PharmD and DPT (discussed later in this chapter)—that is, a professional-level clinical degree.

Several nursing schools have begun developing programs for new practice doctorates. By February 2006, eleven institutions had Doctor of Nursing Practice programs, while 190 institutions were in the process of developing them. Of those 190 institutions in the planning stage, 29 were planning to collaborate with another institution.

There are and will be different entry points for the DNP. Early candidates held master's degrees, and their curriculum was individualized based on education, experience, and choice of specialization. A candidate who enters the program with a baccalaureate degree in nursing or another field would require a more comprehensive and longer program of study, including more clinical experience.

The long-term benefits of acquiring specialized expertise and advanced skill sets via the DNP provide an advantage both to the student (who gains a wider range of opportunities for employment) and society (which gains a corps of nurses with a better understanding of our health care system and how nursing can contribute to it).

## Nutrition

Today's nutritionists are presented with an array of challenges and an expanding field of career options. While the nation's population is living longer, there is a significant increase in obesity, which can result in chronic diseases such as heart disease, cancer, and diabetes. The one thing which health care providers and insurers can agree upon is that prevention is the key to maintaining or reducing health care costs.

Dietitians and nutritionists plan food and nutrition programs in a variety of settings: hospitals, community centers, rehabilitation centers, schools, health spas, corporate wellness programs, fitness centers, and clinics. They help to prevent diseases and treat illnesses by promoting a healthy lifestyle of sound eating habits and exercise. Additionally, they conduct research and promote nutrition through community education via workshops, seminars, and articles for professional journals.

Nutritionists and dietitians need at least a bachelor's degree in dietetics, foods and nutrition, or food service management. Postsecondary nutrition education is available at both the undergraduate and graduate level. The American Dietetic Association (ADA) is the driving force regarding curriculum and accreditation. Colleges and universities offering bachelor's degrees in nutrition are *not* required to offer master's degrees as well.

While a nutritionist can hold either a bachelor's or a master's degree, only a clinical dietitian can practice in a hospital setting which requires RD (registered dietitian) status. The clinical dietitian assesses patient nutritional needs, develops a nutrition plan, and evaluates a patient's progress. He or she confers with medical personnel to coordinate needed patient treatment. Some dietitians specialize in the monitoring and evaluation of specific conditions such as obesity, diabetes, and renal problems.

Management dietitians supervise meal planning in large facilities such as schools, prisons, veteran's centers, and corporate cafeterias. These positions involve budgeting, hiring, enforcing sanitary rules, and preparing reports.

Community dietitians educate people on the best practices to prevent disease. Such settings would include public health clinics, home health agencies, and schools.

Earning the RD includes the completion of specific undergraduate courses and practice experience. The ADA requires the completion of certain prerequisite courses, called "didactic" courses. These courses cover an array of subjects, including but not limited to chemistry, nutrition, statistics, human anatomy and physiology, psychology, and microbiology.

Once a student successfully completes such courses at an authorized college or university—not all institutions have been granted this authority by the ADA—he or she receives a signed Declaration of Intent to Complete CADE (Commission on Accreditation for Dietetics Education) requirements. This form is then included by the student in the ADA application for a national internship, which is required before an individual takes the RD exam. Candidates (with a bachelor's or master's degree) apply for an internship by designating preferred locations, which can be in hospital or college settings. The ADA uses a computer-based program to match a national pool of applicants with internship programs. There is no guarantee that applicants will receive the internship of their choice. Due to the competitive nature of this program, some students are not matched in any given year.

Each internship site is limited to a specific number of interns each year, based on the number of supervisors or faculty and facilities. Some internships are paid, while others are unpaid; some college settings, if they require completion of a course during the internship, charge tuition for the duration of the internship (six to twelve months). Upon completion of the internship, students receive a certificate and take the RD exam a few months later.

More than 50 percent of all nutrition jobs are in hospitals, outpatient or nursing care facilities, or physician's offices. Dietitians with specialized training and a master's degree will experience good employment options. According to the *Occupational Outlook Handbook,* employment in this sector will increase 18 to 26 percent through 2014 (BLS 2007c; 2007d).

A variety of graduate program tracks exist: nutritional geriatrics, international nutrition, nutritional policy, and nutritional wellness. Most programs require two years of full-time enrollment; they may include a research project or thesis. Many candidates interested in a career in nutrition are career-changers.

### Admission Criteria

While an undergraduate degree in nutrition is not required, in most cases an applicant must have completed a series of prerequisite courses before applying to a graduate program. Such courses vary by institution and program. These can include chemistry with labs, human anatomy and physiology with lab, statistics, and certain foundation courses in nutrition. As with other programs discussed in this chapter, a degree from an accredited U.S. college or university or a postsecondary institution abroad—one which is recognized by the Ministry of Education in the home country—is required. Usually, GRE and TOEFL (when applicable) are also required.

### Application Review and Evaluation

Faculty on admission committees seriously consider a candidate's academic achievement in both the prerequisite courses and the overall undergraduate record. Academic performance in science courses is, of course, especially important. Standardized test scores are weighed differently by each institution, but these scores would be especially telling for students who have not had a science background and have not used quantitative skills. Since communicating with clients and with various health care professionals is frequent and necessary in this profession, writing ability is also very important.

### Future of Nutrition Education

As part of an increasing concern to foster greater competency and accountability in the workplace, the American Dietetic Association is continuing to study a new plan for the education and credentialing of registered dieticians. Various models are being considered. One would require a graduate degree in nutrition for eligibility to take the registered dietician exam and for professional entry into dietetics practice; another recommendation would involve the expanding of supervisory practice hour requirements. Other concerns include a better blending of undergraduate and graduate courses, and the need for institutions that currently offer only a bachelor's degree in nutrition to transition to offering a master's program, as well.

## Physical Therapy

Employment in physical therapy is another segment of the health care industry which is expected to increase much faster than average (*i.e.*, by 27 percent or more), according to the U.S. Department of Labor (BLS 2007c; 2007e). Job opportunities will be good in acute care hospitals, rehabilitation centers, and orthopedics sites. In fact, at the current time, many facilities cannot find enough qualified physical therapists and are offering sign-on bonuses, as the nursing profession does. Other employment settings include teaching hospitals, home care agencies, private practice, professional sports teams, and school systems.

Employment requires a degree from an institution accredited by the American Physical Therapy Association (APTA), an accreditor recognized by the U.S. Department of Education and by CHEA. Additionally, physical therapists must be licensed in the state where they choose to practice. Licensure to practice physical therapy does not include degree-specific requirements, only graduation from an accredited program.

Physical therapists provide services that help restore function, improve mobility, relieve pain, and prevent or minimize disabilities from disease or injury. Physical therapists examine, test, measure, and prescribe therapies to improve range of motion, balance, and posture. While physical therapy assistants can perform routine support tasks under the supervision of the physical therapist, the physical therapist has complete autonomy to work with patients.

The physical therapy educational path was initially similar to that of nursing, where people earned diplomas or certificates in hospital settings. Then, programs evolved into being offered in postsecondary institutions. Physical therapy programs at the bachelor's level were five years in length and included one year of clinical rotations. Physical therapy education then transitioned to the master's degree—an additional two to three years of advanced study beyond the four or five year bachelor's degree, depending upon when the individual was enrolled and when the undergraduate degree was conferred.

Bachelor's degrees in physical therapy are no longer offered. Rather, students earn a bachelor's degree in health science/studies if they are in an accelerated undergraduate physical therapy track (see below), or in any other undergraduate discipline, to then obtain either a Master's in Physical Therapy (MSPT) or a Doctorate in Physical Therapy (DPT).

In June 2000, the APTA issued a "Vision 2020" statement *suggesting* that by 2020, all licensed physical therapists have a DPT (Doctor in Physical Therapy)—a postbaccalaureate degree conferred upon successful completion of a doctoral level professional (entry-level) or post-professional education program. The core element of this clinical degree is evidence-based practice. The DPT is not considered in the category of "academic" degrees such as the Ph.D., DSc, or MD.

Since this announcement, colleges and universities offering graduate physical therapy programs either replaced their master's programs in physical therapy (MSPT) with the DPT, continued to offer both the master's and doctorate programs, or transitioned to the accelerated undergraduate track (see below).

## Doctoral Programs

- ACCELERATED DPT PROGRAMS: These are designed for undergraduate students wishing to pursue the bachelor's degree and DPT on a continuous basis and in a reduced period of time. Students would apply as high school seniors or as transfer students to institutions which offer this accelerated track. Upon successful completion of prerequisite courses (attaining a 3.0 GPA) and achieving an overall GPA of 3.0 (commonly required at most institutions) in the junior year, the student would declare his or her intent to pursue the DPT. The student would then "funnel" through the system by taking graduate courses as a senior; he or she would complete the DPT program in two years of full-time study beyond the four-year undergraduate degree program. The student would still receive a bachelor's degree in the discipline designated by the institution (health studies/sciences, kinesiology, etc.), culminating in the DPT. The total length of this program is six years.
- POSTBACCALAUREATE PROGRAMS: These are designed for students who hold an undergraduate degree in any discipline from an accredited U.S. institution, or from an institution abroad which is recognized by the Ministry of Education in the home country. This is a three-year, full-time program, culminating in the awarding of the DPT.
- POST-PROFESSIONAL DPT: This is designed for U.S. licensed and practicing physical therapists who hold certificates, diplomas, or bachelor's or master's degrees in physical therapy. Such "bridge" or "transitional" programs are frequently offered online and are shortened because as practitioners, such individuals have already been exposed to the clinical and research components of a standard DPT program. This program takes into

account the learner's knowledge, skills, and professional experience and builds upon this by adding new elements to the curriculum, thus reflecting developments since the student's graduation from the initial physical therapy program. This degree is often referred to as "transition DPT" or "t DPT." These programs vary considerably in terms of purpose/outcome, scope, breadth of content, length, and cost.

### Application Process

Currently institutions rely on their own print or electronic applications. Within the next year after the publication of this chapter, the APTA may adopt a "common" application process similar to that of the medical schools and the schools of public health. Students will send all required materials to a vendor with a processing fee, and the application and supporting documents would then be sent either via mail or electronically to each institution to which the student wishes to apply. It is not certain, however, whether institutions will have developed the appropriate infrastructure to make use of this process immediately.

### Admission Criteria

For the pathways indicated in item numbers one and two above ("Doctoral Programs"), students must have completed certain prerequisite courses and achieved a certain GPA (usually 3.0) in those courses. While there is no standard series of prerequisite courses required as yet in all graduate PT programs, these are common expectations:

One year of human anatomy and human physiology with lab, one year of chemistry with lab, one year of physics with lab, one semester or one year of biology with lab, one half-year of statistics, one semester of exercise physiology, and two different psychology courses. Some institutions require one year of calculus rather than statistics. Preparation for this profession is not unlike that required for medical school. The APTA is currently considering instituting a common "core" of prerequisite courses for admission.

Additionally, a candidate must hold a bachelor's degree (any discipline) from an accredited U.S. college or university or from a university abroad which is recognized by the Ministry of Education in the home country. Standardized tests are required: GRE and (when applicable) TOEFL.

Applicants must present documentation of paid or unpaid experience or observation in physical therapy or athletic training. The expected number of hours varies by institution, and ranges from 30 to 100 hours in total. For the transitional DPT (the third item under "Doctoral Programs," above), applicants must have a valid, current U.S. physical therapy license and work experience (the number of years required varies by program). Additionally, usually a recent course in statistics is required, and for online programs, access to a computer and comfort in using various software programs is expected. Admission criteria also vary, but the majority of programs will attempt to assess both the work experience of the candidate and his or her clinical competence.

In fact, two application options are frequently available: standard, for recent graduates with little practical experience, or advanced, for physical therapists who have practiced for several years, and have perhaps conducted research and published articles. Such experience can sometimes be used to waive certain courses in the DPT curriculum.

### Application Review and Evaluation

For postbaccalaureate programs (pathway number two above), a solid academic performance in the prerequisite courses is a must. In addition, the admission committee will closely consider the candidate's overall academic performance, the quality of the undergraduate program attended, type and scope of related health care observation or experience, outside interests, and test score results. Quantitative and analytical skills are very important. If a candidate appears strong, he or she will be invited to campus for a personal interview. All of these factors weigh fairly evenly in the decision-making process.

For the DPT bridge program, the most important criteria for admission are U.S. licensure and recent clinical experience.

## Post-Master's Certificates

### CAGS in Health Care Administration

The Certificate in Advanced Graduate Study (CAGS) is designed for individuals who already hold graduate degrees in another discipline and who now want to serve as health care administrators and leaders. This particular academic credential is not offered at all institutions. Professions of typical applicants include social workers, researchers, nurses, and financial officers.

The curriculum offered can differ from one institution to another; while some programs require a specific series of courses, other programs are individually designed to build upon the student's strengths by allowing students to focus on material which is new to them. The curriculum may also include fieldwork, independent research, or a practicum. This certificate can be used as a terminal credential in certain types of employment, although it can also serve as a bridge to a doctoral program for other types of positions. The length of such a program can also vary by institution.

#### ADMISSION CRITERIA

As with applications for other health care-related degrees, the prior degree must have been earned at an accredited institution (or if a non-U.S. institution, from a university which is recognized by the Ministry of Education in that country). Generally speaking, most prior academic disciplines will be considered. While GREs typically are not required, a TOEFL examination (for non-native speakers) is. Work experience showing leadership ability is also expected.

#### APPLICATION REVIEW AND EVALUATION

It is usually expected that the candidate will have achieved an overall GPA of 3.0 in the master's program which the candidate is presenting for this post-master's Certificate. Since the goal of a CAGS program is to develop leaders and managers in the health care arena, evidence of an ability to mentor and lead diverse groups of people, analytical aptitude, and problem-solving skills should be identifiable via references from supervisors, and should also be demonstrated by work experiences. In addition, prior and current employment and future career goals should be compatible with the expected program outcomes.

### CAGS in Nursing

These certificates are designed for individuals seeking specialized advanced education to enhance knowledge, transition to a different nursing specialty area, or to pursue new leadership roles as healthcare trends continue to evolve. Such a certificate can be used as a terminal credential in some specialties, while it can also be a bridge to a doctoral program for others. Program content and length varies by institution.

Concentrations/tracks in nursing range from occupational health nursing, oncology nursing, or health professions education, to family health (adult or pediatric) and psychiatric nursing. Such programs are usually cooperatively designed by the candidate and his or her academic advisor. Such programs are not necessarily offered at institutions offering master's degrees in nursing, especially if the institution offers a Ph.D. or Doctor of Nursing Science (DNSc).

#### ADMISSION CRITERIA

Required: A master's degree from an accredited U.S. college or university, or from a university abroad which is recognized by the Ministry of Education in the home country. Depending on the specialty of the desired certificate, certain master's degrees in particular may be required—for example, a MS in nursing, as well as NP certification. Generally, GREs are not required, but TOEFL would be (where applicable). A minimum overall GPA of 3.0 is typically required in prior master's work.

#### APPLICATION REVIEW AND EVALUATION

Academic performance in the master's program and work experience are two essential factors in the admission decision as to candidates for a Certificate in Advanced Graduate Study. Additionally, research and leadership qualities are important attributes which admission committees seek, since such programs of study work to prepare individuals for leadership positions in the field.

## Summary

In summary, rapid changes in the health care system impact how and where care is delivered, who provides particular services, and the way in which health care is managed and financed. The health care professions urgently require people who are professionally prepared with clinical expertise, leadership abilities, and a holistic view of care and cure. Medical and health professionals with advanced degrees will have ample job opportunities, higher earnings, and greater job flexibility.

The process of ascertaining the appropriate academic foundation of applicants, verifying the rigors and authenticity of undergraduate programs, determining an individual's ability to embark upon graduate studies, and identifying requisite personal attributes needed to succeed in the challenging yet rewarding "calling" of health care can be labor-intensive but gratifying, because the ultimate results are so significant. The graduate programs discussed here represent only a small portion of the many professions which address the needs of those suffering from illness, injury, and disease.

/ CHAPTER THIRTY-SEVEN /

*by Pat Ellison, B.A.*
*Associate Director of Admissions*
*and Assistant Dean for Graduate Studies*
*The University of Texas at Austin*

37

# Graduate Admissions Issues

Regardless of the institution, its size or its mission, graduate schools have much in common when it comes to admissions—both in terms of technology, and goals. As to technology, most graduate schools today use online applications of one kind or another; many offer online application status-checking; and some even inform applicants of decisions by e-mail or via secure Web sites. As to goals, all graduate schools seek excellence in highly-motivated student candidates. After all the transcripts of both U.S. and international applicants have been evaluated, grade point averages calculated, and degree equivalences determined so that faculty may review an application, the desired outcome for all graduate programs is the admission and enrollment of the best and the brightest students.

This chapter will acknowledge the concerns of graduate departments—concerns which often result in a "decentralization to the departments" of the processing of applications at this level of study. Then, the chapter will set out the advantages of a centralized graduate admissions processing "shop." Finally, it will discuss some issues for the future, including staffing and technological needs, and the impact of the "millennial generation," now at the graduate level.

## Centralizing the Application Process

While the *undergraduate* application process is highly centralized and is usually overseen by a high-level official charged with enrollment management, the management of the graduate application process can vary considerably across institutions. In many universities, even though a graduate dean and a faculty governing body preside over the process, the admissions process is in fact confided to the discretion of the individual department. In other universities, however, there is more emphasis on a "centralized admissions" model even for graduate admissions.

Even so, the term "centralized admissions" can mean different things at different institutions. At many institutions, the graduate application process is shoehorned into the undergraduate admissions office. No staff members are dedicated solely to graduate processing. No priority is given to processing graduate applications, and admissions staff members alternate between processing undergraduate and graduate files. It is little wonder that graduate faculty fear this model.

Because of this fear, there is a perception on the part of many graduate faculty that allowing application files to originate in a centralized graduate admissions office merely adds time to the process, and prevents the university from acting quickly upon files of attractive candidates for admission. In short, many graduate departments feel that they are giving up control of the admissions process by allowing application documents to be collected and evaluated by a central processing unit.

In reality, it is important for graduate departments to know that they are able to retain control of the decisions on elements that really matter, such as requirements for admission and appropriate departmental deadlines, but that they can let go of things for which they don't have the staff or the expertise, such as the processing of documents.

Nevertheless, reflecting such concerns, some graduate admissions programs have evolved a confusing dual layer of admissions. In some programs, applicants must send official transcripts and test scores both to the department to which they are applying and to another office on campus, usually the office of the graduate dean or the undergraduate admissions office, thus adding to the expense of applying. While this time-honored level of redundancy seems to offer autonomy to the programs, it can be confusing to the applicant; simply checking the status of one's application can be a challenge. Customer satisfaction is at risk when something as basic as the application process does not work smoothly.

### Advantages of Centralization

Centralizing the graduate application process can offer a number of advantages. First, it provides a hub around which to manage the quality and reputation of an institution. Although applicants will still have to deal with individual graduate programs and provide additional documents in support of their applications, the convenience of sending official transcripts, test scores, and the application itself to a centralized office makes the applicant feel that he or she is working with a single entity. There is less financial burden on the applicant, and less confusion about where documents should be sent. Checking the status of the application is easier for the applicant, and a staff trained in customer service and knowledgeable about the process makes a lasting impression on a prized candidate who has a number of offers of admission from which to choose.

In addition, a centralized staff dedicated to graduate processing can quickly assemble credentials and respond to specific needs in terms of processing flow. The priorities of staff can be adjusted to focus their efforts at various times of the year. As deadlines loom, there are ample hands to open and log the receipt of mail, and at a large university with many graduate applications, this is extremely important. With current technology, it is possible for a centralized admissions office to image paper documents and make them available for review electronically to authorized faculty and staff across campus, cutting down on paper handling by individual graduate program staff members.

Most importantly, credentials are given a uniform evaluation by a trained and educated staff. Without this kind of staffing, it is possible for programs to admit applicants whose grade point averages fall below the University's stated minimum requirements. The evaluation of international credentials requires training and experience. Allowing individual departments to evaluate credentials without proper training and without access to resources on worldwide education systems can result in the admission of international students who do not hold the equivalent of a U.S. bachelor's degree or who hold degrees from institutions which are not properly accredited.[257]

With a uniform evaluation to work from, graduate program faculty and staff know from previous experience that degrees from a given institution are legitimate, and that grade point averages from different institutions abroad can be "translated" into American practice. When this level of experience is not brought to bear, an unequal or uninformed application of standards can cause legal difficulties.

If the application process is not conducted systematically, collecting the final transcripts of applicants who are admitted and who enroll is often erratic at best. Failure to collect final transcripts means that the award of various degrees cannot be confirmed and thus posted to the student's permanent record. At some state institutions this failure to post degrees may result in incorrect classification of students, with an impact on the budget. For state schools, funding to the university can be impacted if graduate students cannot be certified as having undergraduate degrees. A centralized office has the personnel and the duty to follow up with students and to make certain that final credentials are received.

Finally, one of the most important functions that can be performed by a centralized admissions office is the maintenance of application statistics, whether on U.S. or international

[257] There is also a separate issue, not related to accreditation—evaluating the credentials of university graduates from abroad who arguably do not hold the equivalent of a U.S. bachelor's degree. A separate chapter in this volume discusses the ramifications of the Bologna process (three-year degrees from European universities) on U.S. graduate admissions.

students. More and more, graduate programs are asked to provide information about selectivity and yield. The definition of what constitutes a "complete" application becomes an issue. Centralized processing allows for keeping accurate statistics with standardized definitions that can quickly be made available to graduate programs upon request. In a society increasingly interested in the quality of graduate programs, inability to produce this information puts a university at a disadvantage when potential students are trying to compare it to other institutions with similar programs.

The budgetary savings to a university that has a centralized process can be significant. Having a centralized staff dedicated to the processing of credentials allows staff in the individual departmental programs to focus on recruitment and retention. Most importantly, a centralized office can automate processes and applications that benefit the entire university, not just the colleges or departments that have their own resources.

## Collaborating with Program Advisors and Coordinators

Centralized processing works best when there is collaboration and cooperation with the graduate program advisors and their staff coordinators.

The graduate programs, for their part, must have a well-founded faith that the centralized admissions office shares their goals of admitting and enrolling the best graduate students in a timely and efficient manner. To be successful, the centralized graduate admissions office, for its part, must be responsive to the needs and requirements of the graduate programs. A centralized graduate office can do this in a number of ways.

First, such an office can act as the front line in *customer service*, responding to inquires from prospective applicants, answering their inquiries regarding file status, and ultimately informing them of the admission decision. While a central office would never présumé to make decisions or to convey certain types of detailed department-specific information, trained and courteous admissions professionals can nevertheless convey useful general information to applicants while leaving faculty and departmental staff free to review files substantively and to recruit their preferred applicants.

A centralized graduate admissions office can, in addition, deal with *data collection and collation* while leaving the graduate program faculty and coordinators to work with the relationship side of admissions. Freeing department staff from assembling and evaluating admissions files for completeness to focusing on more creative activities involving recruitment can only be a plus. It is hard to imagine that a single department could afford the number of personnel needed to efficiently handle 2,000–2,500 applications annually—a figure which is not uncommon in some larger universities with highly ranked programs. A centralized admissions office with a budget funded from the application fee can shrink and grow as needed during the peak processing cycle.

And finally, a centralized graduate admissions office can bring *technological resources* to the processing arena. The impact of technology affects both scalability (the ability to handle large and growing volumes of paper and electronic documents) and creativity (the ability to create tools that all graduate programs, regardless of their resources, can use).

As one example of a creative application of technology which benefits all departments, a centralized office can develop a Web-based status check that can be used by applicants to all programs. From the candidates' perspective, a centralized status check allows them to see the status of all credentials they have submitted, to both the centralized office and the departmental offices. From the processing perspective, a centralized graduate admissions office no longer needs to rely on inter-campus mail to route documents to reviewers. Instead, a centralized graduate admissions process can develop a central, secure repository for application materials with electronic routing of documents when files are complete. From the faculty perspective, faculty who serve as reviewers or as potential advisors of the candidates can follow the progress of an application and request to review files as they develop. This kind of flexibility is possible because the infrastructure is solid and because there is ultimately a mechanism—and an office—in place to follow up and assemble all necessary and official documents for final review.

## Future Challenges

Having a centralized graduate admissions processing office prepares a university to deal more effectively with many current and foreseeable challenges. These challenges include: electronic reception of documents as a protection against fraud; recruitment needs of the graduate departments; standardized tests; and staffing and technology needs for a new generation of "millennial" students—students who expect greater levels of timely personal attention and results than previous graduate school generations did (Strauss and Howe 2007).

### Electronic Admission Documents

The incidence of fraudulent documents is becoming all too common, and the best way to assure with certainty that required documents are official is to receive them directly from the sending institutions, preferably electronically. This is true of test scores, letters of recommendation, and transcripts. It is especially important for U.S. universities to adopt as standard the sending and receiving of electronic transcripts.[258]

All of these electronic documents will have to be sent to a central receiving computer before they are processed. It is unlikely that individual graduate departments will have the equipment and trained staff required to do this, and where there is no centralized graduate admissions office, this task will fall to the registrar, where processing graduate applications will be only one among many obligations. Instead, this critical responsibility should be handled efficiently by an office dedicated to processing graduate documents.

[258] See Chapter 27, "Developing a New XML Standard."

### Centralizing Recruitment Resources

If centralized graduate admissions offices are to be effective, they must keep pace with the recruitment needs of the graduate departments. Words like "branding" and "marketing" are commonplace on campuses today in response to the fierce competition for highly sought-after students. Many graduate departments will be unable to compete because they lack resources. With centralized record keeping, it is possible for the centralized graduate admissions office to provide departments and deans' offices with information about schools which have served as "feeder schools" to their individual programs. Because accurate selectivity and yield information is available, departments will be better able to assess when their recruitment efforts have been effective.

A centralized graduate admissions office, working with the graduate dean and graduate programs, can thus create a centralized recruitment database. Resources can be pooled to make use of search services and to create glossy publications that can be used by all departments on their recruiting trips. The possibilities are endless, but a centralized graduate admissions office can be critical to the success of recruitment endeavors.

### Changes in Standardized Test Delivery

Most universities still require their applicants to submit a Graduate Record Examination (GRE) score. The Test of English as a Foreign Language (TOEFL) is also required of almost all international graduate applicants, in addition to the GRE.[259]

The nature of the delivery of these tests has changed or is changing, and these changes present a number of issues for the graduate admissions decision makers. Just keeping up with the changes is a major challenge. Without a central office to keep departments informed that the reduced number of testing sites is limiting the number of test takers or that the scale of the score report has changed, it is likely that much of the new information would fall between the cracks. A centralized graduate admissions office can communicate with all of the graduate departments so that they have the information needed to respond to changes, making it possible for them to consider waiving GRE requirements or accepting other tests in lieu of the TOEFL. It is difficult to imagine how individual departments would deal with these challenges alone.

### Standardized Recommendations

The Educational Testing Service (ETS) is considering a product which would ostensibly provide a standardized way for graduate schools to consider students' non-cognitive strengths and weakness. This product, originally to be called a "Standardized Letter of Recommendation," was intended to replace letters of recommendation in their current format. Now re-named

[259] For current TOEFL-related developments, see Chapter 24, "The New TOEFL." See also Chapter 23, "International Students: Marketing and Recruitment.".

the "Personal Potential Index," Jaschik (2007b) reports that this new project (which as of this writing exists in pilot form only), is instead being conceived of as a supplement to regular letters of recommendation.

The ETS expects that most candidates would ask the same people to evaluate them on the Index and in letters of recommendation. Early reaction has been mixed—from approval of trying to get away from an over-reliance on test scores, to skepticism about how personal qualities can be quantified in this fashion (Jaschik 2007b).

## Staffing and Technology

More and more, companies are cropping up to fill the technology needs of graduate departments across the country. Many companies now offer electronic applications for admissions which carry university-specific branding. Such applications make it possible for applicants to submit all credentials to a central entity to be considered by many schools. Such companies also help graduate programs with recruitment by doing targeted mailings and event planning and registration. Graduate programs that have few electronic tools provided by their own campus IT resources are opting to use these companies so that they can have a presence in the electronic world our applicants are accustomed to navigating.

In Texas, the Legislature mandated that all of the public two- and four-year colleges and universities in the state use a common application for *undergraduate* admission. This was aimed at making it easier for Texans to apply for college, but another result was to give colleges and universities a modern tool (for a nominal price) that might have taken years to develop on their own. A number of private colleges have opted in on ApplyTexas because it affords them a place at the electronic table.

Many schools, small and large, outsource the evaluation of international credentials. As yet, we haven't seen a service for graduate programs equivalent to the Law School Data Assembly Service (LSDAS) or the American Medical College Application Service (AMCAS) for those professional programs, but can it be far behind? Graduate programs want to have a simple and coherent method for their top prospects to apply for admission, and unless staffing and technology is provided for them, the departments will seek outside sources.

## Millennials as Graduate Students

In a thoughtful essay in *The Chronicle of Higher Education*, Strauss and Howe (2007) point out that "The first Gen Xers entered the labor force during the 'Reagan Revolution.' In public policy, that meant deregulation, tax cuts, and skimpier safety nets.... Since the late 1970s, adjusted for inflation, the median annual earnings of full-time male workers 15 years and older have failed to grow at all.... As a result, many Gen Xers have taken a pragmatic approach to the education of their children, the Millennial generation. As parents, they have demanded accountability from elementary and secondary schools, as well as bottom-line cash value—the confidence that, in the end, what has been provided has been worth the investment of time and money."

Going on to refer specifically to graduate education, Strauss and Howe state that "members of this generation will want structure, supervision and feedback." The long periods of "drift without supervision for months at a time," together with the accruing of high levels of debt, the length of many graduate programs, and the students' concerns about job placement, all point to a greatly heightened demand for accountability at the graduate level—equivalent, the authors state, to "the same public pressures that undergraduate colleges now confront." Focusing in on one small but specific part of the problem, Strauss and Howe add: "Uninvolved or absentee advisors will become more controversial, perhaps even unacceptable."

## Conclusion

The author of this chapter agrees with the observations of Strauss and Howe that graduate students today are understandably focused on outcomes. When they are denied admission as graduate students, they want to know why, and they want a full critique of their file. Anything which can work to make the specialized and somewhat esoteric process of admission to graduate school more efficient, and perhaps even more transparent, can only be good for all involved.

By organizing a centralized office for processing graduate applications, a college or university can seize the opportunity to promote efficiency, reduce redundancy, and achieve financial benefit while improving its image and creating access to graduate education.

/ CHAPTER THIRTY-EIGHT /

*Introduction by Mary E. Baxton, M.S.*
*The Tseng College of Extended Learning*
*California State University-Northridge*
*Robert Watkins, M.A.*
*Graduate and International Admissions Center*
*The University of Texas at Austin*

38

# Examining the Bologna Process

Graduate admissions professionals have the task of comparing three-year degrees from abroad—both European and non-European—with U.S. undergraduate preparation, and specifically of determining the suitability of the international three-year degrees for graduate study at their institution. The first order of business may be to determine if we are asking the right questions in considering these three-year degrees.[260]

At the outset, it is advisable to consider: What is the purpose of the graduate admissions decision process in the U.S? A full response is three-fold: First, to ensure that the admissions decisions are in line with the philosophy, mission and goals of the university, and of the departmental graduate programs; second, to ensure that admissions decisions are based on a holistic review of the credentials and background of each applicant; and third, to achieve admission of graduate students based on standards that include comparability, quality, and equity.

The Bologna Process represents a fundamental restructuring of higher education in Europe, of which the development of three tiers (cycles)—bachelor, master, and doctoral—in

[260] As Robert Watkins points out later in this chapter, the Bologna Process does not mandate that "first-cycle" postsecondary degrees be three years, but only that they be *at least* three years in duration.

lieu of the traditional long program is one of the more important features. Originally signed in 1999, the Bologna Declaration is an agreement now covering forty-six countries to create a European Higher Education Area (EHEA). In addition to a fundamental restructuring of degree systems, signatories to the Bologna Declaration have agreed to promote quality assurance systems, remove obstacles to the mobility of students, implement a system of easily readable and comparable degrees, and establish a common credit system.

The European signatories to the Bologna Declaration hope to achieve full implementation by 2010. As that year approaches, European and U.S. educators each have their own concerns about the process. Europeans are concerned about making it work, and educators in the U.S. are asking themselves what they are going to do about accepting three-year bachelor or "first cycle" degrees—with an added complication that some three-year degrees emerge out of the Bologna Process countries, while other three-year degrees (such as those from India or Australia) emerge from non-Bologna countries. In addition, some three-year degrees are considered in their home countries to be acceptable for admission to graduate studies in the native country, whereas in other countries, only a four-year "honours degree" is deemed acceptable for graduate admission.

In the fall of 2006, AACRAO[261] sponsored a symposium in Washington on "The Impact of Bologna and Three-Year Degrees on U.S. Admissions." The symposium included data from the Council of Graduate Schools (CGS) showing the impact of international students on U.S. economic competitiveness. Between 1976 and 2002, the number of U.S. citizens and permanent residents attaining doctoral degrees in science and engineering in the U.S. dropped "precipitously," according to the CGS—from more than twenty-five thousand on a yearly basis to fewer than ten thousand annually. That constitutes a drop of 40 percent over the quarter-century studied.

Looked at as a percentage of total doctoral degrees granted in the U.S. in the sciences and engineering in that period, the figures are of equal concern. The percentage of such degrees granted to U.S. citizens and permanent residents now constitutes fewer than 60 percent of such degrees attained in the U.S., as compared to more than 75 percent in 2002. "Without the presence of international students, the number of these degrees attained in the U.S. would fall far below those attained in Europe and Asia" (Baxton *et al.* 2007, p. 21).

The American Council on Education and NAFSA: The Association of International Educators also track Bologna-related matters closely.

For the remainder of this chapter, Robert Watkins traces the development of the Bologna Process; provides an overview of the process and the major changes it is attempting to accomplish; and suggests some strategies for dealing with the Bologna Process and avoiding pitfalls.

[261] AACRAO was joined by three other sponsors: the Australian Department of Education, Science, and Training, the British Council United States, and the German Academic Exchange Service. The proceedings of the symposium have been published by AACRAO and are available at <www.aacrao.org/publications>.

## Development of the Process

When the Ministers of Education of 29 European countries, meeting in Bologna, Italy in June, 1999, sat down to construct the European Higher Education Area (EHEA), they could not foresee how much their deliberations would affect the rest of the world. Their exercise in higher education reform was intended solely to enhance student mobility in Europe. After all, they had successfully dealt with secondary school leaving certificates of differing names, lengths, and content in the mid-1980s by simply declaring them all "equivalent" for purposes of entry into university degree programs across Europe. This particular reform had no ripple effect beyond Europe, but it did enable students with a French *Bachelier de l'Enseignement du Second Degré* after the *Baccalauréat* to enter a German university or a German with a *Zeugnis der Allgemeinen Hochschulreife* after the Abitur exam to be admitted directly into a British bachelor's degree program, among other examples.

The 1999 ministerial meeting in Bologna, however, did have significant repercussions around the world, even if not immediately. Unlike earlier efforts designed primarily to support student mobility in education across Europe, the EHEA—created by what was known as "the Bologna Process"—truly represented a fundamental change in higher education across the continent. The postsecondary degrees and diplomas awarded by the various countries would not simply become "*equivalent;*" they would be eliminated and replaced with an altogether different set of degrees that would be compatible and *consistent across the signatory countries.* It is not going too far to characterize these new degrees as being akin to an educational "Euro." After all most other aspects of common European effort—from trade, to defense, to a common currency—had brought Europe together; why not higher education as well?

In the same way that the Deutschmark, the French franc, and the Italian lira all disappeared, so too would the indigenous degrees of the cooperating countries, though we have now seen that some old nomenclature has been retained in the format of the levels—bachelor, master's, doctorate—promulgated at that first meeting of Bologna countries. A fundamental restructuring of European higher education had been embarked upon, although the purpose was not to enable Europe's university graduates to more easily enter graduate schools around the world. Rather, the primary goal was to finish the work begun in the 1980s when European university entrance credentials were equalized. The purpose of that reform was to align higher education across Europe so as to facilitate seamless movement from one degree to another *within Europe*. Admittedly, some nations, such as Germany, saw an added advantage: expediting student graduation in a higher education system that had heretofore abetted very long paths to degree.

Regardless of intent, the result was much more profound than initially intended. The ripple effect accumulated over time, until eight years after that 1999 meeting, countries around the world, including the United States, began to seriously grapple with the decisions made that day. And what were those decisions? Myths surround the Bologna Process, and so it would be appropriate at this point to enumerate the points agreed on by the ministers before moving on to discuss the effects on the rest of the world. At the end of this chapter, suggestions will be made as to how U.S. Admissions Officers might handle these outcomes.

## Features of the Process

A great deal of information exists on the Bologna Process in as much detail as one is willing to embrace. But for our purposes the salient points are these:

- The ministers agreed on a uniform system of degree levels or cycles from lowest to highest (three in all), with the idea that one degree leads to the next, and then leads to the third. In the early stages the primary focus was on the first two levels, with the third or doctoral level to be fleshed out later. There was no definite length required for these degrees, nor were degree names mandated. *However, the first degree was required to be at least three years in length and the two combined would represent five years total.* Thus, a country such as Russia might choose to stick with the four-plus-one model, while another country could elect to pursue the three-plus-two variant. In fact, most Bologna countries have chosen the latter model. Nomenclature, again, was not fixed, but the majority appear to have adopted the terminology of "bachelor" and "master." Some, however, decided that radical change in structure might be muted somewhat by the retention of traditional names, and thus France kept the *Licence-Maitrise-Doctorat* (referred to there as the L-M-D cycle). Italy also has chosen to keep its traditional *Laurea* though now positioned differently in the system than was the case before Bologna.
- The new degrees would be made more transparent (another desired aspect of the reform) by means of a document designed to illuminate the components of the degree. This document was to be called the *Diploma Supplement*. Again, myth has quickly surrounded this feature, at least insofar as American admissions officers are concerned. The Diploma Supplement is *not* a transcript, even though it is designed to explain an academic degree program undertaken in the same way that a U.S. college transcript does. It is just what the name implies: a supplementary document to the *awarded* diploma. Thus, it is *issued only upon graduation with the degree earned, and not before that time.* This Diploma Supplement, it was agreed, would contain not only the courses, grades, and credits earned but would also include a full description of the country's educational system, in both English and the native language.
- Furthermore, these degrees would be based on a system of credits. The credits would provide a cumulative measure of degree value with each of the courses making up the degree program possessing a credit value. The European Credit Transfer System (ECTS) formulated in 1989 for the Erasmus Mundi program, an earlier entry in the European attempt to enhance student mobility across the continent, was adopted by the ministers meeting in Bologna to meet the need for a credit system. The ECTS *credit system* envisions a full student load per year as 60 ECTS (30 per semester). These credits represent a full range of student experience in higher education including lectures, labs, tutorials, and outside class work time. Given the degree options of either 3+2 or 4+1 for the first two levels of degrees,

a first degree would be worth either 180 ECTS or 240 ECTS. When combined with the second tier, the credit value for the two degrees becomes 300 ECTS either way.

- Quality assurance: The ministers creating the EHEA also determined that some form of quality assurance or accreditation was necessary to aid in establishing true compatibility alongside the other aspects of format, level, and transparency. Given a long-standing tradition in Europe of strong central control of education, accreditation represented a largely alien concept, certainly when compared to the voluntary process found in the United States. The ministers hoped to set up a system of quality control that would encompass institutions, nations, and indeed Area-wide expectations. In 1999 this was a distant concern and only began to take shape slowly, well after the other three features of the EHEA had been firmly set in place.

In addition to these four points, the ministers would continue to meet every two years, with the venue moving among the signatory countries of the EHEA. Subsequent meetings were held in Prague (2001), Berlin (2003), Bergen (2005), and London (2007). The meeting in 2009, the year prior to full implementation, is scheduled for Leuven and Louvain-la-Nueve, Belgium. The meetings are designed to enable the signatory countries to assess progress toward full implementation and to agree on steps requiring action. Reports on progress were generated after each meeting and were labeled Trends Reports (I-V through 2007).

## American Perspective on the Process

Not surprisingly the immediate effect on higher education in the United States centered on the key first point, that of the degree structure. Indeed, the other points represented welcome new features insofar as U.S. higher education administrators were concerned. A document more like the U.S. transcript (though only a final supplement to the degree itself); the use of a credit system for accumulation of credits toward a degree (not traditionally a trait of European higher education except in a few countries); and a procedure for assessing quality—all promised to be of immense help to the international credential evaluator in U.S. institutions. All these advantages paled alongside the formal establishment of a degree structure, however, that institutionalized (at least in many of the EHEA countries, now numbering 46) a system of three-year degrees.

U.S. graduate admissions administrators historically have defined the equivalent of the bachelor's degree, the first and foremost requirement for entry into U.S. graduate programs, as four years of full-time study. The reasons for this interpretation are quite simple. European (and European-style) higher education and U.S. higher education are fundamentally different concepts. In Europe, the curriculum follows an in-depth approach to subject analysis. That is, the European degree is predicated on a very thorough illumination of the chosen field without a preliminary set of general non-field-specific courses. These are assumed to have been covered in upper secondary school, and this coverage also contains an element of streaming not found in U.S. academic high school programs. The U.S. degree is built on a base of general education requirements (distributed over a wide range of important basic subjects across various curricula), which then moves toward specialization. The specialization, or chosen major, in any case does not exceed a given amount, often as little as one-fourth of the overall four-year experience.

Given these diametrically opposed viewpoints, an approach relying on simple internal content comparisons, designed to compare the two types of degrees, breaks down. An added element is that the overseas-educated individual coming to graduate school in the U.S. is seeking a place within the U.S. higher educational construct and therefore, when compared against U.S. applicants, the default has always been in favor of length of study. Consequently, the standard U.S. graduate school response for overseas equivalent degrees is that of possessing a "four-year full-time degree awarded."

Experienced international admissions administrators quickly added other dimensions to the comparison process. While four years of university study is considered the key element, one could also view the overall result in terms of years of total education, to arrive at essentially the same concept. When primary/secondary education exceeded the 12-year U.S. model, as is the case in the United Kingdom for example, the resulting comparison of 13 years of prior education and three years of postsecondary study that resulted in a degree award compared favorably with the standard U.S. 12-plus-four model. Other 13-year primary/secondary systems such as Germany, Italy, etc. were similarly considered acceptable when faced with a three-year first degree situation.

The initial response from U.S. graduate admissions personnel became one of continued "year counting" as the new degrees made it across the Atlantic. A three-year Bologna degree was fine so long as it was preceded by the thirteen years of primary and secondary study prevalent in the United Kingdom. But very few signatory countries possessed this longer pre-tertiary system, and even some that did, began to depart from this model (Germany being the prime example). U.S. admissions officers saw no reason to change their policies to accommodate new degrees in Europe when the 46 signatory countries, even taken collectively, did not constitute the largest student-exporting country. In fact, no single European country came close to the numbers of the Asian educational giants such as India, China, and the Republic of Korea.[262] After all, it was noted stateside, the reform was for enhanced student mobility in Europe, not for added advantage in exporting students beyond that continent.

But the pressure began to build as three factors became evident.

[262] According to Koh and Bhandari (2007), the top five places of origin of the 564,766 international students enrolled in U.S. higher education in 2005-06 are: India (76,503 students or 13.5 percent); China (62,582 students or 11.1 percent); Korea, Republic of (58,487 or 10.4 percent); Japan (38,712 or 6.9 percent); and Canada (28,202 or 5.0 percent). Among the top twenty "Leading Places of Origin," only three are Bologna-signatory countries: Germany at #9, with 8,829 students enrolled in U.S. higher education, or 1.6 percent of the total; the United Kingdom, with 8,274 students, or 1.5 percent; and France, with 6,640 or 1.2 percent, for a total of 4.3 percent Bologna-country students among the top twenty leading countries of origin.

First, the reform efforts in Europe, despite myriad problems, some confusion, and even a little dissent among actual educators, were clearly not going to go away. Europe was committed to the Bologna Process, and slow steady progress continued to be made.

Secondly, world events intervened to cause concern on most American campuses. With the concerns about security resulting in a decided flattening of the international student application numbers, campus administrators not previously involved with or concerned about international student issues suddenly began to take notice of the Bologna Process. For them, the definition of a bachelor's degree took second seat to the issue of application numbers.

Finally, the American sense of egalitarianism, which tended to militate toward equal treatment of applicants regardless of country of origin, brought to the forefront the much larger question of how to deal with three-year degrees from non-European countries. Approaching the new Bologna three-year degrees in a manner different from the handling of three-year degrees in India, Bangladesh, and other countries with twelve years rather than thirteen years of secondary study was felt to be simply unacceptable. And opening the door to potential acceptance of three-year degrees from these countries with their far larger applicant numbers and vast variety of institutions threatened to overwhelm U.S. admissions officers.

## Looming Challenges

With full implementation now just a few short years away, U.S. admissions officers face a growing dilemma. What is the proper response to the Bologna Process in terms of graduate admissions at U.S. institutions? The answer, unfortunately, is not a simple one. First of all, U.S. higher education and the field of international credential evaluation have never spoken with one voice. Schools approach the issue of three-year degrees differently as befits a system that embraces institutional autonomy. Large state schools and smaller highly selective institutions tend to search for ways to exclude, rather than include, based purely on the fact that only limited numbers of the applicants can be admitted each year. Conversely, many private institutions, regardless of size, feeling the keen competition resulting from name recognition or lack thereof, tend to set policy in such a way as to increase the applicant pool and the corresponding number of admits. Many subsist on full fee-paying students, and having fewer restraints on the definition of degree equivalency helps in the recruiting effort.

Historically, international admissions officers have relied on placement recommendations emanating from the National Council on the Evaluation of Foreign Educational Credentials, an inter-associational committee of AACRAO, NAFSA, College Board, IIE (Institute of International Education), CGS (Council of Graduate Schools), ACE (American Council on Education), and AACC (American Association of Community Colleges). The Council was founded in 1955, and in all its country publications, particularly those commissioned by the U.S. government through the then United States Information Agency (USIA), it offered placement recommendations for admissions officers working with the credentials found in the country in question.

The Council tended to provide somewhat conservative placement recommendations, largely reflecting the year-counting approach, so that a three-year degree was invariably seen as insufficient for graduate admission.

The Council, however, disbanded in 2006 when government money dried up and some of the participant organizations began to lose interest in sustaining the committee. In addition, the Council never took up the subject of Bologna, either as part of a single-country review or as part of a broader Area-wide study. The Council *did* address the issue of ECTS credits when it noted that the ECTS credit was comparable to one-half of a U.S. semester hour, which brought the conversion of ECTS credits into line with the U.S. standard model of 30 semester hours per year (compared to the ECTS full annual load of 60). Thus the U.S. international admissions officer no longer has recourse to a body of opinion that had been available in decades past which might have shed some light on possible approaches to the new Bologna degrees.

## Complicating Factors

Before considering some factors that might lead to a viable institutional policy toward Bologna degrees, it would be instructive to first review some of the problems currently permeating the new degree structure in Europe.

### Lack of a Monolithic "Bologna Degree"

First of all, the myth of a monolithic Bologna degree structure needs to be addressed. The Bologna Process, as already noted, did not mandate three year degrees; rather, the agreement was that the first tier of the new degree structure would *not* encompass less than three years. Therefore, the possibility of either a three-year first degree or a four-year first degree demonstrates that one is much more accurate in calling these degrees "Bologna-compliant" degrees rather than Bologna degrees.

In short, there is no "Bologna Degree," only the parameters around which one country might construct successive tiers for their degrees. Clearly the admissions office in the U.S. that looks to overseas degrees in terms of length of time undoubtedly has no difficulty with the four-year first degree that one could expect to see from Russia. Likewise, the three-year degree from a thirteen-year primary/secondary system, such as that found in Germany in the past or Italy currently, poses no problem.

The problem comes in the case of France, Germany in the future, or any other country that *precedes the first three-year degree with a twelve-year primary/secondary system of education.* Therefore, the concept of addressing Bologna-compliant degrees as a whole, rather than by country, carries with it significant problems.

## Non-U.S. "Bachelor's Degrees" Represent Differing Levels of Work

Even more important than the twelve-plus-three sequence is the fact that within the signatory countries, other postsecondary institutions besides the universities are embracing the new degree structure. In the case of Germany, for example, the universities of applied sciences (*fachhochschulen*) now award the new bachelor degree in place of the former *Fachhochschule Diplom*. The universities of applied sciences, in Germany, offer a curriculum which is much less theoretical and more "applied" than their traditional university counterparts (hence their name). A lesser admission criterion exists for these schools, and the course leading to the degree is not as long as the course of studies leading to the university *Diplom*. Even more confusing is the fact that the universities of cooperative education (*berufsakademien*), which have the same entry criteria as regular universities, but contain a substantial work component as well as classroom study within the context of their first degree, have also adopted the Bologna-compliant degree structure. As a result, in one country alone, the same degree title, "bachelor," will be awarded by three very different types of institutions with significantly different curriculum content.

## Length versus Depth of Education

Indeed, it is curriculum content that provides one of the larger questions for many admissions officers examining the new degree structure. In re-crafting the traditional first degrees in a given country into Bologna-compliant format, will content somehow be affected adversely? When a degree such as the *Diplom* or *Magister* from Germany of some five or more years' duration is re-designed into a three-plus-two model, will something be lost in those first three years that a U.S. admissions officer might find significant as he or she prepares to forward the applicant on to a graduate department?

This question arises not just with outsiders attempting to discern quality in the new degree structure, but even can occur as an issue among the very entities that the students hope to join at home—businesses and other organizations in the home country. In Germany, where a first university degree has traditionally been the longer *Diplom* or *Magister*, the corporate sector continues to glance uneasily at the new bachelor's degree, while wondering whether the new graduate indeed has the skills and learning fully in place compared to the graduates of the traditional programs. In-country skittishness naturally exacerbates U.S. admissions officers' anxiety about the new degrees.

Experienced international credential evaluators, whether campus-based or in private evaluation services, have always felt innately that mere counting of years or credits is too simplistic a methodology. And yet, when faced with such highly dissimilar products—European higher education defined as "deep," compared to U.S. higher education often characterized as "broad"—it is only natural to default to length of program. In the case of credits, one is hard pressed to avoid the indisputable fact that a new three-year 180 ECTS degree is just what it appears to be: three years of study and ninety equivalent U.S. semester hours. Europeans point out correctly that learning outcome, rather than simple credit accumulation, is the *sine qua non* of higher education. But U.S. university students participate in a great deal of outside learning activity not contained in the semester credit value structure which codifies strictly time spent in lecture or lab, and such activities are normally considered to be "expected," though not formally part of the credit calculation scheme. The dichotomy is clear between the two concepts and to favor one over the other requires a significant conceptual leap of faith generally not found in U.S. admissions offices, where a strong streak of egalitarian "fair play" tends to be the rule. Indeed, it has even been suggested that favoring the European (or other) degree that is clearly shorter than the U.S. four-year 120-hour-or-more degree during the graduate admission process could conceivably leave a school open to private lawsuits or governmental sanction on the basis of discrimination.

## Approaches to Bologna-Compliant Degrees

It is not too difficult to identify two definitive methods of dealing with the new degrees spawned by the European Higher Education Area. Along with those, a host of middle-ground solutions may be considered.

### Granting Equivalency for All Bologna-Compliant Degrees

One method is to simply accept all of the new degrees from the 46 signatory countries as conceptually comparable to a U.S. bachelor's degree, regardless of length and credit value, and to avoid the pain of attempting to scrutinize or analyze these degrees. Presumably this policy would encompass other three-year degrees around the world, based on a desire for consistency and fairness. This does not address the lingering concern of fairness to U.S. seniors, with ninety or more semester hours, wishing to enter graduate study, but there is an advantage on the part of the three-year degree holder in that they *do* have, in the end, a degree whereas the U.S. student with only ninety semester hours does *not* have that to offer. Quite a number of schools and some private credential evaluation services have, in fact, made this their policy decision.

### Requiring Sixteen Years of Education for Degree Equivalency

Conversely, one may choose the totally opposite approach and affirm that a U.S. bachelor's equivalent is defined purely and simply as a four-year full-time degree awarded. After all, the European Higher Education Area was formulated with mobility and transparency of process within *Europe* as the goal, not (ostensibly anyway) for export to the United States. Since the U.S. was not part of the deliberative process establishing the new degrees, there is certainly no compelling reason to alter institutional policies by default (this argument goes).

In short, in this view, one may accept three-year degrees flowing from a thirteen-year primary/secondary system as in the case of degrees from England, but other degrees (*e.g.*, those from twelve-year systems), would simply not be considered U.S. degree equivalents.

### The Middle Ground

Between those two diametrically opposed viewpoints are all sorts of possibilities. For example, one might accept a three-year Bologna-compliant degree if the applicant applies for the *same* or a *very similar field.* This method operates on the assumption that since European degrees are subject-intensive, the applicant is quite prepared for graduate study in the same field. Alternatively, a graduate major clearly different from the first degree would not receive that same consideration.

Another factor would be institutional origin of the degree. Was the degree awarded by an entity *similar in scope and purpose* to the receiving institution? To return to our German model, the Bologna-compliant degree offered by a traditional university may well suffice within the same field, but the similarly-titled degree from a university of applied science or from one of the *berufsakademien* (professional or vocationally-oriented universities) would *not* suffice, given the very different nature of the degree contents.

An approach that is more holistic in scope entails reviewing not only the entry criteria for the degree in question (was it the university-bound high school diploma or something less?), but also the direction in which the degree leads. Is that three-year degree acceptable for further higher study *every time* in the home country, without question? In Ontario, Canada, for example, the three-year Ordinary degree does *not* lead to graduate study in that Province; it is the four-year Honours degree which is the entrance requirement for master's study. When Bologna-compliant degrees *are* designed to go on to higher education, such degrees would generally pass the test, but three-year degrees in commonwealth-style educational systems where a longer "honours" option exists would not. This consideration should be a major factor in the U.S. admissions officer's deliberations.

Finally, one should always appreciate the stake that graduate departments and their faculty have in the admissions process. If an admissions office contemplates a change in policy that allows for the acceptance of three-year degrees, whether on an automatic or conditional basis, the graduate departments affected should have the opportunity to voice an opinion.

It may be that some would advise altogether against the admission of three-year degrees, out of concern for the quality of the content. Engineering would be a logical field in which a short first degree would be viewed with some suspicion. On the other hand, fields such as communications or journalism may well have a different perspective. Faculty will be the best sources in grappling with the actual curriculum content of a three-year first degree, as compared to what is expected, department by department, of the U.S. degree-holding applicant.

## Conclusion

Without a doubt the Bologna Process has created a real debate within U.S. higher education. Higher education administrators from deans to provosts to presidents are now cognizant of an aspect of international education that heretofore was the sole purview of a handful of professional pundits usually relegated to obscure corners of the Admissions Office.

The real danger lies in the myths concerning, and the over-simplification of, a process that has now gone on for eight years and is not yet complete. To avoid pitfalls, it is also advisable to remember that progress toward the end goal is by no means uniform among the 46 signatory countries, and is still fraught with unanswered questions even among those navigating this process of reform.

The only firm assurance the U.S. admissions officer can expect in this era of radical educational change in Europe is that there is no turning back the clock on these changes and that the more information about what is taking place that one has, the better the potential for crafting a sound policy regarding the admission of international graduate applicants.

/ CHAPTER THIRTY-NINE /

*by Reta Pikowsky, M.Ed.*
*Registrar*
*Georgia Institute of Technology*

39

# Student Data:
## The Relationship Between the Admissions and Registrar's Offices

The relationship between the admissions office and the registrar's office is important for a variety of reasons, not the least of which is the need to ensure effective management and transfer of student data. While physical transfer of hardcopy records still occurs, despite increasingly vigorous calls for admissions offices and registrar's offices to become "paperless," we will focus here on the management of electronic records and the "rollover" of data in the student information system.

We will discuss the transition from applicant to student status and the timing of various activities; loading data from an online application; two common schedules for "rolling the data," thus creating the student record; and managing data in the "grey period" before the semester begins. We will show why effective communication between the two offices—registrar and admissions—is critical to providing good service, by tracking changes in data appropriately. Finally, we will offer some insight into how the quality of the data you have affects the quality of service you can give. In short, the registrar's office and the office of institutional research have much to offer the admissions and enrollment management offices, even in the early stages of the student's enrollment at the institution.

## Transition of Common Data

Regardless of the software products used at your institution to manage recruiting and applicant information, there are aspects of capturing and maintaining data that we in higher education have in common. The *recruiting* database is critical to the admissions and marketing process, but does not affect the registrar's office directly. It is the data captured in the *application* process that affects both offices. In some instances, the only time that certain data elements are captured is in the initial application process, and trying to capture them later on will be a "hit or miss" proposition. Therefore, the registrar's office should be made aware of what is and is not included on the *application for admission* and should be consulted when there are changes or updates.

*Residency status* or tuition classification for the purpose of paying in-state fees can be a very contentious issue, and with college costs rising each year, parents are very concerned about the significant differences between in-state and out-of-state tuition and fees. Typically, the admissions office makes the initial decision about residency, and the registrar's office assumes responsibility for questions and petitions after the student enrolls.

The registrar's office makes use of a residency affidavit of some sort when students wish to request a change in their residency status for the purpose of paying tuition, which means more detailed information is being captured at that point in time. However, reviewing the information provided on the application for admission is sometimes helpful to sort out particularly complex or contentious cases.

*Curriculum* is another area where effective management of the data and effective communication between the two offices is important. The admissions office recruits and admits students well in advance of the start of the semester for which they are seeking entrance. As the admissions office is shaping the next incoming class, the registrar's office is interacting with the curriculum committees as to the usual plethora of changes in courses and majors that arise during any given academic year.

Occasionally, indeed, there are changes in the curriculum that are of particular interest to the admissions office. Degree programs that are discontinued must be coded correctly in the student information system so that the admissions office will not continue admitting students to that major. Discontinuation of a degree program for which students have already been admitted would require a communication strategy to inform such students of any "teach out" plans, or to suggest a change to a different program. Of course, all along the way, there is need to keep track of the related data in such a way that reports can be prepared as needed for decision making and communication.

In some instances, it is the admissions office which does the initial evaluation of transfer credit. This is another critical point in the process when both offices need to be aware of proper procedures to communicate effectively. With good procedures in place, this critical service can be streamlined, and information distributed to the accepted students in a timely manner.

## Loading Online Application Data

Various software products are used to process online applications for admission. As with most software products, there are often limitations in how data is stored. The admissions office and the registrar's office may find mutual cause for concern when there are difficulties in loading certain data elements cleanly into the student information system.

An example of this situation is the relatively common use of campus codes to track where students are enrolled, and tie them to appropriate course sections for their locations. If, on the registrar's side of the house, the campus codes have become so prolific that two digits have become necessary, and the online application for admission can load only one, some action has to be taken to remedy the problem. This kind of problem, as with most others, may require some "give and take" on both sides before a workable solution can be implemented.

## "Rolling" the Data

The previous paragraphs described some of the specific processes that affect both the admissions office and registrar's office as the student transitions from the status of prospect to applicant to enrolled student. An important aspect of this transition is the "rolling" of the data from the admissions system or sub-module to the student module. The timing of this process impacts registration, fee payment, and financial aid.

This "rolling" process creates a general student record for a given term, and enables the student to access registration, fee payment, and financial aid screens. The needs of the various offices do not always coincide, and there is some disagreement as to what kind of schedule works best.

There are two common schedules for "rolling" data from the admissions system or sub-module to the student module of your student information system.

Some institutions prefer a *continuous* roll process that occurs daily or hourly whereby "admitted applicants" data populates the general student record, thus allowing students to register for classes and access other critical services. The registration calendar obviously has an impact on your assessment of the need for this approach. If the institution continues to admit students for fall throughout the spring and summer, and the registrar's office keeps fall registration open, the continuous rolling of records would be required.

Other institutions establish *certain dates* when the admission records are rolled to the student system. This requires the admissions office to complete its work on the incoming class and to be prepared, in cooperation with the registrar's office, to maintain certain changes in data in both areas. In fact, once the general student record is created, regardless of which "rolling" schedule is used, any changes—such as a change in major—should be recorded in both offices. This raises a different question about managing the data, which we will address briefly in the next segment.

The disagreement about which schedule is best for creating the general student record hinges on a determination by all offices involved as to what services and information the admitted applicant can access, and at what point in time. Most student information systems now allow certain types of access to the student who is still only in "admitted" status, but other restrictions on access still remain until the student registers for classes.

Registration cannot occur until the records are rolled. Clearly, the Bursar and the Director of Student Financial Aid have particular interests in this sequence because of deposits and payments of various kinds, and the need to communicate with the student about aid packages. So, aside from concerns about data, there are service and access issues that are involved in this process.

## Managing Data in the "Gray Period"

We have covered very briefly some of the data-related issues as applicants make the transition to student status. There are various changes that may occur in the period of time after the student has been admitted and registered and before the term begins. In some instances, it may be helpful or even essential to track these changes to better inform those who are reviewing and utilizing recruitment and retention data.

Students often change their majors, sometimes with surprising frequency, after submitting the application for admission. Before the admission record is "rolled" to the student module, the admissions office makes the changes as they occur. There may or may not be any value to the institution in keeping track of these pre-matriculation changes, but the issue might bear some further thought, particularly if a school or department that is trying to increase its enrollment starts out strong in the process and then loses admitted students who go to another major.

Information as to addresses and telephone numbers is almost constantly in a state of flux. Where these changes are recorded for incoming students, and how the changes are communicated back and forth between the admissions office and the registrar's office, can impact both offices as well as the students in significant ways.

## Managing No-Shows

Determining whether registered incoming freshmen, or transfer students for that matter, are actually in attendance at the start of the term is another activity which occupies both the admissions office and the registrar's office. Finalizing the list of "no-shows" is an important process for the admissions office both to determine a final count of incoming students and to obtain information, if possible, about where the student actually enrolled if not at your institution. Keeping track of which institutions you are competing with for the students you wish to enroll is an important aspect of the institution's marketing and recruiting strategy.

On the registrar's side of the house, knowledge of actual attendance is important for cancelling registration and freeing up needed space in classes, particularly crowded freshman-level classes. In addition, cancelling registration as early as possible prevents more complications such as the non-attendee remaining registered throughout the term, receiving

F grades in courses, and having a transcript created that can then lead to other difficulties. It is always better to cancel registration than to let the record remain and have to back out the data from the transcript. The increasing trend toward electronic reporting of enrollment data, through the National Student Clearinghouse for example, makes it even more important that students clarify their attendance plans as early in the process as possible to avoid complications on their end and at the institutions where they are registered.

Managing contact information effectively is important in tracking down the potential no-show. The e-mail address, telephone number, and mailing address collected at the point of application for admission remain important if the student is actually not in attendance. The most current contact information is important to cross-check the student's status. Communication using both sets of information is important to increase the chances of reaching the student and making adjustments as necessary with registration, housing, etc. A common practice is for the admissions office to contact the potential no-shows using the contact information on the application for admission. The registrar's office then complements the effort by communicating with the potential no-shows using the most current contact information. Between the two offices, it is likely that one of them will determine the intention of the students on the list to complete the matriculation process. Coordination of this effort is necessary to ensure its effectiveness. One last point: probable "no-shows" can be identified by reviewing the registration audit log to determine if the student has touched his or her schedule and the last day on which it was changed. Any contact with the bursar's office and/or university housing would also be an indicator of the student's intention to enroll.

## Conclusion

Much has been written in recent years about the "cradle to grave" relationship that institutions of higher education attempt to manage these days with potential students. Gathering useful data at critical points in the development of this relationship is essential to good planning and good decision making, and to defining and redefining enrollment goals.

Planning and assessment matrices are more and more necessary, and with increasing calls for accountability both internally and externally, institutions are finding that they need to gather enough data at the right time to answer critical questions.

Because the management of the relationship with the student extends beyond the admissions office, other offices, including the registrar's office and the office of institutional research, must coordinate their efforts, planning, and assessment accordingly, and should play a part in supporting retention efforts.

Ultimately, it is all about the data. Data, efficiently gathered and effectively used, can help you significantly increase the quality of your service and interaction with students—the students whom you have worked so hard to recruit and retain.

/ CHAPTER FORTY /

*by Ira Tyszler, M.A.*
*Dean of Enrollment Management and Institutional Research and Review*
*Touro College*

40

# Accessing IPEDS Data to Shape Marketing

At an open house with parents, one parent says: "I see that your school is down three points in the *U.S. News and World Report* rankings." This is a true statement. What do you say?

Based on IPEDS data, you could point out that at your school, 72 percent (or whatever is the correct figure) of your students receive some kind of financial aid; you could add what percentage of students receive grants—broken out by federal, state, and institutional; what percentage receive loans; what percentage of first-year students continue their studies the following fall, what the graduation rate is...and so on. These are figures which parents are really interested in. The moral is: Fight data with data!

You can then tell the parent that this information comes from the most authoritative source, the U.S. Department of Education—and that they (the parents) can see it for themselves, free and any time, online. Three cheers for IPEDS!

Admissions professionals are constantly faced with the need to make informed and strategic decisions in almost every area of their operations. To be effective in today's demanding environment, it is imperative that decisions be based on the best available data. One of the most comprehensive sources of data about postsecondary institutions is the Integrated Postsecondary Education Data System (IPEDS), available through the National Center for

Education Statistics (NCES) of the U.S. Department of Education. The NCES home page—http://nces.ed.gov/ipeds—contains a wealth of links to information, data, reports, and tools covering the gamut of postsecondary education.

This chapter will provide an overview of IPEDS and explore its relevance to admissions professionals.

IPEDS is the main data collection program of NCES, part of the Department's Institute of Education Sciences. One of the major strengths of the collection is its depth and breadth. Data is collected from virtually every postsecondary entity in the U.S. and is subsequently made available to the public. A wide variety of tools, with comprehensive glossaries and tutorials, are available, as well as numerous opportunities for training, both in person and online. First, however, let us explore the history of IPEDS and examine in greater depth exactly what information is collected, and when, how, and from whom it is gathered.

## IPEDS Background

The *Higher Education Act, in its 1992 reauthorization,* required that all institutions that participate in any of the financial aid programs authorized by Title IV of the Higher Education Act of 1965 [20 U.S.C. 1094 (a) (17)] complete each of the IPEDS surveys. From 1993 to 2000, NCES collected detailed written data from these institutions as it worked to improve its surveys and insure compliance. Beginning in 2000, NCES moved to an online system of collection. Currently, all data must be submitted via the Web for all institutions which participate in Title IV programs. Institutions that do not participate may still complete the online forms on a voluntary basis.

NCES collects a wide range of data through eight web-based IPEDS surveys,[263] each of which is assigned to specific collection periods—Fall, Winter, and Spring—in a given academic year. The individual surveys and their collection periods are shown in Table 40.1.

TABLE 40.1: **Survey Collection Periods**

| Code | Component | Period |
|---|---|---|
| IC | Institutional Characteristics and Price Information | Fall |
| C | Degree Completions | Fall |
| E12 | 12-Month Enrollment and Total Institutional Activity | Fall |
| HR[1] | Human Resources | Winter |
| EF | Enrollment | Available and may be finalized in Winter; must be finalized in Spring |
| F | Finance | Available and may be finalized in Winter; must be finalized in Spring |
| SFA | Student Financial Aid | Spring |
| GRS | Graduation Rates | Spring |

[1] The Human Resources collection has three components, including: Employees by Assigned Position, Fall Staff, and Salaries.

Obviously, familiarity with the data contained in each survey is an important key to effectively and efficiently getting at and managing the data one wishes to obtain. Although the title of each component gives a general idea of its content, a bit of elaboration here will serve as an introduction to the depth of information contained in IPEDS.

[263] The surveys are tweaked from year to year. Occasionally a new survey will be added, or two or more surveys will be consolidated. The listing of surveys above is for 2007–2008. Each summer, NCES announces the new line-up of surveys, and their due dates, on its Web site, <www.nces.ed.gov/ipeds>.

## Component Surveys Overview

### INSTITUTIONAL CHARACTERISTICS (IC)

This component contains not only standard identifying information such as institutional address and the URL of the institution's Web site, but also information on institutional control and affiliation, types of programs and degree, Carnegie classification, admissions criteria, calendar system, and student services, as well as a wide range of information on costs and expenses.

### DEGREE COMPLETIONS (C)

This component quantifies degrees by level, and other awards by length of program, as well as by race/ethnicity and gender of the awardees, and their major.

### GRADUATION RATES (GRS)

The GRS component, by contrast, tracks how many students in an entering cohort complete their degree within 150 percent of normal time-to-degree, and does so by race/ethnicity and gender; it also tracks recipients of athletically-based student aid. In addition, it tracks the number of students who transfer to other schools.

### ENROLLMENT (EF)

The Enrollment survey counts enrolled students by level, race/ethnicity, gender, and type of program enrolled in—credit-hour for degree- or certificate-seeking students, or contact hours for vocational/occupational programs—and by age distribution within level of program. The Enrollment survey also collects data on first-time, first-year students by state of residence. Finally, it also counts those who graduated from high school within the previous twelve months and enrolled in a degree or certificate program.

### STUDENT FINANCIAL AID (SFA)

The Student Financial Aid survey quantifies the number of first-time, full-time degree or certificate students who receive aid, as well as the number of students who receive each type of aid and the average amount received. The survey includes not only Title IV aid, but state and local grants and loans, and institutional aid.

### HUMAN RESOURCES (HR)

The Human Resources collection has three components:

- Employees by Assigned Position (EAP)
- Fall Staff (S)
- Salaries (SA)

*EAP* is primarily a headcount of personnel by function—by full- and part-time status and by faculty status with tenure, where applicable.

*Fall Staff* quantifies the number of full- and part-time employees for institutions with at least fifteen employees. It subdivides faculty and other staff by race/ethnicity and gender. Faculty are further subdivided by contract length, tenure, academic rank, and salary, while administrators and other staff are counted by activity. Part-time staff are categorized as above without regard to salary.

The *Salary* component tracks salary for full-time instructional faculty by rank, gender, and contract length. The Salary survey also captures information about total salary expenditure, including fringe benefits.

#### FINANCE (F)

The Finance survey measures revenues in terms of source, and expenditures by function, physical plant assets and debt, and by endowment. Note: Since public and private institutions use different reporting definitions, comparison between the two types of institution is frequently not possible.

#### 12-MONTH ENROLLMENT AND TOTAL INSTITUTIONAL ACTIVITY (E12)

The most recent IPEDS survey component is the 12-month Enrollment (E12) and Total Institutional Activity survey. Actually E12 is not really new. The dataset it asks for was previously part of the enrollment (EF) component. It is now a stand-alone survey and a part of the Fall collection. This component gathers information on 12-month unduplicated headcounts and total institutional contact-hour or credit-hour activity.

### Data Collection Process

It is important to review the data collection process and its ramification at this point in order to more fully understand the nature of the data in IPEDS. There are a number of important caveats that need to be kept in mind when seeking, querying, or comparing data.

Above all, the IPEDS data collection is constantly changing. Over time, needs for data change, the data collection process itself is tweaked, and accordingly, improvements are implemented.

#### CONTINUITY OF DATA

First, as we have just mentioned, specific surveys and/or data items may have been added or discontinued; even for surveys where there is continuity, data definitions may have changed.

In addition, some data is collected only in alternate years (although some schools, of their own volition, choose to submit the data for all years). Several important examples to keep in mind: Fall Staff is collected in odd years, and "enrollment by age" (a part of the Enrollment survey) is also collected in odd years; but "residence of first-year students" (also a part of the Enrollment survey) is collected in even years. The moral is: Take great care when using such data.

**AVAILABILITY OF DATA**

In general, IPEDS data is available from 1986 through the present, while data from HEGIS[264] (the precursor of IPEDS) is available for 1980, 1984, and 1985. Specific surveys are available as outlined in Table 40.2.

Again, please also keep in mind that some of the above information may change after this volume goes to press. Be sure to check the NCES Web site from time to time for updates—www.nces.ed.gov/ipeds. (*See* Table 40.3, on page 537, for a listing of many other useful IPEDS-related Web sites.)

## Data-Entry and Its Effect on Results

Each institution enters or uploads its data into the web-based collection system during the designated periods (Fall, Winter, Spring) as described above. When all of the data is entered for a given component survey, the individual entering the data runs the submission through a series of web-based edit checks. Once all errors are resolved, an institutional representative called the keyholder locks the data, which verifies that the submission is completed and correct.

NCES then migrates the locked data from the collection system to the analysis system at the collection level. Where there is a risk of releasing personally identifiable small-cell information that is subject to FERPA privacy restrictions, NCES first "perturbs" these values for individual institutions before making the data public or migrating it to the analysis system. The perturbation process is specially designed so that it may or may not change the datum in a particular cell of an institution's submission, but whether it does or does not change, the overall accumulation of data, involving one school in relation to others, remains constant.

TABLE 40.2: **Survey Availability**

| Code | Component | Dates |
|---|---|---|
| IC | Institutional Characteristics | 1990–present |
| EF | Enrollment | 1990–present |
| | Enrollment by Age | 1991–present[1] |
| | Residence of First-Time Freshman | 1992–present[2] |
| C | Completions | 1990–present |
| GRS | Graduation Rates | 1997–present |
| HR | Employees by Assigned Position | 2001–present |
| | Fall Staff | 1991–present[1] |
| | Salaries | 1990–present[3] |
| F | Finance | 1991–present |
| SFA | Financial Aid | 1999–present |
| E12 | 12-Month Enrollment and Total Institutional Activity | Fall 2007–present[4] |

[1] Odd years only
[2] Even years only
[3] Except 2000
[4] Prior data was collected via Enrollment (EF)

The components subject to perturbation are: *Graduation Rates*, *Financial Aid*, *Salaries* and *Fall Staff*. It is a good idea to keep this in mind when evaluating queried data. Your institution's data, in addition to the migrated data from all other institutions that have been similarly migrated, becomes available via passcodes assigned to the institution at the first or *Collection Level*. This data, available only to the institution's keyholder and in-house designees, is preliminary and has not yet been run through NCES's quality control routines—and thus, should be used very cautiously.

[264] HEGIS stands for Higher Education General Information Survey.

At this point, NCES begins to adjudicate the data, running it through several additional quality control procedures. These processes generally take about two months after the data from all institutions have been migrated. In the extremely rare instance where data were not made available, NCES imputes the missing values by using a number of factors such as data from similar institutions and data entered by the institution in preceding years. Imputed data are indicated as such. When this process is complete, data are made available, at the second or *Institution Level*, and are now much more widely accessible; anyone within the institution who has access to the institution's identification number (used as both username and password) can access the data in this preliminarily vetted form. Bear in mind, however, that these are still early release data and are provided for the purpose of peer analysis only. They should not be used to provide aggregate estimates.

After additional checking and analysis, the data are finalized and moved to the *Guest Level* where they are available to the public without the need for user name or password.

### Finding Data with IPEDS Tools

The U.S. Department of Education, acting at the behest of Congress, makes every effort to make the information acquired through the IPEDS surveys accessible not only to professionals in higher education,[265] but to the public. That definitely includes parents and students!

Accordingly, NCES has also designed a number of tools intended to make this treasure trove of information available to every member of the general public who has access to a computer.

Perhaps the most basic of the IPEDS tools, and perhaps of greatest initial interest to admissions personnel, is *College Navigator*.[266]

Navigator is aimed at the general public. It is intended to help prospective students and their parents to compare different colleges and their programs and costs. Congress mandated the creation of this tool to be the primary consumer interface with our institutions, at least in relation to conveying data amassed through IPEDS. Thus, it is certainly advisable that admissions officers familiarize themselves with Navigator—the information it contains, how it is presented, and, ultimately the picture it paints of a school to anyone viewing it. The viewers include the whole spectrum of people interested in your school: not only students and parents, but also high school guidance counselors, and even one's own faculty and administration. We will discuss Navigator more fully below, after briefly presenting the other IPEDS-based tools that are available.

The *Executive Peer Tool* (ExPT) is a tool aimed primarily at college administrators, but is also available to anyone. ExPT is an easy-to-navigate system that enables a comparison of

[265] NCES frequently seeks input through Technical Review Panels and other means as to how to facilitate and simplify access to the data it collects. This is yet another reason to frequently check the AACRAO or NCES Web sites, to ascertain what changes are being considered or announced. In addition, the Association for Institutional Research (AIR), at <www.airweb.org>, serves as a clearinghouse for training materials as to the IPEDS surveys, and offers web-based IPEDS tutorials.

[266] Known until the fall of 2007 as College Opportunities Online (COOL). See <http://nces.ed.gov/collegenavigator/>.

data for a number of institutions. This tool also generates copies of the *IPEDS Data Feedback Report*,[267] sent to the institutional CEO each fall, and it allows users to customize these reports based on a select list of variables for any set of institutions.

Two additional tools for researchers and professionals—though anyone can access them at the guest level—are the *Peer Analysis System* (PAS) and the *Dataset Cutting Tool* (DCT). PAS allows users to compare their (or any) institution to its peers. The tool is extremely flexible and users are able to make use of virtually any data in IPEDS for peer selection and as bases for comparison. Whereas PAS is an analytical instrument, DCT enables the creation of customized data sets for any data in IPEDS that can then be downloaded, saved, and analyzed using a PC-based spreadsheet, databases, and analytical and statistical tools.

College Navigator and ExPT operate largely by means of easy-to-use, drop-down menus for the predetermined and carefully arranged variables available through each of the tools. Both are quite intuitive and easy to use. In contrast, both PAS and DCT require the user to know a bit more about which particular survey component contains the desired data, though a recent feature places the most frequently used variables in one easy-to-find list. The good news is that copious help is available for users at all levels.

## Usefulness of IPEDS Data for Admissions Officers

The introduction to this chapter underlines the idea that the information that is submitted through IPEDS is available to the public, and intended to be used by it. All parties with a stake in higher education need more readily accessible—and readily comparable—data.

These stakeholders range from potential applicants to our institutions, at one end of the spectrum, to policy-makers and administrators, at the other, and all need reliable and accessible data to be able to make better-informed decisions. Whether the issue (for a student) is where to go to college, or whether the issue (for a legislator) is where to target public funding, higher education has increasingly come to be viewed as a commodity, with outcomes which should be knowable and, at least in theory, subject to comparison. In short, in the marketplace, data is vital.

The admissions process has always been competitive in the sense that, in one way or another, each institution competes to enroll the best class that it can and to achieve its enrollment targets. Significant time, energy, and money are expended on this process; large investments are made in market research and advertising; and all sorts of war stories, professional experiences, and anecdotal observations are shared and pondered. Institutional image is studied and constantly refined; newspaper and magazine rankings are reviewed and fretted over. In short, all kinds of factors, tangible and intangible, are brought into the equation each year, as the quest for students is undertaken anew.

[267] The IPEDS Data Feedback Report is discussed Chapter 41, "Tuition Discount Rates: Using IPEDS for Comparative Analysis." See page 548.

Even at the most simplistic level, it is clear that the more the admissions office knows about how its institution compares with its peers, the greater the potential reward. At the very least, as we note in the anecdote which opens this chapter, it is advantageous to be able to anticipate the questions prospective applicants and their families might have, in light of the comparative data readily available to us—and them.

On a somewhat deeper level, using these tools to study institutional data, both within one's own institution and in relation to competitor schools, helps the decision-making process and aids in the efficient allocation of resources. To give just a few examples: comparative information on amounts of financial aid awarded; graduation and retention rates; academic offerings; tuition and fees; dormitory capacity (in the *Institutional Characteristics* survey); and out-of-state enrollees by state are now readily available. Knowing this, one can more wisely invest one's energies and keep priorities in clearer focus.

## Research and Analysis

College Navigator contains a wealth of information and profiles for nearly 7,000 institutions nationwide. Here, one can view information on any of these schools and even compare them side by side. The tool also contains links to additional information not contained within IPEDS, such as institutional mission, crime statistics, accrediting agencies, federal loan default rates, and Web site links. Users are able to select schools based on multiple criteria such as numbers of enrolled students; religious affiliation; location by state, region, or even zip code; major; award level; and institution type. At a glance one could then view data for the institutions selected and compare up to four at a time.

A typical comparison, for example, automatically includes general information such as location and type of school; estimated student expenses for in-state and out-of-state students; all types of financial aid awarded; admissions data such as SAT/ACT score ranges and application fees; undergraduate enrollment data by full- or part-time status; gender and race/ethnicity; retention and graduate rates for first-time, full-time students, including transfer-out rate, where applicable; and information on undergraduate and graduate degrees or certificates awarded. The initial, basic side-by-side comparisons are displayed in columns, but there is always the option to click on details, which display full, detailed information on each school.

College Navigator is intuitive and easy to use, and it assumes no prior knowledge. Two or three mouse clicks yields all of the detailed information outlined above, in an easily digested format. For this reason alone, taking the time to replicate the process which potential applicants and their parents might use can provide admission officers with the exact information their audience can see, and certainly enables us to anticipate concerns and formulate strategic answers to possible questions long before they arise. In short, familiarity with both the data and the format of College Navigator can facilitate the development of recruitment presentations and brochures in a way that addresses potential student concerns or questions very early in the recruitment cycle.

ExPT on the other hand—a simpler and more structured version of PAS—compares institutional data submitted through IPEDS with data submitted by peer institutions. Peer institutions can be selected or defined by the users, either by choosing criteria through a process similar to the one used with College Navigator (*i.e.*, directly by name), or by having the peer group automatically selected through a pre-determined algorithm defined within the ExPT itself. Peer groups, once selected, can be saved, modified, and reused, making subsequent reports extremely easy, especially since the tool works with a maximum of eight variables in any one report.

In addition to constructing customized reports via ExPT, one can print the actual institutional IPEDS Data Feedback Report, which is sent to CEOs each fall for the current or prior year. Although not all items in these reports are directly relevant to the admissions profession, the core Data Feedback Report does allow one the opportunity to see the view of the institution through the same lens as the one used by senior institutional administration.

ExPT allows for short and focused comparisons and analyses. Perhaps the best introduction to the tool is to go to the home page and download the current Data Feedback Report and explore its scope firsthand.[268] The categories of greatest interest to admissions officers, each of which contains several variables, are: Unduplicated 12-month headcount, total FTE, and fall enrollment; percent of students enrolled by race/ethnicity and gender; tuition and fees; percent of full-time, first-time undergraduates receiving financial aid by type of aid, and average amounts of aid received; graduation rates by race/ethnicity; graduation rate cohort as a percent of all undergraduates and of total entering students; transfer-out rate and retention rate; and number of degrees awarded by level. ExPT also compares data on revenue by source, expenditures by FTE enrollment, staff, and salaries.

While ExPT, like College Navigator, is still easy to use, the analytical comparisons provided by ExPT in graphical format are far deeper and more thorough than Navigator's, allowing for user-targeted variables and comparing more institutions in each table. Users are limited to the most recent IPEDS year and can choose from a list of sixty-five pre-selected variables, though only eight variables can be used at a time. One can learn a great deal of valuable and useful information about one's institution and how it compares to its peers. This is helpful not only in anticipating and being able to answer questions from applicants and others but in designing marketing tools and planning a recruitment strategy. Similarly, patterns of enrollment and issues of affordability as well as financial aid awards, graduation rates, degree conferral, and financial data provide background information and perspective that can be quite useful in framing a picture of an institution—especially within the context of the ongoing public dialogue on affordability, accessibility, and outcomes. More and more, these issues are very much in the public eye, and knowing all one can is vital when articulat-

[268] As previously mentioned, a sample and discussion of an IPEDS Data Feedback Report appears at the end of the following chapter, on Using the IPEDS Peer Analysis System to Compare Tuition Discount Rates.

ing the needs and value of the institution to the public, whether alumni or legislators. Certainly the data provide a solid baseline for strategic planning internally (*i.e.*, in the campus context) as well as externally.

So far the tools that we have covered were intended for generalists. While they are intuitive and easy to navigate, they do not allow for complete analytical control, nor do they provide immediate access to the entire impressive range of data that IPEDS collects. To custom-design analytical reports and comparative rankings, one needs to use PAS to manipulate the entire wealth of data available from within the tool itself, or the DCT to cut and download entire, customized institutional datasets to a PC to be analyzed with local software. Whereas in ExPT data comparisons can be copied and pasted into a spreadsheet, with DCT one can also generate fully-labeled SAS or SPSS code to convert downloaded files into SAS or SPSS system files. DCT enables creation of comparison groups of schools by entering or uploading a list of Unit ID numbers or by using criteria based on a group of select variables. DCT is extremely flexible, allowing users to choose entire surveys or merely sections, or even just variables of interest for download.

Of all the tools, the most flexible and comprehensive is PAS. In comparison with the other tools, PAS has very few limitations. It is comprehensive in its approach and scope. In using PAS, the user has to make three initial choices: Select a *focus institution*, select a group of *comparison institutions* against which the focus school is to be compared, and then select the *group of variables* that will serve as the basis for the comparison or ranking.

Like DCT, PAS allows for the creation of comparison groups in several ways, and like ExPT, one can choose an auto-generated group of peers; however, the algorithm for auto-generating groups is different in each tool. PAS allows the user not only to select defining variables from virtually any field in any of the IPEDS component surveys, but also allows for the use of calculated variables from existing data fields. Moreover, variables can be calculated recursively using previously calculated values. This is also true for the data fields one selects for comparison. The calculations can be based on addition, difference, or ratio, allowing for a very wide range of criteria for institutional selection or data comparison.

PAS has a number of other interesting features, and the list of enhancements grows all the time. For example, in addition to merely being able to download query results to spreadsheets or databases, PAS has a built-in Forms Facsimile feature which allows an institution to produce a matrix version of its previously submitted data reports that resemble the old ink-and-paper submission forms in appearance. PAS also has an ever-growing inventory of template-based reports and frequently used variables, for convenience. It is always a good idea to check what is already available *before* beginning, since it could prove to be a time saver and eliminate a lot of searching.

Many of the report templates are either specifically designed for admissions or, at least, directly relevant to the profession. For example, for non-open enrollment institutions, there are reports for admissions, admission trends, and SAT and ACT test scores. Additionally, there are templates for student financial aid (selected years) and price trends, as well as all sorts of reports on enrollments, completions, and graduation rates. All that is needed to run any of these reports is to select a year.

PAS has several other report modalities in addition to Forms Facsimile and pre-built report templates. When retrieving data one can also choose a ranking report for one variable, with values sorted in descending order. For retrieving multiple variables, perhaps from multiple files, the institution's data report is appropriate. To trace a variable across a range of years, for a group of institutions, there is the trend report. Finally, PAS has a statistical summary report feature, with optional graphs, to report basic descriptive statistics.

TABLE 40.3: **IPEDS Resources on the Web**[1]

| Resource | URL(s) |
|---|---|
| **General Help and Information** | |
| About NCES | http://nces.ed.gov/ |
| About IPEDS | http://nces.ed.gov/ipeds/<br>http://nces.ed.gov/ipeds/about |
| **Data Help**[2] | |
| Finding Data Elements | http://nces.ed.gov/ipeds/surveys/ |
| Understanding Data Elements | http://nces.ed.gov/ipeds/glossary/ |
| **Tools Help**[2] | |
| Finding the Right Tool | http://nces.ed.gov/ipeds/tool_matrix/<br>http://nces.ed.gov/ipeds/tool_matrix/tool_matrix.asp |
| PAS and DCT | http://nces.ed.gov/ipedspas/firsttime.asp |
| **Tools** | |
| PAS, DCT | http://nces.ed.gov/ipedspas |
| ExPT | http://nces.ed.gov/ipedspas/Expt |
| College Navigator | http://nces.ed.gov/ipeds/compare_colleges/College Navigator_summary.asp |
| DAS | http://nces.ed.gov/dasol/ |
| **Training and Trainers**[3] | |
| Live Training Workshops | http://www.airweb.org/?page=411 |
| List of IPEDS Trainers | http://www.airweb.org/?page=474 |
| Web-Based Tutorials and Courses | http://www.airweb.org/?page=838 |

[1] All information, except as otherwise noted, is contained on the Web site of the U.S. Department of Education, Institute of Education Sciences, National Center for Education Statistics.
[2] Help on specific problems or general questions is also available from the IPEDS Help Desk by phone: (877) 225-2568 or e-mail: ipedshelp@rti.org.
[3] NCES has partnered with the Association for Institutional Research (AIR) to provide IPEDS training. The links cited are to the AIR Web site.

Data can be chosen across several years for both comparisons and rankings. For this reason, it is important to understand the distinction between a *data* year and a *collection* year. A "collection year" is the academic year in which data are collected. "Data year" refers to the year for which data are reported. Thus, most collection year data in the Institutional Characteristics, Salaries, Fall Staff, Enrollment, and Employees by Assigned Position components are collected for the current collection year, while Completions, Financial Aid, and Finance are collected for the prior year. Since within a data year, all data pertain to the year for which the data are reported, enrollment data collected in 2005–2006 is data from 2005 whereas completions data for 2005–2006 is not collected until 2006–2007.

There is no question about the fact that IPEDS data and the various tools that provide access to the data are extremely useful. Indeed, this vast trove of information is not only useful, it is vital in today's climate where consumers are encouraged to comparison shop, so to speak—and to choose a college based not only on "sticker price," but on value—added qualities and how it measures up against its competitors. The entirely understandable curiosity of students and parents is only part of a larger drive toward accountability. Legislatures at the state and federal levels are relying on the increased availability of data to press institutions to demonstrate their effectiveness.

Where do admissions professionals fit into this new equation? It was not all that long ago that successful admissions directors or recruiters were measured chiefly by having met the goal of bringing in a diverse freshman class that met both quantitative and qualitative targets set by the institution. Ideally, the students were a good match for the school, and all available seats were filled. Now this equation may very well have changed. One can easily envision the same person now being hauled onto the carpet for bringing in exactly the same class. If, as has been widely discussed, one of the institutional outcome measures would involve graduation rates, and if institutions were to find that their accreditation, funding, and eligibility to award Federal financial aid would be tied to these rates, our hypothetical director could be deemed a failure six years after the admission of a cohort when the "ideal" class failed, for whatever reason external to the admissions process, to graduate in sufficient numbers. Future individual and institutional success might thus very well hinge on criteria that are not, at present, even looked at. Stated another way, the data that admission decisions are based on would need to be broadened, and the process that formulates policies, criteria, and strategies for recruitment may need to consider many additional factors.

## Basic Strategies and Approaches

The remainder of this chapter will focus mainly on PAS, since it is a somewhat more complex tool than the others, and provides the most flexibility and the greatest data access.

Locating and managing variables are arguably the two most challenging aspects of using the IPEDS tools. Fortunately there are many ways of locating variables. First, there is *no substitute for familiarity* with the data elements of the component surveys. The best starting point is http://nces.ed.gov/ipeds/ipedssurveys.asp, which provides the IPEDS survey screens or forms from 1994 to the present. A rather small investment in time here can provide huge rewards when later using the tools, enabling the user to see and better understand not only where to look for individual data elements but also how each survey is structured and how the survey's data interrelate. It is also a tremendous help to peruse the IPEDS Glossary, which provides precise definitions for each data element, at http://nces.ed.gov/ipeds/glossary/. PAS also provides a search function to locate variables by key word, as well as a clickable "info" button beside each data item that leads to a definition for that item.

Another good idea is to *map out* the variables that will be needed either during the search for information or in the selection of peer institutions. The Frequently Used/Derived Variables List is a good starting point for mapping data. This list is the first option one sees when clicking on any of the *variables* links available on the first PAS screen. Many needed data items are already at one's fingertips, obviating the need to search for them.

Once chosen, PAS keeps all data variables in a Master Variable List (MVL). The MVL enables the user to utilize the same variables, even modify them, for subsequent activities. The MVL is cumulative and remains available any time during a session prior to log off, to manual deletion, or to starting a new session. MVLs may also be stored on the NCES site for up to 30 days and may be downloaded to one's desktop. Power users (anyone can become a power user by following the directions in PAS) may also upload locally stored MVLs to be used over and over again in each new session. The same can be done for peer institution lists.

Even for PAS, the learning curve is not steep. A small investment in time is all that one would need to get started. Many of the tools are highly intuitive, and anyone with the ability to click a mouse button should find them extremely easy to use. Remember, however, that each of the tools is designed to be best for specific types of tasks, as discussed above. After using each once or twice, the best tool for each task will become clear.

Here are a few sample exercises for ExPT, DCT, and PAS with step-by-step solutions, as well as some suggestions for possible inquiries via Navigator, ExPT, DCT, and PAS. The Navigator exercise asks you to compare different groups of institutions within 50 miles of your institution, via selected characteristics, and see how your institution compares as seen through the eyes of a prospective student or parent.

## Sample IPEDS Tool Exercises

All exercises begin at the following URL: http://nces.ed.gov/ipedspas.

### Exercise 1: Using ExPT

The following instructions provide practice in using the Executive Peer Tool:

- Step 1: Click the *Executive Peer Tool* link. Click *"I agree to the terms above."*
- Step 2: Type in the name of your institution in the Focus institution box and click *Next step*.
- Step 3: You now have the option of either downloading a previous IPEDS Data Feedback Report (in PDF format) for the institution you selected or you may choose one of four self-explanatory methods for creating a peer group for custom comparisons. The last two options will probably not suit your purposes, since both involve pre-selected groups. However, both lists, though neither might completely satisfy your criteria, can be modified by deleting selected institutions and adding new ones by name. When adding peers by name, partial names may be added and you will be given a list from which to choose the institutions you would like to keep.

  Choose *Select your peer list* and click *next step*.

  You are now presented with a screen that allows you to choose criteria from drop-down lists and check boxes. Select all items that will most closely yield the peer group that you desire. The drop-down list allows the use of the Shift + Click, or you may Ctrl + Click to select a range of items or any number of items from within the same drop-down list. After selecting the appropriate criteria, click *next step.*

At this point, you may de-select any institutions you do not want and add more peers by name if you desire. Once this is done, click *next step*. Now, confirm that the list is correct and either modify or save the list. Once you have done the confirmation click *next step*.

- Step 4: Now you may select up to eight variables that will serve as the basis for comparison with your peers. For the purposes of this particular report, check all four items under *Percent of Full-Time, First-Time, Degree/Certificate-Seeking Undergraduate students receiving financial aid, by type of aid,* and *Types and average amounts of financial aid received by full-time, first-time, degree/certificate seeking undergraduates* and click *next step*.
- Step 5: You now see the reported comparison in tabular form, which can be saved by copying and pasting the data into a spreadsheet. By clicking the Graph link, you can get the same comparison done as a printable graph in PDF format. Clicking the Comparison Group Data link yields a table of all of the underlying actual data fields supporting your table, which also can be copied and pasted into a spreadsheet. The modify variables link allows you to compare the same schools using different variables while the start over link takes you back to step 2 where you can begin a new comparison using a new set of institutions.

### Exercise 2: Using DCT

The following instructions provide practice in using the Dataset Cutting Tool.

You will need to log into the system at one of the three levels, explained in the chapter. We will use Institution Level, reached by clicking the provided link on the page and accepting the terms by clicking on the *I agree to the terms* above link. At the Institution Level, the user ID and password are *both* the Institution Unit ID, which may be obtained from College Navigator, also explained earlier in the chapter (http://nces.ed.gov/collegenavigator/). The Dataset Cutting Tool (DCT) is accessible via the link at the bottom of the DCT column on the right. Newcomers may elect to read the introduction and tutorial, linked near the top of the page.

At this point, you may click on the download data files link, which allows you to download complete raw data files in several formats by choosing years and surveys from a drop-down menu and clicking on *get*. For more customized data, we will create a custom dataset by selecting a year from the drop-down menu and selecting schools in one of four self-explanatory ways. In addition, as explained in the chapter, we must also choose the way we want to view the data, by choosing either Collection or Data Year. Clicking the *View data by* link provides an explanation and a table describing the two viewing choices. We will select schools using specific criteria by clicking the appropriate radio button. We will keep the default year, leave the *imputation flags* box unchecked, leave the collection year radio button selected, and click *continue*.

We are now presented with a screen of drop-down menus and check boxes similar to what we used in step 2 of the ExPT exercise above. Choosing the *continue* button will display a list of up to 1,000 individually displayed schools from which to select or de-select all or some. At least one school must be selected. Click *continue.* You are then asked to select *collection (or data) years from which to get data.* Next you are asked to choose the surveys you wish from each year you chose. Click *continue.*

You are then asked to select the sections of each report containing the data you seek. Select what you need and click *continue.*

You will then need to select the variables that you require either by checking appropriate boxes and then by clicking on the various Select links in the surveys for which you have checked boxes. This will give you a drop-down menu from which to choose additional variables. Once you have selected appropriate values from these menus, choose the *save and close* link. Click *continue.*

DCT will present a page summarizing the selections you have made and offer you various download options or the option to view the data online.

### Exercise 3: Sample Admissions/Enrollment Problem Using PAS

Since the IPEDS Peer Analysis System (PAS) has the greatest complexity of tools, the following exercise is specific. Feel free to substitute a more current year or modify other variables accordingly.

- TASK: Look at the percent of undergraduate applicants admitted, the full-time admissions yield (percent of undergraduates admitted who enrolled full-time), and the fall-to-fall retention rate of full-time first-time undergraduate students at public research universities in the mideast (U.S.) region using the various reports available in the PAS.
- SOLUTION: Go to Peer Analysis System
  1] Log in at the *institution level* and agree to the data usage terms
  2] Type 195809 as both UserID and password
  3] Click *Use my institution* to designate your focus institution
  4] Create a *Comparison group—click Comparison Group* from the menu on the right side of the page
  5] Select *institutions by variable*
  6] Open *Frequently used/derived variables.* Click "+"
  7] Open *Institutions*
  8] Tag *Geographic region, Sector of institution, Carnegie*
  9] *Classification 2005 Basic,* click *Continue*
  10] Tag *2006–07,* click *Continue*
  11] Click *Go to the query form*
  12] Choose *Mideast* for Geographic region
  13] Choose *Private not-for-profit four-year or above* for sector

14] Make two choices for Carnegie: *Master's college and Universities (larger programs)* and *Doctoral/Research* (CTRL – click)
15] *Submit* (comparison group = 56 institutions)
16] Choose additional *Variables* – Click *Variables*
17] Click *Select more variables*
18] Open *Frequently used/derived variables*
19] Open *Selectivity and admissions yield*, click "+"
20] Tag *Percent admitted total* (Click on *Info* button for info)
21] Tag *Admissions yield full-time*
22] Open *Fall enrollment/retention rates*, click "+"
23] Tag *Full-time retention rate*
24] Click *Continue*
25] Tag *2006–07* for Selectivity and admissions yield (or modified year)
26] Tag *Fall 2005* for Fall enrollment/retention rates (or modified year)
27] *Continue.*

**SEE YOUR DATA:**

28] *Click Reports & Stats*

- Choose *Ranking report*
- Click *Admissions yield full-time* to see institution list in ranked order
- Click *Previous*

29] Choose *Trend Report*

- Tag *Full-time retention rate, Continue*
- Tag all three years that are available, *Submit* (notice *Download* button)
- Click *Previous*

30] *Reports & Stats*

- Choose *Institutions data*
- Select *Percent admitted total, Admissions yield full-time, full-time retention rate*
- Click *Finished selection*
- Tag *Download in comma-separated format*, click *Continue*
- Click *Open* to open in spreadsheet program. Format nicely.

31] *Reports & Stats*

- Choose *Report Templates*
- Click *Admissions and Test scores*
- Click *Admissions*
- Click *Display*

(Try out other templates)

## Additional Exercises

### NAVIGATOR

- Compare different groups of institutions within 50 miles of your institution, with selected characteristics and see how your institution compares through the eyes of a prospective student or parent.
- Do a full review of all information for your school for accuracy and for the image it projects.

### EXPT

- Compare your institution against its peers for: tuition and fees, graduation rates by race/ethnicity, graduation rate by cohort, full-time equivalent staff, and enrollment by race/ethnicity.
- Copy and paste the result for the report(s) into a spread sheet and produce a graph directly from ExPT. Do the same for the underlying group's data.

### DCT

- Download a select data file and import the data into a spreadsheet, statistics package, or database.
- Create and download custom datasets using admissions-related parameters of your choice. Use a spreadsheet program to format the data so that your colleagues can utilize them as briefing sheets when recruited.

### PAS

- Do a study of selectivity for a group of your peers.
- Analyze your out-of-state competitors. How many first-year students from your state enroll in institutions outside your state?
- Compare graduation-rate data for students by gender and race/ethnicity for various majors with your peer group.
- Compare average amounts of institutional, federal, and state aid for institutions in your state and for your peers.
- Compare price of attendance for various groups of students with your peers.
- Familiarize yourself with the numerous pre-existing templates and frequently used variables. You will find a wealth of information at your fingertips requiring an absolutely minimal investment in time.

/ CHAPTER FORTY-ONE /

*by Michael B. Duggan, Ed.D.*
*Director, Enrollment Research and Planning*
*Suffolk University*
*Rebecca Mathews, M.Ed.*
*Associate Director, Enrollment Research and Planning*
*Suffolk University*

41

# Tuition Discount Rates:
## Using IPEDS for Comparative Analysis

Tuition discounting is the practice of reducing the cost of attendance to individual students by replacing portions of their tuition with institutional student aid (Allan 2001). The discount rate is generally calculated by either dividing total institutional aid by total tuition revenue, or by calculating the average institutional aid award as a percent of tuition. For example, if a university charges $20,000 for tuition, but gives its students an average of $5,000 in institutional grant aid, the discount rate is 25 percent ($5,000/$20,000 = 25%). Another way of looking at the discount is in terms of net price. For the same school charging $20,000 in tuition but offering an average grant of $5,000, the *net price* is $15,000.

Tuition discounting began to be widespread when the number of high school seniors experienced a decrease in the 1980s, sparking what has been called an "arms race" (Goral 2003). In the 1990s discounting became widely used for enrollment management, and discount rates rose sharply as colleges rushed to apply this new tool (June 2006a). During that time financial aid was the fastest growing expenditure for most four-year private colleges (Redd 2000). Between 2003 and 2005 overall discount rates stayed level, but the percent of students receiving a discount continued to grow (June 2006a).

The practice of tuition discounting has been subject to widespread criticism. Those concerned with widening access to higher education have been concerned that discounts are not based solely on financial need, but have become an enrollment management tool. Growth in aid to wealthy students has outpaced growth in aid to needy students (Redd 2000). In 1995, the average grant aid for higher-income undergraduate students at private colleges and universities was 39 percent of that for lower-income ($1,359 vs. $3,446). Just four years later the average grant for higher-income students equaled 82 percent of the average grant for lower-income students (Goral 2003). Aid at public colleges and universities has seen similar increases.

A second source of concern is the impact that widespread discounts have on the fiscal health of colleges. Tuition discounts were originally funded by endowments and gifts. Today schools are increasingly redirecting tuition revenue to fund discounts. This practice has the potential to undermine the financial stability of an institution, not to mention limiting funds for instruction, academics, and student support (Goral 2003). Doing so can even threaten an institution's bond rating, and bond rating agencies have called for greater attention to the financial risks discounting can pose (June 2006a).

Finally, there is doubt as to whether tuition discounts are actually an effective enrollment management tool. Institutions hoping to meet their enrollment management goals by increasing their discounts have not necessarily succeeded (Kurz and Scannell 2005).

Schools that have used tuition discounting effectively have done so through a careful analysis of data. One important piece of data involves knowing the discount rates of an institution's peers. Until recently the most common source of tuition discounting data has been the NACUBO survey of tuition discounting, currently done in conjunction with the College Board. While the findings from the NACUBO study (Hubbell and Lapovsky 2005) are interesting as an overview of tuition discounting, they are of limited utility. Hubbell and Lapovsky sent their survey to accredited, independent four-year institutions and 450 institutions responded. According to the National Center for Education Statistics (Knapp *et al.* 2005, p. 4), a unit of the U.S. Department of Education, there were 1,913 private, degree-granting, four-year institutions in 2004–2005. Based on these statistics, it would appear that about 24 percent of eligible institutions participated in the NACUBO study. Based on this comparatively low response rate, it is not clear whether the results of the Hubbell and Lapovsky study are generalizeable.

In contrast, the IPEDS Peer Analysis System (PAS) can provide access to the vast majority of the 1900+ independent, four-year institutions (exceptions being institutions that did not respond to IPEDS or did not respond fully to the surveys). The IPEDS PAS offers a much richer source for mining tuition discounting data than is currently available through other means. This article will explain exactly how to use the PAS to access this data.

### Accessing Freshmen Discounting Data

The federal government, through the Integrated Postsecondary Education Data System (IPEDS), collects a variety of data from higher education institutions. The data that are collected are made available to the higher education community and the public through the IPEDS Peer Analysis System (PAS). There are three levels of access to the PAS: guest level, institution level, and collection level.[269] This chapter will focus on data available using the institution level login. The Peer Analysis System allows users to compare an institution (called a focus institution in PAS) with other colleges and universities (peer group).

We have used the IPEDS PAS data to generate estimates of the freshmen discount rate for a group of other institutions to compare with those of our own institution.

We do not have space enough in this chapter to discuss methods for navigating the Peer Analysis System. Readers are urged to visit the Web site of the Association for Institutional Research for information as to opportunities for training on IPEDS at the AACRAO and AIR annual meetings, and at regional conferences, as well as online.[270]

For the rest of this chapter, we will assume that readers have successfully logged in at the institution level. The next step is selecting the focus institution and the peer group of colleges and universities to compare it with. As an example, we have used Suffolk University as our focus institution and have selected a group of private, non-profit, four-year or above institutions with the Carnegie Classification of Masters Colleges and Universities (larger programs) as the peer group. In the next section, we will discuss how the freshman discount rate is calculated and then, rather than going through a step-by-step process for selecting data from the PAS to generate the discount rate, we will list the variables that we used.

### Calculating the Freshman Discount Rate

Basically, to calculate the freshman discount rate for a new cohort of freshmen, one needs the institutional grant aid awarded to those new freshmen and the gross tuition revenues generated by the new cohort. The discount rate is the ratio of the total institutional grant aid divided by gross tuition revenue.

In order to get these two pieces from the IPEDS PAS, we have to pull several variables and then do some manipulating of the data. The data are taken from the *Institutions Data* selection in the *Reports & Stats* menu.

The first set of data comes from the *Institutional Characteristics/Admissions/Student Charges* section. In this section, we can select the tuition rate for the year or years we are interested in (referred to as "Student charges—Institutions reporting by academic year"). Next, we go the *Student Financial Aid* survey data and look at the student financial aid for full-time first-time degree/certificate-seeking students category. In this section, we pull data

[269] For more information on levels of access, interested readers can visit <http://nces.ed.gov/ipedspas/>.

[270] See < www.airweb.org >.

on the average amount of institutional grant aid awarded to new full-time, first-time students, the number of these students who were awarded aid, and the number of new freshmen in that year's cohort. (Note: Data for this article reflect the academic year 2004–2005.)

Table 41.1 shows the raw data that were pulled from the PAS. We have eliminated a few institutions that had blank or incomplete data and we also eliminated schools with a new freshman class of less than 100.

Table 1 includes:

1. The name of each school;
2. The fall 2004 freshman tuition rate;
3. The number of new fall 2004 freshmen receiving institutional grant aid;
4. The average institutional grant aid awarded to these new freshmen;
5. The number of students in the fall 2004 new freshmen cohort;
6. Total freshmen institutional grant aid;
7. Total freshmen tuition revenue; and
8. Freshmen discount rate.

To get total institutional grant aid awarded to new freshmen, we have to multiply the data in Item #3 with the data in Item #4 (the number of students receiving institutional grant aid multiplied by the average institutional grant award). To get gross freshmen tuition revenue, we have to multiply #2 by #5 (the fall 2004 tuition rate multiplied by the fall 2004 freshmen cohort). Then, we divide the total institutional grant aid by the total freshmen tuition revenue to get the freshman discount rate.

**How do I find my institution's Data Feedback Report?**

To find your institution's Data Feedback Report, go to http://nces.ed.gov/ipedspas/ and click on Executive Peer Tool. This will take you to the NCES Data Usage Agreement. Read the statement and if you agree, click on I agree to the terms. You will then be prompted to enter the name of the focus institution that you want information on. Enter the name of the institution and click Next Step. If there are multiple institutions with that name, you will have a list of schools to select from; otherwise, you will have one choice listed. In either case, click on the name of the institution you want. This will take you to a page with the option of IPEDS Data Feedback Report Downloads. At this point, you can download copies of your 2006 and 2007 Data Feedback Reports (as examples of what is possible).

## IPEDS Data Feedback Report

Each fall, winter, and spring, staff of institutions of higher education gather data to submit to the Integrated Postsecondary Education Data System (IPEDS) of the National Center for Education Statistics (NCES). The NCES has a variety of tools to access the IPEDS data, as well as offering reports on IPEDS data. One of the more interesting reports (from an institutional perspective) and perhaps one of the less well-known is the IPEDS Data Feedback Report.

The IPEDS Data Feedback Report is an eight-page report that is customized for each institution. Each fall, the report is sent to the president of each higher education institution. It is also available on the NCES Web site.

The report presents twelve charts showing data for the institution and a set of comparison institutions. It includes comparisons of your institution and the comparison group over a

TABLE 41.1: Sample Analysis of 2004–2005 Student Financial Aid Data for New Freshmen

| 1 | 2 | 3 | 4 | 5 | 6 | 7 | 8 |
|---|---|---|---|---|---|---|---|
| Institution Name | Tuition ($) | Grants Awarded (n) | Avg. Grant Awarded ($) | Cohort (n) | Total Aid ($) | Gross Tuition Revenue for Cohort ($) | Freshman Discount Rate (%) |
| Arcadia University | 22,440 | 470 | 10,349 | 477 | 4,864,030 | 10,703,880 | 45 |
| Ashland University | 18,394 | 518 | 8,709 | 573 | 4,511,262 | 10,539,762 | 43 |
| Aurora University | 14,750 | 284 | 7,021 | 294 | 1,993,964 | 4,336,500 | 46 |
| Baldwin-Wallace College | 19,494 | 555 | 9,350 | 711 | 5,189,250 | 13,860,234 | 37 |
| Bellarmine University | 19,250 | 411 | 10,300 | 434 | 4,233,300 | 8,354,500 | 51 |
| Bellevue University | 3,720 | 38 | 1,131 | 121 | 42,978 | 450,120 | 10 |
| Belmont University | 15,360 | 484 | 5,989 | 727 | 2,898,676 | 11,166,720 | 26 |
| Benedictine University | 17,800 | 304 | 7,466 | 312 | 2,269,664 | 5,553,600 | 41 |
| Bentley College | 25,330 | 580 | 15,525 | 927 | 9,004,500 | 23,480,910 | 38 |
| Bradley University | 17,600 | 941 | 7,472 | 1,013 | 7,031,152 | 17,828,800 | 39 |
| Brenau University | 14,610 | 188 | 9,099 | 198 | 1,710,612 | 2,892,780 | 59 |
| California Lutheran University | 21,820 | 387 | 11,971 | 402 | 4,632,777 | 8,771,640 | 53 |
| Cambridge College | 11,700 | 27 | 2,770 | 127 | 74,790 | 1,485,900 | 5 |
| Canisius College | 20,910 | 860 | 10,665 | 879 | 9,171,900 | 18,379,890 | 50 |
| Cardinal Stritch University | 15,360 | 117 | 6,901 | 193 | 807,417 | 2,964,480 | 27 |
| Chaminade University of Honolulu | 13,850 | 243 | 5,697 | 246 | 1,384,371 | 3,407,100 | 41 |
| Chapman University | 25,500 | 686 | 13,691 | 829 | 9,392,026 | 21,139,500 | 44 |
| College of Notre Dame of Maryland | 19,900 | 139 | 10,250 | 149 | 1,424,750 | 2,965,100 | 48 |
| College of St Catherine | 15,474 | 353 | 7,616 | 382 | 2,688,448 | 5,911,068 | 45 |
| Columbia College | 17,690 | 257 | 9,266 | 261 | 2,381,362 | 4,617,090 | 52 |
| Concordia University-Wisconsin | 16,370 | 300 | 8,975 | 382 | 2,692,500 | 6,253,340 | 43 |
| Converse College | 19,960 | 195 | 12,248 | 197 | 2,388,360 | 3,932,120 | 61 |
| Cumberland University | 12,130 | 269 | 5,158 | 308 | 1,387,502 | 3,736,040 | 37 |
| Dallas Baptist University | 11,610 | 275 | 6,316 | 324 | 1,736,900 | 3,761,640 | 46 |
| DeSales University | 19,000 | 349 | 7,790 | 364 | 2,718,710 | 6,916,000 | 39 |
| Doane College | 15,620 | 297 | 8,218 | 305 | 2,440,746 | 4,764,100 | 51 |
| Dominican University | 18,900 | 258 | 3,692 | 271 | 952,536 | 5,121,900 | 19 |
| Dowling College | 12,168 | 393 | 4,901 | 456 | 1,926,093 | 5,548,608 | 35 |
| Drake University | 20,200 | 621 | 10,550 | 643 | 6,551,550 | 12,988,600 | 50 |
| D'Youville College | 14,690 | 194 | 6,012 | 227 | 1,166,328 | 3,334,630 | 35 |
| Eastern University | 17,700 | 421 | 7,777 | 422 | 3,274,117 | 7,469,400 | 44 |
| Emerson College | 22,976 | 331 | 10,057 | 700 | 3,328,867 | 16,083,200 | 21 |
| Fairfield University | 27,930 | 507 | 11,378 | 856 | 5,768,646 | 23,908,080 | 24 |
| Fairleigh Dickinson University-College at Florham | 22,876 | 556 | 11,021 | 601 | 6,127,676 | 13,748,476 | 45 |
| Fairleigh Dickinson University-Metropolitan Campus | 21,224 | 441 | 12,828 | 505 | 5,657,148 | 10,718,120 | 53 |
| Fontbonne University | 15,100 | 178 | 6,869 | 187 | 1,222,682 | 2,823,700 | 43 |

TABLE 41.1: **Sample Analysis of 2004–2005 Student Financial Aid Data for New Freshmen**

| 1 Institution Name | 2 Tuition ($) | 3 Grants Awarded (n) | 4 Avg. Grant Awarded ($) | 5 Cohort (n) | 6 Total Aid ($) | 7 Gross Tuition Revenue for Cohort ($) | 8 Freshman Discount Rate (%) |
|---|---|---|---|---|---|---|---|
| Friends University | 14,430 | 138 | 6,026 | 198 | 831,588 | 2,857,140 | 29 |
| Gannon University | 17,550 | 501 | 8,093 | 523 | 4,054,593 | 9,178,650 | 44 |
| Gardner-Webb University | 14,960 | 280 | 6,953 | 400 | 1,946,840 | 5,984,000 | 33 |
| Gonzaga University | 21,730 | 926 | 9,619 | 973 | 8,907,194 | 21,143,290 | 42 |
| Hamline University | 21,280 | 297 | 5,545 | 445 | 1,646,865 | 9,469,600 | 17 |
| Harding University | 10,380 | 805 | 4,500 | 965 | 3,622,500 | 10,016,700 | 36 |
| Hawaii Pacific University | 10,922 | 178 | 7,618 | 656 | 1,356,004 | 7,164,832 | 19 |
| Holy Family University | 15,990 | 215 | 7,200 | 255 | 1,548,000 | 4,077,450 | 38 |
| Indiana Wesleyan University | 15,204 | 619 | 5,736 | 1344 | 3,550,584 | 20,434,176 | 17 |
| Iona College | 18,990 | 838 | 8,240 | 895 | 6,905,120 | 16,996,050 | 41 |
| John Carroll University | 22,108 | 677 | 9,798 | 734 | 6,633,246 | 16,227,272 | 41 |
| Johnson & Wales University | 16,650 | 2017 | 4,572 | 2303 | 9,221,724 | 38,344,950 | 24 |
| Lawrence Technological University | 13,626 | 202 | 4,557 | 269 | 920,514 | 3,665,394 | 25 |
| Le Moyne College | 19,640 | 460 | 10,371 | 473 | 4,770,660 | 9,289,720 | 51 |
| Lesley University | 20,925 | 143 | 11,994 | 214 | 1,715,142 | 4,477,950 | 38 |
| Lewis & Clark College | 25,938 | 422 | 14,159 | 537 | 5,975,098 | 13,928,706 | 43 |
| Lewis University | 16,906 | 454 | 7,346 | 509 | 3,335,084 | 8,605,154 | 39 |
| Liberty University | 12,600 | 2080 | 6,934 | 2094 | 14,422,720 | 26,384,400 | 55 |
| Lindenwood University | 11,200 | 876 | 6,585 | 917 | 5,768,460 | 10,270,400 | 56 |
| Long Island University-Brooklyn Campus | 21,150 | 827 | 3,292 | 931 | 2,722,484 | 19,690,650 | 14 |
| Loyola College in Maryland | 26,803 | 502 | 14,213 | 953 | 7,134,926 | 25,543,259 | 28 |
| Loyola Marymount University | 25,266 | 651 | 10,652 | 1390 | 6,934,452 | 35,119,740 | 20 |
| Loyola University New Orleans | 22,812 | 747 | 12,241 | 808 | 9,144,027 | 18,432,096 | 50 |
| Madonna University | 9,700 | 285 | 2,616 | 590 | 745,560 | 5,723,000 | 13 |
| Manhattanville College | 23,620 | 252 | 9,088 | 403 | 2,290,176 | 9,518,860 | 24 |
| Marian College of Fond du Lac | 15,500 | 254 | 5,572 | 270 | 1,415,288 | 4,185,000 | 34 |
| Marist College | 19,540 | 815 | 8,117 | 955 | 6,615,355 | 18,660,700 | 35 |
| Marymount University | 16,952 | 303 | 8,968 | 414 | 2,717,304 | 7,018,128 | 39 |
| Maryville University of Saint Louis | 16,000 | 298 | 7,068 | 313 | 2,106,264 | 5,008,000 | 42 |
| Marywood University | 19,600 | 330 | 9,725 | 332 | 3,209,250 | 6,507,200 | 49 |
| McDaniel College | 24,500 | 315 | 11,845 | 357 | 3,731,175 | 8,746,500 | 43 |
| Medaille College | 14,010 | 229 | 4,522 | 305 | 1,035,538 | 4,273,050 | 24 |
| Mercer University | 22,050 | 586 | 12,243 | 635 | 7,174,398 | 14,001,750 | 51 |
| Mercy College-Main Campus | 11,230 | 483 | 1,810 | 736 | 874,230 | 8,265,280 | 11 |
| Metropolitan College of New York | 17,856 | 180 | 1,933 | 270 | 347,940 | 4,821,120 | 7 |
| MidAmerica Nazarene University | 12,630 | 233 | 4,939 | 249 | 1,150,787 | 3,144,870 | 37 |
| Monmouth University | 19,108 | 810 | 6,435 | 948 | 5,212,350 | 18,114,384 | 29 |

TABLE 41.1: **Sample Analysis of 2004–2005 Student Financial Aid Data for New Freshmen**

| 1 | 2 | 3 | 4 | 5 | 6 | 7 | 8 |
|---|---|---|---|---|---|---|---|
| **Institution Name** | **Tuition ($)** | **Grants Awarded (n)** | **Avg. Grant Awarded ($)** | **Cohort (n)** | **Total Aid ($)** | **Gross Tuition Revenue for Cohort ($)** | **Freshman Discount Rate (%)** |
| Nazareth College of Rochester | 18,040 | 447 | 8,146 | 449 | 3,641,262 | 8,099,960 | 45 |
| New York Institute of Technology-Manhattan Campus | 17,840 | 217 | 6,503 | 269 | 1,411,151 | 4,798,960 | 29 |
| New York Institute of Technology-Old Westbury | 17,840 | 437 | 8,006 | 525 | 3,498,622 | 9,366,000 | 37 |
| Niagara University | 17,700 | 710 | 9,889 | 731 | 7,021,190 | 12,938,700 | 54 |
| Notre Dame de Namur University | 21,350 | 140 | 9,979 | 161 | 1,397,060 | 3,437,350 | 41 |
| Oklahoma City University | 15,200 | 290 | 9,738 | 316 | 2,824,020 | 4,803,200 | 59 |
| Olivet Nazarene University | 14,900 | 622 | 6,322 | 699 | 3,932,284 | 10,415,100 | 38 |
| Our Lady of the Lake University-San Antonio | 15,594 | 214 | 5,559 | 221 | 1,189,626 | 3,446,274 | 35 |
| Pfeiffer University | 14,570 | 175 | 6,848 | 188 | 1,198,400 | 2,739,160 | 44 |
| Piedmont College | 13,500 | 109 | 6,417 | 167 | 699,453 | 2,254,500 | 31 |
| Providence College | 23,180 | 696 | 11,229 | 1036 | 7,815,384 | 24,014,480 | 33 |
| Quinnipiac University | 21,540 | 933 | 8,369 | 1335 | 7,808,277 | 28,755,900 | 27 |
| Regis University | 22,200 | 354 | 8,152 | 390 | 2,885,808 | 8,658,000 | 33 |
| Rider University | 21,820 | 819 | 9,312 | 892 | 7,626,528 | 19,463,440 | 39 |
| Rivier College | 19,200 | 218 | 7,523 | 235 | 1,640,014 | 4,512,000 | 36 |
| Robert Morris University | 14,226 | 648 | 4,770 | 678 | 3,090,960 | 9,645,228 | 32 |
| Roberts Wesleyan College | 17,182 | 248 | 6,491 | 254 | 1,609,768 | 4,364,228 | 37 |
| Rochester Institute of Technology | 22,056 | 1860 | 8,925 | 2250 | 16,600,500 | 49,626,000 | 33 |
| Rockhurst University | 17,950 | 271 | 6,215 | 305 | 1,684,265 | 5,474,750 | 31 |
| Rollins College | 26,910 | 261 | 15,399 | 486 | 4,019,139 | 13,078,260 | 31 |
| Roosevelt University | 16,080 | 164 | 6,033 | 238 | 989,412 | 3,827,040 | 26 |
| Sacred Heart University | 21,990 | 765 | 7,066 | 877 | 5,405,490 | 19,285,230 | 28 |
| Saint Ambrose University | 17,565 | 479 | 8,002 | 485 | 3,832,958 | 8,519,025 | 45 |
| Saint Bonaventure University | 18,650 | 567 | 9,324 | 574 | 5,286,708 | 10,705,100 | 49 |
| Saint Edward's University | 15,960 | 509 | 7,375 | 601 | 3,753,875 | 9,591,960 | 39 |
| Saint Francis University | 19,390 | 303 | 9,712 | 326 | 2,942,736 | 6,321,140 | 47 |
| Saint John Fisher College | 18,200 | 507 | 8,540 | 530 | 4,329,780 | 9,646,000 | 45 |
| Saint Joseph's University | 25,770 | 1003 | 8,244 | 1211 | 8,268,732 | 31,207,470 | 26 |
| Saint Marys College of California | 25,000 | 421 | 11,669 | 611 | 4,912,649 | 15,275,000 | 32 |
| Saint Peters College | 19,200 | 502 | 10,256 | 515 | 5,148,512 | 9,888,000 | 52 |
| Saint Thomas University | 17,010 | 159 | 5,987 | 191 | 951,933 | 3,248,910 | 29 |
| Saint Xavier University | 17,150 | 402 | 6,011 | 408 | 2,416,422 | 6,997,200 | 35 |
| Santa Clara University | 27,135 | 916 | 10,586 | 1170 | 9,696,776 | 31,747,950 | 31 |
| Seattle Pacific University | 20,139 | 549 | 7,948 | 633 | 4,363,452 | 12,747,987 | 34 |
| Seattle University | 21,285 | 592 | 9,496 | 719 | 5,621,632 | 15,303,915 | 37 |
| Shenandoah University | 19,090 | 178 | 5,950 | 329 | 1,059,100 | 6,280,610 | 17 |

TABLE 41.1: **Sample Analysis of 2004-2005 Student Financial Aid Data for New Freshmen**

| 1 | 2 | 3 | 4 | 5 | 6 | 7 | 8 |
|---|---|---|---|---|---|---|---|
| Institution Name | Tuition ($) | Grants Awarded (n) | Avg. Grant Awarded ($) | Cohort (n) | Total Aid ($) | Gross Tuition Revenue for Cohort ($) | Freshman Discount Rate (%) |
| Simmons College | 23,760 | 319 | 7,926 | 393 | 2,528,394 | 9,337,680 | 27 |
| Southern New Hampshire University | 18,984 | 478 | 8,405 | 542 | 4,017,590 | 10,289,328 | 39 |
| Southern Wesleyan University | 14,300 | 99 | 6,309 | 122 | 624,591 | 1,744,600 | 36 |
| Southwest Baptist University | 11,800 | 362 | 5,343 | 390 | 1,934,166 | 4,602,000 | 42 |
| Spring Arbor University | 15,700 | 297 | 6,418 | 298 | 1,906,146 | 4,678,600 | 41 |
| Springfield College | 20,160 | 470 | 9,949 | 556 | 4,676,030 | 11,208,960 | 42 |
| St Marys University | 17,256 | 394 | 6,312 | 464 | 2,486,928 | 8,006,784 | 31 |
| Suffolk University | 19,790 | 561 | 4,653 | 1014 | 2,610,333 | 20,067,060 | 13 |
| The College of New Rochelle | 16,500 | 255 | 6,709 | 1091 | 1,710,795 | 18,001,500 | 10 |
| The College of Saint Rose | 16,230 | 508 | 5,897 | 563 | 2,995,676 | 9,137,490 | 33 |
| The College of Saint Scholastica | 20,630 | 431 | 9,586 | 445 | 4,131,566 | 9,180,350 | 45 |
| The University of Findlay | 19,996 | 556 | 10,694 | 581 | 5,945,864 | 11,617,676 | 51 |
| Touro College | 10,200 | 1600 | 4,000 | 1807 | 6,400,000 | 18,431,400 | 35 |
| Trinity Washington University | 16,700 | 143 | 7,577 | 144 | 1,083,511 | 2,404,800 | 45 |
| Union University | 14,850 | 340 | 5,452 | 375 | 1,853,680 | 5,568,750 | 33 |
| University of Dallas | 18,582 | 234 | 8,547 | 243 | 1,999,998 | 4,515,426 | 44 |
| University of Detroit Mercy | 20,400 | 442 | 8,774 | 455 | 3,878,108 | 9,282,000 | 42 |
| University of Indianapolis | 17,200 | 641 | 7,142 | 680 | 4,578,022 | 11,696,000 | 39 |
| University of Mary | 9,990 | 413 | 3,906 | 413 | 1,613,178 | 4,125,870 | 39 |
| University of New England | 20,225 | 487 | 9,007 | 490 | 4,386,409 | 9,910,250 | 44 |
| University of New Haven | 21,120 | 454 | 9,737 | 571 | 4,420,598 | 12,059,520 | 37 |
| University of Redlands | 25,224 | 532 | 13,206 | 604 | 7,025,592 | 15,235,296 | 46 |
| University of St Francis | 17,310 | 155 | 8,926 | 157 | 1,383,530 | 2,717,670 | 51 |
| University of St Thomas | 16,200 | 215 | 6,814 | 298 | 1,465,010 | 4,827,600 | 30 |
| University of the Incarnate Word | 15,600 | 323 | 5,471 | 474 | 1,767,133 | 7,394,400 | 24 |
| Villanova University | 27,175 | 822 | 15,669 | 1654 | 12,879,918 | 44,947,450 | 29 |
| Viterbo University | 15,570 | 298 | 6,877 | 310 | 2,049,346 | 4,826,700 | 42 |
| Webster University | 16,250 | 415 | 7,341 | 452 | 3,046,515 | 7,345,000 | 41 |
| Western New England College | 20,570 | 687 | 7,812 | 799 | 5,366,844 | 16,435,430 | 33 |
| Wheaton College | 20,000 | 349 | 8,501 | 595 | 2,966,849 | 11,900,000 | 25 |
| Wheelock College | 22,000 | 102 | 8,139 | 151 | 830,178 | 3,322,000 | 25 |
| Wilkes University | 19,428 | 547 | 9,824 | 551 | 5,373,728 | 10,704,828 | 50 |
| William Carey University | 7,800 | 152 | 4,800 | 163 | 729,600 | 1,271,400 | 57 |
| William Woods University | 14,300 | 193 | 8,812 | 195 | 1,700,716 | 2,788,500 | 61 |
| Worcester Polytechnic Institute | 29,550 | 659 | 16,088 | 747 | 10,601,992 | 22,073,850 | 48 |
| Xavier University | 20,100 | 786 | 9,827 | 878 | 7,724,022 | 17,647,800 | 44 |

range of topics from enrollment to retention and graduation to fiscal matters. In the 2006 report, for example, the following charts were included:

- Unduplicated twelve-month headcount, total FTE enrollment (academic year 2004–05) and full- and part-time enrollment (Fall 2005).
- Percent of all students enrolled by race/ethnicity, and percent women (Fall 2005).
- Academic year tuition and required fees for full-time, first time degree/certificate-seeking undergraduates (2003–04 through 2005–06).
- Percent of full-time, first time degree/certificate-seeking undergraduates receiving financial aid by type of aid (2004–05).
- Types and average amounts of financial aid received by full-time, first time degree/certificate-seeking undergraduates receiving financial aid by type of aid (2004–05).
- Graduate rates of full-time, first time degree/certificate-seeking undergraduates within 150 percent of normal time to program completion, by race/ethnicity (1999 cohort).
- Graduate rate cohort as a percent of all undergraduates and as a percent of total entering students (Fall 2005); Graduation rate and transfer-out rate (1999 cohort); and retention rates (Fall 2005).
- Number of degrees awarded by level (academic year 2004–05).
- Percent distribution of core revenues by source (FY 2005).
- Core expenses by FTE student by function (FY 2005).
- Full-time equivalent staff by assigned position (Fall 2005).
- Average salaries of full-time instructional faculty equated to 9-month contracts by academic ranks (Academic year 2005–06).

As Figure 41.1 (on page 554) illustrates, the Data Feedback Report presents institutional and comparison group data in a comparatively easy to understand manner.

### Your Comparison Group

The Data Feedback Report has a comparison group of other colleges and universities that were selected based on your institutional characteristics. The group was selected based on type of institution, control, Carnegie Classification, and geographic region. It is possible to change your comparison group. There is a tutorial on the Web at http://nces.ed.gov/ipeds/comp_gp.asp that provides a step-by-step process for changing your institution's comparison group.

If you want to see how you compare to another group of institutions *without* formally changing your comparison group, use the NCES Executive Peer Tool, accessible at http://nces.ed.gov/ipedspas/ExPT/ or http://nces.ed.gov/ipeds/find_data/exec_peer_summary.asp.

## Conclusion

The majority of private institutions of higher education are concerned with (or should at least be aware of) their freshman tuition discount rate. The discount rate can influence the

FIGURE 41.1

Third Page from Sample IPEDS Data Feedback Report

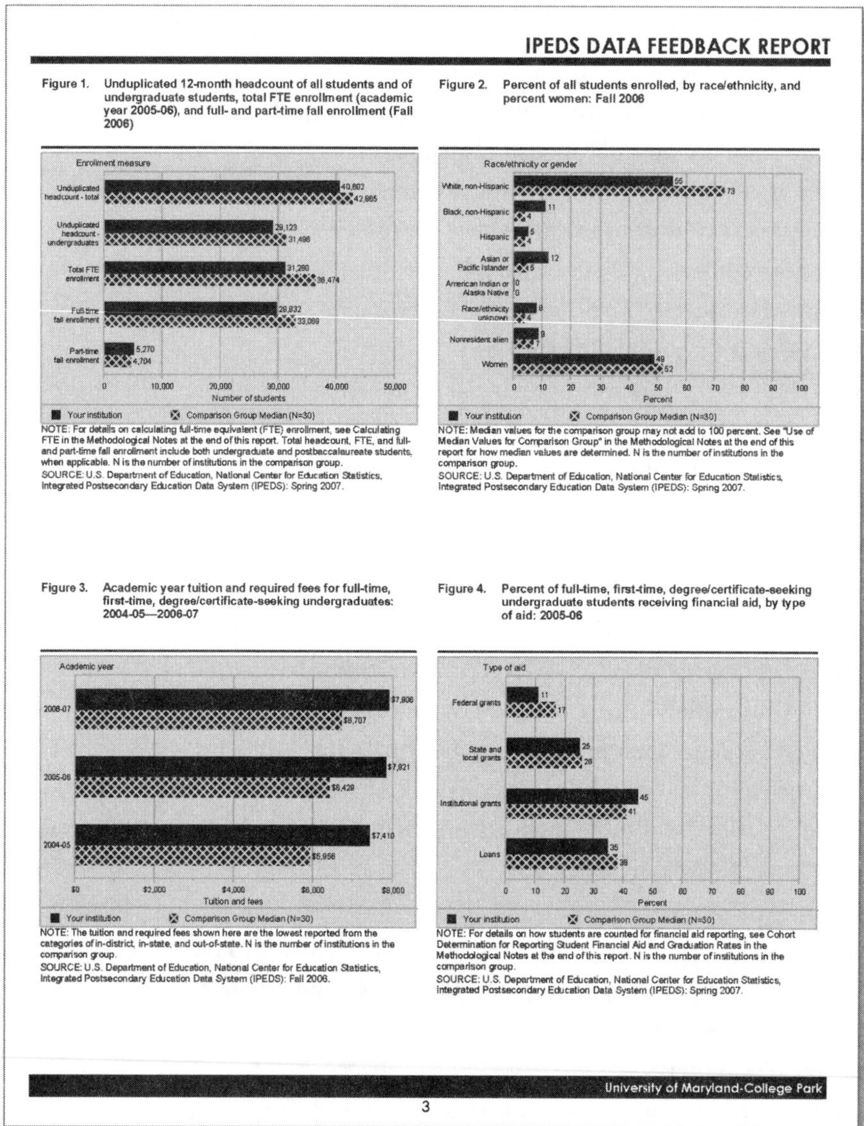


decision of accepted students as to which college to enroll in, and if tuition revenue is directed to fund discounts, it can impact an institution's bottom line.

As this chapter has shown, the data to produce estimates of freshman discount rates are already gathered by the National Center for Education Statistics. With a few comparatively straightforward steps, a researcher can generate the discount rate for her institution and for a group of peer institutions. This information is highly useful for enrollment management planning, strategic planning, and also for accreditation reviews.

/ CHAPTER FORTY-TWO /

*by Tony Campeau, B.A.*
*Montana Tech of the University of Montana*

*Lynn Gurganus, M.Ed.*
*University of Montevallo*

*Rob Hoover, M.B.A.*
*Emory University*

42

# So You Want to be a Director of Admissions?

Obviously not everyone who works in college admissions is cut out to be a Director of Admissions. As you have seen evidenced in your experience in the profession, a number of recent college graduates spend a year or two on the road before they seek that initial "real job." It's often joked that one should not waste time getting to know new roadrunners, because so few will be around next year. It seems that, somewhere around the five-year mark though, the real separation occurs.

Those who have a real affinity for admissions work begin to distance themselves professionally from those who are just "doing a job." One group seems not to see the applicability of experiences from their current situation, while the other group realizes that all of their experiences during those first few years are serving to prepare them for a job that will come open five or ten years from now. The simple (and crucial) truth is simply that the perfect job opportunity comes to those who are prepared.

## Scope of the Position

The role of the Director of Admissions and the scope of the job will vary by institution. In some situations the focus of the responsibility is almost entirely on recruitment. In others the primary focus is on application processing. Most positions will have responsibility for both areas. Orientation and other new student initiatives may also come under the oversight of the Director of Admissions. In many cases, the position will fall within the realm of Enrollment Management, and include either significant knowledge of or oversight of financial aid and other student enrollment resources.

Since it stands to reason that not every vacant position will be a good opportunity for you (and conversely, that you would not be a good hire for every institution), it becomes very important to get as accurate a picture as possible of the entire position. The right admissions management position is heavenly. The wrong position can be, well, not heavenly. Be mindful that, sometimes, the best career decisions end up being the job offers that were declined. Before seriously considering an opportunity, you should have your concerns answered about (among other things):

- **EXPECTATIONS:** What are the expectations of the position? Are there specific expectations of outcomes? Are there specific expectations as to processes? If you will not be answering directly to the President, does the person to whom you will answer share the same institutional vision as the President? For that matter, does the institution have a discernible institutional vision? What is the institutional evaluation process? Will you be given the opportunity for a periodic evaluation of how your performance is meeting expectations? In short, the institution will have very definite expectations of you. Since you will be responsible for meeting these expectations, you want to understand as many of them as possible going in.
- **ENVIRONMENT:** Does the physical environment of the place appeal to you? How important is it to you for the institution to fit a certain physical or institutional image? While experiences at varied types of institutions can be a very significant asset in preparation for a position, coming from and going to extremes in institutional size, emphases, physical location, and student body makeup can lead to an initial experience of culture shock (if not shell shock) for admissions professionals going to work for an institution which operates at the edge of (or beyond) their collective comfort zones.
- **THE HISTORY OF THE POSITION:** Why is the position vacant? What is the life expectancy of the position of Director of Admissions at this institution? Where have those who have left the position gone? Would you be following a dearly beloved icon who "always did it this way," or would you be following someone who was run out of town on a rail? There is a big difference in how the individuals walking into those two situations are viewed. Would you be maintaining and enhancing, or would you be rebuilding? Was there an in-house candidate who did not get the position and will now be on your staff?
- **PERSONNEL:** What is the current staffing situation? What changes will you need to make? How much authority do you have to make any such changes? Would you be walking into a situation where you have personal knowledge of staff abilities, or would the entire staff be new to you? What are their current responsibilities, and how would they be amenable to changes in responsibility? What is the current pay structure, and

how much influence would you have as to salary issues? Are there significant in-house tensions that would need to be dealt with early on? (One note: Although far more time and emphasis is usually placed on evaluating professional positions, you would do well to pay special attention to the support staff. Most of them know how to do everything in the office and many of them have skills that are more difficult to replace than those of your professional staff.)

- BUDGET: What is the actual budget for the office? How much is fixed and how much is discretionary? How much control would you have over budget decisions for the office? Based upon the level of budgetary experience you have, what assistance will you need in overseeing this area?

As a final thought for those interested in moving into Director's positions, keep in mind that your behavior in your first few years can have a great impact on job opportunities available to you in the future. Especially for those seeking a position at another institution in their own state or region, their cumulative past actions, behaviors, and perceived professionalism greatly impact whether or not they are granted an interview. A decision *not* to interview a particular candidate may be arrived at, based upon actions from years before, in light of situations that may have occurred in or outside of work. In short, from the day you begin in this profession, you are always interviewing for a Director's position. Whether or not you ever choose to apply for a position is inconsequential. Every day in admissions is preparation for a job as Director of Admissions.

## First Year on the Job

After a thoughtful selection process you find yourself as the new Director of Admissions. Now what? In this section we will break down your first year and a half into three sections, mirroring a typical semester system. The following outline for your first year is meant to present ideas and processes you can accomplish in addition to running the daily operations of the admissions office. They should even help you be more efficient as you work to meet the many demands of your new job.

These guidelines and perspectives are generalized in consideration of the differing roles of an admissions office. As mentioned earlier, some colleges separate recruitment from application processing, and the administrative role of the Director of Admissions can vary drastically depending on the size and profile of an institution. These guidelines are designed to be generally applicable. Please use the guidelines as exactly that, guidelines. Consult your personal professional network, talk with your new supervisor, and engage in professional development opportunities to tailor these guidelines to fit your unique situation.

## Semester 1: Be a Student

You are part of an institution of higher education. Assume the role of student and learn as much as you can. As a student of your new position and possibly a new institution, recall and implement those skills that have helped you in your previous formal education. Not the late-night cram sessions and term paper all-nighters, but the analytical problem-solving skills and organizational techniques needed to be a successful student.

Learn the history of the institution, in particular the history and role of your new office. Take notes! The personnel who work for you and those who have previously been in the office (if you have access to them) can be instrumental in helping you more thoroughly understand the *context* of your role and your office. In your first month, set aside at least one hour to interview each of these people. Keep the interview informal, but organized. We recommend that you prepare a set of questions or topics that you want to discuss with each team member. Again, take notes. Do this even if you have worked in the same office for years. You will be surprised at what you learn.

### SAMPLE QUESTIONS/TOPICS

- What do you see the role of the admissions office at Great University in Perfect Setting, USA?
- How would you define your role in this admissions office?
- What do you see as the major strengths/weaknesses of this office/University?
- If you could change three things about Great University, what would they be?
- What are your personal/professional goals, and how can I help you accomplish them?

Finally, these interviews are your opportunity to communicate your ideas and framework while seeking feedback. This can help clarify expectations for everyone and establish a communication channel for the future.

Next, tailor the above questions for interviews with your extended campus network. Identify the five to twenty people on campus whom you will be working with most closely, and schedule the time to interview each of them. They may be members of the enrollment management team, or perhaps the other directors in the student services area on campus. Discuss with your staff and supervisor whom you should interview. Who are the people most key to your (office's) success?

Read. Read the catalog—cover to cover. This may not be the most engaging part of your new job. But in your effort to be a subject matter expert, reading this document may be one of the best uses of your time. While you read, take notes. Mark up the catalog. Make sure that you read with a critical eye. You will likely find errors and omissions; make note of them. Discuss your questions with the editor of the catalog. Give the editor the first opportunity to discuss discrepancies with the people responsible for the content. And then, keep reading. Read the most recent versions of your alumni mailings, your admissions publications, Web site, vision document, strategic plan, reports to the governing board, and each of the letters in your communication plan. Again, as a good student, take notes.

Finally, in regard to your "first semester learning curriculum," take the time to understand the technical tools of your new position. If the office has a student information system (SIS) different from the one you are used to, this learning process can be demanding. If the SIS system is similar, the learning curve will be less steep, but even so you may need to relearn parts of the system, depending on how your new university applies the system.

**Organizational Tip**

Gather twelve folders and label them by month. Keep copies of important documents that come up in the current month. Even if you fully understand and trust a current filing system, take the time to duplicate some effort here. You may be able to do this electronically, but if your office is not completely paperless, take the time to make hard copies of important e-mails and store them in these files. Make sure you put any policy documents in this file. Also be sure to include notes on any admission office events like visitation days and any new notifications you send to students (deadline reminders, invitations to special events, etc.). This file system becomes your memory of your first year. Give yourself a break and have the discipline to maintain this file system for at least one year. Then you will not have to reinvent the wheel next time around.

### ENGAGE YOURSELF IN CAMPUS CULTURE

Attend as many community events as you can. You will be exceptionally busy in your new job, and you need to make sure you do not become isolated. Some non-mandatory campus events are mandatory for you. Athletic events, student performances, open lecturers/forums, student government meetings, and alumni gatherings are examples of some of the events you should try to attend. You do not have to attend all of them, and you do not even have to stay for the entire event. But you need to make an effort to engage yourself across campus cultures.

This is important for two reasons. First, it is a good political move. Being seen as engaged in campus culture increases your credibility. Perhaps more importantly, this is an extension of your education. You will learn about and know first-hand the details of your community. In order to accurately convey the "feel" of your campus to prospective students, it helps if you can speak from recent experience.

Warning! Do not overextend yourself. Be cautious of volunteering to help with each of the above-mentioned events or to serve on extraneous committees. Your first job is Director of Admissions, and you need to focus on that. Further, after a year of observation you will better know where you may want to insert yourself to enhance your campus culture.

### FINAL THOUGHT ON THE FIRST SEMESTER

At first, make only those changes that are necessary. You should be careful to avoid making changes in order to "put your mark" on the fundamental operations of the admission office until you have time to fully appreciate the current system. If you start making what are perceived to be unnecessary changes early on, you may find reluctance from your staff when you want to make more crucial changes down the road. Also, by limiting the number and scope of changes you make early in your tenure, you may avoid having to revise or upgrade those changes in a few months. Of course, if you recognize a fundamental flaw in your office, it is your responsibility to make the appropriate change.

## Semester 2: Staffing

Engage yourself in actively managing your staff. This does not mean you need to micromanage your staff. Rather, you need to appropriately participate in the operations of your office. Take the time to be a good manager. Often, Directors of Admission are so busy with their own projects that they forget one of the most important aspects of the job: helping their staff operate as efficiently as possible. Use your own management style, techniques, and system, but make the time to actively engage as a manager. Hopefully, you will have adopted and implemented a reporting evaluation structure (either yours or the institution's) in the first semester. Now you need to take this a step further. Do not rely on quarterly evaluations as your opportunity to manage. Take the interviews from the first semester and review them. Are there issues you can address? If so, now is the time to do it. Show your staff that you were listening to them and that you are there to support them.

### PLAN YOUR VISION

We warned against making unnecessary changes in your first semester. Now is the time to plan the changes you may want to make. Picture the office in two years. What do you want it to look like? How should it be operating? Start with a broad perspective and your own vision statement for your office. Then begin to fill in the blanks. What is it going to take to make the necessary changes? Be sure to include the effective parts of the current office operations. In the end you will create a document that you can share with your staff and the campus leadership. Be sure to talk to both of these constituencies about this document before you unveil it (next semester). By including these constituencies you will help build ownership and you will be able to recognize any potential conflicts.

Be careful not to try to do this all at once. Instead, set aside a little time (once a week perhaps) that you can make note of your thoughts for that week. Also keep track of the details. If you want to use a new software product that you see at a conference, make note of its cost. Take the time to reflect. If you try to do this all at once your vision could end up tainted by the most pressing topic of that particular week. By working on this a little each week, you keep your plan fresh and comprehensive. This should be a fun project for you. Keep it that way. Just because it is fun does not mean it is not important. Make a little time to work on this each week.

### RESEARCH

Yes that's right, more research. In the first semester you researched what was already out there. Now you need to take a good look at what you *know* and determine what you *do not know*. What are the institutional questions that are not answered?

Use a process similar to that of developing your vision. Set aside a little time each week to make note of what information is not readily available. Depending on your school, you may have resources to find this information relatively quickly. Regardless of the methodology for institutional research at your school, try to approach this process with the big picture in mind. Rather than asking for a new report each week, take your time to figure out what information you really need and how it ties together. Then discuss this with the appropriate people on campus. Maybe the information is already available; it is just spread out over several offices.

Engage the other constituencies (again similar to creating your vision) who are the purveyors of institutional knowledge. If you are lucky enough to have an office of institutional research on your campus, buy them some doughnuts. They will be key to your ability to make effective decisions. If you do not have such an office, find individuals who may be in need of the same type of information, and get them together with you and the people who can gather that information. Buy them all lunch and discuss how you can most easily get the data you need.

In the end, make sure you have good data (specific to the decisions you need to make) that is well organized.

### Semester 3: Transitioning

It is probably safe to assume that if you have successfully navigated the first year as a director, then you have been focused and busy. While you probably have not had a lot of time to evaluate results, you are hopefully beginning to see some of your work making an impact. Your vision will be well thought out, and people will recognize that you did your homework before you insisted on making the changes necessary to move your office and the institution forward. You move from a transitional stage to truly making this your office.

## The Second Year and Beyond

The second year, in comparison, is the time to look up and look ahead. This is the time to capitalize on all of the foundation-building that you have done to this point, and to formulate longer-term strategies. This shift of your focus will help you become a more successful leader as you expand your role.

A good way to frame this progression into the second year is to focus on developing four areas: *evaluation*, *implementation of long-term strategic plans*, *refinement of your leadership role*, and *advocacy for your office*. Admittedly, if you had a wildly successful first year, some of these may just be continuations of what you have already started. More than likely though, you have not had time to address these issues as deeply as one should.

Useful evaluation in the second year should piggy-back on the review that has already been done as part of the first year. As you try to measure your own success, a good question to ask is, "Are my strengths serving the job well?" The hope is that you have been able to notice some of your abilities moving the staff and office forward. If you sense that you have been able to build trust, develop a sense of direction, and accomplish several goals in the first year, your unique qualities and leadership style are probably adding value. If that is not the case, you need to refocus your efforts and make adjustments that will increase your value as a leader. Generally this means simplifying: do a few things and do them right.

You should also be able to see points where your judgment has been accurate and beneficial, furthering the goals of the office. It is entirely possible that some of your decisions were misguided—or even just plain wrong. Moving into the second year is a great time to acknowledge any missteps and to make necessary adjustments to minimize the chances of that happening as you move ahead.

As you evaluate yourself, the progress of the office should be evaluated as well. Hopefully, you were able to set some specific goals for staff development and expectations early in your tenure. If so, use those as benchmarks to review the growth of the entire unit. If no objectives were laid out, then an evaluation based on some new, clear criteria can still be useful. The key is to show areas within the office that have improved; demonstrate characteristics of the staff that have been strengthened; and marshal evidence that the entire program has generally moved forward. The bottom line is, if the office is better than when you got there, then you are doing some things right.

In addition to evaluating yourself and the office, the second year is an excellent time to evaluate the institution and how you and your office fit into its strategy. Unless you were fortunate enough to walk into a place that already had a great strategy and understanding of its own identity, you probably have based a lot of your work on information pieced together as necessary. By the second year, though, you should have a good idea of what the institution is all about. Now you can begin to define and segment markets, gain an understanding of what brings those key constituents to your school, and review the various messages that are being delivered across the many parts of the campus. The goal here is to find additional areas in which to build consensus and improve continuity. If you find that your office is moving in a direction that supports the university as a whole and with a clear purpose, you should feel good about the work that you have done and continue to build on that momentum.

These evaluations should help you to become extremely knowledgeable and familiar with your institution. That awareness of yourself and your surroundings, coupled with the trust that you have built across campus, will help you as you continue putting in place a plan that will distinguish you and your office. Your strategy should be distinct and uniquely formulated to fit the needs of your current institution. The tendency at times can be to implement familiar ideas and use the same tactics that previous institutions implemented. And sometimes the easy mistake is to use a competitor's strategy that does not quite fit your own school. But to maximize your value and to create a leading admissions office, your decisions should be based on a unique identity, defined and developed through your thoughtful examination of the institution.

As you continue to evaluate and move toward developing the long-term strategy, you will probably notice something different about your schedule. You will more than likely find yourself trying to balance the time required to do the daily work and the long-term strategic thinking. Most people who advance to these positions are able to do so because they have been hard workers and have had very result-oriented success. In other words, you probably have been promoted to this position because you work hard, can solve problems, can clearly communicate, and get things done.

Now that you are the director those daily things remain important, but you also have to be able to give some of that up now. You no longer can only be a productive worker. You now have to schedule "thought" time. It can be difficult to split time between the work and the development of ideas. For example, if you have been a problem-solver, it can be very difficult to not be the first to solve a problem. But proper training of staff and delegation can help. If you prepare your staff to assume more of those responsibilities and give them the autonomy to do it their way, then you will be able to commit more time to development, planning, and strategic thinking. If you are not able to make that transition, then you risk not being able to provide the leadership and direction that you should. If you spend too much of your time in the role of solving the immediate problems, you will fail in fulfilling your role as leader and strategic planner.

As you continue to transition into the position of leadership, you will also find that an important part of your role is to advocate for your office. You should be as good at marketing your own office and the work that you do as you are at marketing your institution. This advocacy could start by being as simple as keeping others informed about your office's challenges and successes. It also can include bringing proposals to upper administration that will improve your office—do not be afraid to suggest improvements. The most obvious reason to do this is that it develops a level of trust within the office that will create loyalty within the office staff. It also can gain the respect of administrators for you and your office. They will hopefully see that your goals are in line with the institution's goals and that your efforts are improving the institution from "the middle." Their support and trust will make your job easier down the road.

As you push to move the objectives of your office, you need to collaborate with others across campus so as to gain more opportunities to share your vision for the entire institution. You need to introduce your vision to your boss and the admissions office staff. Then you should make the time to meet with the other change agents on campus. This can be done formally (in campus forums, committee meetings, etc.) or informally (in the hall, over coffee). Every chance you get, pitch your vision and the steps required to get there to anyone who will listen. Talk to the faculty, staff in other offices, cooks, and security personnel. All of them are part of the picture.

*Your goal is to align as many resources across campus as you need to implement the changes you need to make.* The faculty will better understand how their visits with prospective students affect enrollment. The cooks will understand why you may make special requests on visitation days. The security contingent will be sympathetic to parking issues during major events. Find those who buy into your vision and give them a role. Let them get excited and involved. Focus on the big picture and let others manage the details (as much as possible).

Understanding where and who you are by evaluating what you do is necessary to develop meaningful long-term strategy. A thoughtful long-term game-plan, with purposes and methods that are suited to your institution, can help your office work with relative ease toward common goals. Accomplishing those goals as part of your strategy will give you the opportunity to build more bridges across campus, and will help add resources for more success down the road. All of these efforts should create an environment in which success is the norm, and your value to the institution is without question.

/ CHAPTER FORTY-THREE /

*by Lisa Kujawa, M.A.*
*Assistant Provost*
*Lawrence Technological University*

*Jane Rohrback, M.A.*
*Director of Admissions*
*Lawrence Technological University*

43

# Creating a Career Ladder:
## Motivating and Developing Staff

Lawrence Technological University (LTU) is an independent, coeducational accredited university founded in 1932 and offering over sixty academic programs at the associate, baccalaureate, master's, and doctoral degree level. The University is composed of the Colleges of Architecture and Design, Arts and Sciences, Engineering, and Management. Approximately five thousand students are enrolled in full-time, part-time, and non-credit programs.

We should begin with a little history of the admissions office. Before we can describe our current office dynamic, we need to describe how it used to be. Each admissions counselor position was focused to service a specific type of student or service (*e.g.*, freshman, transfer, graduate or international, campus programming), which resulted in silos within the admissions office and the campus community. Counselors were knowledgeable and accountable only for what was related to their specific responsibility—for example, there was one admissions counselor responsible for on-campus programming. This counselor met with deans, associate deans, and student service offices to coordinate all activities for successful programs. Since this counselor was the only counselor who directly interacted with the campus community, the general belief was that this was the best counselor on staff, and that other counselors were "wasting university resources" traveling to promote academic programs for which they appeared to lack knowledge or enthusiasm.

As another example of the silos within the admissions office, one counselor was assigned to graduate admissions, and another counselor was assigned to international students. If a student needing counseling for an international or graduate admissions issue entered the admissions office at a time when those admissions counselors were not present, he or she would be informed that the counselor who handled those students was not available. This not only frustrated the prospective student; it also frustrated the counselor, who was concerned for his or her population. A change was needed to bring a culture of student service and cross-training to the existing counselors.

The office was restructured with the idea that all admissions counselors need to build campus-wide relationships. In order to address this problem and prepare the admissions office for the future, new positions were created and job descriptions were revamped. The first major change was the creation of an Assistant Director position as a liaison between counselors and the director. A second Assistant Director of Admissions position was created four years later to help manage data entry and support staff. In addition, the job descriptions of the Admissions Counselors were redesigned to provide those positions with more breath and depth in all of the admissions functions.

The Admissions office now consists of forty individuals:

- Twenty student assistants
- Ten admissions counselors (levels one and two plus senior ACs)
- Three application specialists
- One transfer articulation specialist
- One part-time data entry specialist
- One part-time evening receptionist
- One receptionist
- Two assistant directors
- One director

The admissions office is responsible for recruitment and admissions for undergraduate students, graduate students, international students, English as a Second Language (ESL) programs, and evaluation of transfer credit for our transfer students. It also coordinates the orientation and registration programs, including conducting placement assessments for new students. The redesigned admissions counselor positions have an active role in every facet of the admissions process. Their responsibilities are listed below:

#### MICHIGAN HIGH SCHOOL TERRITORY

- Visit high schools
- Attend college nights

- Process all applications

**OUT-OF-STATE TERRITORY**

- Attend National Association of College Admissions Counselors (NACAC) fairs
- Develop strategies to manage territory
- Process applications
- Visit high schools

**UNDERGRADUATE TRANSFER APPLICATIONS**

- Accept applications in assigned major and create transfer credit evaluation
- Meet with department chair to review transfer evaluations
- Build relationships with department and report back any new program information to the office

**GRADUATE PROGRAM**

- Communicate with assigned graduate program director about applications
- Build relationships with department and report back any new program information to the office
- Answer any inquiries, via e-mail or phone, related to assigned graduate program

**ON-CAMPUS PROGRAMMING**

- Plan and organize recruitment programs
- Communicate with academic departments for campus involvement
- Execute program and create report of results

**APPOINTMENT BLOCKS**

- Set aside one evening per week to cover office appointments and phone calls
- Be confident in providing information about LTU in the following:
  - Undergraduate programs
  - Transfer of undergraduate credit
  - Graduate programs
  - ESL programs
  - International students

## The Admissions Career Ladder

The admissions ladder at Lawrence Tech is unique in comparison with many other universities. The levels at LTU are somewhat more informal than elsewhere, but their titles can be equated to standard titles in any admissions office, as we do just below. Accordingly, we describe in detail the five levels of admissions professionals, with comparisons to common levels established at other universities. (*See* Table 43.1.)

In the rest of the chapter, for ease of reference, we will refer to the positions by the commonly used titles in the column above left, rather than by the LTU titles.

### Admissions Counselor I (Entry Level/New Hire)

For Lawrence Tech this is typically a new hire to the admissions field.

At this level, the counselor is usually an individual who either recently graduated with an undergraduate degree or is someone looking for a career change to admissions. Some responsibilities and characteristics of such a person are:

- Requires supervision
- Useful for basic but necessary tasks
- Low level skills; rote activities
- No essential knowledge needed
- Recruitment territory trips
- Self-taught college materials
- Lack of understanding of the "big picture"
- No real commitment or (as yet) desire for development of a career
- Lack of broad understanding of the profession
- Beginners who stay beginners

TABLE 43.1: **Admissions Ladder**

| Common Title | LTU Title |
|---|---|
| Admissions Counselor 1 | Entry Level/New Hire |
| Admissions Counselor 2 | Admissions Counselor |
| Assistant Director | Senior Admissions Counselor |
| Associate Director | Assistant Director |
| Director | Director |

Our office has three Admissions Counselors in this level. Typically new hires stay at this stage for approximately one year, a complete recruitment cycle. One of the main indicators of this level is the amount of supervision needed to complete all assignments. Another indicator can be an inability to make decisions independently, without a sign-off from an Assistant Director or Director. The new counselors may also have difficulty managing multiple responsibilities. However, these are all skills that we can help new counselors develop. This is where the understanding of the "big picture" can be assessed. Does the counselor meet the expectation set by the director for all duties, or does he or she focus only on the areas he is confident in? An example of the latter situation is a counselor who only focuses on the local territory and does not strategically research his or her out-of-state market to identify new markets for the university. Although not all counselors make the transition to the next level at the same speed, it is more of a priority at this stage to identify which counselors are not moving forward (or who are content to remain at this stage). In the past we have, in fact, had instances when the occasional counselor has chosen to remain at this stage for many years.

That was the era when an admissions counselor simply visited schools, attended college nights, maintained office hours, and evaluated files. However, with the admissions field evolving and requiring counselors to do much more than recruiting, it is essential that they progress and move beyond this basic level.

### Admissions Counselor II (Admissions Counselor)

This employee has an understanding of the admissions field. The counselor at this stage can be expected to have the following attributes:

- Loyalty
- Understanding of the "big picture"
- Dedication
- Knowledge
- Developing leadership role
- Requires only limited supervision

Our office has three counselors at this level. At this stage, admissions counselors are confident in their responsibilities. They are contributing to the office in their assigned tasks. Less supervision is required, but supervision is still needed to verify that duties are being completed. In this stage, the counselor is learning more about the admissions field and is now identifying it as a possibility for a career. This counselor is interested in taking on additional one-time special assignments (*e.g.*, planning an impromptu recruitment event if inquiries are lagging or creating a flyer for a new recruitment event).

### Assistant Director (Senior Admissions Counselor)

- Develops strategies for territory management
- "Out of the box" thinker
- Works autonomously
- Leader within the admissions office

Our office has four counselors at this level. At this stage admission counselors are active contributors to the office. They understand the admissions strategic plan, and are making suggestions to improve our processes. They also will identify processes in the office that need improvement and can provide solutions to make them run more smoothly. Another key attribute at this stage is the ability to work autonomously. These counselors are seen as leaders within the office and the campus community. They are excellent multi-taskers and have the ability to take on additional responsibilities while successfully completing their regular requirements (*e.g.*, updating content on our admissions Web site).

### Associate Director (Assistant Director)

- Supervision experience
- Management of projects/plans
- Office management

At this stage the Assistant Director has supervision responsibilities. Training is a major responsibility of anyone functioning at this stage. The Assistant Director works with the counselors at all levels and spends quality time with the level one counselors to ensure they are meeting the expectations of the Director. In addition such a director must follow the progress and challenge the counselors at all other levels, to stimulate their growth in the admissions field. At this level, the Assistant Director must have the ability to address issues as they arise, so as to mentor admissions counselors and improve processes within the admissions office. It is essential that he or she has the ability to lead multiple projects and make certain they are successful. The Assistant Director spends a great deal of time with the Director to make sure all projects are aligned with the university and department strategic plan.

### Director

Typically more than five years of admissions experience is needed for this stage. The Director must be able to manage the entire admissions office. This encompasses the staff, budget, and overseeing the quality and quantity of the students recruited. The Director must work with campus academic leadership as well, so as to coordinate an effective recruitment plan. He or she must also initiate agreements with community colleges and work with the campus community to develop articulation agreements. Generally he or she must manage all agreements with third party partners to assist in improving the yield of our enrolled students via such arrangements.

The Director serves as the main liaison for the admissions office to the campus community, by informing the campus community of the activities and successes of the admissions office and of the recent trends in admissions. The Director must actively work on guiding the admissions office to meet the strategic goals of the university. A successful Director is one who has the ability to focus the recruitment strategy a year prior—to ensure that the groundwork has been laid for the level of future enrollment expected by the institution.

## Building the Ladder

Building the ladder for the admissions counselor rungs begins at the search for a new counselor. After a posting for a new counselor position, we can receive up to one hundred applications from a wide range of candidates—from new graduates to applicants with over ten years of experience, or retired professors, or high school teachers.[269]

[269] Although it is the Director of Admissions who receives the applications, the Director reports to the Assistant Provost, and we have collaborated in writing this chapter. Hence, "we."

A typical college student does not aspire to be an admissions counselor. He or she might have worked in the admissions office while attending college, but would not have considered it for a profession until they saw a posting for the job in the newspaper or online. There are many qualified individuals who are capable of performing the list of duties that we have presented earlier. All candidates usually state that they had a wonderful college experience and want to share that with others exploring college. They will also mention how they were so confused with the admissions process when they were searching for the best school to attend that they can use their experiences to help parents and potential students. Candidates are savvy and well trained to tell us what we want to hear. So it is not about identifying the candidate who can do the job. The key to building the ladder for your organization is to find the right fit in a candidate. You must identify who will make the maximum contribution to your team. One individual can compromise an effective team.

It has taken some to time to build our current, very effective team. We have developed quite an intensive three-step interviewing process to make sure we continue to assemble the effective team. The interviews are structured as follows:

- FIRST—A phone interview conducted by the Director
- SECOND—An interview with the Associate Director and Director of Admissions
- THIRD—The candidate gives a five-minute presentation to the entire admissions office about any topic, and answers questions the office has designed for the new hires.

The first interview answers "why" the candidate is interested in the position. As Director of Admissions, I believe it is important to speak to the candidate in an informal setting to verify if his or her prior employment and experiences align with our goals. During this stage I explain the position and inform them of the responsibilities of the position. This first interview typically lasts approximately fifteen minutes. I do inform the candidates of the salary range, to identify and discourage those who have an unrealistic expectation of our noble profession.

The second interview helps us to answer what we want to know about the "ability" and "fit" of the candidate. Our Director of Career Services has developed questions that pinpoint the qualities I look for in an admissions counselor. For an Admissions Counselor I want to hire someone who is dedicated, hard working, a multi-tasker, trustworthy, and dependable. The questions devised by our Director of Career Services are shown in Table 43.2 (on page 572).

These questions were very successful in segmenting our candidates; many were not able to pass to the third interview. Although using these questions often required posting the position again and interviewing more candidates, we were able to confidently choose, for a third interview, candidates who would complement our admissions team.

The third interview involves the entire admissions staff in interviewing at least three candidates and observing the candidates' five- minute presentation. All candidates are qualified for the position, and the Director and Associate Director would feel comfortable hiring any of them. This interview is really for the staff to have input as to who will be a part of their team. The staff will prepare questions for the candidates about such issues as how the person works in a team, and qualities of dependability and loyalty. After the third interview, the staff discusses how well the candidate would fit into our team and work environment. After all interviews have taken place, we meet one more time as a team to discuss and decide who is the best fit for our office. Although the process is long, it has proven to be extremely successful.

TABLE 43.2: **Interview Questions**

| |
|---|
| **How does this job align with your career goals?** |
| **Describe a method you use to plan your daily activities.**<br>—How did you develop this method over the years?<br>—How has this method changed over the years? |
| **Describe a situation when you helped a team member with a task.**<br>—Why did you feel it was important to help this individual?<br>—What was the outcome of your efforts? |
| **Tell me about a time when you had to meet a deadline which did not seem to allow enough time.**<br>—How did you proceed?<br>—What was the outcome? |
| **Describe a situation where you had to pick up slack for a team member who was ill, unavailable, or not performing.** |
| **Describe how you deal with unexpected events on the job.**<br>—Let's say a supervisor gives you a new project and you have a previous deadline to meet. How did you handle it? |
| **Describe a time when you had to take work home or put in long hours to complete an assignment on schedule.**<br>—What could you have done differently to better manage your time?<br>—How did the assignment turn out? |
| **Describe a situation where your decisions were challenged by your supervisor.**<br>—How did you react?<br>—What was the outcome? |
| **Describe a time when you got others to assist you in completing a task.**<br>—How did you get them to help out?<br>—What was the outcome? |
| **What impresses you the most about LTU?** |
| **Describe the most significant job-related pressure situation you have experienced in the last five years.**<br>—How did you cope with it?<br>—What effect did it have on your performance? |
| **Tell me about a time when you failed to meet a deadline.**<br>—Why did you fail to meet the deadline?<br>—What were the repercussions?<br>—What did you learn? |
| **Describe a time when you had a personal conflict with a co-worker.**<br>—How did you resolve the conflict?<br>—What was the outcome? |
| **Give me an example of a time when an idea of yours paid off in a big way.**<br>—What was the idea?<br>—What effect did it have? |
| **What interests you the most about LTU?** |

## Expectations

It is very important to set the stage for expectations on the first day. This gives the new hire some basic facts that will make their employment a success. Items discussed seem basic but are essential for the employee to hear. I preface this exchange with the statement that I will discuss items I hope not to have to address in the future. (Since they are a new employee, no poor work habits have been formed.) Items covered are the dress code, conduct on campus within the office or campus community, conduct required when traveling for recruitment or attending a conference, use of Internet and phone for personal use, the director's pet peeves, and the probationary period. These items are presented so that the new employee understands from the beginning why not abiding by these ground rules breaks down the team which we have worked so hard to create. This is said not to threaten, but to let employees know my expectations. There have been times when I had to bring an employee back to my office after a few months to discuss performance on an issue discussed above, but such occasions have been few.

## Training

The training program designed for new counselors is integral to their development and serves as an introduction for them to the office and the campus community; in addition it is also very important for the growth and professional development of our existing counselors.

A handbook was created to train new admissions counselors. It is updated prior to the new staff member's first day of work for both the new counselor and the current counselors; all are expected to use it as a reference guide. During the interview phase, the Associate Director asks for input from all counselors about ways to improve the manual. This is beneficial because it allows the counselors to review the current processes to verify that they are up-to-date, and it also serves as a reminder to all of the correct procedures.

The Associate Director trains and supervises all new staff members and carefully reviews the manual to make sure that information is provided in a consistent manner. The counselor will use this document repeatedly in the first weeks on the job. The following is a list of information outlined in the Admissions Counselor Training Handbook with a limited sample of topics:

- Policies relating to students who are "First time in any college"—How to recompute GPA, admissions decisions, scholarship information
- Transfer student policies—How to compute GPA, make admissions decisions, and award transfer credit
- Graduate student policies—Procedures to complete application, contact information
- International student policies—How to make an admissions decision, F1 information, J1 information, I-20, general information
- Canadian student policies—Grading system
- General information—Financial aid, tours, Friday tour program, education centers, housing, advising
- Placement assessments procedures
- Dual degrees
- Admissions office policies—Calling in, time off, time sheets, laptops, dress code, overtime, office hours/flextime, expectations as to appointment coverage, application processing, phone procedures, lunch time, mailing procedures, inquiry requests, giveaways, professional organizations, education benefits
- Recruitment—Expectations as to office appointments, high school visits, college nights
- On campus programs—How to plan them
- Travel—Airline tickets, car rental, check requests, comp time, mileage reimbursement, schedules, travel advance, travel emergencies, travel reimbursements, out of state recruitment
- Banner—How to use our student management system

## Team Mentoring

As prospective students come to campus to find out more information, current counselors have the new counselor join them during office appointments. It is very important that the new counselor observe each different counselor as they meet with prospective students and parents. Also, it is important that they get an opportunity to experience an office visit with each of the major categories of students: traditional undergraduate, non-traditional undergraduate, international, and graduate.

I feel it is one of the most valuable experiences for the new counselor to see all of our "admissions counselor styles" of servicing students. We have a great set of counselors who each have a different but effective style in counseling our prospective students. It is important for the new counselors to experience those differences and to make use of elements of each in creating their own styles of serving students.

For the existing counselors, their participation in this kind of demonstration furthers their own professional development through their willingness to support a new team member and teach him or her about the profession. Typically, the senior level counselors tend to mentor the new counselors at a higher level than those at the "admissions counselor one" level, regardless of their tenure in the field.

During this time, the new counselor will be trained in making a decision on applications, creating an evaluation for the transfer student, and acquiring detailed knowledge of the Lawrence Tech academic programs. Student assistants are also given a role in the development of the new admissions counselor. The new counselor is required to go on several detailed tours conducted by different students to get a feel for what prospective students experience on a campus visit.

Before an admissions counselor will be allowed to work independently, the Associate Director will verify that he or she is knowledgeable in all of the different aspects of the job. In addition, before new counselors can take appointments, they must first give an admissions presentation to the Director and Associate Director to make certain that they are ready to be on their own. Even after this early immersion is nearly complete, the Associate Director (AD) may allow the counselor to see students in the office, make phone calls, or process freshman files—but may still require the new counselor to show all transfer credit evaluations to the AD for approval, since transfer credit evaluation is a complex process, with many ramifications if not completed accurately.

## Faculty Mentoring

Lawrence Technological University is a very agile university; programs are often updated based on suggestions from a faculty/business/industry advisory board. Lawrence Tech is well known for engineering programs and its new labs and equipment, and courses are added to accommodate growing trends in technology. To keep the admissions counselors current in their information, faculty are invited to attend staff meetings periodically and to share program updates appropriate for prospective students. The admissions counselors visit facilities, labs, or projects valuable for that particular program as part of the update. Listening to individuals who are knowledgeable and passionate about a program provides the counselors the energy and excitement to evoke enthusiasm in prospective students.

## Common Service Philosophy

The admissions office is located in the new Alfred A. Taubman Student Service Center. The building is home to all the student service offices on campus which were once housed in many different buildings throughout campus. The admissions office shares the floor with the University's One Stop Center which consists of the registrar, financial aid, and student accounting offices.

Our admissions counselors are also required to have a functional knowledge of each of those offices. The directors of those offices acknowledge the reality that bricks and mortar alone will not change how students are serviced. So together we created a common student service philosophy as a new way of approaching our customers—a cohort which includes prospective students, parents, current students, faculty, staff, and alumni. This philosophy aims to improve the customer service provided to all. The values that determined the design of the building also form the core of our service philosophy—

*In order to insure the success of our students, we will*
+ *Provide consistent high-level service*
+ *Focus on customer satisfaction*
+ *Create an environment of teamwork and improvement*
+ *Commit to a never-ending search for a better way*

To provide a better service to our incoming students, the admissions office was cross-trained with the registrar's office to advise new students, process overrides, and add students into closed courses. The registrar's office also works with the academic departments to provide cross-training to ensure we can service our new students at a consistently high level.

This higher level of service eliminates the statements "I do not handle that" or "our office does not answer those questions, please go stand in that line." If it concerns an admissions issue, it is an expectation that a student will receive a high level of service. If it is an issue concerning one of the offices of the One Stop Center, we have common consultation rooms so that a member of one of those offices can quickly join the appointment for better service and the counselor's own professional development.

## Merit Increases

Performance reviews are conducted on a yearly basis. It is important to be realistic, honest, and goal-oriented when writing a performance review. The more information provided to employees in a constructive manner, the better they will understand the expectations for their professional development. The first step in our performance review is a self-assessment completed by the admissions staff member. This provides a period of self-reflection on the year's performance, and it also is an opportunity for the Director and Associate Director to review self-reported accomplishments. The rating scale for our performance reviews is shown in Table 43.3, on page 576.

Prior to the completion of the self-assessments or performance reviews, I discuss my expectations and let all staff members know that a "three" is required in each category for a merit increase. I am not one to provide an outstanding score for each category, even for the top performers. I want the outstanding scores to have meaning and value to those who do receive them, and I think providing them without merit diminishes the distinction. It is difficult when counselors give themselves high scores in their self-assessment, and the self-assessment does not accord with the evaluations of the Associate Director and Director. In this situation it is important for the counselor to provide specific examples throughout his or her review to substantiate the scores submitted. To assist me in remembering situations, the Assistant Director keeps files to remember successes and failures.

TABLE 43.3: **Performance Rating Scale**

| Points | Rating | Rating Description |
|---|---|---|
| 5 | Outstanding performance requirements | Achieves performance levels that are judged to substantially exceed normal expectations; overall performance is clearly exceptional; consistently performs above and beyond normal expectations. |
| 4 | Exceeds performance requirements | Achieves objectives and consistently exceeds normal expectations. |
| 3 | Meets performance requirements | Performs in a competent and fully satisfactory manner; meets objectives that are in line with good solid performance and major job responsibilities. |
| 2 | Meets some performance requirements | Performs some job responsibilities in a satisfactory way but not all; may be new in the position; requires improvement to meet university standards. |
| 1 | Fails to meet performance requirements | Does not achieve major job responsibilities and objectives; this performance level is not acceptable for continued employment. |

Each of the categories listed in Table 43.4 (on page 577) are the opportunities the Director and Associate Director have to discuss both positive work performance and areas that need improvement. A score of one to five must be awarded for each category.

These performance reviews are time-consuming to write, but if written constructively they can provide counselors with valuable information on their job performance. This is the time we can discuss their level of performance, and where the last year's performance places them in the admissions ladder, whether they are performing as an Admissions Counselor I or II or as a Senior Admissions Counselor.

Also discussed are goals for the next year in recruitment, territory management, and professional development opportunities. After the review is written and the merit increase is provided, it is important to reference the specific goals contained in the reviews. All goals set are specific to each counselor, and in addition, are tailored to specific obligations regarding territory and other aspects of strategic initiatives. We provide this information to encourage the counselors to go back to that review and refer to it throughout the year, to reinforce what has been written concerning their performance and future goals.

## Merit Alternatives

Although merit increases are not very large at Lawrence Tech, it is important to recognize stellar individual and group performance. Appreciation rewards do not necessarily need to cost money to be valued by the recipients. The following are some ways to reward with only minimal cost:

- After a weekday on-campus program send everyone home early! The Director or Associate Director then stay behind and answer the phone and take care of appointments for the rest of the day.
- If there is a holiday coming up, have the office choose the day before or after to get an extra day off—yes, with pay! Example: If Independence Day is on a Wednesday, allow counselors to take one day off during that week to increase their holiday time off. As long as the time frame is restricted to one week and admissions responsibilities are being covered, this arrangement should not pose any problem.
- To reward going above and beyond the normal call of duty, a day off with pay can be provided to an Admissions Counselor.

TABLE 43.4: **Areas of Performance**

| Category | Requirement |
|---|---|
| Customer Focus | Displays courtesy and sensitivity in dealing with both internal and external customers; initiates timely response to customer needs; solicits customer feedback. |
| Job Knowledge | Competent and knowledgeable in required job skills; able to learn and apply new skills; effective computer skills; awareness of current developments; understands relationships to other departments/functions. |
| Problem Solving/ Decision Making | Demonstrates originality and sensitivity in handling problems; has a direct objective approach to tackling problems; makes timely, well-considered decisions. |
| Productivity/Quality | Establishes and manages priorities; organizes work to improve output; completes work in a timely manner; demonstrates accuracy, thoroughness and commitment to excellence; seeks ways to improve and promote quality; uses feedback to improve performance. |
| Adaptability/Initiative | Adapts to changes in the work environment; accepts constructive criticism and feedback; willingness to change approach or method to best fit the situation; acts quickly to take advantage of opportunities; aggressively advocates a new service, procedure, or approach that benefits the department and the university; volunteers to lead difficult and challenging work efforts. |
| Dependability/ Accountability | Responds to requests for service and assistance; able to follow instructions and guidelines; responds to management direction; accepts accountability; schedules out-of-office time appropriately; begins workday on time; absences follow guidelines; meetings and appointments attended; accepts responsibility for all actions and decisions; handles situations in a responsible, professional manner; admits mistakes readily and corrects them quickly. |
| Teamwork | Balances team and individual responsibilities; functions as an effective team member; shows objectivity and openness to others' views; supports team success above own interests. |
| Interpersonal Skills/ Communication | Establishes and maintains effective relations; is tactful and considerate of others; offers assistance and support to co-workers; participates in problem solving and conflict resolution; is viewed as an asset to the department by co-workers; communicates ideas verbally and in writing; demonstrates good listening skills; selects and uses appropriate communication methods; disseminates appropriate information |

We use other appreciation methods that require some dollars, but which do not put a big dent in the budget.

- It is a well known fact that admissions departments love food, and it is one of the best ways to show appreciation. I use food as a reward frequently, such as:
  - Lunch for a staff meeting
  - Ice cream treats on a hot day...or any day
  - Host a Cinco de Mayo celebration with authentic food and virgin Margaritas
  - Provide subs for lunch; counselors are responsible for their own drinks
- Gift cards—The Director has gift cards in the amounts of fifteen, twenty and twenty-five dollars used for great performances, or in-office work competitions.

Acknowledgement of hard work or consistent work is always welcome and appreciated; sometimes it is the little things that are most appreciated.

There is another type of appreciation that can often be the most meaningful, but is not as easily defined. It is more of an intrinsic appreciation and greater sense of respect and trust that allows the counselor to have more of a direct effect on the goals of the admissions office, along with the Director and Associate Director. This type of appreciation was more stumbled upon than planned, but it arose because we have some great counselors on staff interested in taking on additional duties, while still effectively managing their assigned duties. The Associate Director and I first assigned a task to an admissions counselor during my second year as Director. Initially it was a temporary assignment; we assigned a counselor to assist with our Web site content management. The Associate Director and I were very impressed with the counselor's ability to work on the temporary project and yet continue to excel in her assigned responsibilities, and we made the project permanent. Since then the Associate Director has been assigning tasks to those counselors who have been very successful in managing multiple projects. We call this technique of rewarding good performers with work which broadens their perspectives and responsibilities the "intrinsic appreciation method."

## Raises

I have made a conscious decision when hiring new admissions counselors to bring them in at the Admissions Counselor I level. My goal is to hire new counselors who have some experience, while starting them at the entry level salary range. I do not feel comfortable hiring a new admissions counselor, without any previously demonstrated loyalty to our team, at a higher salary than those currently on staff. I have been successful in cost savings from this salary policy, while directing raises to high-performing counselors. The Lawrence Tech administration has agreed that our successes are driven by the team in our office, and have supported the Director and Associate Director in rewarding our existing counselors.

## Performance Improvement Plans

If counselors fail to meet and address expectations outlined in the performance review or policies outlined in the Admissions Counselor Manual, the Director and Associate Director meet to discuss the problem. Together we discuss the flaws in performance that have occurred, and monitor them to see if a minor problem gets worse. It is important to address performance deficits as they occur, because they may continue and then result in a larger performance problem in the future.

If performance does not improve after discussions with the staffer in question, we draw up a performance improvement plan, both to document formally the behavior in question and to provide a timeline and consequences. Below are the categories of the plan used by our admissions office.

- Level of Correction:
  - Verbal Warning
  - Written Warning/Probation

- ▶ Final Warning/Probation
- ▶ Investigatory Leave
- ▶ Final Written Warning/Termination

- Subject; Nature of Issue(s):
  - ▶ Policy/Procedure Violation
  - ▶ Performance Transgression
  - ▶ Behavior/Conduct Infraction
  - ▶ Absenteeism/Tardiness

The behavior is documented with dates to clearly describe the unwanted behavior, and contains a re-statement of expectations required in this situation. The counselor is able to write comments and the Plan is signed by all. These last steps are important, for this type of documentation shows the counselor the seriousness of the behaviors in question, the nature of the consequences to be expected if there is no improvement, and the final consequence of termination.

If you initiate a performance improvement plan, it is important that you followed up on it and not ignore it. The counselor must understand that this situation is serious and will be persistently addressed, with appropriate documentation. It is also important to contact your human resources office to review your performance improvement plan before you put it before the employee.

## Conclusion

We believe that everyone comes to work every day wanting to do the right things to be successful. It is the Director's job to provide an environment that teaches the entire staff within the Office of Admissions that there is more to the profession of admissions then just high school visits and college fairs.

Based on our experience, we believe that the most successful admissions offices create this sense of achievement—of professional growth—by developing a ladder of success when one is not otherwise apparent. This creation of a career ladder allows the more experienced members of the office to communicate a sense of progression from level to level. That sense of progression allows all within the office to try and achieve a more advanced level—and, just as important, to understand their role so it can be embraced in even the worst times.

Nurturing successful admissions professionals equates to healthy enrollments, because members of a staff where there is an emphasis on attaining higher levels of responsibility and recognition better understand their role within the enrollment process, and the benefits that they bring to their colleges or universities. Directors of Admissions need to set the tone for collaboration and communication—with the deans, the faculty, and with their own staff. The best way to accomplish that is to set a tone of service for others and to develop adaptable and enterprising admissions staff trained in every aspect of the admissions process.

Creating successful admissions ladders correlates with enhanced morale and enhanced results in a critical department. Far too often, when there is not any documented progression from a first year recruiter to an assistant director or a seasoned admissions professional, employees do not understand their role or see the context in which they are exercising their skills. They only see their functions as evaluating files, visiting high schools, and bringing inquiry cards back to the office. They perform tasks instead of developing strategy; they take direction instead of initiating ideas and solutions; and they look at their work as just a job and not a career or profession. If there is not a documented ladder, create one. Create a strategic plan and tie it to your overall university plan. Create goals and hold people accountable. Explain and communicate how everyone's contribution makes a difference.

Healthy enrollments do not just happen. That good outcome is the result of a systematic approach to leading and developing an admissions staff—an approach that is interconnected to the broader campus community. Creating this kind of interactive structure with clear progressions will ensure success at all levels of the organization.

/ CHAPTER FORTY-FOUR /

*by Brian Williams, M.A.*
*Vice President for Enrollment*
*John Carroll University*

44

# Engaging the Greater College Community

It is all too easy to become disconnected from the campus community. Yet being connected and engaged with the campus community is so critical to doing the job well. The focus of our work is understandably external; we concentrate most on prospective students and their families, guidance counselors, and traveling. However, it is incumbent on the leaders within the admissions structure of the office to ensure that this external focus does not turn into isolation.

Regardless of where admissions may fall on the organizational chart—whether as part of academic affairs, student affairs, or in an enrollment management division—the admissions staff must go beyond its own structural boundaries to be "part of the main." This chapter will take a very colloquial approach to understanding the various ways in which admissions officers can and must interact with the whole.

Learning about the campus is essential for various reasons such as the ability to:

- Learn about the university you are promoting;
- Educate the academic community about admissions efforts and challenges;
- Help the other members of the community in their efforts, so that, in turn, they will attend your events or help when you need calls, letters, or speakers to aid in the recruitment process;

- Develop as a professional; and
- Become a true member of the institution rather than just a "seller" of it.

For their own benefit, as well as that of the institution, admissions officers should gain experience in other parts of the campus community in order to support their development into an enrollment professional later. Getting beyond a one-dimensional existence is essential for progressing in a complex three-dimensional profession.

This chapter will provide a rubric for different levels of engagement in relation to the various facets of campus life with which admissions officers should gain at least a passing familiarity: financial aid; student accounts / bursar; orientation; residential life; student affairs; academic advising; academic community; business and financial matters; and advancement / development.

## Stages of Engagement

### Engaging the College Community

Campus politics and reporting lines differ greatly from institution to institution. Even within one institution, it may be easy or difficult to join committees or otherwise "break through" the culture of different divisions. This section will discuss six roles an admissions officer may choose to explore, in order to grow as a professional.

This is about *how* to engage the college community, with a little bit in each instance about *why* this is necessary. Obviously, your approach may need to change and develop over time, and in any event, each of these approaches may need to be adapted to the particular culture of your institution.

#### THE OBSERVER

Colleges and universities are rich centers of cultural activity and learning. The most basic way of getting involved is to attend and support events on campus. Being a visible member of the community achieves many goals at once.

- It breaks down the perception of the administration as being an abstract or elusive entity, by being seen to be supporting the academic endeavors of the school.
- It dispels the myth and stigma of admissions staff as "always on the road," or else hiding in an office reading essays.
- It provides you with stories from campus to enhance view books, newsletters, group information sessions, and all our interactions with prospective students.

*The campus is a dynamic, organic place, not a one-time "thing" that can be memorized.*
We must compel ourselves to at least observe and engage rather than just reading about the campus that is just outside our doors. Our presence, at times, is a political as well as a profes-

sional necessity. Simply going to see a show, getting tickets to sporting events, and attending guest lectures and symposia can make you an active and visible observer of the campus.

### THE LISTENER

The admissions process is a mystery to many on campus; it is seen almost as a black box profession. When we are not connected and vocal across campus our profession is at best, vague—and at worst, invisible—to many across the community. I have found that, in general, the community has many questions about what we do and how we represent our institutions. Some questions that are in their minds are:

- What high schools do you visit?
- What do you do when you are at a college fair?
- What kind of psychology major do you have?
- What type of students do you look for?

The most valuable role we can play in the community is to listen. We can meet with faculty and others in their own settings—and/or invite them to our own staff meetings. This focused listening is critical in our work. Even when enrollment goals are met for our campuses, there will always be some programs that are suffering low enrollments, programs that feel underrepresented in our print publications. Be assured that the representatives of such programs will be vocal. Hearing about what is not done well comes with the territory when venturing across campus. It is important to understand the justification for criticism; not being defensive is essential. In listening to the community you need to remember the old adage: You were given two ears and only one tongue—in other words, you should listen twice as much as you speak!

### THE LIAISON

Watching and listening can quickly evolve into the more formal role of liaison. On many campuses, the office of admissions and the faculty must work in concert with each other through more concrete and established channels than mere discussion. The liaison role requires that one or more members of the admissions staff maintain connections with other units on campus—most typically with academics and athletics. The liaison role is a two-way process: bringing information acquired back to our admissions colleagues *and* educating the campus about our admissions efforts. Liaisons should inform the campus directly of the trends in admission applications; of upcoming visits and events; and of other plans and trends which can help the faculty play a useful role in the admissions cycle, whether at open houses or other events. An additional benefit to the admissions officer is that by talking about reports, numbers, trends, and challenges in the recruitment process, you may stumble across solutions and suggestions from among your own faculty and coaches. Faculty are typically an untapped resource on a campus. Chapter 11 in this book is devoted exclusively to "Faculty's Role in Recruitment."

### THE SUPPORT CENTER

The admissions office, with its typically larger staff and larger budget, may be viewed with envy by smaller units on the campus. However, an admissions staff can use this as an opportunity to create strong allies and consistent practices across campus by leveraging its resources in creative ways. There are many times when other offices on campus are limited by their time, energy, or resources. For example, when the admissions staff has software tools that can e-mail tens of thousands of students, why not absorb a few more e-mails to support an academic department's needs? We also work with various graphics and publication firms; so we could, within the limits of accomplishing our own work, help departments by aiding in their printing needs. Small things like sharing our digital photo repository to increase a department's Web site images can go a long way in strengthening relationships. If we are in service to departments, we create cheerleaders for our efforts, making it easier when we turn to them and ask for support at recruitment events. It is the essence of *quid pro quo*. We can help each other meet our distinct and common goals.

### THE INFLUENCER

Influencers impact the community and are involved in the *decision-making* process. Committee work is an endeavor where we can influence the decisions and processes on campus. As admissions professionals we are in touch with future students, and we have some sense of what they expect to find on our campus. So when we serve on committees, we should use the opportunity to influence decisions that will make our campuses more responsive to the needs of future students.

### THE CHAMPION

When energy and effort come together, it is possible for the admissions office to help shape the vision—the self-concept and the aspirations—of the institution. Speaking to the Board and leadership of the institution provides opportunities for championing student access and affordability. These opportunities to influence institutional decisions do not happen every day, but when they do, they should be embraced.

## Engaging Various Offices on Campus

An analysis of these various stages of engagement serves as the basis for interacting with various offices across the institution, based on your own personal goals of professional development and the needs of your office and institution. In the remainder of this chapter, let us consider various offices across the campus community and how these stages of engagement can help create a context for admissions professionals to play a productive role. We will look at each of the stages of engagement and their implications for each area of the campus. We will move in chronological order, in the same order that the student moves through the enrollment process and through the various offices that they reach.

## Financial Aid

While in most cases admissions and financial can share reporting lines and physical space, the two offices may not always interact as closely as might be ideal. Linking with aid is crucial in the enrollment process because the enrollment decision for families is so linked to cost factors.

### THE OBSERVER

Admissions staff tend to receive general questions about financial aid, and perhaps appeals from families for more aid. But, if you sit even for a short time at the front desk of a financial aid office, you will quickly see how the nature of the questions changes. Deeper questions about affordability arise; more detailed questions about how to pay for school surface. Observing the questions that the financial aid office must field, and the numbers of students they interact with—future, current, and former—is a very useful experience for an admissions officer. Additionally, if your financial aid office allows it, observing entrance and exit loan interviews with students helps you to see the process as experienced by the students.

### THE LISTENER

Engage your financial aid colleagues with discussions about parent and student phone calls they receive. Members of that staff deal with families over a series of semesters, in ways that admissions staff generally do not, once a student enrolls. For example, consider a family that had a less than ideal financial aid package. Admissions staff will work with this student once, while the financial aid staff will see this family repeatedly over the next four to six years. Listening to the financial aid staff can help inform freshmen awarding strategies in very profound and specific ways. We may begin to see flaws in our communication with families and identify certain types of students who present particular patterns of difficulty once enrolled on our campus. This information can be used to improve our communication with families earlier in the admissions cycle.

### THE LIAISON

A good liaison role between admissions and financial aid can be established to help package freshmen financial aid. Building a FAFSA award from the bottom up is something every admissions counselor should be able to do. As liaison roles develop, you begin to notice the financial aid cycle—that financial aid is busy with returning student financial aid awards right around the same time that freshmen awarding is at its peak in March and April. So, another area of helping the aid office could involve having an admissions professional be involved in financial aid appeals among freshmen packaging. Other possibilities for useful liaisons between the two offices can involve developing a cross-training program for both staffs; and having financial aid officers attend group presentations, high school visits, and other admissions events. As the affordability of higher education continues to be a major issue to most parents, having the financial aid staff visible in the process early on may be very useful, both for the institution and the prospective students.

#### THE SUPPORT CENTER

The financial aid office usually has fewer resources allocated to it than the admissions office. But, despite this fact, students process all communications as coming from "the college"—and, all too often the process can appear discontinuous to them. Specifically, when the same students were applicants, they were recruited with slick brochures, great Web pages, and so forth. Then, all the attractive parts stop when the student receives a text-heavy, rules-laden financial aid letter. My contention is that the "recruiting" should continue. The financial aid (FA) award should be treated as the next view book, the next piece in the admissions cycle. Admissions should be involved in the presentation and formatting. To address this part of the cycle in a broader perspective, it would be fair to say that when we do not treat FA mailings as part of the recruitment cycle, we lose valuable marketing opportunities to continue to influence the enrollment decision.

#### THE CHAMPION

Affordability is taking center stage in federal and state policy as student borrowing, student debt, and escalating college costs become a main part of the political agenda. Forging links with financial aid will allow admissions staff to be more aware of all dimensions of the issues—and will strengthen our ability to engage the leadership of the institution, if we choose to do so, in discussions about affordability, escalating costs, and the impact on families.

### Student Accounts/Bursar

There is an inherent disconnect in our work with student accounts: typically student accounts reports to a different vice president than the admissions office, and we perform our roles in different ways. For example, colleges generally mail out financial aid awards with a focus on "cost of attendance," but tuition statements focus on direct cost. These two approaches—what aid is awarded and what is owed—are conveyed in two different mailings with very little coordination between them. Aid awards and billing statements thus come through in disjointed ways. Consider: What office should you call if a loan is not showing on your account?

#### THE OBSERVER

It takes a while to understand that the first semester bill is perhaps one of the most important publications that is sent to prospective students. The true cost of education and sacrifices that some families might have to make finally becomes real. Yet very often the bill is sent as a distinct mailing without much supporting information and without a recruitment focus. The clarity, or lack of clarity, with which we communicate to families about their financial aid package and financial planning for the next four years can contribute greatly to retaining students throughout the "summer melt" phase before move-in. Orientation is a good place to watch what information is shared with families about payment plans and billing due dates. Another good time to observe the billing process is during registration for the spring semester—does your institution block students from registration who have an unpaid balance? What unpaid dollar amount triggers this action?

#### THE LISTENER

When you sit with your bursar, you begin to hear the stories of students who have a hard time affording your institution. You learn which students have difficulty paying—and you can ask what challenges exist in the process.

#### THE LIAISON

By partnering with student accounts, you will come to understand fee structures, billing cycles, and tuition policies. Knowledge at this level of detail is critical to developing financial aid budgets, and in sharing that knowledge with families early in their decision process.

#### THE SUPPORT CENTER

The first semester bill is one of the most important mailings that can leave your college campus in the enrollment cycle. The more expensive the college or the larger the amount due, the more humbling the moment is when a family looks at a statement and sees a figure listed after two anxiety-producing words: amount due. The billing statement should be seen as a yield/recruitment opportunity in order to prevent summer "melt" of students. Through the billing cycle, an admissions-centric focus can identify opportunities to bundle additional information with the bill. Are there ways to link the bill to other information? Can you use consistent graphics to make the information easier to follow? Remember that the message is about the value and worth of the college degree as opposed to a bare-bones mailing that simply says, pay this amount now.

#### THE CHAMPION

Payment options and the importance of saving for college are critical for schools to talk about as early in the recruitment process as possible. Many schools have realized this and are bringing financial aid and billing into new structural models such as Student Financial Services, student planning, and other campus-specific approaches that make the billing process easier for families. It is more about financial planning than it is about financial aid. New models are pointing the way to where institutions need to be in relation to enhanced student services, but admissions offices have not yet been fully incorporated into this model.

## Orientation

The passing of the baton in the summer to Orientation staff is a critical time during which admissions work is still important. Families will continue to ponder whether they made the right choice. In an era of double depositing, Summer Orientation has become the ultimate admissions Open House—and the place where students will seek affirmation of their enrollment decisions. While May 1st stands as a candidate reply date, it has not been a time of closure for admissions staffs for quite a long time. Admissions work is not done until the first day of classes, if that. The continued enrollment of a student is a precious relationship that must always be celebrated, nurtured, and never taken for granted.

### THE OBSERVER

Attending orientation is an essential task for an admissions staff. It is too easy to shift our mindset to the next class of rising high school seniors and summer group information sessions, and neglect the process happening right in front of us. Yet, these are the students who were admitted, who just experienced the admissions cycle. Orientation is the best focus group we have, a ready-made opportunity to see how well you did as a staff in selecting students.

A different way to observe during orientation is to actually watch how students register for classes. At two different institutions, I have watched as students sign up for courses online. It is amazing to watch them alternate between browser windows showing the school registration pages and *ratemyprofessor.com* while, at the same time, instant messaging with friends! You will see first hand how students use technology and be amazed by how resourceful they are—it makes you reconsider the tools we use to communicate with students in the admissions process.

### THE LISTENER

Having lunch with families at Orientation or creating informal focus groups is a great way to inform and enhance your processes. *What made you choose our institution?* That is typically the only question you need to ask in order to start the ball rolling with families in this setting. Sitting at lunch or assisting at check-in, any way you can help will open opportunities to see the fruits of those late nights and calls with families.

### THE LIAISON

You should ensure that someone from the admissions staff is on any formal Orientation/Registration planning committees on campus. Being able to discuss the projected size of the freshman and transfer classes and having ongoing communication with the campus administration is critical to a successful program. Conversely, the admissions office needs to know—early—the dates and key information about Orientation, so that information can be shared in the recruitment cycle. Being isolated from this information can result in a large disservice to our students and families. Working with orientation staff helps them to understand the nature of the class you are recruiting and handing off to them, and can ensure a consistent and smooth transition for families.

#### THE SUPPORT CENTER

Depending on funding and the desire for consistent branding and messaging, the admissions office can play a role in printing orientation brochures as part of the admissions mail flow. One unified look and feel is important, so that once students choose to enroll, they do not experience "marketing whiplash" and witness an identity crisis. Many times orientation sessions are branded on our campus; are the colors and themes consistent with what we have told students throughout the rest of the recruitment cycle? If the admissions office is involved in the communication, consistency can be ensured. Consider having a composite packet mailed on May 1st or any time someone deposits. Indeed, the tools and functionality of admissions can and should be utilized throughout the orientation period. The interaction can flow both ways: online event reservation tools purchased for use in advancing admissions events can be used by Orientation as well. In some cases, admissions functionality is more advanced than what is available to other parts of the university, and understandably so. In most schools, orientation occurs only twice a year, and purchasing or investing in online solutions for that level of use is not necessarily cost effective. But admissions tools can be "borrowed" by others on campus, and can extend the admission functionality throughout the summer.

#### THE CHAMPION

Admissions staff know the profile and characteristics of the incoming class. Meetings with orientation staff can help to celebrate the students who have chosen to attend your institution. You can convey to the orientation staff the context and "personality" of the class. Efforts such as this can reinforce the hand-off of responsibility and care that is needed.

### Residence Life

The quality of residence life is an important factor in the admissions process. Where students live, how they interact outside the classroom, and the support given to residents all come together to define the life of the campus. It begins with the room: not showing a residence hall room on our campus tours would raise suspicion among our campus visitors. But residence life is more than just a bed; it truly becomes the home that students will live in for four years, and admissions needs to learn the experience from top to bottom.

#### THE OBSERVER

Tour your campus often. Beyond learning about options in the residence halls, each year you will see how students decorate their rooms—what the new trends are, what future upgrades might be needed for students. By monitoring trends, it might help you identify new photos for admissions view books, find rooms to show on campus tours, and more. Walking the campus provides an opportunity for informal quality checks. If there is hall damage or issues on the tour route used for campus visitors, you can take responsibility for reporting these problems, thereby accelerating repairs.

#### THE LISTENER

Speaking to residential life staff and new student resident assistants/hall directors throughout the year is a good part of your ongoing education. *What do students do on the weekends? Who leaves on the weekends?* The answers change every year, and it is important to stay on top of this so that these infamous questions can be answered at college fairs and in sessions with families.

#### THE LIAISON

Sharing numbers with Residence Life is critical. The size of the freshman class and its gender ratio has a profound impact on residential space planning and the need to change floors and room configurations. I recall one recent year where an incoming freshman male student was in a wheel chair, and it impacted the conversion of a female floor to a male floor in a hall. These changes take time. So, sharing specifics of the incoming class and keeping the lines of communication open must be a year-round commitment. The closer it comes to the beginning of the semester the more important the dialogue becomes, based on the institution and its ability to accept late applicants. At the end of the cycle, move-in day is a highly therapeutic experience. Carrying boxes and comforters up and down stairs is a great closure to recruiting the incoming class and is a humbling experience! It is a wonderful way to welcome the class just recruited, as admissions staff finalize the fall travel visits and get ready to leave the campus for a few months.

#### THE SUPPORT CENTER

Admissions and residence life can partner together for developing a "show room" for use on campus tours. Having a dedicated show room is a great way to partner—decorating a room and sharing ownership of its maintenance. Also, in the admissions cycle, housing deposits and mailings are one of the first post-deposit contacts that we encounter. This mailing should represent a continuation of the look and feel established by the admissions staff, just like orientation mentioned earlier.

#### THE CHAMPION

The admissions staff plays a large role in understanding competitor housing options. It should be the responsibility of the admissions office to keep abreast of these trends and to provide organized feedback as to visitor impressions of living options, costs of room and board at competitor institutions, and related topics.

## Student Affairs

At four-year institutions, the admissions staff is responsible for replacing nearly 25 percent of the student population each year. The newly-recruited group then storms the campus and charts new directions for the campus to take in fulfilling its mission. You can get some new ideas for helping the campus stay ahead of the curve by carefully observing and appropriately participating in student life. After all, you helped to choose these students just a year or so earlier! When an admissions officer overhears current students say "There's nothing to do here," we should take part of the blame to the extent that, since the time we brought students to campus, we have not helped to transform the campus.

### THE OBSERVER

Read the student newspaper regularly—you will learn the key issues and trends among current students. Purchase tickets to sponsored events. Participate in events for fun—many opportunities arise, such as judging a campus lip sync contest, where you can be an active observer even while being an active participant. By going to events and keeping your eyes open on campus, you can find students to profile in future publications and on the Web, beyond those students who are the most immediately apparent to administrators—*i.e.*, tour guides and other campus leaders.

### THE LISTENER

Listen to students as much as you can. Tour guides work in your office; work study students are filing and processing applications in various ways. There are very few excuses not to stay connected with the campus through students in our work. More intentionally, interaction can come from meetings with student government, editors of the newspaper, and with heads of other campus activities and organizations. Listen to the student affairs staff, as well. Meeting with them can give you some insight into the types of students on your campus who can be successful outside the classroom. These are the stories we need to tell in the recruitment process.

### THE LIAISON

Allies on the student newspaper are a must! Prospective students and their families can easily read newspapers online or pick them up while walking on campus tours. The voice of the student newspaper will carry great weight with families and, if negative, will cancel out all the optimism that a tour guide can muster. Other allies can be found through your support of other campus events as well. Major weekends for Student Affairs like Homecoming, Parents' Weekend, and athletic events can tend to overlap with key visitor weekends for admission. However, rather than seeing these events as conflicting and vying for campus space, turn it into an opportunity. Partnering with Student Affairs not only can create opportunities to better use campus space for events, but it can also begin to tie events together in creative ways.

Visitors will see a vibrant campus: you can invite athletes to their specific events; theatre majors can visit campus when productions are occurring; and so on. I have often been amazed at the ways we neglect to connect current events with our prospective students as much as we could. Our current students have younger siblings. So, further, homecoming or Parents' Weekend are opportunities to link student affairs to enrollment in such simple ways.

#### THE SUPPORT CENTER

Campus events can be planned to serve the purposes of both the admissions office and student affairs. Campus guest lectures, student plays and productions, and athletic events are all great venues to invite local students to—or to coordinate overnight programs around.

#### THE CHAMPION

More selective campuses have a responsibility to meet the needs of the campus beyond the purely academic. Shaping the class is the responsibility we have—*to identify and select students who will advance, and benefit from, the broad mission of the institution*. Student Affairs is in tune with the co-curricular needs of the campus, and can best identify those needs. By linking with Student Affairs, Admissions may be able to play a role in helping to shape the timing of key events on campus, so that the energy generated by each office results in the better performance of the activities of both. Imagine a great debate team composed entirely of college seniors—the next year, the debate team has no one left to pass the torch, and subsequently withers for a time. Therefore, it is the responsibility of the admissions staff to support each and every campus organization and "fill those holes" each year. This extreme example shows how profound a role the admissions office can play in shaping the future student life of the campus.

### Academic Advising

Many times there can be tension or misunderstanding between the administrative and academic sectors on a college campus. So the admissions office must seek credibility in working with the academic life of a college campus. We are more alike than most advisors like to admit. In fact, admissions staff are trained to understand high school curricula, student ability, test scores, transfer credit, and AP credit in order to ensure student success in the classroom. Academic advising is manifest in every decision to admit, deny, or wait list a student in the admissions cycle—the advising process begins with the admissions staff.

#### THE OBSERVER

Orientation is where advising begins. Admissions staff should take care to observe how students are counseled into various classes, based on their preparation. When we see the advice that students are given, that can impact the way we talk to similar students in the future, can inform our admissions decisions, and more.

#### THE LISTENER

Having meetings with academic advisors is an excellent way to gain a sense of the interests and concerns of students. What are students frustrated with? What courses do they want to take? Your discussions with advisors about course options and student frustrations will provide useful information for you to incorporate into your own work. Sometimes, for example, advisors are the first to know which students are having a hard time with courses, and struggling with their academic lives, generally. You can listen and then backtrack to the admissions application. Trying to understand patterns of student success and risk is an essential component of admissions work. This concept of informing the admissions process—of understanding patterns that may emerge after the fact—is different from retention. The admissions and advising offices may work with many of the same materials, but with a different emphasis and purpose. Admissions can determine factors of success to inform who might be offered acceptance in the first place, while advisors can focus on the support students need to graduate.

#### THE LIAISON

Liaison models involving partnerships between academic affairs, advising, and admissions can create productive new ways of enhancing students' ability to benefit from the curriculum. The understanding that the admissions staff has of a freshmen class, for example, can help assign students to the *right* advisor. Great links with advising help ensure student success. Additionally, we may have borderline admissions cases—students who may be at risk for any number of factors. By establishing formal relationships with Academic Advising, admissions staff can flag students as at-risk and make sure that support is in place for student success— such as requiring a lighter course load, or postponing a given course.

#### THE SUPPORT CENTER

Information and profiles of advisees are sometimes best culled from the members of an admissions staff, rather than from other offices. We are familiar with the students and can provide good information to make an advisor's job easier, whether at Orientation or later. If there is information about students that surfaces in our admissions review, we can consider the best ways to ensure that advisors have this information to work with in their contact with students.

#### THE CHAMPION

Advisors can be "filled in" about each new class of students and their academic background—admissions staff should consider developing a newsletter or report regarding the profile of the class, and of each student, prior to orientation. You could share information with advisors about the high school curriculum patterns of the new class, for example, and help them consider the support and needs of each new class.

## Academic Community

Beyond academic advising lies a greater mystery: the world of the faculty. It is a vague world for many admissions professionals. We see a small cross-section of faculty in our work—that dedicated group of professors and deans who speak at open houses, open their classrooms to student visits, or are profiled in our publications. Yet so much more happens in the academic life of our institutions that most admissions professionals do not get to see.

### THE OBSERVER

One of the best ways to understand the academic community is to attend Faculty Senate or Faculty Forum meetings. This is typically where new courses and majors are proposed and developed and where faculty are at their philosophical– and political—best! While admissions staff will almost inevitably not have a "voice" in the meeting, your attendance will be useful to give the office an early indicator of what is coming, and to affirm a commitment to being an active participant in the community. You will hear new majors discussed and approved, and then your office can make sure that that information is included in the appropriate admissions applications, view books, and information sessions.

### THE LISTENER

Attending department meetings or inviting faculty to admissions staff meetings is very useful. You will learn about recent successes for faculty and students—their research, new courses, internships, and job placement. These are all critical to our work. Learning about each program improves each contact with the students we have, and hope to have.

### THE LIAISON

Between teaching, research, committee work, advising, and countless other roles on campus, faculty are stretched in many different directions. Understandably, recruiting new students often does not make the top of the list. Thus, on many campuses, the practice of having liaison persons in admissions work directly with academic departments evolved as a fairly common way of coping with this situation. The partnership can be as informal as the admissions office learning which programs have the capacity to grow in enrollment, and having admissions gain a better understanding as to what types of students a given department is looking for (*e.g.*, learning that a biology department has been seeking too many pre-med students and not enough students interested in genetics). Service as an academic department liaison also provides a vehicle for faculty to participate in the enrollment cycle—whether via classroom visits, providing mock lectures at open houses, or participating in phoning nights. A formal liaison role can ensure that faculty feel like partners in the enrollment cycle and that admissions is helping to meet their classroom needs.

#### THE SUPPORT CENTER

Academic departments often have limited budgets, and the admissions office can help. There have been times this past year when our admissions budget has supported Web site changes and provided financial assistance to help create brochures for various departments across our campus. While any given department may have only a limited need to promote its program on campus, admissions invariably has a larger ability to use brochures at college fairs and in our mailing cycle. So helping to support a larger print run of a brochure can both drive down the total cost and add a robust mailing piece to the admissions arsenal. Some would call that a win-win situation.

#### THE CHAMPION

The admissions staff needs to be seen as the trend-watcher and the forecaster of likely enrollment in the majors offered at our institutions. We know what careers students are interested in pursuing, or even those which are currently fashionable. We can track interest in various subjects from the standardized test national data. Is our campus ready for the next trend? Admissions staff should strive to be in the dialogue regarding curriculum development and the evolution of majors.

### Business and Finance

#### THE OBSERVER

College costs are under severe scrutiny in the media and with families. The admissions officer should understand the components of tuition and price structure. Appreciation of the commodification of higher education is critical in the decision-making process.

#### THE LISTENER

Listening to families is an invaluable skill when it comes to finances. A college education is one of the larger "purchases" a family will make. Therefore we must hear concerns with grace and sincerity in the decision process. In conversations with others on campus, from financial aid staff to the Bursar, the admissions office can try to understand which families present challenges in payment and affordability. There can be trends that the admissions staff may be able to spot earlier in the admissions cycle and thus be better able to understand the situations that arise for an institution, and the challenges that arise for families.

#### THE LIAISON

The admissions office can help monitor endowed funds and the spectrum of scholarships available to students. If various funds are set up for certain types of students—whether by geography, major, or other criteria—admissions is best positioned to find and identify those students. Without links to funds and fund balances, as well as knowledge of which funds are available, it is very difficult to ensure that we are good stewards of a donor's funds. Obviously, the structure of financial aid available is a topic which admissions officers should be informed about—not perhaps in as specific detail as financial aid officers can muster, but enough to not need to transfer student and parent phone calls every time there is a question about aid.

#### THE SUPPORT CENTER

When admissions staff can partner with business and finance staff, the office of admissions can gain a strong ally when it comes to budget and salary decisions. Admissions offices tend to have one of the largest single budgets on a college campus, and bring in a large amount of the revenue for the institution. So it is quite important to forge these relationships.

#### THE CHAMPION

The admissions office can perform an important service by sharing data, internally, about the impact of tuition increases on the recruitment and admissions process. Sharing "facts on the ground" can help to ensure that students have a voice at the table before tuition increases are decided. Fiscal planning for an institution should not be isolated to one office. In most cases admissions staff are not at the board level determining tuition rates. But the ability to recruit students is closely tied to the cost of tuition, room, and board.

### Advancement/Alumni

The students whom the admissions office brings to campus are the future alumni of the institution, the future donors, the future names that will be on new campus buildings many years from now. In the long view of enrollment management, it is incumbent upon an admissions staff to accept the simple premise that it is their job *to recruit alumni*; to find those students who will graduate and successfully be ambassadors of our story well into the future.

#### THE OBSERVER

Alumni are testimony that our process has worked. Working directly with alumni staff and with other recent graduates, we can see the outgrowth of all our efforts. It is why we are here. Attending reunion events is crucial—to watch, listen, and be present. We want the loyalty of our graduates: both to encourage their children to attend and to contribute to the institution in a variety of ways—financially, as mentors, or (depending on your school) as alumni interviewers of prospective students.

#### THE LISTENER

Learn about the advancement and fundraising cycle. Knowing early on what major campaigns are in development can help to shape the admissions messages (*e.g.*, a gift for a named school of business might change how much you promote business and other programs). Talk to alumni about their experiences. At reunion one usually only needs to ask *what did you love about your experience with us*? And you will be regaled with stories of late night bonding with friends, great faculty, and more from people who are passionate about the institution. These are the stories that can then enrich our admissions presentations, become marginalia in a future brochure, and identify those alumni who can represent us at receptions, college fairs, and other forums.

#### THE LIAISON

Joint meetings of the admissions and alumni offices make great sense. Some areas where this is especially useful include endowed scholarship planning, as well as discussion of "special interest" and legacy applications before a powerful alumni child is denied. Other situations where information-sharing is useful include college fairs and campus visits. Many times children of alumni will apply for admission, and this may be off the radar of the alumni staff. When alumni children come for a campus tour, how much more appealing it can be when you meet the parent by saying "Welcome back" to the alumnus or alumna during the visit.

#### THE SUPPORT CENTER

Admissions staff can volunteer to help with alumni magazines and literature. When you consider the audience for this literature as the parents of future applicants, you begin to realize that the need for an admissions voice in these brochures increases dramatically. We can become an informative and trusted voice to help parents in the college process, whether or not their children ultimately enroll at our institution. Examples of articles and advice to share can range from the role of 529 college-savings plans (subject of a separate chapter in this book), to an inside look at the admission/selection process, to more institution-specific topics. Each campus will dictate the voice, presence, and frequency of such articles. In addition, by working closely with alumni staff, you will learn when alumni are holding events in various cities. These can sometimes become open opportunities for both offices to partner together; alumni regional events may be able to incorporate an admissions event at the same time. A social event before a basketball game in a regional city can be a powerful way to link events together that span the enrollment cycle. You will gain support for recruiting in distant regions and can also provide the opportunity for alumni volunteers to participate in the recruitment process in these cities.

#### THE CHAMPION

The end goal for an admissions staff is to recruit alumni—to find those students who will enroll and graduate from our institutions. Alumni who have made it through the process are our most precious resource in helping to support our efforts to find more people like them to shape future graduating classes. By sharing the challenges and trends with alumni you can gain support (recruiting, fiscal, and otherwise) to aid your efforts—not just to "get the class" but to also graduate it!

## Conclusions

There are so many offices and voices on a college campus. The admissions office interacts with just a sliver of the total campus; a handful of tour guides; and a dedicated group of go-to faculty who speak at events. But, as you begin to consider all these various ways of engaging the community, without knowing it, you will begin to embrace a deeper and more substantial Strategic Enrollment Management (SEM) philosophy from your corner of your institution. At heart, SEM is a process focused on students, but it is also a disciplined way to understand the systems that students use to navigate an institution. Regardless of the route you take, engagement with the wider community will stretch you as a professional. When upward mobility in your office may not be possible, this horizontal development will give you the depth you need as a professional.

By embracing a spirit of engagement, you will not only find the best way to navigate your current campus, but will also understand the full interaction of different approaches, as staff changes or professional development brings you to new responsibilities. By considering the role admissions plays in the larger community, you will begin to intuitively function as an enrollment professional and not just as a recruiter. You will grow. And your office, your campus, and the profession will benefit from your engagement.

# Appendix A: Student and Parent FAQs

*Dewey Holleman*
*Higher Education Practice Consultant, Ciber, Inc.*
*(Former Admissions Counselor, Assistant and Associate Director of Admissions, and Director of Admissions)*

Reprinted from AACRAO's *College Recruiters' Quick Guide*

Some of the most frequently asked questions college admissions counselors receive from students, parents and school counselors follow. You should be prepared to answer all of these, or know how your institution would like you to respond to them, before you represent your institution at an event.

## Admissions Policy

- What is the application fee?
- Do you require a minimum SAT or ACT score?
- Do you accept both the SAT and ACT?
- Is an interview required for admissions?
- Do I have to write an essay for admissions?
- Do I need to send letters of reference? If so, how many?
- Do I have to have a physical examination prior to admission?
- Do I have to submit immunization records?
- Is there a required set of high school level courses I must complete to be eligible for admission?
- Do you calculate the grade point average only on certain courses in high school? If so, how do you do it?
- How do you look at AP or IB or AICE courses?
- How will you honor CLEP scores? What credit will I get?
- Do you accept the GED?
- Are there certain GED scores required for admission?
- Will you honor a home study program or a diploma from an unaccredited high school?
- How will the college evaluate or use two or more sets of SAT/ACT scores?
- Do you offer an Early Admission Program?
- What are the transfer admission requirements?
- Is admission open to any freshman or transfer student in any semester or quarter?
- Do you offer a joint/dual enrollment program?
- Do you offer remedial or developmental studies?
- Will "D's" transfer to your college?

- Is physical education required? If so, can it be waived?
- Is it easier to get in the summer term than the fall term?

### Admissions Process

- Is there an application deadline, and if so, when is it?
- How long does it take to process an application and when will the acceptance letter be mailed?
- Can I apply to your school online?
- Can I pay my application fee online?
- Can I look at my application status online?
- What do I have to send with my application?
- Is there a waiting list used for admissions, and how does it work?

### Advising

- When must I declare a major?

### Athletics

- With what athletic division and conference is the college affiliated?
- What sports do you have?
- What intramural sports do you have?
- Do you have junior varsity or varsity cheerleading? When are try-outs?
- Do you have a dance team?
- Do you have baton twirlers?
- What athletic facilities are available to regular students?

### Curriculum

- What is the core curriculum? The general education requirements?
- How many majors do you offer?
- How many degrees do you offer?
- Are internships, cooperative study or study abroad programs offered? Required?
- What is the difference between the semester system and the quarter system?
- What are your college's strongest majors?
- For what programs of study is your college known?
- Does your college offer graduate courses?
- Is there a mini-term or summer school?
- Is there an ROTC program available?
- What is the class attendance policy?

## Financial Aid

- Are academic scholarships available?
- Are there talent scholarships?
- Are there athletic scholarships?
- Does out-of-state tuition apply?
- How much are books?
- How do I apply for financial aid?
- Will I get a bill or how can I find out how much I owe?
- Do you take credit cards? Can I pay on-line?
- What is the refund policy?

## General Facts

- What is your freshman class size?
- How many courses are considered a full load?
- What is the percentage of undergraduates who earn degrees and then go on to graduate school?
- How long does it take to graduate?
- What agencies accredit your college?
- What is the student/faculty ratio?
- How many, or what percentage, of full-time faculty members are employed? How many, or what percentage, of faculty members hold a doctorate or terminal degree?
- How large is the campus acreage?
- How many buildings do you have?
- What year was the college founded and what is the brief history?
- From where do most of the out-of-state students come?
- In what size town is the college located?
- What are the major attractions close to the college?
- What is the minority enrollment by ethnicity?
- What is the international student enrollment?
- Where can students cash out-of-town checks?
- Are there banks on campus? Where are the ATMs?
- What is the ratio of males to females on campus?
- Who are some well-known graduates of your college?
- How does the college compare in size to the other colleges in the state?
- Does the college have a toll-free number or will you accept collect calls from prospective students?
- What is the placement rate of bachelor degree graduates?
- What big name companies recruit students at your school?

## Health Services

- Is there an infirmary or health services center available to students?

## Housing

- What appliances can I bring to my dorm room?
- Can freshman live off campus?
- May students have private rooms on campus?
- How many students share a room?
- Are the dorms air-conditioned?
- Is there a deposit required to reserve a dorm room? If so, how much is it?
- Do the dorms have laundry facilities?
- Do the dorms have private baths or hall baths?
- Is there a curfew?
- When are the doors locked at night?
- What are the current expenses for room, board, tuition and fees?
- Do you provide overnight housing for prospective students?

## Orientation

- Do you have an orientation program? When? Do I have to attend?

## Registration

- Do you offer pre-registration via telephone or the Web?

## Residency

- How do I qualify for residency in your state?

## Safety

- Do you have police on campus?
- How secure is the campus?

## Student Life

- May freshman have cars on campus?
- Do you have national fraternities and sororities?
- Do I have to purchase a meal plan?
- Is there a dress code?
- What campus organizations emphasize religious activities?
- What music groups can I join? Marching bands, choral, symphony?
- Are jobs available on your campus?

### Student Support

- Does your college offer a tutorial program?
- What computer access is available to students?
- What type of computer must I have to be successful at your school?
- How accessible or ADA compliant would you say the campus is?
- Do you have counseling services for students?
- What if I have a special diet I have to follow?
- Do you have a Career Services Office/Center?

### Visiting the Campus

- When can I visit your school?
- Is there an Open House event?

# Appendix B: College Fair Do's and Don'ts

*Dewey Holleman*
*Higher Education Practice Consultant, Ciber, Inc.*
*(Former Admissions Counselor, Assistant and Associate Director of Admissions, and Director of Admissions)*

Reprinted from AACRAO's *College Recruiters' Quick Guide*

## Do:

- Arrive 30 minutes early to allow yourself time to find and set up your table;
- Remember that you are a guest of the college fair host and should abide by their rules;
- Maintain a high level of personal and professional conduct at all times;
- Make all confirmations of attendance and cancellations as far in advance as possible;
- Stay for the entire program; and
- Use only that technology which is allowed by the host and be sure that sound does not interfere with that of other institutions.

## Don't:

- Ask to relocate;
- Interfere with other institutions' space, information or technology;
- Leave your table for extended periods of time;
- Roam around and ask attendees to visit your table;
- Eat or drink at your table during an event;
- Provide promotional items or food at your table; or
- Leave an event early.

# Appendix C: Working with High School Counselors

*Dewey Holleman*
*Higher Education Practice Consultant, Ciber, Inc.*
*(Former Admissions Counselor, Assistant and Associate Director of Admissions, and Director of Admissions)*

Reprinted from AACRAO's *College Recruiters' Quick Guide*

Below are the top 11 questions you should ask of the high school counselor before you set up your recruitment operations:

- How are you? (get to know the counselor)
- Has anyone expressed an interest in [XYZ] college/university? If so, what are their names?
- How large is the senior class? Junior class? Sophomore class?
- How much time will I be allowed at your school? (get beginning and ending time)
- Do students sign up or do you make a general announcement?
- What college do the majority of your students attend?
- What percentage of students continue their education past high school?
- Does the high school provide a Financial Aid seminar? Who conducts it?
- How long will it take to get from [XYZ] high school to your school?
- How do I get to your high school?
- Do you need any materials sent to you before my visit?

**Other questions you may want to ask:**

- Is there a TV/VCR/DVD available? (if you need it)
- Are there other colleges/universities scheduled to visit that day?
- In what type of room will I be meeting with students? (office, classroom, conference room, auditorium, lunchroom)
- Is your school on a block schedule with alternating day schedules (red day, white day)? If so, what happens if a day of school is cancelled prior to my visit?
- How are your students currently attending my college/university doing? (This works especially well at smaller high schools; be sure you know that a recent graduate from the high school is attending before you ask.)
- Do you need information about special events/visit opportunities at my college/university?
- May I have your current e-mail address?

# References


AACC. *See* American Association of Community Colleges.

AACN. *See* American Association of Colleges of Nursing.

AAMC. *See* Association of American Medical Colleges.

Adams, D.W. 1988. Fundamental considerations: The deep meaning of Native American schooling, 1880–1900. *Harvard Educational Review*. 58(1): 1–28.

Adams, T.A. 2005. Establishing intellectual space for Black students in predominantly White universities through black studies. *Negro Educational Review*. 56(4): 285–299.

Adelman, C. 1998. *Women and Men of the Engineering Path: A Model for Analyses of Undergraduate Careers.* Washington, D.C.: U.S. Department of Education. Available at: <www.eric.ed.gov/ERICWebPortal/contentdelivery/servlet/ERICServlet?accno=ED419696>.

———. 1999. *Answers in the Toolbox: Academic Intensity, Attendance Patterns, and Bachelor's Degree Attainment.* Washington, D.C.: U.S. Department of Education. Available at: <www.eric.ed.gov/ERICWebPortal/contentdelivery/servlet/ERICServlet?accno=ED431363>.

———. 2002. The relationship between urbanicity and educational outcomes. In *Increasing Access to College: Extending Possibilities for All Students*, edited by L. Hagedorn and W. Tierney. Albany: State University of New York Press.

———. 2006. *The Toolbox Revisited: Paths to Degree Completion from High School through College.* Washington, D.C.: U.S. Department of Education. Available at: <www.ed.gov/rschstat/research/pubs/toolboxrevisit/toolbox.pdf>.

Alberts, B.M. 2006. *Campus Wide Retention Planning: The Six-Minute "Read."* Retrieved Sept. 1, 2007 from: <www.nacada.ksu.edu/Clearinghouse/AdvisingIssues/retention-what-works.htm>.

Alexander, K., A. Pallas, and S. Holupka. 1987. Consistency and change in educational stratification: Recent trends regarding social background and college access. *Research in Social Stratification and Mobility*. 6: 161–185.

Allan, R.G. 2001. A background briefing on tuition discounting. *NASFAA's Student Aid Transcript.* Fall: 56–59.

Allen, W. 1992. The color of success: African American college student outcomes at predominately White and historically Black colleges. *Harvard Educational Review*. 6(2): 26–44.

Allen, W.R., U.M. Jayakumar, K.A. Griffin, W.S. Korn, and S. Hurtado. 2005. *Black Undergraduates from Bakke to Grutter: Freshman Status, Trends, and Prospects, 1971–2004*. Los Angeles: Higher Education Research Institute, UCLA.

American Association of Colleges of Nursing. 2007. *Nursing Shortage* (Fact Sheet). Available at: <www.aacn.nche.edu/media/factsheets/nursingshortage.htm>.

American Association of Community Colleges. 2007. *Facts 2007*. Available at: <www2.aacc.nche.edu/pdf/factsheet2007_updated.pdf>.

Anyon, J. 1997. *Ghetto Schooling: A Political Economy of Urban Educational Reform.* New York: Teachers College Press.

AP. See *Associated Press.*

Appleman, H. 2003. College savings plans: You'll need a scorecard. *The New York Times*. Feb. 16, Business Section. Available at: <http://query.nytimes.com/gst/fullpage.html?res=9904EFDD123AF935A25751C0A9659C8B63>.

Ashburn, E. 2006. State Department to bring foreign students to community colleges. *The Chronicle of Higher Education*. 52(35): A51. Available at: <http://chronicle.com/weekly/v52/i35/35a05103.htm>.

*Associated Press*. 2006. New course to help teachers relate to American Indian students. July 13. Available at: <www.diverseeducation.com/artman/publish/article_6015.shtml>.

———. 2007. High schoolers get early start on college careers. March 30. Available at: <www.communitycollegetimes.com/article.cfm?TopicId=52&ArticleId=170>.

Association of American Medical Colleges. 2005a. *AAMC Endorses Criminal Background Checks* (Press Release). Aug. 25. Washington, D.C.: AAMC. Available at: <www.aamc.org/newsroom/pressrel/2005/050826.htm>.

———. 2005b. *Medical Educational Costs and Student Debt, A Working Group Report to the AAMC Governance.* Washington, D.C.: AAMC. <https://services.aamc.org/Publications/showfile.cfm?file=version35.pdf&prd_id=121&prv_id=137&pdf_id=35>.

———. 2007a. *Medical School Admission Requirements (MSAR) 2008–2009.* Washington, D.C.: AAMC.

———. 2007b. *Tuition and Student Fees Reports: Private Medical School—Tuition and Fees First Year Medical Students 2006–2007.* Washington, D.C.: AAMC. <http://services.aamc.org/tsfreports/report.cfm?select_control=PRI&year_of_study=2007>.

———. 2007c. *Tuition and Student Fees Reports: Public Medical Schools—Tuition And Fees First Year Medical Students 2006–2007.* Washington, D.C.: AAMC. <http://services.aamc.org/tsfreports/report.cfm?select_control=PUB&year_of_study=2007>.

Atkinson, R. C. 2001/2002. Achievement versus aptitude in college admissions. *Issues in Science and Technology.* 18(2): 31–36.

Baggaley, A. R. 1974. Academic prediction at an Ivy League college, moderated by demographic variables. *Measurement and Evaluation in Guidance.* 6: 232–235.

Baird, K. 2007. Access to college: The role of tuition, financial aid, scholastic preparation, and college supply in public college enrollments. *Journal of Student Financial Aid.* 36(3).

Baker, C. 2002. Tuition crunch; States increase prepaid college tuition plans to offset weak economy. *The Washington Times.* Dec. 3.

Barefoot, B.O. 2004. Higher education's revolving door: Confronting the problem of student drop-out in U.S. colleges and universities. *Open Learning.* 19(1): 9–18.

Baron, J., and M. Norman. 1992. SATs, achievement tests, and high-school class rank as predictors of college performance. *Educational and Psychological Measurement.* 52(4): 1047–1055.

Baum, S., and L. Lapovsky. 2006. *Tuition Discounting: Not Just a Private College Practice.* New York: College Entrance Examination Board.

Baum, S. and K. Payea. 2005. *Education Pays Update—A Supplement to Education Pays, 2004: The Benefits of Higher Education for Individuals and Society.* New York: The College Board.

Baxton, M., S.O. Ikenberry, A.M.Koenig, S. Levine, and L. Rosenberg. 2007. *The Impact of Bologna and Three-Year Degrees on U.S. Admissions.* Washington, D.C.: AACRAO.

Bell, D. 2007. Desegregation's demise. *The Chronicle of Higher Education.* 53(45): B11. Available at: <http://chronicle.com/weekly/v53/i45/45b01101.htm>.

Berker, A., and L. Horn. 2003. *Work First, Study Second: Adult Undergraduates Who Combine Employment and Postsecondary Enrollment.* NCES Publication No. 2003167. Washington, D.C.: U.S. Department of Education, National Center for Education Statistics. Accessed online at <http://nces.ed.gov/pubs2003/2003167.pdf>.

Biglan, A. 1973. The characteristics of subject matter in different academic areas. *Journal of Applied Psychology.* 57(3): 195–203.

Blackburn, R.T., and J.H. Lawrence. 1995. *Faculty at Work: Motivation, Expectation, Satisfaction.* Baltimore, MD: Johns Hopkins University Press.

Blimling, G.S. 2001. Diversity makes you smarter. *Journal of College Student Development.* 42: 517–19.

Block, S. 2002. States forced to rethink prepaid tuition plans. *USA Today.* Dec. 26: A1.

BLS. *See* Bureau of Labor Statistics.

Blumenstyk, G. 2006. The military market: As more colleges pursue service members as students, concerns grow about overly aggressive tactics. *The Chronicle of Higher Education.* 52(44): A2. Available at: <http://chronicle.com/weekly/v52/i44/44a02501.htm>.

Boggs, G.R. 2004. Community colleges in a perfect storm. *Change.* 36(6): 6.

Bontrager, B. 2006. *The Brave New World of Strategic Enrollment Management.* Preconference paper for the 16th Annual AACRAO Strategic Enrollment Management Conference, Phoenix, AZ.

Boyd, W.M, II. 1980. Black students outperform their SAT scores. Excellent secondary preparation can impart important knowledge and attitudes. *Independent School.* 39: 35–37.

Bracey, G.W. 1980. The SAT, college admissions, and the concept of talent: Unexamined myths, unexplained perceptions, needed explorations. *Phi Delta Kappan.* 62(3): 197–199.

———. 2002a. Stratification among the haves. *Phi Delta Kappan.* 3(9): 656–657.

———. 2002b. The SAT elite. *Phi Delta Kappan.* 83(5): 351–352.

Bradburn, E.M. 2002. *Short-Term Enrollment in Postsecondary Education: Student Background and Institutional Differences in Reasons for Early Departure, 1996–98.* NCES Publication No. 2003153. Washington, D.C.: U.S. Department of Education, National Center for Education Statistics. Available at: <http://nces.ed.gov/pubs2003/2003153.pdf>.

Brayboy, B.M. 1999. *Climbing the Ivy: Examining the Experiences of Academically Successful Native American Indian Undergraduates at Two Ivy League Universities.* Unpublished Dissertation, University of Pennsylvania.

Brigham, C.C. 1929. *Personal Communication.* New York.

Britz, J.D. 1998. Maguire reviews the past, forecasts the future. *The Lawlor Review.* VI(3).

Brown, J.A. 2004. Marketing and retention strategies for adult degree programs. In *Developing and Delivering Adult Degree Programs, New Directions for Adult and Continuing Education.* 103: 51–60.

Bruno, A. 2007. *Unauthorized Alien Students: Issues and "DREAM Act" Legislation.* Washington, D.C.: Library of Congress, Congressional Research Service. Available at: <www.opencrs.com/rpts/RL33863_20070130.pdf>.

Bryant, A.L. 1996. Affirmative action: 'Are we there yet?' *The Journal of College Admission.* 152/153: 48–51.

Bulkeley, D. 2006. A law granting in-state tuition to undocumented students is legally sound. *Deseret Morning News.* Feb. 2: A1. Available at: <http://deseretnews.com/dn/view/0,1249,635181044,00.html>.

Burd, S. 2006. As the volume of private loans soars, students feel the pinch. *The Chronicle of Higher Education.* 53(5): A20.

Burdman, P. 2001. A call to discard the SAT. *Black Issues in Higher Education.* 18(2): 12.

Bureau of Labor Statistics. 2008a. Health care. In *Career Guide to Industries, 2008–09 Edition.* Washington, D.C.: U.S. Department of Labor. Retrieved Jan. 31 from: <www.bls.gov/oco/cg/cgs035.htm>.

———. 2008b. Registered nurses. In *Occupational Outlook Handbook, 2008–09 Edition.* Washington, D.C.: U.S. Department of Labor. Retrieved Jan. 31 from: <www.bls.gov/oco/ocos083.htm>.

———. 2008c. Key phrases in the handbook. In *Occupational Outlook Handbook, 2008–09 Edition.* Washington, D.C.: U.S. Department of Labor. Retrieved Jan. 31 from: <www.bls.gov/oco/oco20016.htm>.

———. 2008d. Dietitians and nutritionists. In *Occupational Outlook Handbook, 2008–09 Edition.* Washington, D.C.: U.S. Department of Labor. Retrieved Jan. 31 from: <www.bls.gov/oco/ocos077.htm>.

———. 2008e. Physical therapists. In *Occupational Outlook Handbook, 2008–09 Edition.* Washington, D.C.: U.S. Department of Labor. Retrieved Jan. 31 from <www.bls.gov/oco/ocos080.htm>.

Burnham, P.S., and B.A. Hewitt. 1971. Advanced Placement scores: Their predictive validity. *Educational and Psychological Measurement.* 31: 939–945.

Burton, N.W., and L. Ramist. 2001. *Predicting Success in College: SAT Studies of Classes Graduating Since 1980.* New York: The College Board.

Cabrera, A.F., and S.M. LaNasa. 2000a. Three critical tasks America's disadvantaged face on their path to college. In *Understanding the College Choice of Disadvantaged Students,* edited by A.F. Cabrera and S.M. LaNasa. San Francisco: Jossey-Bass.

———. 2000b. Understanding the college choice process. In *Understanding the College Choice of Disadvantaged Students,* edited by A.F. Cabrera and S.M. LaNasa. San Francisco: Jossey-Bass.

Camara, W., and V. Sathy. 2004. *College Board Response to Harvard Educational Review Article by Freedle.* New York: The College Board. Available at: <www.collegeboard.com/research/pdf/051425Harvard_050406.pdf>.

Campanella, F.B. 1974. *Papers of J. Maguire.* Boston, MA.

Carnegie Foundation for the Advancement of Teaching. 1990. *Campus Life: In Search of Community.* Princeton: Princeton University Press.

———. 2001. *The Carnegie Classification of Institutions of Higher Education,* 2000 Edition. Menlo Park, CA: Carnegie Publications. Available at: <www.carnegiefoundation.org/dynamic/downloads/file_1_341.pdf>.

Carney, C.M. 1999. *Native American Higher Education in the United States.* New Brunswick, NJ: Transaction Publishers.

Castillo, J. 1982. Spiritual foundations of Indian success. *American Indian Culture and Research Journal.* 6(3): 15–34.

Cavanagh, S. 2002. Colleges increasingly look to attract gay, lesbian applicants. *Education Week.* 21(41): 12.

CAWMSET. *See* Commission on the Advancement of Women and Minorities in Science, Engineering and Technology Development.

Champagne, D., and J. Stauss. 2002. *Native American Studies in Higher Education: Models for Collaboration Between Universities and Indigenous Nations.* Walnut Creek: Alta Mira Press.

Chapman, D.W. 1981. A model of student college choice. *The Journal of Higher Education.* 52(2): 490–505.

CHEA. *See* Council for Higher Education Accreditation.

Choy, S.P. 2000. *Low-Income Students: Who They Are and How They Pay for Their Education*. NCES Publication No. 2000169. Washington, D.C.: U.S. Department of Education, National Center for Education Statistics. Available at: <http://nces.ed.gov/pubs2000/2000169.pdf>.

———. 2001. *Students Whose Parents Did Not Go to College: Postsecondary Access, Persistence, and Attainment*. NCES Publication No. 2001126. Washington, D.C.: U.S. Department of Education, National Center for Education Statistics. Available at: <http://nces.ed.gov/pubs2001/2001126.pdf>.

———. 2004. *Paying for College: Changes between 1990 and 2000 for Full-time Dependent Undergraduates*. NCES Publication No. 2004075. Washington, D.C.: U.S. Department of Education, National Center for Educational Statistics. Available at: <http://nces.ed.gov/pubs2004/2004075.pdf>.

Choy, S.P., L. Horn, A. Nunez, and X. Chen. 2000. Transition to college: What helps at-risk students and students whose parents did not attend college. In *Understanding the College Choice of Disadvantaged Students*, edited by A.F. Cabrera and S.M. LaNasa. San Francisco: Jossey-Bass.

Ciffarelli, P., and M. Cullen. 2004. Technology and student marketing. In *Student Marketing for Colleges and Universities*, edited by Richard Whiteside. Washington, D.C.: AACRAO.

Clark, A. 2006. *Letters and Sciences Retreat Explores Effect of Privatization on Public Universities*. Sept. 1, News Release. University of Wisconsin-Whitewater. Available at: <www.uww.edu/marketingandmedia/news_releases/2006_09_letters_and_sciences_r.html>.

Clark, K. 2006. Uncovering the many secrets of financial aid. *U.S. News & World Report*. Sept. 18, Money & Business Section. Available at: <www.usnews.com/usnews/biztech/articles/060910/18main.htm>.

———. 2007. *Who, How and Why to Evaluate Offer Letters*. Available at: <www.financialaidletter.com>.

Cokely, K.O. 2001. Gender differences among African American students in the impact of racial identity on academic psychosocial development. *Journal of College Student Development* 42(5): 480–487.

Coleman, A.R., and S.R. Palmer. 2007. A more circuitous path to racial diversity. *The Chronicle of Higher Education*. 53(45): B10. Available at: <http://chronicle.com/weekly/v53/i45/45b01001.htm>.

College Board and NASFAA. 2002. *Financial Aid Professionals at Work in 1999–2000: Results from the 2001 Survey of Undergraduate Financial Aid Policies, Practices, and Procedures*. New York and Washington, D.C.: College Board and National Association of Student Aid Administrators.

College Board. 1997. *A Report on the College Board Colloqium on the Role of Ethics in Enrollment Management and Financial Aid*. New York: College Entrance Examination Board.

———. 2003. *Challenging times, clear choices: An action agenda for college access and success*. Available at: <www.pathwaystocollege.net/pdf/NDSFA_ActionAgenda.pdf>.

———. 2004a. *2004 College Bound Seniors: A Profile of SAT Program Test Takers*. Available from <www.collegeboard.com/prod_downloads/about/news_info/cbsenior/yr2004/2004_CBSNR_total_group.pdf>.

———. 2004b. *Average SAT Scores Vary with Parental Education*. Retrieved January 11, 2005 from <www.collegeboard.com/prod_downloads/about/news_info/cbsenior/yr2004/graph_14_average_sat_scores_parental_education.pdf>.

———. 2005a. *Trends in Student Aid*. New York: College Entrance Examination Board.

———. 2005b. *Trends in College Pricing*. New York: College Entrance Examination Board.

———. 2005c. *SAT Reasoning Test*. Available at: <www.collegeboard.com/prof/counselors/tests/sat/about/about_sat.html>.

———. 2006a. *Trends in Student Aid*. New York: College Board. Available at: <www.collegeboard.com/prod_downloads/press/cost06/trends_aid_06.pdf>.

———. 2006b. *Trends in College Pricing*. New York: College Board. Available at: <www.collegeboard.com/prod_downloads/press/cost06/trends_college_pricing_06.pdf>.

———. 2006c. *Access and Diversity Collaborative*. Available at: <www.collegeboard.com/highered/ad/best/best/html>.

———. 2007. *The College Board Announces States' Results in the 2007 Advanced Placement Report to the Nation: A Larger Percentage of High School Graduates Achieve High AP® Standards*. Available at: <www.collegeboard.com/press/releases/152694.html>.

———. 2008a. *AP: Fees* (Web page). Retrieved Jan. 28 from: <www.collegeboard.com/about/news_info/ap/faqs.html>.

———. 2008b. *AP Course Audit Information* (Web page). Retrieved Jan. 28 from: <http://apcentral.collegeboard.com/apc/public/courses/teachers_corner/46361.html>.

Collins, J. 2001. *Good to Great*. New York: Harper Business.

Con, W.H., and J. Hardy. 1978. School university network: Toward a model of articulation. *North Carolina Association Quarterly*.

Conner, J.D. 1979. History and responsibilities of the American Association of Collegiate Registrars and Admissions Officers. In *Admissions, Academic Records, and Registrar Services,* edited by C.J. Quann, San Francisco: Jossey-Bass.

Connerly, W. 2000/2002. *Creating Equal.* San Francisco: Encounter Books.

Constance, C.L. 1973. *Historical Review of the Association.* Washington, D.C.: AACRAO.

Cook, J.D. 2002. Searching for gay-friendly colleges: How guidance counselors can help their gay students. *Journal of College Admission*. 177: 9–12.

Cooper, P.P. 2002. Billions flow into 529 accounts, as returns flunk math for college. *The Philadelphia Inquirer*. Nov. 3: E1.

Cornwell, C., and D.B. Mustard. 2005. *Merit Aid and Sorting: The Effects of HOPE-Style Scholarships on College Ability Stratification*. Research Paper, University of Georgia Terry College of Business, October.

Cornwell, C., D.B. Mustard, and J.S. Deeper. 2006. The enrollment effects of merit-based financial aid: Evidence from Georgia's HOPE program. *Journal of Labor Economics*. 24(4): 761–786.

Council for Higher Education Accreditation. 2005. *Almanac of External Quality Review 2005*. Washington, D.C.: CHEA.

Craig, T. 2007. Virginia Republican bill would bar illegal immigrants from college. *The Washington Post*. August 30: A1. Available at: <www.washingtonpost.com/wp-dyn/content/article/2007/08/29/AR2007082901619_pf.html>.

Creighton, S., and L. Hudson. 2002. *Participation Trends and Patterns in Adult Education: 1991–1999*. NCES Publication No. 2002119. Washington, D.C.: U.S. Department of Education, National Center for Education Statistics. Available at: <http://nces.ed.gov/pubs2002/2002119.pdf>.

Crouse, J. 1985. Does the SAT help colleges make better admissions decisions? *Harvard Educational Review*. 55: 195–219.

Crouse, J., and D. Trusheim. 1988. *The Case Against the SAT*. Chicago: The University of Chicago Press.

———. 1991. How colleges can correctly determine selection benefits from the SAT. *Harvard Educational Review*. 61(2): 125–147.

CRUX Research. 2007. *College Admissions Officers Research Summary*. Honeoye Falls, NY: Crux.

Cubin, D., G. May, and E. Babcock. 2006. Diversifying the engineering workforce. *Journal of Engineering Education*. 94: 73–86.

Cuyjet, M.J. 1997. African American men on college campuses: Their needs and their perceptions. In *Helping African American Men Succeed in College: New Directions for Student Services*, No. 80, edited by M.J. Cuyjet. San Francisco: Jossey-Bass.

———. 2006. African American college men: Twenty-first-century issues and concerns. In *African American Men in College*, edited by M.J. Cuyjet. San Francisco: Jossey-Bass.

Dale, A. 2007. Kiddie tax hits college, law that shuts a loophole spurs shift to 529 plans. *The Wall Street Journal*. June 16: B2.

Dale, M. 2003. IRS OKs new type of tuition savings plan, *Associated Press*. Feb. 15.

Danenberg, M. 2007. *Private Loans*. Available at: <www.newamerica.net/blogs/2006/11/buried_data_on_student_loan_borrowing >.

Dartmouth College. 2006. *Native American Program*, (Web page). Available at: <www.dartmouth.edu/~nap/>.

Davis, R.J. 2000. *Status of Admissions Policies and Practices at Four-Year Public Institutions of Higher Education in Virginia Implemented to Evaluate Home School Applicants*. Dissertation Abstracts International (UMI No. 9974201). Available at: <http://scholar.lib.vt.edu/theses/available/etd-04212000-14230017/>.

Davis, R.D. 2004. *Black Students' Perceptions: The Complexity of Persistence to Graduation at an American University*. New York: Peter Lang.

DeBerard, M.S., G.I. Spielmans, and D.L. Julka. 2004. Predictors of academic achievement and retention among college freshman: A longitudinal study. *College Student Journal*. 38(1): 66–80.

*Deficit Reduction Act of 2004*, Pub. L. 109–171, 29 Stat. 4 (2006).

*DeFunis v. Odegaard*, 416 U.S. 312 (1974).

Deming, W.E. 1986. *Out of the Crisis*. Cambridge, MA: MIT Press.

Dennis, M.J. 1998. *A Practical Guide to Enrollment and Retention Management in Higher Education*. Westport: Bergin & Garvey.

Dew, J.R., and M.M. Nearing. 2004. *Continuous Quality Improvement in Higher Education*. Westport, CT: American Council on Education/Praeger Series on Higher Education.

Deyhle, D. 1995. Navajo youth and Anglo racism: Cultural integrity and resistance. *Harvard Educational Review.* 65(3): 403–444.

Deyhle, D., and K. Swisher. 1997. Research in American Indian and Alaska Native education: From assimilation to self-determination. *Review of Research in Education.* 22(1): 113–194.

DiPaolo, T. 2006. Transfer and articulation. In *The Registrar's Guide: Evolving Best Practices in Records and Registration,* edited by B. Lauren. Washington, D.C.: American Association of Collegiate Registrars and Admissions Officers.

Dixon, G., and R. Kanoy. 2005. A collaborative effort to improve access to higher education: A successful state-wide approach. AACRAO 91st Annual Meeting, New York.

Dodd, B.G., S.J. Fitzpatrick, R.J. De Ayala, and J.A. Jennings. 2002. *An Investigation of the Validity of AP Grades of 3 and a Comparison of AP and Non-AP Student Groups.* Report No. 2002–9. New York: College Board. Available at: <www.collegeboard.com/research/pdf/Research%20Report%202002–9%20v2.pdf>.

Dolence, M.G. 1993. *Strategic Enrollment Management: A Primer for Campus Administrators.* Washington, D.C.: American Association of Collegiate Registrars and Admissions Officers.

———. 1999. Phone interview with S.E. Henderson. Cincinnati, OH.

Dorans, N.J. 2004. Further comment. *Harvard Educational Review.* 74(1): 62.

Dougherty, C., L. Mellor, and S. Jiana. 2006. *The Relationship between Advanced Placement and College Graduation.* Austin, TX: National Center for Educational Accountability. Available at: <www.just4kids.org/en/files/Publication-The_Relationship_between_Advanced_Placement_and_College_Graduation-02-09-06.pdf>.

Doyle, W.R., J.A. Delaney, and B.A. Naughton. 2004. Institutions amplifying state policy: How public colleges award institutional aid. *Change.* 36(4): 36–41.

Drucker, P. 1998. *Peter Drucker on the Profession of Management.* Cambridge, MA: Harvard Business School Press.

Duderstadt, J.J. 2005. *The Crisis in Financing Public Higher Education—and a Possible Solution: A 21st C Learn Grant Act.* Available at: <http://milproj.ummu.umich.edu/publications/financing_pub_univ/>.

Dungy, G.J. 1996. Community & diversity: A compelling interest. *The Journal of College Admission.* 152/153: 52–57.

Dynarski, S.M. 2002. The behavioral and distributional implications of aid for college. *American Economic Review.* 92(2): 279–285.

Dynarski, S.M. 2004. The new merit aid. In *College Choices: the Economics of Where to Go, When to Go, and How to Pay for It,* edited by C.M. Hoxby. Chicago: University of Chicago Press.

Dynarski, S.M., and J.E. Scott-Clayton. 2006. *The Feasibility of Delivering Aid for College through the Tax System.* National Tax Association Annual Conference, Nov. 17.

ED. *See* U.S. Department of Education.

The Education Trust. 1999. Ticket to nowhere: The gap between leaving high school and entering college and high-performance jobs. *Thinking K–16.* 3(2): 10.

Einhaus, C. 2000. *The Q & A for LBGTAs at Western Michigan University* (pamphlet). Fort Collins, CO: Colorado State University.

———. 2001. *Searching for a Gay-Friendly College: Measuring the Campus Climate for Bisexual, Gay, Lesbian, Transgender and Ally Students* (pamphlet). Fort Collins, CO: Colorado State University.

———. 2003. *Admissions Comes Out: Recruiting Lesbian, Bisexual, Gay and Transgender Students.* Presented at the American Association of College Registrars and Admissions Officers international meeting, Washington, D.C., April 6–9.

Elliott, R., and A. C. Strenta. 1988. Effects of improving the reliability of the GPA on prediction generally and on comparative predictions for gender and race particularly. *Journal of Educational Measurement.* 25: 333–347.

Evans, A.J. 2003. How and why to admit home-educated students. *SACRAO Journal.* 16: 27–30.

———. 2005. *A Case Study of the Benefits of Accreditation for Home Study Programs for Access to Higher Education in Georgia.* Doctoral dissertation submitted to the Graduate School of The University of Georgia. Available at: <www.kennesaw.edu/admissions/presentations/Angela%20Evans%20Dissertation%20PDF.pdf>.

Ewing, M. 2006. The AP Program and student outcomes: A summary of research. *Research Notes.* RN-29(November). New York: The College Board. Available at: <www.collegeboard.com/research/pdf/RN-29.pdf>.

Experience, Inc. 2006. *Sharing Photos and Writing Blogs: How College Students are Using the Internet.* July 19, Press Release. Available at: <www.experience.com/corp/press_release?id=press_release_1152733240076&channel_id=about_us&page_id=media_coverage_news&tab=cn1>.

Farmer-Hinton, R., and T.L. Adams. 2006. Social capital and college preparation: Exploring the role of counselors in a college prep school for Black students. *The Negro Educational Review.* 57(1/2): 101–116.

Farrell, E.F. 2007. Tangled up in tech: Admissions people grapple with the promises and pitfalls of electronic recruiting. *The Chronicle of Higher Education.* 53(28). Available at: <www.chronicle.com/weekly/v53/i28a03601.htm>.

Farver, A., W. Sedlacek, and G. Brooks. 1975. Longitudinal prediction of university grades for Blacks and Whites. *Measurement and Evaluation in Guidance*. 7: 243–250.

Felder, R.M., G.N. Felder, M. Mauney, C.E. Hamrin, and E.J. Dietz. 1994. *Gender Differences in Student Performances and Attitudes: A Longitudinal Study of Engineering Student Performance and Retention*. Report No. NCSU-94A. Raliegh: North Carolina State University. Available at: <www.eric.ed.gov/ERICWebPortal/contentdelivery/servlet/ERICServlet?accno=ED368553>.

Fine, B. 1956. Advance [sic] Placement Program for freshmen in colleges promises several advantages. *The New York Times*. July 29: E9.

Fischer, K. 2005. Washington Legal Foundation challenges immigrant-tuition laws. *The Chronicle of Higher Education*. 52(5): A34. Available at: <http://chronicle.com/weekly/v52/i05/05a03401.htm>.

Fishman, J.A. 1958. Some social psychological theory for selecting and guiding college students. In *The American College: A Psychological and Social Interpretation of Higher Learning*, edited by N. Sanford. New York: John Wiley and Sons.

Fleming, J., and N. Garcia. 1998. Are standardized tests fair to African Americans? Predictive validity of the SAT in Black and White colleges. *Journal of Higher Education*. 69: 471–495.

Flowers, L.A. 2004. Retaining African-American students in higher education: An integrative review. *Journal of College Student Retention*. 6(1): 23–35.

Floyd, D.L., M.L. Skolnik, and K.P. Walker. 2005. *The Community College Baccalaureate: Emerging Trends and Policy Issues*. Sterling, VA: Stylus Publications.

Fox, M.J.T., S.C. Lowe, and G.S. McClellan. 2005. *Serving Native American Students: New Directions for Student Services*, No. 109. San Francisco: Jossey-Bass.

Frankie, C. 2002. Saving for college not as simple as 5–2–9. *Mutual Fund Market News*. Dec. 9.

Freedle, R.O. 2003. Correcting the SAT's ethnic and social-class bias: A method for reestimating SAT scores. *Harvard Educational Review*. 73(1): 1–43.

Fritz, W. 2001. *Enrollment Management Strategic Plan 2001*. Retrieved Jan. 11, 2005 from: <http://www2.gsu.edu/~wwwugs/EMGStrategicPlan.htm>.

Fry, R. 2003. *Hispanics in College: Participation and Degree Attainment*. ERIC Digest No. 187. New York, NY: ERIC Clearinghouse on Urban Education. Available at: <www.eric.ed.gov/ERICWebPortal/contentdelivery/servlet/ERICServlet?accno=ED480917>.

Fuerbringer, J. 2003. Yes, bonds trumped stocks, again, savor it and move on. *The New York Times*. Jan. 2: C8. Available at: <http://query.nytimes.com/gst/fullpage.html?res=9C0oE6D6133FF931A35752C0A9659C8B63>.

Galloway, R.A.S. 1995. *Home Schooled Adults: Are They Ready for College?* Paper presented at the Annual Meeting of the American Educational Research Association, San Francisco, CA.

Gandara, P., and J. Moreno. 2002. Introduction: The Puente Project: Issues and perspectives on preparing Latino youth for higher education. *Educational Policy*. 16(4): 463–473.

Garay, A. 2007. Immigrant veterans suing over denial of tuition waiver. *Associated Press*. June 29. Available at: <http://parentstudentloans.wordpress.com/2007/06/29/>.

Garrett, M.T., and E.F. Pichette. 2000. Red as an apple: Native American acculturation and counseling with or without reservation. *Journal of Counseling & Development*. 78(1): 3–13.

Gay, Lesbian and Straight Education Network. 2002a. *Finding an LGBT Friendly Campus: A Guide for LBGT Students Pursuing Higher Education*. New York: GLSEN. Available at: <www.glsen.org/binary-data/GLSEN_ATTACHMENTS/file/200-1.pdf>.

———. 2002b. *Finding an LGBT-Friendly Campus: A Guide for Counselors Advising LGBT Students Pursuing Higher Education*. New York: GLSEN. Available at: <www.glsen.org/binary-data/GLSEN_ATTACHMENTS/file/199-1.pdf>.

Gay, Lesbian and Straight Education Network and American Civil Liberties Union. 2001. *Common Questions and Answers About Gay-Straight Alliances*. GLSEN website. Available at: <www.glsen.org/binary-data/GLSEN_ATTACHMENTS/file/170-1.pdf>.

Geiser, S., and V. Santelices. 2004. *The Role of Advanced Placement and Honors Courses in College Admissions*. Berkeley: University of California. Available at: <www.eric.ed.gov/ERICWebPortal/contentdelivery/servlet/ERICServlet?accno=ED492533>.

Georgia Home Education Association. 2007. *Georgia State Laws* (Web page). Brooks, GA: GHEA. Retrieved Jan. 13 from: <www.ghea.org/pages/resources/stateLaw.php>.

Gerald, D.E., and W.J. Hussar. 2002. *Projections of Education Statistics to 2012*. NCES Publication No. 2002030. Washington, D.C.: U.S. Department of Education, National Center for Education Statistics. Available at: <http://nces.ed.gov/pubs2002/2002030.pdf>.

Gertner, J. 2006. Forgive us our student debts. *New York Times Magazine*. June 11: 60–68.

GHEA. *See* Georgia Home Education Association.

Gilmour, D.J. 2000. Challenges and costs rise for colleges. *Community College Week*. 13(9): 4.

Gladieux, L.E. 2004. Low-income students and the affordability of higher education. In *America's Untapped Resource: Low-Income Students in Higher Education*, edited by R.D. Kahlenberg. New York: Century Foundation.

Glater, J.D. 2007. Colleges charging more for some majors. *The Seattle Times*. July 29, Nation & World section. Available at: <http://seattletimes.nwsource.com/html/nationworld/2003810981_tuition290.html>.

Glover, J.R., J.L. Ruchhoeft, J.M. Trenor, S.A. Long, and F.J. Claydon. 2005. *Girls Reaching and Demonstrating Excellence (GRADE) Camps: An Innovative Recruiting Strategy at the University of Houston to Increase Female Representation in Engineering*. Proceedings of the 2005 American Society for Engineering Education Annual Conference and Exhibition, Portland, OR (June).

GLSEN. *See* Gay, Lesbian and Straight Education Network.

Glynn, J.G., P.L. Sauer, and T.E. Miller. 2003. Signaling student retention with prematriculation data. *NASPA Journal*. 41(1): 41–67.

Golden, D. 2006. *The Price of Admission*. New York: Crown Publishers.

Gonzalez, K.P., C. Stone, and J.E. Jovel. 2003. Examining the role of social capital in access to college for Latinas: Toward a college opportunity framework. *Journal of Hispanic Higher Education*. 2: 166–170.

Goodman, I., and C. Cunningham. 2002. *Final Report of the Women's Experiences in College Engineering (WECE) Project*. Cambridge, MA: Goodman Research Group, Inc. Available at: <www.grginc.com/WECE_FINAL_REPORT.pdf>.

Goral, T. 2003. Is discounting dangerous? *University Business*. 6(8): 22–27.

Gray, D.W. 1998. *A Study of the Academic Achievements of Homeschooled Students Who Have Matriculated into Post-Secondary Institutions*. DAI, 59, 021, 0418. Doctoral Dissertation, University of Sarasota, Sarasota, FL.

Green, C.A. 1990. Targeting new markets. In *Managing Change in Higher Education: New Directions for Higher Education*, No. 71, pp. 79–89, edited by D.W. Steeples. San Francisco: Jossey-Bass.

Green, P., B. Dugoni, and S. Ingels. 1995. *Trends Among High School Seniors, 1972–1992*. NCES Publication No. 95380. Washington, D.C.: U.S. Department of Education, National Center for Education Statistics. Available at: <http://nces.ed.gov/pubs95/95380.pdf>.

Groner, J. 2003. In 'Grutter v. Bollinger' amicus avalanche, one brief stood out. *Legal Times*. July 2. Available at <www.law.com/jsp/article.jsp?id=1056139919083>.

Grose, T.K. 2006. Trouble on the horizon. *Prism*. 16(2): 26–31.

*Grutter v. Bollinger*, 539 U.S. 306 (2003).

*Grutter v. Bollinger*, Civil Action No. 97-CV-75928-DT (2001).

Guiffrida, D. 2005. To break away or strengthen ties to home: A complex issue for African American college students attending a predominantly White institution. *Equity and Excellence in Education*. 38(1): 49–60.

HACU. *See* Hispanic Association of Colleges and Universities.

Hadfield, J. 2003. Recruiting and Retaining Adult Students. In *Meeting the Special Needs of Adult Students: New Directions for Student Services*, No. 102, edited by D. Kilgore and P.J. Rice. San Francisco: Jossey-Bass.

Hagedorn, L.S. 2005. Square pegs: Adult students and their "fit" in postsecondary institutions. *Change*. 37(1): 22–28.

Hand, C.A., and J.E. Prather. 1985. *The Predictive Validity of Scholastic Aptitude Test Scores for Minority College Students*. Paper presented at the annual meeting of the American Educational Research Association, in Chicago, IL.

Harris, P.M., N.A. Jones. 2005. *We the People: Pacific Islanders in the United States*. Washington, D.C.: U.S. Census Bureau. Available at: <www.census.gov/prod/2005pubs/censr-26.pdf>.

Hatfield, K.M. 2003. Funding higher education for adult students. In *Meeting the Special Needs of Adult Students: New Directions for Student Services*, No. 102, edited by D. Kilgore and P.J. Rice. San Francisco: Jossey-Bass.

Haycock, K. 2006. *Promise Abandoned: How Policy Choices and Institutional Practices Restrict College Opportunities*. Washington, D.C.: The Education Trust. Available at: <www2.edtrust.org/NR/rdonlyres/B6772F1A-116D-4827-A326-F8CFAD33975A/0/PromiseAbandonedHigherEd.pdf>.

Head, J.F., and T.M. Hughes. 2004. Freshman Admissions Predictor: An interactive self-help web counseling service. *College and University*. 80(2): 49–52.

Head, J.F., and A.J. Evans. 2000. Adventures with home schoolers: A decade of non-traditional admissions. *On Target*. 12(Fall): 27–31.

Hearn, J.C. 2001. The paradox of growth in federal aid for college students: 1965–1990. In *The Finance of Higher Education: Theory, Research, Policy, and Practice*, edited by M.B. Paulsen and J.C. Smart. New York: Agathon.

Hebel, S. 2003. Percentage admission plans fall short as substitutes for affirmative action, Harvard Reports Say. *The Chronicle of Higher Education*. Feb. 11. Available at: <http://chronicle.com/daily/2003/02/2003021102n.htm>.

———. 2006. California judge rejects challenge to the state's immigration law. *The Chronicle of Higher Education*. Available at: <http://chronicle.com/daily/2006/10/2006101102n.htm>.

Hegen, D. 2007. *Overview of State Legislation Related to Immigration and Immigrants in 2007*. April 18. Washington, D.C.: National Conference of State Legislatures. Retrieved Jan. 16, 2008 from: <www.ncsl.org/programs/immig/2007StateLegislationImmigration.htm>.

Heller, D.E. 2006. The elephant in the student aid office. *Inside Higher Ed*. Sept. 25. Available at: <http://insidehighered.com/views/2006/09/25/heller>.

Henderson, S.E. 1998. A historical view of an admissions dilemma: Seeking quantity or quality in the student body. In *Handbook for the College Admissions Profession*, edited by C.C. Swann and S.E. Henderson. Westport, CT: Greenwood Press.

———. 2001. On the brink of a profession. In *The Strategic Enrollment Management Revolution*, edited by J. Black. Washington, D.C.: American Association of Collegiate Registrars and Admissions Officers.

———. 2005. Refocusing enrollment management: Losing structure and finding the academic context. *College and University*. 80(3): 3–8.

Henig, S. 2007. Colleges reach out to American Indians. *The Chronicle of Higher Education*. 53(4): A39. Available at: <http://chronicle.com/weekly/v53/i04/04a03901.htm>.

Henriksen, J.A.S. 1995. *The Influence of Race and Ethnicity on Access to Postsecondary Education and the College Experience*. ERIC Digest ED386242. Available at: <www.eric.ed.gov/ERICWebPortal/contentdelivery/servlet/ERICServlet?accno=ED386242>.

Herdt, G.H., and A. Boxer. 1996. *Children of the Horizons*, 2nd Edition. Boston: Beacon Press.

Herrnstein, R., and C. Murray. 1994. *Bell Curve: Intelligence and Class Structure in American Life*. New York: The Free Press.

Hill, C.B., and G.C. Winston. 2006. How scarce are high-ability, low-income students? In *College Access: Opportunity or Privilege?*, edited by M.S. McPherson and M.O. Schapiro. New York: College Board.

Hill, M. 2002. Pennsylvania's pledge to back college-tuition plan is not a guarantee. *Philadelphia Inquirer*. Nov. 3: E2.

Hilliard, A. 1990. Limitations of current academic achievement measures. In *Going to School: The African American Experience*, edited by K. Lomotley. Albany, New York: State University of New York Press.

Hispanic Association of Colleges and Universities. 1997. *HSI & Percentage of Hispanics* (Web page). San Antonio, TX: HACU. Retrieved 10 Jan. from: <www.hacu.net/hacu/HSI__Percentage_of_Hispanics_EN.asp?SnID=2061312409>.

———. 2002. *The Increasing Presence of Hispanics and Hispanic-Serving Institutions*. San Antonio, TX: The Hispanic Association of Colleges and Universities.

———. 2007. *Hispanic-Serving Institution Definitions*, Web page. San Antonio, TX: HACU. Retrieved 10 Jan. from: <www.hacu.net/hacu/HSI_Definition_EN.asp?SnID=1890560310>.

Hofmeister, S.1995. A bankruptcy peculiar to California. *The New York Times*. Jan. 6: D1. Available at: <http://query.nytimes.com/gst/fullpage.html?res=990CEED9143DF935A35752C0A963958260>.

Holsendolph, E. 2005. The costly college game. *Black Issues in Higher Education*. 22(6): 22–24.

Home School Legal Defense Association. 2007a. *You Can Homeschool—The Big Questions* (Web page). Purcellville, VA: HSLDA. Retrieved Jan. 13 from: <www.youcanhomeschool.org/starthere/questions.asp>.

———. 2007b. *Home School Laws* (Web page). Purcellville, VA: HSLDA. Retrieved Jan. 13 from: <www.hslda.org/laws/>.

Hopfensperger, J. 2007. Immigration proposals clash; The Governor and DFL lawmakers offered differing views on issues involving the state's immigrants. *(Minneapolis) Star Tribune*. February 15: 5B.

Horn, L., E.M. Cataldi, E. Forrest, and A. Sikora. 2005. *Waiting to Attend College: Undergraduates Who Delay Their Postsecondary Enrollment*. NCES Publication No. 2005152. Washington, D.C.: U.S. Department of Education, National Center for Education Statistics. Available at: <http://nces.ed.gov/pubs2005/2005152.pdf>.

Hossler, D. 1986. *Creating Effective Enrollment Management Systems*. New York: College Entrance Examination Board.

———. 2000. Effective admissions recruitment. In *Promising Practices in Recruitment, Remediation, and Retention: New Directions for Higher Education*, No. 108, edited by G.H. Gaither. San Francisco: Jossey-Bass.

———. 2006. Students and families as revenue: The impact on institutional behaviors. In *Privatization and Public Universities*, edited by D.M. Priest and E.P. St. John. Bloomington: Indiana University Press.

Hossler, D., and K.S. Gallager. 1987. Studying student college choice: A three-phase model and the implications for policymakers. *College and University.* 62(3): 207–221.

Hossler, D., J. Braxton, and G. Coopersmith. 1989. Understanding student college choice. In *Higher Education: Handbook of Theory and Research*, Vol. V, edited by J.C. Smart. New York: Agathon Press.

Hossler, D., J. Schmit, and N. Vesper. 1999. *Going to College: How Social, Economic and Educational Factors Influence the Decisions Students Make.* Baltimore: The Johns Hopkins Press.

Hossler, D., and J.P. Bean and Associates. 1990. *The Strategic Planning of College Enrollments.* San Francisco: Jossey-Bass.

Hrabe, F.L. 2002. Is the welcome mat out? *College and University.* 77(4): 35–7.

Hrabowski, F.A., III, K.I. Maton, and G.L. Greif. 1998. *Beating the Odds: Raising Academically Successful African American Males.* New York: Oxford University Press.

Hrabowski, F.A., III., K.I. Maton, M.L. Greene, and G.L. Greif. 2002. *Overcoming the Odds: Raising Academically Successful African American Young Women.* New York: Oxford University Press.

HSLDA. *See* Home School Legal Defense Association.

Hubbard, L. 1999. College aspirations among low-income African American high school students: Gendered strategies for success. *Anthropology & Education Quarterly.* 30(3): 363–383.

Hubbell, L.L., and Lapovsky, L. 2005. *Tuition Discounting: 15 Years in Perspective.* Washington, D.C.: National Association of College and University Business Officers. Retrieved from: <www.nacubo.org/x6363.xml>.

Hudson, L. 2003. *Racial/Ethnic Differences in the Path to a Postsecondary Credential.* NCES Publication No. 2003005. Washington, D.C.: U.S. Department of Education, National Center for Educational Statistics. Available at: <http://nces.ed.gov/pubs2003/2003005.pdf>.

Hughes, S. 2005. Utah 529 plan settles SEC charges. *Wall Street Journal.* Aug. 5: A1.

Hugo, E. 2001. Dual enrollment for underrepresented student populations. In *Systems for Offering Concurrent Enrollment at High Schools and Community Colleges: New Directions for Community Colleges*, No. 113, edited by P.F. Robertson, B.G. Chapman, and F. Gaskin. San Francisco, CA: Jossey-Bass.

Hunter, J., and W. Samter. 2000. A college admission test protocol to mitigate the effects of false negative SAT scores. *Journal of College Admission.* (168): 22–29.

Hurley, D. 2007. The path to prosperity: A policy of investment. *Policy Matters.* May. Available at: <www.aascu.org/policy_matters/pdf/may2007.pdf>.

Hurley, J.F. 2001. 529 and Medicaid. *529 E-ditorial* (No. 01–4). May 18. Available at: <www.savingforcollege.com/top-tip/editorial.php?editorial_id=27>.

———. 2002a. *The Best Way to Save for College: A Complete Guide to 529 Plans.* Pittsford, NY: Bonacom Publications.

———. 2002b. Whither individual funds? *529 E-ditorial* (No. 02–8). Oct. 17. Available at: <www.savingforcollege.com/529_monthly_columns/editorial.php?editorial_id=43>.

———. 2002c. *The Hurley Report on College Investing.* Issue 3 (Oct.).

———. 2002d. *The Hurley Report on College Investing.* Issue 6 (Dec.).

———. 2002e. Making the right year-end moves. *529 E-ditorial* (No. 02–9). Nov. 20. Available at: <www.savingfor college.com/529_monthly_columns/editorial.php?editorial_id=44>.

———. 2007. *The Best Way to Save for College: A Complete Guide to 529 Plans*, 7th Edition. Pittsford, NY: Savingforcollege.com, LLC.

Hurtado, S. 1997. Differences in college access and choice among racial-ethnic groups: Identifying continuing barriers. *Research in Higher Education.* 38(1): 43–75.

Hurtado, S., K.K. Inkelas, C. Brigs, and B. Rhee. 1997. Differences on college access and choice among racial/ethnic groups: Identifying continuing barriers. *Research in Higher Education.* 38(1): 43–71.

Husson, W.J., and T. Kennedy. Developing and maintaining accelerated degree programs within traditional institutions. In *The University's Role in Economic Development: From Research to Outreach: New Directions for Adult and Continuing Education*, No. 97, edited by J.P. Pappas. San Francisco: Jossey-Bass.

IBO. *See* International Baccalaureate Organization.

Ihlanfeldt, W. 1980. *Achieving* Optimal Enrollments and Tuition Revenues. San Francisco: Jossey-Bass.

Internal Revenue Service. 2007. *Tax Benefits for Education.* Publication 970, Cat. No. 25221V. Washington, D.C.: U.S. Department of the Treasury, IRS. Available at: <www.irs.gov/pub/irs-pdf/p970.pdf>.

International Baccalaureate Organization. 2002a. *A Basis for Practice: The Diploma Programme.* Geneva: IBO. Available at: <www.ibo.org/diploma/documents/basis_diploma.pdf>.

———. 2002b. *Schools Guide to The Diploma Programme*. Geneva: IBO. Available at: <www.ibo.org/diploma/documents/schools_guide_diploma.pdf>.

———. 2006a. *U.S. Department of Education Awards IBNA $1.08 Million* (News Release). September 13, 2006. See <www.ibo.org/media/pressreleasesep1306.cfm>.

———. 2006b. *A Guide to the IB Diploma Programme for Universities & Colleges*. New York: IBO. Available at: <www.ibo.org/diploma/recognition/guide/documents/UniversityGuideToDP.pdf>.

———. 2006c. *IBNA Examination Review & Data Summary 2006: Profile of Diploma Programme Test Takers*. New York: IBO. Available at: <www.ibo.org/ibna/elibrary/documents/IB_data_summary_06.pdf>.

———. 2007. *IBNA Examination Review & Data Summary 2007: Profile of Diploma Programme Test Takers*. New York: IBO. Available at: <www.ibo.org/ibna/elibrary/documents/DataSummary.2007.FINAL_000.pdf>.

———. 2008. *Mission and Strategy* (Web page). Retrieved Jan. 30 from: <www.ibo.org/mission/>.

IRS. See Internal Revenue Service.

Jackson, J. 2000. Speech made at the 2000 National Democratic Convention, Los Angeles, CA, August 15, 2000. *Cable News Network*. Available at: <www.cnn.com/ELECTION/2000/conventions/democratic/transcripts/u060815.html>.

Jackson, S.A. 2002. *The Quiet Crisis: Falling Short in Producing American Scientific and Technical Talent*. Available at: <www.bestworkforce.org/PDFdocs/Quiet_Crisis.pdf>.

Jacobs, W. R. 1995. Is the SAT fair? Journal of College Admis*sions*. 146(Winter): 22–31.

Jaschik, S. 2007a. Rebound in higher ed support. *Inside Higher Ed*. March 8. Available at: <http://insidehighered.com/news/2007/03/08/sheeo>.

———. 2007b. New standard for getting in. *Inside Higher Ed*. July 6. Available at: <http://insidehighered.com/news/2007/07/06/ppi>.

Jencks, C., and J. Crouse. 1985. Aptitude vs. achievement: Should we replace the SAT? *The Public Interest*. (67): 21–35.

Jenkins, T.P. 1998. *The Performance of Home Schooled Students in Community Colleges*. Doctoral Dissertation, Texas A&M University–Commerce.

Jennings, B.M., and M.A. Olivas. 2000. *Prepaying & Saving for College: Opportunities and Issues*. Policy Perspectives No. 3. New York: College Board. Available at: <www.eric.ed.gov/ericwebportal/contentdelivery/servlet/ericservlet?accno=ed440567>.

Jolliffe, D.A. 2007. Personal communication. June 27.

Joly, K. 2006. License to recruit? *University Business*. August. Available at: <www2.universitybusiness.com/ViewArticle.aspx?articleid=281>.

Jones, L. 2001. Creating an affirming culture to retain African-American students during the post affirmative action era in higher education. In *Retaining African Americans in Higher Education: Challenging Paradigms for Retaining Students, Faculty and Administrators*, edited by L. Jones. Sterling, VA: Stylus.

Jones, P., and G. Gloeckner. 2004. First-year college performance: A study of home school graduates and traditional school graduates. *Journal of College Admission*. 183(Spring): 17–20. Available at: <www.eric.ed.gov/ERICWebPortal/contentdelivery/servlet/ERICServlet?accno=EJ682484>.

Jorgensen, A. 1993. *Resistance Strategies of Successful Native American Community College Students*. Unpublished dissertation, Arizona State University.

*Journal of Blacks in Higher Education*. 2006a. A large black-white scoring gap persists on the SAT. 53(Autumn): 72–76.

———. 2006b. The persisting racial gap in ACT college admission test scores. 53(Autumn): 17–18.

———. 2006c. The grievous shortfall in financial aid for most African-American college students. 54(Winter 2006/2007): 24.

———. 2007a. Black enrollments in advanced placement programs: The news is mixed. 55(Spring): 85–89.

———. 2007b. Comparing Black and White college enrollment rates of the high school class of 2005. 55(Spring): 43.

June, A.W. 2006a. Tuition-discount rate holds steady. *The Chronicle of Higher Education*. 53(2): A55. Available at: <http://chronicle.com/weekly/v53/i02/02a05501.htm>.

———. 2006b. College classifications get an overhaul. *The Chronicle of Higher Education*. 52(26): A25. Available at: <http://chronicle.com/weekly/v52/i26/26a02501.htm>.

Kahlenberg, R.R. 2004. Easing admission, or at least anxiety. *The Washington Post*. September 28: C.09. Available at: <www.washingtonpost.com/ac2/wp-dyn/A55480-2004Sep27>.

Kanter, R.M. 1983. *The Change Masters*. New York: Simon & Schuster.

Kantrowitz, M. 2007. *Pell Grant Historical Figures* (Web page). Cranberry Township, PA: FinAid Page, LLC. Retrieved Jan. 15 from: <www.finaid.org/educators/pellgrant.phtml>.

———. 2008. *Financial Aid and Scholarships for Undocumented Students*. Cranberry Township, PA: FinAid Page, LLC. Retrieved Jan. 15 from: <www.finaid.org/otheraid/undocumented.phtml>.

Kasworm, C.E. 2003. Setting the stage: Adults in higher education. In *Meeting the Special Needs of Adult Students: New Directions for Student Services*, No. 102, edited by D. Kilgore and P.J. Rice. San Francisco: Jossey-Bass.

Kay, M., and S. Jyson. 2003. UT, A&M admissions cap up for vote, law makers to weigh limiting entry under top ten percent rule. *The Austin American-Statesman*. May 23: B1.

Keller, C. 1997. *Recruiting on Campus: Utilizing Faculty, Students, and Alumni in the Admissions Process*. Cedar Rapids, IA: Stamats.

Kemerer, F.R. 1985. The role of deans, department chairs, and faculty in enrollment management. *College Board Review*. 134: 4–8, 28–29.

Keng, L., and B. Dodd. n.d. *An Investigation of College Performance of AP and Non-AP Student Groups*. (in press).

Kennesaw State University. 2007. *From Home School to Higher Education: An Admissions Guide for Home Educated Applicants*. Retrieved Jan. 13 from: <www.kennesaw.edu/admissions/pdfs/2007%20Admissions%20Package%20for%20Home%20Educated%20Applicants.pdf>.

Kimelman, J. 2002. Investing: A rush to safety on college savings. *The New York Times*. Dec. 1, Business Section. Available at: <http://query.nytimes.com/gst/fullpage.html?res=9B02E5DD1338F932A35751C1A9649C8B63>.

Kleiner, B., L. Lewis, and B. Greene. 2005. *Dual Enrollment of High School Students at Post-secondary Institutions: 2002–2003*. NCES Publication No. 2005008. Washington, D.C.: U.S. Department of Education, National Center for Education Statistics. Available at: <http://nces.ed.gov/pubs2005/2005008.pdf>.

Knapp, L.G., J.E. Kelly-Reid, R.W. Whitmore, J. Cong, B. Levine, M. Berzofsky, and S.G. Broyles. 2005. *Postsecondary Institutions in the United States: Fall 2004 and Degrees and Other Awards Conferred: 2003–04*. NCES Publication No. 2005182. Washington, D.C.: U.S. Department of Education, National Center for Education Statistics. Available at: <http://nces.ed.gov/pubs2005/2005182.pdf>.

Koh, H. 2007. *The Impact of Community Colleges on International Education* (Web page). New York: Institute of International Education. Retrieved Jan. 14 from: <http://opendoors.iienetwork.org/?p=42055>.

Koh, H., and R. Bhandari. 2007. *Open Doors 2006: Report on International Educational Exchange*. New York: Institute of International Education.

Kotter, J.P. 1996. *Leading Change*. Boston: Harvard Business Press.

Krecek, J. 2006. Department of Veterans Affairs: Educational benefits and certification. In *The Registrar's Guide: Evolving Best Practices in Records and Registration*, edited by B. Lauren. Washington, D.C.: American Association of Collegiate Registrars and Admissions Officers.

Kreutner, L., and E.S. Godfrey. 1980. Enrollment management: A new vehicle for institutional renewal. *College Board Review*. 118: 6–9, 29.

Kristof, K.M. 2002. Saving for college is made easier with tax breaks; State-sponsored 529 plans are gaining in popularity, but choosing among various offerings can be daunting. *Los Angeles Times*. Dec. 8, Business Section: C3.

Krueger, A., J. Rothstein, and S. Turner. 2005. *Race, Income, and College in 25 Years: The Continuing Legacy of Segregation and Discrimination*. NBER Working Paper No. 11445. Cambridge, MA: National Bureau of Economic Research.

Krueger, C. 2006. *In-state Tuition for Undocumented Immigrants*. Denver: Education Commission of the States. Available at: <http://ecs.org/clearinghouse/61/00/6100.pdf>.

KSU. *See* Kennesaw State University.

Kuh, G.D., and G.H. Wallman. 1986. Outcomes-oriented marketing. In *Managing College Enrollments: New Directions for Higher Education*, No. 53, edited by D. Hossler. San Francisco: Jossey-Bass.

Kurdi, H. 2002. Colorado prepaid tuition plan at risk, families must decide whether or not to stay with risky investment. *The Daily Texan*. Dec. 4. Available at: <http://media.www.dailytexanonline.com/media/storage/paper410/news/2002/12/04/University/Colorado.Prepaid.Tuition.Plan.At.Risk-497296.shtml>.

Kurtz, K., and J. Scannell. 2005. Repositioning price. *University Business*. 8(1): 23–25.

Lauricella, T. 2003. Parent trap: Plan to promote college saving stirs financial feuds. *The Wall Street Journal*. May 27: A1.

Law School Admission Council. *Legal Education Statistics*. Newtown, PA: LSAC. Available at: <www.lsac.org/pdfs/2007–2008/LegalEducationStatistics.pdf>.

Lawlor, S., S. Richman, and C. Richman. 1997. The validity of using the SAT as a criterion for Black and White students' admission to college. *College Student Journal*. 31(4): 507–516.

Layzell, D.T. 1997. *Forecasting and Managing Enrollment Revenue: An Overview of Current Trends, Issues, and Methods: New Directions for Institutional Research,* No. 93. San Francisco: Jossey-Bass.

Lederman, D. 2006. A new way for need-based aid. *Inside Higher Ed.* Oct. 2. Available at: <http://insidehighered.com/news/2006/10/02/oregon>.

Ledlow, S. 1992. Is cultural discontinuity an adequate explanation for dropping out? *Journal of American Indian Education.* 31(3): 21–36.

Lee, S.J., and K.K. Kumashiro. 2005. *A Report on the Status of Asian Americans and Pacific Islanders in Education: Beyond the 'Model Minority' Stereotype.* Washington, D.C.: National Education Association. Available at: <www.nea.org/teachexperience/images/aapireport.pdf>.

Lehman, J.S. 1990. Social irresponsibility, actuarial assumptions, and wealth redistribution: Lessons about public policy from a pre-paid tuition program. *Michigan Law Review.* 88: 1035–1141.

———. 1993. The distribution of benefits from prepaid tuition programs: New empirical evidence about the effects of program design on participant demographics. In *Prepaid College Tuition Plans: Promise and Problems,* edited by M.A. Olivas. New York: College Board.

Lemann, N. 1999. *The Big Test: The Secret History of the American Meritocracy.* New York: Farrar Straus & Giroux.

Leppel, K. 2005. College persistence and student attitudes toward financial success. *College Student Journal.* 39(2): 223–241.

Lindsey, D. 1995. *Indians at Hampton Institute, 1877–1923.* Urbana: University of Illinois.

Lippman, L., S. Burns, and E. MacArthur. 1996. *Urban Schools: The Challenge of Location and Poverty.* NCES Publication No. 96864. Washington, D.C.: U.S. Department of Education, National Center for Education Statistics. Available at: <http://nces.ed.gov/pubs/96864.pdf>.

Long, B.T. 2006. *College Tuition Pricing and Federal Financial Aid: Is there a Connection?* Testimony before the U.S. Senate Committee on Finance, Dec. 5. Washington, D.C. Available at: <www.senate.gov/~finance/hearings/testimony/2005test/120506bltest.pdf>.

Longanecker, D. 2002. Is merit-based aid really trumping need-based aid? *Change.* 34(2): 30–37.

———. 2006. A tale of two pities: The story of public higher education finance in America. *Change.* 38(1): 14–25.

LSAC. *See* Law School Admission Council.

Lucozzi, E.A. 1998. A far better place: Institutions as allies. In *Working with Lesbian, Gay, Bisexual, and Transgender College Students: A Handbook for Faculty and Administrators,* edited by R.L. Sanlo. Westport, CT: Greenwood Press.

Luebchow, L. 2007. *Colorado State Does Student Loans Right.* Available at: <www.newamerica.net/blogs/education_policy/2007/08/colorado_state>. Washington, D.C.: The New America Foundation.

Lunneborg, C. E., and P. W. Lunneborg. 1986. Beyond prediction: The challenge of minority achievement in higher education. *Journal of Multicultural Counseling and Development.* 14(2): 77–84.

Lyall, K.C., and K.R. Sell. 2005. *The True Genius of America at Risk: Are We Losing Our Public Universities to De Facto Privatization?* Westport, CT: Praeger Publishers.

Maehl, W.H. 2004. Adult degrees and the learning society. *In Developing and Delivering Adult Degree Programs: New Directions for Adult and Continuing Education,* No. 103, edited by J.P. Pappas, J. Jerman. San Francisco: Jossey-Bass.

Maguire, J. 1976. To the organized go the students. *Bridge Magazine.* 39(1): 16–20. Available at: <www.financialaid-services.org/whatsnew/bridgemag.htm>.

———. 1999. Phone interview with S.E. Henderson. Cincinnati, OH.

Mangan, K. 2007. Some New Orleans colleges predict bigger enrollments this fall. *The Chronicle of Higher Education.* 53(37): A2. Available at: <http://chronicle.com/free/v53/i37/37a03201.htm>.

Marcus, R. 2006. Immigration's scrambled politics. *The Washington Post.* April 4: A23. Available at: <www.washingtonpost.com/wp-dyn/content/article/2006/04/03/AR2006040301618.html>.

Marklein, M.B. 2004. Colleges grow gay-friendlier. *USA Today.* June 22, Education Section. Available at: <www.usatoday.com/news/education/2004-06-21-lgbt-main_x.htm>.

Maryland Independent College and University Association. 2007. *The Sellinger Program: Supporting Higher Education in the Maryland Tradition.* Annapolis, MD: MICUA. Available at: <www.micua.org/eSellinger.pdf>.

McArdle, J.J. 1994. Structural factor analysis experiments with incomplete data. *Multivariate Behavioral Research.* 29: 409–454.

McArdle, J.J., and F. Hamagami. 1992. Modeling incomplete longitudinal and cross-sectional data using latent growth structural models. *Experimental Aging Research.* 18(3): 145–166.

McDonough, P. 2006. *Counseling and College Counseling in America.* Alexandria, VA: NACAC.

McDonough, P.M. 1997. *Choosing Colleges: How Social Class and Schools Structure Opportunity*. Albany, NY: State University of New York Press.

McPherson, M.S., and M.O. Schapiro. 2006. Watch what we do (and not what we say). In *College Access: Opportunity or Privilege?*, edited by M.S. McPherson and M.O. Schapiro. New York: College Board.

MCRC. *See* Michigan Civil Rights Commission.

Meade, J. 1991. The missing piece. *Prism*. (Sept.): 19–22.

Messer, K.L. 2006. African American male college athletes. In *African American Men in College*, edited by M.J. Cuyjet. San Francisco: Jossey-Bass.

Mettler, S. 2005. *Soldiers to Citizens: The G.I. Bill and the Making of the Greatest Generation*. Oxford; New York: Oxford University Press.

Michigan Civil Rights Commission. 2007. *"One Michigan" at the Crossroads: An Assessment of the Impact of Proposal 06-02*. Available at: <www.michigan.gov/documents/mdcr/FinalCommissionReport3-07_1_189266_7.pdf>.

MICUA. *See* Maryland Independent College and University Association.

Mitchell, J.S. 2000. College counseling for gays comes out of the closet. *College Board Review*. 189/190: 12–19.

Mittelstadt, M. 2005. In-state rates for illegal immigrants challenged. *Dallas Morning News*. August 13.

Moffatt, G.K. 1993. *The Validity of the SAT as a Predictor of Grade Point Average for Nontraditional College Students*. Paper presented at the annual meeting of the Eastern Educational Research Association, Clearwater, FL.

Morgan, K.C. 2002. *The Use of AP Examination Grades by Students in College*. New York: Roper ASW.

Morgan, R., and B. Mancekshana. 2000. *AP Students in College: An Investigation of Their Course-Taking Patterns and College Majors*. Report No. SR-2000-09. Princeton, NJ: Educational Testing Service. Available at: <http://cbweb2s.collegeboard.org/ap/pdf/validity2.pdf>.

Morgan, R., and C. Crone. 1993. *Advanced Placement Examinees at the University of California: An Investigation of the Freshman-Year Courses and Grades of Examinees in Biology, Calculus AB, and Chemistry*. ETS Statistical Report 93–210. Princeton, NJ: Educational Testing Service.

Morgan, R., and L. Ramist. 1998. *Advanced Placement Students in College: An Investigation of Course Grades at 21 Colleges*. Report No. SR-98-13. Princeton, NJ: Educational Testing Service. Available at: <www.collegeboard.com/ap/pdf/sr-98-13.pdf>.

Morial, M.H. 2007. Financial aid gets Blacks through college. *The Broward Times*. Jan. 5: p. 7. Retrieved Sept. 16, 2007 from: Ethnic NewsWatch database, document ID: 1215404161.

Morse, A., A. Blott, and L. Speasmaker. 2006. *2006 State Legislation Related to Immigration: Enacted, Vetoed, and Pending Gubernatorial Action*. July 3. Washington, D.C.: National Conference of State Legislatures. Retrieved Jan. 16, 2008 from: <www.ncsl.org/programs/immig/06ImmigEnactedLegis2.htm>.

Morse, R.J., and S.M. Flanigan. 2005. Using the rankings. *U.S. News & World Report*. Retrieved Jan. 11, 2005 from: <www.usnews.com/usnews/edu/college/rankings/about/05rank_brief.php>.

Mortenson, T.G. 2002 . Time for a fundamental re-evaluation of the bad policy decisions of the 1990s. *Postsecondary Education Opportunity*. 125(Nov): 1–5. Available at: <www.eric.ed.gov/ERICWebPortal/contentdelivery/servlet/ERICServlet?accno=ED473779>.

———. 2005. Family income and higher education opportunity, 1970–2003. *Postsecondary Education Opportunity*. 156(June).

Muraskin, L., J. Lee, A. Wilner, and W.S. Swail. 2004. *Raising the Graduation Rates of Low-Income College Students*. Washington, D.C.: The Pell Institute for the Study of Opportunity in Higher Education. Available at: <www.eric.ed.gov/ERICWebPortal/contentdelivery/servlet/ERICServlet?accno=ED490856>.

n.a. 1957. College work in the high schools. *The New York Times*. Dec.15.

n.a. 2006. College enrollment by racial and ethnic group, selected years. *The Chronicle of Higher Education 2005–6 Almanac*. 52(1): 15. Available at: <http://chronicle.com/weekly/almanac/2005/nation/0101503.htm>.

n.a. 2007. *The Gay and Lesbian Guide to College Life*. Princeton, NJ: Princeton Review.

NAFSA. *See* NAFSA: Association of International Educators.

NAFSA: Association of International Educators. 2002. *NAFSA's Principles of Good Practice for the Recruitment and Admissions of International Students* (Web page). New York: NAFSA. Available at: <www.nafsa.org/about.sec/governance_leadership/ethics_standards/nafsa_s_principles_of>.

———. 2007. *An International Education Policy for U.S. Leadership, Competitiveness, and Security*. New York: NAFSA. Available at: <www.nafsa.org/_/File/_/neip_rev.pdf>.

———. 2008. *Financial Aid for Undergraduate International Students* (Web page). New York: NAFSA. Retrieved Jan. 14 from: <www.nafsa.org/students.sec/financial_aid_for_undergraduate>.

NASFAA. *See* National Association of Student Financial Aid Administrators.

National Association of Student Financial Aid Administrators. 1999. *Statement of Ethical Principles*. Washington, D.C.: NASFAA.

National Consortium of Directors of LGBT Resources in Higher Education. 2003. *Evaluating Colleges: A Good Fit for LGBT Students?* (Web page). Available at: <www.lgbtcampus.org/faq/assessing_colleges.html>.

———. 2002. *Bibliography: "Campus Climate Reports"* (Web page). Available at: <www.lgbtcampus.org/resources/campus_climate.html>.

National Council of La Raza. 2008. *DREAM Act*. Retrieved Jan. 15 from: <www.nclr.org/content/policy/detail/1331/>.

NCLR. *See* National Council of La Raza.

Neal, D. 2005. *Why Has Black-White Skill Convergence Stopped?* NBER Working Paper No. 11090. Cambridge, MA: National Bureau of Economic Research.

Nettles, M.T., R. Thoeny, and E.J. Grossman. 1986. Comparative and predictive analyses of Black and White students' college achievement and experiences. *Journal of Higher Education*. 57: 289–318.

Nissimov, R. 2002. UT's giant fee hike results in apology, legal confusion. *The Houston Chronicle*. Mar. 6: A1. Available at: <www.chron.com/CDA/archives/archive.mpl?id=2002_3524376>.

Noel-Levitz. 2006a. *Cost of Recruiting Poll Results* (News Release). March 2. Iowa City: Noel-Levitz, Inc. Available at: <www.noellevitz.com/About+Us/In+the+News/News+Item/Cost+of+Recruiting+Poll+Results.htm>.

———. 2006b. 2006 *Admissions Funnel Report for Four-year Public and Private Institutions*. Available at: <https://www.noellevitz.com/search/Click.aspx?/cgi-bin/MsmGo.exe?grab_id=0&page_id=643&query=2006%20Admissions%20Funnel%20Report>.

Nora, A. 2002. A theoretical and practical view of student adjustment and academic achievement. In *Increasing Access to College: Extending Possibilities for All Students*, edited by L.S. Hagedorn and W.G. Tierney. Albany: State University of New York Press.

Olivas, M.A. 1988. Administering intentions: Law, theory, and practice in postsecondary residency requirements. *Journal of Higher Education*. 59(3): 263–290.

———. 1993. *Prepaid College Tuition Plans: Promise and Problems*. New York: College Board.

———. 1995. Storytelling out of school: Undocumented college residency, race, and reaction. *Hastings Constitutional Law Quarterly*. 22(Summer): 1019–1086.

———. 1997. Constitutional criteria: The social science and common law of admissions decision in higher education. University of Colorado Law Review, 68(40): 1065–1122.

———. 2003. State college savings and prepaid tuition plans: A reappraisal and review. *Journal of Law & Education*. 32(Oct.): 475–514.

———. 2004. IRRIRA, the DREAM Act, and undocumented college student residency. *Journal of College & University Law*. 30: 435.

Opdyke, J.D. 2003. College savings 101: How we chose. *The Wall Street Journal*. Feb. 22: 2.

Oregon State University. 2005a. *IR [Insight Resume] Process Summary*.

———. 2005b. *IR [Insight Resume] Summary Statement*.

———. 2006. *Fall Enrollment Summary 2006*. Corvallis, OR: OSU Office of Institutional Research. Available at: <http://oregonstate.edu/admin/aa/ir/enrollment/ES_Fall_2006.pdf>.

———. 2008. *Credit Opportunities: Earning Advanced Standing Credit* (Web page). Retrieved Jan. 30 from: <http://oregonstate.edu/admissions/firstyear/apibclep.html>.

OSU. *See* Oregon State University.

Overland, M.A. 2006a. Shattered dreams in the Philippines: Collapse of education-savings plans leaves nearly a million students unable to pay for college. *The Chronicle of Higher Education*. 52(26): A40. At http://chronicle.com/weekly/v52/i26/26a04001.htm>.

———. 2006b. Education bailout makes for strange bedfellows. *The Chronicle of Higher Education*. 52(26): A42. Available at: <http://chronicle.com/weekly/v52/i26/26a04201.htm/>.

Padgett, J. 2007. *Identifying Low Income Families—Going Beyond the AGI*. College Board presentation paper, Eastern Association of Student Financial Aid Administrators. Niagara Falls, May.

Palazesi, L.M., and B.L. Bower. 2006. Self-identity modification: Baby Boomers reinvent themselves using the community college. *Community College Review*. 34(1): 44–67.

Pappas, J.P., and J. Jerman. 2004. Future considerations. In *Developing and Delivering Adult Degree Programs: New Directions for Adult and Continuing Education*, No. 103, edited by J.P. Pappas and J. Jerman. San Francisco: Jossey-Bass.

Pascarella, E., B. Palmer, M. Moye, and C. Pierson. 2001. Do diversity experiences influence the development of critical thinking? *Journal of College Student Development.* 42: 257–271.

Paulsen, M.B., and E.P. St. John. 2002. Social class and college costs: Examining the financial nexus between college choice and persistence. *The Journal of Higher Education.* 73(2): 189–227.

Pavel, D.M., R.R. Skinner, E. Farris, M. Cahalan, J. Tippeconnic, and W. Stein. 1998. *American Indians and Alaskan Natives in Postsecondary Education.* NCES Publication No. 98291. Washington, D.C.: U.S. Department of Education, National Center for Education Statistics. Available at: <http://nces.ed.gov/pubs98/98291.pdf>.

*Pension Protection Act of 2006*, Pub. L. 109–280, 120 Stat. 780 (2006).

Peppers, D., M. Rogers, and B. Dorf. 1999. *The One to One Fieldbook: The Complete Toolkit for Implementing a 1 to 1 Marketing Program.* New York: Currency.

Perna, L. 2000. Racial and ethnic group differences in college enrollment decisions. In *Understanding the College Choice of Disadvantaged Students: New Directions for Institutional Research*, No. 107, edited by A.F. Cabrera and S.M. LaNasa. San Francisco: Jossey-Bass.

Peter, K., and E.F. Cataldi. 2005. *The Road Less Traveled? Students Who Enroll in Multiple Institutions.* NCES Publication No. 2005157. Washington, D.C.: U.S. Department of Education, National Center for Education Statistics. Available at: <http://nces.ed.gov/pubs2005/2005157.pdf>.

Pew Hispanic Center. 2004. *Latinos in California, Texas, New York, Florida and New Jersey* (Survey Brief). From <http://pewhispanic.org/files/factsheets/10.pdf>.

Pewewardy, C. 2004. You think you hired an 'Indian' faculty member? In *Indigenizing the Academy: Transforming Scholarship and Empowering Communities,* edited by D.A. Mihesuah and A.C. Wilson. Lincoln: University of Nebraska Press.

PHC. *See* Pew Hispanic Center.

Pook, G. 2004. *Diploma Programme Assessment: Principles and Practice.* Cardiff, Wales, UK: International Baccalaureate Organization. Available at: <www.ibo.org/diploma/assessment/documents/d_x_dpyyy_ass_0409_1_e.pdf>.

Pottinger, R. 1989. Disjunction to higher education: American Indian students in the southwest. *Anthropology & Education Quarterly. 20*(4): 326–344.

Powers, E. 2006. Public hearing, take 2. *Inside Higher Ed.* March 21. Available at: <www.insidehighered.com/news/2006/03/21/commission>.

Powers, S. 2002. College students may lose out; 2 tuition programs face cutbacks. *Orlando Sentinel.* Dec. 4: B1.

Princiotta, D., and S. Bielick. 2006. *Homeschooling in the United States: 2003.* NCES Publication No. 2006042. Washington, D.C.: U.S. Department of Education, National Center for Education Statistics. Available at: <http://nces.ed.gov/pubs2006/2006042.pdf>.

Prue, I. 1997. *A Nation-Wide Survey of College Admissions Personnel's Knowledge, Attitudes, and Experiences with Home-Schooled Applicants.* Unpublished doctoral dissertation, The University of Georgia, Athens.

Quann, C.J. 1979. *Admissions, Academic Records and Registrar Services: A Handbook of Policies and Procedures.* San Francisco: Jossey-Bass.

Quirk, M. 2005. The best class money can buy. *The Atlantic Monthly.* 294(4).

Ramsey, F., and D. Schafer. 2002. *The Statistical Sleuth: A Course in Methods of Data Analysis*, 2nd Edition. Pacific Grove, CA: Duxbury Press.

Randall, K. 2007. *AP Students "Significantly Outperform" Peers According to Two Landmark Studies by University of Texas at Austin Researchers* (Web page). University of Texas at Austin, Office of Public Affairs, March 26. Available at: <www.edb.utexas.edu/education/news/2007/APstudents.php>.

Ray, B.D. 1998. *Home Education Research Fact Sheet* (IIc). Salem, OR: National Home Education Research Institute.

Redd, K.E. 2000. Discounting toward disaster: Tuition discounting, college finances, and enrollment of low-income undergraduates. *New Agenda Series.* 3(2): 1–38. Available at: <www.eric.ed.gov/ERICWebPortal/contentdelivery/servlet/ERICServlet?accno=ED447775>.

Redden, E. 2007. A new tack for the DREAM Act. *Inside Higher Ed.* July 19. Available at: <www.insidehighered.com/news/2007/07/19/dream>.

Reed, D.S. 2001. *On Equal Terms: The Constitutional Politics of Equal Opportunity.* Princeton, NJ: Princeton University Press.

Reeves, T., and C. Bennett. 2003. *The Asian and Pacific Islander Population in the United States: March 2002.* Washington, D.C.: U.S. Census Bureau. Available at: <www.census.gov/prod/2003pubs/p20-540.pdf>.

———. 2004. *We the People: Asians in the United States.* Washington, D.C.: U.S. Census Bureau. Available at: <www.census.gov/prod/2004pubs/censr-17.pdf>.

Reich, R.B. 1997. *Locked in the Cabinet.* New York: Knopf.

Rendón, L.I., R.E. Jalomo, and A. Nora. 2000. Theoretical considerations in the study of minority student retention in higher education. In *Reworking the Student Departure Puzzle,* edited by J.M. Braxton. Nashville: Vanderbilt University Press.

Reuben, J.A. 2001. Merit, mission and minority students: The history of debate over special admission programs. In *A Faithful Mirror: Reflections on the College Board and Education in America,* edited by M.C. Johanek. New York: College Board.

Reyhner, J. 1992. American Indians out of school: A review of school- based causes and solutions. *Journal of American Indian Education.* 31(3): 37–56.

Riley, R.W. 2000. *The Growing Importance of International Education.* Remarks as prepared for delivery by U.S. Secretary of Education Richard W. Riley, La Maison Francaise, Washington, D.C., April 19. Available at: <www.eric.ed.gov/ERICWebPortal/contentdelivery/servlet/ERICServlet?accno=ED440543> and <www.ed.gov/Speeches/04–2000/000419.html>.

Rimando, R. 2007. E-mail correspondence with author, M. Mitsui.

Rizzo, M.J., and R.G. Ehrenberg. 2004. Resident and nonresident tuition at flagship state universities. In *College Choices: the Economics of Where to Go, When to Go, and How to Pay for It,* edited by C.M. Hoxby. Chicago: University of Chicago Press.

Robison, C. 2003. Committee in Senate OKs rise in tuition. *The Houston Chronicle.* May 21: A27. Available at: <www.chron.com/CDA/archives/archive.mpl?id=2003_3656062>.

Robison, C., and R.G. Ratcliffe. 2007. Perry to stick by law giving tuition breaks to illegal immigrants. *The Houston Chronicle.* Jan. 12, Top Stories section. Available at: <www.chron.com/disp/story.mpl/front/4465325.html>.

Rooney, P., W. Hussar, M. Planty, S. Choy, G. Hampden-Thompson, S. Provasnik, M.A. Fox, B. Kridl, and A. Livingston. 2006. *The Condition of Education 2006.* NCES Publication No. 2006071. Washington, D.C.: U.S. Department of Education, National Center for Education Statistics. Available at: <http://nces.ed.gov/pubs2006/2006071.pdf>.

Rosigno, V.J. 1998. Race and reproduction of educational disadvantage. *Social Forces.* 76(3): 1033–1061.

Rothstein, J., and C.E. Rouse. 2007. *Constrained after College: Student Loans and Early Occupational Career Choice.* NBER Working Paper No. 13117. Princeton University and National Bureau of Economic Research, May 7.

Rudolph, F. 1962. *The American College and University.* New York: Vintage Books.

———. 1990. *The American College and University: A History.* New York: A. Knopf.

Ryan, C., and D. Futterman. 1998. *Lesbian and Gay Youth: Care and Counseling.* New York: Columbia Press.

Sacks, P. 2001. *Standardized Minds: The High Price of America's Testing Culture and What We Can Do to Change It.* Philadelphia: DaCapo Press.

Sadler, P.M., and R.H. Tai. 2007. Weighting for recognition: Accounting for Advanced Placement and honors courses when calculating high school grade point average. *NASSP Bulletin.* 91(1): 5–32.

Saenz, V.B. 2002. *Hispanic Students and Community Colleges: A Critical Point for Intervention.* ERIC Document No. ED477908. Los Angeles: ERIC Clearinghouse for Community Colleges. Available at: <www.eric.ed.gov/ERICWebPortal/contentdelivery/servlet/ERICServlet?accno=ED477908>.

Sanko, J.J. 2002. State's prepaid college fund could come up short; With tuitions rising, returns down, program gives investors an out. *Rocky Mountain News.* Nov. 22: 13B.

Saunders, J. 2000. Regents unanimous for one Florida. *The Florida Times Union.* Feb. 18. Available at: <www.jacksonville.com/tu-online/stories/021800/met_2171246.html>.

Scannell, J. 1999. Phone interview with S.E. Henderson. Cincinnati, OH.

Schmidt, P. 1998. Oregon voters reject measure needed for prepaid tuition plan. *The Chronicle of Higher Education.* 45(16): A53. Available at: <http://chronicle.com/weekly/v45/i16/16a05302.htm>.

———. 2003. Thousands of families abandon Colorado's prepaid tuition plan. *The Chronicle of Higher Education.* 49(26): A24. Available at: <http://chronicle.com/weekly/v49/i26/26a02402.htm>.

———. 2004. Noted higher-education researcher urges admissions preferences for the poor. *The Chronicle of Higher Education.* 50(32): A26. Available at: <http://chronicle.com/weekly/v50/i32/32a02601.htm>

———. 2006. Ward Connerly names states that may be his next targets for bans on Affirmative Action preferences. *The Chronicle of Higher Education.* Dec. 14.

———. 2007. Inflation eats into recent growth in state spending on student aid. *The Chronicle of Higher Education.* 53(45): A20. Available at: <http://chronicle.com/weekly/v53/i45/45a02001.htm>.

———. 2007a. Justice O'Connor sees 'muddy' future for Affirmative Action. *The Chronicle of Higher Education.* 53(33): A28. Available at: <http://chronicle.com/weekly/v53/i33/33a02802.htm>.

———. 2007b. *Color and Money: How Rich White Kids Are Winning the War over College Affirmative Action*. New York: Palgrave Macmillan.

———. 2007c. 5 More states may curtail Affirmative Action. *The Chronicle of Higher Education*. 54(8): A1. Available at: <http://chronicle.com/weekly/v54/i08/08a00101.htm>.

———. 2007d. Defense Dept. may cut U.S. service academies' affirmative action efforts. *The Chronicle of Higher Education*. 53(37). Available at: <http://chronicle.com/weekly/v53/i37/37a01901.htm>.

———. 2007e. Dow Jones Fund opens journalism programs to white students after lawsuit. *The Chronicle of Higher Education*. 53(25): Available at: <http://chronicle.com/weekly/v53/i25/25a01801.htm>.

Schwanhausser, M. 2003. Puzzling tax credits for college are worth study. *Philadelphia Inquirer*. Mar. 24: C1.

Schwartz, N.D., and R. Nixon. 2007. Some States consider leasing lotteries. *The New York Times*. October 14, Business section. Available at: <www.nytimes.com/2007/10/14/business/14private.html?/em&ex=1192593600&en=ac84ed361dd64a9d&ei=5987%0A>.

Sedlacek, W. 2004. *Beyond the Big Test*. San Francisco: Jossey-Bass.

Seidman, A. 2005. Minority student retention: Resources for practitioners. In *Minority Retention: What Works?*, edited by G.H. Gaither. San Francisco: Jossey-Bass.

Selingo, J. 2000. Facing new missions and rivals, state colleges seek a makeover. *The Chronicle of Higher Education*. 47(12): A40. Available at: <http://chronicle.com/weekly/v47/i12/12a04001.htm>.

———. 2005. Michigan: Who really won? Colleges' cautious reaction to the Supreme Court's affirmative-action decisions may have snatched defeat from the jaws of victory. *The Chronicle of Higher Education*. 51(19): A21. Available at: <http://chronicle.com/weekly/v51/i19/19a02101.htm>.

Sevier, R.A. 1992. Recruiting African-American undergraduates: A national survey of the factors that affect institutional choice. *College and University*. 68(1): 48–52.

———. 1996. Those important things: What every college president needs to know about marketing and student recruiting. *College and University*. 71(4): 9–16.

Seymour, E., and N. Hewitt. 1997. *Talking About Leaving: Why Undergraduates Leave the Sciences*. Boulder, CO: Westview Press.

Shah, N. 2002. Final rush on for prepaid college tuition plan. *Palm Beach Post*. Jan. 31: 1A.

Shapira, I.. 2006. Educators, parents eager for an edge opt for IB classes in grade schools. *The Washington Post*. Dec. 17: A01. See <www.washingtonpost.com/wp-dyn/content/article/2006/12/16/AR2006121600954.html>.

Sheehan, F.R. 1988. The role of state boards of higher education in influencing access and retention of minorities in higher education. *Peabody Journal of Education*. 66(1): 20–31.

Sherrill, J., and C.A. Hardesty. 1994. *The Gay, Lesbian, and Bisexual Students' Guide to Colleges, Universities, and Graduate Schools*. New York and London: New York University.

Sidoti, L. 2002. Downturn threatens prepaid tuition plans; Florida's investments are solid, avoiding the woes of other states, officials said. *Orlando Sentinel*. Nov. 30: A28.

Sjogren, C., and P. Campbell. 2003. The International Baccalaureate: A diploma of quality, depth and breadth. *College and University*. 79(2): 55–58.

Slack, W., and D. Porter. 1980. The scholastic aptitude test: A critical appraisal. *Harvard Educational Review*. 50(2): 154–175.

Smith, C. 2007. Finding the academic context: The SEM role for faculty. *SEM Brief*. June 29. Available at: <http://consulting.aacrao.org/2007/06/29/the-sem-role-for-faculty/>.

Smith, J.E. 1998. Recruitment: Student outreach strategies. In *Handbook for the College Admissions Profession*, edited by C.C. Swann and S.E. Henderson. Westport, CT: Greenwood Press.

Smith, L. 2007. The 2007–8 almanac. *The Chronicle of Higher Education*. 54(1): 62. Available at: <http://chronicle.com/weekly/almanac/2007/states/ma.htm>.

Snyder, T.D., A.G. Tan, and C.M. Hoffman. 2006. *Digest of Education Statistics: 2005*. NCES Publication No. 2006030. Washington, D.C.: U.S. Department of Education, National Center for Education Statistics. Available at: <http://nces.ed.gov/pubs2006/zip/2006030.zip>.

———. 2007. *Digest of Education Statistics: 2006*. NCES Publication No. 2007017. Washington, D.C.: U.S. Department of Education, National Center for Education Statistics. Available at: <http://nces.ed.gov/pubs2007/2007017.pdf>.

Somers, P., S. Woodhouse, and J. Cofer. 2004. Pushing the boulder uphill: The persistence of first-generation college students. *NASPA Journal*. 41(3): 418–435.

Sonderup, L. 2006. *Hispanic Marketing: A Critical Marketing Segment* (Web page). Golden, CO: CSC Publishing & Glen Emerson Morris. Available at: <www.ad-mkt-review.com/public_html/docs/fs075.html>.

STAMATS. 2006. TeenTalk Study. *Stamats 2006 TeensTALK®: A Review of College-Bound Teen Trends, Attitudes, Lifestyles, and Knowledge.* Webinar: October 26, presented by S. Kappler.

StatSoft, Inc.. 2008. Discriminant function analysis (Web page). In *Statistics: Methods and Applications* (Electronic Version). Tulsa, OK: StatSoft. Retrieved Jan. 25 from: <www.statsoft.com/textbook/stdiscan.html>.

Steele, C.M. 1997. A Threat in the air: How stereotypes shape intellectual identity and performance. *The American Psychologist.* 52(6): 613–630.

Steele, C.M., and J. Aronson. 1995. Stereotype threat and the intellectual test performance of African Americans. *Journal of Personality and Social Psychology.* 69(5): 797–812.

Stephens, S., and S. Theis. 2003. Lawmakers fear loss in value of prepaid tuition. *The Plain Dealer* (Cleveland). June 12: C1.

Stern, G.J., P.F. Drucker, and F. Hesselbein. 1998. *The Drucker Foundation Self-Assessment Tool: Process Guide* (Revised Edition). San Francisco: Jossey-Bass.

Sternberg, R.J. 1997. *Successful Intelligence.* New York: Plume.

———. 1999. The theory of successful intelligence. *Review of General Psychology.* 3: 292–316.

Sternberg, R.J., and The Rainbow Project Collaborators. 2006. The Rainbow Project: Enhancing the SAT through assessments of analytical, practical, and creative skills. *Intelligence.* 34: 321–350.

Sternberg, R.J., B. Torff, and E.L. Grigorenko. 1998. Teaching triarchically improves school achievement. *Journal of Educational Psychology.* 90: 374–384.

Sternberg, R.J., G.B. Forsythe, J. Hedlund, J. Horvath, S. Snook, W.M. Williams, R.K. Wagner, and E.L. Grigorenko. 2000. *Practical Intelligence in Everyday Life.* New York: Cambridge University Press.

Sternberg, R.J., M. Ferrari, P.R. Clinkenbeard, and E.L. Grigorenko. 1996. Identification, instruction, and assessment of gifted children: A construct validation of a triarchic model. *Gifted Child Quarterly.* 40(3): 129–137.

Sternberg, R.J., The Rainbow Project Collaborators, and University of Michigan Business School Project Collaborators. 2004. Theory based university admissions testing for a new millennium. *Educational Psychologist.* 39(3): 185–198.

Stewart, D. 1992. *College Admission Policies in the 1990s: A Look Toward the Future.* New York: College Board.

Stewart, E., and D. Bulkeley. 2007. Students fear repeal of the in-state tuition perk. *Deseret Morning News.* Jan. 29. Available at: <http://deseretnews.com/dn/view/0%2C1249%2C655192144%2C00.html>.

Stowe, S. 2007. Bill giving illegal residents Connecticut tuition rates is vetoed by the Governor. *The New York Times.* June 27, N.Y./Region section. Available at: <www.nytimes.com/2007/06/27/nyregion/27veto.html>.

Strauss, W., and N. Howe. 2007. Millennials as graduate students. *The Chronicle of Higher Education.* 53(30). Available at: <http://chronicle.com/weekly/v53/i30/30b01601.htm>.

Stricker, L.J., D. Rock, and N. Burton. 1996. Using the SAT and high school record in academic guidance. *Educational and Psychological Measurement.* 56(4): 626–641.

Suthers, J.W. 2007. *Formal Opinion of John W. Suthers, Attorney General.* No. 07–03, August 14. State of Colorado Department of Law, Office of the Attorney General.

Swail, W.S, A.F. Cabrera, and C. Lee. 2004. *Latino Youth and the Pathway to College.* Washington, D.C.: Pew Hispanic Center.

Swann, C.C., and S.E. Henderson. 1998. *Handbook for the College Admissions Profession.* Westport, CT: Greenwood Press.

*Tax Increase Prevention and Reconciliation Act of 2005*, Pub. L. 109–222, 120 Stat. 345 (enacted 2006) Illinois HB 376 (August 6, 2007).

Tergesen, A. 2006. What price college admission? Parents are spending tens of thousands on advisers to shape their kids' game plans. *BusinessWeek.* June 10, Personal Finance section. Available at: <www.businessweek.com/print/magazine/content/06_25/b3989109.htm>.

Texas Tech University. 2008. Market position. In *Enrollment Management Plan* (Electronic Version). Lubbock, TX: Office of Institutional Research and Information Management, Texas Tech University. Retrieved Jan. 25 from: <www.ttu.edu/administration/enrmgt/emplan/ch2.php>.

Tierney, W.G. 1992. *Official Encouragement, Institutional Discouragement: Minorities in Academe—The Native American Experience.* Norwood: Ablex Publishing Corporation.

———. 1999. Models of minority college-going and retention: Cultural integrity versus cultural suicide. *Journal of Negro Education.* 68(1): 80–91.

———. 2005. The changing landscape of higher education: The future of college admission. In *State of College Admission*, edited by D.A. Hawkins and J. Lautz. Alexandria, VA: NACAC. Available at: <www.nacacnet.org/NR/rdonlyres/AF40D947-D5B0-4199-A032-5C7A3C5D0F49/0/SoCA_Web.pdf>.

Ting, S. R. 2000. Predicting Asian Americans' academic performance in the first year of college: An approach combining SAT scores and non-cognitive variables. *Journal of College Student Development*. 41: 442–449.

———. 2003. A longitudinal study of non-cognitive variables in predicting academic success of first-generation college students. *College and University*. 78(4): 27–31.

Tinto, V. 1975. Dropout from higher education: A theoretical synthesis of recent research. *Review of Educational Research*. 45: 89–125.

———. 1987. *Leaving College: Rethinking the Causes and Cures of Student Attrition*. Chicago: University of Chicago Press.

———. 1993. *Leaving College: Rethinking the Causes and Cures of Student Attrition*, 2nd Edition. Chicago: University of Chicago Press.

———. 2004. *Student Retention and Graduation: Facing the Truth, Living with the Consequences*. Occasional Paper 1. The Pell Institute for the Study of Opportunity in Higher Education.

Tomsho, R. 2002. Prepaid college tuition plans are falling short. *The Wall Street Journal*. Dec. 16: B1.

———. 2006. Amid rising costs and criticisms, some college cut back merit aid. *The Wall Street Journal*. Oct. 11. Available at: <http://online.wsj.com/article/SB116052998822488903.html>.

Toobin, J. 2006. Gerald Ford's affirmative action. *The New York Times*. Dec. 30, Opinion section. Available at: <www.nytimes.com/2006/12/30/opinion/30toobin.html>.

Tornatzky, L.G., E.E. Macias, and S. Jones. 2002. *Latinos and Information Technology: The Promise and the Challenge*. Claremont, CA: Tomas Rivera Policy Institute. Available at: <www.ibm.com/ibm/ibmgives/downloads/Latinos_and_IT.pdf>.

Torres, C., and A. Marquez. 2005. *Reaching Higher Ground: Parental Outreach Programs at the Postsecondary Level*. Los Angeles: The Tomas Rivera Policy Institute.

Tremblay, C., J. Shearer, and D. Stephens. 2006. *Today's Efforts, Tomorrow's Program*. AACRAO Strategic Enrollment Management Conference (SEM XVI), Phoenix, AZ.

Trenor, J.M., C. Madubike, and F.J. Claydon. 2006. *Establishing a Women in Engineering Program at an Urban University*. Proceedings of the 2006 WEPAN National Conference, Pittsburgh, PA.

Troiden, R.R. 1998. Homosexual identity development. *Journal of Adolescent Health*. 9: 105.

U. S. Census Bureau. 2000. *School Enrollment—Social and Economic Characteristics of Students: October 2000*. PPL-148. Available at: <www.census.gov/population/socdemo/school/ppl-148/tab05.xls>.

———. 2001. *Difference in Population by Race and Hispanic or Latino Origin for the United States: 1990 to 2000*. PHC-T-1. Available at: <www.census.gov/population/cen2000/phc-t1/tab04.pdf>.

———. 2002. *Current Population Survey, 2002*. Available at: <www.census.gov/population/socdemo/hispanic/ppl-165/tab07-1.pdf>.

———. 2003. *Statistical Abstract of the United States 2003*. Available at: <www.census.gov/prod/2004pubs/03statab/educ.pdf>.

———. 2004a. *U. S. Interim Projections by Age, Sex, Race, and Hispanic Origin*. Available at: <www.census.gov/ipc/www/usinterimproj/>.

———. 2004b. *Current Population Survey, 2004*. Available at: <www.census.gov/population/socdemo/hispanic/ASEC2004/2004CPS_tab7.1.html>.

———. 2005a. *Annual Estimates of the Population by Sex, Race, and Hispanic or Latino Origin for the United States: April 1, 2000 to July 1, 2005*. NC-EST2005-03. Available at: <www.censusbureau.biz/popest/national/asrh/NC-EST2005/NC-EST2005-03.xls>.

———. 2006a. *Facts for Features: Hispanic Heritage Month 2006: Sept. 15–Oct. 15*. Available at: <www.census.gov/Press-Release/www/releases/archives/facts_for_features_special_editions/007173.html>.

———. 2006b. *American Fact Finder Glossary*. Retrieved Dec. 7, 2006 from: <http://factfinder.census.gov/home/en/epss/glossary_a.html>.

———. 2007. *Percent of the Total Population Who Are American Indian and Alaska Native Alone: 2006*. R0203. Available at: <http://factfinder.census.gov/servlet/GRTTable?format=US-30&geo_id=01000US&ds_name=ACS_2006_EST_G00_&_box_head_nbr=R0203>.

U.S. Department of Defense. 2003. *Voluntary Education Programs* (Web page). Available at: <www.voled.doded.mil/voled_Web/VolEdProgramScope-text.htm>.

U.S. Department of Education. 2007a. *Tech Prep Education* (Web page). Retrieved Dec. 27 from: <www.ed.gov/about/offices/list/ovae/pi/cte/tpreptopic.html>.

———. 2007b. *Migrant Education—College Assistance Migrant Program*. Retrieved Jan. 10 from: <www.ed.gov/programs/camp/>.

———. 2007c. *Federal TRIO Programs* (Home page). Retrieved Jan. 10 from: <www.ed.gov/about/offices/list/ope/trio/>.

———. 2008. *Accreditation in the United States*. <www.ed.gov/admins/finaid/accred/accreditation_pg8.html>.

U.S. House. 1998. *Higher Education Amendments of 1998*. 155th Cong., 2nd sess. P.L. 105–244, H.R. 6. Available at: <www.ed.gov/policy/highered/leg/hea98/HR6.pdf>.

U.S. Secretary of Education's Commission on the Future of Higher Education. 2006. Final draft report, August 9. Washington, D.C.: U.S. Department of Education.

UNI. *See* University of Northern Iowa.

University of Iowa. 2008. *Carver College of Medicine Student Handbook: Miscellaneous Other Policies* (Web page). Carver College of Medicine. Available at: <www.medicine.uiowa.edu/OSAC/administration/miscpolicies.htm>.

University of Northern Iowa. 2007. *Transfer Plan-It* (Web page). Retrieved Jan. 13 from: <https://access.uni.edu/cgi-bin/transfer/transferPlanIt.cgi>.

Vaughan, G.V. 2004. How to keep open access in community colleges. *Education Digest*. 69(6): 52–59.

Veysey, L. 1965. *The Emergence of the American University*. Chicago: University of Chicago Press.

Wallis, C., and S. Steptoe. 2006. How to bring our schools out of the 20th century. *Time*. Dec. 10. Available at: <www.time.com/time/magazine/article/0,9171,1568480,00.html>.

Walton, M. 1986. *The Deming Management Method*. New York: Perigee.

Warburton, E.C., R. Bugarin, and A. Nunez. 2001. *Bridging the Gap: Academic Preparation and Postsecondary Success of First-Generation Students*. NCES Publication No. 2001153. Washington, D.C.: U.S. Department of Education, National Center for Education Statistics. Available at: <http://nces.ed.gov/pubs2001/2001153.pdf>.

Waterman, S.J. 2007. A complex path to Haudenosaunee degree completion. *Journal of American Indian Education*. 46(1): 20–40.

Webb, J., and C. Hagel. 2007. A post-Iraq G.I. Bill. *The New York Times*. Nov. 9, Opinion section. Available at: <www.nytimes.com/2007/11/09/opinion/09webb.html?_r=3&oref=slogin&oref=slogin>.

Weber, B. 2007. The residential college: Colleges across the country are engaged in a grand social experiment to fuse academic and social life. *The New York Times*. July 29, Education Life Supplement: 18–19, 36. Available at: <www.nytimes.com/2007/07/29/education/edlife/cornellweber3.html?_r=1&adxnnlx=1199459096-BbZOlTnYW92kA8wGz6tySw&pagewanted=all>.

Weitzman, R. 1982. The prediction of college achievement by the scholastic aptitude test and the high school record. *Journal of Educational Measurement*. 19(3): 179–191.

WEPAN. *See* Women in Engineering Programs and Advocates Network.

Western Interstate Commission for Higher Education. 2003. *Knocking at the College Door, 1988–2018*. Boulder, CO: WICHE.

WICHE. *See* Western Interstate Commission for Higher Education.

Wikipedia. 2008a. *Total Quality Management*. Retrieved Jan. 22 from: <http://en.wikipedia.org/wiki/total_quality_management>.

———. 2008b. *Six Sigma*. Retrieved Jan. 22 from: <http://en.wikipedia.org/wiki/six_sigma>.

Wilkins, D.E. 2003. A tour of Indian peoples and lands. In *Rethinking the Color Line: Readings in Race and Ethnicity*, 2nd Edition, edited by C.A. Gallagher. New York: McGraw Hill.

Wilkinson, R. 2005. *Aiding Students, Buying Students: Financial Aid in America*. Nashville: Vanderbilt University Press.

———. 2007. Reading a commissioner—A review of "Going broke by degree: Why college costs too much. *Journal of Student Financial Aid*. 36(3): 39–44. Available at: <www.nasfaa.org/annualpubs/journal/vol36n3/rupertwilkinson.pdf>.

Williams, D., II. 1993. Taxation of prepaid tuition plans and other forms of college expense assistance. In *Prepaid College Tuition Plans: Promise and Problems*, edited by M.A. Olivas. New York: College Board.

Williams, L.B. 2004. Critical issues in advising transfer students: Student retention begins before matriculation. In *The College Transfer Student in America: The Forgotten Student*, edited by B.C. Jacobs, B. Lauren, M.T. Miller, and D.P. Nadler. Washington, D.C.: American Association of Collegiate Registrars and Admissions Officers.

Willingham, W.W., and L. Ramist. 1982. The SAT debate: Do Trusheim and Crouse add useful information? *Phi Delta Kappan*. 64(3): 207–208.

Windmeyer, S.L. 2006. *The Advocate College Guide for LGBT Students*. New York: Alyson Books.

Wingett, Y. 2007. Arizona's colleges struggle to enforce new tuition statute. *The Arizona Republic*. January 3: A1. Available at: <www.azcentral.com/arizonarepublic/news/articles/0103prop300-students.html>.

Wingett, Y., and M. Benson. 2007. Migrant law blocks benefits to thousands; Prop. 300 denying college aid, child care. *The Arizona Republic*. August 2: A1.

Wingett, Y., and R. Ruelas. 2007. ASU helps migrants find tuition. *The Arizona Republic*. Sept. 8. Available at: <www.azcentral.com/arizonarepublic/news/articles/0908studentmoney0908.html>.

Winzenburg, S.M. 2006. The faculty role in admissions. *The Chronicle of Higher Education*. 53(9): C1. Available at: <http://chronicle.com/weekly/v53/i09/09c00101.htm>.

Wolfe, R.N., and S.D. Johnson. 1995. Personality as a predictor of college performance. *Educational and Psychological Measurement*. 55(2): 177–185.

Women in Engineering Programs and Advocates Network. 2006. *Engaging America's Intellectual Talent: The Status of Women and Minorities in Engineering*. Denver, CO: Commission on Professionals in Science and Technology.

Wright, B., and W.G. Tierney. 1991. American Indians in higher education: A history of cultural conflict. *Change*. 23(2): 11–18.

Yip, P. 2003. Closing the tuition gap; Rising costs endanger state plans for savings. *Dallas Morning News*. Mar. 18: L9.

Young, J.W. 1994. Differential prediction of college grades by gender and by ethnicity: A replication study. *Educational and Psychological Measurement*. 54: 1022–1029.

———. 2001. *Differential Validity, Differential Prediction, and College Admission Testing: A Comprehensive Review and Analysis.* New York: College Board.

Zarate, M.E., and H.P. Pachon. 2006. *Perceptions of Financial Aid Among California Latino Youth*. Los Angeles: The Tomas Rivera Policy Institute. Available at: <www.trpi.org/PDFs/Financial_Aid_Surveyfinal6302006.pdf>.

Zia, H. 2000. *Asian American Dreams: The Emergence of an American People New York.* New York: Farrar, Straus, Giroux.

Zwick, R. 2002. Is the SAT a "wealth test?" *Phi Delta Kappan*. 84(4): 307–311.

# Index

## A

## B



## C

## D



## E



## F

## G



## H



## I

## N



## O



## P



## R

## S

## T



## U



## V



## W



## Y